חומש קורן מקראות הדורות
THE KOREN MIKRAOT HADOROT

פרשת נח
PARASHAT NOAḤ

קורן ירושלים

THE ROHR FAMILY EDITION

חומש קורן מקראות הדורות
THE KOREN MIKRAOT HADOROT

THE ZAHAVA AND MOSHAEL STRAUS EDITION OF SEFER BERESHIT

פרשת נח עם רש״י
PARASHAT NOAḤ WITH RASHI

TORAH TRANSLATION BY

Rabbi Lord Jonathan Sacks שליט״א

RASHI'S COMMENTARY TRANSLATED BY

Rabbi Jonathan Mishkin

•

KOREN PUBLISHERS JERUSALEM

The Koren Mikraot HaDorot, The Rohr Edition
Volume 2: Parashat Noaḥ
First Edition, 2022

Koren Publishers Jerusalem Ltd.
POB 4044, Jerusalem 9104001, ISRAEL
POB 8531, New Milford, CT 06776, USA

www.korenpub.com

The Tanakh translation is excerpted from the Magerman Edition of The Koren Tanakh.

The creation of this work was made possible with the generous support of the Jewish Book Trust Inc.

Printed in ISRAEL

ISBN 978 965 7760 57 4

KMDNO01

The Rohr Family Edition of
The Koren Mikraot HaDorot
pays tribute to the memory of

Mr. Sami Rohr ז״ל
ר׳ שמואל ב״ר יהושע אליהו ז״ל

who served his Maker with joy
and whose far-reaching vision, warm open hand, love of Torah,
and love for every Jew were catalysts for the revival and growth of
vibrant Jewish life in the former Soviet Union
and in countless communities the world over

and to the memory of his beloved wife

Mrs. Charlotte Rohr (née Kastner) ע״ה
שרה בת ר׳ יקותיאל יהודה ע״ה

who survived the fires of the Shoah to become
the elegant and gracious matriarch,
first in Colombia and later in the United States,
of three generations of a family
nurtured by her love and unstinting devotion.
She found grace in the eyes of all those whose lives she touched.

Together they merited to see all their children
build lives enriched by faithful commitment
to the spreading of Torah and *Ahavat Yisrael*.

Dedicated with love by
The Rohr Family
NEW YORK, USA

עֲטֶרֶת זְקֵנִים בְּנֵי בָנִים
(משלי יז, ו)

Grandchildren
are the crowning glory of the aged
(Proverbs 17:6)

May the learning and traditions of our people
be strengthened by our future generations.
In honor of our wonderful grandchildren

Zahava and Moshael Straus

CONTENTS

Publisher's Preface
xi

A Note on the Translation of Rashi
xv

PARASHAT NOAḤ WITH RASHI
1

HAFTAROT

Haftarat Noaḥ
49

Maftir and Haftara for Shabbat Rosh Ḥodesh
51

FOR PARASHAT NOAḤ WITH COMMENTARIES AND THE BIBLICAL IMAGINATION
TURN TO THE OTHER END OF THIS VOLUME.

PUBLISHER'S PREFACE

The genius of Jewish commentary on the Torah is one of huge and critical import. Jewish life and law for millennia have been directed by our interpretations of the Torah, and each generation has looked to its rabbinic leadership for a deeper understanding of its teachings, its laws, its stories.

For centuries, *Mikraot Gedolot* have been a core part of understanding the Ḥumash; the words of Rashi, Ibn Ezra, Ramban, Rashbam, Ralbag, and other classic commentators illuminate and help us understand the Torah. But traditional editions of *Mikraot Gedolot* present only a slice in time and a small selection of the corpus of Jewish commentators. Almost every generation has produced rabbinic scholars who speak to their times, from Philo and Onkelos two thousand years ago, to Rabbi Joseph B. Soloveitchik, Rabbi Aharon Kotler, the Lubavitcher Rebbe, and Nehama Leibowitz in ours.

The Koren Mikraot HaDorot – Scriptures or Interpretations for the Generations – brings two millennia of Torah commentary into the hands and homes of Jews around the world. Readers will be able to encounter not only the classic commentators, but to gain a much broader sense of the issues that scholars grappled with in their time and the inspiration they drew from the ancient texts. We see, for example, how Philo speaks to an assimilating Greek Jewish audience in first-century Alexandria, and how similar yet different it is from Rabbi Samson Raphael Hirsch's approach to an equally assimilating nineteenth-century German readership; how the perspectives of Rabbi Soloveitchik and Rabbi Kotler differ in a post-Holocaust world; how Rav Se'adya Gaon interpreted the Torah for the Jews of Babylonia. It is an exciting journey through Jewish history via the unchanging words of the Torah.

◀

The text of the Torah features the exceptional new translation of Rabbi Lord Jonathan Sacks, together with the celebrated and meticulously accurate Koren Hebrew text. Of course, with the exception of Rashi – for whom we present an entirely new translation in full – the commentaries are selected. We offer this anthology not to limit our reader's exploration but rather as a gateway for further learning of Torah and its commentaries on a broader and deeper level than space here permits. We discuss below how to use this book.

We must thank **Pamela and George Rohr** of New York, who recognized the unique value of the *Koren Mikraot HaDorot* and its ability to communicate historical breadth and context to the reader. For my colleagues here at Koren, we thank you; for the many generations of users who will find this a continuing source of new learning, we are forever in your debt.

We also are indebted to **Zahava and Moshael Straus**, true leaders of this Jewish generation in so many fields, who have invested not only in *Parashat Noaḥ* but the entire book of Bereshit. Together, we were thus able to launch this innovative and unique project.

We are honored to acknowledge and thank **Debra and David Magerman**, whose support for the Koren Ḥumash with Rabbi Sacks's exemplary translation and commentary laid the foundation for the core English text of this work.

Finally, I must personally thank **Rabbi Marvin Hier**, with whom I had a special breakfast some years ago at the King David Hotel. During the meal, he raised the problem that so few people knew the writings of Rabbi Joseph B. Soloveitchik and Rabbi Aharon Kotler on the Torah; and I, who had just read some of Philo's work, had the same reaction. From that conversation came the seed for this project.

HOW TO USE THE KOREN MIKRAOT HADOROT

The Koren Mikraot HaDorot will be a fifty-five-volume edition of the Ḥumash (one for each *parasha* plus a companion volume). Each of the fifty-four volumes of the *parashot* can be read from right to left (Hebrew opening side), and left to right (English opening side).

Opening from the Hebrew side offers:

- the full Torah text, the translation of Rabbi Sacks, and the full commentary of Rashi in both Hebrew and the new English translation

◀

- all *haftarot* associated with the *parasha* of the volume, including Rosh Ḥodesh and special readings, both in Hebrew and English

Opening from the English side presents four sections:

- **THE TIME OF THE SAGES** – includes commentaries from the Second Temple period and the talmudic period
- **THE CLASSIC COMMENTATORS** – quotes selected explanations by Rashi as well as most of the commentators found in traditional *Mikraot Gedolot*
- **CONFRONTING MODERNITY** – selects commentaries from the eighteenth century to the close of the twentieth century
- **THE BIBLICAL IMAGINATION** – features essays surveying some of the broader conceptual ideas as a supplement to the linear, text-based commentary

The first three of these sections each feature the relevant verses, in Hebrew and English, on the page alongside their respective commentaries, in chronological order, providing the reader with a single window onto the text without excessive page turning.

In addition to being a valuable resource in a Jewish home or synagogue library, we conceived of these volumes as a weekly accompaniment in the synagogue. There is scope for the reader to study each *parasha* on a weekly basis in preparation for the reading on Shabbat. One may select a particular group of commentators for study that week, or perhaps alternate between ancient and modern viewpoints. Some readers may choose to delve into the text through verse-by-verse interpretation, while others may prefer a conceptual perspective on the *parasha* as a whole. The broad array of options for learning means this is a series which can be returned to year after year, always presenting new insights and new approaches to understanding the text.

ACKNOWLEDGMENTS

The creation of this book was possible only thanks to the small but exceptional team here at Koren Jerusalem. We are grateful to:

- Rabbi Tzvi Hersh Weinreb, שליט״א, who conceptualized the structure of the project and provides both moral and halakhic leadership at Koren
- Rabbi Shai Finkelstein, whose encyclopedic knowledge of Torah and its interpreters is equaled only by his community leadership, formerly in Memphis and today in Jerusalem
- Rabbi Yedidya Naveh, whose knowledge, organizational skills, and superb leadership brought the disparate elements together

- Rabbi Jonathan Mishkin, translator of the commentaries, who crafted a fluent, accurate, and eloquent English translation

Our design, editing, typesetting, and proofreading staff, including Tani Bayer, Esther Be'er, Tomi Mager, Adina Luber, Dr. Yoel Finkelman, and Carolyn Budow Ben David, enabled an attractive, user-friendly, and accurate edition of these works.

> "One silver basin" (Numbers 7:13) was brought as a symbol of the Torah, which has been likened to wine, as the verse states: "And drink of the wine which I have mingled" (Proverbs 9:5). Because it is customary to drink wine in a basin – as we see in the verse "that drink wine in basins" (Amos 6:6) – he therefore brought a basin. "Of seventy shekels, after the shekel of the sanctuary" (Numbers 7:13). Why? Because just as the numerical value of "wine" [*yayin*] is seventy, so there are seventy modes of expounding the Torah. (Bemidbar Rabba 13:16)

Each generation produces exceptional rabbinic, intellectual leadership. It has been our purpose to enable all Jews to taste the wine of those generations, in the hope of expanding the breadth and depth of their knowledge. Torah is our greatest treasure, and we need the wisdom of those generations to better understand this bountiful gift from God. We hope that we at Koren can deepen that understanding for all who seek it.

Matthew Miller, Publisher
Jerusalem, 5781 (2021)

A NOTE ON THE TRANSLATION OF RASHI

The translation of Rashi's commentary provided here is complete and unabridged, following the meticulously researched Hebrew version of the commentary published by Koren. This version omits some material published in other editions that was found likely to have been added later by Rashi's students and other authors. We have included all of Rashi's numerous grammatical and linguistic discussions, even though these tend to be of less interest to the English-speaking reader, for two reasons: First, we felt it important for the readership to be confident that they are holding a complete version of Rashi's commentary and to know that they are not missing any matter of potential interest it might contain. Second, we wished to impress upon the reader that the elegant Sacks translation of the Torah included in this volume represents only one reading among many possible interpretations. Rashi's inquiries into the meanings of individual words and phrases emphasize the ambiguity of the verses and the potential of any passage to be interpreted in several different ways. This multifaceted nature of the Torah is a central theme of *The Koren Mikraot HaDorot.*

The inclusion of these discussions – often technical and sometimes confusing – bears implications for the translation. Here the translator was often forced to insert himself into the discussion to clearly establish the grammatical difficulty or ambiguity in the Hebrew text that is troubling Rashi. Since these difficulties are not always conveyed in the Sacks verse translation, the reader will find bracketed editorial comments used more aggressively in these discussions. The editor's notes also serve to supply the English-speaking reader with relevant details regarding Hebrew grammar that Rashi assumes to be known to his audience, which are necessary to understanding his point.

◀

Here at the outset, we will provide a very brief overview of the Hebrew system of *binyanim*, or Hebrew verb forms, which is central to so many of Rashi's grammatical arguments.

Hebrew verbs, which are always conjugated by number, person, gender, and tense, are also divided into seven categories of verbs called *binyanim*. Three of these are in the active voice, three passive, and one in a reflexive voice that is neither active nor passive. In theory, any three-letter root (*shoresh*) in Hebrew can be conjugated in any one of these forms, with slightly different meanings in each one, though few roots exist in all forms. Readers who encounter one of Rashi's discourses analyzing to which class a given verb belongs can refer to the following chart to orient themselves.

BINYAN NAME	EXAMPLE (PAST/FUTURE)	VOICE	
Paal (Kal) – פָּעַל (קל)	*Katav/Yikhtov* – write	Active	Simple
Hifil – הִפְעִיל	*Hikdish/Yakdish* – consecrate	Active	Causative
Pi'el – פִּעֵל	*Giddel/Yegaddel* – promote or exalt	Active	Intensive
Hitpael – הִתְפַּעֵל	*Hitgaddel/Yitgaddel* – become great	Reflexive	Intensive
Pual – פֻּעַל	*Guddal/Yeguddal* – be promoted or exalted	Passive	Intensive
Hufal – הֻפְעַל	*Hukdash/Yukdash* – be consecrated	Passive	Causative
Nifal – נִפְעַל	*Nikhtav/Yikkatev* – be written	Passive	Simple

Each of the three active conjugations pairs with one of the passive ones, as seen in the above chart, such that the seven *binyanim* can be simplified into three more basic forms. The simple form (*paal/nifal*) denotes simple actions. The causative form (*hifil/hufal*) is reserved for actions induced by the subject in the object, e.g., to cause something to become holy (consecrate). The intensive form (*pi'el/pual*) describes a special form of the action, usually more significant or intense. The reflexive form is considered a third subgroup of the intensive form and is used for actions done to oneself.

Rashi's grammatical discussions also focus on the vocalization (*nikkud,* or vowel marks) of the Hebrew text. The reader can review the names of the vowel marks in the following chart, as well as see how these vowels are transliterated in this edition.

VOWEL MARK	NAME	TRANSLITERATION
בְּ	*Sheva* (*Ḥataf* when combined with a *segol, pataḥ,* or *kamatz*)	*e* or silent
בֶּ	*Segol* (in Rashi's language: *Pataḥ Katan*)	*e*
בַּ	*Pataḥ*	*a*
בָּ	*Kamatz*	*a* or *o*
בִּ	*Ḥirik*	*i*
בֵּ	*Tzerei* (in Rashi's language, also: *Kamatz Katan*)	*e* or *ei*
בֹ	*Ḥolam* (in Rashi's language: *Melafum*)	*o*
בֻּ	*Kubbutz* (in Rashi's language: *Shuruk*)	*u*
בוּ	*Shuruk*	*u*

For Rashi's terms in Old French, we have been guided by Yisrael Gukovitzky's dictionary *Targum HaLaaz* (1985).

Yedidya Naveh, Managing Editor
Jerusalem, 5781 (2021)

פרשת נח
PARASHAT NOAḤ

חומש עם רש״י
THE ḤUMASH WITH RASHI

6 9 This is the story of Noaḥ. Noaḥ was a righteous man, a person
10 of integrity in his generation; Noaḥ walked with God. And
11 Noaḥ had three sons: Shem, Ḥam, and Yefet. The earth had
12 become corrupt in God's sight, full of violence. And when
God saw how corrupt the earth had become, all flesh corrupt-
13 ing its ways upon the earth, God said to Noaḥ, "The
end of all flesh has come before Me, for the earth is full of violence because of them. I am about to destroy them, along with

ו ט | אֵלֶּה תּוֹלְדֹת נֹחַ נֹחַ אִישׁ צַדִּיק. הוֹאִיל וְהִזְכִּירוֹ סִפֵּר בְּשִׁבְחוֹ, שֶׁנֶּאֱמַר: "זֵכֶר צַדִּיק לִבְרָכָה" (משלי י, ז). דָּבָר אַחֵר, לְמֶדְךָ שֶׁעִקַּר תּוֹלְדוֹתֵיהֶם שֶׁל צַדִּיקִים מַעֲשִׂים טוֹבִים:

6 9 | אֵלֶּה תּוֹלְדֹת נֹחַ נֹחַ אִישׁ צַדִּיק – *This is the story of Noaḥ. Noaḥ was a righteous man:* Because the text began this passage with Noaḥ's name, it proceeds to praise him, as the verse states: *The mention of the righteous is a blessing* [Proverbs 10:7. Rashi is troubled by the gap between the word *toledot* which suggests that the text is about to discuss Noaḥ's lineage, and the actual presentation of his sons which does not occur until the next verse]. Another interpretation: This verse teaches that a person's most important descendants are in fact his good deeds.

בְּדֹרֹתָיו. יֵשׁ מֵרַבּוֹתֵינוּ דּוֹרְשִׁים אוֹתוֹ לְשֶׁבַח: כָּל שֶׁכֵּן אִלּוּ הָיָה בְּדוֹר צַדִּיקִים הָיָה צַדִּיק יוֹתֵר. וְיֵשׁ שֶׁדּוֹרְשִׁים אוֹתוֹ לִגְנַאי: לְפִי דוֹרוֹ הָיָה צַדִּיק, וְאִלּוּ הָיָה בְּדוֹרוֹ שֶׁל אַבְרָהָם לֹא הָיָה נֶחְשָׁב לִכְלוּם:

בְּדֹרֹתָיו – *In his generation:* Some of our Rabbis interpret this phrase to Noaḥ's credit: The man was virtuous in his generation [despite living in a negative environment]; imagine how admirable he would have been had he lived in a society with other righteous people. But some scholars see this phrase as critical of Noaḥ: Although Noaḥ was considered exemplary within his own generation, had he lived in the time of Avraham he would not have stood out at all.

אֶת־הָאֱלֹהִים הִתְהַלֶּךְ־נֹחַ. וּבְאַבְרָהָם הוּא אוֹמֵר: "אֲשֶׁר הִתְהַלַּכְתִּי לְפָנָיו" (להלן כד, מ), נֹחַ הָיָה צָרִיךְ סַעַד לְתָמְכוֹ, אֲבָל אַבְרָהָם הָיָה מִתְחַזֵּק וּמְהַלֵּךְ בְּצִדְקוֹ מֵאֵלָיו:

אֶת־הָאֱלֹהִים הִתְהַלֶּךְ־נֹחַ – *Noaḥ walked with God:* In comparison to this description, Avraham said, *The Lord before whom I have walked* (Genesis 24:40). This indicates that Noaḥ required the assistance of God to support him ["with" God], whereas Avraham was strong enough in his virtue to walk by himself ["before" God].

הִתְהַלֶּךְ. לְשׁוֹן עָבָר. וְזֶהוּ שִׁמּוּשָׁהּ שֶׁל לָמֶ"ד בִּלְשׁוֹן כָּבֵד, מְשַׁמֶּשֶׁת לְהַבָּא וּלְשֶׁעָבַר בִּלְשׁוֹן אֶחָד: "קוּם הִתְהַלֵּךְ" (להלן יג, יז) לְהַבָּא, "הִתְהַלֶּךְ נֹחַ" לְשֶׁעָבַר; "הִתְפַּלֵּל בְּעַד עֲבָדֶיךָ"

הִתְהַלֶּךְ – *Walked:* The form of this verb, *hithallekh*, connotes the past tense – Noaḥ would walk with God. This is the function of the letter *lamed* in the heavy conjugation [of the verb *hithallekh*, which is in the *hitpa'el* form]: it reflects both the future imperative and the past tense. For example, *get up and walk through [hithallekh] the length and breadth of the*

◀

ו ט אֵלֶּה תּוֹלְדֹת נֹחַ נֹחַ אִישׁ צַדִּיק תָּמִים הָיָה בְּדֹרֹתָיו ה
י אֶת־הָאֱלֹהִים הִתְהַלֶּךְ־נֹחַ׃ וַיּוֹלֶד נֹחַ שְׁלֹשָׁה בָנִים
יא אֶת־שֵׁם אֶת־חָם וְאֶת־יָפֶת׃ וַתִּשָּׁחֵת הָאָרֶץ לִפְנֵי
יב הָאֱלֹהִים וַתִּמָּלֵא הָאָרֶץ חָמָס׃ וַיַּרְא אֱלֹהִים אֶת־
הָאָרֶץ וְהִנֵּה נִשְׁחָתָה כִּי־הִשְׁחִית כָּל־בָּשָׂר אֶת־דַּרְכּוֹ
יג עַל־הָאָרֶץ׃ וַיֹּאמֶר אֱלֹהִים לְנֹחַ קֵץ כָּל־
בָּשָׂר בָּא לְפָנַי כִּי־מָלְאָה הָאָרֶץ חָמָס מִפְּנֵיהֶם וְהִנְנִי

(שמואל א' יב, יט) לְהַבָּא, "וּבָא וְהִתְפַּלֵּל אֶל הַבַּיִת הַזֶּה" (מלכים א' ח, מב) לְשׁוֹן עָבָר, אֶלָּא שֶׁהַוָּי"ו שֶׁבְּרֹאשׁוֹ הוֹפְכוֹ לְהַבָּא:

land (13:17) represents a command for the future, whereas the current verse, *Noaḥ walked [hithallekh] with God* describes the past. Again, when the people turn to Shmuel, they request of him, *pray [hitpallel] on your servants' behalf to the Lord your God* (I Samuel 12:19) which is a request for the future. Whereas in Shlomo's dedication of the Temple he petitions God, *having heard of Your great name and Your mighty hand and Your outstretched arm; should [the foreigner] come and pray [vehitpallel] at this House* (I Kings 8:42) connoting the past, although the prefix letter *vav* transforms the verb into the future.

יא | וַתִּשָּׁחֵת. לְשׁוֹן עֶרְוָה וַעֲבוֹדָה זָרָה, כְּמוֹ: "פֶּן תַּשְׁחִתוּן" (דברים ד, טז), "כִּי הִשְׁחִית כָּל בָּשָׂר" (להלן פסוק יב):

11 | וַתִּשָּׁחֵת – *Had become corrupt:* The verb connotes licentiousness and idolatry, as in the warning *not to act in self-destruction [tashḥitun], making yourselves any idol, an image of any shape, any form of man or of woman* (Deuteronomy 4:16), and the following verse: *All flesh corrupting [hishḥit] its ways upon the earth* (6:12).

וַתִּמָּלֵא הָאָרֶץ חָמָס. גָּזֵל:

וַתִּמָּלֵא הָאָרֶץ חָמָס – *Full of violence: [Ḥamas* refers specifically to] robbery.

יב | כִּי־הִשְׁחִית כָּל־בָּשָׂר. אֲפִלּוּ בְּהֵמָה חַיָּה וָעוֹף נִזְקָקִין לְשֶׁאֵינָן מִינָן:

12 | כִּי־הִשְׁחִית כָּל־בָּשָׂר – *All flesh corrupting its ways:* [It was not just humans who were misbehaving, but] even cattle, wild beasts, and the birds. For these were copulating with representatives of other species.

יג | קֵץ כָּל־בָּשָׂר. כָּל מָקוֹם שֶׁאַתָּה מוֹצֵא זְנוּת, אַנְדְּרָלָמוּסְיָא בָּאָה לָעוֹלָם וְהוֹרֶגֶת טוֹבִים וְרָעִים:

13 | קֵץ כָּל־בָּשָׂר – *The end of all flesh:* Whenever immorality runs rampant in society, indiscriminate punishment is unleashed against the world, killing both the innocent and the guilty. [This explains the adjective "all".]

◀

14 all the earth. So make yourself an ark of cypress wood. Make
15 it with compartments and coat it in pitch inside and out. This
is how you shall make it: the ark shall be three hundred cubits
16 long, fifty cubits wide, and thirty cubits high. Make a window
for the ark, and taper the latter to within a cubit of the top.
Put a door in the side of the ark and make lower, middle, and

כִּי־מָלְאָה הָאָרֶץ חָמָס. לֹא נֶחְתַּם גְּזַר דִּינָם אֶלָּא עַל הַגָּזֵל:

כִּי־מָלְאָה הָאָרֶץ חָמָס – *For the earth is full of violence:* The fate of the world was decreed in response to the robbery.

אֶת־הָאָרֶץ. כְּמוֹ מִן הָאָרֶץ, וְדוֹמֶה לוֹ: "כְּצֵאתִי אֶת הָעִיר" (שמות ט, כט) מִן הָעִיר. "חָלָה אֶת רַגְלָיו" (מלכים א׳ טו, כג) מִן רַגְלָיו. דָּבָר אַחֵר, "אֶת הָאָרֶץ", עִם הָאָרֶץ, שֶׁאַף שְׁלֹשָׁה טְפָחִים שֶׁל עֹמֶק הַמַּחֲרֵשָׁה נִמּוֹחוּ וְנִטַּשְׁטְשׁוּ:

אֶת־הָאָרֶץ – *Along with all the earth:* The particle *et* [which has no English equivalent and usually introduces a direct object] should be understood as *min* ["from"]. That is: I am about to destroy them, [removing them] from the earth. We find a similar usage of the term in the verse, *As I leave the city [et ha'ir], I will spread out my hands to the Lord* (Exodus 9:29), suggesting: As I leave from the city; and in the verse, *in his old age, however, he suffered from a foot disease [ḥala et raglav]* (I Kings 15:23), meaning that Asa became ill from his legs. Another interpretation: the phrase *et haaretz* connotes "with the earth" [that is, even the ground itself will be destroyed]. For the soil of the earth was dissolved and washed away to a depth of three handbreadths, which is as far as the plow digs.

יד | עֲשֵׂה לְךָ תֵּבַת. הַרְבֵּה רֶוַח וְהַצָּלָה לְפָנָיו, וְלָמָּה הִטְרִיחוֹ בְּבִנְיָן זֶה? כְּדֵי שֶׁיִּרְאוּהוּ אַנְשֵׁי דּוֹר הַמַּבּוּל עָסוּק בָּהּ מֵאָה וְעֶשְׂרִים שָׁנָה וְשׁוֹאֲלִין אוֹתוֹ: מַה זֹּאת לְךָ? וְהוּא אוֹמֵר לָהֶם: עָתִיד הַקָּדוֹשׁ בָּרוּךְ הוּא לְהָבִיא מַבּוּל לָעוֹלָם, אוּלַי יָשׁוּבוּ:

14 | **עֲשֵׂה לְךָ תֵּבַת** – *So make yourself an ark:* Considering that God has at His disposal many means and methods of rescue, why did He trouble Noaḥ to build the ark? God hoped that during the one hundred and twenty years that it took Noaḥ to construct the vessel, the people of his time would see him occupied with the project and would ask him what he was doing. Then Noaḥ would say: The Holy One, blessed be He, plans on releasing a flood against the world [to punish you for your sins]. Perhaps when they heard that, they would repent.

עֲצֵי־גֹפֶר. כָּךְ שְׁמוֹ. וְלָמָּה מִמִּין זֶה? עַל שֵׁם גָּפְרִית שֶׁנִּגְזַר עֲלֵיהֶם לִמָּחוֹת בּוֹ:

עֲצֵי־גֹפֶר – *Cypress wood:* The name of the tree is *gofer*. Why did God specify that this type of wood be used? The name of the tree was associated with the *gofrit* ["sulfur"] that God would rain down upon the earth to wipe out humankind.

קִנִּים. מְדוֹרִים לְכָל בְּהֵמָה וְחַיָּה:

קִנִּים – *Compartments:* Noaḥ was instructed to build separate chambers for each of the cattle and animal species.

בַּכֹּפֶר. זֶפֶת בִּלְשׁוֹן אֲרַמִּי. וּמָצִינוּ בַּתַּלְמוּד 'כּוּפְרָא'. בְּתֵבָתוֹ שֶׁל מֹשֶׁה,

בַּכֹּפֶר – *In pitch: Kofer* is the Hebrew term for the Aramaic *zefet* [pitch]; in the Talmud, this substance is referred to as *kufra*.

יד מַשְׁחִיתָם אֶת־הָאָרֶץ: עֲשֵׂה לְךָ תֵּבַת עֲצֵי־גֹפֶר
קִנִּים תַּעֲשֶׂה אֶת־הַתֵּבָה וְכָפַרְתָּ אֹתָהּ מִבַּיִת וּמִחוּץ
טו בַּכֹּפֶר: וְזֶה אֲשֶׁר תַּעֲשֶׂה אֹתָהּ שְׁלֹשׁ מֵאוֹת אַמָּה
אֹרֶךְ הַתֵּבָה חֲמִשִּׁים אַמָּה רָחְבָּהּ וּשְׁלֹשִׁים אַמָּה
טז קוֹמָתָהּ: צֹהַר | תַּעֲשֶׂה לַתֵּבָה וְאֶל־אַמָּה תְּכַלֶּנָּה
מִלְמַעְלָה וּפֶתַח הַתֵּבָה בְּצִדָּהּ תָּשִׂים תַּחְתִּיִּם שְׁנִיִּם

עַל יְדֵי שֶׁהָיוּ הַמַּיִם תָּשִׁים, דַּיָּהּ בְּחֹמֶר מִבִּפְנִים וְזֶפֶת מִבַּחוּץ, וְעוֹד כְּדֵי שֶׁלֹּא יָרִיחַ רֵיחַ רַע שֶׁל זֶפֶת, אֲבָל כָּאן מִפְּנֵי חֹזֶק הַמַּיִם זִפְתָהּ מִבַּיִת וּמִחוּץ:

[Now, why was Noaḥ ordered to cover both the inside and the outside of his ark with pitch, whereas Yokheved covered] Moshe's ark [with pitch only on the outside]? Since Moshe's life raft was placed in calm waters, it was sufficient to cover the inside of the vessel with clay and the outside with pitch. Furthermore, by reserving the pitch for the exterior of Moshe's ark, his mother ensured that the righteous baby would not have to smell the foul odor of the substance. However, in the current instance, the ark would face strong waves and currents. Therefore, it had to be fully coated on the inside as well as the outside with pitch [in order to prevent leaks].

טז | צֹהַר. יֵשׁ אוֹמְרִים חַלּוֹן, וְיֵשׁ אוֹמְרִים אֶבֶן טוֹבָה הַמְּאִירָה לָהֶם:

16 | **צֹהַר** – *A window:* Some commentators claim that the *tzohar* was a window, whereas other scholars maintain that it was a precious light-producing stone which illuminated the boat's interior.

וְאֶל־אַמָּה תְּכַלֶּנָּה מִלְמַעְלָה. כִּסּוּיָהּ מְשֻׁפָּע וְעוֹלֶה עַד שֶׁהוּא קָצָר מִלְמַעְלָה וְעוֹמֵד עַל אַמָּה, כְּדֵי שֶׁיָּזוּבוּ הַמַּיִם לְמַטָּה מִכָּאן וּמִכָּאן:

וְאֶל־אַמָּה תְּכַלֶּנָּה מִלְמַעְלָה – *And taper the latter to within a cubit of the top:* The roof of the ark slanted upward until it narrowed at the top, with a horizontal section of a cubit remaining. In this way the water would run down either side of the roof.

בְּצִדָּהּ תָּשִׂים. שֶׁלֹּא יִפְּלוּ גְּשָׁמִים בָּהּ:

בְּצִדָּהּ תָּשִׂים – *Put in the side:* Noaḥ was to build the door on the side of the ark [and not the top] to prevent the rain from falling inside.

תַּחְתִּיִּם שְׁנִיִּם וּשְׁלִשִׁים. שָׁלֹשׁ עֲלִיּוֹת זוֹ עַל גַּב זוֹ, עֶלְיוֹנִים לָאָדָם אֶמְצָעִיִּים לְמָדוֹר הַבְּהֵמוֹת תַּחְתִּיִּים לְזֶבֶל:

תַּחְתִּיִּם שְׁנִיִּם וּשְׁלִשִׁים – *Lower, middle, and upper decks:* The ark was divided into three floors, one atop the other. Noaḥ and his family were assigned to the upper story, the middle level was occupied by the animals, and the bottom deck was reserved for waste.

17 upper decks. ⬥ And I – I am about to bring floodwaters over the earth to destroy all flesh that has within it the breath of life
18 under the heavens. Everything on earth will die. But I will establish My covenant with you, and you will enter the ark – you,
19 your sons, your wife, and your sons' wives with you. And you shall take two of each living creature, male and female, into
20 the ark to keep alive with you. ⬥ Of every kind of bird, animal,
21 and wild beast, bring two to keep alive. As for you, take all the food to be eaten and store it: it will be for food for you and for
22 them." Noah did so: all that God commanded him, he ful-
7 1 filled. ⬥ Then the Lord said to Noah, "Enter the ark, you and   SHENI

יז | וַאֲנִי הִנְנִי מֵבִיא. הִנְנִי מוּכָן לְהַסְכִּים עִם אוֹתָם שֶׁזְּרָזוּנִי כְּבָר: "מָה אֱנוֹשׁ כִּי תִזְכְּרֶנּוּ" (תהלים ח, ה):

מַבּוּל. שֶׁבִּלָּה אֶת הַכֹּל, שֶׁבִּלְבֵּל אֶת הַכֹּל, שֶׁהוֹבִיל אֶת הַכֹּל מִן הַגָּבוֹהַּ לַנָּמוּךְ. וְזֶהוּ שֶׁתִּרְגֵּם אוּנְקְלוֹס: "טוֹפָנָא", שֶׁהֵצִיף אֶת הַכֹּל וְהֵבִיאָם לְבָבֶל שֶׁהִיא עֲמוּקָה, לְכָךְ נִקְרֵאת 'שִׁנְעָר', שֶׁכָּל מֵתֵי מַבּוּל נִנְעֲרוּ לְשָׁם:

יח | וַהֲקִמֹתִי אֶת־בְּרִיתִי. בְּרִית הָיָה צָרִיךְ עַל הַפֵּרוֹת שֶׁלֹּא יִרְקְבוּ וְיֵעָפְשׁוּ, וְשֶׁלֹּא יַהַרְגוּהוּ רְשָׁעִים שֶׁבַּדּוֹר:

אַתָּה וּבָנֶיךָ וְאִשְׁתְּךָ. הָאֲנָשִׁים לְבַד וְהַנָּשִׁים לְבַד, מִכָּאן שֶׁנֶּאֶסְרוּ בְּתַשְׁמִישׁ הַמִּטָּה:

יט | וּמִכָּל־הָחַי. אֲפִלּוּ שֵׁדִים:

---

17 | וַאֲנִי הִנְנִי מֵבִיא – *And I – I am about to bring:* I am now prepared to agree with those who long ago tried to sway Me, saying what are mortals, that You should be mindful of them; human beings, that You should take note of them? (Psalms 8:5).

מַבּוּל – *Floodwaters:* There are three reasons why the deluge is called a *mabbul*. Firstly, the water destroyed [*billa*] everything; it confused [*bilbel*] the world; and it brought [*hovil*] everything down from a high level to a lower position. Thus, Targum Onkelos renders the word *mabbul* as *tofana*, which means that the waters caused everything to float to Babylonia. The latter is a low land, which is also called *Shinar* since everybody who died in the flood was shaken out [*nin'aru*] there.

18 | וַהֲקִמֹתִי אֶת־בְּרִיתִי – *But I will establish My covenant:* Noah required an assurance that the fruit he brought aboard would not rot or decay during the flood. God also promised him that the wicked men of his time would not kill him.

אַתָּה וּבָנֶיךָ וְאִשְׁתְּךָ – *You, your sons, your wife:* The men entered the ark by themselves and the women entered by themselves. We learn from this that sexual intimacy was forbidden on the ark.

19 | וּמִכָּל־הָחַי – *Of each living creature:* This phrase refers to the demons [who were also rescued on the ark. The Hebrew text contains two phrases: *umikkol haḥai* – of each living creature, and *umikkol basar* – of each animal of flesh. Rashi seems to be explaining the apparent repetition by suggesting that the first term included non-animal creatures.]

יז וּשְׁלִשִׁים תַּעֲשֶׂהָ: וַאֲנִי הִנְנִי מֵבִיא אֶת־הַמַּבּוּל
מַיִם עַל־הָאָרֶץ לְשַׁחֵת כָּל־בָּשָׂר אֲשֶׁר־בּוֹ רוּחַ חַיִּים
יח מִתַּחַת הַשָּׁמָיִם כֹּל אֲשֶׁר־בָּאָרֶץ יִגְוָע: וַהֲקִמֹתִי
אֶת־בְּרִיתִי אִתָּךְ וּבָאתָ אֶל־הַתֵּבָה אַתָּה וּבָנֶיךָ
יט וְאִשְׁתְּךָ וּנְשֵׁי־בָנֶיךָ אִתָּךְ: וּמִכָּל־הָחַי מִכָּל־בָּשָׂר
שְׁנַיִם מִכֹּל תָּבִיא אֶל־הַתֵּבָה לְהַחֲיֹת אִתָּךְ זָכָר
כ וּנְקֵבָה יִהְיוּ: מֵהָעוֹף לְמִינֵהוּ וּמִן־הַבְּהֵמָה לְמִינָהּ
מִכֹּל רֶמֶשׂ הָאֲדָמָה לְמִינֵהוּ שְׁנַיִם מִכֹּל יָבֹאוּ אֵלֶיךָ
כא לְהַחֲיוֹת: וְאַתָּה קַח־לְךָ מִכָּל־מַאֲכָל אֲשֶׁר יֵאָכֵל
כב וְאָסַפְתָּ אֵלֶיךָ וְהָיָה לְךָ וְלָהֶם לְאָכְלָה: וַיַּעַשׂ נֹחַ
ז א כְּכֹל אֲשֶׁר צִוָּה אֹתוֹ אֱלֹהִים כֵּן עָשָׂה: וַיֹּאמֶר יהוה שני

שְׁנַיִם מִכֹּל. מִן הַפְּחוּתִין שֶׁבָּהֶם לֹא פָּחֲתוּ מִשְּׁנַיִם, אֶחָד זָכָר וְאֶחָד נְקֵבָה:

שְׁנַיִם מִכֹּל – *Two of each:* The least numerous of the creatures were represented by two animals – one male and one female [whereas more than two specimens were brought for the pure species of animal].

כ | **מֵהָעוֹף לְמִינֵהוּ.** אוֹתָן שֶׁדָּבְקוּ בְּמִינֵיהֶם וְלֹא הִשְׁחִיתוּ דַּרְכָּם; וּמֵאֲלֵיהֶן בָּאוּ, וְכָל שֶׁהַתֵּבָה קוֹלַטְתּוֹ הִכְנִיס בָּהּ:

20 | **מֵהָעוֹף לְמִינֵהוּ** – *Of every kind of bird:* All those birds which had mated only with their own kind and had not corrupted their ways. The animals came of their own accord [and did not have to be gathered by Noaḥ]. And Noaḥ took in whichever beasts the ark was willing to accept. [The vessel miraculously rejected those animals that had mated with other species.]

כב | **וַיַּעַשׂ נֹחַ.** זֶה בִּנְיַן הַתֵּבָה:

22 | **וַיַּעַשׂ נֹחַ** – *Noaḥ did so:* This refers to the construction of the ark [as opposed to verse 7:5, which refers to his boarding the vessel].

ז א | **רָאִיתִי צַדִּיק.** וְלֹא נֶאֱמַר 'צַדִּיק תָּמִים', מִכָּאן שֶׁאוֹמְרִים מִקְצָת שִׁבְחוֹ שֶׁל אָדָם בְּפָנָיו וְכֻלּוֹ שֶׁלֹּא בְּפָנָיו:

7 1 | **רָאִיתִי צַדִּיק** – *For I have seen you to be righteous:* Here God describes Noaḥ as righteous, whereas above, the text refers to him as *a righteous man, a person of integrity* (6:9). This teaches us that it is appropriate to partially compliment a man to his face, but to fully praise him when he is not present.

all your household, for I have seen you alone to be righteous
2 before Me in this generation. Take seven and seven of every
pure animal, seven pairs, and two of every animal that is not
3 pure, of each kind a pair. Also take seven pairs of each kind
of bird, male and female, to keep their kind alive across the
4 earth. For in seven days' time I will send rain on the earth for
forty days and forty nights, and I will wipe from the face of
5 the earth every living creature I have made." Noaḥ did all
6 that the Lord commanded him. Noaḥ was six hundred
7 years old when the floodwaters came upon the earth. Noaḥ,
with his sons, his wife, and his sons' wives, came into the ark
8 to escape the waters of the flood. The pure animals, the animals that were not pure, the birds, and all that walked the

ב | **הַטְּהוֹרָה.** הָעֲתִידָה לִהְיוֹת טְהוֹרָה לְיִשְׂרָאֵל, לָמַדְנוּ שֶׁלָּמַד נֹחַ תּוֹרָה:

2 | **הַטְּהוֹרָה** – *Pure animal:* These are animals that the nation of Israel will eventually refer to as pure [kosher]. This point confirms that Noaḥ learned Torah [and thus knew the distinction between kosher and unkosher animals].

שִׁבְעָה שִׁבְעָה. כְּדֵי שֶׁיַּקְרִיב מֵהֶם קָרְבָּן בְּצֵאתוֹ:

שִׁבְעָה שִׁבְעָה – *Seven and seven:* Noaḥ took multiple pure animals onto the ark so that he could sacrifice them when he exited the ark [following the flood, in 8:20].

ג | **גַּם מֵעוֹף הַשָּׁמַיִם וְגוֹ׳.** בַּטְּהוֹרִים דִּבֵּר הַכָּתוּב, וְיִלָּמֵד סָתוּם מִן הַמְפֹרָשׁ:

3 | **גַּם מֵעוֹף הַשָּׁמַיִם** – *Also of each kind of bird:* This instruction was limited to the pure species. We can infer the unstated from the stated. [Even though this verse does not specify that the *seven pairs of each kind of bird* refers to just the pure species, this point which is made obvious with the animals applies to the birds as well.]

ד | **כִּי לְיָמִים עוֹד שִׁבְעָה.** אֵלּוּ שִׁבְעַת יְמֵי אֶבְלוֹ שֶׁל מְתוּשֶׁלַח הַצַּדִּיק, שֶׁחָס הַקָּדוֹשׁ בָּרוּךְ הוּא עַל כְּבוֹדוֹ וְעִכֵּב אֶת הַפֻּרְעָנוּת. צֵא וַחֲשֹׁב שְׁנוֹתָיו שֶׁל מְתוּשֶׁלַח וְתִמְצָא שֶׁהֵם כָּלִים בִּשְׁנַת שֵׁשׁ מֵאוֹת שָׁנָה לְחַיֵּי נֹחַ:

4 | **כִּי לְיָמִים עוֹד שִׁבְעָה** – *For in seven days' time:* These seven days represent the mourning period over the death of Metushelaḥ the righteous. Because the Holy One, blessed be He, wished to honor that man, He delayed the punishment until the week of mourning had passed. If one works out the age of Metushelaḥ, he will find that this person reached the end of his life when Noaḥ was six hundred years old [which was when the flood occurred].

כִּי לְיָמִים עוֹד. מַהוּ "עוֹד"? זְמַן אַחַר זְמַן זֶה, נוֹסָף עַל מֵאָה וְעֶשְׂרִים שָׁנָה:

כִּי לְיָמִים עוֹד – *For in…days' time:* What is the significance of the term *od* ["more"]? God added additional time [seven days] to the hundred and twenty years [mentioned in 6:3], after which the decree was meant to be carried out.

◀

לְנֹחַ בֹּא־אַתָּה וְכָל־בֵּיתְךָ אֶל־הַתֵּבָה כִּי־אֹתְךָ
ב רָאִיתִי צַדִּיק לְפָנַי בַּדּוֹר הַזֶּה: מִכֹּל | הַבְּהֵמָה
הַטְּהוֹרָה תִּקַּח־לְךָ שִׁבְעָה שִׁבְעָה אִישׁ וְאִשְׁתּוֹ וּמִן־
הַבְּהֵמָה אֲשֶׁר לֹא טְהֹרָה הִוא שְׁנַיִם אִישׁ וְאִשְׁתּוֹ:
ג גַּם מֵעוֹף הַשָּׁמַיִם שִׁבְעָה שִׁבְעָה זָכָר וּנְקֵבָה לְחַיּוֹת
ד זֶרַע עַל־פְּנֵי כָל־הָאָרֶץ: כִּי לְיָמִים עוֹד שִׁבְעָה אָנֹכִי
מַמְטִיר עַל־הָאָרֶץ אַרְבָּעִים יוֹם וְאַרְבָּעִים לָיְלָה
וּמָחִיתִי אֶת־כָּל־הַיְקוּם אֲשֶׁר עָשִׂיתִי מֵעַל פְּנֵי
ה ו הָאֲדָמָה: וַיַּעַשׂ נֹחַ כְּכֹל אֲשֶׁר־צִוָּהוּ יְהוָה: וְנֹחַ בֶּן־
ז שֵׁשׁ מֵאוֹת שָׁנָה וְהַמַּבּוּל הָיָה מַיִם עַל־הָאָרֶץ: וַיָּבֹא
נֹחַ וּבָנָיו וְאִשְׁתּוֹ וּנְשֵׁי־בָנָיו אִתּוֹ אֶל־הַתֵּבָה מִפְּנֵי
ח מֵי הַמַּבּוּל: מִן־הַבְּהֵמָה הַטְּהוֹרָה וּמִן־הַבְּהֵמָה
אֲשֶׁר אֵינֶנָּה טְהֹרָה וּמִן־הָעוֹף וְכֹל אֲשֶׁר־רֹמֵשׂ עַל־

אַרְבָּעִים יוֹם – *For forty days:* The forty-day period corresponds to the time it takes for the formation of a fetus. This alludes to the sin of that generation, which had forced the Creator to fashion illegitimate children.

אַרְבָּעִים יוֹם. כְּנֶגֶד יְצִירַת הַוָּלָד, שֶׁקִּלְקְלוּ לְהַטְרִיחַ לְיוֹצְרָם לָצוּר צוּרַת מַמְזֵרִים:

5 | **וַיַּעַשׂ נֹחַ** – *Noaḥ did:* This verse [as opposed to 6:22] refers to Noaḥ's entry into the ark.

ה | **וַיַּעַשׂ נֹחַ.** זֶה בִּיאָתוֹ לַתֵּבָה:

7 | **נֹחַ וּבָנָיו** – *Noaḥ, with his sons:* The verse emphasizes that the men and women entered the ark separately. The two groups kept apart from each other because intimacy was forbidden as long as the outside world was suffering its torments.

ז | **נֹחַ וּבָנָיו.** הָאֲנָשִׁים לְבַד וְהַנָּשִׁים לְבַד, לְפִי שֶׁנֶּאֶסְרוּ בְּתַשְׁמִישׁ הַמִּטָּה מִפְּנֵי שֶׁהָעוֹלָם שָׁרוּי בְּצַעַר:

מִפְּנֵי מֵי הַמַּבּוּל – *To escape the waters of the flood:* Noaḥ was a man of little faith, and even he only partially believed that God was going to flood the entire world. Hence Noaḥ only entered the ark when the rising waters forced him inside.

מִפְּנֵי מֵי הַמַּבּוּל. אַף נֹחַ מִקְּטַנֵּי אֲמָנָה הָיָה, מַאֲמִין וְאֵינוֹ מַאֲמִין שֶׁיָּבֹא הַמַּבּוּל, וְלֹא נִכְנַס לַתֵּבָה עַד שֶׁדְּחָקוּהוּ הַמַּיִם:

9 earth came two by two to Noaḥ into the ark, male and female,
10 as God had commanded Noaḥ. Thus, after seven days the
11 floodwaters came upon the earth. In the six hundredth year of
Noaḥ's life, in the second month, on the seventeenth of the
month – on that day, all the wellsprings of the great deep
12 burst, and the heavens' floodgates opened. The rain fell on the
13 earth for forty days and forty nights. On that very day, Noaḥ,
his sons, Shem, Ḥam, and Yefet, Noaḥ's wife, and his sons'
14 three wives entered the ark. With them came every kind of
wild beast, every kind of animal, every creeping, crawling
creature of the land, every kind of flying creature, every bird,

9 | **שְׁנַיִם שְׁנַיִם** – *Two by two:* [Although some of the species came in sets of seven pairs, the verse refers to] the lowest number of animals which came from any given species.

ט | **שְׁנַיִם שְׁנַיִם.** כֻּלָּם הֻשְׁווּ בְּמִנְיָן זֶה, מִן הַפָּחוּת הָיוּ שְׁנַיִם:

בָּאוּ אֶל־נֹחַ – *They came to Noaḥ:* Of their own accord.

בָּאוּ אֶל־נֹחַ. מֵאֲלֵיהֶן:

11 | **בַּחֹדֶשׁ הַשֵּׁנִי** – *In the second month:* Rabbi Eliezer taught: This was the month of Marḥeshvan [counting Tishrei as the first month in the year]; whereas Rabbi Yehoshua maintained that this was the month of Iyar [thereby counting Nisan as the first month].

יא | **בַּחֹדֶשׁ הַשֵּׁנִי.** רַבִּי אֱלִיעֶזֶר אוֹמֵר: זֶה מַרְחֶשְׁוָן, רַבִּי יְהוֹשֻׁעַ אוֹמֵר: זֶה אִיָּר:

נִבְקְעוּ – *Burst:* To release their waters.

נִבְקְעוּ. לְהוֹצִיא מֵימֵיהֶן:

תְּהוֹם רַבָּה – *Of the great deep:* Humanity's punishment was thus served to them in a manner that was measure for measure: They sinned in a way that was described as *great wickedness* (6:5), and hence they were stricken with water from *the great deep*.

תְּהוֹם רַבָּה. מִדָּה כְּנֶגֶד מִדָּה, הֵם חָטְאוּ בְּ"רַבָּה רָעַת הָאָדָם" (לעיל ו, ה) וְלָקוּ בִּ"תְהוֹם רַבָּה":

12 | **וַיְהִי הַגֶּשֶׁם עַל־הָאָרֶץ** – *The rain fell on the earth:* In contrast to this description, a later verse states, the flood came upon the earth [7:17. This difference in terminology is explained as follows]: At the outset of the flood, God brought down rains with a touch of compassion so that if the people repented, the precipitation would turn into rains of blessings. However, since humanity did not abandon its wickedness, the rain turned into a flood.

יב | **וַיְהִי הַגֶּשֶׁם עַל־הָאָרֶץ.** וּלְהַלָּן (פסוק יז) הוּא אוֹמֵר: "וַיְהִי הַמַּבּוּל"? אֶלָּא כְּשֶׁהוֹרִידָן הוֹרִידָן בְּרַחֲמִים, שֶׁאִם יַחְזְרוּ יִהְיוּ גִּשְׁמֵי בְרָכָה, כְּשֶׁלֹּא חָזְרוּ הָיוּ לְמַבּוּל:

אַרְבָּעִים יוֹם – *For forty days:* The first day of rains was not included in the period of forty days, since no rain fell during the night preceding it. We know this to be so, since the verse states: *On that day, all the wellsprings of the great deep burst* [7:11.

אַרְבָּעִים יוֹם וְגוֹ'. אֵין יוֹם רִאשׁוֹן מִן הַמִּנְיָן, לְפִי שֶׁאֵין לֵילוֹ עִמּוֹ, שֶׁהֲרֵי כָּתוּב: "בַּיּוֹם הַזֶּה נִבְקְעוּ כָּל מַעְיְנֹת" (לעיל פסוק יא), נִמְצְאוּ

◀

ט הָאֲדָמָה: שְׁנַיִם שְׁנַיִם בָּאוּ אֶל־נֹחַ אֶל־הַתֵּבָה זָכָר
י וּנְקֵבָה כַּאֲשֶׁר צִוָּה אֱלֹהִים אֶת־נֹחַ: וַיְהִי לְשִׁבְעַת
יא הַיָּמִים וּמֵי הַמַּבּוּל הָיוּ עַל־הָאָרֶץ: בִּשְׁנַת שֵׁשׁ־
מֵאוֹת שָׁנָה לְחַיֵּי־נֹחַ בַּחֹדֶשׁ הַשֵּׁנִי בְּשִׁבְעָה־עָשָׂר
יוֹם לַחֹדֶשׁ בַּיּוֹם הַזֶּה נִבְקְעוּ כָּל־מַעְיְנוֹת תְּהוֹם רַבָּה
יב וַאֲרֻבֹּת הַשָּׁמַיִם נִפְתָּחוּ: וַיְהִי הַגֶּשֶׁם עַל־הָאָרֶץ
יג אַרְבָּעִים יוֹם וְאַרְבָּעִים לָיְלָה: בְּעֶצֶם הַיּוֹם הַזֶּה בָּא
נֹחַ וְשֵׁם־וְחָם וָיֶפֶת בְּנֵי־נֹחַ וְאֵשֶׁת נֹחַ וּשְׁלֹשֶׁת נְשֵׁי־
יד בָנָיו אִתָּם אֶל־הַתֵּבָה: הֵמָּה וְכָל־הַחַיָּה לְמִינָהּ וְכָל־
הַבְּהֵמָה לְמִינָהּ וְכָל־הָרֶמֶשׂ הָרֹמֵשׂ עַל־הָאָרֶץ

אַרְבָּעִים יוֹם כָּלִים בְּכ״ח בְּכִסְלֵו לְרַבִּי אֱלִיעֶזֶר, שֶׁהֶחֳדָשִׁים נִמְנִין כְּסִדְרָן אֶחָד מָלֵא וְאֶחָד חָסֵר, הֲרֵי שְׁנֵים עָשָׂר מִמַּרְחֶשְׁוָן וְעֶשְׂרִים וּשְׁמוֹנָה מִכִּסְלֵו:

Since a day of twenty-four hours begins with the night and continues during the subsequent daylight, the first full day of the rains began after the daytime when the *great deep burst*]. Now according to Rabbi Eliezer, this meant that the forty days ended on the twenty-eighth of the month of Kislev, because the months of the year alternate between being full months [of thirty days] and incomplete months [of twenty-nine days. Thus, Tishrei was full, and Marḥeshvan was deficient. Now according to verse 11 the rains started on the seventeenth of the month, but as Rashi has argued, the forty days should be counted from the eighteenth of the month.] This leaves twelve days in the month of Marḥeshvan, and twenty-eight days in the month of Kislev [for a total of forty].

יג | **בְּעֶצֶם הַיּוֹם הַזֶּה.** לִמֶּדְךָ הַכָּתוּב שֶׁהָיוּ בְּנֵי דוֹרוֹ אוֹמְרִים: אִלּוּ אָנוּ רוֹאִים אוֹתוֹ נִכְנָס לַתֵּבָה אָנוּ שׁוֹבְרִין אוֹתָהּ וְהוֹרְגִין אוֹתוֹ. אָמַר הַקָּדוֹשׁ בָּרוּךְ הוּא: אֲנִי מַכְנִיסוֹ לְעֵינֵי כֻלָּם, וְנִרְאֶה דְּבַר מִי יָקוּם:

13 | **בְּעֶצֶם הַיּוֹם הַזֶּה** – *On that very day:* The people of Noaḥ's generation boasted that when they would see Noaḥ entering the ark they would break down the door and kill the man. But the Holy One, blessed be He, responded: Watch while I bring Noaḥ into the boat in full view of everybody [that is, in broad daylight], and then we'll see whose plan is realized!

יד | **צִפּוֹר כָּל־כָּנָף.** דָּבוּק הוּא, צִפּוֹר שֶׁל כָּל מִין כָּנָף, לְרַבּוֹת חֲגָבִים:

14 | **צִפּוֹר כָּל־כָּנָף** – *Every kind of flying creature:* The term *tzippor* appears here as a construct: every kind of winged creature. This includes locusts.

15 and each winged thing. They came to Noaḥ, to the ark, two by
16 two, of all flesh that had within it the breath of life. They came,
male and female of all flesh, as God had commanded him.
17 Then the LORD shut him in. For forty days the flood came SHELISHI
upon the earth. The waters swelled, lifting the ark so that it
18 rose above the land. The waters surged, swelling enormously
on the earth, and the ark began to drift on the surface of the
19 water. The waters surged ever more, until all the high moun-
20 tains beneath all the heavens were covered. Fifteen cubits
above them the waters surged as the mountains were covered.
21 All flesh that moved upon the earth perished – birds, animals,
wild beasts, and all the creatures that swarm on the earth,
22 and all humankind. Everything on dry land that had breath of
23 life in its nostrils died. Every living thing on the face of the

טז | **וַיִּסְגֹּר יהוה בַּעֲדוֹ.** הֵגֵן עָלָיו שֶׁלֹּא שְׁבָרוּהָ, הִקִּיף הַתֵּבָה דֻּבִּים וַאֲרָיוֹת וְהָיוּ הוֹרְגִים בָּהֶם. וּפְשׁוּטוֹ שֶׁל מִקְרָא, סָגַר כְּנֶגְדּוֹ מִן הַמַּיִם, וְכֵן כָּל 'בְּעַד' שֶׁבַּמִּקְרָא לְשׁוֹן 'כְּנֶגֶד' הוּא: "בְּעַד כָּל רֶחֶם" (להלן כ, יח), "בַּעֲדֵךְ וּבְעַד בָּנַיִךְ" (מלכים ב' ד, ד), "עוֹר בְּעַד עוֹר" (איוב ב, ד), "מָגֵן בַּעֲדִי" (תהלים ג, ד), "הִתְפַּלֵּל בְּעַד עֲבָדֶיךָ" (שמואל א' יב, יט), כְּנֶגֶד עֲבָדֶיךָ:

16 | **וַיִּסְגֹּר יהוה בַּעֲדוֹ** – *Then the LORD shut him in:* God protected Noaḥ by preventing his wicked neighbors from smashing the ark. How did He do so? He surrounded the boat with bears and lions who proceeded to maul any attackers. Nevertheless, the straightforward meaning of *baado* is that God closed the door of the ark against the waters. Indeed, every usage of *be'ad* in Scripture implies "in front of", as in the verse, *for the LORD had blocked off [be'ad] all the wombs* (20:18). Other cases include, *when you come back in, close the door behind you [baadekh] and your sons* (II Kings 4:4); *skin for [be'ad] skin* (Job 2:4); *a shield in front of me [baadi]* (Psalms 3:4); and *pray on behalf of [be'ad] your servants* (I Samuel 12:19). [In all these cases the word can be understood of to mean "in front" in a general or metaphorical sense.]

יז | **וַתָּרָם מֵעַל הָאָרֶץ.** מְשֻׁקַּעַת הָיְתָה בַּמַּיִם אַחַת עֶשְׂרֵה אַמָּה, כִּסְפִינָה טְעוּנָה שֶׁמְּשֻׁקַּעַת מִקְצָתָהּ בַּמַּיִם, וּמִקְרָאוֹת שֶׁלְּפָנֵינוּ יוֹכִיחוּ:

17 | **וַתָּרָם מֵעַל הָאָרֶץ** – *So that it rose above the land:* The ark sunk eleven cubits beneath the surface of the water like a heavily laden ship, part of which descends below the waves. The following passages will support this calculation.

יח | **וַיִּגְבְּרוּ.** מֵאֲלֵיהֶן:

18 | **וַיִּגְבְּרוּ** – *Surged:* Of their own accord [independent of the rainfall.]

כ | **חֲמֵשׁ עֶשְׂרֵה אַמָּה מִלְמַעְלָה.** לְמַעְלָה שֶׁל גֹּבַהּ כָּל הֶהָרִים לְאַחַר שֶׁהֻשְׁווּ הַמַּיִם לְרָאשֵׁי הֶהָרִים:

20 | **חֲמֵשׁ עֶשְׂרֵה אַמָּה מִלְמַעְלָה** – *Fifteen cubits above them:* After the water level had reached the height of the mountains, it continued to rise an additional fifteen cubits. [That is, the

טו לְמִינֵהוּ וְכָל־הָעוֹף לְמִינֵהוּ כֹּל צִפּוֹר כָּל־כָּנָף: וַיָּבֹאוּ
אֶל־נֹחַ אֶל־הַתֵּבָה שְׁנַיִם שְׁנַיִם מִכָּל־הַבָּשָׂר אֲשֶׁר־
טז בּוֹ רוּחַ חַיִּים: וְהַבָּאִים זָכָר וּנְקֵבָה מִכָּל־בָּשָׂר בָּאוּ
יז כַּאֲשֶׁר צִוָּה אֹתוֹ אֱלֹהִים וַיִּסְגֹּר יְהוָה בַּעֲדוֹ: וַיְהִי שלישי
הַמַּבּוּל אַרְבָּעִים יוֹם עַל־הָאָרֶץ וַיִּרְבּוּ הַמַּיִם וַיִּשְׂאוּ
יח אֶת־הַתֵּבָה וַתָּרָם מֵעַל הָאָרֶץ: וַיִּגְבְּרוּ הַמַּיִם וַיִּרְבּוּ
יט מְאֹד עַל־הָאָרֶץ וַתֵּלֶךְ הַתֵּבָה עַל־פְּנֵי הַמָּיִם: וְהַמַּיִם
גָּבְרוּ מְאֹד מְאֹד עַל־הָאָרֶץ וַיְכֻסּוּ כָּל־הֶהָרִים
כ הַגְּבֹהִים אֲשֶׁר־תַּחַת כָּל־הַשָּׁמָיִם: חֲמֵשׁ עֶשְׂרֵה
כא אַמָּה מִלְמַעְלָה גָּבְרוּ הַמָּיִם וַיְכֻסּוּ הֶהָרִים: וַיִּגְוַע
כָּל־בָּשָׂר ׀ הָרֹמֵשׂ עַל־הָאָרֶץ בָּעוֹף וּבַבְּהֵמָה וּבַחַיָּה
כב וּבְכָל־הַשֶּׁרֶץ הַשֹּׁרֵץ עַל־הָאָרֶץ וְכֹל הָאָדָם: כֹּל
אֲשֶׁר נִשְׁמַת־רוּחַ חַיִּים בְּאַפָּיו מִכֹּל אֲשֶׁר בֶּחָרָבָה
כג מֵתוּ: וַיִּמַח אֶת־כָּל־הַיְקוּם ׀ אֲשֶׁר ׀ עַל־פְּנֵי הָאֲדָמָה

figure fifteen should not be calculated from the surface of the ground, but from the top of the mountains.]

כב | נִשְׁמַת־רוּחַ חַיִּים. נְשָׁמָה שֶׁל רוּחַ חַיִּים:

22 | נִשְׁמַת־רוּחַ חַיִּים – *Breath of life:* [The phrase might be understood to mean "living breath." Rashi clarifies that it means:] The breath of life.

אֲשֶׁר בֶּחָרָבָה. וְלֹא דָגִים שֶׁבַּיָּם:

אֲשֶׁר בֶּחָרָבָה – *On dry land:* Only the animals on dry land perished; this excludes the fish in the sea.

כג | וַיִּמַח. לְשׁוֹן וַיִּפְעַל הוּא וְאֵינוֹ לְשׁוֹן וַיִּפָּעֵל, וְהוּא מִגִּזְרַת ׳וַיִּפֶן׳ ׳וַיִּבֶן׳. כָּל תֵּבָה שֶׁסּוֹפָהּ הֵ״א, כְּגוֹן בָּנָה, מָחָה, קָנָה, כְּשֶׁהוּא נוֹתֵן וָי״ו יוּ״ד בְּרֹאשָׁהּ נָקוּד בְּחִירִיק תַּחַת הַיּוּ״ד:

23 | וַיִּמַח – *Was wiped out:* The verb *vayimaḥ* represents the *kal* [simple] form, not the passive *nifal*. [That is, this is an active verb, meaning that water, or perhaps God, wiped out every living thing.] The verb is similar in form to *vayifen* ["he turned"] and *vayiven* ["he built"]. Every verb ending with a *heh*, such as the verb *kana* ["to acquire"], *maḥa* ["to destroy"], *bana* ["to build"] is vocalized with a *ḥirik* when there is a *vav* or a *yod* at the beginning.

◀

earth was wiped out: from humans to animals, from creeping
creatures to winged birds of the heavens, all were wiped from
the earth. Only Noaḥ and those with him in the ark survived.
24 For one hundred fifty days, the waters surged over the earth.
8 1 Then God remembered Noaḥ and all the wild beasts and animals with him in the ark. God sent a wind over the earth, and
2 the waters began to subside. The wellsprings of the deep and
heavens' floodgates closed, and the heavens' rains were reined
3 in. The water steadily receded from the earth, and by the end

אַךְ־נֹחַ. לְבַד נֹחַ, זֶהוּ פְּשׁוּטוֹ. וּמִדְרַשׁ אַגָּדָה, גּוֹנֵחַ וְכוֹהֶה דָּם מִטֹּרַח הַבְּהֵמוֹת וְהַחַיּוֹת. וְיֵשׁ אוֹמְרִים שֶׁאִחֵר מְזוֹנוֹת לָאֲרִי וְהִכִּישׁוֹ, וְעָלָיו נֶאֱמַר: "הֵן צַדִּיק בָּאָרֶץ יְשֻׁלָּם" (משלי יא, לא):

אַךְ־נֹחַ – *Only Noaḥ:* The straightforward meaning of the word *akh* is "only." However, the Midrash suggests that Noaḥ was groaning and spitting blood because of the trouble that the cattle and wild beasts were giving him. [That is, the word *akh* was Noaḥ's guttural response to his situation.] Some Sages write [in the Midrash] that one day Noaḥ was late serving the lion its food and the big cat bit him. Such does the verse state: *If the righteous person is repaid on earth, certainly the wicked and the sinner will be* [Proverbs 11:31, referring to good people being punished for their infractions].

ח א | **וַיִּזְכֹּר אֱלֹהִים.** זֶה הַשֵּׁם מִדַּת הַדִּין הוּא, וְנֶהֶפְכָה לְמִדַּת רַחֲמִים עַל יְדֵי תְּפִלַּת הַצַּדִּיקִים. וּרְשָׁעָתָן שֶׁל רְשָׁעִים הוֹפֶכֶת מִדַּת רַחֲמִים לְמִדַּת הַדִּין, שֶׁנֶּאֱמַר: "וַיַּרְא ה' כִּי רַבָּה רָעַת הָאָדָם וְגוֹ' וַיֹּאמֶר ה' אֶמְחֶה" (לעיל ו, ה-ז), וְהוּא שֵׁם מִדַּת רַחֲמִים:

8 1 | **וַיִּזְכֹּר אֱלֹהִים** – *Then God remembered:* Even though the name *Elohim* is generally associated with God's attribute of Justice, the text uses the term here to indicate that justice can be transformed into mercy by the prayers of the righteous. Conversely, the wickedness of evil people changes God's sense of mercy to that of justice, as the text states: *The Lord saw how great man's wickedness was upon the earth.... The Lord said, "I will erase My creation, humankind, from the face of the land"* (6:5–7). The name "Lord" appears in that verdict despite generally indicating God's compassion.

וַיִּזְכֹּר אֱלֹהִים אֶת־נֹחַ וְגוֹ'. מַה זָּכַר לָהֶם לַבְּהֵמוֹת? זְכוּת שֶׁלֹּא הִשְׁחִיתוּ דַּרְכָּם קֹדֶם לָכֵן, וְשֶׁלֹּא שִׁמְּשׁוּ בַּתֵּבָה:

וַיִּזְכֹּר אֱלֹהִים אֶת־נֹחַ – *Then God remembered Noaḥ:* [The verse states that God remembered the animals as well.] What did God remember with regard to the animals? God recalled that the animals had not corrupted their ways before the flood, nor did they copulate while in the ark.

וַיַּעֲבֵר אֱלֹהִים רוּחַ. רוּחַ תַּנְחוּמִין וַהֲנָחָה עָבְרָה לְפָנָיו:

וַיַּעֲבֵר אֱלֹהִים רוּחַ – *God sent a wind:* A wind of comfort and relief passed before Him.

עַל־הָאָרֶץ. עַל עִסְקֵי הָאָרֶץ:

עַל־הָאָרֶץ – *Over the earth:* [The earth was submerged in water. This phrase actually means:] "Because of what had happened on the earth."

מֵאָדָם עַד־בְּהֵמָה עַד־רֶמֶשׂ וְעַד־עוֹף הַשָּׁמַיִם וַיִּמָּחוּ
כד מִן־הָאָרֶץ וַיִּשָּׁאֶר אַךְ־נֹחַ וַאֲשֶׁר אִתּוֹ בַּתֵּבָה: וַיִּגְבְּרוּ
ח א הַמַּיִם עַל־הָאָרֶץ חֲמִשִּׁים וּמְאַת יוֹם: וַיִּזְכֹּר אֱלֹהִים ו
אֶת־נֹחַ וְאֵת כָּל־הַחַיָּה וְאֶת־כָּל־הַבְּהֵמָה אֲשֶׁר אִתּוֹ
בַּתֵּבָה וַיַּעֲבֵר אֱלֹהִים רוּחַ עַל־הָאָרֶץ וַיָּשֹׁכּוּ הַמָּיִם:
ב וַיִּסָּכְרוּ מַעְיְנֹת תְּהוֹם וַאֲרֻבֹּת הַשָּׁמָיִם וַיִּכָּלֵא הַגֶּשֶׁם
ג מִן־הַשָּׁמָיִם: וַיָּשֻׁבוּ הַמַּיִם מֵעַל הָאָרֶץ הָלוֹךְ וָשׁוֹב

וַיָּשֹׁכּוּ – *Began to subside:* The verb *vayashokku* is similar to its use in the verse *King Aḥashverosh's rage had subsided [keshokh]* (Esther 2:1), and it connotes the waning of anger.

וַיָּשֹׁכּוּ. כְּמוֹ: "כְּשֹׁךְ חֲמַת הַמֶּלֶךְ" (אסתר ב, א), לְשׁוֹן הֲנָחַת חֵמָה:

2 | **וַיִּסָּכְרוּ מַעְיְנֹת** – *The wellsprings of the deep closed:* When the water was released, the text states, *on that day, all the wellsprings of the great deep burst, and the heavens' floodgates opened* (7:11), whereas in the current verse the Torah omits the adjective "all." This is because those springs which are necessary for the world remained open. These include the hot springs of Tiberias and the like.

ב | וַיִּסָּכְרוּ מַעְיְנֹת. כְּשֶׁנִּפְתְּחוּ כְּתִיב: "כָּל מַעְיְנוֹת" (לעיל ז, יא) וְכָאן אֵין כְּתִיב 'כָּל', לְפִי שֶׁנִּשְׁתַּיְּרוּ מֵהֶם אוֹתָן שֶׁיֵּשׁ בָּהֶם צֹרֶךְ לָעוֹלָם, כְּגוֹן חַמֵּי טְבֶרְיָא וְכַיּוֹצֵא בָּהֶן:

וַיִּכָּלֵא – *Were reined in:* The rain was prevented from falling. The verb *vayikkale* appears similarly in the verse *As for You, Lord, do not withhold [tikhla] Your compassion from me* (Psalms 40:12), and in the verse *None of us will refuse [yikhleh] you his tomb to bury your dead"* (Genesis 23:6).

וַיִּכָּלֵא. וַיִּמָּנַע, כְּמוֹ: "לֹא תִכְלָא רַחֲמֶיךָ" (תהלים מ, יב), "לֹא יִכְלֶה מִמְּךָ" (להלן כג, ו):

3 | **מִקְצֵה חֲמִשִּׁים וּמְאַת יוֹם** – *By the end of one hundred fifty days:* The waters began to recede on the first day of the month of Sivan. How is this date calculated? The rains ceased on the twenty-seventh of Kislev. Add to the last three days of Kislev [28–30] the twenty-nine days of Tevet for a total of thirty-two days. The month of Shevat [which is full with thirty days], the month of Adar [which is deficient with twenty-nine days], the month of Nisan [that is full with thirty days], and the month of Iyar [deficient with twenty-nine] add up to one hundred and eighteen days. [With the addition of the thirty-two days from Kislev and Tevet] we reach a total of one hundred and fifty days. [Although Rashi writes here that the rain stopped falling on the twenty-seventh of Kislev, in his explanation to

ג | מִקְצֵה חֲמִשִּׁים וּמְאַת יוֹם. הִתְחִילוּ לַחְסֹר, וְהוּא אֶחָד בְּסִיוָן, כֵּיצַד? בְּעֶשְׂרִים וְשִׁבְעָה בְּכִסְלֵו פָּסְקוּ הַגְּשָׁמִים, הֲרֵי שְׁלֹשָׁה מִכִּסְלֵו וְעֶשְׂרִים וְתִשְׁעָה מִטֵּבֵת הֲרֵי שְׁלֹשִׁים וּשְׁנַיִם, וּשְׁבָט וַאֲדָר וְנִיסָן וְאִיָּר מֵאָה וּשְׁמוֹנָה עָשָׂר, הֲרֵי מֵאָה וַחֲמִשִּׁים:

4 of one hundred fifty days, the water had abated. In the seventh
month, on the seventeenth day of the month, the ark came to
5 rest on the mountains of Ararat. The water continued to abate
until the tenth month, and on the first day of the tenth month,

7:12 he maintains that the rain stopped on the twenty-eighth of that month. Various theories have been offered to reconcile these two positions.]

ד | **בַּחֹדֶשׁ הַשְּׁבִיעִי.** סִיוָן, וְהוּא שְׁבִיעִי לְכִסְלֵו שֶׁבּוֹ פָּסְקוּ הַגְּשָׁמִים:

4 | **בַּחֹדֶשׁ הַשְּׁבִיעִי** – *In the seventh month:* This refers to the month of Sivan, which is the seventh month counting from Kislev [although Sivan is the ninth month counting from Tishrei] for the rains ceased to fall in the month of Kislev.

בְּשִׁבְעָה־עָשָׂר יוֹם. מִכָּאן אַתָּה לָמֵד שֶׁהָיְתָה הַתֵּבָה מְשֻׁקַּעַת בַּמַּיִם אַחַת עֶשְׂרֵה אַמָּה, שֶׁהֲרֵי כְּתִיב: "בָּעֲשִׂירִי בְּאֶחָד לַחֹדֶשׁ נִרְאוּ רָאשֵׁי הֶהָרִים", זֶה אָב שֶׁהוּא עֲשִׂירִי לְמַרְחֶשְׁוָן לִירִידַת גְּשָׁמִים, וְהֵם הָיוּ גְּבוֹהִים עַל הֶהָרִים חֲמֵשׁ עֶשְׂרֵה אַמָּה, וְחָסְרוּ מִיּוֹם אֶחָד בְּסִיוָן עַד אֶחָד בְּאָב חֲמֵשׁ עֶשְׂרֵה אַמָּה לְשִׁשִּׁים יוֹם, הֲרֵי אַמָּה לְאַרְבָּעָה יָמִים, נִמְצָא שֶׁבְּשִׁשָּׁה עָשָׂר שֶׁל סִיוָן לֹא חָסְרוּ אֶלָּא אַרְבַּע אַמּוֹת, וְנָחָה הַתֵּבָה לְיוֹם הַמָּחֳרָת, לָמַדְתָּ שֶׁהָיְתָה מְשֻׁקַּעַת אַחַת עֶשְׂרֵה אַמָּה בַּמַּיִם שֶׁעַל רָאשֵׁי הֶהָרִים:

בְּשִׁבְעָה־עָשָׂר יוֹם – *On the seventeenth:* This verse teaches that the ark was submerged beneath the water to a depth of eleven cubits, a fact reached through the following reasoning. The next verse states: *On the first day of the tenth month, the mountaintops became visible* (8:5), referring to the month of Av, which is the tenth month counting from Marḥeshvan, the month when the rains began. [According to 7:11, the rain began to fall on the seventeenth of the second month, Marḥeshvan. Av comes ten months later, although Av is usually considered the eleventh month when counting from Tishrei.] Now because the water rose fifteen cubits above the mountains [as stated in 7:20], and the waters decreased from the first of Sivan [as Rashi argues above] until the first of Av, that means that the waters receded fifteen cubits over a span of sixty days. [Adding Sivan's thirty days to Tamuz's twenty-nine days and the first of Av yields a total of sixty.] Hence, the water drained at a rate of one cubit every four days. What emerges is that on the sixteenth of the month of Sivan the water had gone down just four cubits. And since on the next day the ark came to rest [on the mountains of Ararat], we learn that the ark was submerged eleven cubits in the water on top of the mountains. [That is, the bottom of the boat landed on the mountaintop on the seventh of Av, but there were still eleven cubits of water rising from the mountain top to the surface. The water began to recede on the first of Sivan and continued to abate until the first of Av. But in the meantime, the ark came to rest on the seventeenth of Sivan.]

ה | **בָּעֲשִׂירִי... נִרְאוּ רָאשֵׁי הֶהָרִים.** זֶה אָב שֶׁהוּא עֲשִׂירִי לְמַרְחֶשְׁוָן שֶׁהִתְחִיל הַגֶּשֶׁם. וְאִם תֹּאמַר, הוּא

5 | **בָּעֲשִׂירִי... נִרְאוּ רָאשֵׁי הֶהָרִים** – *Of the tenth month, the mountaintops became visible:* This refers to the month of Av, which is the tenth month counting from Marḥeshvan, when the rain

◀

ד וַיַּחְסְרוּ הַמַּיִם מִקְצֵה חֲמִשִּׁים וּמְאַת יוֹם: וַתָּנַח
הַתֵּבָה בַּחֹדֶשׁ הַשְּׁבִיעִי בְּשִׁבְעָה־עָשָׂר יוֹם לַחֹדֶשׁ
ה עַל הָרֵי אֲרָרָט: וְהַמַּיִם הָיוּ הָלוֹךְ וְחָסוֹר עַד הַחֹדֶשׁ
הָעֲשִׂירִי בָּעֲשִׂירִי בְּאֶחָד לַחֹדֶשׁ נִרְאוּ רָאשֵׁי הֶהָרִים:

started falling [on the seventeenth. Usually, Av is considered the eleventh month of the year]. Now, one might argue that perhaps this verse refers to Elul, which is the tenth month counting from Kislev, the month when the rain ceased to fall [on the twenty-seventh, as Rashi writes in comments to 8:3]. For one could imagine that just as when verse 4 states that *in the seventh month the ark came to rest*, that reckoning is worked out from Kislev, when the rain ceased to fall, [similarly, in the current verse, the calculation should start from Kislev and hence the tenth month should be Elul. In this way the counting would be uniform throughout the passage. Rashi proceeds to refute this argument.] We cannot say [that both verses count from Kislev]. We must count seven months [mentioned in verse 4] from the end of the rains [in Kislev, and not from their start in Marḥeshvan], since the text has already stated above that the forty days of rainfall combined with the one hundred and fifty days that the water prevailed on the earth take us to the first of Sivan [a conclusion Rashi explains in comments to verse 3. Now if we claim that the seventh month referred to in verse 4 is] the seventh month from when the rains started [on the seventeenth of Marḥeshvan, that] takes us not to Sivan [but to Iyar, the month preceding Sivan, and we cannot argue that the ark came to rest while the waters were still surging over the planet]. Conversely, the tenth month mentioned in verse 5 must be counted from when the rains started [in Marḥeshvan]. For if we suggest that the text means the tenth month from when the rains ceased [in Kislev, and that the mountains became visible on the first of] Elul, the subsequent verse makes no sense when it states: *By the first day of the first month…the water on the earth dried up* (8:13). This is due to the following calculation. *After forty days* (8:6) had elapsed from when the mountaintops had become visible [as stated in 8:5] Noaḥ *sent a raven forth* (8:7), and after waiting twenty-one days he released the dove. [Seven days after Noaḥ sent out the raven, he dispatched the dove for the first time. The dove returned to him and seven days later he sent it out

אֱלוּל וַעֲשִׂירִי לְכִסְלֵו שֶׁפָּסַק הַגֶּשֶׁם, כְּשֵׁם שֶׁאַתָּה אוֹמֵר "בַּחֹדֶשׁ הַשְּׁבִיעִי" סִיוָן וְהוּא שְׁבִיעִי לַהַפְסָקָה – אִי אֶפְשָׁר לוֹמַר כֵּן, עַל כָּרְחֲךָ שְׁבִיעִי אִי אַתָּה מוֹנֶה אֶלָּא לַהַפְסָקָה, שֶׁהֲרֵי לֹא כָּלוּ אַרְבָּעִים יוֹם שֶׁל יְרִידַת גְּשָׁמִים וּמֵאָה וַחֲמִשִּׁים שֶׁל תִּגְבֹּרֶת הַמַּיִם עַד אֶחָד בְּסִיוָן. וְאִם אַתָּה אוֹמֵר שְׁבִיעִי לַיְּרִידָה אֵין זֶה סִיוָן. וְהָעֲשִׂירִי אִי אֶפְשָׁר לִמְנוֹת אֶלָּא לַיְּרִידָה, שֶׁאִם אַתָּה אוֹמֵר לַהַפְסָקָה וְהוּא אֱלוּל, אִי אַתָּה מוֹצֵא "בָּרִאשׁוֹן בְּאֶחָד לַחֹדֶשׁ חָרְבוּ הַמַּיִם מֵעַל הָאָרֶץ" (להלן פסוק יג), שֶׁהֲרֵי מִקֵּץ אַרְבָּעִים יוֹם מִשֶּׁנִּרְאוּ רָאשֵׁי הֶהָרִים שִׁלַּח אֶת הָעוֹרֵב, וְעֶשְׂרִים וְאַחַת יוֹם הוֹחִיל בִּשְׁלִיחוּת הַיּוֹנָה, הֲרֵי שִׁשִּׁים יוֹם מִשֶּׁנִּרְאוּ רָאשֵׁי הֶהָרִים עַד שֶׁחָרְבוּ פְּנֵי הָאֲדָמָה. וְאִם תֹּאמַר בֶּאֱלוּל נִרְאוּ, נִמְצָא שֶׁחָרְבוּ בְּמַרְחֶשְׁוָן, וְהוּא קוֹרֵא אוֹתוֹ רִאשׁוֹן?! וְאֵין זֶה אֶלָּא תִּשְׁרֵי שֶׁהוּא רִאשׁוֹן לִבְרִיאַת עוֹלָם, וּלְרַבִּי יְהוֹשֻׁעַ הוּא נִיסָן:

6 the mountaintops became visible. After forty days Noaḥ
7 opened the window he had made in the ark and sent a raven
forth. It flew to and fro until the water on the earth had dried.
8 After that he sent forth a dove to see whether the water had
9 subsided from the face of the land. But the dove found no
resting place to plant its foot, and so it returned to him, to the
ark, for water still covered the face of the earth completely. He
reached out his hand and brought the dove back to him, into
10 the ark. Then he waited another seven days, and again he sent

again. This second time it came back with an olive branch. The third mission took place after an additional seven days, for a total of twenty-one days.] This means that sixty full days passed between the time that *the mountaintops became visible* (8:5) and the point that the earth became dry [counting the fortieth day as the first of the subsequent twenty-one days]. Were we to argue that the mountaintops only became visible in Elul [that is, that we should consider the tenth month mentioned in verse 5 as the tenth from Kislev] that would mean that the earth would not have become dry until Marḥeshvan [of the second year, sixty days after the mountaintops had been cleared of water]. Now, why would that month be called the first month in the text? It is only the month of Tishrei which can be referred to the first month, since that is when the world was created – although Rabbi Yehoshua holds that that was Nisan. [Therefore, we must conclude that the mountaintops already became visible in Av, the tenth month after Marḥeshvan, and not in Elul, the tenth month after Kislev, since that would push off the drying of the earth to the second Marḥeshvan, which verse 13 would not have referred to as the first month.]

ו | מִקֵּץ אַרְבָּעִים יוֹם. מִשֶּׁנִּרְאוּ רָאשֵׁי הֶהָרִים:

6 | **מִקֵּץ אַרְבָּעִים יוֹם** – *After forty days:* The verse refers to forty days after the mountaintops became visible.

אֶת־חַלּוֹן הַתֵּבָה אֲשֶׁר עָשָׂה. לְצֹהַר, וְלֹא זֶה פֶּתַח הַתֵּבָה הֶעָשׂוּי לְבִיאָה וִיצִיאָה:

אֶת־חַלּוֹן הַתֵּבָה אֲשֶׁר עָשָׂה – *The window he had made in the ark:* This refers to the *tzohar* window [mentioned in 6:16, which Noaḥ put in the ark to provide light], and not to the door of the vessel made for coming in and going out.

ז | יָצוֹא וָשׁוֹב. הוֹלֵךְ וּמַקִּיף סְבִיבוֹת הַתֵּבָה, וְלֹא הָלַךְ בִּשְׁלִיחוּתוֹ, שֶׁהָיָה חוֹשְׁדוֹ עַל בַּת זוּגוֹ, כְּמוֹ שֶׁשָּׁנִינוּ בְּאַגָּדַת 'חֵלֶק' (סנהדרין קח ע״ב):

7 | **יָצוֹא וָשׁוֹב** – *To and fro:* The raven flew around and around the ark, refusing to leave on its mission. This was because the bird suspected that Noaḥ had designs on its mate as we learn from the midrash in tractate Sanhedrin (108b).

ו וַיְהִי מִקֵּץ אַרְבָּעִים יוֹם וַיִּפְתַּח נֹחַ אֶת־חַלּוֹן הַתֵּבָה
ז אֲשֶׁר עָשָׂה׃ וַיְשַׁלַּח אֶת־הָעֹרֵב וַיֵּצֵא יָצוֹא וָשׁוֹב
ח עַד־יְבֹשֶׁת הַמַּיִם מֵעַל הָאָרֶץ׃ וַיְשַׁלַּח אֶת־הַיּוֹנָה
ט מֵאִתּוֹ לִרְאוֹת הֲקַלּוּ הַמַּיִם מֵעַל פְּנֵי הָאֲדָמָה׃ וְלֹא־
מָצְאָה הַיּוֹנָה מָנוֹחַ לְכַף־רַגְלָהּ וַתָּשָׁב אֵלָיו אֶל־
הַתֵּבָה כִּי־מַיִם עַל־פְּנֵי כָל־הָאָרֶץ וַיִּשְׁלַח יָדוֹ וַיִּקָּחֶהָ
י וַיָּבֵא אֹתָהּ אֵלָיו אֶל־הַתֵּבָה׃ וַיָּחֶל עוֹד שִׁבְעַת יָמִים

עַד־יְבֹשֶׁת הַמַּיִם – *Until the water on earth had dried:* The straightforward meaning of the clause is its literal sense. [The raven continued to fly around until the land dried up.] But the homiletic interpretation is as follows. The raven was selected for a different mission that was required when the earth dried up in the days of Eliyahu. There we read: *The ravens brought [Eliyahu] bread and meat each morning and bread and meat each evening* (I Kings 17:6).

עַד־יְבֹשֶׁת הַמַּיִם. פְּשׁוּטוֹ כְּמַשְׁמָעוֹ. אֲבָל מִדְרַשׁ אַגָּדָה: מוּכָן הָיָה הָעוֹרֵב לִשְׁלִיחוּת אַחֶרֶת בַּעֲצִירַת גְּשָׁמִים בִּימֵי אֵלִיָּהוּ, שֶׁנֶּאֱמַר: "וְהָעֹרְבִים מְבִיאִים לוֹ לֶחֶם וּבָשָׂר" (מלכים א' יז, ו):

8 | **וַיְשַׁלַּח אֶת־הַיּוֹנָה** – *After that he sent forth a dove:* Seven days after [the raven's flight, Noaḥ released the dove. We can infer that a week had passed because the text subsequently states] *Then he waited another seven days* (8:10). Since the latter verse claims that Noaḥ waited an additional seven days, that implies that he initially waited seven days before first sending out the dove.

ח | וַיְשַׁלַּח אֶת־הַיּוֹנָה. לְסוֹף שִׁבְעָה יָמִים, שֶׁהֲרֵי כְּתִיב (להלן פסוק י): "וַיָּחֶל עוֹד שִׁבְעַת יָמִים אֲחֵרִים", מִכְּלָל זֶה אַתָּה לָמֵד שֶׁאַף בָּרִאשׁוֹנָה הוֹחִיל שִׁבְעָה יָמִים:

וַיְשַׁלַּח – *After that he sent:* The verb does not mean that Noaḥ sent the bird out on a mission, but that he threw the bird out of the boat to go on its way. As such, Noaḥ would be able to determine *whether the water had subsided.* For if the bird found a place to rest, it would not return to the ark. [In other words, Noaḥ did not send the bird out with the job of ascertaining the state of the world, as the dove was incapable of accepting a mission. Noaḥ just sent the bird out of the ark to fly about naturally, so that Noaḥ himself could learn if the waters had receded.]

וַיְשַׁלַּח. אֵין זֶה לְשׁוֹן שְׁלִיחוּת אֶלָּא לְשׁוֹן שִׁלּוּחַ, שִׁלְּחָהּ לָלֶכֶת לְדַרְכָּהּ, וּבְזוֹ יִרְאֶה אִם קַלּוּ הַמַּיִם, שֶׁאִם תִּמְצָא מָנוֹחַ לֹא תָשׁוּב אֵלָיו:

10 | **וַיָּחֶל** – *Then he waited:* The verb *vayaḥel* connotes waiting, as in the verse *They listened to me and waited [veyiḥellu]* (Job 29:21). There are many such usages in Scripture.

י | וַיָּחֶל. לְשׁוֹן הַמְתָּנָה, וְכֵן: "לִי שָׁמְעוּ וְיִחֵלּוּ" (איוב כט, כא), וְהַרְבֵּה יֵשׁ בַּמִּקְרָא:

11 the dove forth from the ark. The dove came back to him in
the evening – and in its beak was a freshly picked olive leaf.
Noaḥ knew then that the water had subsided from the earth.
12 He waited another seven days and again sent forth the
13 dove – and it returned to him no more. So it was that, by the
first day of the first month of Noaḥ's six hundred and first
year, the water on the earth dried up. Noaḥ removed the cov-
14 ering of the ark and saw that the face of the land was dry. By
the twenty-seventh day of the second month, the earth had
15 16 dried completely. Then God said to Noaḥ, "Leave REVI'I
the ark – you, and your wife, your sons, and your sons' wives
17 with you. And every living thing with you – birds, animals,

יא | **טָרָף בְּפִיהָ.** אוֹמֵר אֲנִי שֶׁזָּכָר הָיָה, לְכָךְ הוּא קוֹרֵהוּ פְּעָמִים לְשׁוֹן זָכָר וּפְעָמִים לְשׁוֹן נְקֵבָה, לְפִי שֶׁכָּל יוֹנָה שֶׁבַּמִּקְרָא לְשׁוֹן נְקֵבָה, כְּמוֹ: "כְּיוֹנֵי הַגֵּאָיוֹת כֻּלָּם הֹמוֹת" (יחזקאל ז, טז), וְכֵן: "כְּיוֹנָה פוֹתָה" (הושע ז, יא):

11 | **טָרָף בְּפִיהָ** – *In its beak, freshly picked:* [The term *befiha*, literally, "in her mouth," suggests that the noun *yona*, dove, is feminine.] Now I maintain that the bird Noaḥ dispatched was a male, which explains why the text sometimes refers to it in the masculine form, and sometimes in the feminine. For every appearance of the term "dove" in Scripture presents it as feminine, as in the verse, *like doves of the valley, crying [homot], all of them* [Ezekiel 7:16; the verb *homot* is a feminine construction, where the masculine would be *homim*], and in the verse, *like an easily wooed, witless [fota] dove* [Hosea 7:11, instead of *foteh*. Rashi is teaching that the species of animal is referred to in the feminine regardless of whether the specimen under discussion is male or female.]

טָרָף. חָטַף. וּמִדְרַשׁ אַגָּדָה לְשׁוֹן מָזוֹן, וְדָרְשׁוּ "בְּפִיהָ" לְשׁוֹן מַאֲמָר, אָמְרָה: יִהְיוּ מְזוֹנוֹתַי מְרוּרִין כְּזַיִת זוֹ וּבְיָדוֹ שֶׁל הַקָּדוֹשׁ בָּרוּךְ הוּא וְאַל יִהְיוּ מְתוּקִים כִּדְבַשׁ וּבְיַד בָּשָׂר וָדָם:

טָרָף – *Picked:* The verb *taraf* means that the dove plucked the leaf from the tree [as opposed to finding it lying on the ground or floating on the water]. Now according to the Midrash, the term *taraf* means "food", whereas the word *befiha* connotes "speech" [that is, the bird was asking for food]. For the dove said: I would rather have bitter food like the leaf of an olive tree if it is provided by the Holy One, blessed be He, than food that is sweet like honey but served by human beings.

יב | **וַיִּיָּחֶל.** הוּא לְשׁוֹן 'וַיָּחֶל' (לעיל פסוק י), אֶלָּא שֶׁזֶּה לְשׁוֹן וַיִּפְעַל וְזֶה לְשׁוֹן וַיִּתְפַּעֵל, 'וַיָּחֶל' וַיַּמְתֵּן, 'וַיִּיָּחֶל' וַיִּתְמַתֵּן:

12 | **וַיִּיָּחֶל** – *He waited:* The term *vayiyyaḥel* means the same as the word *vayaḥel* [in verse 10]. However, that construct represents the simple form ["he waited"], whereas the current word suggests the reflexive ["he made himself wait"]. Thus, *vayaḥel* is the equivalent of *vayamten* ["he waited"], and *vayiyyaḥel* corresponds to *vayitmatten* [in the reflexive *hitpael* form.]

יא אֲחֵרִים וַיֹּסֶף שַׁלַּח אֶת־הַיּוֹנָה מִן־הַתֵּבָה: וַתָּבֹא
אֵלָיו הַיּוֹנָה לְעֵת עֶרֶב וְהִנֵּה עֲלֵה־זַיִת טָרָף בְּפִיהָ
יב וַיֵּדַע נֹחַ כִּי־קַלּוּ הַמַּיִם מֵעַל הָאָרֶץ: וַיִּיָּחֶל עוֹד
שִׁבְעַת יָמִים אֲחֵרִים וַיְשַׁלַּח אֶת־הַיּוֹנָה וְלֹא־יָסְפָה
יג שׁוּב־אֵלָיו עוֹד: וַיְהִי בְּאַחַת וְשֵׁשׁ־מֵאוֹת שָׁנָה
בָּרִאשׁוֹן בְּאֶחָד לַחֹדֶשׁ חָרְבוּ הַמַּיִם מֵעַל הָאָרֶץ
וַיָּסַר נֹחַ אֶת־מִכְסֵה הַתֵּבָה וַיַּרְא וְהִנֵּה חָרְבוּ פְּנֵי
יד הָאֲדָמָה: וּבַחֹדֶשׁ הַשֵּׁנִי בְּשִׁבְעָה וְעֶשְׂרִים יוֹם לַחֹדֶשׁ
טו יָבְשָׁה הָאָרֶץ: וַיְדַבֵּר אֱלֹהִים אֶל־נֹחַ ז רביעי
טז לֵאמֹר: צֵא מִן־הַתֵּבָה אַתָּה וְאִשְׁתְּךָ וּבָנֶיךָ וּנְשֵׁי־
יז בָנֶיךָ אִתָּךְ: כָּל־הַחַיָּה אֲשֶׁר־אִתְּךָ מִכָּל־בָּשָׂר בָּעוֹף

13 | בָּרִאשׁוֹן – *By the first:* According to Rabbi Eliezer, the first month mentioned here refers to Tishrei, whereas Rabbi Yehoshua maintains it is Nisan.

יג | בָּרִאשׁוֹן. לְרַבִּי אֱלִיעֶזֶר הוּא תִּשְׁרֵי וּלְרַבִּי יְהוֹשֻׁעַ הוּא נִיסָן:

חָרְבוּ – *Dried up:* The earth became like mud with a hard crust on its surface [while remaining moist beneath.]

חָרְבוּ. נַעֲשָׂה כְּמִין טִיט, שֶׁקָּרְמוּ פָּנֶיהָ שֶׁל מַעְלָה:

14 | יָבְשָׁה – *Had dried: By the twenty-seventh day of the second month* the soil had returned to its natural state. Now the rains first started to fall on the seventeenth of the second month [one year before, as reported in 7:11]. The extra eleven days represent the eleven-day difference between the length of the solar year [365 days] and that of the lunar year [354 days], for the punishment meted out to the generation of the flood lasted a full year.

יד | יָבְשָׁה. נַעֲשֵׂית גָּרִיד כְּהִלְכָתָהּ. "בְּשִׁבְעָה וְעֶשְׂרִים", וִירִידָתוֹ בַּחֹדֶשׁ הַשֵּׁנִי בְּשִׁבְעָה עָשָׂר, אֵלּוּ אַחַד עָשָׂר יָמִים שֶׁהַחַמָּה יְתֵרָה עַל הַלְּבָנָה, שֶׁמִּשְׁפַּט דּוֹר הַמַּבּוּל שָׁנָה תְּמִימָה הָיָה:

16 | אַתָּה וְאִשְׁתְּךָ – *You and your wife:* Man and wife were permitted to exit the ark together, indicating that once the inhabitants left the boat they were permitted sexual intimacy.

טז | אַתָּה וְאִשְׁתְּךָ וְגוֹ'. אִישׁ וְאִשְׁתּוֹ, כָּאן הִתִּיר לָהֶם תַּשְׁמִישׁ הַמִּטָּה:

17 | **הוצא** – *Bring them out:* The verb here is written with a *vav* [*hotze*] but it is read as if written with a *yod* [*haytze*]. This anomaly suggests that Noaḥ was to instruct the animals to leave the ark, but if they refused to go out, he was to lead them out – *hotze* – against their will.

יז | **הוצא**. כְּתִיב, 'הַיְצֵא' קְרִי. "הַיְצֵא" – אֱמֹר לָהֶם שֶׁיֵּצְאוּ, "הוֹצֵא" – אִם אֵין רוֹצִים לָצֵאת הוֹצִיאֵם אַתָּה:

and all wild beasts that walk the earth – bring them out with
you. Let them swarm again on the earth and be fertile and
18 multiply upon it." So Noaḥ came out with his sons, his wife,
19 and his sons' wives. Every beast, creeping thing, winged creature, everything that creeps across the earth, emerged from
20 the ark by families. Then Noaḥ built an altar to the LORD and,
taking of each of the kinds of pure animals and pure birds, sac-
21 rificed burnt offerings on the altar. The LORD smelled the fragrant aroma and said in His heart, "Never again will I curse
the land because of man; the devisings of the human heart are
evil from its youth. And never again will I destroy all life as I
22 have done. As long as earth and time endure – sowing time
and harvest, cold and heat, summer, winter, day, and night will

וְשָׁרְצוּ בָאָרֶץ. וְלֹא בַּתֵּבָה, מַגִּיד שֶׁאַף הַבְּהֵמָה וְהָעוֹף נֶאֶסְרוּ בְּתַשְׁמִישׁ:

וְשָׁרְצוּ בָאָרֶץ – *Let them swarm again on the earth:* The animals are not permitted to procreate while still on board the ark. We learn from this emphasis that the birds and the animals as well [in addition to the humans] were forbidden to be intimate during the flood.

יט | **לְמִשְׁפְּחֹתֵיהֶם.** קִבְּלוּ עֲלֵיהֶם עַל מְנָת לְדָבֵק בְּמִינָן:

19 | **לְמִשְׁפְּחֹתֵיהֶם** – *By families:* When the animals left the ark, they agreed to God's condition to cleave to their own species.

כ | **מִכֹּל הַבְּהֵמָה הַטְּהֹרָה.** אָמַר: לֹא צִוָּה לִי הַקָּדוֹשׁ בָּרוּךְ הוּא לְהַכְנִיס מֵאֵלּוּ שִׁבְעָה שִׁבְעָה אֶלָּא כְּדֵי לְהַקְרִיב קָרְבָּן מֵהֶם:

20 | **מִכֹּל הַבְּהֵמָה הַטְּהֹרָה** – *Each of the kinds of pure animals:* Said Noaḥ: The only reason that the Holy One, blessed be He, ordered me to take seven pairs of the pure animals onto the ark, was to later offer them as sacrifices.

כא | **מִנְּעֻרָיו.** 'מִנְּעָרָיו' כְּתִיב, מִשֶּׁנִּנְעַר לָצֵאת מִמְּעֵי אִמּוֹ נִתַּן בּוֹ יֵצֶר הָרָע:

21 | **מִנְּעֻרָיו** – *From its youth:* The term *mine'urav* ["from his youth"] is written without a *vav* [after the *ayin*] and as such, appears like *mine'arav*. This indicates that when a fetus moves itself [*nin'ar*] to emerge from its mother's womb, its evil inclination has already taken hold.

לֹא אֹסִף... וְלֹא־אֹסִף. כָּפַל הַדָּבָר לִשְׁבוּעָה, הוּא שֶׁכָּתוּב (ישעיה נד, ט): "אֲשֶׁר נִשְׁבַּעְתִּי מֵעֲבֹר מֵי נֹחַ", וְלֹא מָצִינוּ בָּהּ שְׁבוּעָה אֶלָּא זוֹ שֶׁכָּפַל דְּבָרָיו וְהִיא שְׁבוּעָה, וְכֵן דָּרְשׁוּ חֲכָמִים בְּמַסֶּכֶת שְׁבוּעוֹת (דף לו ע"א):

לֹא אֹסִף... וְלֹא־אֹסִף – *Never again... never again:* God repeats His determination here as an oath. Thus, when the verse states: *I swore that the waters of Noaḥ would never sweep again over the earth* (Isaiah 54:9), it is referring to this repeated statement, as there was no explicit oath. This is the interpretation of our Sages in tractate Shevuot (36a).

◀

וּבַבְּהֵמָה וּבְכׇל־הָרֶמֶשׂ הָרֹמֵשׂ עַל־הָאָרֶץ הוֹצֵא הַיְצֵא
יח אִתָּךְ וְשָׁרְצוּ בָאָרֶץ וּפָרוּ וְרָבוּ עַל־הָאָרֶץ: וַיֵּצֵא־נֹחַ
יט וּבָנָיו וְאִשְׁתּוֹ וּנְשֵׁי־בָנָיו אִתּוֹ: כׇּל־הַחַיָּה כׇּל־הָרֶמֶשׂ
וְכׇל־הָעוֹף כֹּל רוֹמֵשׂ עַל־הָאָרֶץ לְמִשְׁפְּחֹתֵיהֶם יָצְאוּ
כ מִן־הַתֵּבָה: וַיִּבֶן נֹחַ מִזְבֵּחַ לַיהוָה וַיִּקַּח מִכֹּל ׀
הַבְּהֵמָה הַטְּהֹרָה וּמִכֹּל הָעוֹף הַטָּהֹר וַיַּעַל עֹלֹת
כא בַּמִּזְבֵּחַ: וַיָּרַח יהוה אֶת־רֵיחַ הַנִּיחֹחַ וַיֹּאמֶר יהוה
אֶל־לִבּוֹ לֹא אֹסִף לְקַלֵּל עוֹד אֶת־הָאֲדָמָה בַּעֲבוּר
הָאָדָם כִּי יֵצֶר לֵב הָאָדָם רַע מִנְּעֻרָיו וְלֹא־אֹסִף עוֹד
כב לְהַכּוֹת אֶת־כׇּל־חַי כַּאֲשֶׁר עָשִׂיתִי: עֹד כׇּל־יְמֵי הָאָרֶץ
זֶרַע וְקָצִיר וְקֹר וָחֹם וְקַיִץ וָחֹרֶף וְיוֹם וָלַיְלָה לֹא

כב | עֹד כׇּל־יְמֵי הָאָרֶץ וְגוֹ׳ לֹא יִשְׁבֹּתוּ. שִׁשָּׁה עִתִּים הַלָּלוּ, שְׁנֵי חֳדָשִׁים לְכׇל אֶחָד וְאֶחָד, כְּמוֹ שֶׁשָּׁנִינוּ: חֲצִי תִּשְׁרֵי וּמַרְחֶשְׁוָן וַחֲצִי כִּסְלֵו – זֶרַע, חֲצִי כִּסְלֵו וְטֵבֵת וַחֲצִי שְׁבָט – קֹר וְכוּ׳, כִּבְבָא מְצִיעָא (דף קו ע״ב):

22 | עֹד כׇּל־יְמֵי הָאָרֶץ... לֹא יִשְׁבֹּתוּ. – *As long as earth and time endure... will not cease:* The six periods listed here [aside from day and night] represent the entire length of the year – each of the terms signifies two months. This is taught in Bava Metzia (106b): The second half of the month of Tishrei, together with the month of Marḥeshvan and the first half of the month of Kislev comprise the sowing season. The second half of Kislev combined with month of Tevet and the first half of Shevat constitute the cold season, and so forth.

קֹר. קָשֶׁה מֵחֹרֶף:

קֹר – *Cold:* The term *kor* signifies harsher weather than mere winter [*ḥoref*].

וָחֹרֶף. עֵת זֶרַע שְׂעוֹרִים וְקִטְנִיּוֹת הַחֲרִיפִין לְהִתְבַּשֵּׁל מַהֵר, וְהוּא חֲצִי שְׁבָט וַאֲדָר וַחֲצִי נִיסָן.

וָחֹרֶף – *And winter:* During the winter, barley and pungent beans are sown – these ripen quickly. This season begins in the second half of Shevat and runs through Adar and the first half of Nisan.

קַיִץ. הוּא זְמַן לְקִיטַת תְּאֵנִים וּזְמַן שֶׁמְּיַבְּשִׁין אוֹתָן בַּשָּׂדוֹת, וּשְׁמוֹ קַיִץ, כְּמוֹ: ״וְהַלֶּחֶם וְהַקַּיִץ לֶאֱכוֹל הַנְּעָרִים״ (שמואל ב׳ טז, ב):

קַיִץ – *Summer:* [This is the time covered by the second half of Sivan, the month of Tamuz, and the first half of Av.] During this season, the figs are harvested and laid out to dry in the fields. These fruits are referred to as *kayitz*, as the verse states: *The bread and summer fruit [vehakayitz] are for the young men to eat* (II Samuel 16:2).

◀

9 1 not cease." Then God blessed Noaḥ and his sons, saying to
2 them, "Be fertile, multiply, fill the earth. Fear and dread of you
shall fall upon all beasts of the earth, upon all winged creatures of the heavens, upon all that creeps upon the land and all
3 fish of the sea. Into your hand they are given. Every moving
thing that lives shall be food for you; I allow them all to you,
4 like green plants. But flesh with its lifeblood still in it you may
5 not eat. And for your own lifeblood I will demand account; I
will demand it from every wild beast. For human life I will

חֹם. הוּא סוֹף יְמוֹת הַחַמָּה, חֲצִי אָב וֶאֱלוּל וַחֲצִי תִּשְׁרֵי, שֶׁהָעוֹלָם חַם בְּיוֹתֵר, כְּמוֹ שֶׁשָּׁנִינוּ בְּמַסֶּכֶת יוֹמָא (דף כט ע״א) שִׁלְהֵי קַיְטָא קָשֵׁי מִקַּיְטָא:

חֹם – *Heat:* This season, *ḥom*, takes place at the end of the summer days [*yemot haḥama*]. It begins in the second half of Av, continues through Elul, and ends with the first half of Tishrei. This period is called *ḥom* because this is when the world is at its hottest [*ḥam*], as the Talmud states in Yoma (page 29a): The end of the summer is more severe than the summer itself.

וְיוֹם וָלַיְלָה לֹא יִשְׁבֹּתוּ. מִכְּלָל שֶׁשָּׁבְתוּ כָּל יְמוֹת הַמַּבּוּל, שֶׁלֹּא שִׁמְּשׁוּ הַמַּזָּלוֹת וְלֹא נִכַּר בֵּין יוֹם וְלַיְלָה:

וְיוֹם וָלַיְלָה לֹא יִשְׁבֹּתוּ – *Day and night will not cease:* [God's guarantee promising that day and night will never again cease] implies that the shift from one to the other was interrupted during the flood. This is because during the deluge the celestial spheres were not operative, and hence there was no distinction between day and night.

לֹא יִשְׁבֹּתוּ. לֹא יִפְסְקוּ כָּל אֵלֶּה מִלְּהִתְנַהֵג כְּסִדְרָן:

לֹא יִשְׁבֹּתוּ – *Will not cease:* These seasons will never stop functioning the way that they are meant to.

ט ב | **וְחִתְּכֶם.** וְאֵימַתְכֶם, כְּמוֹ: "תִּרְאוּ חֲתַת" (איוב ו, כא). וְאַגָּדָה: לְשׁוֹן חִיּוּת, שֶׁכָּל זְמַן שֶׁתִּינוֹק בֶּן יוֹמוֹ חַי אֵין צָרִיךְ לְשָׁמְרוֹ מִן הָעַכְבָּרִים, עוֹג מֶלֶךְ הַבָּשָׁן מֵת צָרִיךְ לְשָׁמְרוֹ מִן הָעַכְבָּרִים, שֶׁנֶּאֱמַר: "וּמוֹרַאֲכֶם וְחִתְּכֶם יִהְיֶה", אֵימָתַי יִהְיֶה מוֹרַאֲכֶם עַל הַחַיּוֹת? כָּל זְמַן שֶׁאַתֶּם חַיִּים:

9 2 | **וְחִתְּכֶם** – *And dread of you:* The word *ḥatat* means "fear," as in the verse *You see my terror [ḥatat] and stand aghast* (Job 6:21). According to the Midrash, the term is related to *ḥiyyut* ["life"]. Note that as long as even a day-old child is alive, he need not be protected against mice [which are afraid of living people], whereas no mice would fear Og the [giant] king of Bashan were he to be lying dead. Thus, when the verse states: *Fear and dread of you shall fall upon all beasts of the earth*, it means that animals shall flee your presence as long as you are alive.

ג | **לָכֶם יִהְיֶה לְאָכְלָה.** שֶׁלֹּא הִרְשֵׁיתִי לְאָדָם הָרִאשׁוֹן לֶאֱכֹל בָּשָׂר אֶלָּא יֶרֶק עֵשֶׂב, וְלָכֶם – "כְּיֶרֶק עֵשֶׂב" שֶׁהִפְקַרְתִּי לְאָדָם הָרִאשׁוֹן "נָתַתִּי לָכֶם אֶת כֹּל":

3 | **לָכֶם יִהְיֶה לְאָכְלָה** – *Shall be food for you:* I did not allow the first man to eat meat; his diet was restricted to vegetation. However, just as I granted Adam license to eat *green plants*, you may now eat everything.

ט א יִשְׁבֹּתוּ׃ וַיְבָרֶךְ אֱלֹהִים אֶת־נֹחַ וְאֶת־בָּנָיו וַיֹּאמֶר
ב לָהֶם פְּרוּ וּרְבוּ וּמִלְאוּ אֶת־הָאָרֶץ׃ וּמוֹרַאֲכֶם וְחִתְּכֶם
יִהְיֶה עַל כָּל־חַיַּת הָאָרֶץ וְעַל כָּל־עוֹף הַשָּׁמָיִם בְּכֹל
אֲשֶׁר תִּרְמֹשׂ הָאֲדָמָה וּבְכָל־דְּגֵי הַיָּם בְּיֶדְכֶם נִתָּנוּ׃
ג כָּל־רֶמֶשׂ אֲשֶׁר הוּא־חַי לָכֶם יִהְיֶה לְאָכְלָה כְּיֶרֶק
ד עֵשֶׂב נָתַתִּי לָכֶם אֶת־כֹּל׃ אַךְ־בָּשָׂר בְּנַפְשׁוֹ דָמוֹ לֹא
ה תֹאכֵלוּ׃ וְאַךְ אֶת־דִּמְכֶם לְנַפְשֹׁתֵיכֶם אֶדְרֹשׁ מִיַּד
כָּל־חַיָּה אֶדְרְשֶׁנּוּ וּמִיַּד הָאָדָם מִיַּד אִישׁ אָחִיו אֶדְרֹשׁ

ד | **בְּנַפְשׁוֹ דָמוֹ.** אָסַר לָהֶם אֵבֶר מִן הַחַי, כְּלוֹמַר כָּל זְמַן שֶׁנַּפְשׁוֹ בְּדָמוֹ לֹא תֹאכְלוּ הַבָּשָׂר:

4 | **בְּנַפְשׁוֹ דָמוֹ** – *Flesh with its lifeblood:* With this statement God forbade humanity to eat limbs torn from living animals. In other words, people may not eat an animal's flesh as long as its soul is still in it.

בְּנַפְשׁוֹ דָמוֹ. בְּעוֹד נַפְשׁוֹ בּוֹ:

בְּנַפְשׁוֹ דָמוֹ – *Flesh with its lifeblood:* As long as its soul is in it. [The emphasis is not on the consumption of blood, but on the presence of life in the animal.]

בָּשָׂר בְּנַפְשׁוֹ לֹא תֹאכֵלוּ. הֲרֵי אֵבֶר מִן הַחַי, וְאַף "דָּמוֹ לֹא תֹאכֵלוּ" הֲרֵי דָּם מִן הַחַי:

בָּשָׂר בְּנַפְשׁוֹ לֹא תֹאכֵלוּ – *But flesh with its lifeblood still in it you may not eat:* The words *basar benafsho lo tokhelu* prohibit eating a limb or flesh from an animal that still lives. [The full clause reads *basar benafasho damo lo tokhelu*, where the middle word *damo* – "its blood" – seems superfluous.] This teaches us that it is also forbidden to drink the blood of an animal while its blood [soul] is still in the animal [that is, while it is still alive. Later, Torah law will forbid to Jews the consumption of animal blood even once its host is dead].

ה | **וְאַךְ אֶת־דִּמְכֶם.** אַף עַל פִּי שֶׁהִתַּרְתִּי לָכֶם נְטִילַת נְשָׁמָה בִּבְהֵמָה, "אֶת דִּמְכֶם... אֶדְרֹשׁ" – הַשּׁוֹפֵךְ דַּם עַצְמוֹ, "לְנַפְשֹׁתֵיכֶם" – אַף הַחוֹנֵק עַצְמוֹ, אַף עַל פִּי שֶׁלֹּא יָצָא מִמֶּנּוּ דָּם:

5 | **וְאַךְ אֶת־דִּמְכֶם** – *And for your own lifeblood:* Even though I have allowed you to take the lives of animals, *for your own lifeblood I will demand account* – I will demand the blood of a person who takes his own life. The term *lenafshoteikhem* [literally, "for your lives," appearing within the phrase *et dimkhem lenafshoteikhem* – "for your own lifeblood"] emphasizes that God holds an individual accountable for suicide even if he strangles himself and no blood is actually spilled.

6 demand account, of every man toward his fellow man: One
who sheds the blood of man – by man shall his blood
7 `be shed, for in God's image man was made. As for you, be
fertile and multiply, abound on earth and become many on
8 it."   Then God said to Noaḥ and to his sons with   HAMISHI
9 him: "I – I am about to establish My covenant with you and
10 your descendants after you, and with every living creature
that is with you – the birds, the animals, and all the wild

מִיַּד כָּל־חַיָּה. לְפִי שֶׁחָטְאוּ דּוֹר הַמַּבּוּל וְהֻפְקְרוּ לְמַאֲכַל חַיּוֹת רָעוֹת לִשְׁלֹט בָּהֶן, שֶׁנֶּאֱמַר: "נִמְשַׁל כַּבְּהֵמוֹת נִדְמוּ" (תהלים מט, כא), לְכָךְ הֻצְרַךְ לְהַזְהִיר עֲלֵיהֶן אֶת הַחַיּוֹת:

וּמִיַּד הָאָדָם. מִיַּד הַהוֹרֵג בְּמֵזִיד וְאֵין עֵדִים, אֲנִי אֶדְרֹשׁ:

מִיַּד אִישׁ אָחִיו. שֶׁהוּא אוֹהֵב לוֹ כְּאָח וַהֲרָגוֹ שׁוֹגֵג, אֲנִי אֶדְרֹשׁ אִם לֹא יִגְלֶה וִיבַקֵּשׁ עַל עֲוֹן לִמְחֹל, שֶׁאַף הַשּׁוֹגֵג צָרִיךְ כַּפָּרָה, וְאִם אֵין עֵדִים לְחַיְּבוֹ גָּלוּת וְהוּא אֵינוֹ נִכְנָע הַקָּדוֹשׁ בָּרוּךְ הוּא דּוֹרֵשׁ מִמֶּנּוּ, כְּמוֹ שֶׁדָּרְשׁוּ רַבּוֹתֵינוּ "וְהָאֱלֹהִים אִנָּה לְיָדוֹ" (שמות כא, יג) בְּמַסֶּכֶת מַכּוֹת (דף י ע"ב): הַקָּדוֹשׁ בָּרוּךְ הוּא מְזַמְּנָן לְפֻנְדָּק אֶחָד וְכוּ':

מִיַּד כָּל־חַיָּה – *From every wild beast:* As a consequence of the sins of the generation of the flood, humanity became prey to wild beasts who dominate them, as the verse states: *Like the beasts that perish* [Psalms 49:21; human beings have become like cattle which predators do not fear]. Hence the wild animals need to be specifically warned not to kill people.

וּמִיַּד הָאָדָם – *Of every man:* I will hold accountable anyone who murders another unobserved.

מִיַּד אִישׁ אָחִיו – *Toward his fellow man:* [Literally, "his brother."] If a person inadvertently kills his fellow man whom he loves like a brother, I will hold him responsible if he is not exiled [to one of the designated cities of refuge] and does not seek forgiveness for his transgression – for even a person who kills accidentally requires atonement. When there are no witnesses to the event who can testify that it was an accident and have him sentenced to exile, and if he does not willingly submit to justice, the Holy One, blessed be He, will ensure that such punishment shall come about. This is how our Sages in tractate Makkot (10b) interpret the verse *It came about by an act of God* [Exodus 21:13. The Talmud describes a situation where two men have taken the lives of other people: One murdered his victim intentionally, the other killed unintentionally. However, in neither case were witnesses present who could testify to either man's culpability. Hence the first man cannot be executed by the court, nor can the second man be exiled to live in the city of refuge. In order to right these wrongs] the Holy One, blessed be He, arranges for both individuals to visit the same inn at the same time. [While they are there, the murderer finds himself sitting beneath a ladder that the accidental killer is descending. The latter slips and falls, crushing the former to death. Thus, the villain who deserved to be put to death indeed dies, while the

ו אֶת־נֶפֶשׁ הָאָדָם׃ שֹׁפֵךְ דַּם הָאָדָם בָּאָדָם דָּמוֹ יִשָּׁפֵךְ
ז כִּי בְּצֶלֶם אֱלֹהִים עָשָׂה אֶת־הָאָדָם׃ וְאַתֶּם פְּרוּ וּרְבוּ
ח שִׁרְצוּ בָאָרֶץ וּרְבוּ־בָהּ׃ וַיֹּאמֶר אֱלֹהִים חמישי
ט אֶל־נֹחַ וְאֶל־בָּנָיו אִתּוֹ לֵאמֹר׃ וַאֲנִי הִנְנִי מֵקִים אֶת־
י בְּרִיתִי אִתְּכֶם וְאֶת־זַרְעֲכֶם אַחֲרֵיכֶם׃ וְאֵת כָּל־נֶפֶשׁ
הַחַיָּה אֲשֶׁר אִתְּכֶם בָּעוֹף בַּבְּהֵמָה וּבְכָל־חַיַּת הָאָרֶץ

negligent man who should have been exiled for his previous mishap is now sentenced to that fate anyway. This is how God ensures that punishment is meted out to one who takes the life *of his fellow man*, even when he had meant no harm.]

ו | **בָּאָדָם דָּמוֹ יִשָּׁפֵךְ.** אִם יֵשׁ עֵדִים הֲמִיתוּהוּ אַתֶּם, לָמָּה? "כִּי בְּצֶלֶם אֱלֹהִים עָשָׂה אֶת־הָאָדָם", וְזֶה מִקְרָא חָסֵר: עָשָׂה הָעוֹשֶׂה אֶת הָאָדָם, וְכֵן הַרְבֵּה בַּמִּקְרָא:

6 | **בָּאָדָם דָּמוֹ יִשָּׁפֵךְ** – *By man shall his blood be shed:* If there are witnesses to the murder, you [the court] must put the perpetrator to death [and the matter is taken out of God's hands unlike in the previous case]. Now why is the shedding of human blood so serious? Because *in God's image man was made*. This last clause is missing its subject [literally, "for – made man in God's image"], for it should be understood as: The Maker made man in God's image. There are many such cases of incomplete phrasing in Scripture.

ז | **וְאַתֶּם פְּרוּ וּרְבוּ.** לְפִי פְּשׁוּטוֹ, הָרִאשׁוֹנָה לִבְרָכָה וְכָאן לְצִוּוּי. וּלְפִי מִדְרָשׁוֹ, לְהַקִּישׁ מִי שֶׁאֵינוֹ עוֹסֵק בִּפְרִיָּה וּרְבִיָּה לְשׁוֹפֵךְ דָּמִים:

7 | **וְאַתֶּם פְּרוּ וּרְבוּ** – *As for you, be fertile and multiply:* According to the straightforward meaning of the text, the first appearance of these words [in 9:1] represents a blessing to man to be populous, whereas the current instance suggests a commandment. However, the homiletic interpretation of the repetition teaches that when one ignores his obligation to procreate, that neglect is tantamount to murder.

ט | **וַאֲנִי הִנְנִי.** מַסְכִּים אֲנִי עִמְּךָ; שֶׁהָיָה נֹחַ דּוֹאֵג לַעֲסֹק בִּפְרִיָּה וּרְבִיָּה עַד שֶׁהִבְטִיחוֹ הַקָּדוֹשׁ בָּרוּךְ הוּא שֶׁלֹּא לְשַׁחֵת הָעוֹלָם עוֹד, וְכֵן עָשָׂה. בָּאַחֲרוֹנָה אָמַר לוֹ: הִנְנִי מַסְכִּים לַעֲשׂוֹת קִיּוּם וְחִזּוּק בְּרִית לְהַבְטָחָתִי וְאֶתֵּן לְךָ אוֹת:

9 | **וַאֲנִי הִנְנִי** – *I, I am about:* I sympathize with you. Initially Noaḥ was afraid to have children [lest they be wiped out in a future disaster] unless the Holy One, blessed be He, assured him that He would never again destroy the world. And hence God did so. God reinforced this promise by saying: I hereby agree to establish a covenant and to secure it by giving you a sign to confirm the matter.

י | **חַיַּת הָאָרֶץ אִתְּכֶם.** הֵם הַמִּתְהַלְּכִים עִם הַבְּרִיּוֹת:

10 | **חַיַּת הָאָרֶץ אִתְּכֶם** – *The wild beasts of earth that are with you:* This refers to the animals that walk with human beings.

beasts of earth that are with you, everything that left the ark,
11 every living creature on earth. I will establish My covenant
with you, that never again may all life be destroyed by the waters of a flood; never again will there be a flood to destroy the
12 earth." God said, "This is the sign of the covenant I am making
between Me and you – and every living creature with you – for
13 all generations to come. I have laid down My bow in the
clouds to be the sign of the covenant between Me and the
14 earth. Whenever I bring clouds over the earth and the rain-
15 bow appears in the clouds, I will remember My covenant that
binds Me and you and every living creature of all flesh so that
never again will the waters become a flood to destroy all life.
16 The rainbow will be there in the cloud, and I will see it, remembering the eternal covenant between God and every liv-
17 ing creature, all flesh upon the earth." So said God to Noaḥ:
"This is the sign of the covenant that I have established between Me and all flesh that is on earth."

מִכֹּל יֹצְאֵי הַתֵּבָה. לְהָבִיא שְׁקָצִים וּרְמָשִׂים:

לְכֹל חַיַּת הָאָרֶץ. לְהָבִיא הַמַּזִּיקִין שֶׁאֵינָן בִּכְלַל "הַחַיָּה אֲשֶׁר אִתְּכֶם", שֶׁאֵין הִלּוּכָן עִם הַבְּרִיּוֹת:

יא | **וַהֲקִמֹתִי.** אֶעֱשֶׂה קִיּוּם לִבְרִיתִי, וּמַהוּ קִיּוּמוֹ? אוֹת הַקֶּשֶׁת, כְּמוֹ שֶׁמְּסַיֵּם וְהוֹלֵךְ:

יב | **לְדֹרֹת עוֹלָם.** נִכְתָּב חָסֵר, שֶׁיֵּשׁ דּוֹרוֹת שֶׁלֹּא הֻצְרְכוּ לְאוֹת לְפִי שֶׁצַּדִּיקִים גְּמוּרִים הָיוּ, כְּמוֹ דּוֹרוֹ שֶׁל חִזְקִיָּהוּ מֶלֶךְ יְהוּדָה וְדוֹרוֹ שֶׁל רַבִּי שִׁמְעוֹן בֶּן יוֹחַאי:

מִכֹּל יֹצְאֵי הַתֵּבָה – *Everything that left the ark:* The phrase includes all detested and crawling creatures.

לְכֹל חַיַּת הָאָרֶץ – *Every living creature on earth:* These final words include the demons. These entities are not within the category of *every living creature that is with you*, for they do not walk with humans.

11 | **וַהֲקִמֹתִי** – *I will establish:* "I will give a confirmation [*kiyyum*] of my covenant." And what is that confirmation? The sign of the rainbow, as the verses proceed to describe.

12 | **לְדֹרֹת עוֹלָם** – *For all generations to come:* The word *ledorot* is written in deficient form [without the letter *vav* after the *resh*] to indicate that not all generations are served by this sign. Indeed, in eras when completely righteous individuals live, the token in the sky is not required [since it is then clear that there is no threat of destruction]. Such was the time of Ḥizkiyahu, king of Yehuda, and the generation of Rabbi Shimon ben Yoḥai.

◀

בראשית | פרק ט

יא אִתְּכֶ֑ם מִכֹּ֖ל יֹצְאֵ֣י הַתֵּבָ֑ה לְכֹ֖ל חַיַּ֥ת הָאָֽרֶץ: וַהֲקִמֹתִ֤י
אֶת־בְּרִיתִי֙ אִתְּכֶ֔ם וְלֹֽא־יִכָּרֵ֧ת כָּל־בָּשָׂ֛ר ע֖וֹד מִמֵּ֣י
יב הַמַּבּ֑וּל וְלֹֽא־יִהְיֶ֥ה ע֛וֹד מַבּ֖וּל לְשַׁחֵ֥ת הָאָֽרֶץ: וַיֹּ֣אמֶר
אֱלֹהִ֗ים זֹ֤את אֽוֹת־הַבְּרִית֙ אֲשֶׁר־אֲנִ֣י נֹתֵ֗ן בֵּינִי֙ וּבֵ֣ינֵיכֶ֔ם
יג וּבֵ֕ין כָּל־נֶ֥פֶשׁ חַיָּ֖ה אֲשֶׁ֣ר אִתְּכֶ֑ם לְדֹרֹ֖ת עוֹלָֽם: אֶת־
קַשְׁתִּ֕י נָתַ֖תִּי בֶּעָנָ֑ן וְהָ֣יְתָה֙ לְא֣וֹת בְּרִ֔ית בֵּינִ֖י וּבֵ֥ין
יד הָאָֽרֶץ: וְהָיָ֕ה בְּעַֽנְנִ֥י עָנָ֖ן עַל־הָאָ֑רֶץ וְנִרְאֲתָ֥ה הַקֶּ֖שֶׁת
טו בֶּעָנָֽן: וְזָכַרְתִּ֣י אֶת־בְּרִיתִ֗י אֲשֶׁ֤ר בֵּינִי֙ וּבֵ֣ינֵיכֶ֔ם וּבֵ֛ין
כָּל־נֶ֥פֶשׁ חַיָּ֖ה בְּכָל־בָּשָׂ֑ר וְלֹֽא־יִהְיֶ֨ה ע֤וֹד הַמַּ֨יִם֙
טז לְמַבּ֔וּל לְשַׁחֵ֖ת כָּל־בָּשָֽׂר: וְהָֽיְתָ֥ה הַקֶּ֖שֶׁת בֶּעָנָ֑ן
וּרְאִיתִ֗יהָ לִזְכֹּר֙ בְּרִ֣ית עוֹלָ֔ם בֵּ֣ין אֱלֹהִ֔ים וּבֵין֙ כָּל־נֶ֣פֶשׁ
יז חַיָּ֔ה בְּכָל־בָּשָׂ֖ר אֲשֶׁ֥ר עַל־הָאָֽרֶץ: וַיֹּ֥אמֶר אֱלֹהִ֖ים
אֶל־נֹ֑חַ זֹ֤את אֽוֹת־הַבְּרִית֙ אֲשֶׁ֣ר הֲקִמֹ֔תִי בֵּינִ֕י וּבֵ֥ין
כָּל־בָּשָׂ֖ר אֲשֶׁ֥ר עַל־הָאָֽרֶץ:

---

14 | בְּעַֽנְנִי עָנָן – *When I bring clouds:* When I contemplate bringing darkness [Rashi's interpretation of the word *anan*] and destruction to the world.

16 | בֵּין אֱלֹהִים וּבֵין כָּל־נֶפֶשׁ חַיָּה – *Between God and every living creature:* The covenant has been forged between the celestial attribute of Justice [alluded to in the word *Elohim*] and you. For this verse could have employed the same phrasing as the previous verse and said: "Between Me" [instead of "between *Elohim*"] and every living creature. However, the choice of wording teaches that when the attribute of Justice levels accusations against you and demands that you be destroyed, I will see the sign and remember our agreement.

17 | זֹאת אוֹת־הַבְּרִית – *This is the sign of the covenant:* God showed Noaḥ the rainbow and said to him: This is the sign that I have been talking about.

יד | בְּעַנְנִי עָנָן. כְּשֶׁתַּעֲלֶה בְמַחֲשָׁבָה לְפָנַי לְהָבִיא חֹשֶׁךְ וַאֲבַדּוֹן לָעוֹלָם:

טז | בֵּין אֱלֹהִים וּבֵין כָּל־נֶפֶשׁ חַיָּה. בֵּין מִדַּת הַדִּין שֶׁל מַעְלָה וּבֵינֵיכֶם, שֶׁהָיָה לוֹ לִכְתֹּב: "בֵּינִי וּבֵין כָּל נֶפֶשׁ חַיָּה", אֶלָּא זֶהוּ מִדְרָשׁוֹ: כְּשֶׁתָּבֹא מִדַּת הַדִּין לְקַטְרֵג עֲלֵיכֶם לְחַיֵּב אֶתְכֶם, אֲנִי רוֹאֶה אֶת הָאוֹת וְנִזְכָּר:

יז | זֹאת אוֹת־הַבְּרִית. הֶרְאֵהוּ הַקֶּשֶׁת וְאָמַר לוֹ: הֲרֵי הָאוֹת שֶׁאָמַרְתִּי:

18 Noaḥ's sons who came out from the ark were Shem, Ḥam, and SHISHI
19 Yefet. Ḥam was the father of Kenaan. These three were Noaḥ's
20 sons; and from them all the world branched out. Noaḥ began
21 to be a man of the land, and he planted a vineyard. He drank
some of the wine, became drunk, and lay uncovered in his
22 tent. Ḥam, father of Kenaan, saw his father's nakedness and
23 told his two brothers who were outside. Shem and Yefet then
took a cloak and put it over both their shoulders. They walked
backward and covered their father's nakedness, averting their

יח | **וְחָם הוּא אֲבִי כְנָעַן.** לָמָּה הֻצְרַךְ לוֹמַר כָּאן? לְפִי שֶׁהַפָּרָשָׁה עֲסוּקָה וּבָאָה בְּשִׁכְרוּתוֹ שֶׁל נֹחַ שֶׁקִּלְקֵל בָּהּ חָם וְעַל יָדוֹ נִתְקַלֵּל כְּנַעַן, וַעֲדַיִן לֹא כָּתַב תּוֹלְדוֹת חָם וְלֹא יָדַעְנוּ שֶׁכְּנַעַן בְּנוֹ, לְפִיכָךְ הֻצְרַךְ לוֹמַר כָּאן: "וְחָם הוּא אֲבִי כְנָעַן":

18 | **וְחָם הוּא אֲבִי כְנָעַן** – *Ḥam was the father of Kenaan:* Why is this fact pointed out here? The following passage deals with Noaḥ's drunkenness and the sin perpetrated against him by Ḥam. That act in turn leads to Kenaan being cursed. And so, because the lineage of Ḥam has not yet been recorded and the reader has no idea that Kenaan is Ḥam's son [making Noaḥ's outburst in verse 25 inexplicable], the text saw fit to preface the story with *Ḥam was the father of Kenaan*.

כ | **וַיָּחֶל.** עָשָׂה עַצְמוֹ חֻלִּין, שֶׁהָיָה לוֹ לַעֲסֹק תְּחִלָּה בִּנְטִיעָה אַחֶרֶת:

20 | **וַיָּחֶל** – *Began:* The verb vayaḥel means that Noaḥ made himself profane [*ḥullin*, by first planting a vineyard], for he should have begun his agricultural efforts with a different type of crop.

אִישׁ הָאֲדָמָה. אֲדוֹנֵי הָאֲדָמָה, כְּמוֹ: "אִישׁ נָעֳמִי" (רות א, ג):

אִישׁ הָאֲדָמָה – *A man of the land:* The term *ish* connotes "master" of the land, as in the phrase *Naomi's husband [ish]* (Ruth 1:3).

וַיִּטַּע כָּרֶם. כְּשֶׁנִּכְנַס לַתֵּבָה הִכְנִיס עִמּוֹ זְמוֹרוֹת וְיִחוּרֵי תְאֵנִים:

וַיִּטַּע כָּרֶם – *And he planted a vineyard:* When Noaḥ first entered the ark he took with him vine cuttings and fig shoots.

כא | **אָהֳלֹה.** "אָהֳלָהּ" כְּתִיב, רֶמֶז לַעֲשָׂרָה שְׁבָטִים שֶׁנִּקְרְאוּ עַל שֵׁם שׁוֹמְרוֹן שֶׁנִּקְרֵאת אָהֳלָה, שֶׁגָּלוּ עַל עִסְקֵי יַיִן, שֶׁנֶּאֱמַר: "הַשֹּׁתִים בְּמִזְרְקֵי יַיִן" (עמוס ו, ו):

21 | **אָהֳלֹה** – *His tent:* The way the word *oholo* is written [in the Torah scroll without vowels] it should be pronounced *ohola* [since the final letter is unusually a *heh* and not a *vav*]. This is an allusion to the ten tribes of Israel [that is, the kingdom of Israel formed when most of the nation split from the tribes of Binyamin and Yehuda]. This confederacy was known as Shomron [after the kingdom's capital city] which in turn is called Ohola [in Ezekiel 23:4]. For these ten tribes were eventually exiled from their land due to their preoccupation with wine, as the verse states: *Who guzzle wine from bowls… therefore, you will now be the first of exiles* [Amos 6:6–7; these tribes will be exiled – *yiglu* – first, a term that recalls the word *vayitgal* in the current verse].

◀

יח וַיִּהְיוּ בְנֵי־נֹחַ הַיֹּצְאִים מִן־הַתֵּבָה שֵׁם וְחָם וָיָפֶת וְחָם ח ששי
יט הוּא אֲבִי כְנָעַן: שְׁלֹשָׁה אֵלֶּה בְּנֵי־נֹחַ וּמֵאֵלֶּה נָפְצָה
כ כָּל־הָאָרֶץ: וַיָּחֶל נֹחַ אִישׁ הָאֲדָמָה וַיִּטַּע כָּרֶם: וַיֵּשְׁתְּ
כא מִן־הַיַּיִן וַיִּשְׁכָּר וַיִּתְגַּל בְּתוֹךְ אָהֳלֹה: וַיַּרְא חָם אֲבִי
כב כְנַעַן אֵת עֶרְוַת אָבִיו וַיַּגֵּד לִשְׁנֵי־אֶחָיו בַּחוּץ: וַיִּקַּח
כג שֵׁם וָיֶפֶת אֶת־הַשִּׂמְלָה וַיָּשִׂימוּ עַל־שְׁכֶם שְׁנֵיהֶם
וַיֵּלְכוּ אֲחֹרַנִּית וַיְכַסּוּ אֵת עֶרְוַת אֲבִיהֶם וּפְנֵיהֶם

וַיִּתְגַּל – *And lay uncovered:* The verb *vayitgal* appears in the reflexive *hitpael* construction [meaning that Noaḥ uncovered himself].

וַיִּתְגַּל. לְשׁוֹן וַיִּתְפַּעֵל:

22 | **וַיַּרְא חָם אֲבִי כְנַעַן** – *Ḥam, father of Kenaan, saw:* [Since it was Ḥam who acted inappropriately here, why is the name of his son mentioned at all?] Some of our Sages claim that it was Kenaan who saw his grandfather's nakedness and told his father about it. This explains why Kenaan appears in this verse, and why Noaḥ curses him.

כב | **וַיַּרְא חָם אֲבִי כְנַעַן.** יֵשׁ מֵרַבּוֹתֵינוּ אוֹמְרִים, כְּנַעַן רָאָה וְהִגִּיד לְאָבִיו, לְכָךְ הֻזְכַּר עַל הַדָּבָר וְנִתְקַלֵּל:

וַיַּרְא... אֵת עֶרְוַת אָבִיו – *He saw his father's nakedness:* According to one approach Ḥam castrated his father, while another opinion claims that he sodomized him.

וַיַּרְא... אֵת עֶרְוַת אָבִיו. יֵשׁ אוֹמְרִים סֵרְסוֹ, וְיֵשׁ אוֹמְרִים רְבָעוֹ:

23 | **וַיִּקַּח שֵׁם וָיֶפֶת** – *Shem and Yefet then took:* The verse does not use the plural form *vayikḥu* but the singular *vayikkaḥ* to teach that it was Shem who made more of an effort to protect his father's honor than did Yefet. It was because of this devotion that Shem's descendants [that is, the people of Israel] were privileged to wear garments with fringes, whereas, the offspring of Yefet were rewarded with a burial place, as the verse states: *And it will happen on that day: I will grant Gog a burial-place there in Israel* [Ezekiel 39:11. In 10:2 Magog is listed as a son of Yefet, while Gog is the king of Magog]. Meanwhile, Ḥam who disgraced his father will be punished, as the verse states regarding his descendants: *Just so will it be when the king of Assyria leads away the captives of Egypt, the exiles of Kush* [Isaiah 20:4. Kush is named as a son of Ḥam in 10:6].

כג | **וַיִּקַּח שֵׁם וָיֶפֶת.** אֵין כְּתִיב ׳וַיִּקְחוּ׳ אֶלָּא ״וַיִּקַּח״, לִמֵּד עַל שֵׁם שֶׁנִּתְאַמֵּץ בַּמִּצְוָה יוֹתֵר מִיֶּפֶת, לְכָךְ זָכוּ בָּנָיו לְטַלִּית שֶׁל צִיצִית, וְיֶפֶת זָכָה לִקְבוּרָה לְבָנָיו, שֶׁנֶּאֱמַר: ״אֶתֵּן לְגוֹג מְקוֹם שָׁם קֶבֶר״ (יחזקאל לט, יא). וְחָם שֶׁבִּזָּה אֶת אָבִיו, נֶאֱמַר בְּזַרְעוֹ: ״כֵּן יִנְהַג מֶלֶךְ אַשּׁוּר אֶת שְׁבִי מִצְרַיִם וְאֶת גָּלוּת כּוּשׁ נְעָרִים וּזְקֵנִים עָרוֹם וְיָחֵף וַחֲשׂוּפַי שֵׁת״ וְגוֹ׳ (ישעיה כ, ד):

24 faces so as not to see the nakedness of their father. Noaḥ woke
from his wine and realized what his youngest son had done to
25 him. He said, "Cursed be Kenaan! The lowest of slaves shall
26 he be to his brothers." Then he said, "Blessed be the Lord,
27 God of Shem; Kenaan shall be his slave. May God enlarge Yefet, and let him dwell in the tents of Shem; Kenaan shall be
28 his slave." After the flood Noaḥ lived three hundred and fifty
29 years. Noaḥ lived a total of nine hundred and fifty years, and
he died.
10 1 These are the descendants of Noaḥ's sons, Shem, Ḥam, and
2 Yefet; after the flood, children were born to them. Yefet's
sons were Gomer, Magog, Madai, Yavan, Tuval, Meshekh,
3 and Tiras. Gomer's sons were Ashkenaz, Rifat, and Togarma.

וּפְנֵיהֶם אֲחֹרַנִּית. לָמָּה נֶאֱמַר פַּעַם שְׁנִיָּה? לְלַמֵּד שֶׁכְּשֶׁקָּרְבוּ אֶצְלוֹ וְהֻצְרְכוּ לַהֲפֹךְ עַצְמָם לְכַסּוֹתוֹ, הָפְכוּ פְּנֵיהֶם אֲחוֹרַנִּית:

וּפְנֵיהֶם אֲחֹרַנִּית – *Averting their faces:* Why does the verse repeat the description *ufneihem aḥorannit*, literally, "they turned their faces backward," after stating, *they walked backward*? We learn from here that when they approached their father, they were forced to turn around in order to cover him up. They then once again turned their faces backward [away from their father so as not to look at him in his state of shame.]

כד | **בְּנוֹ הַקָּטָן.** הַפָּסוּל וְהַבָּזוּי, כְּמוֹ: "הִנֵּה קָטֹן נְתַתִּיךָ בַּגּוֹיִם בָּזוּי" (ירמיה מט, טו; עובדיה א, ב):

24 | **בְּנוֹ הַקָּטָן** – *His youngest son:* The adjective *hakatan* describes Ḥam as Noaḥ's rejected and despised son, as in the verse *Look, I have made you small [katon] among nations, scorned by humanity* (Jeremiah 49:15 and Obadiah 1:2).

כה | **אָרוּר כְּנָעַן.** אַתָּה גָּרַמְתָּ לִי שֶׁלֹּא אוֹלִיד בֵּן רְבִיעִי אַחֵר לְשַׁמְּשֵׁנִי, אָרוּר בִּנְךָ הָרְבִיעִי לִהְיוֹת מְשַׁמֵּשׁ אֶת זַרְעָם שֶׁל אֵלּוּ הַגְּדוֹלִים שֶׁהֻטַּל עֲלֵיהֶם טֹרַח עֲבוֹדָתִי מֵעַתָּה. וּמָה רָאָה חָם שֶׁסֵּרְסוֹ? אָמַר לָהֶם לְאֶחָיו: אָדָם הָרִאשׁוֹן שְׁנֵי בָנִים הָיוּ לוֹ, וְהָרַג זֶה אֶת זֶה בִּשְׁבִיל יְרֻשַּׁת הָעוֹלָם, וְאָבִינוּ יֵשׁ לוֹ שְׁלֹשָׁה בָנִים וְעוֹדֶנּוּ מְבַקֵּשׁ בֵּן רְבִיעִי:

25 | **אָרוּר כְּנָעַן** – *Cursed be Kenaan:* Said Noaḥ to Ḥam: Because you castrated me and robbed me of the opportunity to father a fourth son who would have served me, it is your fourth son [Kenaan – see 10:6] who is now cursed and destined to serve the descendants of those better men [Shem and Yefet]. For it is because of you that they are now compelled to serve me from now on. Now what drove Ḥam to castrate his father? Said Ḥam to his brothers: You know, the first man had two sons and one of them murdered the other in order to inherit the entire world. Now look – our father already has three sons, and he is intent on having a fourth!

כו | **בָּרוּךְ יהוה אֱלֹהֵי שֵׁם.** שֶׁעָתִיד לִשְׁמֹר הַבְטָחָתוֹ לְזַרְעוֹ לָתֵת לָהֶם אֶת אֶרֶץ כְּנַעַן:

26 | **בָּרוּךְ יהוה אֱלֹהֵי שֵׁם** – *Blessed be the Lord, God of Shem:* Blessed be the Lord who will preserve His promise to the descendants of Shem [Israel] and give them the land of Canaan.

כד אֲחֹרַנִּית וְעֶרְוַת אֲבִיהֶם לֹא רָאוּ: וַיִּיקֶץ נֹחַ מִיֵּינוֹ
כה וַיֵּדַע אֵת אֲשֶׁר־עָשָׂה לוֹ בְּנוֹ הַקָּטָן: וַיֹּאמֶר אָרוּר
כו כְּנָעַן עֶבֶד עֲבָדִים יִהְיֶה לְאֶחָיו: וַיֹּאמֶר בָּרוּךְ יהוה
כז אֱלֹהֵי שֵׁם וִיהִי כְנַעַן עֶבֶד לָמוֹ: יַפְתְּ אֱלֹהִים לְיֶפֶת
כח וְיִשְׁכֹּן בְּאׇהֳלֵי־שֵׁם וִיהִי כְנַעַן עֶבֶד לָמוֹ: וַיְחִי־נֹחַ
אַחַר הַמַּבּוּל שְׁלֹשׁ מֵאוֹת שָׁנָה וַחֲמִשִּׁים שָׁנָה:
כט וַיְהִי כׇּל־יְמֵי־נֹחַ תְּשַׁע מֵאוֹת שָׁנָה וַחֲמִשִּׁים שָׁנָה
וַיָּמֹת:
י א וְאֵלֶּה תּוֹלְדֹת בְּנֵי־נֹחַ שֵׁם חָם וָיָפֶת וַיִּוָּלְדוּ לָהֶם בָּנִים
ב אַחַר הַמַּבּוּל: בְּנֵי יֶפֶת גֹּמֶר וּמָגוֹג וּמָדַי וְיָוָן וְתֻבָל
ג וּמֶשֶׁךְ וְתִירָס: וּבְנֵי גֹּמֶר אַשְׁכְּנַז וְרִיפַת וְתֹגַרְמָה:

וִיהִי. לָהֶם כְּנַעַן לְמַס עוֹבֵד:

וִיהִי – *Shall be:* Kenaan shall be a vassal to them.

כז | **יַפְתְּ אֱלֹהִים לְיֶפֶת.** מְתֻרְגָּם: "יַפְתֵּי", יַרְחִיב:

27 | **יַפְתְּ אֱלֹהִים לְיֶפֶת** – *May God enlarge Yefet:* The Targum renders the verb *yaft* as *yaftei* ["to expand"] – God will extend Yefet's domain.

וְיִשְׁכֹּן בְּאׇהֳלֵי־שֵׁם. יַשְׁרֶה שְׁכִינָתוֹ בְּיִשְׂרָאֵל. וּמִדְרַשׁ חֲכָמִים, אַף עַל פִּי שֶׁ"יַּפְתְּ אֱלֹהִים לְיֶפֶת", שֶׁבָּנָה כּוֹרֶשׁ שֶׁהָיָה מִבְּנֵי יֶפֶת בַּיִת שֵׁנִי, לֹא שָׁרְתָה בּוֹ שְׁכִינָה; וְהֵיכָן שָׁרְתָה? בְּמִקְדָּשׁ רִאשׁוֹן שֶׁבָּנָה שְׁלֹמֹה שֶׁהָיָה מִבְּנֵי שֵׁם:

וְיִשְׁכֹּן בְּאׇהֳלֵי־שֵׁם – *And let him dwell in the tents of Shem:* God's Divine Presence will rest among Israel. According to the Sages [the entire verse refers to Shem] and this clause means that although God will indeed enlarge Yefet's territory [even so, God will only dwell within Israel's midst.] For when Cyrus, King of Persia, who was a descendant of Yefet [see 10:2], built the Second Temple, God's Divine Presence did not dwell there as it had in the First Temple that Shlomo constructed. And Shlomo of course was a descendant of Shem.

וִיהִי כְנַעַן עֶבֶד. אַף מִשֶּׁיִּגָּלוּ בְּנֵי שֵׁם יִמָּכְרוּ לָהֶם עֲבָדִים מִבְּנֵי כְנַעַן:

וִיהִי כְנַעַן עֶבֶד – *Kenaan shall be his slave:* Even if the descendants of Shem are exiled from their land, the sons of Kenaan will still be sold to them as slaves.

י ב | **וְתִירָס.** זוֹ פָּרַס:

10 2 | **וְתִירָס** – *And Tiras:* This is Persia.

4 Yavan's sons were Elisha, Tarshish, Kitim, and Dodanim.
5 From these the seagoing nations spread out to their territories, each with its own language, by their clans and their
6 nations. Ḥam's sons were Kush, Mitzrayim, Put, and Ke-
7 naan. Kush's sons were Seva, Ḥavila, Savta, Raama, and
8 Savtekha. Raama's sons were Sheva and Dedan. Kush was
9 the father of Nimrod, the first mighty warrior on earth. He
was a mighty hunter before the Lord, which is why people
still say, "Like Nimrod, a mighty hunter before the Lord."
10 His kingdom began with Babylon, Erekh, Akad, and Kalneh
11 in the land of Shinar. From that land, Ashur went out and
12 built Nineveh, Reḥovot Ir, Kalaḥ, and Resen between
13 Nineveh and Kalaḥ; that is the great city. Mitzrayim fa-
14 thered the Ludim, Anamim, Lehavim and Naftuḥim, Patrusim, Kasluḥim – from whom the Philistines descended –
15 and the Kaftorim. Kenaan fathered Tzidon, his first-
16 born, and Ḥet, and the Jebusites, Amorites, and Girgashites,

ח | לִהְיוֹת גִּבֹּר. לְהַמְרִיד כָּל הָעוֹלָם עַל הַקָּדוֹשׁ בָּרוּךְ הוּא בַּעֲצַת דּוֹר הַפַּלָּגָה:

8 | לִהְיוֹת גִּבֹּר – *Mighty warrior:* Nimrod led all of humanity in rebellion [*lehamrid*, evoking *Nimrod*] against the Holy One, blessed be He. For it was he who suggested that they construct the Tower of Babel.

ט | גִּבֹּר־צַיִד. צָד דַּעְתָּן שֶׁל בְּרִיּוֹת בְּפִיו וּמַטְעָן לִמְרֹד בַּמָּקוֹם:

9 | גִּבֹּר־צַיִד – *A mighty hunter:* This man captured men's imagination with his words, and misled them in revolt against God.

לִפְנֵי יהוה. מִתְכַּוֵּן לְהַקְנִיטוֹ עַל פָּנָיו:

לִפְנֵי יהוה – *Before the Lord:* It was Nimrod's intention to provoke God to His face.

עַל־כֵּן יֵאָמַר. עַל כָּל אָדָם מַרְשִׁיעַ בְּעַזּוּת פָּנִים, יוֹדֵעַ רִבּוֹנוֹ וּמִתְכַּוֵּן לִמְרֹד בּוֹ, יֵאָמֵר: זֶה כְּנִמְרֹד גִּבּוֹר צַיִד:

עַל־כֵּן יֵאָמַר – *Which is why people still say:* Regarding somebody who brazenly sins, and despite recognizing His Master means to rebel against Him, people say: This man is like Nimrod who was a mighty hunter.

יא | מִן־הָאָרֶץ. כֵּיוָן שֶׁרָאָה אַשּׁוּר אֶת בָּנָיו שׁוֹמְעִין לְנִמְרוֹד וּמוֹרְדִין בַּמָּקוֹם לִבְנוֹת הַמִּגְדָּל, יָצָא מִתּוֹכָם:

11 | מִן־הָאָרֶץ – *From that land:* When Ashur saw that his sons were listening to Nimrod's advice by agreeing to rebel against God and build the tower, he moved away from them.

◄

ד ה וּבְנֵי יָוָן אֱלִישָׁה וְתַרְשִׁישׁ כִּתִּים וְדֹדָנִים: מֵאֵלֶּה
נִפְרְדוּ אִיֵּי הַגּוֹיִם בְּאַרְצֹתָם אִישׁ לִלְשֹׁנוֹ לְמִשְׁפְּחֹתָם
ו ז בְּגוֹיֵהֶם: וּבְנֵי חָם כּוּשׁ וּמִצְרַיִם וּפוּט וּכְנָעַן: וּבְנֵי
כוּשׁ סְבָא וַחֲוִילָה וְסַבְתָּה וְרַעְמָה וְסַבְתְּכָא וּבְנֵי
ח רַעְמָה שְׁבָא וּדְדָן: וְכוּשׁ יָלַד אֶת־נִמְרֹד הוּא הֵחֵל
ט לִהְיוֹת גִּבֹּר בָּאָרֶץ: הוּא־הָיָה גִבֹּר־צַיִד לִפְנֵי יהוה
י עַל־כֵּן יֵאָמַר כְּנִמְרֹד גִּבּוֹר צַיִד לִפְנֵי יהוה: וַתְּהִי
רֵאשִׁית מַמְלַכְתּוֹ בָּבֶל וְאֶרֶךְ וְאַכַּד וְכַלְנֵה בְּאֶרֶץ
יא שִׁנְעָר: מִן־הָאָרֶץ הַהִוא יָצָא אַשּׁוּר וַיִּבֶן אֶת־נִינְוֵה
יב וְאֶת־רְחֹבֹת עִיר וְאֶת־כָּלַח: וְאֶת־רֶסֶן בֵּין נִינְוֵה
יג וּבֵין כָּלַח הִוא הָעִיר הַגְּדֹלָה: וּמִצְרַיִם יָלַד אֶת־
לוּדִים וְאֶת־עֲנָמִים וְאֶת־לְהָבִים וְאֶת־נַפְתֻּחִים:
יד וְאֶת־פַּתְרֻסִים וְאֶת־כַּסְלֻחִים אֲשֶׁר יָצְאוּ מִשָּׁם
טו פְּלִשְׁתִּים וְאֶת־כַּפְתֹּרִים: וּכְנַעַן יָלַד אֶת־
טז צִידֹן בְּכֹרוֹ וְאֶת־חֵת: וְאֶת־הַיְבוּסִי וְאֶת־הָאֱמֹרִי

12 | הָעִיר הַגְּדֹלָה – *The great city:* The adjective refers to Nineveh, as the verse states: *Nineveh was an immensely great city* (Jonah 3:3).

13 | לְהָבִים – *Lehavim:* These people were so called because their faces resembled flames [*lehavim*, in their color].

14 | וְאֶת־פַּתְרֻסִים וְאֶת־כַּסְלֻחִים אֲשֶׁר יָצְאוּ מִשָּׁם פְּלִשְׁתִּים – *Patrusim, Kasluḥim – from whom the Philistines descended:* [The Hebrew phrasing gives the impression that] the Philistines descended from both of these peoples. For the Patrusim and Kasluḥim would sleep with each other's wives. The Philistines were born of these women [and their paternity was uncertain].

יב | הָעִיר הַגְּדֹלָה. הִיא נִינְוֵה, שֶׁנֶּאֱמַר: "וְנִינְוֵה הָיְתָה עִיר גְּדוֹלָה לֵאלֹהִים" (יונה ג, ג):

יג | לְהָבִים. שֶׁפְּנֵיהֶם דּוֹמִים לְלַהַב:

יד | וְאֶת־פַּתְרֻסִים וְאֶת־כַּסְלֻחִים אֲשֶׁר יָצְאוּ מִשָּׁם פְּלִשְׁתִּים. מִשְּׁנֵיהֶם יָצְאוּ, שֶׁהָיוּ פַּתְרוּסִים וְכַסְלוּחִים מַחֲלִיפִין מִשְׁכַּב נְשׁוֹתֵיהֶם אֵלּוּ לָאֵלּוּ, וְיָצְאוּ מֵהֶם פְּלִשְׁתִּים:

17 18 the Hivites, Arkites, and Sinites, the Arvadites, Zemarites, and
19 Hamatites. Later, the Canaanite families were dispersed. The
Canaanite borders were from Sidon toward Gerar near Aza,
and toward Sedom, Amora, Adma, and Tzevoyim, near Lasha.
20 These were the descendants of Ḥam, by their clans and their
21 languages, with their lands and their nations. Sons
were also born to Shem. The older brother of Yefet, he was the
22 ancestor of all the sons of Ever. Shem's sons were Elam, Ashur,
23 Arpakhshad, Lud, and Aram. Aram's sons were Utz, Ḥul,
24 Geter, and Mash. Arpakhshad was the father of Shelaḥ, and
25 Shelaḥ was the father of Ever. To Ever, two sons were born.
One was named Peleg, for in his time the earth was divided.

יח | וְאַחַר נָפֹצוּ. מֵאֵלֶּה נָפוֹצוּ מִשְׁפָּחוֹת הַרְבֵּה:

18 | וְאַחַר נָפֹצוּ – *Were dispersed:* Many families emerged from these groups.

יט | גְּבוּל הַכְּנַעֲנִי. גְּבוּל סוֹף אַרְצוֹ. כָּל 'גְּבוּל' לְשׁוֹן סוֹף וְקָצֶה:

19 | גְּבוּל הַכְּנַעֲנִי – *The Canaanite borders:* The description in this verse details the edge of the Canaanites' territory. For the term *gevul* always refers to the outer reaches of an area, or its end.

בֹּאֲכָה. שֵׁם דָּבָר. וְלִי נִרְאֶה, כְּאָדָם הָאוֹמֵר לַחֲבֵרוֹ: גְּבוּל זֶה מַגִּיעַ עַד אֲשֶׁר תָּבֹא לְמָקוֹם פְּלוֹנִי:

בֹּאֲכָה – *Toward :* The term *boakha* represents the infinitive in noun form ["coming"]. It seems to me that the sense is like the construct used when a person says to his fellow: This border continues until you come to a particular place.

כ | לִלְשֹׁנֹתָם בְּאַרְצֹתָם. אַף עַל פִּי שֶׁנֶּחְלְקוּ לִלְשׁוֹנוֹת וַאֲרָצוֹת, כֻּלָּם בְּנֵי חָם הֵם:

20 | לִלְשֹׁנֹתָם בְּאַרְצֹתָם – *By their languages, with their lands:* Even though these peoples became dispersed into different languages and lands, they were all descendants of Ḥam.

כא | אֲבִי כָּל־בְּנֵי־עֵבֶר. הַנָּהָר, הָיָה שֵׁם:

21 | אֲבִי כָּל־בְּנֵי־עֵבֶר – *He was the ancestor of all the sons of Ever:* Shem was the ancestor of all those who lived across [*me'ever*] the river. [According to Rashi, the present verse does not refer to the man named "Ever" who is introduced in 10:24, since this would be stating the obvious. Rather, the word *ever* connotes a preposition, with the phrase *benei ever* meaning: "Those who live across the river."]

אֲחִי יֶפֶת הַגָּדוֹל. אֵינִי יוֹדֵעַ אִם יֶפֶת הַגָּדוֹל אִם שֵׁם. כְּשֶׁהוּא אוֹמֵר: "שֵׁם בֶּן מְאַת שָׁנָה וְגוֹ' שְׁנָתַיִם אַחַר הַמַּבּוּל" (להלן יא, י), הֱוֵי אוֹמֵר יֶפֶת

אֲחִי יֶפֶת הַגָּדוֹל – *The older brother of Yefet:* This verse leaves me unsure whether Yefet was the oldest of Noaḥ's sons [and hence the phrase *aḥi Yefet hagadol* should be understood as: "The brother of Yefet the elder"], or whether Shem is the

◀

יז וְאֶת הַגִּרְגָּשִׁי: וְאֶת־הַחִוִּי וְאֶת־הָעַרְקִי וְאֶת־הַסִּינִי:
יח וְאֶת־הָאַרְוָדִי וְאֶת־הַצְּמָרִי וְאֶת־הַחֲמָתִי וְאַחַר נָפֹצוּ
יט מִשְׁפְּחוֹת הַכְּנַעֲנִי: וַיְהִי גְּבוּל הַכְּנַעֲנִי מִצִּידֹן בֹּאֲכָה
גְרָרָה עַד־עַזָּה בֹּאֲכָה סְדֹמָה וַעֲמֹרָה וְאַדְמָה וּצְבֹיִם
כ עַד־לָשַׁע: אֵלֶּה בְנֵי־חָם לְמִשְׁפְּחֹתָם לִלְשֹׁנֹתָם
כא בְּאַרְצֹתָם בְּגוֹיֵהֶם: וּלְשֵׁם יֻלַּד גַּם־הוּא
כב אֲבִי כָּל־בְּנֵי־עֵבֶר אֲחִי יֶפֶת הַגָּדוֹל: בְּנֵי שֵׁם עֵילָם
כג וְאַשּׁוּר וְאַרְפַּכְשַׁד וְלוּד וַאֲרָם: וּבְנֵי אֲרָם עוּץ וְחוּל
כד וְגֶתֶר וָמַשׁ: וְאַרְפַּכְשַׁד יָלַד אֶת־שָׁלַח וְשֶׁלַח יָלַד
כה אֶת־עֵבֶר: וּלְעֵבֶר יֻלַּד שְׁנֵי בָנִים שֵׁם הָאֶחָד פֶּלֶג

older one [and the verse should be taken as translated in this edition]. However, a later text relates that *when Shem was one hundred years old, he had a son, Arpakhshad, two years after the flood* (11:10). This proves that Yefet was the oldest brother, as follows. Noaḥ was five hundred years old when he first became a father [as attested in 5:32], and the flood began when the man was six hundred years old [as reported in 7:11]. This means that Noaḥ's oldest son was one hundred years old when the rains destroyed the world. But Shem only reached the age of one hundred two years after the flood. [This proves that he could not have been Noaḥ's firstborn.]

הַגָּדוֹל, שֶׁהֲרֵי בֶּן חֲמֵשׁ מֵאוֹת שָׁנָה הָיָה נֹחַ כְּשֶׁהִתְחִיל לְהוֹלִיד, וְהַמַּבּוּל הָיָה בִּשְׁנַת שֵׁשׁ מֵאוֹת שָׁנָה, נִמְצָא שֶׁהַגָּדוֹל בְּבָנָיו הָיָה בֶּן מֵאָה שָׁנָה, וְשֵׁם לֹא הִגִּיעַ לְמֵאָה עַד שְׁנָתַיִם אַחַר הַמַּבּוּל:

אֲחִי יֶפֶת – *The brother of Yefet:* Shem is described as Yefet's brother and not as Ḥam's. For Shem and Yefet acted respectfully toward their father, while Ḥam disgraced him.

אֲחִי יֶפֶת. וְלֹא אֲחִי חָם, שֶׁאֵלּוּ שְׁנֵיהֶם כִּבְּדוּ אֶת אֲבִיהֶם וְזֶה בִּזָּהוּ:

25 | **נִפְלְגָה** – *Was divided:* In Peleg's time human language became mixed up. The people spread out from the valley where they had settled and were divided [*nitpallegu*] across the world. We learn from this that Ever was a prophet who named his son after future events. [The civilization who built the Tower of Babel is commonly known as *dor hapalaga* – the generation of the dispersal. The father Ever anticipated this upheaval, and so named his son Peleg.] Indeed, the work Seder ◀

כה | נִפְלְגָה. נִתְבַּלְבְּלוּ הַלְּשׁוֹנוֹת וְנָפוֹצוּ מִן הַבִּקְעָה וְנִתְפַּלְּגוּ בְּכָל הָעוֹלָם. לָמַדְנוּ שֶׁהָיָה עֵבֶר נָבִיא, שֶׁקָּרָא שֵׁם בְּנוֹ עַל שֵׁם הֶעָתִיד. וְשָׁנִינוּ בְּסֵדֶר עוֹלָם שֶׁבְּסוֹף יָמָיו נִתְפַּלְּגוּ, שֶׁאִם תֹּאמַר בִּתְחִלַּת יָמָיו, הֲרֵי יָקְטָן אָחִיו צָעִיר מִמֶּנּוּ וְהוֹלִיד

26 His brother was named Yoktan. Yoktan was the father of Al-
27 modad, Shelef, Ḥatzarmavet, Yeraḥ, Hadoram, Uzal, Dikla,
28 29 Oval, Avimael, Sheva, Ofir, Ḥavila, and Yovav; all these were
30 Yoktan's sons. Their settlements extended from Mesha toward
31 Sefar, in the eastern hill country. These were the descendants
of Shem, by their clans and their languages, with their lands
32 and their nations. These, then, are the clans of the sons of
Noaḥ, by their lines, in their nations. And from these, the nations spread out across the earth after the flood.
11 1 The whole world spoke the same language, the same words. SHEVI'I
2 And as the people migrated from the east they found a valley

כַּמָּה מִשְׁפָּחוֹת קֹדֶם לָכֵן, שֶׁנֶּאֱמַר: "וְיָקְטָן יָלַד" וְגוֹ' (להלן פסוק כו) וְאַחַר כָּךְ: "וַיְהִי כָל הָאָרֶץ שָׂפָה אֶחָת" (להלן יא, א). וְאִם תֹּאמַר בְּאֶמְצַע יָמָיו, לֹא בָּא הַכָּתוּב לִסְתֹּם אֶלָּא לְפָרֵשׁ; הָא לָמַדְתָּ שֶׁבִּשְׁנַת מוֹת פֶּלֶג נִתְפַּלְּגוּ:

Olam maintains [in chapter 1] that the scattering of humanity took place only at the end of Peleg's life. Now the incident could not have happened when he was young [and the impetus for his name] due to the following reasoning: Peleg had a younger brother named Yoktan who had fathered several families before the event of the tower. To start, verse 26 reports: *Yoktan was the father of Almodad, Shelef, Ḥatzarmavet, Yeraḥ*, and only then do we read that *the whole world spoke the same language* [11:1, before humanity was dispersed; hence Yoktan was already an adult at the time of the dispersal, and all the more so his older brother Peleg]. And the reader should not suggest that God scattered the people sometime during the middle of Peleg's life [whereupon his name was changed to reflect the event]. For the purpose of the text is not to obscure [the chronology] but to clarify it. We must therefore infer that humanity was scattered in the exact year of his death.

יָקְטָן. שֶׁהָיָה עָנָו וּמַקְטִין עַצְמוֹ, לְכָךְ זָכָה לְהַעֲמִיד כָּל הַמִּשְׁפָּחוֹת הַלָּלוּ:

יָקְטָן – *Yoktan:* Yoktan was so called because he was modest man who belittled [*hiktin*] himself. As a reward for this humility, he was privileged to establish all of these families.

כו | חֲצַרְמָוֶת. עַל שֵׁם מְקוֹמוֹ, דִּבְרֵי אַגָּדָה:

26 | **חֲצַרְמָוֶת** – *Ḥatzarmavet:* [Literally, "Death's Court."] According to the Midrash, this man was named after the place where he lived.

יא א | שָׂפָה אֶחָת. לְשׁוֹן הַקֹּדֶשׁ:

11 1 | **שָׂפָה אֶחָת** – *The same language:* The holy tongue [Hebrew].

כו כִּי בְיָמָיו נִפְלְגָה הָאָרֶץ וְשֵׁם אָחִיו יָקְטָן׃ וְיָקְטָן יָלַד
אֶת־אַלְמוֹדָד וְאֶת־שָׁלֶף וְאֶת־חֲצַרְמָוֶת וְאֶת־יָרַח׃
כז כח וְאֶת־הֲדוֹרָם וְאֶת־אוּזָל וְאֶת־דִּקְלָה׃ וְאֶת־עוֹבָל
כט וְאֶת־אֲבִימָאֵל וְאֶת־שְׁבָא׃ וְאֶת־אוֹפִר וְאֶת־חֲוִילָה
ל וְאֶת־יוֹבָב כָּל־אֵלֶּה בְּנֵי יָקְטָן׃ וַיְהִי מוֹשָׁבָם מִמֵּשָׁא
לא בֹּאֲכָה סְפָרָה הַר הַקֶּדֶם׃ אֵלֶּה בְנֵי־שֵׁם לְמִשְׁפְּחֹתָם
לב לִלְשֹׁנֹתָם בְּאַרְצֹתָם לְגוֹיֵהֶם׃ אֵלֶּה מִשְׁפְּחֹת בְּנֵי־נֹחַ
לְתוֹלְדֹתָם בְּגוֹיֵהֶם וּמֵאֵלֶּה נִפְרְדוּ הַגּוֹיִם בָּאָרֶץ
אַחַר הַמַּבּוּל׃

יא א ב וַיְהִי כָל־הָאָרֶץ שָׂפָה אֶחָת וּדְבָרִים אֲחָדִים׃ וַיְהִי ט שביעי
בְּנָסְעָם מִקֶּדֶם וַיִּמְצְאוּ בִקְעָה בְּאֶרֶץ שִׁנְעָר וַיֵּשְׁבוּ

וּדְבָרִים אֲחָדִים – *The same words:* All of humanity shared the same plan. Everyone came together and said: It is not right that God should retain the upper realm for Himself! Let us ascend to the heavens and wage war against Him. Another interpretation: The people spoke against the single [*yaḥid*] Master of the Universe. Another interpretation: The assembled masses believed that once every 1,650 years the firmament would collapse, as it did during the flood [which took place in the year 1656 after creation]. Thus, they decided to build scaffolding to support the sky. This idea is presented in Bereshit Rabba (38:6).

2 | **בְּנָסְעָם מִקֶּדֶם** – *As the people migrated from the east:* All of humanity had settled in the east, as the earlier verse states: *Their settlements extended from Mesha toward Sefar, in the eastern hill country* (10:30). From there they set out to find a place that could sustain them all, finding only Shinar to be suitable.

וּדְבָרִים אֲחָדִים. בָּאוּ בְּעֵצָה אַחַת וְאָמְרוּ: לֹא כָּל הֵימֶנּוּ שֶׁיָּבֹר לוֹ אֶת הָעֶלְיוֹנִים, נַעֲלֶה לָרָקִיעַ וְנַעֲשֶׂה עִמּוֹ מִלְחָמָה. דָּבָר אַחֵר, עַל יְחִידוֹ שֶׁל עוֹלָם. דָּבָר אַחֵר, "וּדְבָרִים אֲחָדִים", אָמְרוּ: אַחַת לְאֶלֶף וְתרנ"ו שָׁנִים הָרָקִיעַ מִתְמוֹטֵט כְּשֵׁם שֶׁעָשָׂה בִּימֵי הַמַּבּוּל, בֹּאוּ וְנַעֲשֶׂה לוֹ סְמוֹכוֹת. בְּרֵאשִׁית רַבָּה (לח, ו):

ב | **בְּנָסְעָם מִקֶּדֶם.** שֶׁהָיוּ יוֹשְׁבִים שָׁם, כִּדְכְתִיב לְמַעְלָה: "וַיְהִי מוֹשָׁבָם וְגוֹ' הַר הַקֶּדֶם" (לעיל י, ל), וְנָסְעוּ מִשָּׁם לָתוּר לָהֶם מָקוֹם לְהַחֲזִיק אֶת כֻּלָּם, וְלֹא מָצְאוּ אֶלָּא שִׁנְעָר:

◀

3 in the land of Shinar and settled there. They said to each other, "Come, let us make bricks, let us bake them thoroughly."
4 They used bricks for stone and tar for mortar. And they said,
"Come, let us build ourselves a city and a tower that reaches
the heavens, and make a name for ourselves. Otherwise we
5 will be scattered across the face of the earth." But the Lord
came down to see the city and the tower being built by the
6 children of men. The Lord said, "If, as one people with one
language, they have begun to do this, nothing they plan to do

ג | **אִישׁ אֶל־רֵעֵהוּ.** אֻמָּה לְאֻמָּה, מִצְרַיִם לְכוּשׁ וְכוּשׁ לְפוּט וּפוּט לִכְנַעַן:

3 | **אִישׁ אֶל־רֵעֵהוּ** – *To each other:* The verse [does not mean that individuals suggested the plan to each other, but that] each nation discussed it with the other groups: Mitzrayim consulted with Kush, who talked it over with Put, who in turned raised the issue with Kenaan.

הָבָה. הַזְמִינוּ עַצְמְכֶם. כָּל 'הָבָה' לְשׁוֹן הַזְמָנָה הוּא, שֶׁמְּכִינִים עַצְמָן וּמִתְחַבְּרִים לִמְלָאכָה אוֹ לְעֵצָה אוֹ לְמַשָּׂא. הָבָה – הַזְמִינוּ, אפריילי"ר בְּלַעַז:

הָבָה – *Come:* The people told each other to prepare themselves for the task ahead. The term *hava* represents an invitation [rather than a command] to individuals who arrange themselves into working groups, advisory committees, or to undertake some burden. The term in Old French is *apareillier* ["to prepare"].

לְבֵנִים. שֶׁאֵין אֲבָנִים בְּבָבֶל, שֶׁהִיא בִּקְעָה:

לְבֵנִים – *Bricks:* Since Babylon is situated in a valley, there are no rocks there [that is, there is no quarry from which stones can be hewn].

וְנִשְׂרְפָה לִשְׂרֵפָה. כָּךְ עוֹשִׂין הַלְּבֵנִים שֶׁקּוֹרִים טיוול"ש, שׂוֹרְפִים אוֹתָן בְּכִבְשָׁן:

וְנִשְׂרְפָה לִשְׂרֵפָה – *Let us bake them thoroughly:* This is the process for producing bricks known as *tiules* ["tiles"] in Old French – the materials are baked in a kiln.

לַחֹמֶר. לָטוּחַ הַקִּיר:

לַחֹמֶר – *For mortar:* For plastering the wall.

ד | **פֶּן־נָפוּץ.** שֶׁלֹּא יָבִיא עָלֵינוּ שׁוּם מַכָּה לַהֲפִיצֵנוּ מִכָּאן:

4 | **פֶּן־נָפוּץ** – *Otherwise we will be scattered:* Let us act to prevent God from striking us with some plague that will force us to disperse from here.

ה | **וַיֵּרֶד יהוה לִרְאֹת.** לֹא הֻצְרַךְ לְכָךְ, אֶלָּא לְלַמֵּד לַדַּיָּנִים שֶׁלֹּא יַרְשִׁיעוּ הַנִּדּוֹן עַד שֶׁיִּרְאוּ וְיָבִינוּ. מִדְרַשׁ רַבִּי תַּנְחוּמָא (יח):

5 | **וַיֵּרֶד יהוה לִרְאֹת** – *But the Lord came down to see:* God did not actually need to descend in order to see the developing project [since He is of course omniscient]. Rather, the language of the text is meant to teach judges not to convict a defendant until they have properly investigated and understood the matter. This interpretation is found in Midrash Tanḥuma [chapter 18].

◀

ג שָׁם׃ וַיֹּאמְרוּ אִישׁ אֶל־רֵעֵהוּ הָבָה נִלְבְּנָה לְבֵנִים
וְנִשְׂרְפָה לִשְׂרֵפָה וַתְּהִי לָהֶם הַלְּבֵנָה לְאָבֶן וְהַחֵמָר
ד הָיָה לָהֶם לַחֹמֶר׃ וַיֹּאמְרוּ הָבָה ׀ נִבְנֶה־לָּנוּ עִיר
וּמִגְדָּל וְרֹאשׁוֹ בַשָּׁמַיִם וְנַעֲשֶׂה־לָּנוּ שֵׁם פֶּן־נָפוּץ
ה עַל־פְּנֵי כָל־הָאָרֶץ׃ וַיֵּרֶד יהוה לִרְאֹת אֶת־הָעִיר
ו וְאֶת־הַמִּגְדָּל אֲשֶׁר בָּנוּ בְּנֵי הָאָדָם׃ וַיֹּאמֶר יהוה
הֵן עַם אֶחָד וְשָׂפָה אַחַת לְכֻלָּם וְזֶה הַחִלָּם לַעֲשׂוֹת

בְּנֵי הָאָדָם – *The children of men:* Obviously the people involved in this enterprise were children of men – who else would they be, the offspring of donkeys and camels? The choice of words teaches that these individuals descended from the first man who had similarly expressed ingratitude [and whose character the current society had inherited]. For just as Adam had defended himself by saying: *The woman you put here with me – she gave me fruit from the tree and I ate* (3:12), these people were similarly ungrateful to God for rescuing them from the flood. They were thus perfectly willing to rebel against God who had extended them such grace.

בְּנֵי הָאָדָם. אֶלָּא בְּנֵי מִי? שֶׁמָּא בְּנֵי חֲמוֹרִים וּגְמַלִּים?! אֶלָּא בְּנֵי אָדָם הָרִאשׁוֹן שֶׁכָּפָה אֶת הַטּוֹבָה וְאָמַר: "הָאִשָּׁה אֲשֶׁר נָתַתָּה עִמָּדִי" (לעיל ג, יב), אַף אֵלּוּ כָּפוּ בַטּוֹבָה לִמְרֹד בְּמִי שֶׁהִשְׁפִּיעָם טוֹבָה וּמִלְּטָם מִן הַמַּבּוּל:

6 | **הֵן עַם אֶחָד** – *If, as one people:* Even though these people hold all the benefits of a sound society, as they are united as a single nation with a common language, they still are plotting to do this.

ו | **הֵן עַם אֶחָד.** כָּל טוֹבָה זוֹ יֵשׁ עִמָּהֶם, שֶׁעַם אֶחָד הֵם וְשָׂפָה אַחַת לְכֻלָּם, וְדָבָר זֶה הֵחֵלּוּ לַעֲשׂוֹת:

הַחִלָּם – *They have begun:* The form of the word haḥillam is [a verbal noun] similar to that of *omram* ["their saying"], and *asotam* ["their doing"]. It means "their beginning".

הַחִלָּם. כְּמוֹ 'אָמְרָם' 'עֲשׂוֹתָם', לְהַתְחִיל הֵם לַעֲשׂוֹת:

לֹא־יִבָּצֵר – *Will be impossible:* The term should be understood as a rhetorical question [that is, "Shall nothing be impossible for them?"], and the verb *lehibbatzer* means "to be prevented," as Targum Onkelos translates it. A similar usage appears in the verse, *He withholds [yivtzor] the spirits of princes* (Psalms 76:13).

לֹא־יִבָּצֵר. בִּתְמִיָּה. "יִבָּצֵר" לְשׁוֹן מְנִיעָה כְּתַרְגּוּמוֹ, וְדוֹמֶה לוֹ: "יִבְצֹר רוּחַ נְגִידִים" (תהלים עו, יג):

◀

7 will be impossible for them. Let us go down and confuse their
language so that one will not understand the speech of an-
8 other." From there the Lord scattered them all over the earth,
9 and they abandoned the building of the city. That is why it was
called Bavel, because it was there that the Lord confused the
language of all the earth; and from there the Lord scattered
them all across the face of the earth.
10 These are the descendants of Shem. When Shem was one
hundred years old, he had a son, Arpakhshad, two years after
11 the flood. After Arpakhshad was born, Shem lived five hun-
12 dred years and had other sons and daughters. When
Arpakhshad was thirty-five years old, he had a son, Shelaḥ.
13 After Shelaḥ was born, Arpakhshad lived four hundred and

ז | **הָבָה נֵרְדָה.** בְּבֵית דִּינוֹ נִמְלַךְ מֵעַנְוְתָנוּתוֹ יְתֵרָה:

7 | **הָבָה נֵרְדָה** – *Let us go down:* Because of His great humility, God now consulted with His court.

הָבָה. מִדָּה כְּנֶגֶד מִדָּה, הֵם אָמְרוּ: "הָבָה נִבְנֶה", וְהוּא כְּנֶגְדָּם מָדַד וְאָמַר: "הָבָה נֵרְדָה":

הָבָה – *Let us:* God's response to the human plan represented a measure for measure reaction to the people's proclamation. After the masses had declared: *Let us build ourselves a city and a tower* (11:4), God responded with *Let us go down and confuse their language*.

וְנָבְלָה. וּנְבַלְבֵּל, נוּ"ן מְשַׁמֵּשׁ בִּלְשׁוֹן רַבִּים, וְהֵ"א אַחֲרוֹנָה יְתֵרָה כְּהֵ"א שֶׁל 'נֵרְדָה':

וְנָבְלָה – *And let us confuse:* The verb *venavela* means "let us mix up." The initial letter *nun* signals the plural form, while the final letter *heh* is superfluous, just as it is at the end of the word *nereda* ["let us go down." The *heh* does not indicate a feminine object: We will confuse her or it.]

לֹא יִשְׁמְעוּ. זֶה שׁוֹאֵל לְבֵנָה וְזֶה מֵבִיא טִיט, וְזֶה עוֹמֵד עָלָיו וּפוֹצֵעַ אֶת מוֹחוֹ:

לֹא יִשְׁמְעוּ – *So that one will not understand:* [As a result of the confusion] one worker will ask another for a brick, but his colleague will deliver mortar to him. In response, the first man will bash the other's head in.

ח | **וַיָּפֶץ יהוה אֹתָם מִשָּׁם.** בָּעוֹלָם הַזֶּה. מַה שֶּׁאָמְרוּ "פֶּן נָפוּץ" (לעיל פסוק ד) נִתְקַיֵּם עֲלֵיהֶם, הוּא שֶׁאָמַר שְׁלֹמֹה: "מְגוֹרַת רָשָׁע הִיא תְבוֹאֶנּוּ" (משלי י, כד):

8 | **וַיָּפֶץ יהוה אֹתָם מִשָּׁם** – *From there the Lord scattered them:* The people were spread out across this world. For since they had feared that they would *be scattered across the face of the earth* (11:4), God punished them in just that way. This is an example of what Shlomo writes: *That which the wicked man dreads will befall him* (Proverbs 10:24).

ט | **וּמִשָּׁם הֱפִיצָם.** לִמֵּד שֶׁאֵין לָהֶם חֵלֶק לָעוֹלָם הַבָּא. וְכִי אֵי זוֹ

9 | **וּמִשָּׁם הֱפִיצָם** – *And from there He scattered them:* [The previous verse already described the fate of the people in this world.

ז וְעַתָּה לֹא־יִבָּצֵר מֵהֶם כֹּל אֲשֶׁר יָזְמוּ לַעֲשׂוֹת: הָבָה
נֵרְדָה וְנָבְלָה שָׁם שְׂפָתָם אֲשֶׁר לֹא יִשְׁמְעוּ אִישׁ שְׂפַת
ח רֵעֵהוּ: וַיָּפֶץ יהוה אֹתָם מִשָּׁם עַל־פְּנֵי כָל־הָאָרֶץ
ט וַיַּחְדְּלוּ לִבְנֹת הָעִיר: עַל־כֵּן קָרָא שְׁמָהּ בָּבֶל כִּי־
שָׁם בָּלַל יהוה שְׂפַת כָּל־הָאָרֶץ וּמִשָּׁם הֱפִיצָם יהוה
עַל־פְּנֵי כָּל־הָאָרֶץ:
י אֵלֶּה תּוֹלְדֹת שֵׁם שֵׁם בֶּן־מְאַת שָׁנָה וַיּוֹלֶד אֶת־
יא אַרְפַּכְשָׁד שְׁנָתַיִם אַחַר הַמַּבּוּל: וַיְחִי־שֵׁם אַחֲרֵי
הוֹלִידוֹ אֶת־אַרְפַּכְשָׁד חֲמֵשׁ מֵאוֹת שָׁנָה וַיּוֹלֶד בָּנִים
יב וּבָנוֹת: וְאַרְפַּכְשַׁד חַי חָמֵשׁ וּשְׁלֹשִׁים
יג שָׁנָה וַיּוֹלֶד אֶת־שָׁלַח: וַיְחִי אַרְפַּכְשַׁד אַחֲרֵי הוֹלִידוֹ

קָשֶׁה, שֶׁל דּוֹר הַמַּבּוּל אוֹ שֶׁל דּוֹר הַפַּלָּגָה? אֵלּוּ לֹא פָּשְׁטוּ יָד בָּעִקָּר וְאֵלּוּ פָּשְׁטוּ יָד בָּעִקָּר לְהִלָּחֵם בּוֹ, וְאֵלּוּ נִשְׁטְפוּ וְאֵלּוּ לֹא נֶאֶבְדוּ מִן הָעוֹלָם! אֶלָּא שֶׁדּוֹר הַמַּבּוּל הָיוּ גַּזְלָנִים וְהָיְתָה מְרִיבָה בֵּינֵיהֶם, וְאֵלּוּ הָיוּ נוֹהֲגִים אַהֲבָה וְרֵעוּת בֵּינֵיהֶם, שֶׁנֶּאֱמַר: "שָׂפָה אֶחָת וּדְבָרִים אֲחָדִים" (לעיל פסוק א). לָמַדְתָּ שֶׁשָּׂנְאוּי הַמַּחֲלֹקֶת וְגָדוֹל הַשָּׁלוֹם:

Hence the present sentence] teaches that these people would not receive any share in the next world either. Now which sin was more severe – that of the people of the flood, or that perpetrated by the generation of the dispersal? Note that the first group had not tried to attack God, whereas the later society attempted to wage war against Him, so to speak. And yet, the earlier civilization was wiped off the face of the earth, and the later one was not! However, the people of the deluge were thieves who thrived on conflict amongst themselves, while the tower builders worked together in love and unity, as is attested to in the first verse of the narrative: *The whole world spoke the same language, the same words* (11:1). We learn from here that God despises dissension but values peace.

י | שֵׁם בֶּן־מְאַת שָׁנָה. כְּשֶׁהוֹלִיד אֶת אַרְפַּכְשַׁד שְׁנָתַיִם אַחַר הַמַּבּוּל:

10 | **שֵׁם בֶּן־מְאַת שָׁנָה** – *When Shem was one hundred years old:* [The adverb "when" is not represented in the Hebrew. Thus, in the original text, the first clause, *Shem was one hundred years old*, and the second, *And he had a son, Arpakhshad*, appear to have no connection. Hence Rashi explains] that *Shem was one hundred years old* when he fathered *Arpakhshad, two years after the flood.*

◄

14 three years and had other sons and daughters. When
15 Shelaḥ was thirty years old, he had a son, Ever. After Ever was
born, Shelaḥ lived four hundred and three years and had oth-
16 er sons and daughters. Ever lived thirty-four years
17 and then had a son, Peleg. After Peleg was born, Ever lived
four hundred and thirty years and had other sons and daugh-
18 ters. Peleg lived thirty years and then had a son, Reu.
19 After Reu was born, Peleg lived two hundred and nine years
20 and had other sons and daughters. Reu lived thirty-
21 two years and then had a son, Serug. After Serug was born,
Reu lived two hundred and seven years and had other sons
22 and daughters. Serug lived thirty years and then had
23 a son, Naḥor. After Naḥor was born, Serug lived two hundred
24 years and had other sons and daughters. Naḥor lived
25 twenty-nine years and then had a son, Teraḥ. After Teraḥ was
born, Naḥor lived one hundred and nineteen years and had
26 other sons and daughters. Teraḥ lived seventy
27 years and fathered Avram, Naḥor, and Haran.These are the
descendants of Teraḥ. Teraḥ was the father of Avram, Naḥor,
28 and Haran, and Haran had a son, Lot. While his father Teraḥ

כח | **עַל־פְּנֵי תֶּרַח אָבִיו.** בְּחַיֵּי אָבִיו. וּמִדְרַשׁ אַגָּדָה אוֹמֵר, שֶׁעַל יְדֵי אָבִיו מֵת, שֶׁקָּבַל תֶּרַח עַל אַבְרָם בְּנוֹ לִפְנֵי נִמְרוֹד עַל שֶׁכִּתֵּת אֶת צְלָמָיו, וְהִשְׁלִיכוֹ לְכִבְשַׁן הָאֵשׁ, וְהָרָן יוֹשֵׁב וְאוֹמֵר בְּלִבּוֹ: אִם אַבְרָם נוֹצֵחַ אֲנִי מִשֶּׁלּוֹ, וְאִם נִמְרוֹד נוֹצֵחַ אֲנִי מִשֶּׁלּוֹ. וּכְשֶׁנִּצַּל אַבְרָם אָמְרוּ לוֹ לְהָרָן: מִשֶּׁל מִי אַתָּה? אָמַר לָהֶם הָרָן: מִשֶּׁל אַבְרָם אֲנִי. הִשְׁלִיכוּהוּ לְכִבְשַׁן הָאֵשׁ וְנִשְׂרַף, וְזֶהוּ: "אוּר כַּשְׂדִּים". וּמְנַחֵם פֵּרֵשׁ "אוּר" בִּקְעָה, וְכֵן: "בָּאֻרִים כַּבְּדוּ ה'" (ישעיה כד, טו), וְכֵן: "מְאוּרַת צִפְעוֹנִי" (שם יא, ח), כָּל חוֹר וּבֶקַע עָמֹק קָרוּי 'אוּר':

28 | **עַל־פְּנֵי תֶּרַח אָבִיו** – *While Teraḥ his father was still alive:* [Literally, "In the presence of Teraḥ his father."] Haran died while his father was still alive. The Midrash [presents an alternative interpretation,] that Haran died because of his father. Teraḥ had brought a complaint against his son Avram before Nimrod for having smashed the father's idols. As a result, Nimrod cast Avram into a fiery furnace. While this was happening, Haran, who was present, said to himself: If Avram emerges victorious from this debate, I will side with him; whereas if Nimrod wins, I will support him. After Avram was rescued from death [having escaped unscathed from the furnace], the court turned to Haran and said: "Well, which do you support [the faith of Avram or that of Nimrod]?" Said Haran: "I am on Avram's side!" Immediately he was thrown into the fiery furnace, where he perished. This is the source of the name *Ur Kasdim* ["the fire of Kasdim"]. Meanwhile, Menaḥem ben Saruq explains the term *ur* as denoting a valley, as in the verse *Out of the crevices*

◀

אֶת־שֶׁלַח שָׁלֹשׁ שָׁנִים וְאַרְבַּע מֵאוֹת שָׁנָה וַיּוֹלֶד
יד בָּנִים וּבָנוֹת׃ וְשֶׁלַח חַי שְׁלֹשִׁים שָׁנָה
טו וַיּוֹלֶד אֶת־עֵבֶר׃ וַיְחִי־שֶׁלַח אַחֲרֵי הוֹלִידוֹ אֶת־
עֵבֶר שָׁלֹשׁ שָׁנִים וְאַרְבַּע מֵאוֹת שָׁנָה וַיּוֹלֶד בָּנִים
טז וּבָנוֹת׃ וַיְחִי־עֵבֶר אַרְבַּע וּשְׁלֹשִׁים שָׁנָה
יז וַיּוֹלֶד אֶת־פָּלֶג׃ וַיְחִי־עֵבֶר אַחֲרֵי הוֹלִידוֹ אֶת־
פֶּלֶג שְׁלֹשִׁים שָׁנָה וְאַרְבַּע מֵאוֹת שָׁנָה וַיּוֹלֶד בָּנִים
יח וּבָנוֹת׃ וַיְחִי־פֶלֶג שְׁלֹשִׁים שָׁנָה וַיּוֹלֶד אֶת־
יט רְעוּ׃ וַיְחִי־פֶלֶג אַחֲרֵי הוֹלִידוֹ אֶת־רְעוּ תֵּשַׁע שָׁנִים
כ וּמָאתַיִם שָׁנָה וַיּוֹלֶד בָּנִים וּבָנוֹת׃ וַיְחִי
כא רְעוּ שְׁתַּיִם וּשְׁלֹשִׁים שָׁנָה וַיּוֹלֶד אֶת־שְׂרוּג׃ וַיְחִי רְעוּ
אַחֲרֵי הוֹלִידוֹ אֶת־שְׂרוּג שֶׁבַע שָׁנִים וּמָאתַיִם שָׁנָה
כב וַיּוֹלֶד בָּנִים וּבָנוֹת׃ וַיְחִי שְׂרוּג שְׁלֹשִׁים שָׁנָה
כג וַיּוֹלֶד אֶת־נָחוֹר׃ וַיְחִי שְׂרוּג אַחֲרֵי הוֹלִידוֹ אֶת־נָחוֹר
כד מָאתַיִם שָׁנָה וַיּוֹלֶד בָּנִים וּבָנוֹת׃ וַיְחִי
כה נָחוֹר תֵּשַׁע וְעֶשְׂרִים שָׁנָה וַיּוֹלֶד אֶת־תָּרַח׃ וַיְחִי
נָחוֹר אַחֲרֵי הוֹלִידוֹ אֶת־תֶּרַח תְּשַׁע־עֶשְׂרֵה שָׁנָה
כו וּמְאַת שָׁנָה וַיּוֹלֶד בָּנִים וּבָנוֹת׃ וַיְחִי־תֶרַח
שִׁבְעִים שָׁנָה וַיּוֹלֶד אֶת־אַבְרָם אֶת־נָחוֹר וְאֶת־הָרָן׃
כז וְאֵלֶּה תּוֹלְדֹת תֶּרַח תֶּרַח הוֹלִיד אֶת־אַבְרָם אֶת־
כח נָחוֹר וְאֶת־הָרָן וְהָרָן הוֹלִיד אֶת־לוֹט׃ וַיָּמָת הָרָן

[ba'urim] they will glorify the Lord (Isaiah 24:15), and the verse *And an infant's hand will explore the viper's nest [me'urat]* (Isaiah 11:8). For a hole or a deep fissure is called an *ur*.

◀

was still alive, Haran died in the land of his birth, Ur Kas-
29 dim. Avram and Naḥor married; the name of Avram's wife MAFTIR
was Sarai, and the name of Naḥor's wife was Milka. She
30 was the daughter of Haran, father of Milka and Yiska. And
31 Sarai was barren – she had no child. Teraḥ took his son
Avram, and his grandson Lot, son of Haran, and his daughter-in-law Sarai, his son Avram's wife, and together they set
out from Ur Kasdim to go to the land of Canaan. But when
32 they arrived at Ḥaran, they settled there. Teraḥ lived two
hundred and five years, and he died in Ḥaran.

כט | **יִסְכָּה.** זוֹ שָׂרָה, עַל שֵׁם שֶׁסּוֹכָה בְּרוּחַ הַקֹּדֶשׁ, וְשֶׁהַכֹּל סוֹכִין בְּיָפְיָהּ, וּלְשׁוֹן נְסִיכוּת, כְּמוֹ 'שָׂרָה' לְשׁוֹן שְׂרָרָה:

29 | **יִסְכָּה** – *Yiska:* Yiska is another name for Sara. She was so called because she would look [*sokha* into the future] using divine inspiration. Alternatively, all people would look [*sokhin*] at her beauty. A third possibility: The name Yiska is connected to nobility [*nesikhut*], just as the term Sara represents authority [*serara*].

לא | **וַיֵּצְאוּ אִתָּם.** וַיֵּצְאוּ תֶּרַח וְאַבְרָם עִם לוֹט וְשָׂרַי:

31 | **וַיֵּצְאוּ אִתָּם** – *Together they set out:* The subjects of the verb *vayetze'u*, "set out," are Teraḥ and Avram, who left Ur Kasdim with Lot and Sarai.

לב | **וַיָּמָת תֶּרַח בְּחָרָן.** לְאַחַר שֶׁיָּצָא אַבְרָם מֵחָרָן וּבָא לְאֶרֶץ כְּנַעַן, הָיָה תֶּרַח יוֹתֵר מִשִּׁשִּׁים שָׁנָה, שֶׁהֲרֵי כָּתוּב: "וְאַבְרָם בֶּן חָמֵשׁ שָׁנִים וְשִׁבְעִים שָׁנָה בְּצֵאתוֹ מֵחָרָן"

32 | **וַיָּמָת תֶּרַח בְּחָרָן** – *And Teraḥ died in Ḥaran:* It was only after Avram left Ḥaran for the land of Canaan [in the following *parasha*] and had lived there for more than sixty years that Teraḥ died. This deduction is based on the following reasoning. The next chapter states: *Avram was seventy-five years old when he left Ḥaran* (12:4). We also know that Teraḥ was seventy years old

◀

עַל־פְּנֵ֖י תֶּ֣רַח אָבִ֑יו בְּאֶ֥רֶץ מֽוֹלַדְתּ֖וֹ בְּא֥וּר כַּשְׂדִּֽים:
כט וַיִּקַּ֨ח אַבְרָ֧ם וְנָח֛וֹר לָהֶ֖ם נָשִׁ֑ים שֵׁ֨ם אֵֽשֶׁת־אַבְרָם֙ מפטיר
שָׂרָ֔י וְשֵׁ֤ם אֵֽשֶׁת־נָחוֹר֙ מִלְכָּ֔ה בַּת־הָרָ֥ן אֲבִֽי־מִלְכָּ֖ה
וַֽאֲבִ֥י יִסְכָּֽה: ל וַתְּהִ֥י שָׂרַ֖י עֲקָרָ֑ה אֵ֥ין לָ֖הּ וָלָֽד: לא וַיִּקַּ֨ח
תֶּ֜רַח אֶת־אַבְרָ֣ם בְּנ֗וֹ וְאֶת־ל֤וֹט בֶּן־הָרָן֙ בֶּן־בְּנ֔וֹ
וְאֵת֙ שָׂרַ֣י כַּלָּת֔וֹ אֵ֖שֶׁת אַבְרָ֣ם בְּנ֑וֹ וַיֵּֽצְא֨וּ אִתָּ֜ם מֵא֣וּר
כַּשְׂדִּ֗ים לָלֶ֨כֶת֙ אַ֣רְצָה כְּנַ֔עַן וַיָּבֹ֥אוּ עַד־חָרָ֖ן וַיֵּ֥שְׁבוּ
שָֽׁם: לב וַיִּֽהְי֣וּ יְמֵי־תֶ֔רַח חָמֵ֥שׁ שָׁנִ֖ים וּמָאתַ֣יִם שָׁנָ֑ה וַיָּ֥מָת
תֶּ֖רַח בְּחָרָֽן:

(להלן יב, ז), וְתֶ֫רַח בֶּן שִׁבְעִים שָׁנָה הָיָה כְּשֶׁנּוֹלַד אַבְרָם, הֲרֵי קמ"ה לְתֶ֫רַח כְּשֶׁיָּצָא אַבְרָם מִמֶּנּוּ; נִשְׁאֲרוּ מִשְּׁנוֹתָיו הַרְבֵּה! וְלָמָּה הִקְדִּים הַכָּתוּב מִיתָתוֹ שֶׁל תֶּ֫רַח לִיצִיאָתוֹ שֶׁל אַבְרָם? שֶׁלֹּא יְהֵא הַדָּבָר מְפֻרְסָם לַכֹּל, וְיֹאמְרוּ: לֹא קִיֵּם אַבְרָהָם כִּבּוּד אָבִיו שֶׁהִנִּיחוֹ זָקֵן וְהָלַךְ לוֹ. לְפִיכָךְ קְרָאוֹ הַכָּתוּב מֵת, שֶׁהָרְשָׁעִים אַף בְּחַיֵּיהֶם קְרוּיִים מֵתִים, וְהַצַּדִּיקִים בְּמִיתָתָן קְרוּיִים חַיִּים:

when Avram was born [as stated in 11:26]. Adding these two facts together, we conclude that Teraḥ was one hundred and forty-five years old when Avram left Ḥaran. And yet, the father still had a long time to live. [Teraḥ lived another sixty years until the age of two hundred and five.] Why then does the text mention Teraḥ's death before Avram's departure [related at the start of chapter 12]? The goal of the Torah was to avoid publicizing how Avram left Teraḥ when the old man was still alive; the reader might have accused Avram of neglecting his filial obligation to respect his father. Furthermore, the text refers to Teraḥ as a dead man [although he lived for another sixty years], because even when alive, the wicked are considered dead, whereas the righteous are considered alive even when they die. Thus, the verse states: *Benayahu son of Yehoyada was the son of a living man* (II Samuel 23:20).

HAFTARAT NOAḤ

On Rosh Ḥodesh Marḥeshvan read the maftir and haftara on page 51.

54 1 Barren woman, never a mother, rejoice; break out in joyful song though ISAIAH
you have not given birth, for the children of the forsaken woman will
2 outnumber those of the wife, so says the LORD. Broaden the site of your
tent; stretch out your canvas home; do not hold back; lengthen your tent
3 cords, and strengthen its pegs: you shall overflow rightward and left, your
4 children possessing nations, and filling forsaken towns with life. Do not
fear – you will not be shamed; fear not, for none can disgrace you. You
will forget your youthful abjection; the debasement of your widowhood
5 you will call no more to mind, for your husband, He who made you – the
LORD of Hosts is His name, and your redeemer, Israel's Holy One – will
6 be named God of all the world, for as a woman abandoned, of sorrowful
spirit, the LORD has called to you: Can the young bride ever be rejected?
7 says your God; for one small moment I left you; with infinite care shall I
8 gather you back; in the flash of My fury I hid My face from you for just
a moment, and in everlasting love will I care for you now. So speaks the
9 LORD, your redeemer. For these are the waters of Noaḥ to Me,
and I swore that the waters of Noaḥ would never sweep again over the
earth. And so did I swear no more to be furious with you, no more to
10 rebuke you. For mountains may move, hills may crumble away; but My *Sepharadim end here*
love for you will not be moved, nor My pact of peace crumble. So speaks
11 the LORD, who cares for you. Oppressed and storm swept, never comforted; behold: I am paving your ground with garnet, lapis lazuli
12 your foundations. I am fitting your windows with rubies, your gates with
13 glowing granite, marking your borders with stones men covet. All your
children will be students of the LORD, and great will be your children's
14 peace. On righteousness will you be founded; stay far from oppression;
15 you will not fear, and terror will never come near you. No strife can arise
without My assent; who among you fears one who could come upon you?
16 For I create the craftsman who blows the charcoal fire and brings forth the
17 tools of his trade; I create also the destroyer to do harm. No weapon made
to harm you can prevail; any tongue that calls you into judgment, you
will prove its fault. This is the birthright of the LORD's servants, for their
55 1 innocence is Mine; so says the LORD. You who are thirsty, all,
come to water; you who have no silver, come, take food and eat; come and
2 take food without silver, wine and milk without cost, for why should you
weigh out your silver for no bread, your labor bringing you no fullness?
Listen – listen to Me: let goodness nourish you, and let your souls delight

הפטרת נח

בראש חודש מרחשון קוראים את המפטיר ואת ההפטרה בעמ' 51.

ישעיה

נד א רָנִּי עֲקָרָה לֹא יָלָדָה פִּצְחִי רִנָּה וְצַהֲלִי לֹא־חָלָה כִּי־רַבִּים
ב בְּנֵי־שׁוֹמֵמָה מִבְּנֵי בְעוּלָה אָמַר יהוה: הַרְחִיבִי ׀ מְקוֹם אָהֳלֵךְ וִירִיעוֹת מִשְׁכְּנוֹתַיִךְ יַטּוּ אַל־תַּחְשֹׂכִי הַאֲרִיכִי מֵיתָרַיִךְ וִיתֵדֹתַיִךְ
ג חַזֵּקִי: כִּי־יָמִין וּשְׂמֹאול תִּפְרֹצִי וְזַרְעֵךְ גּוֹיִם יִירָשׁ וְעָרִים נְשַׁמּוֹת
ד יוֹשִׁיבוּ: אַל־תִּירְאִי כִּי־לֹא תֵבוֹשִׁי וְאַל־תִּכָּלְמִי כִּי לֹא תַחְפִּירִי כִּי בֹשֶׁת עֲלוּמַיִךְ תִּשְׁכָּחִי וְחֶרְפַּת אַלְמְנוּתַיִךְ לֹא תִזְכְּרִי־עוֹד:
ה כִּי בֹעֲלַיִךְ עֹשַׂיִךְ יהוה צְבָאוֹת שְׁמוֹ וְגֹאֲלֵךְ קְדוֹשׁ יִשְׂרָאֵל אֱלֹהֵי
ו כָל־הָאָרֶץ יִקָּרֵא: כִּי־כְאִשָּׁה עֲזוּבָה וַעֲצוּבַת רוּחַ קְרָאָךְ יהוה
ז וְאֵשֶׁת נְעוּרִים כִּי תִמָּאֵס אָמַר אֱלֹהָיִךְ: בְּרֶגַע קָטֹן עֲזַבְתִּיךְ
ח וּבְרַחֲמִים גְּדֹלִים אֲקַבְּצֵךְ: בְּשֶׁצֶף קֶצֶף הִסְתַּרְתִּי פָנַי רֶגַע מִמֵּךְ
ט וּבְחֶסֶד עוֹלָם רִחַמְתִּיךְ אָמַר גֹּאֲלֵךְ יהוה: כִּי־מֵי נֹחַ זֹאת לִי אֲשֶׁר נִשְׁבַּעְתִּי מֵעֲבֹר מֵי־נֹחַ עוֹד עַל־הָאָרֶץ כֵּן נִשְׁבַּעְתִּי

הספרדים מסיימים כאן

י מִקְּצֹף עָלַיִךְ וּמִגְּעָר־בָּךְ: כִּי הֶהָרִים יָמוּשׁוּ וְהַגְּבָעוֹת תְּמוּטֶינָה וְחַסְדִּי מֵאִתֵּךְ לֹא־יָמוּשׁ וּבְרִית שְׁלוֹמִי לֹא תָמוּט אָמַר מְרַחֲמֵךְ
יא יהוה: עֲנִיָּה סֹעֲרָה לֹא נֻחָמָה הִנֵּה אָנֹכִי מַרְבִּיץ בַּפּוּךְ
יב אֲבָנַיִךְ וִיסַדְתִּיךְ בַּסַּפִּירִים: וְשַׂמְתִּי כַּדְכֹד שִׁמְשֹׁתַיִךְ וּשְׁעָרַיִךְ
יג לְאַבְנֵי אֶקְדָּח וְכָל־גְּבוּלֵךְ לְאַבְנֵי־חֵפֶץ: וְכָל־בָּנַיִךְ לִמּוּדֵי יהוה וְרַב
יד שְׁלוֹם בָּנָיִךְ: בִּצְדָקָה תִּכּוֹנָנִי רַחֲקִי מֵעֹשֶׁק כִּי־לֹא תִירָאִי וּמִמְּחִתָּה
טו כִּי לֹא־תִקְרַב אֵלָיִךְ: הֵן גּוֹר יָגוּר אֶפֶס מֵאוֹתִי מִי־גָר אִתָּךְ עָלַיִךְ
טז יִפּוֹל: הֵן אָנֹכִי בָּרָאתִי חָרָשׁ נֹפֵחַ בְּאֵשׁ פֶּחָם וּמוֹצִיא כְלִי לְמַעֲשֵׂהוּ הִנֵּה

יז וְאָנֹכִי בָּרָאתִי מַשְׁחִית לְחַבֵּל: כָּל־כְּלִי יוּצַר עָלַיִךְ לֹא יִצְלָח וְכָל־לָשׁוֹן תָּקוּם־אִתָּךְ לַמִּשְׁפָּט תַּרְשִׁיעִי זֹאת נַחֲלַת עַבְדֵי יהוה
נה א וְצִדְקָתָם מֵאִתִּי נְאֻם־יהוה: הוֹי כָּל־צָמֵא לְכוּ לַמַּיִם וַאֲשֶׁר אֵין־לוֹ כָּסֶף לְכוּ שִׁבְרוּ וֶאֱכֹלוּ וּלְכוּ שִׁבְרוּ בְּלוֹא־כֶסֶף וּבְלוֹא
ב מְחִיר יַיִן וְחָלָב: לָמָּה תִשְׁקְלוּ־כֶסֶף בְּלוֹא־לֶחֶם וִיגִיעֲכֶם בְּלוֹא לְשָׂבְעָה שִׁמְעוּ שָׁמוֹעַ אֵלַי וְאִכְלוּ־טוֹב וְתִתְעַנַּג בַּדֶּשֶׁן נַפְשְׁכֶם:

3 in plenty. Turn your ear to Me and come; listen, that your souls may live; *Yemenites*
let Me forge an everlasting covenant with you, like David's faithful prom- *end here*
4 5 ises, for I make him a witness to nations, a leader, a ruler of nations; for
you shall call out, call, to a people you know not, and a people who know
you not will come running out to you for the sake of the LORD your God,
the Holy One of Israel, your glory.

MAFTIR FOR SHABBAT ROSH ḤODESH

8 9 On the Sabbath day: two yearling sheep without blemish and two-tenths NUMBERS
10 of fine flour as a grain offering, mixed with oil, and its libation. This is the
burnt offering for every Sabbath, in addition to the regular daily burnt
offering and its libation.

11 On your new moons you shall present a burnt offering to the LORD: two
12 young bulls, one ram, and seven yearling sheep, all without blemish. With
each bull, there shall be a grain offering of three-tenths of fine flour mixed
with oil, a grain offering of two-tenths of fine flour mixed with oil for each
13 ram, and a grain offering of one-tenth of fine flour mixed with oil for each
lamb. This shall be a burnt offering of pleasing aroma, a fire offering to
14 the Lord. Their libations shall be half a hin of wine for a bull, a third of
a hin of wine for a ram, and a quarter of a hin of wine for a lamb. This is
15 the monthly burnt offering for each new moon of the year. There shall be
one male goat as a sin offering to the Lord in addition to the regular burnt
offering and its libation.

HAFTARA FOR SHABBAT ROSH ḤODESH

6 1 Thus speaks the LORD: The heavens are My throne, the world, My foot- ISAIAH
stool. What House, then, would You build for Me, where could I rest?
2 My own hands made all this, all these are Mine, so says the LORD. And
these are the ones I look toward: the poor, of humbled spirit, trembling to
3 heed My words. While he, killing his ox is like a murderer of men, the one
who offers up a lamb, might so well behead a dog, the offering brought
may just as well be pigs' blood; and his remembrance incense is a blessing
of sin. These men, they choose their paths, their souls desire disgusting
4 things, and so I too will choose – will choose their torments, and bring
to them what they most fear; for I called out – no one answered, I spoke;
but none was listening. They did what was evil in My sight, and chose

ג הַטּוּ אָזְנְכֶם וּלְכוּ אֵלַי שִׁמְעוּ וּתְחִי נַפְשְׁכֶם וְאֶכְרְתָה לָכֶם בְּרִית התימנים מסיימים כאן
ד עוֹלָם חַסְדֵי דָוִד הַנֶּאֱמָנִים: הֵן עֵד לְאוּמִּים נְתַתִּיו נָגִיד וּמְצַוֵּה
ה לְאֻמִּים: הֵן גּוֹי לֹא־תֵדַע תִּקְרָא וְגוֹי לֹא־יְדָעוּךָ אֵלֶיךָ יָרוּצוּ לְמַעַן
יהוה אֱלֹהֶיךָ וְלִקְדוֹשׁ יִשְׂרָאֵל כִּי פֵאֲרָךְ:

מפטיר לשבת ראש חודש

כח ט וּבְיוֹם הַשַּׁבָּת שְׁנֵי־כְבָשִׂים בְּנֵי־שָׁנָה תְּמִימִם וּשְׁנֵי עֶשְׂרֹנִים סֹלֶת במדבר
י מִנְחָה בְּלוּלָה בַשֶּׁמֶן וְנִסְכּוֹ: עֹלַת שַׁבַּת בְּשַׁבַּתּוֹ עַל־עֹלַת הַתָּמִיד
וְנִסְכָּהּ:
יא וּבְרָאשֵׁי חָדְשֵׁיכֶם תַּקְרִיבוּ עֹלָה לַיהוה פָּרִים בְּנֵי־בָקָר שְׁנַיִם
יב וְאַיִל אֶחָד כְּבָשִׂים בְּנֵי־שָׁנָה שִׁבְעָה תְּמִימִם: וּשְׁלֹשָׁה עֶשְׂרֹנִים
סֹלֶת מִנְחָה בְּלוּלָה בַשֶּׁמֶן לַפָּר הָאֶחָד וּשְׁנֵי עֶשְׂרֹנִים סֹלֶת מִנְחָה
יג בְּלוּלָה בַשֶּׁמֶן לָאַיִל הָאֶחָד: וְעִשָּׂרֹן עִשָּׂרוֹן סֹלֶת מִנְחָה בְּלוּלָה
יד בַשֶּׁמֶן לַכֶּבֶשׂ הָאֶחָד עֹלָה רֵיחַ נִיחֹחַ אִשֶּׁה לַיהוה: וְנִסְכֵּיהֶם
חֲצִי הַהִין יִהְיֶה לַפָּר וּשְׁלִישִׁת הַהִין לָאַיִל וּרְבִיעִת הַהִין לַכֶּבֶשׂ
טו יָיִן זֹאת עֹלַת חֹדֶשׁ בְּחָדְשׁוֹ לְחָדְשֵׁי הַשָּׁנָה: וּשְׂעִיר עִזִּים אֶחָד
לְחַטָּאת לַיהוה עַל־עֹלַת הַתָּמִיד יֵעָשֶׂה וְנִסְכּוֹ:

הפטרת שבת ראש חודש

סו א כֹּה אָמַר יהוה הַשָּׁמַיִם כִּסְאִי וְהָאָרֶץ הֲדֹם רַגְלָי אֵי־זֶה בַיִת אֲשֶׁר ישעיה
ב תִּבְנוּ־לִי וְאֵי־זֶה מָקוֹם מְנוּחָתִי: וְאֶת־כָּל־אֵלֶּה יָדִי עָשָׂתָה וַיִּהְיוּ
כָל־אֵלֶּה נְאֻם־יהוה וְאֶל־זֶה אַבִּיט אֶל־עָנִי וּנְכֵה־רוּחַ וְחָרֵד
ג עַל־דְּבָרִי: שׁוֹחֵט הַשּׁוֹר מַכֵּה־אִישׁ זוֹבֵחַ הַשֶּׂה עֹרֵף כֶּלֶב מַעֲלֵה
מִנְחָה דַּם־חֲזִיר מַזְכִּיר לְבֹנָה מְבָרֵךְ אָוֶן גַּם־הֵמָּה בָּחֲרוּ בְּדַרְכֵיהֶם
ד וּבְשִׁקּוּצֵיהֶם נַפְשָׁם חָפֵצָה: גַּם־אֲנִי אֶבְחַר בְּתַעֲלֻלֵיהֶם וּמְגוּרֹתָם
אָבִיא לָהֶם יַעַן קָרָאתִי וְאֵין עוֹנֶה דִּבַּרְתִּי וְלֹא שָׁמֵעוּ וַיַּעֲשׂוּ הָרַע
ה בְּעֵינַי וּבַאֲשֶׁר לֹא־חָפַצְתִּי בָּחָרוּ: שִׁמְעוּ דְּבַר־

5 what I never desired. You who tremble at His word – listen to
the LORD's word: Your brothers said; the ones who hated you, who cast
you out because of My name, "Let us see, then, your joy –" they will be
6 shamefaced. A voice roaring out from the city – a voice, from the Sanctu-
7 ary – a voice – it is the LORD's – as He repays His enemies. Before she
had writhed in labor she gave birth; before the agonies took her she had
8 delivered a boy. Who ever heard of anything like this? Who ever saw anything like this? Can the land give birth in a day? Can a nation be born at
9 a single step? Yet Zion has labored, and has birthed her children. "Would
I bring on the labor and not deliver?" So the LORD speaks. "Would I who
10 fathered, close the womb?" So your God speaks. Bring
Jerusalem joy, exult in her, all of you who love her; celebrate her joy with
11 her, all of you who mourned her; That you may suck your fill from the
bosom of her comforting; may suckle, take delight in the brilliance of her
12 glory. For thus says the LORD: See Me make peace flow to her
like a river, the wealth of nations like a rushing brook, and you shall suckle.
13 You will be borne on hips, playing upon loving laps – as a man is consoled
by his mother, just so shall I comfort you, and in Jerusalem, you shall be
14 consoled. You shall look on, your heart rejoicing, while your bones grow
vigorous, like grass, and the hand of the LORD becomes known to His
15 servants, and His rage known to all His enemies. For see: the LORD is
coming in fire, His chariots like a storm-wind, to slake His fury in rage,
16 His rebuke in flames of fire. For in fire, the LORD comes to judgment,
and by the sword, to all flesh, and many are those the LORD will execute.
17 Those in the gardens, sanctifying and purifying themselves, one after the
other in the midst of it, while eating the flesh of pigs and pests and mice,
18 they will all be gathered in together: so the LORD has spoken. For I know
their works, their thoughts; and time will come, to gather all nations and
19 tongues, and they will come, and look upon My glory. I shall place a sign
among them, send out survivors from them to all nations, to Tarshish,
Pul and Lud, to the great archers, Tuval, Yavan, to the distant coastlands
where none ever heard tell of Me or saw My glory, and they will tell of My
20 glory to the nations. And they will bring back all your brothers from in
among all nations, an offering to the LORD, on horseback and on chariot,
on camels, mules and dromedaries, to My holy mount, Jerusalem: so says
the LORD – just as the children of Israel would bring up their offerings
21 in pure vessels, to the LORD's House – and from among them also I shall
22 take priests and Levites: so says the LORD. For as just as the new heavens,
the new earth that I am now forming, will stand forever before Me, so says

יְהֹוָה הַחֲרֵדִים אֶל־דְּבָר֑וֹ אָמְרוּ֩ אֲחֵיכֶ֨ם שֹׂנְאֵיכֶ֜ם מְנַדֵּיכֶ֗ם לְמַ֤עַן
שְׁמִי֙ יִכְבַּ֣ד יְהֹוָ֔ה וְנִרְאֶ֥ה בְשִׂמְחַתְכֶ֖ם וְהֵ֥ם יֵבֹֽשׁוּ: ק֤וֹל שָׁאוֹן֙ מֵעִ֔יר
ק֖וֹל מֵהֵיכָ֑ל ק֣וֹל יְהֹוָ֔ה מְשַׁלֵּ֥ם גְּמ֖וּל לְאֹיְבָֽיו: בְּטֶ֥רֶם תָּחִ֖יל יָלָ֑דָה
בְּטֶ֨רֶם יָב֥וֹא חֵ֛בֶל לָ֖הּ וְהִמְלִ֥יטָה זָכָֽר: מִֽי־שָׁמַ֣ע כָּזֹ֗את מִ֤י רָאָה֙
כָּאֵ֔לֶּה הֲי֤וּחַל אֶ֨רֶץ֙ בְּי֣וֹם אֶחָ֔ד אִם־יִוָּ֥לֵֽד גּ֖וֹי פַּ֣עַם אֶחָ֑ת כִּי־חָ֛לָה
גַּם־יָלְדָ֥ה צִיּ֖וֹן אֶת־בָּנֶֽיהָ: הַאֲנִ֥י אַשְׁבִּ֛יר וְלֹ֥א אוֹלִ֖יד יֹאמַ֣ר יְהֹוָ֑ה
אִם־אֲנִ֧י הַמּוֹלִ֛יד וְעָצַ֖רְתִּי אָמַ֥ר אֱלֹהָֽיִךְ: שִׂמְח֧וּ אֶת־
יְרוּשָׁלִַ֛ם וְגִ֥ילוּ בָ֖הּ כָּל־אֹהֲבֶ֑יהָ שִׂ֤ישׂוּ אִתָּהּ֙ מָשׂ֔וֹשׂ כָּל־הַמִּתְאַבְּלִ֖ים
עָלֶֽיהָ: לְמַ֤עַן תִּֽינְקוּ֙ וּשְׂבַעְתֶּ֔ם מִשֹּׁ֖ד תַּנְחֻמֶ֑יהָ לְמַ֧עַן תָּמֹ֛צּוּ
וְהִתְעַנַּגְתֶּ֖ם מִזִּ֥יז כְּבוֹדָֽהּ: כִּי־כֹ֣ה ׀ אָמַ֣ר יְהֹוָ֗ה הִנְנִ֨י
נֹטֶֽה־אֵ֠לֶ֠יהָ כְּנָהָ֨ר שָׁל֜וֹם וּכְנַ֧חַל שׁוֹטֵ֛ף כְּב֥וֹד גּוֹיִ֖ם וִינַקְתֶּ֑ם עַל־צַד֙
תִּנָּשֵׂ֔אוּ וְעַל־בִּרְכַּ֖יִם תְּשָׁעֳשָֽׁעוּ: כְּאִ֕ישׁ אֲשֶׁ֥ר אִמּ֖וֹ תְּנַחֲמֶ֑נּוּ כֵּ֤ן אָנֹכִי֙
אֲנַ֣חֶמְכֶ֔ם וּבִירֽוּשָׁלַ֖ם תְּנֻחָֽמוּ: וּרְאִיתֶם֙ וְשָׂ֣שׂ לִבְּכֶ֔ם וְעַצְמוֹתֵיכֶ֖ם
כַּדֶּ֣שֶׁא תִפְרַ֑חְנָה וְנוֹדְעָ֤ה יַד־יְהֹוָה֙ אֶת־עֲבָדָ֔יו וְזָעַ֖ם אֶת־אֹיְבָֽיו:
כִּֽי־הִנֵּ֤ה יְהֹוָה֙ בָּאֵ֣שׁ יָב֔וֹא וְכַסּוּפָ֖ה מַרְכְּבֹתָ֑יו לְהָשִׁ֤יב בְּחֵמָה֙ אַפּ֔וֹ
וְגַעֲרָת֖וֹ בְּלַהֲבֵי־אֵֽשׁ: כִּ֤י בָאֵשׁ֙ יְהֹוָ֣ה נִשְׁפָּ֔ט וּבְחַרְבּ֖וֹ אֶת־כָּל־בָּשָׂ֑ר
וְרַבּ֖וּ חַֽלְלֵ֥י יְהֹוָֽה: הַמִּתְקַדְּשִׁ֨ים וְהַמִּֽטַּהֲרִ֜ים אֶל־הַגַּנּ֗וֹת אַחַ֤ר
אַחַת֙ בַּתָּ֔וֶךְ אֹֽכְלֵי֙ בְּשַׂ֣ר הַחֲזִ֔יר וְהַשֶּׁ֖קֶץ וְהָעַכְבָּ֑ר יַחְדָּ֥ו יָסֻ֖פוּ
נְאֻם־יְהֹוָֽה: וְאָנֹכִ֗י מַעֲשֵׂיהֶם֙ וּמַחְשְׁבֹ֣תֵיהֶ֔ם בָּ֕אָה לְקַבֵּ֥ץ אֶת־
כָּל־הַגּוֹיִ֖ם וְהַלְּשֹׁנ֑וֹת וּבָ֖אוּ וְרָא֥וּ אֶת־כְּבוֹדִֽי: וְשַׂמְתִּ֨י בָהֶ֜ם א֗וֹת
וְשִׁלַּחְתִּ֣י מֵהֶ֣ם ׀ פְּלֵיטִ֡ים אֶֽל־הַגּוֹיִ֡ם תַּרְשִׁ֨ישׁ פּ֥וּל וְל֛וּד מֹ֥שְׁכֵי
קֶ֖שֶׁת תֻּבַ֣ל וְיָוָ֑ן הָאִיִּ֣ים הָרְחֹקִ֗ים אֲשֶׁ֨ר לֹֽא־שָׁמְע֤וּ אֶת־שִׁמְעִי֙
וְלֹא־רָא֣וּ אֶת־כְּבוֹדִ֔י וְהִגִּ֥ידוּ אֶת־כְּבוֹדִ֖י בַּגּוֹיִֽם: וְהֵבִ֣יאוּ אֶת־כָּל־
אֲחֵיכֶ֣ם מִכָּל־הַגּוֹיִ֣ם ׀ מִנְחָ֣ה ׀ לַֽיהֹוָ֡ה בַּסּוּסִ֡ים וּ֠בָרֶ֠כֶב וּבַצַּבִּ֨ים
וּבַפְּרָדִ֜ים וּבַכִּרְכָּר֗וֹת עַ֣ל הַ֥ר קָדְשִׁ֛י יְרוּשָׁלַ֖ם אָמַ֣ר יְהֹוָ֑ה כַּאֲשֶׁ֣ר
יָבִיאוּ֩ בְנֵ֨י יִשְׂרָאֵ֧ל אֶת־הַמִּנְחָ֛ה בִּכְלִ֥י טָה֖וֹר בֵּ֥ית יְהֹוָֽה: וְגַם־מֵהֶ֥ם
אֶקַּ֛ח לַכֹּהֲנִ֥ים לַלְוִיִּ֖ם אָמַ֥ר יְהֹוָֽה: כִּ֣י כַאֲשֶׁ֣ר הַשָּׁמַ֣יִם הַחֲדָשִׁ֡ים
וְהָאָ֜רֶץ הַחֲדָשָׁ֗ה אֲשֶׁ֨ר אֲנִ֥י עֹשֶׂ֛ה עֹמְדִ֥ים לְפָנַ֖י נְאֻם־יְהֹוָ֑ה כֵּ֛ן יַעֲמֹ֥ד

23 the LORD, so will stand your children, your name. And it shall be – every
new moon, every Sabbath – all flesh will come to worship Me: so says the
24 LORD. Going out, they will see the bodies of those people who sinned
against Me, for the worms will not die nor the fire be quenched, and they
will be repugnant to all flesh.

And it shall be – every new moon, every Sabbath, all flesh will come to worship Me: so says the LORD.

If Rosh Ḥodesh continues on Sunday, Sepharadim add the following two verses.

I SAMUEL

20 18 Jonathan then said to David, "Tomorrow is the New Month, and you shall
be missed, for your seat will be empty."

42 "Go in peace," Jonathan said to David, "for the two of us have sworn in the
name of the LORD, 'May the Lord be between me and you, and between
my seed and your seed, forever.'"

כג זַרְעֲכֶם וְשִׁמְכֶם: וְהָיָה מִדֵּי־חֹ֙דֶשׁ֙ בְּחָדְשׁ֔וֹ וּמִדֵּ֥י שַׁבָּ֖ת בְּשַׁבַּתּ֑וֹ
כד יָב֥וֹא כָל־בָּשָׂ֛ר לְהִשְׁתַּחֲוֺ֥ת לְפָנַ֖י אָמַ֥ר יהוה: וְיָצְא֣וּ וְרָא֔וּ בְּפִגְרֵי֙ הָאֲנָשִׁ֔ים הַפֹּשְׁעִ֖ים בִּ֑י כִּ֣י תוֹלַעְתָּ֞ם לֹ֣א תָמ֗וּת וְאִשָּׁם֙ לֹ֣א תִכְבֶּ֔ה וְהָי֥וּ דֵרָא֖וֹן לְכָל־בָּשָֽׂר:

וְהָיָ֗ה מִדֵּי־חֹ֙דֶשׁ֙ בְּחָדְשׁ֔וֹ וּמִדֵּ֥י שַׁבָּ֖ת בְּשַׁבַּתּ֑וֹ יָב֤וֹא כָל־בָּשָׂר֙ לְהִשְׁתַּחֲוֺ֣ת לְפָנַ֔י אָמַ֖ר יהוה:

אם ר"ח חל בשבת וראשון הספרדים מוסיפים פסוק ראשון ואחרון מהפטרת 'מָחָר חֹדֶשׁ'.

שמואל א

כ יח וַיֹּֽאמֶר־ל֥וֹ יְהוֹנָתָ֖ן מָחָ֣ר חֹ֑דֶשׁ וְנִפְקַ֕דְתָּ כִּ֥י יִפָּקֵ֖ד מוֹשָׁבֶֽךָ:
מב וַיֹּ֧אמֶר יְהוֹנָתָ֣ן לְדָוִ֗ד לֵ֣ךְ לְשָׁל֑וֹם אֲשֶׁר֩ נִשְׁבַּ֨עְנוּ שְׁנֵ֜ינוּ אֲנַ֗חְנוּ בְּשֵׁ֤ם יהוה֙ לֵאמֹ֔ר יהו֞ה יִֽהְיֶ֣ה ׀ בֵּינִ֣י וּבֵינֶ֗ךָ וּבֵ֥ין זַרְעִ֛י וּבֵ֥ין זַרְעֲךָ֖ עַד־עוֹלָֽם:

For the complete Rashi and haftara turn to the right side of this volume.

חומש קורן מקראות הדורות
THE KOREN MIKRAOT HADOROT

פרשת נח
PARASHAT NOAḤ

KOREN

THE ROHR FAMILY EDITION

חומש קורן מקראות הדורות
THE KOREN MIKRAOT HADOROT

THE ZAHAVA AND MOSHAEL STRAUS EDITION OF SEFER BERESHIT

פרשת נח עם מפרשים

PARASHAT NOAḤ WITH COMMENTARIES

TORAH TRANSLATION BY

Rabbi Lord Jonathan Sacks שליט״א

COMMENTARIES COLLECTED AND ABRIDGED BY

Rabbi Shai Finkelstein, EDITOR-IN-CHIEF

COMMENTARIES TRANSLATED BY

Rabbi Jonathan Mishkin

MANAGING EDITOR

Rabbi Yedidya Naveh

•

KOREN PUBLISHERS JERUSALEM

The Koren Mikraot HaDorot, The Rohr Edition
Volume 2: Parashat Noaḥ
First Edition, 2022

Koren Publishers Jerusalem Ltd.
POB 4044, Jerusalem 9104001, ISRAEL
POB 8531, New Milford, CT 06776, USA

www.korenpub.com

The Tanakh translation is excerpted from the Magerman Edition of The Koren Tanakh.

The creation of this work was made possible with the generous support of the Jewish Book Trust Inc.

Printed in ISRAEL

ISBN 978 965 7760 57 4

KMDNO01

The Rohr Family Edition of
The Koren Mikraot HaDorot
pays tribute to the memory of

Mr. Sami Rohr ז״ל
ר׳ שמואל ב״ר יהושע אליהו ז״ל

who served his Maker with joy
and whose far-reaching vision, warm open hand, love of Torah,
and love for every Jew were catalysts for the revival and growth of
vibrant Jewish life in the former Soviet Union
and in countless communities the world over

and to the memory of his beloved wife

Mrs. Charlotte Rohr (née Kastner) ע״ה
שרה בת ר׳ יקותיאל יהודה ע״ה

who survived the fires of the Shoah to become
the elegant and gracious matriarch,
first in Colombia and later in the United States,
of three generations of a family
nurtured by her love and unstinting devotion.
She found grace in the eyes of all those whose lives she touched.

Together they merited to see all their children
build lives enriched by faithful commitment
to the spreading of Torah and *Ahavat Yisrael*.

Dedicated with love by
The Rohr Family
NEW YORK, USA

עֲטֶרֶת זְקֵנִים בְּנֵי בָנִים
(משלי יז, ו)

Grandchildren
are the crowning glory of the aged
(Proverbs 17:6)

May the learning and traditions of our people
be strengthened by our future generations.
In honor of our wonderful grandchildren

Zahava and Moshael Straus

CONTENTS

Publisher's Preface
xi

Editor's Introduction
xv

A Note on the Translation
xviii

PARASHAT NOAḤ WITH COMMENTARIES

THE TIME OF THE SAGES
1

THE CLASSIC COMMENTATORS
67

CONFRONTING MODERNITY
157

THE BIBLICAL IMAGINATION

The Flood and Its Significance
235

The Eternal Dialectic
239

Educational Challenges in the Modern World
243

FOR THE COMPLETE RASHI AND HAFTARA
TURN TO THE OTHER END OF THIS VOLUME.

PUBLISHER'S PREFACE

The genius of Jewish commentary on the Torah is one of huge and critical import. Jewish life and law for millennia have been directed by our interpretations of the Torah, and each generation has looked to its rabbinic leadership for a deeper understanding of its teachings, its laws, its stories.

For centuries, *Mikraot Gedolot* have been a core part of understanding the Ḥumash; the words of Rashi, Ibn Ezra, Ramban, Rashbam, Ralbag, and other classic commentators illuminate and help us understand the Torah. But traditional editions of *Mikraot Gedolot* present only a slice in time and a small selection of the corpus of Jewish commentators. Almost every generation has produced rabbinic scholars who speak to their times, from Philo and Onkelos two thousand years ago, to Rabbi Joseph B. Soloveitchik, Rabbi Aharon Kotler, the Lubavitcher Rebbe, and Nehama Leibowitz in ours.

The Koren Mikraot HaDorot – Scriptures or Interpretations for the Generations – brings two millennia of Torah commentary into the hands and homes of Jews around the world. Readers will be able not only to encounter the classic commentators, but to gain a much broader sense of the issues that scholars grappled with in their time and the inspiration they drew from the ancient texts. We see, for example, how Philo speaks to an assimilating Greek Jewish audience in first-century Alexandria, and how similar yet different it is from Rabbi Samson Raphael Hirsch's approach to an equally assimilating nineteenth-century German readership; how the perspectives of Rabbi Soloveitchik and Rabbi Kotler differ in a post-Holocaust world; how Rav Se'adya Gaon interpreted the Torah for the Jews of Babylonia. It is an exciting journey through Jewish history via the unchanging words of the Torah.

The text of the Torah features the exceptional new translation of Rabbi Lord Jonathan Sacks, together with the celebrated and meticulously accurate Koren Hebrew text. Of course, with the exception of Rashi – for whom we present an entirely new translation in full – the commentaries are selected. We offer this anthology not to limit our reader's exploration but rather as a gateway for further learning of Torah and its commentaries on a broader and deeper level than space here permits. We discuss below how to use this book.

We must thank **Pamela and George Rohr** of New York, who recognized the unique value of *The Koren Mikraot HaDorot* and its ability to communicate historical breadth and context to the reader. For my colleagues here at Koren, we thank you; for the many generations of users who will find this a continuing source of new learning, we are forever in your debt.

We also are indebted to **Zahava and Moshael Straus**, true leaders of this Jewish generation in so many fields, who have invested not only in *Parashat Noaḥ* but the entire book of Bereshit. Together, we were thus able to launch this innovative and unique project.

We are honored to acknowledge and thank **Debra and David Magerman**, whose support for the Koren Ḥumash with Rabbi Sacks's exemplary translation and commentary laid the foundation for the core English text of this work.

Finally, I must personally thank **Rabbi Marvin Hier**, with whom I had a special breakfast some years ago at the King David Hotel. During the meal, he raised the problem that so few people knew the writings of Rabbi Joseph B. Soloveitchik and Rabbi Aharon Kotler on the Torah; and I, who had just read some of Philo's work, had the same reaction. From that conversation came the seed for this project.

HOW TO USE *THE KOREN MIKRAOT HADOROT*

The Koren Mikraot HaDorot will be a fifty-five-volume edition of the Ḥumash (one for each *parasha* plus a companion volume). Each of the fifty-four volumes of the *parashot* can be read from right to left (Hebrew opening side), and left to right (English opening side).

Opening from the Hebrew side offers:

- the full Torah text, the translation of Rabbi Sacks, and the full commentary of Rashi in both Hebrew and the new English translation
- all *haftarot* associated with the *parasha* of the volume, including Rosh Ḥodesh and special readings, both in Hebrew and English

Opening from the English side presents four sections:

- **THE TIME OF THE SAGES** – includes commentaries from the Second Temple period and the talmudic period
- **THE CLASSIC COMMENTATORS** – quotes selected explanations by Rashi as well as most of the commentators found in traditional *Mikraot Gedolot*
- **CONFRONTING MODERNITY** – selects commentaries from the eighteenth century to the close of the twentieth century
- **THE BIBLICAL IMAGINATION** – features essays surveying some of the broader conceptual ideas as a supplement to the linear, text-based commentary

The first three of these sections each feature the relevant verses, in Hebrew and English, on the page alongside their respective commentaries, in chronological order, providing the reader with a single window onto the text without excessive page turning.

In addition to being a valuable resource in a Jewish home or synagogue library, we conceived of these volumes as a weekly accompaniment in the synagogue. There is scope for the reader to study each *parasha* on a weekly basis in preparation for the reading on Shabbat. One may select a particular group of commentators for study that week, or perhaps alternate between ancient and modern viewpoints. Some readers may choose to delve into the text through verse-by-verse interpretation, while others may prefer a conceptual perspective on the *parasha* as a whole. The broad array of options for learning means this is a series which can be returned to year after year, always presenting new insights and new approaches to understanding the text.

ACKNOWLEDGMENTS

The creation of this book was possible only thanks to the small but exceptional team here at Koren Jerusalem. We are grateful to:

- Rabbi Tzvi Hersh Weinreb, שליט"א, who conceptualized the structure of the project and provides both moral and halakhic leadership at Koren
- Rabbi Shai Finkelstein, whose encyclopedic knowledge of Torah and its interpreters is equaled only by his community leadership, formerly in Memphis and today in Jerusalem
- Rabbi Yedidya Naveh, whose knowledge, organizational skills, and superb leadership brought the disparate elements together
- Rabbi Jonathan Mishkin, translator of the commentaries, who crafted a fluent, accurate, and eloquent English translation

Our design, editing, typesetting, and proofreading staff, including Tani Bayer, Esther Be'er, Tomi Mager, Adina Luber, Dr. Yoel Finkelman, and Carolyn Budow Ben David, enabled an attractive, user-friendly, and accurate edition of these works.

> "One silver basin" (Numbers 7:13) was brought as a symbol of the Torah, which has been likened to wine, as the verse states: "And drink of the wine which I have mingled" (Proverbs 9:5). Because it is customary to drink wine in a basin – as we see in the verse "that drink wine in basins" (Amos 6:6) – he therefore brought a basin. "Of seventy shekels, after the shekel of the sanctuary" (Numbers 7:13). Why? Because just as the numerical value of "wine" [*yayin*] is seventy, so there are seventy modes of expounding the Torah. (Bemidbar Rabba 13:16)

Each generation produces exceptional rabbinic, intellectual leadership. It has been our purpose to enable all Jews to taste the wine of those generations, in the hope of expanding the breadth and depth of their knowledge. Torah is our greatest treasure, and we need the wisdom of those generations to better understand this bountiful gift from God. We hope that we at Koren can deepen that understanding for all who seek it.

Matthew Miller, Publisher
Jerusalem, 5781 (2021)

EDITOR'S INTRODUCTION

Over the course of millennia, the Jewish people have watched while the surrounding society and its values have changed unceasingly. For the Jews, the steadfast response to an evolving world has always been the study of Torah, specifically engagement with the weekly *parasha*. Devotees of Jewish learning have always looked to the weekly Torah portion for spiritual and intellectual guidance through life's challenges. And in every generation, commentaries on the Ḥumash have debated the precise interpretation of the verses therein. These scholars have continuously asked what message God is trying to convey to Israel and the world through the Torah's narratives and laws. Their explanations have struggled to identify the correct ways to apply its lessons to our daily lives.

Throughout, all these authors have approached the Torah text from their own unique perspectives, shaped in no small measure by the eras and environments they lived in. Naturally, the pantheon of commentaries present widely different styles in their writings. Occasionally the commentators will subject a particular verse to piercing scrutiny as a self-contained unit. At other times they present interpretations that seem to stray from the straightforward meaning of the text. Ultimately, all commentaries demand that a verse provide readers with theological meaning and direction for communal and social life.

Recognition of the wisdom embedded in the vast literature of commentary on the Torah spanning the various eras of Jewish history planted the seeds of the project whose fruit you now hold. We have called this publication ***Mikraot HaDorot*** – Readings of the Generations. This window into the world of Torah commentaries is not simply an upgrade of the classical *Mikraot Gedolot* collections, which give readers merely a handful of familiar

interpretations. *The Koren Mikraot HaDorot* instead presents a plethora of exegetical contributions, with more than forty scholars spanning Jewish teachings from the past two thousand years represented on its pages.

Each volume of the *Koren Mikraot HaDorot* series can be opened from both the right (Hebrew) side and left (English) side. The Hebrew opening side includes the Hebrew and a new English text of the *parasha,* translated by Rabbi Lord Jonathan Sacks, with a full, new translation of Rashi and the *haftarot.* The English opening side contains the bulk of the commentaries, and is divided into four parts: The first, THE TIME OF THE SAGES, comprises commentaries from antiquity – ranging from Philo to the Yalkut Shimoni. These figures lived mainly in the land of Israel, Egypt, and Babylonia. The second, THE CLASSIC COMMENTATORS, contains interpretations from the Middle Ages – starting from Rav Se'adya Gaon and Rashi and continuing through time to the work of Rabbi Shlomo Efrayim of Luntschitz, author of the *Keli Yakar.* The authors included here represent the rich traditions of both Sephardic (Spanish and North African) and Ashkenazic (central and eastern European) schools of exegesis. The third section, CONFRONTING MODERNITY, offers the work of both Old World and New World scholars who lived between the eighteenth and twentieth centuries. Before each of these three sections we include a time line that specifies the chronological relationships between the commentators and the places they lived.

In the final section, THE BIBLICAL IMAGINATION, we provide three in-depth investigations of particular ideas through the writings of the various commentaries. There are several goals to these essays. First, we aim to reveal common threads weaving across the generations of Torah scholarship. Second, we hope to illustrate how the various authors were influenced by their lives and times, and that the lessons they transmitted to their communities reflected their environments. Finally, each essay highlights for the reader some central issues that the commentaries have grappled with. We trust that this tool will facilitate the reader's understanding of the words of the commentaries themselves.

Three principles have governed the decision making in our work on *The Koren Mikraot HaDorot*:

- Chronological order: We have striven to sketch out the historical development of Torah exegesis, an enterprise that has occupied innumerable communities of Jews in far-flung lands for centuries.

- Economy of selection: In compiling the excerpts used in this work, we have gone through the authors' works and isolated those sections which most directly address the particular question, issue, or difficulty that confronted the scholar.
- Objectivity of presentation: This book presents ideas of the commentaries authentically, never censoring them or smoothing them over in light of our own positions or perspectives. We always strove to faithfully transmit the legal, conceptual, social, and ethical messages of the commentators.

The modern world constantly challenges us as individuals, as a society, and as communal leaders, teachers, and parents. The values and culture of the society that surrounds us force thinking Jews to seriously consider and reconsider their ideas and priorities on a regular basis as we struggle to find the correct path through life. Furthermore, we constantly must ask ourselves what teachings we wish to transmit to future generations. It is our hope that the *Koren Mikraot HaDorot* project will help guide its readers as they grapple with these very real problems. The world of Torah commentary is wide and deep beyond measure. It contains innumerable answers to the questions that face the individual, the family, the generation, and indeed all of humanity.

Rabbi Shai Finkelstein, Editor-in-Chief
Jerusalem, 5781 (2021)

A NOTE ON THE TRANSLATION

The terse writing style prevalent in Jewish scholarship over most of history can be difficult for the modern reader to decipher. Since our goal in the *Koren Mikraot HaDorot* series is to make thousands of years of Torah commentary accessible to a modern, English-speaking audience, we have opted for a relatively loose translation style that accurately presents the content of the Hebrew commentary while not necessarily mirroring its exact syntax. We have also resorted occasionally to paraphrase in instances where a literal translation would be opaque in English. As any student of Torah exegesis will recognize, draconian insistence on a word-for-word translation would result in an English text that was unreadable and that preserved neither the clarity nor the majesty of the original Hebrew.

Many of the commentaries' discussions focus on the meanings of words and phrases that are ambiguous in the Hebrew text of the *parasha*. The beautiful new translation of the Torah by Rabbi Lord Jonathan Sacks that we include here often dispels these ambiguities in the interest of clarity, necessarily coming down on one side or the other of a disagreement between commentators. The reader of the commentaries should therefore view the Torah translation presented here as one possible reading of the often-cryptic Hebrew original. In a similar vein, the significance of certain interpretations may seem unclear, or their points obvious, until one encounters another commentary with a starkly different read of the same verse. These contrasts, and the realization that themes and meanings we thought to be clear are actually ambiguous and multifaceted, are the essence of *The Koren Mikraot HaDorot*.

We have, as far as possible, allowed each text to speak for itself, and have left editorial comments to a minimum. Nevertheless, the commentaries

often assume the reader's knowledge of other biblical episodes, midrashim, or Hebrew grammar beyond what might be expected from the English-speaking public today. To ensure clarity, we have therefore interpolated brief editor's notes where we deemed it necessary, setting them off from the original text in square brackets.

Throughout Jewish history, the text of the Tanakh has been viewed as the apogee of the Hebrew language. For many commentators, especially those of the Middle Ages, it served as a fountain of language from which they drew numerous idioms and phrases. The result is that the Hebrew text of many commentaries is shot through with snippets of biblical prose or poetry to such an extent that almost every sentence can be viewed as a quote or allusion. Marking and citing all of these would make for a cluttered translation and would hinder rather than enhance the reader's understanding. We have therefore opted to cite only those quotes which are brought by the author as explicit evidence to further the point being made, and not those that supply only a turn of phrase.

The Hebrew side of this volume contains a complete and unabridged translation of Rashi's commentary. For those who wish to follow the *parasha* on the English side of the book, we have also reprinted many of Rashi's explanations alongside those of the other classic commentators. This will allow the reader to compare Rashi's interpretation to those of Rashbam, Ibn Ezra, and others, as well as appreciate how Rashi's commentary often serves to define the issues that will be addressed by later exegetes.

The text of the commentaries is of course abridged. We have not included ellipses to mark every point where text has been omitted, to maintain a clutter-free translation. However, we have included ellipses at points where the subject of discussion would otherwise appear to have changed abruptly and inexplicably, to save the reader confusion. We have also not adhered strictly to the original heading, or s.v. (*dibbur hamatḥil*) of every text, changing it in instances where it would help to focus the reader on those words that are the actual subject of discussion, and adding it to texts that did not originally have it.

Most of the commentaries that we quote in this series were originally organized by chapter and verse. Therefore, anyone who wishes to consult the original Hebrew text of a given commentary can simply open to the verse in question. However, not all sources are organized this way. The midrashim in particular are often ordered loosely; an important interpretation of a verse in Exodus might be found in a midrash on Deuteronomy. For the reader's convenience in locating the original Hebrew source, we have

provided citations for those works not organized sequentially, as well as for commentaries originally composed on verses other than the one under discussion. These citations can be found outside of the final punctuation at the end of the excerpt in question.

Our translation has generally relied upon the Hebrew text found in the Bar-Ilan Responsa Project and the online compendia Sefaria and AlHatorah.org, as well as the standard printed editions of commentaries not found in any of these. The Responsa Project contains more than one edition of several midrashim (Midrash Tanḥuma, Midrash Rabba, and Avot Derabbi Natan). For these works, our citations should be understood as referring to the standard editions published in Vilna and Warsaw unless otherwise indicated. Aside from this, please note:

- Passages from Philo are quoted with permission from *Torah from Alexandria: Philo as a Biblical Commentator,* edited by Rabbi Michael Leo Samuel (New York: Kodesh Press, 2015).
- Selected commentaries of Rabbi Joseph B. Soloveitchik are printed with permission from *Chumash Mesoras HaRav,* edited by Dr. Arnold Lustiger (New York: OU Press and Ohr Publishing Inc., 2017).
- The commentaries of the Lubavitcher Rebbe are quoted from *The Torah, with an Interpolated Translation and Commentary Based on the Works of the Lubavitcher Rebbe,* edited by Rabbi Chaim Nochum Cunin and Rabbi Moshe Yaakov Wisnefsky (New York: Kehot Publication Society, 2017).
- The commentaries of Nehama Leibowitz are quoted, with generous permission, from *Studies in Shemot (Exodus),* translated by Aryeh Newman (Jerusalem: World Zionist Organization Department for Torah Education and Culture in the Diaspora, 1981).

While we have thus done our best to aid the reader in finding and consulting the original Hebrew text of the commentaries we have translated, we emphasize that this is not a critical edition, and the scope and readership of the series do not permit us to fully cite every allusion and internal reference that authors make to midrashim and other commentaries. Still, we have made a supreme effort to provide citations of talmudic passages, and of course biblical verses, quoted or referred to in the material included here.

Yedidya Naveh, Managing Editor
Jerusalem, 5781 (2021)

1ST CENTURY BCE

PHILO, 25 BCE – 50 CE

1ST CENTURY CE

2ND CENTURY

3RD CENTURY

MISHNA, 3RD CENTURY

HALAKHIC MIDRASHIM, 3RD CENTURY (MEKHILTA, SIFRA, SIFREI)

4TH CENTURY

TALMUD YERUSHALMI, 3RD – 5TH CENTURY

TALMUD BAVLI, 3RD – 6TH CENTURY

5TH CENTURY

MIDRASH TANḤUMA, 5TH CENTURY

6TH CENTURY

7TH CENTURY

8TH CENTURY

AVOT DERABBI NATAN, 7TH – 9TH CENTURY

9TH CENTURY

MIDRASH RABBA, 5TH – 12TH CENTURY

10TH CENTURY

11TH CENTURY

MIDRASH LEKAḤ TOV, 11TH CENTURY

12TH CENTURY

MIDRASH AGGADA, 12TH – 13TH CENTURY

13TH CENTURY

YALKUT SHIMONI, 13TH CENTURY

פרשת נח

PARASHAT NOAḤ

THE TIME OF THE SAGES

ו ט אֵלֶּה תּוֹלְדֹת נֹחַ נֹחַ אִישׁ צַדִּיק תָּמִים הָיָה בְּדֹרֹתָיו אֶת־ ה
י הָאֱלֹהִים הִתְהַלֶּךְ־נֹחַ׃ וַיּוֹלֶד נֹחַ שְׁלֹשָׁה בָנִים אֶת־שֵׁם
יא אֶת־חָם וְאֶת־יָפֶת׃ וַתִּשָּׁחֵת הָאָרֶץ לִפְנֵי הָאֱלֹהִים וַתִּמָּלֵא

CHAPTER 6, VERSE 9

TALMUD BAVLI

נֹחַ אִישׁ צַדִּיק תָּמִים – *Noaḥ was a righteous man, a person of integrity:* Rabbi Yirmeya ben Elazar taught: One should be reserved when praising a person in his presence, but fully extol his virtues when he is not there. Hence we find that when God addresses Noaḥ, He simply calls him "righteous." (7:1). However, the Torah describes the man more effusively when it states: *Noaḥ was a righteous man, a person of integrity in his generation*. (Eruvin 18b)

בְּדֹרֹתָיו – *In his generation:* Rabbi Yoḥanan taught: Noaḥ was surely a man of integrity within his own [sinful] generation, but he was less impressive compared to other generations. However, Reish Lakish maintained: Since Noaḥ was a leader in his generation [despite the evil influences all around him], had he lived in another time he would have been even greater. Rabbi Ḥanina responded: Rabbi Yoḥanan's position can be illustrated with the following metaphor. Consider a barrel of wine that is stored in a cellar filled with bottles of vinegar. In that location the odor of the wine is fragrant compared to the other smell. And yet, were the wine to be placed elsewhere its scent would be less noticeable. To this Rabbi Oshaya answered: Reish Lakish's interpretation can be compared to a vial of perfume sitting in a garbage heap. If the perfume's fragrance is strong enough to be smelled in that location, how much more so would it be detected in a less offensive space. (Sanhedrin 108a)

TANḤUMA

נֹחַ נֹחַ... נֹחַ – *Noaḥ. Noaḥ...Noaḥ:* Why is Noaḥ's name mentioned three times in this verse? It hints that Noaḥ was one of three men who lived to see three worlds: Noaḥ, Daniel, and Iyov. Noaḥ saw the world settled as it was at first, he saw the world destroyed by the flood, and he saw it rebuilt following that cataclysm. Daniel saw the First Temple in its glory, he witnessed its destruction, and he lived to see the Second Temple constructed in its place. Iyov had a family whom he enjoyed. He then saw his children die, and yet he lived to see the establishment of a new family. When a person troubles himself to sustain life created by God, he is referred to as a *tzaddik* [a righteous man]. Scripture speaks of two such men: Noaḥ and Yosef. For we read regarding Yosef: *They sold the righteous [tzaddik] for silver and the poor for the price of shoes* (Amos 2:6). And Yosef sustained his family, as the text reports: *Yosef provided his father, his brothers, and all his father's household with food* (47:12). (Noaḥ 5)

BERESHIT RABBA

נֹחַ אִישׁ צַדִּיק – *Noaḥ was a righteous man:* Three men were drawn to work the soil and failed in their efforts: Kayin, Noaḥ, and Uziyahu [the tenth king of Yehuda]. Regarding the first of these, the verse states: *Kayin was a worker of the land* (4:2). The Torah similarly relates: *Noaḥ began to be a man of the land* (9:20). And in describing Uziyahu, the text informs us: *He had farmers and vinedressers in the hills and the fertile lands, for he had a deep*

6 9 This is the story of Noaḥ. Noaḥ was a righteous man, a person
10 of integrity in his generation; Noaḥ walked with God. And
11 Noaḥ had three sons: Shem, Ḥam, and Yefet. The earth had

BERESHIT RABBA *(cont.)*

love for the soil (II Chronicles 26:10). Noaḥ is called a "man of the land" because he revived the land [which had just been devastated by the flood]. Furthermore, it was due to Noaḥ's merits that rain fell to water the land, and he proceeded to cover the surface of the ground with vegetation. Rabbi Berekhya taught: Moshe was even more beloved than Noaḥ. Noaḥ was first called "a righteous man," and in his later years "a man of the land." [Implied is a certain spiritual degradation over the course of his life.] Moshe, however, was first identified as an Egyptian man [by Yitro's daughters in Exodus 2:19], and is at the end of his life called a man of God [in Deuteronomy 33:1]. (Noaḥ 36:3)

VERSE 10

BERESHIT RABBA

וַיּוֹלֶד נֹחַ שְׁלֹשָׁה בָנִים – *And Noaḥ had three sons:* Rabbi Yudan taught: Why did all the previous generations of men father children when they were one hundred or two hundred years old, but Noaḥ only had his sons when he reached the age of five hundred? The Holy One, blessed be He, declared: If I allow Noaḥ to have sons earlier, they may turn out to be wicked, and I do not wish to destroy them in the flood. However, if Noaḥ's descendants end up being righteous [and grow to have their own children and grandchildren before the flood], the family's patriarch will have to build a whole host of arks to rescue them all from the deluge. Therefore God withheld children from Noaḥ until he was five hundred years old [so they would be young when the flood began]. (Bereshit 26:2)

VERSE 11

TALMUD BAVLI

וַתִּשָּׁחֵת הָאָרֶץ – *The earth had become corrupt:* The school of Rabbi Yishmael taught: Whenever the Torah refers to corruption, it connotes licentiousness and idol worship. An example of the former is the verse *All flesh corrupting its ways [darko] upon the earth* [6:12; the word "way" – *derekh* – can allude to sexual activity]. An example of the latter is the verse *Take great care for your own sake not to act corruptly, making yourselves any idol, an image of any shape, any form of man or of woman* (Deuteronomy 4:15–16). (Sanhedrin 57a)

LEKAḤ TOV

וַתִּשָּׁחֵת הָאָרֶץ – *The earth had become corrupt:* Whenever human beings sin, it is the earth itself which is stricken as a consequence. This may be compared to a student who becomes corrupt – it is his teacher who is rebuked for the failure. We find this to be so both with Adam and Kayin [whose actions led to the land being cursed in Genesis 3–4]. **לִפְנֵי הָאֱלֹהִים** – *In God's sight:* The humans believed that they could conceal their behavior from the Holy One, blessed be He. But Scripture attests that this is impossible when it states: *He knows their actions, they are crushed when the night is over* (Job 34:25).

יב הָאָ֖רֶץ חָמָֽס׃ וַיַּ֧רְא אֱלֹהִ֛ים אֶת־הָאָ֖רֶץ וְהִנֵּ֣ה נִשְׁחָ֑תָה כִּֽי־
יג הִשְׁחִ֧ית כָּל־בָּשָׂ֛ר אֶת־דַּרְכּ֖וֹ עַל־הָאָֽרֶץ׃ וַיֹּ֨אמֶר
אֱלֹהִ֜ים לְנֹ֗חַ קֵ֤ץ כָּל־בָּשָׂר֙ בָּ֣א לְפָנַ֔י כִּֽי־מָלְאָ֥ה הָאָ֛רֶץ חָמָ֖ס
יד מִפְּנֵיהֶ֑ם וְהִנְנִ֥י מַשְׁחִיתָ֖ם אֶת־הָאָֽרֶץ׃ עֲשֵׂ֤ה לְךָ֙ תֵּבַ֣ת עֲצֵי־
גֹ֔פֶר קִנִּ֖ים תַּעֲשֶׂ֣ה אֶת־הַתֵּבָ֑ה וְכָפַרְתָּ֥ אֹתָ֛הּ מִבַּ֥יִת וּמִח֖וּץ
טו בַּכֹּֽפֶר׃ וְזֶ֕ה אֲשֶׁ֥ר תַּעֲשֶׂ֖ה אֹתָ֑הּ שְׁלֹ֧שׁ מֵא֣וֹת אַמָּ֗ה אֹ֚רֶךְ

VERSE 12

PHILO

כָּל־בָּשָׂר – *All flesh:* The term "flesh" is a metaphor for the love of self and self-indulgence. These traits characterize anyone who lives an uncultivated life of virtue, which proved to be the root cause of that generation's moral corruption.

TALMUD BAVLI

כִּי־הִשְׁחִית כָּל־בָּשָׂר אֶת־דַּרְכּוֹ עַל־הָאָרֶץ – *All flesh corrupting its ways upon the earth:* Rabbi Yoḥanan taught: Note the destructive power of violence. For although the generation of the flood committed all manner of sin, their fate was only sealed once armed robbery became commonplace. Thus the verse states: *For the earth is full of violence because of them. I am about to destroy them, along with all the earth* (6:13). (Sanhedrin 108a)

TANḤUMA

וַיַּרְא אֱלֹהִים אֶת־הָאָרֶץ וְהִנֵּה נִשְׁחָתָה – *And when God saw how corrupt the earth had become:* In the middle of the story, the Torah reports that *God remembered Noaḥ and all the wild beasts and animals with him in the ark* (8:1). Granted that God paid attention to the fate of the humans, but why does the Torah note His care for the animals and the cattle that were with them? The Holy One, blessed be He, never withholds the reward due to any creature. For even the mouse on the ark maintained its fidelity to its own kind and did not copulate with other species. But all the people of that sinful generation had fornicated with each other's wives, as the verse states: *God saw how corrupt the earth had become.*

LEKAḤ TOV

כִּי־הִשְׁחִית כָּל־בָּשָׂר אֶת־דַּרְכּוֹ עַל־הָאָרֶץ – *All flesh corrupting its ways upon the earth:* The language of this verse teaches that it was not just the humans who acted immorally, but also the animals, the cattle, and the birds. This they did by mating with species other than their own. Now how do we know that such behavior was forbidden, and that the beasts were commanded to avoid it? From the verse *Then God said, "Let the land produce every kind of living thing: all the different species of cattle, crawling things and wild animals of the earth." And so it was* [1:24; it was God's intention that each animal species maintain its distinction].

12 become corrupt in God's sight, full of violence. And when God
saw how corrupt the earth had become, all flesh corrupting its
13 ways upon the earth, God said to Noaḥ, "The end of
all flesh has come before Me, for the earth is full of violence
because of them. I am about to destroy them, along with all the
14 earth. So make yourself an ark of cypress wood. Make it with
15 compartments and coat it in pitch inside and out. This is how
you shall make it: the ark shall be three hundred cubits long,

VERSE 13

LEKAḤ TOV

וְהִנְנִי מַשְׁחִיתָם אֶת־הָאָרֶץ – *I am about to destroy them, along with all the earth:* Rav Huna and Rav Yirmeya taught in the name of Rav Kahana son of Rav Malkiya: In the flood, the earth's soil was ruined to a depth of three handbreadths, which is how deep the plow cuts when it prepares a field. Thus was fulfilled God's threat to destroy all life on the planet *along with all the earth*.

YALKUT SHIMONI

כִּי־מָלְאָה הָאָרֶץ חָמָס מִפְּנֵיהֶם – *For the earth is full of violence because of them:* The term *ḥamas* is used to describe a theft of something worth at least a *peruta* [the smallest unit of currency], whereas *gezel* refers to stealing something that is worth less even than that [for which there is no legal redress]. Here is what the people in that generation would do. Picture a man who has arrived at the market with a basket full of lupines [a kind of legume] for sale. People around him would come along and each help themselves to a pea or two, which amounted to less than a *peruta*, until he was ruined. And the owner could not sue any individual for theft! The Holy One, blessed be He, declared: You have acted badly; I too will treat you badly. (51)

VERSE 14

MIDRASH AGGADA

עֲשֵׂה לְךָ תֵּבַת עֲצֵי־גֹפֶר – *So make yourself an ark of cypress wood:* Why was Noaḥ instructed to build the ark out of cypress [*gofer*] wood? The generation of the flood was punished with burning sulfur [*gofrit*]. Indeed, Noaḥ too should have suffered the same fate as his neighbors. However because *Noaḥ found favor in the Lord's sight* (6:8), God commanded him to build his boat out of *gofer* in order to help him atone [for the sins he had committed].

VERSE 15

PHILO

שְׁלֹשׁ מֵאוֹת אַמָּה אֹרֶךְ הַתֵּבָה חֲמִשִּׁים אַמָּה רָחְבָּהּ – *Three hundred cubits long, fifty cubits wide*: Noaḥ makes the ark in the figure of a box, so that wherever it is placed, it will remain steady and firm.

טז הַתֵּבָה חֲמִשִּׁים אַמָּה רׇחְבָּהּ וּשְׁלֹשִׁים אַמָּה קוֹמָתָהּ׃ צֹהַר ׀
תַּעֲשֶׂה לַתֵּבָה וְאֶל־אַמָּה תְּכַלֶנָּה מִלְמַעְלָה וּפֶתַח הַתֵּבָה
יז בְּצִדָּהּ תָּשִׂים תַּחְתִּיִּם שְׁנִיִּם וּשְׁלִשִׁים תַּעֲשֶׂהָ׃ וַאֲנִי הִנְנִי
מֵבִיא אֶת־הַמַּבּוּל מַיִם עַל־הָאָרֶץ לְשַׁחֵת כׇּל־בָּשָׂר אֲשֶׁר־
בּוֹ רוּחַ חַיִּים מִתַּחַת הַשָּׁמָיִם כֹּל אֲשֶׁר־בָּאָרֶץ יִגְוָע׃
יח וַהֲקִמֹתִי אֶת־בְּרִיתִי אִתָּךְ וּבָאתָ אֶל־הַתֵּבָה אַתָּה וּבָנֶיךָ
יט וְאִשְׁתְּךָ וּנְשֵׁי־בָנֶיךָ אִתָּךְ׃ וּמִכׇּל־הָחַי מִכׇּל־בָּשָׂר שְׁנַיִם מִכֹּל
כ תָּבִיא אֶל־הַתֵּבָה לְהַחֲיֹת אִתָּךְ זָכָר וּנְקֵבָה יִהְיוּ׃ מֵהָעוֹף
לְמִינֵהוּ וּמִן־הַבְּהֵמָה לְמִינָהּ מִכֹּל רֶמֶשׂ הָאֲדָמָה לְמִינֵהוּ
כא שְׁנַיִם מִכֹּל יָבֹאוּ אֵלֶיךָ לְהַחֲיוֹת׃ וְאַתָּה קַח־לְךָ מִכׇּל־מַאֲכָל

VERSE 16

TALMUD BAVLI

תַּחְתִּיִּם שְׁנִיִּם וּשְׁלִשִׁים תַּעֲשֶׂהָ – *Make lower, middle, and upper decks:* The lowest level of the boat held the waste, the middle deck housed the animals, and the top area was reserved for the people. (Sanhedrin 108b)

BERESHIT RABBA

צֹהַר תַּעֲשֶׂה לַתֵּבָה – *Make a window for the ark:* [The word *tzohar* is obscure.] Rabbi Ḥoniya, Rabbi Pinḥas, Rabbi Ḥanin, and Rabbi Hoshaya all found themselves unable to explain what this *tzohar* was. But Rabbi Abba bar Kahana and Rabbi Levi did offer interpretations for the term. According to Rabbi Abba bar Kahana, the *tzohar* feature of the ark was a window placed in its side. Rabbi Levi, however, maintained that the term refers to a precious stone. Rabbi Pinḥas taught in the name of Rabbi Levi: During the twelve months that Noaḥ was ensconced in the ark, he never required sunlight during the day, nor moonlight at night. Rather, the family had brought a brilliant gem with them into the ark, where they hung it up. When the stone was dim, Noaḥ knew that it was daytime, and when it shone brightly, he understood that it was night outside. (Noaḥ 31:11)

VERSE 17

BERESHIT RABBA

וַאֲנִי הִנְנִי מֵבִיא אֶת־הַמַּבּוּל מַיִם – *And I, I am about to bring floodwaters:* [The first "I," *vaani,* appears superfluous. The Midrash fills in the missing sentence:] Said God: And I concur with the angels, who claim: *What are mortals, that You should be mindful of them; human beings, that You should take note of them?* (Psalms 8:5). The phrase "floodwaters" [*hamabbul mayim*] also seems repetitive. For at first what fell was ordinary water, however once it hit the earth it became a devastating flood. These rains threatened *to destroy all flesh.... Everything on earth will die*, suggests that everything [even food] would dry up and wither.

16 fifty cubits wide, and thirty cubits high. Make a window for the
ark, and taper the latter to within a cubit of the top. Put a door
in the side of the ark and make lower, middle, and upper decks.
17 And I – I am about to bring floodwaters over the earth to destroy all flesh that has within it the breath of life under the heav-
18 ens. Everything on earth will die. But I will establish My covenant with you, and you will enter the ark – you, your sons, your
19 wife, and your sons' wives with you. And you shall take two of
each living creature, male and female, into the ark to keep alive
20 with you. Of every kind of bird, animal, and wild beast, bring
21 two to keep alive. As for you, take all the food to be eaten and

BEREHSIT RABBA *(cont.)*

But, God promised Noaḥ: *I will establish My covenant with you*, guaranteeing that the fruit Noaḥ brought into the ark to feed himself and the animals would not rot and would become neither moldy nor desiccated. Furthermore, there were mighty men at that time who were able to dam up the opening from the deep [through which the water was welling up]. At the same time these giants tried to force themselves into the ark through its window. And yet, these enemies became all twisted up, as the verse states: *The giants tremble under the waters and their denizens!* (Job 26:5). Similarly, when lions attempted to storm the ark, their teeth were knocked loose, as the verse states: *The lion may roar, and he may howl, but his teeth will break* (Job 4:10). (Noaḥ 31:12)

VERSE 20

LEKAḤ TOV

מֵהָעוֹף לְמִינֵהוּ וּמִן־הַבְּהֵמָה לְמִינָהּ – *Of every kind of bird, animal, and wild beast:* This verse teaches that all the creatures on the ark were forbidden to engage in sexual relations during the flood. And yet, three individuals violated this rule and they were all punished: Ḥam, the raven, and the dog.

VERSE 21

BERESHIT RABBA

וְאַתָּה קַח־לְךָ מִכָּל־מַאֲכָל – *As for you, take all the food:* Rabbi Abba bar Kahana taught: Noaḥ brought pressed figs with him into the ark. It was taught in the name of Rabbi Neḥemya: Most of the food stores were indeed pressed figs. Rabbi Abba bar Kahana further taught: Noaḥ stocked up on branches to feed to the elephants, shrubs for the deer, and glass for the ostriches. [Ostriches often swallow hard and shiny objects such as gizzard stones.] According to Rabbi Levi, Noaḥ took with him vine cuttings to plant after the ordeal, fig shoots to plant fig trees, and olive shoots to plant olive trees. Thus, in Rabbi Abba bar Kahana's view, the clause *It will be for food for you*, refers to food that was suitable for both Noaḥ and the animals [the dried figs could be enjoyed by all the passengers]. But Rabbi Levi maintained that the verse emphasized that Noaḥ's interests were to take precedent. [Noaḥ was required to collect specific food that each particular animal was accustomed to, starting

כב אֲשֶׁר יֵאָכֵל וְאָסַפְתָּ אֵלֶיךָ וְהָיָה לְךָ וְלָהֶם לְאָכְלָה: וַיַּעַשׂ נֹחַ
ז א כְּכֹל אֲשֶׁר צִוָּה אֹתוֹ אֱלֹהִים כֵּן עָשָׂה: וַיֹּאמֶר יהוה לְנֹחַ שני
בֹּא־אַתָּה וְכָל־בֵּיתְךָ אֶל־הַתֵּבָה כִּי־אֹתְךָ רָאִיתִי צַדִּיק
ב לְפָנַי בַּדּוֹר הַזֶּה: מִכֹּל ׀ הַבְּהֵמָה הַטְּהוֹרָה תִּקַּח־לְךָ שִׁבְעָה
שִׁבְעָה אִישׁ וְאִשְׁתּוֹ וּמִן־הַבְּהֵמָה אֲשֶׁר לֹא טְהֹרָה הִוא
ג שְׁנַיִם אִישׁ וְאִשְׁתּוֹ: גַּם מֵעוֹף הַשָּׁמַיִם שִׁבְעָה שִׁבְעָה זָכָר

BERESHIT RABBA *(cont.)*

with his own preferences.] The words "and store it" [literally, "and store it for you"] teach that a person should only collect things that he might eventually need. (Noaḥ 31:14)

VERSE 22

LEKAḤ TOV

וַיַּעַשׂ נֹחַ כְּכֹל אֲשֶׁר צִוָּה אֹתוֹ אֱלֹהִים – *Noaḥ did all that God commanded him:* Noaḥ did nothing extra. Nor did he do anything less than what he had been instructed.

CHAPTER 7, VERSE 1

PHILO

צַדִּיק לְפָנַי בַּדּוֹר הַזֶּה – *Righteous before Me in this generation:* There is ample evidence that shows how one just and worthy man can be instrumental in saving many people simply because of their relationship to the just and virtuous person. We know from sailors and soldiers, along with their armies, how one good captain or one skillful and experienced general can save the lives of his regiments. Secondly, God praises the just man who acquires virtue not only for himself, but also for his entire family.

TANḤUMA

בֹּא־אַתָּה וְכָל־בֵּיתְךָ אֶל־הַתֵּבָה – *Enter the ark, you and all your household:* What does the book of Ecclesiastes mean when it describes *a small town. Few people in it. A great king came and surrounded it and built great siege works all around* (Ecclesiastes 9:14). The small town is an allusion to the world, while the few people in it were the generation of the flood. The great king is the King of Kings, the Holy One, blessed be He. The siege alludes to God's plan to *erase [His] creation, humankind, from the face of the land* (Genesis 6:7). The subsequent verse in Ecclesiastes states: *And one poor wise man was there to be found, able to save the whole town by his wisdom. And not a soul remembered that poor man* (Ecclesiastes 9:15). The "one poor wise man" was Noaḥ. He was able to save the whole town by his wisdom – when God told him to *enter the ark, you and all your household*. Yet, *not a soul remembered that poor man*. Said the Holy One, blessed be He: "Nobody remembers Noaḥ except for Me," as the verse states: *Then God remembered Noaḥ* (8:1). (Vayigash 1)

22 store it: it will be for food for you and for them." Noaḥ did so:
7 1 all that God commanded him, he fulfilled. Then the LORD said SHENI
to Noaḥ, "Enter the ark, you and all your household, for I have
seen you alone to be righteous before Me in this generation.
2 Take seven and seven of every pure animal, seven pairs, and
3 two of every animal that is not pure, of each kind a pair. Also
take seven pairs of each kind of bird, male and female, to keep

VERSE 2

TALMUD BAVLI

שִׁבְעָה שִׁבְעָה אִישׁ וְאִשְׁתּוֹ – *Seven pairs:* [Literally, "seven, seven, man and wife."] Are animals bound by marriage then? Rabbi Shmuel bar Naḥmani taught in the name of Rabbi Yonatan: The terminology in the verse is meant to convey that these were animals who had not mated with members of other species [see Lekaḥ Tov on 6:12]. Now how did Noaḥ know which animals had not engaged in such licentiousness? Rav Ḥisda explained: Noaḥ led the animals in front of the ark. If the animal was able to enter the ark, it was clear that that specimen had not sinned. But if the ark rejected an animal, that was a sign that it had behaved inappropriately. Rabbi Abbahu says: Noaḥ gathered into the ark only those animals that came on their own. [That is, God selected the righteous animals and sent them forward to be saved.]

TANḤUMA

מִכֹּל הַבְּהֵמָה הַטְּהוֹרָה תִּקַּח־לְךָ – *Take…of every pure animal:* When the verse states: *Teach a wise man, and he will become yet wiser; inform a righteous person, and he will add to his learning* (Proverbs 9:9), that is an allusion to Noaḥ building the ark. The Holy One, blessed be He, instructed Noaḥ to bring along with him *seven and seven of every pure animal*, and when Noaḥ finally left the ark, those were the animals he sacrificed to God [see 8:20]. For Noaḥ reasoned to himself: It must have been for this purpose that the Almighty told me to put seven pairs of pure animals into the ark [since only one pair would have been sufficient to repopulate the world]. (Vayakhel 9)

BERESHIT RABBA

וּמִן־הַבְּהֵמָה אֲשֶׁר לֹא טְהֹרָה – *Of every animal that is not pure:* [It would have been simpler to say "impure" – *tameh*.] Rabbi Yudan taught in the name of Rabbi Yoḥanan, Rabbi Berekhya taught in the name of Rabbi Eliezer, and Rabbi Yaakov of Kefar Ḥanin taught in the name of Rabbi Yehoshua ben Levi: The Holy One, blessed be He, used delicate language and added extra words in order to avoid sounding coarse. (Noaḥ 32:4)

VERSE 3

LEKAḤ TOV

גַּם מֵעוֹף הַשָּׁמַיִם שִׁבְעָה שִׁבְעָה – *Also take seven pairs of each kind of bird:* There were thus fourteen specimens of each type of bird. Do not suggest that there were seven individuals from every species [even though the Hebrew could be understood this way], since that would have left one bird without a mate.

ד וּנְקֵבָה לְחַיּוֹת זֶרַע עַל־פְּנֵי כָל־הָאָרֶץ׃ כִּי לְיָמִים עוֹד שִׁבְעָה
אָנֹכִי מַמְטִיר עַל־הָאָרֶץ אַרְבָּעִים יוֹם וְאַרְבָּעִים לָיְלָה
וּמָחִיתִי אֶת־כָּל־הַיְקוּם אֲשֶׁר עָשִׂיתִי מֵעַל פְּנֵי הָאֲדָמָה׃
ה ו וַיַּעַשׂ נֹחַ כְּכֹל אֲשֶׁר־צִוָּהוּ יהוה׃ וְנֹחַ בֶּן־שֵׁשׁ מֵאוֹת שָׁנָה
ז וְהַמַּבּוּל הָיָה מַיִם עַל־הָאָרֶץ׃ וַיָּבֹא נֹחַ וּבָנָיו וְאִשְׁתּוֹ וּנְשֵׁי־
ח בָנָיו אִתּוֹ אֶל־הַתֵּבָה מִפְּנֵי מֵי הַמַּבּוּל׃ מִן־הַבְּהֵמָה
הַטְּהוֹרָה וּמִן־הַבְּהֵמָה אֲשֶׁר אֵינֶנָּה טְהֹרָה וּמִן־הָעוֹף וְכֹל
ט אֲשֶׁר־רֹמֵשׂ עַל־הָאֲדָמָה׃ שְׁנַיִם שְׁנַיִם בָּאוּ אֶל־נֹחַ אֶל־
י הַתֵּבָה זָכָר וּנְקֵבָה כַּאֲשֶׁר צִוָּה אֱלֹהִים אֶת־נֹחַ׃ וַיְהִי

VERSE 4

BERESHIT RABBA

אַרְבָּעִים יוֹם וְאַרְבָּעִים לָיְלָה – *Forty days and forty nights:* Rabbi Shimon bar Yoḥai taught: Because humanity transgressed the Torah, which was given [to Moshe] over a span of forty days, civilization was therefore destroyed by rains which fell for forty days and forty nights. Rabbi Yoḥanan ben Zakkai taught: Those people corrupted the divine image of man, which is formed in utero within forty days. They were therefore drowned by forty days and nights of rain. (Noaḥ 32:5)

LEKAḤ TOV

כִּי לְיָמִים עוֹד שִׁבְעָה – *For in seven days' time:* Why was there a delay of seven days before the onset of the flood? Rav explained: These days represented the week of mourning for Metushelaḥ, who had just died. [It is understood that Metushelaḥ was the last righteous man other than Noaḥ, and the flood was delayed until after his death out of respect for him.] We learn from here that even eulogies for the righteous can delay punishment. Another interpretation: An additional week's respite was given to mankind following the stay of a hundred and twenty years that God had granted them [in 6:3].

VERSE 7

TANḤUMA

וּבָנָיו וְאִשְׁתּוֹ וּנְשֵׁי־בָנָיו – *With his sons, his wife, and his sons' wives:* The family that was rescued on the ark was not permitted to engage in any sexual activity during the flood, nor were the cattle, the animals, or the birds. We learn this from the sequence of the passengers who boarded the boat: *Noaḥ, with his sons, his wife, and his sons' wives came into the ark.* In other words, the men came into the ark together, followed by the women who stayed within their group. And so did this division remain throughout the time on the ark; Noaḥ and his sons and everyone else on the ark were barred from intimacy. For the Holy One, blessed be He, said to them: Would it be appropriate for you procreate and to thereby

4 their kind alive across the earth. For in seven days' time I will
send rain on the earth for forty days and forty nights, and I will
wipe from the face of the earth every living creature I have
5 6 made." Noaḥ did all that the LORD commanded him. Noaḥ was
six hundred years old when the floodwaters came upon the
7 earth. Noaḥ, with his sons, his wife, and his sons' wives, came
8 into the ark to escape the waters of the flood. The pure animals,
the animals that were not pure, the birds, and all that walked
9 the earth came two by two to Noaḥ into the ark, male and fe-
10 male, as God had commanded Noaḥ. Thus, after seven days the

TANḤUMA *(cont.)*

build new worlds while My anger is raging outside and destroying the planet? However, once the flood is over, you will be required to repopulate the earth. Indeed, after the land had dried up, God told Noaḥ: *Leave the ark you, and your wife, your sons, and your sons' wives with you* [8:16; here the order indicates that the couples were reunited] for everybody was now permitted to engage in procreation – the humans, the cattle, the animals, and the birds. (Noaḥ 17)

BERESHIT RABBA

וַיָּבֹא נֹחַ – *Noaḥ came:* Rabbi Yoḥanan taught: Noaḥ lacked faith that God would really flood the world. For had the waters not begun to swirl around his ankles, he would not have entered the ark at all. (Noaḥ 32:6)

VERSE 10

PHILO

וַיְהִי לְשִׁבְעַת הַיָּמִים – *Thus, after seven days:* God wished to allow the space of the week for the sinners of that generation to repent. God hoped that when seeing the ark, replete with all its animals, the people would believe the predictions of the forthcoming deluge that awaited them. The number seven recalls the creation of the world, as if to say: "I am the Creator of the world. I am He who is now about to destroy the world with a great flood. But the original cause of the creation of the world was the goodness which is Me." God offers them the opportunity to make their entreaty, not with mouth and tongue, but rather with the heart of amendment and penitence.

AVOT DERABBI NATAN

וַיְהִי לְשִׁבְעַת הַיָּמִים – *Thus, after seven days:* For a time, the Holy One, blessed be He, altered the usual course of nature for humanity, making the sun rise in the west and set in the east. God did this to get the people's attention and to strike fear into their hearts, with the hope that they would repent. Unfortunately, the masses failed to take notice of the anomaly. This is the explanation for the verse *Thus, after seven days the floodwaters came upon the earth.* [The seven days allude to the week of creation, when the laws of the universe were put in place.] (32)

יא לְשִׁבְעַת הַיָּמִים וּמֵי הַמַּבּוּל הָיוּ עַל־הָאָרֶץ׃ בִּשְׁנַת שֵׁשׁ־
מֵאוֹת שָׁנָה לְחַיֵּי־נֹחַ בַּחֹדֶשׁ הַשֵּׁנִי בְּשִׁבְעָה־עָשָׂר יוֹם
לַחֹדֶשׁ בַּיּוֹם הַזֶּה נִבְקְעוּ כָּל־מַעְיְנוֹת תְּהוֹם רַבָּה וַאֲרֻבֹּת
יב הַשָּׁמַיִם נִפְתָּחוּ׃ וַיְהִי הַגֶּשֶׁם עַל־הָאָרֶץ אַרְבָּעִים יוֹם

BERESHIT RABBA

וַיְהִי לְשִׁבְעַת הַיָּמִים – *Thus, after seven days:* Rabbi Yehoshua ben Levi taught: The Holy One, blessed be He, mourned for seven days over His world before plunging it into destruction. For the verse states [of God, before the flood]: *And His heart was touched with sorrow* (6:6), and "sorrow" refers to mourning, as a later verse reads: *The king was sorrowful for his son* (II Samuel 19:3). Rabbi Yosei ben Durmaskit taught: Because humanity sinned with their eyes [by coveting other people's possessions] and eyes are compared to water [because of the tears they produce], so did the Holy One, blessed be He, punish them with water. (Noaḥ 32:7)

VERSE 11

TANḤUMA

נִבְקְעוּ כָּל־מַעְיְנוֹת תְּהוֹם רַבָּה – *All the wellsprings of the great deep burst:* The psalmist writes: *Your justice is like the mighty mountains, Your judgment like the great deep* (Psalms 36:7), regarding which Rabbi Yehuda bar Simon taught: That verse refers to the righteousness that God extended to Noaḥ in the ark – it was equivalent to *the mighty mountains*. For at the end of the flood we read: *The ark came to rest on the mountains of Ararat* (8:4). At the same time, God judged the generation of the flood strictly, examining every detail of their behavior, down to the greatest depths, as we read: *On that day, all the wellsprings of the great deep burst*. (Emor 6)

BERESHIT RABBA

נִבְקְעוּ כָּל־מַעְיְנוֹת תְּהוֹם רַבָּה – *All the wellsprings of the great deep burst:* When the Torah states that the unformed earth *was void and desolate* (1:2) that is an allusion to the first man, who was reduced to nothing [as a result of his sin], and to his son Kayin who sought to return the world to that desolate state [through his act of murder]. That verse continues: *There was darkness* – a reference to the sinful generation of Enosh, regarding whom the prophet uses similar language: *Gone, those who think to go deeper than the Lord to hide their counsel; in the darkness of their deeds, "Who sees us?" they say. "Who will know?"* (Isaiah 29:15). And the last words of that description, *On the face of the deep*, alludes to the generation of the flood, the start of which is described using the same word: *On that day, all the wellsprings of the great deep burst*. (Bereshit 2:3)

LEKAḤ TOV

בַּחֹדֶשׁ הַשֵּׁנִי – *In the second month:* The second month is Marḥeshvan [sometimes called simply Ḥeshvan], since the world was created in the month of Tishrei [the preceding month]. This explains why Marḥeshvan is known as the *month of Bul* (I Kings 6:38) – for it was then

11 floodwaters came upon the earth. In the six hundredth year of
Noaḥ's life, in the second month, on the seventeenth of the
month – on that day, all the wellsprings of the great deep burst,
12 and the heavens' floodgates opened. The rain fell on the earth

LEKAḤ TOV *(cont.)*

that the world experienced the flood [*mabbul*]. The initial letter *mem* [with a numerical value of forty] was dropped from the name to illustrate the forty days lost to the world. **בְּשִׁבְעָה־עָשָׂר יוֹם לַחֹדֶשׁ** – *On the seventeenth of the month:* The text records Noaḥ's age as well as the specific date when the flood took place to teach that Noaḥ and his family spent a full year inside the ark. During those long months, Noaḥ kept track of time using methods that the Holy One, blessed be He, had taught Adam, and which had been passed down to him. **נִבְקְעוּ כׇּל־מַעְיְנוֹת תְּהוֹם רַבָּה** – *All the wellsprings of the great deep burst:* First the waters welled up from beneath the ground until they rose to the height of the mountain peaks. Following that, the *heavens' floodgates opened*, which elevated the water an additional fifteen cubits so that the hilltops were covered as well.

YALKUT SHIMONI

בְּשִׁבְעָה־עָשָׂר יוֹם לַחֹדֶשׁ – *On the seventeenth of the month:* Rabbi Eliezer taught: On the seventeenth of Marḥeshvan, the Pleiades constellation rose in the day, causing the wellsprings of the great deep to become overwhelmed. And since this celestial cluster altered its behavior, the Holy One, blessed be He, took two stars out of the group and brought a flood upon the world [through the gaps left in the firmament]. Rabbi Yehoshua said: The date was actually the seventeenth of Iyar [counting Nisan as the first month and not Tishrei], when the Pleiades constellation descends in the day, thereby causing the wellsprings of the great deep to diminish in strength. But because the people of that generation had acted in an unnatural way, the Holy One, blessed be He, changed the laws of nature. He elevated the star group during the day, removed two stars from the constellation, and brought a flood upon the world. (56)

VERSE 12

BERESHIT RABBA

וַיְהִי הַגֶּשֶׁם עַל־הָאָרֶץ – *The rain fell on the earth:* At the start of the world, praise of God came only from the waters [which was all that existed before creation; see 1:2], as the verse states: *From the sounds of many waters, from the mighty waves of the sea, the Lord is on high* (Psalms 93:4). Said the Holy One, blessed be He: If these which have no mouths, no ability to reason, and no faculty of speech, nevertheless praise me, then when I create human beings, who will possess all of those features, how much more will I be extolled! Subsequently however, the generation of the flood rebelled against God; the generation of Enosh similarly turned on Him, as did the civilization of the Tower of Babel. Said the Holy One, blessed be He: Let these people be cleared away, and the water which was here before them be brought in to take their place. Thus the verse states: *The rain fell on the earth for forty days and forty nights.* (Bereshit 5:1)

יג וְאַרְבָּעִ֖ים לָֽיְלָה׃ בְּעֶ֨צֶם הַיּ֤וֹם הַזֶּה֙ בָּ֣א נֹ֔חַ וְשֵׁם־וְחָ֥ם וָיֶ֖פֶת בְּנֵי־נֹ֑חַ וְאֵ֣שֶׁת נֹ֗חַ וּשְׁלֹ֧שֶׁת נְשֵֽׁי־בָנָ֛יו אִתָּ֖ם אֶל־הַתֵּבָֽה׃
יד הֵ֜מָּה וְכָל־הַֽחַיָּ֣ה לְמִינָ֗הּ וְכָל־הַבְּהֵמָה֙ לְמִינָ֔הּ וְכָל־הָרֶ֛מֶשׂ הָרֹמֵ֥שׂ עַל־הָאָ֖רֶץ לְמִינֵ֑הוּ וְכָל־הָע֣וֹף לְמִינֵ֔הוּ כֹּ֖ל צִפּ֥וֹר כָּל־כָּנָֽף׃
טו וַיָּבֹ֥אוּ אֶל־נֹ֖חַ אֶל־הַתֵּבָ֑ה שְׁנַ֤יִם שְׁנַ֙יִם֙ מִכָּל־הַבָּשָׂ֔ר אֲשֶׁר־בּ֖וֹ ר֥וּחַ חַיִּֽים׃
טז וְהַבָּאִ֗ים זָכָ֨ר וּנְקֵבָ֤ה מִכָּל־בָּשָׂר֙ בָּ֔אוּ כַּֽאֲשֶׁ֛ר צִוָּ֥ה אֹת֖וֹ אֱלֹהִ֑ים וַיִּסְגֹּ֥ר יְהֹוָ֖ה בַּֽעֲדֽוֹ׃ שלישי
יז וַיְהִ֧י הַמַּבּ֛וּל אַרְבָּעִ֥ים י֖וֹם עַל־הָאָ֑רֶץ וַיִּרְבּ֣וּ הַמַּ֗יִם וַיִּשְׂאוּ֙ אֶת־הַתֵּבָ֔ה וַתָּ֖רָם מֵעַ֥ל הָאָֽרֶץ׃
יח וַיִּגְבְּר֥וּ הַמַּ֛יִם וַיִּרְבּ֥וּ מְאֹ֖ד עַל־

VERSE 13

MIDRASH TANNA'IM DEVARIM

בְּעֶצֶם הַיּוֹם הַזֶּה – *On that very day*: [Alternatively, "at midday."] The Torah states: *On that very day the Lord spoke to Moshe* [Deuteronomy 32:48. The verse occurs at the end of Moshe's life just as he is given a glimpse of the land of Israel.] There are four instances in the Torah which employ the phrase "On that very day." At the start of the flood, the text reads: *On that very day, Noah…entered the ark*. After Avraham was commanded to circumcise his household, the verse reports that on *that very day, Avraham and his son Yishmael were circumcised* (17:26). When the nation of Israel left Egypt, the text states: *At the end of four hundred thirty years, on that very day, all the Lord's battalions left Egypt* (Exodus 12:41). The verse describing Moshe's death constitutes the fourth example. What is the function of the phrase in the Noah narrative? Said the Holy One, blessed be He: If I bring Noah onto the ark in the dead of the night, the people around him will claim that I was trying to conceal his escape, and had Noah tried to board his ship in the daytime they would have stopped him. And so the Holy One, blessed be He, said: Watch while I lead Noah onto the ark at high noon! Whoever thinks he can stop Me, let him come and try. Thus the verse states: *On that very day, Noah…entered the ark*. What is the function of the phrase in the Avraham story? Said the Holy One, blessed be He: If I instruct Avraham to circumcise himself in the dead of the night, the people around him will claim that had they been aware of what Avraham was up to, they would have stopped him from doing so [for his act defied their own customs]. And so the Holy One, blessed be He, said: Watch while Avraham performs this ritual in broad daylight! Whoever thinks he can stop this ceremony from happening, let him come and try. Thus the verse states: *That very day, Avraham and his son Yishmael were circumcised*. What is the function of the phrase in the account of the exodus? Said the Holy One, blessed be He: If I lead Israel out of Egypt in the dead of the night, the oppressors will all claim that had they been aware that the Hebrews were escaping, they would have prevented their liberation, taking up arms and

13 for forty days and forty nights. On that very day, Noaḥ, his
sons, Shem, Ḥam, and Yefet, Noaḥ's wife, and his sons' three
14 wives entered the ark. With them came every kind of wild
beast, every kind of animal, every creeping, crawling creature
of the land, every kind of flying creature, every bird, and each
15 winged thing. They came to Noaḥ, to the ark, two by two, of all
16 flesh that had within it the breath of life. They came, male and
female of all flesh, as God had commanded him. Then the
17 Lord shut him in. For forty days the flood came upon the SHELISHI
earth. The waters swelled, lifting the ark so that it rose above
18 the land. The waters surged, swelling enormously on the earth,

MIDRASH TANNA'IM DEVARIM *(cont.)*

waging war against the slaves. And so the Holy One, blessed be He, said: Watch while I rescue the Israelites in full view of the whole world! Whoever thinks he can stop this redemption from happening, let him come and try. Thus the verse states: *At the end of four hundred thirty years, to the very day, all the Lord's battalions left Egypt*. What is the function of the phrase as Moshe prepared to die? Said the Holy One, blessed be He: If I direct Moshe into a cave in the dead of the night, the people will complain that had they realized that Moshe was being taken from them, they would have protested and stopped his demise. They would claim: Would we really have allowed Moshe to leave us – he who took us out of Egypt, who split the sea on our behalf, who brought us water to drink and manna and quails to eat, and who performed innumerable wonders and miracles for our benefit? And so the Holy One, blessed be He, said: Behold, I plan on taking Moshe's life in the middle of day! Whoever thinks he can save the leader's life, let him come and try! Thus the verse states: *On that very day the Lord spoke to Moshe*. (32:48)

VERSE 16

LEKAḤ TOV

וְהַבָּאִים זָכָר וּנְקֵבָה מִכָּל־בָּשָׂר בָּאוּ – *They came, male and female of all flesh:* The animals gathered at the ark on their own initiative. **וַיִּסְגֹּר יהוה בַּעֲדוֹ** – *Then the Lord shut him in:* God protected Noaḥ from the wicked masses who tried to overturn the ark. To keep the villains at bay, the Holy One, blessed be He, sent bears and lions to surround the vessel.

YALKUT SHIMONI

וַיִּסְגֹּר יהוה בַּעֲדוֹ – *Then the Lord shut him in:* The Holy One, blessed be He, extinguished the sun and the moon and these bodies did not shine for a full twelve months, as the verse states: *At His command, the sun will not rise, and the stars will seal themselves shut* (Job 9:7). How then did Noaḥ function without light? God provided him with a precious jewel which illuminated his journey.

יט הָאָרֶץ וַתֵּלֶךְ הַתֵּבָה עַל־פְּנֵי הַמָּיִם׃ וְהַמַּיִם גָּבְרוּ מְאֹד מְאֹד
עַל־הָאָרֶץ וַיְכֻסּוּ כָּל־הֶהָרִים הַגְּבֹהִים אֲשֶׁר־תַּחַת כָּל־
כ הַשָּׁמָיִם׃ חֲמֵשׁ עֶשְׂרֵה אַמָּה מִלְמַעְלָה גָּבְרוּ הַמָּיִם וַיְכֻסּוּ
כא הֶהָרִים׃ וַיִּגְוַע כָּל־בָּשָׂר ׀ הָרֹמֵשׂ עַל־הָאָרֶץ בָּעוֹף וּבַבְּהֵמָה
כב וּבַחַיָּה וּבְכָל־הַשֶּׁרֶץ הַשֹּׁרֵץ עַל־הָאָרֶץ וְכֹל הָאָדָם׃ כֹּל
אֲשֶׁר נִשְׁמַת־רוּחַ חַיִּים בְּאַפָּיו מִכֹּל אֲשֶׁר בֶּחָרָבָה מֵתוּ׃

VERSE 19

LEKAḤ TOV

וְהַמַּיִם גָּבְרוּ מְאֹד מְאֹד עַל־הָאָרֶץ – *The waters surged ever more:* [Literally, "surged greatly over the earth."] During the Torah's account of creation we read: *Then God said, "Let an expanse stretch through the water, let it separate water from water"* (1:6). This refers to the waters that initially covered the earth, as the earlier verse states: *And the spirit of God moved over the waters* (1:2). Thus when God divided the waters, He delineated the upper waters and the lower waters – some of it resting above the expanse, and some of it beneath. For the Almighty knew that in the future, the generation of the flood would sin and corrupt their ways; and in order to punish them with the water, he elevated it to the heavens, as the verse states: *With these, He judges nations* (Job 36:31). Later, in His greatness, God would turn the sea into dry ground, as the verse states: *So the Israelites walked through the sea on dry land* (Exodus 14:22), and conversely turn the earth into sea, as our verse states: *The waters surged greatly over the earth.*

VERSE 20

TALMUD BAVLI

חֲמֵשׁ עֶשְׂרֵה אַמָּה מִלְמַעְלָה גָּבְרוּ הַמָּיִם – *Fifteen cubits above them the waters surged:* Rabbi Tarfon, Rabbi Yishmael, and the elders were sitting and discussing the Torah passage about the manna, and Rabbi Elazar Hamoda'i was sitting with them. Rabbi Elazar Hamoda'i said to the company: The manna that fell for the Israelites piled up on the ground to a height of sixty cubits. Rabbi Tarfon said to him: Moda'i, how long will you merely collect words and cite teachings that have no basis? Rabbi Elazar responded: But Rabbi, I am interpreting a verse. With regard to the flood the text states: *Fifteen cubits above them the waters surged as the mountains were covered.* Now, can the verse be suggesting that the waters stood fifteen cubits above the valleys, fifteen cubits above the plains, and fifteen cubits above the mountains? That would mean that the water stood as though in layers, conforming to the height of the lands below it! Furthermore, how would the Ark have been able to sail over water that flowed at different levels? Rather, *on that day, all the wellsprings of the great deep burst* (7:11), until the water rose and was level with the mountains. Once it reached that height, the water continued to rise until it reached *fifteen cubits above…the mountains.* Rabbi Elazar Hamoda'i continued: Now, which attribute is greater – the attribute of Compassion or the attribute of Justice? We must assume the former is greater than the latter. With

19 and the ark began to drift on the surface of the water. The waters surged ever more, until all the high mountains beneath all
20 the heavens were covered. Fifteen cubits above them the waters
21 surged as the mountains were covered. All flesh that moved
upon the earth perished – birds, animals, wild beasts, and all
22 the creatures that swarm on the earth, and all humankind. Everything on dry land that had breath of life in its nostrils died.

TALMUD BAVLI *(cont.)*

regard to the attribute of Justice, during the flood, the verse states: *And heavens' floodgates [or "windows"] opened* (7:11). Whereas with regard to the attribute of Compassion, in the case of the manna, the verse states: *But He commanded the skies above and opened the doors of heaven* (Psalms 78:23). Let us work out the following calculation: The area of how many windows is equal to that a door? The size of a door is equivalent to four windows. However, since the verse uses the plural term "doors," add another four, for a total area of eight windows. [Hence the manna fell at a rate four times that of the flood's rains. Since the water of the flood reached a depth of fifteen cubits], it turns out that the manna that fell for the nation of Israel was piled up sixty cubits high. (Yoma 76a)

VERSE 21

TANḤUMA

וַיִּגְוַע כָּל־בָּשָׂר – *All flesh perished:* Rabbi Berekhya taught: The people who died in the flood were hardy and great of stature, as the verse states: *These were the heroes of old, men of legends* (6:4). Had God not punished these giants with fire from above, no person could have withstood them, as the verse states: *You see! They were obliterated; fire has devoured their abundance!* (Job 22:20). When the Holy One, blessed be He, saw that these supermen could not be drowned, He brought fire upon them from the sky. Furthermore, God turned the birds, the cattle, and the beasts against them, and they devoured them. Our verse could be understood to mean: "All flesh that moved upon the earth perished at the hands of the birds, animals, wild beasts, and all the creatures that swarm on the earth." (Yalkut Talmud Torah, Bereshit 36)

LEKAḤ TOV

וַיִּגְוַע כָּל־בָּשָׂר – *All flesh perished:* Not all of the creatures died at the same time. For example, the birds were able to survive longer by flying above the waves. This step-by-step destruction is suggested by the verb *gevi'a* ["perish," instead of the more usual verb *mita* – "die"].

VERSE 22

TALMUD BAVLI

כֹּל אֲשֶׁר נִשְׁמַת־רוּחַ חַיִּים בְּאַפָּיו – *Everything that had breath of life in its nostrils:* Rabbi Akiva maintains: A person's life is dependent mainly on his nose [that is, his respiratory system], whereas Rabbi Eliezer believes: A person's life depends mainly on his navel

כג וַיִּמַח אֶת־כָּל־הַיְקוּם ׀ אֲשֶׁר ׀ עַל־פְּנֵי הָאֲדָמָה מֵאָדָם עַד־
בְּהֵמָה עַד־רֶמֶשׂ וְעַד־עוֹף הַשָּׁמַיִם וַיִּמָּחוּ מִן־הָאָרֶץ וַיִּשָּׁאֶר
כד אַךְ־נֹחַ וַאֲשֶׁר אִתּוֹ בַּתֵּבָה: וַיִּגְבְּרוּ הַמַּיִם עַל־הָאָרֶץ
ח א חֲמִשִּׁים וּמְאַת יוֹם: וַיִּזְכֹּר אֱלֹהִים אֶת־נֹחַ וְאֵת כָּל־הַחַיָּה ו
וְאֶת־כָּל־הַבְּהֵמָה אֲשֶׁר אִתּוֹ בַּתֵּבָה וַיַּעֲבֵר אֱלֹהִים רוּחַ

TALMUD BAVLI *(cont.)*

[that is, his digestive system]. Shall we say that these *tanna'im* share the same debate as another pair of rabbis who discuss which point of an embryo serves as its basis? One *tanna* argues that an embryo is built from its head, as the verse states: *From my mother's womb You brought me out [gozi]* (Psalms 71:6), and we know that *gozi* hints at the head from the verse *Shear [gozi] your hair and throw it away* (Jeremiah 7:29). Abba Sha'ul, however, believes that an embryo is formed from its navel, and branches out from that spot. No, we can in fact say that both Rabbi Akiva and Rabbi Eliezer agree with Abba Sha'ul. For Abba Sha'ul states his opinion only with regard to the forming of an embryo – that when an embryo is formed, it is formed from its middle. However, with regard to sustaining life, both *tanna'im* [that is, even Abba Sha'ul] will agree that this is the function of the nose, since the story of the flood tells us: *Everything that had breath of life in its nostrils died.*

LEKAḤ TOV

כֹּל אֲשֶׁר נִשְׁמַת־רוּחַ חַיִּים בְּאַפָּיו – *Everything that had breath of life in its nostrils died:* This excludes the fish in the sea, who were not sentenced to die. The fish had not corrupted their ways, and hence they were saved.

VERSE 23

MEKHILTA DERABBI YISHMAEL

מֵאָדָם עַד־בְּהֵמָה – *From humans to animals:* He who sins first is always the first to be punished. (Massekhta Defisḥa 7)

TALMUD BAVLI

וַיִּמַח אֶת־כָּל־הַיְקוּם – *Every living thing was wiped out:* The Sages taught in a *baraita*: The people of the generation of the flood have no share in the World to Come, as the verse states: *Every living thing on the face of the earth was wiped out* – that refers to life in this world; *All were wiped from the earth* – that refers to life in the World to Come. Such is the opinion of Rabbi Akiva. Rabbi Yehuda ben Beteira said: The people of the generation of the flood will neither live again nor be judged, as the verse states: *My spirit will not forever judge [yadon] man; he is of flesh* (6:3), meaning that they will neither stand in judgment, nor shall their souls be restored to them. Alternatively, the verse suggests that these people's souls will not return to their sheaths [*nadan*, that is, to their bodies]. Rabbi Menaḥem son of Rabbi Yosef taught: Even when the Holy One, Blessed be He, one day restores souls to lifeless corpses, those belonging to the people of the flood will be afflicted harshly as if they were in Gehinom, as the verse states: *Conceive chaff, give birth to straw; your spirit – fire will*

23 Every living thing on the face of the earth was wiped out: from
humans to animals, from creeping creatures to winged birds of
the heavens, all were wiped from the earth. Only Noaḥ and
24 those with him in the ark survived. For one hundred fifty days,
8 1 the waters surged over the earth. Then God remembered Noaḥ
and all the wild beasts and animals with him in the ark. God

TALMUD BAVLI *(cont.)*

consume it (Isaiah 33:11).... The verse states: *Every living thing was wiped out: from humans to animals, from creeping creatures to winged birds of the heavens, all were wiped from the earth.* Now granted that the human beings sinned; however in what manner did the animal kingdom act corruptly that it too warranted destruction? It was taught in the name of Rabbi Yehoshua ben Korḥa: Let us explain the matter with a parable. Consider a man who fashioned a wedding canopy for his son and prepared all sorts of food for the wedding feast. Sometime before the wedding the son died. What did the man do? He got up and dismantled his son's wedding canopy. He said: The only reason I built the canopy was for my son; now that he has died, what use have I for a wedding canopy? So too said the Holy One, Blessed be He: The only reason I created cattle and wild beasts was for people to make use of them. Now that the people have sinned and been sentenced to destruction, what use have I for cattle and wild animals? (Sanhedrin 108a)

LEKAḤ TOV

וַיִּשָּׁאֶר אַךְ־נֹחַ – *Only Noaḥ survived:* The term *akh* ["only"] also expresses anguish [as in a wordless exclamation of misery]; for Noaḥ was coughing up blood because of the cold.

CHAPTER 8, VERSE 1

TANḤUMA

וַיִּזְכֹּר אֱלֹהִים אֶת־נֹחַ – *Then God remembered Noaḥ:* Picture a man sailing on the high seas when a storm whips up. If he has animals and tools with him, he throws those possessions overboard in order to save his life. For no compassion is due to animals or other objects when a person's life is in danger. However, the Holy One, blessed be He, has mercy for the animals just as He does for people, as the verse states: *His compassion extends to all His works* (Psalms 145:9). And thus we read that *God remembered Noaḥ and all the wild beasts and animals with him in the ark.* (Noaḥ 6)

BERESHIT RABBA

וַיִּזְכֹּר אֱלֹהִים אֶת־נֹחַ – *Then God remembered Noaḥ:* How fortunate are the righteous of this world who are able to transform the attribute of Justice into the attribute of Compassion. For whenever the Torah employs the name *Elohim,* that indicates that God's dimension of Justice is at work, as in the verse *Do not curse a judge [elohim]* (Exodus 22:27), and *Both parties' claims shall be brought to the court [ha'elohim]* (Exodus 22:8). And yet that name also appears in the following contexts: *God [Elohim] listened to Leah, and she became pregnant and bore Yaakov a fifth son* (30:17), *And God [Elohim] heard their groaning, and remembered His*

ב עַל־הָאָרֶץ וַיָּשֹׁכּוּ הַמָּיִם: וַיִּסָּכְרוּ מַעְיְנֹת תְּהוֹם וַאֲרֻבֹּת
ג הַשָּׁמָיִם וַיִּכָּלֵא הַגֶּשֶׁם מִן־הַשָּׁמָיִם: וַיָּשֻׁבוּ הַמַּיִם מֵעַל
הָאָרֶץ הָלוֹךְ וָשׁוֹב וַיַּחְסְרוּ הַמַּיִם מִקְצֵה חֲמִשִּׁים וּמְאַת יוֹם:
ד וַתָּנַח הַתֵּבָה בַּחֹדֶשׁ הַשְּׁבִיעִי בְּשִׁבְעָה־עָשָׂר יוֹם לַחֹדֶשׁ עַל
ה הָרֵי אֲרָרָט: וְהַמַּיִם הָיוּ הָלוֹךְ וְחָסוֹר עַד הַחֹדֶשׁ הָעֲשִׂירִי
ו בָּעֲשִׂירִי בְּאֶחָד לַחֹדֶשׁ נִרְאוּ רָאשֵׁי הֶהָרִים: וַיְהִי מִקֵּץ
אַרְבָּעִים יוֹם וַיִּפְתַּח נֹחַ אֶת־חַלּוֹן הַתֵּבָה אֲשֶׁר עָשָׂה:
ז וַיְשַׁלַּח אֶת־הָעֹרֵב וַיֵּצֵא יָצוֹא וָשׁוֹב עַד־יְבֹשֶׁת הַמַּיִם מֵעַל

BERESHIT RABBA *(cont.)*

covenant (Exodus 2:24), and *Then God [Elohim] remembered Noaḥ*. [The righteous people in question were able to access God's love and mercy even through his attribute of Justice.] (Vayetze 73:3) **וַיִּזְכֹּר אֱלֹהִים אֶת־נֹחַ** – *Then God remembered Noaḥ*: What exactly did God remember? That Noaḥ fed and sustained the animals for twelve long months in the ark. (Noaḥ 33:3)

LEKAḤ TOV

וַיִּזְכֹּר אֱלֹהִים אֶת־נֹחַ – *Then God remembered Noaḥ:* The psalmist writes: *Your justice is like the mighty mountains* (Psalms 36:7). This verse is illustrated by the story of Noaḥ. For when the Holy One, blessed be He, showed mercy toward Noaḥ, the mountains benefited as well, as the verse states: *The mountaintops became visible* (8:5). That verse continues: *Your judgment like the great depths* – a claim also demonstrated by the flood. For when the Holy One, blessed be He, executed justice toward that generation of sinners, it was not just they but the depths of the oceans who suffered, as the verse states: *On that day, all the wellsprings of the great deep burst* (7:11). Finally, the verse concludes: *O Lord, You save both human and beast.* For when the Holy One, blessed be He, remembered Noaḥ on his boat, it was not just the humans whom God recalled, as the verse states: *God remembered Noaḥ and all the wild beasts and animals with him in the ark.*

VERSE 2

BERESHIT RABBA

וַיִּסָּכְרוּ מַעְיְנֹת תְּהוֹם – *The wellsprings of the deep closed:* Rabbi Elazar taught: When speaking of humanity's punishment, the text states: *All the wellsprings of the great deep burst* (7:11). But in connection with their reprieve, the text states: *The wellsprings of the deep closed.* The word "all" [*kol*] is omitted from the latter verse. This is because the springs of Tiberias, Avlonis, and the Banyas [hot springs in the north of the land of Israel] remained open. (Vayetze 73:4)

2 sent a wind over the earth, and the waters began to subside. The
wellsprings of the deep and heavens' floodgates closed, and the
3 heavens' rains were reined in. The water steadily receded from
the earth, and by the end of one hundred fifty days, the water
4 had abated. In the seventh month, on the seventeenth day of
the month, the ark came to rest on the mountains of Ararat.
5 The water continued to abate until the tenth month, and on the
first day of the tenth month, the mountaintops became visible.
6 After forty days Noaḥ opened the window he had made in the
7 ark and sent a raven forth. It flew to and fro until the water on

VERSE 4

BERESHIT RABBA

וַתָּנַח הַתֵּבָה – *The ark came to rest:* Rabbi Yoḥanan taught: During the twelve months of the flood, the constellations came to a standstill. Said Rabbi Yonatan to him: The constellations were in motion, but their influence was suppressed. Rabbi Eliezer countered this by citing God's later promise, *As long as earth and time endure – sowing time and harvest, cold and heat, summer, winter, day, and night will not cease* [8:22, implying that the celestial spheres' motions are constant]. But Rabbi Yehoshua responded: Since God promised that the movements of the heavens would never again never cease, that suggests that they indeed stopped during the time of the flood. (Albeck, Bereshit 25)

VERSE 5

LEKAḤ TOV

וְהַמַּיִם הָיוּ הָלוֹךְ וְחָסוֹר – *The water continued to abate:* The tops of the mountains became visible on the first of the month of Av. This took place forty-four days after the ark came to rest on the mountains of Ararat. [That had happened on the seventeenth day of Sivan, the seventh month, as reported in 8:4.] The waters drained at a rate of ten cubits per day.

VERSE 6

TANḤUMA,

וַיִּפְתַּח נֹחַ אֶת־חַלּוֹן – *Noaḥ opened the window:* Rabbi Shimon ben Lakish taught: When Noaḥ built the ark he put a window in the upper deck. Whoever looked out of this window could see from one end of the world to the other. (Yalkut Talmud Torah, Bereshit 39)

LEKAḤ TOV

וַיְהִי מִקֵּץ אַרְבָּעִים יוֹם – *After forty days:* Noaḥ opened the window on the tenth of Elul. Since the rains had ceased falling, Noaḥ felt safe in opening the window. This is why some commentators maintain that the *tzohar* [mentioned in 6:16] was a window.

VERSE 7

TALMUD BAVLI

וַיְשַׁלַּח אֶת־הָעֹרֵב – *And he sent a raven forth:* Reish Lakish says: The raven argued with Noaḥ, refusing to leave the ark. It said to him: "Your Master [God] hates me, and you hate me. I

ח הָאָֽרֶץ׃ וַיְשַׁלַּ֥ח אֶת־הַיּוֹנָ֖ה מֵאִתּ֑וֹ לִרְאוֹת֙ הֲקַ֣לּוּ הַמַּ֔יִם מֵעַ֖ל
ט פְּנֵ֥י הָאֲדָמָֽה׃ וְלֹא־מָצְאָה֩ הַיּוֹנָ֨ה מָנ֜וֹחַ לְכַף־רַגְלָ֗הּ וַתָּ֤שָׁב
אֵלָיו֙ אֶל־הַתֵּבָ֔ה כִּי־מַ֖יִם עַל־פְּנֵ֣י כָל־הָאָ֑רֶץ וַיִּשְׁלַ֤ח יָדוֹ֙

TALMUD BAVLI *(cont.)*

know that Your Master hates me because although He commanded you to take aboard seven pairs of the kosher species, only two specimens from the non-kosher species were saved. And I know that you hate me since you are ignoring all of those seven pairs of kosher birds, and instead insist on dispatching me – one of the two non-kosher birds! What if the angel of heat or the angel of cold attacks me out there and I die? Will the world not be lacking one species of creature [since there were only two ravens left in the world]? Or perhaps you are trying to get rid of me because it is my wife that you want for yourself!" Noaḥ said to the raven: "Wicked animal! If I am now forbidden to the woman who is generally permitted to me [my human wife], then surely I am forbidden from such intercourse with the animals, who have always been prohibited to me!" And how do we know that all sexual activity was prohibited to the ark's passengers as long as they were on board? We learn this from the verse which states: *You will enter the ark – you, your sons, your wife, and your sons' wives with you* [6:18; that is, when the people boarded the ark, the men came in together, and the women came in separately]. However, when they left the ark, God commanded: *Leave the ark – you, and your wife, your sons, and your sons' wives with you* [8:16; hence when they exited the craft, the couples were reunited]. Thus Rabbi Yoḥanan taught: We learn from here that all sex was prohibited while the people were on the ark. (Sanhedrin 108b)

LEKAḤ TOV

וַיְשַׁלַּח אֶת־הָעֹרֵב – *And he sent a raven forth:* Our Sages taught: The raven complained to Noaḥ: "Not only does your Master despise me, but you hate me as well. How do I know that God loathes me? Look at what He commanded you: *Take seven and seven of every pure animal, seven pairs, and two of every animal that is not pure, of each kind a pair* (7:2) – and here I am, an impure species. And then you Noaḥ ask me to leave the ark and fly across the desolate world; what if I die from exposure – my kind will disappear from the world forever!" Noaḥ responded in anger to the disgruntled bird: "Of what use are you to the world? You can't be eaten, and you can't be sacrificed!" But the Holy One, blessed be He, said to Noaḥ: You ought to reconsider your opinion of this bird. For the world will soon dry out, and centuries later there will rise a righteous man who will dry it even further, and that man will require the services of the ravens. Thus we read in the story of Eliyahu: *The ravens brought him bread and meat each morning and bread and meat each evening, and he drank from the stream* (I Kings 17:6). Rav taught: The ravens fed Eliyahu with meat from King Aḥav's kitchen. And our verse: *It flew to and fro [vashov] until the water on the earth had dried* (8:7), indicates that the raven repented [did *teshuva*].

8 the earth had dried. After that he sent forth a dove to see
9 whether the water had subsided from the face of the land. But
the dove found no resting place to plant its foot, and so it returned to him, to the ark, for water still covered the face of the
earth completely. He reached out his hand and brought the

YALKUT SHIMONI

וַיְשַׁלַּח אֶת־הָעֹרֵב – *And he sent a raven forth:* Noaḥ dispatched the raven to scout out the world. The bird flew about and found human carcasses scattered on the mountain tops. Content with the food it had discovered, the raven did not return to the ark. Noaḥ therefore sent out the dove, which did eventually return from its mission. Based on this, it has become common wisdom that employing an impure person as a messenger is akin to using a fool. [The raven is an impure, i.e., non-kosher, bird.] But a pure person can be trusted as a loyal envoy. (58)

VERSE 8

PHILO

וַיְשַׁלַּח אֶת־הַיּוֹנָה – *After that he sent forth a dove:* These birds contrast two traits: wickedness and virtue. For the raven, there is no house nor habitation nor city that can satisfy it, since is an insolent unsociable bird. The dove, in contrast, symbolizes virtue. The bird has a regard to humanity and for the public good. In an allegorical sense, the virtuous man sends that bird forth as his ambassador for desirable and salutary objects, wishing to receive from it desirable information; and it, like an ambassador, brings us back genuine pleasure so that what is hurtful may be guarded against, and what is useful may be diligently and carefully admitted.

BERESHIT RABBA

וַיְשַׁלַּח אֶת־הַיּוֹנָה – *After that he sent forth a dove:* Yehuda bar Naḥman taught in the name of Rabbi Shimon: Had the dove found a place to rest, it would not have returned to the ark. Similarly, a later verse states: *Oppression has exiled Yehuda, oppression and the harshness of her labor. Confined among nations, she finds no resting place* (Lamentations 1:3) – had the exiled Israelites found respite and peace among the nations, they would have never returned to their land. And again we read: *Yet even among those nations you shall find no ease, no resting place for the sole of your foot. There the Lord will give you a trembling heart, pining eyes, and a languishing spirit* (Deuteronomy 28:65). This is God's prediction: The Jewish people will never feel comfortable in the Diaspora, lest they refuse to come back to the land of Israel. (Noaḥ 33:6)

YALKUT SHIMONI

וַיְשַׁלַּח אֶת־הַיּוֹנָה – *After that he sent forth a dove:* [Literally, "sent forth a dove from next to him." The term "from next to him" – *me'itto* – is absent from his sending of the raven.] We learn from this episode that pure birds tend to make their homes in the vicinity of righteous people. (58)

י וַיִּקָּחֶהָ וַיָּבֵא אֹתָהּ אֵלָיו אֶל־הַתֵּבָה׃ וַיָּחֶל עוֹד שִׁבְעַת יָמִים
יא אֲחֵרִים וַיֹּסֶף שַׁלַּח אֶת־הַיּוֹנָה מִן־הַתֵּבָה׃ וַתָּבֹא אֵלָיו
הַיּוֹנָה לְעֵת עֶרֶב וְהִנֵּה עֲלֵה־זַיִת טָרָף בְּפִיהָ וַיֵּדַע נֹחַ כִּי־
יב קַלּוּ הַמַּיִם מֵעַל הָאָרֶץ׃ וַיִּיָּחֶל עוֹד שִׁבְעַת יָמִים אֲחֵרִים
יג וַיְשַׁלַּח אֶת־הַיּוֹנָה וְלֹא־יָסְפָה שׁוּב־אֵלָיו עוֹד׃ וַיְהִי בְּאַחַת
וְשֵׁשׁ־מֵאוֹת שָׁנָה בָּרִאשׁוֹן בְּאֶחָד לַחֹדֶשׁ חָרְבוּ הַמַּיִם מֵעַל

VERSE 10

LEKAḤ TOV

וַיָּחֶל עוֹד שִׁבְעַת יָמִים – *Then he waited another seven days:* Noaḥ tarried an additional seven days. We find a similar usage of the verb [*vayaḥel*] in the verse *Wait [toḥel] for seven days until I come to you; then I will inform you what you are to do* (I Samuel 10:8). We can infer from this verse that Noaḥ had previously waited seven days after the raven's departure before sending out the dove – for our verse states that Noaḥ waited "another" seven days. That indicates that he had initially waited a first week before moving on to this second bird.

VERSE 11

VAYIKRA RABBA

וְהִנֵּה עֲלֵה־זַיִת טָרָף בְּפִיהָ – *And in its beak was a freshly picked olive leaf:* The verse states: *Command the Israelites to bring you pure oil from crushed olives for the light, to kindle the lamp, every night* (Leviticus 24:2). Rabbi Ḥiyya taught: The candelabrum must be lit with oil made from olives, and not from sesame seeds or extracted from walnuts. This oil may not come from radishes or from almonds – only oil squeezed from olives is acceptable. Rabbi Avin explored the matter with the following metaphor: There was a king who suffered a rebellion of his entire army; only one of his divisions remained loyal to the monarch. Said the king: The men of that division who stayed faithful to me shall be made commanders, lieutenants, and military governors. Similarly did the Holy One, blessed be He, reward the olive tree, who brought light to the world in the time of Noaḥ, as the verse states: *The dove came back to him in the evening – and in its beak was a freshly picked olive leaf.* (Emor 31)

LEKAḤ TOV

וְהִנֵּה עֲלֵה־זַיִת טָרָף בְּפִיהָ – *And in its beak was a freshly picked olive leaf:* From where did the dove bring the olive leaf? Rabbi Levi taught: The bird flew to the land of Israel and plucked it from a tree growing there, for that land had not been inundated by the flood. And so states the prophet: *You are a land not cleansed, not swept with rain on the day of rage* (Ezekiel 22:24). Rabbi Kirai taught: The gates were opened to the Garden of Eden on behalf of the dove, and the bird flew in and snatched a leaf from a tree that was there. Why did the dove bring Noaḥ a leaf from an olive tree? With this choice, the dove showed that it preferred the bitter taste of the olive when it could take it for itself, over the food it was forced to accept from human hands while it was stuck on the ark.

10 dove back to him, into the ark. Then he waited another seven
11 days, and again he sent the dove forth from the ark. The dove
came back to him in the evening – and in its beak was a freshly
picked olive leaf. Noaḥ knew then that the water had subsided
12 from the earth. He waited another seven days and again sent
13 forth the dove – and it returned to him no more. So it was
that, by the first day of the first month of Noaḥ's six hundred
and first year, the water on the earth dried up. Noaḥ removed

YALKUT SHIMONI

וְהִנֵּה עֲלֵה־זַיִת טָרָף בְּפִיהָ – *And in its beak was a freshly picked olive leaf:* Said the dove to the Holy One, blessed be He: "Master of the Universe! I would rather that my food always be as bitter as olives as long as it is You who feed me, rather than sweet as honey if I have to depend upon human beings for my sustenance." And why do we say that the word *taraf* suggests a creature's sustenance? For a later verse states: *Give me neither poverty nor wealth; nourish me [hatrifeni] with my fixed portion of bread* (Proverbs 30:8). (58)

VERSE 12

LEKAḤ TOV

וַיִּיָּחֶל עוֹד שִׁבְעַת יָמִים אֲחֵרִים – *He waited another seven days:* The verb *vayiyyaḥel* is written here with two *yods* [in contrast to the word's appearance in verse 10, where it has a single *yod*]. This indicates that these later seven days weighed upon Noaḥ like a full two weeks. Another interpretation: The phrase *another seven days* suggests that there were three weeks of seven days altogether. [Noaḥ waited one week in between the raven's mission and the dove's first dispatch, one week between the dove's first and second flight, and another seven days before the bird's final trip. Thus the first *vayaḥel* in verse 10 indicates a wait of one week, and the second *vayiyyaḥel* with two *yod*'s indicates an additional two weeks' wait.] Corresponding to this duration, the prophet Daniel fasted for three weeks [see Daniel 10:2].

VERSE 13

BERESHIT RABBA

בָּרִאשׁוֹן בְּאֶחָד לַחֹדֶשׁ – *By the first day of the first month:* We learn that the punishment imposed upon the generation of the flood lasted for twelve months. How can this be calculated? The first description of the flood states: *In the six hundredth year of Noaḥ's life, in the second month, on the seventeenth of the month – on that day, all the wellsprings of the great deep burst, and heavens' floodgates opened* [7:11; the date is the seventeenth of Marḥeshvan]. We next read that *the rain fell on the earth for forty days and forty nights* (7:12), which accounts for the rest of the month of Marḥeshvan and the month of Kislev. The narrative continues to report that *for one hundred fifty days, the waters surged over the earth* (7:24), thereby covering the months of Tevet, Shevat, Adar, Nisan, and Iyar. At that point, *in the seventh month, on the seventeenth day of the month, the ark came to rest on the mountains of Ararat* (8:4). The seventh month refers [not to the standard way of reckoning which considers Nisan the seventh month but] to the month of Sivan which is the seventh month

הָאָרֶץ וַיָּסַר נֹחַ אֶת־מִכְסֵה הַתֵּבָה וַיַּרְא וְהִנֵּה חָרְבוּ
יד פְּנֵי הָאֲדָמָה: וּבַחֹדֶשׁ הַשֵּׁנִי בְּשִׁבְעָה וְעֶשְׂרִים יוֹם לַחֹדֶשׁ
טו יָבְשָׁה הָאָרֶץ: וַיְדַבֵּר אֱלֹהִים אֶל־נֹחַ לֵאמֹר: ז רביעי
טז יז צֵא מִן־הַתֵּבָה אַתָּה וְאִשְׁתְּךָ וּבָנֶיךָ וּנְשֵׁי־בָנֶיךָ אִתָּךְ: כָּל־
הַחַיָּה אֲשֶׁר־אִתְּךָ מִכָּל־בָּשָׂר בָּעוֹף וּבַבְּהֵמָה וּבְכָל־הָרֶמֶשׂ

BERESHIT RABBA *(cont.)*

following the end of the rains [in Kislev]. Now the waters abated for sixteen days [from the first of Sivan to the seventeenth of that month] at the rate of one cubit every four days [as will later be shown], which is equal to one and a half handbreadths per day. [And if the waters' high point was fifteen cubits above the mountaintops, as reported in 7:20, and it receded as a rate of one cubit every four days, then after sixteen days it would have receded four cubits, remaining eleven cubits above the tops of the mountains. If at this point the bottom of the ark rested on Mount Ararat,] we can thus conclude that the bottom of the ark was immersed eleven cubits below the water level. And we know that all the water was drained from the earth after sixty days, as the verse states: *The water continued to abate until the tenth month* (8:5), the month of Av, which fell ten months after the start of the rains. [If the waters receded from the first of Sivan – at the end of the 150 days culminating with the end of Iyar – until the first of Av, that yields sixty days altogether to rid the earth of the fifteen cubits of water. Hence the calculation that the water dissipated at a speed of one cubit every four days. As for this text's opening statement, according to verse 8:14, the earth was dried out completely *by the twenty-seventh day of the second month* – Marḥeshvan. Thus because the rains began *in the second month, on the seventeenth of the month* (7:11) of the previous year, the entire ordeal lasted for a year and ten days.] (Noaḥ 33:7)

LEKAḤ TOV

בְּאַחַת וְשֵׁשׁ־מֵאוֹת שָׁנָה – *Of Noaḥ's six hundred and first year:* The language of this verse proves that even one day of a year can be considered a full year. For the verse states: *By the first day of the first month*, referring to the month of Tishrei, meaning that the year was only one day old, and yet the text calls this a new year. [The opening of the verse calls this time *Noaḥ's six hundred and first year* – when really the date was just one day into that year.] The flood ran from the beginning of the year until the first of Tishrei. The term *rishon* ["the first month"] refers to the reckoning of the flood, since the months of the deluge are counted from Tishrei, thereby making the second month Marḥeshvan.

VERSE 15

PHILO

וַיְדַבֵּר אֱלֹהִים אֶל־נֹחַ לֵאמֹר – *Then God said to Noaḥ:* A reverent man follows God more than the guidance of his own reason. Just as it was fitting that he entered the ark by the command of God, so too he refuses to leave the ark except by the command of God as well.

the covering of the ark and saw that the face of the land was dry.
14 By the twenty-seventh day of the second month, the earth had
15 16 dried completely. Then God said to Noaḥ, "Leave the REVI'I
ark – you, and your wife, your sons, and your sons' wives with
17 you. And every living thing with you – birds, animals, and all
wild beasts that walk the earth – bring them out with you. Let

BERESHIT RABBA

וַיְדַבֵּר אֱלֹהִים אֶל־נֹחַ לֵאמֹר – *Then God said to Noaḥ:* The psalmist writes, *Set me free from this confinement so that I may give thanks to Your name; the righteous will gather around me when You are good to me* (Psalms 142:8). This is an allusion to Noaḥ, who was shut up in the ark for twelve months. Upon his release, Noaḥ expressed his gratitude to God for being good to him and setting him free. (Noaḥ 34:1)

VERSE 16

TANḤUMA

צֵא מִן־הַתֵּבָה – *Leave the ark:* Once the waters abated, Noaḥ understood that the time had come to leave the ark. However, the survivor reasoned to himself: Because the Holy One, blessed be He, instructed me to enter the ark, as the verse states: *Enter the ark, you and all your household* (7:1), it is only with God's permission that I will leave its confines. At that point the Holy One, blessed be He, did reveal Himself to Noaḥ, as the text states: *Then God said to Noaḥ, "Leave the ark – you, and your wife"*. (Noaḥ 8) **צֵא מִן־הַתֵּבָה** – *Leave the ark:* Rabbi Levi taught: Neither Noaḥ nor his sons slept a wink during the twelve months they were ensconced in the ark, for they were constantly working to feed all the cattle, the wild animals and the birds. Rabbi Akiva taught: In preparation for their maritime sojourn, the family stocked up on branches for the elephants and glass for the ostriches. Now there are some animals which are accustomed to eating in the second hour of the night, while other species eat an hour later. And hence the human beings were busy around the clock taking care of their charges. Rabbi Yoḥanan taught in the name of Rabbi Eliezer son of Rabbi Yosei the Galilean: Once Noaḥ was busy feeding the lion when the animal attacked him, causing him to limp thereafter. Hence the verse states: *Only [akh] Noaḥ and those with him in the ark survived* (7:23). The word *akh* [which usually reflects some sort of limitation or deficiency] suggests that Noaḥ was no longer in perfect condition. Because he was blemished, he was barred from offering sacrifices to God after the flood. Therefore his son Shem had to perform the service in his stead. (Noaḥ 8)

VERSE 17

BERESHIT RABBA

וְשָׁרְצוּ בָאָרֶץ – *Let them swarm again on the earth:* The animals were now given license to be fertile and multiply *on the earth*, whereas they had not been permitted to procreate in the ark. (Noaḥ 34:8)

הָרֹמֵשׂ עַל־הָאָרֶץ הוֹצֵא אִתָּךְ וְשָׁרְצוּ בָאָרֶץ וּפָרוּ וְרָבוּ הַיְצֵא
יח עַל־הָאָרֶץ: וַיֵּצֵא־נֹחַ וּבָנָיו וְאִשְׁתּוֹ וּנְשֵׁי־בָנָיו אִתּוֹ:
יט כָּל־הַחַיָּה כָּל־הָרֶמֶשׂ וְכָל־הָעוֹף כֹּל רוֹמֵשׂ עַל־הָאָרֶץ
כ לְמִשְׁפְּחֹתֵיהֶם יָצְאוּ מִן־הַתֵּבָה: וַיִּבֶן נֹחַ מִזְבֵּחַ לַיהוָה וַיִּקַּח
מִכֹּל ׀ הַבְּהֵמָה הַטְּהֹרָה וּמִכֹּל הָעוֹף הַטָּהוֹר וַיַּעַל עֹלֹת
כא בַּמִּזְבֵּחַ: וַיָּרַח יְהוָה אֶת־רֵיחַ הַנִּיחֹחַ וַיֹּאמֶר יְהוָה אֶל־לִבּוֹ
לֹא אֹסִף לְקַלֵּל עוֹד אֶת־הָאֲדָמָה בַּעֲבוּר הָאָדָם כִּי יֵצֶר לֵב
הָאָדָם רַע מִנְּעֻרָיו וְלֹא־אֹסִף עוֹד לְהַכּוֹת אֶת־כָּל־חַי כַּאֲשֶׁר

VERSE 19

TANḤUMA

לְמִשְׁפְּחֹתֵיהֶם יָצְאוּ מִן־הַתֵּבָה – *Emerged from the ark by families:* Do animals then have families? Rather, what the verse emphasizes is that it was only those animals which had not corrupted themselves by mating with other species which were admitted to the ark. As such, the Holy One, blessed be He, describes these animals as if their lineage were significant. Now if the text so praises the cattle, the wild animals, and the birds – creatures of no importance – and they are granted such status, how much more so were Noaḥ and his sons credited. Thus the text proceeds to name the family when it states: *Noaḥ's sons who came out from the ark were Shem, Ḥam, and Yefet* (9:18). (Noaḥ 18)

VERSE 20

BERESHIT RABBA

וַיִּבֶן נֹחַ מִזְבֵּחַ לַיהוָה – *Then Noaḥ built an altar:* The word *vayiven* can be understood as if it were *vayaven*, "Noaḥ understood." Noaḥ thought to himself: Why did the Holy One, blessed be He, command me to take more pure [kosher] animals onto the ark than impure ones? God must have intended for me to offer some of these as sacrifices. Hence the verse states: *Then Noaḥ built an altar to the Lord and, taking of each of the kinds of pure animals and pure birds, sacrificed burnt offerings on the altar.* Rabbi Elazar ben Yaakov taught: Noaḥ burned these sacrifices on the great altar in Jerusalem [that is, on the site of the Temple Mount]. Indeed, that was the very spot where Adam had brought his own offerings. (Noaḥ 34:9)

VERSE 21

TALMUD YERUSHALMI

יֵצֶר לֵב הָאָדָם רַע – *The devisings of the human heart are evil:* When reciting the *Shema*, one must distance oneself at least four cubits from the excrement of any child old enough to eat an olive's worth of grain. But no such measure need be taken if the child cannot consume that much. Rabbi Avuh explained: "The reason for this rule is that even children have evil thoughts." The students argued: "But are they not children?" He answered: "Is it not written:

them swarm again on the earth and be fertile and multiply
18 upon it." So Noaḥ came out with his sons, his wife, and his sons'
19 wives. Every beast, creeping thing, winged creature, everything
that creeps across the earth, emerged from the ark by families.
20 Then Noaḥ built an altar to the LORD and, taking of each of the
kinds of pure animals and pure birds, sacrificed burnt offerings
21 on the altar. The LORD smelled the fragrant aroma and said in
His heart, "Never again will I curse the land because of man;
the devisings of the human heart are evil from its youth. And

TALMUD YERUSHALMI *(cont.)*

The devisings of the human heart are evil from its youth? And Rabbi Yudan interpreted this to mean: The character of a human being is tainted from the time that he moves [*nin'ar*] to enter into the world." (Berakhot 3:5)

TALMUD BAVLI

יֵצֶר לֵב הָאָדָם רַע – *The devisings of the human heart are evil:* The Sages taught: So insidious is the evil inclination that even its Creator called it "evil," as the verse states: *The devisings of the human heart are evil from its youth.* (Kiddushin 30b)

SHEMOT RABBA

יֵצֶר לֵב הָאָדָם רַע – *The devisings of the human heart are evil:* The nation of Israel said to the Holy One, blessed be He: "Master of the Universe! You have created people with an evil inclination, as the verse states: *The devisings of the human heart are evil from its youth* – it is this force within us which has caused us to sin! And yet You do not remove it. We beg of You to rid our character of this craving for transgression so that we may serve You faithfully." God responded: "Indeed, I plan on doing just that in the future, as the verse states: *On that day, so says the LORD: I will gather the lame, draw close those driven away and any I have afflicted [hare'oti]* (Michah 4:6)." That text is an allusion to the evil inclination which God has installed in man, as the verse states: *The devisings of the human heart are evil [ra] from its youth.* (Ki Tisa 46:4)

LEKAḤ TOV

וַיָּרַח יהוה אֶת־רֵיחַ הַנִּיחֹחַ – *The LORD smelled the fragrant aroma:* The Holy One, blessed be He, accepted Noaḥ's sacrifices. **וַיֹּאמֶר יהוה אֶל־לִבּוֹ** – *The LORD said in His heart:* God spoke to His own glory. **יֵצֶר לֵב הָאָדָם רַע מִנְּעֻרָיו** – *The devisings of the human heart are evil from its youth:* The wickedness of human beings starts from the moment they first stir [*nin'ar*] in the world. This point is reflected in a conversation that Rabbi Yehuda Hanasi had with the emperor Antoninus. The ruler asked the Sage: When does the evil inclination enter a person – is it at the moment of his conception, or at the time of his birth? Rabbi Yehuda Hanasi tried to argue that evil is introduced conception, but Antoninus disagreed. Eventually, Rabbi Yehuda Hanasi admitted that Antoninus was correct,

כב עֲשִׂיתִי: עֹד כָּל־יְמֵי הָאָרֶץ זֶרַע וְקָצִיר וְקֹר וָחֹם וְקַיִץ וָחֹרֶף
ט א וְיוֹם וָלַיְלָה לֹא יִשְׁבֹּתוּ: וַיְבָרֶךְ אֱלֹהִים אֶת־נֹחַ וְאֶת־בָּנָיו
ב וַיֹּאמֶר לָהֶם פְּרוּ וּרְבוּ וּמִלְאוּ אֶת־הָאָרֶץ: וּמוֹרַאֲכֶם וְחִתְּכֶם
יִהְיֶה עַל כָּל־חַיַּת הָאָרֶץ וְעַל כָּל־עוֹף הַשָּׁמָיִם בְּכֹל אֲשֶׁר
ג תִּרְמֹשׂ הָאֲדָמָה וּבְכָל־דְּגֵי הַיָּם בְּיֶדְכֶם נִתָּנוּ: כָּל־רֶמֶשׂ
אֲשֶׁר הוּא־חַי לָכֶם יִהְיֶה לְאָכְלָה כְּיֶרֶק עֵשֶׂב נָתַתִּי לָכֶם

LEKAḤ TOV *(cont.)*

since the verse states: *The devisings of the human heart are evil from its youth [minne'urav]*, meaning: from the time that a child makes his movement [*nin'ar*] to enter the world.

VERSE 22

BERESHIT RABBA

עֹד כָּל־יְמֵי הָאָרֶץ – *As long as earth and time endure:* Rabbi Yudan taught in the name of Rabbi Shmuel: Did the sons of Noaḥ believe that the covenant that God was forging with them would last forever? No; it will last only as long as the heavens and the earth exist. But when the day arrives described in this verse *Lift your eyes to the heavens and gaze at the earth below: the heavens fade away like smoke; like an old cloak, the land wears out* (Isaiah 51:6), then *yes, on that day it will be annulled* (Zechariah 11:11). Rabbi Aḥa taught: God said: What was the cause of the human sin against Me? Was it not that they planted but did not reap, i.e., they gave birth but did not bury their dead? [People's exceptionally long lives and expanding populations made them proud.] From this point forward, *sowing time and harvest will not cease* – they shall both bear children and bury their dead. (Noaḥ 34:11)

CHAPTER 9, VERSE 1

BERESHIT RABBA

וַיְבָרֶךְ אֱלֹהִים אֶת־נֹחַ וְאֶת־בָּנָיו – *Then God blessed Noaḥ and his sons:* This blessing was a reward for the sacrifices that Noaḥ offered [at the end of the previous chapter]. (Noaḥ 34:12)

LEKAḤ TOV

פְּרוּ וּרְבוּ וּמִלְאוּ אֶת־הָאָרֶץ – *Be fertile, multiply, fill the earth:* The commandment to procreate devolves upon both men and women, however men have more of an obligation to do so. For so we find that our patriarch Avraham told his servant: *There you will find a wife for my son* (24:7). [Apparently Avraham was more preoccupied with his son's obligation to build a family than with that of any daughters he might have had.]

VERSE 2

LEKAḤ TOV

וּמוֹרַאֲכֶם וְחִתְּכֶם – *Fear and dread of you:* After the flood the animals once again feared and dreaded humanity. However, the "dominion" that man was granted at creation [as

22 never again will I destroy all life as I have done. As long as earth
and time endure – sowing time and harvest, cold and heat,
9 1 summer, winter, day, and night will not cease." Then God
blessed Noaḥ and his sons, saying to them, "Be fertile, multiply,
2 fill the earth. Fear and dread of you shall fall upon all beasts of
the earth, upon all winged creatures of the heavens, upon all
that creeps upon the land and all fish of the sea. Into your hand
3 they are given. Every moving thing that lives shall be food for

LEKAḤ TOV *(cont.)*

expressed in 1:28] did not return. And ever since, while a day-old child need not be protected against mice who would pluck out his eyes, dead bodies must be guarded against such a threat, even if they are as imposing as the giant Og, king of Bashan.

VERSE 3

TANḤUMA

כָּל־רֶמֶשׂ אֲשֶׁר הוּא־חַי – *Every moving thing that lives:* A later verse states: *Who can purify the defiled? No one [lo eḥad]!* (Job 14:4). The Holy One, blessed be He, allowed Israel to eat the flesh of a cow, but forbade consumption of camel meat. Now, who can turn the pure [kosher] animal into the impure [non-kosher]; who can make what is forbidden into something permitted? No one – not even the One [*eḥad*] God! At the start of the world [that is, after the flood], everything could be eaten, as the verse states: *Every moving thing that lives shall be food for you; I allow them all to you, like green plants.* Subsequently, when the nation of Israel stood at Mount Sinai, God bestowed the Torah upon them, and provided them with many commandments through which they could earn great reward. Why then did God not outline for Adam which animals were kosher? Said the Holy One, blessed be He: I gave the first man one simple commandment and he soon transgressed it; how could he possibly master all of the other obligations? Rabbi Yehuda ben Pedaya said: Adam! Who will clear the dust away from your eyes? You were unable to withstand temptation for one hour, yet your descendants are governed by a whole host of rules and they manage to observe them. Consider the Jew who plants seeds – he hoes and weeds, then he prunes and toils and waters his vegetation. And then, when the fruits of his labor emerge, and the farmer sees the produce and longs just to taste it, he refrains, in deference to the commandment *When you enter the land and plant any tree for food, you shall regard its fruit as forbidden. For three years it shall be forbidden to you; it must not be eaten* (Leviticus 19:23). But you, Adam, were told: *You are free to eat from any tree in the garden. But the Tree of Knowledge of good and evil – you may not eat from that* (Genesis 2:16–17), and you could not even manage that one restriction. Yet Your descendants Israel are guided by a whole range of laws and they are able to observe them. (Shemini 13)

ד ה אֶת־כֹּל׃ אַךְ־בָּשָׂר בְּנַפְשׁוֹ דָמוֹ לֹא תֹאכֵלוּ׃ וְאַךְ אֶת־דִּמְכֶם
לְנַפְשֹׁתֵיכֶם אֶדְרֹשׁ מִיַּד כָּל־חַיָּה אֶדְרְשֶׁנּוּ וּמִיַּד הָאָדָם מִיַּד
ו אִישׁ אָחִיו אֶדְרֹשׁ אֶת־נֶפֶשׁ הָאָדָם׃ שֹׁפֵךְ דַּם הָאָדָם בָּאָדָם

VERSE 4

BERESHIT RABBA

אַךְ־בָּשָׂר בְּנַפְשׁוֹ דָמוֹ – *But flesh with its lifeblood still in it:* Rabbi Yosei bar Ivo taught in the name of Rabbi Yoḥanan: Because Adam was not permitted to eat meat, he was not warned against eating a limb torn from a living animal. However, since the descendants of Noaḥ were allowed to eat animal flesh, they had to be prohibited from eating meat taken from an animal that was still alive. (Noaḥ 34:13)

LEKAḤ TOV

אַךְ־בָּשָׂר בְּנַפְשׁוֹ דָמוֹ – *But flesh with its lifeblood still in it:* This verse prohibits the consumption of flesh from a living animal.

VERSE 5

TALMUD BAVLI

וְאַךְ אֶת־דִּמְכֶם לְנַפְשֹׁתֵיכֶם אֶדְרֹשׁ – *And for your own lifeblood I will demand account:* It is forbidden for a person to cause injury to himself. On the other hand, some rabbis maintain that one is allowed to cause injury to himself. Who is the *tanna* who holds the first opinion? One might suppose it is the authority in the following *baraita*: The verse states: *And for your own lifeblood I will demand account*, which Rabbi Elazar interprets as: I will hold you accountable for spilling your own blood – since perhaps killing is different. [Since Rabbi Elazar believes that it is prohibited specifically to take one's own life, it might be inferred that he holds that it is permitted to merely injure oneself.] (Bava Kamma 91b)

LEKAḤ TOV

וְאַךְ אֶת־דִּמְכֶם לְנַפְשֹׁתֵיכֶם אֶדְרֹשׁ – *And for your own lifeblood I will demand account:* [Literally, "and yet, etc."] This prohibition [understood to be a proscription against suicide] includes strangulation [even though no blood actually leaves the body]. We might have thought that Sha'ul's death was similarly forbidden. [I Samuel 31 tells the story of Sha'ul's imminent capture by the Philistines, and of his decision to fall on his sword rather than be taken alive.] We also might have thought that the actions of Ḥananya, Mishael, and Azarya were similarly outlawed. [Chapter 3 in the book of Daniel describes the willingness of these three youths to be cast into a fiery furnace rather than to betray God.] To counter this supposition, the verse employs the term "yet." [The word hints that the rule here is contrasted to some form of suicide that is permitted; here the author argues that the acts of the characters above were not prohibited form of suicide.] מִיַּד כָּל־חַיָּה אֶדְרְשֶׁנּוּ – *I will demand it from every wild beast:* This alludes to the four kingdoms who have been compared to wild beasts. [The traditional four enemies who dominated Israel are Babylonia, Persia, Greece, and Rome; they were all ultimately destroyed in punishment for their murderous

4 you; I allow them all to you, like green plants. But flesh with its
5 lifeblood still in it you may not eat. And for your own lifeblood
I will demand account; I will demand it from every wild beast.
For human life I will demand account, of every man toward his
6 fellow man: One who sheds the blood of man – by man shall

LEKAḤ TOV *(cont.)*

behavior.] **וּמִיַּד הָאָדָם** – *Of every man:* This refers to the people of Israel, as the verse states: *You, My sheep, sheep of My tending, are people [adam], and I am your God, declares the Lord God* (Ezekiel 34:31). **מִיַּד אִישׁ אָחִיו** – *Toward his fellow man:* [Literally, "toward each man's brother"]: This is allusion to the descendants of Esav [who threatened his brother Yaakov], as the verse states: *Rescue me, I pray, from my brother's hand, from the hand of Esav* (32:12). **אֶדְרֹשׁ אֶת־נֶפֶשׁ הָאָדָם** – *For human life I will demand account:* In some future time. [The Romans were traditionally viewed as descendants of Esav. The implication here is that Israel's enemies will one day be held to account for their behavior toward the Jewish people.]

VERSE 6

MISHNA

כִּי בְּצֶלֶם אֱלֹהִים עָשָׂה אֶת־הָאָדָם – *For in God's image man was made:* Rabbi Akiva used to say: Beloved is humankind, for we were created in the image of God. As a gesture of special love, it was made known to us that we were created in the image of God, when He told Noaḥ: *For in God's image man was made.* (Avot 3:14)

TALMUD BAVLI

שֹׁפֵךְ דַּם הָאָדָם – *One who sheds the blood of man:* Rabbi Eliezer taught: If an individual does not fulfill his obligation to procreate, he is considered to have shed blood. For the text first states: *One who sheds the blood of man – by man shall his blood be shed*, a sentence that is followed immediately by the order *As for you, be fertile and multiply*. Rabbi Yaakov says: If a person ignores that commandment, it as if he diminishes the divine image, for the text states: *For in God's image man was made*, just before demanding: *As for you, be fertile and multiply*. Ben Azzai taught: Such a person is considered to have shed blood and to have diminished the divine image [since verse 6 refers to both murder and to the divine image of humankind, and verse 7 states:] *As for you, be fertile and multiply*. The Rabbis said to ben Azzai: "There is a type of scholar who expounds well and fulfills his own teachings, and another who fulfills his teachings, but does not expound well. But you expound well on the importance of procreation, and yet you do not fulfill your own teachings [never having fathered children]." Ben Azzai answered them: "What can I do, as my soul yearns for Torah [and I have no desire for anything else]. Let the world be maintained by other people [who do fulfill the obligation to procreate]." (Yevamot 63b) **בָּאָדָם דָּמוֹ יִשָּׁפֵךְ** – *By man shall his blood be shed:* Rabbi Yaakov bar Aḥa found the following written in a book of *aggadot* in the study hall of Rav: [Contrary to the halakha regard Jews,] a descendant of Noaḥ [a gentile] can be executed in a court consisting of one judge, and by the testimony of even one witness, and without being given forewarning before committing the transgression. [Capital cases regarding Jews are judged by a

ז דָּמוֹ יִשָּׁפֵךְ כִּי בְּצֶלֶם אֱלֹהִים עָשָׂה אֶת־הָאָדָם׃ וְאַתֶּם פְּרוּ
ח וּרְבוּ שִׁרְצוּ בָאָרֶץ וּרְבוּ־בָהּ׃ וַיֹּאמֶר אֱלֹהִים חמישי
ט אֶל־נֹחַ וְאֶל־בָּנָיו אִתּוֹ לֵאמֹר׃ וַאֲנִי הִנְנִי מֵקִים אֶת־בְּרִיתִי
י אִתְּכֶם וְאֶת־זַרְעֲכֶם אַחֲרֵיכֶם׃ וְאֵת כָּל־נֶפֶשׁ הַחַיָּה אֲשֶׁר
אִתְּכֶם בָּעוֹף בַּבְּהֵמָה וּבְכָל־חַיַּת הָאָרֶץ אִתְּכֶם מִכֹּל יֹצְאֵי

TALMUD BAVLI *(cont.)*

court of twenty-three judges, the defendant must have two witnesses arrayed against him, and he must be forewarned.] And although women cannot testify against a gentile [any more than they can against a Jew], even a relative may judge his case or testify against him. [Jews cannot be judged by familial relations.] The Sages taught in the name of Rabbi Yishmael: A descendant of Noaḥ can be executed even for killing a fetus. Now from where are these matters derived? Rav Yehuda says: They are derived from the verse *And for your own lifeblood I will demand account* – even on the basis of even one judge's verdict. Furthermore, the verse continues: *I will demand it from every wild beast*, meaning that one can be executed even without forewarning. [Just as an animal need not be warned prior to acting for it to be held liable, so too most human beings.] The next clause states: *For human life I will demand account,* hinting that justice must be done even based on only one witness's testimony. The verse concludes: *Of every man toward his fellow man*. That teaches that judgment and testimony must be at the hand of a man, but not at the hand of a woman. And finally, the term *fellow man* [literally, "every man's brother"] teaches that for most of humanity, the testimony of a witness can be accepted even if he is a relative of the defendant. What is Rabbi Yishmael's reasoning for holding a person accountable for killing a fetus? That Sage interprets the verse: *One who sheds the blood of man – by man* [*baadam,* literally, "in a person"] *shall his blood be shed*. [The term *baadam* is interpreted homiletically:] Who is a person that is "in a person?" We must say this refers to a fetus in its mother's womb. (Sanhedrin 57b)

LEKAḤ TOV

שֹׁפֵךְ דַּם הָאָדָם – *One who sheds the blood of man:* Rabbi Yoḥanan taught: God issued seven commandments to the first man [and by extension to all of humanity]. When the verse states: *And the Lord God commanded the man* (2:16), the word "command" is firstly an allusion to the obligation to establish a system of justice. For we later read concerning Avraham: *For I have chosen him so that he may command his children and his household after him to keep the way of the Lord by doing what is right and just* (18:19). Secondly, the name "Lord" in that verse indicates that it is forbidden to curse the name of God, as a later verse declares: *And anyone who blasphemes the Lord's name shall be put to death* (Leviticus 24:16). Furthermore, the name "God" in that verse alludes to the prohibition of idolatry [even for gentiles], as Israel was told directly: *Have no other gods than Me* (Exodus 20:3). The word "man" in the verse, is a reference to the prohibition of murder, as a subsequent verse states: *One who sheds the blood of man – by man shall his blood be shed*. The term "saying" represents a warning against illicit sexual unions, as we later read: *Say: if a man sent away his wife, and she walked away*

7 his blood be shed, for in God's image man was made. As
for you, be fertile and multiply, abound on earth and become
8 many on it." Then God said to Noaḥ and to his sons ḤAMISHI
9 with him: "I – I am about to establish My covenant with you
10 and your descendants after you, and with every living creature
that is with you – the birds, the animals, and all the wild beasts
of earth that are with you, everything that left the ark, every

LEKAḤ TOV *(cont.)*

from him and married another man, would he return to her again? (Jeremiah 3:1). Next, although man was given permission *to eat from any tree in the garden* (Genesis 2:16), he was warned then not to steal. Additionally, while he was allowed to eat the fruit, license was not granted him to eat any limb from a living animal [the seventh of the Noahide laws]. Now all of these rules are reasonable laws, and had the Torah which demands their observance not been given to Israel, human civilization would have intuited this basic code of behavior on its own. (Bereshit 2:15)

VERSE 8

BERESHIT RABBA

וַיֹּאמֶר אֱלֹהִים אֶל־נֹחַ וְאֶל־בָּנָיו – *Then God said to Noaḥ and his sons:* Why does God address Noaḥ and his sons? Rabbi Yehuda and Rabbi Neḥemya disagreed on the matter. According to Rabbi Yehuda, God was displeased with Noaḥ for ignoring [His commandment to procreate, as stated in 9:7], and therefore Noaḥ was shamed [by having to share God's favor with his sons]. However, Rabbi Neḥemya maintained that Noaḥ acted appropriately and in a holy manner [by continuing with the celibacy that had been demanded while he was on the ark]. As a reward for that, God granted even Noaḥ's sons communion with the Divine Spirit. (Noaḥ 35:1)

VERSE 9

LEKAḤ TOV

אֶת־בְּרִיתִי – *My covenant:* Our passage mentions the term "covenant" seven times, corresponding to the seven days of the week. These references are as follows: *I am about to establish My covenant with you* (9:9); *I will establish My covenant with you* (9:11); *God said, "This is the sign of the covenant"* (9:12); *The sign of the covenant between Me and the earth* (9:13); *I will remember My covenant* (9:15); *Remembering the eternal covenant between God and every living creature* (9:16); *This is the sign of the covenant that I have established* (9:17).

VERSE 10

LEKAḤ TOV

וְאֵת כָּל־נֶפֶשׁ הַחַיָּה אֲשֶׁר אִתְּכֶם – *And with every living creature that is with you:* This verse emphasizes that the whole of the animal kingdom was created for the benefit of humankind.

יא הַתֵּבָה לְכֹל חַיַּת הָאָרֶץ׃ וַהֲקִמֹתִי אֶת־בְּרִיתִי אִתְּכֶם וְלֹא־
יִכָּרֵת כָּל־בָּשָׂר עוֹד מִמֵּי הַמַּבּוּל וְלֹא־יִהְיֶה עוֹד מַבּוּל
יב לְשַׁחֵת הָאָרֶץ׃ וַיֹּאמֶר אֱלֹהִים זֹאת אוֹת־הַבְּרִית אֲשֶׁר־אֲנִי
נֹתֵן בֵּינִי וּבֵינֵיכֶם וּבֵין כָּל־נֶפֶשׁ חַיָּה אֲשֶׁר אִתְּכֶם לְדֹרֹת
יג עוֹלָם׃ אֶת־קַשְׁתִּי נָתַתִּי בֶּעָנָן וְהָיְתָה לְאוֹת בְּרִית בֵּינִי וּבֵין
יד הָאָרֶץ׃ וְהָיָה בְּעַנְנִי עָנָן עַל־הָאָרֶץ וְנִרְאֲתָה הַקֶּשֶׁת בֶּעָנָן׃
טו וְזָכַרְתִּי אֶת־בְּרִיתִי אֲשֶׁר בֵּינִי וּבֵינֵיכֶם וּבֵין כָּל־נֶפֶשׁ חַיָּה
בְּכָל־בָּשָׂר וְלֹא־יִהְיֶה עוֹד הַמַּיִם לְמַבּוּל לְשַׁחֵת כָּל־בָּשָׂר׃
טז וְהָיְתָה הַקֶּשֶׁת בֶּעָנָן וּרְאִיתִיהָ לִזְכֹּר בְּרִית עוֹלָם בֵּין אֱלֹהִים

VERSE 11

PHILO

וְלֹא־יִהְיֶה עוֹד מַבּוּל לְשַׁחֵת הָאָרֶץ – *Never again will there be a flood to destroy the earth:* The statement clearly implies there will be many floods in the future, but that there shall never be one of such character as to be able to change the whole earth into a lake or sea.

YALKUT SHIMONI

וְלֹא־יִכָּרֵת כָּל־בָּשָׂר עוֹד – *Never again may all life be destroyed:* Rabbi Yehuda Hanasi taught: This declaration only asserts that no flood will ever destroy all of earth's life. However, individuals can still perish in such natural disasters. How might this happen? If a man falls into the sea and drowns, or should his boat sink in the ocean, killing him – those would be personal floods. Rabbi Yehuda says: Although God promises never to flood the world with water, He might still flood it with fire or sulfur, as we see with the city of Sedom. Furthermore, God might unleash a torrent of plague against the gentile nations in messianic times. (61)

VERSE 12

BERESHIT RABBA

לְדֹרֹת עוֹלָם – *For all generations to come:* Rabbi Yudan taught: the term *ledorot* is written defectively [that is, without the letter *vav*, which could have appeared twice] to indicate that the sign of the rainbow was unnecessary in two generations. Neither the time of King Ḥizkiyahu nor that of the Men of the Great Assembly were ever under any threat of destruction [since the people living then were wholly righteous]. Rabbi Ḥizkiya disagreed with this assessment of the era of the Men of the Great Assembly, arguing that the second blameless time was that of Rabbi Shimon bar Yoḥai. (Noaḥ 35:2)

VERSE 14

LEKAḤ TOV

וְהָיָה בְּעַנְנִי עָנָן עַל־הָאָרֶץ – *Whenever I bring clouds over the earth:* We learn from this that the heavenly Accuser only ever prosecutes during a time of actual danger. [It is only

11 living creature on earth. I will establish My covenant with you,
that never again may all life be destroyed by the waters of a
flood; never again will there be a flood to destroy the earth."
12 God said, "This is the sign of the covenant I am making between Me and you – and every living creature with you – for all
13 generations to come. I have laid down My bow in the clouds to
14 be the sign of the covenant between Me and the earth. Whenever I bring clouds over the earth and the rainbow appears in
15 the clouds, I will remember My covenant that binds Me and
you and every living creature of all flesh so that never again will
16 the waters become a flood to destroy all life. The rainbow will
be there in the cloud, and I will see it, remembering the eternal
covenant between God and every living creature, all flesh upon

LEKAḤ TOV *(cont.)*

during such times that the wicked are punished; divine retribution does not issue from a clear blue sky.]

YALKUT SHIMONI

וְנִרְאֲתָה הַקֶּשֶׁת בֶּעָנָן – *And the rainbow appears in the clouds:* At the approach of Rabbi Yehoshua ben Levi, the prophet Eliyahu proclaimed: Clear the way for the son of Levi! As Rabbi Yehoshua ben Levi walked along, he encountered Rabbi Shimon bar Yoḥai sitting on thirteen stools of gold. The latter asked Rabbi Yehoshua: Are you the son of Levi? Said he: I am. Tell me, asked Rabbi Shimon bar Yoḥai: Has a rainbow ever appeared in your lifetime? Said he: It has. But Rabbi Shimon responded: If so, you cannot be *the* son of Levi [whose arrival Eliyahu had announced. No rainbow would have been seen in the sky while such a righteous individual lived; his virtue alone would spare the world from destruction]. The truth is that there really had not been a rainbow in Rabbi Yehoshua ben Levi's lifetime, however the Sage was too humble to take credit for it. (61)

VERSE 15

LEKAḤ TOV

וְזָכַרְתִּי אֶת־בְּרִיתִי – *I will remember My covenant:* Great is the covenant which endures forever, which sustained the patriarchs, which supported the nation of Israel, and which lasts through David and his descendants.

VERSE 16

LEKAḤ TOV

הַקֶּשֶׁת – *The rainbow:* For I drew my bow taut to unleash the flood upon the earth. Now, however, you will see that my bow is loose and unthreatening. **לִזְכֹּר בְּרִית עוֹלָם** – *Remembering the eternal covenant:* I will thereby recall never to lay waste to the world again.

יז וּבֵין כָּל־נֶפֶשׁ חַיָּה בְּכָל־בָּשָׂר אֲשֶׁר עַל־הָאָרֶץ: וַיֹּאמֶר
אֱלֹהִים אֶל־נֹחַ זֹאת אוֹת־הַבְּרִית אֲשֶׁר הֲקִמֹתִי בֵּינִי וּבֵין
כָּל־בָּשָׂר אֲשֶׁר עַל־הָאָרֶץ:
יח וַיִּהְיוּ בְנֵי־נֹחַ הַיֹּצְאִים מִן־הַתֵּבָה שֵׁם וְחָם וָיָפֶת וְחָם הוּא ח ששי
יט אֲבִי כְנָעַן: שְׁלֹשָׁה אֵלֶּה בְּנֵי־נֹחַ וּמֵאֵלֶּה נָפְצָה כָל־הָאָרֶץ:
כ כא וַיָּחֶל נֹחַ אִישׁ הָאֲדָמָה וַיִּטַּע כָּרֶם: וַיֵּשְׁתְּ מִן־הַיַּיִן וַיִּשְׁכָּר

LEKAḤ TOV *(cont.)*

וּבֵין כָּל־נֶפֶשׁ חַיָּה – And between every living creature: God struck His covenant with humanity as well as with the cattle and the wild animals.

VERSE 17

LEKAḤ TOV

זֹאת אוֹת־הַבְּרִית – *This is the sign of the covenant:* The rainbow will serve as a sign that people can view, and the covenant is what that sign represents.

VERSE 18

BERESHIT RABBA

בְּנֵי־נֹחַ הַיֹּצְאִים מִן־הַתֵּבָה – *Noaḥ's sons who came out from the ark:* A later verse which states: *He makes silence; who can breach it? He hides His face; who can see Him? He sees nation and one man* (Job 34:29), refers to the "nation" of the generation of the flood, and to Noaḥ as the man. Noaḥ is called "one" since the entire world was founded by him. God can establish all of civilization from one nation, and out of a single individual. Thus the verse states: *Noaḥ's sons who came out of the ark.* (Noaḥ 36:1)

LEKAḤ TOV

וַיִּהְיוּ – *Were:* The sons of Noaḥ were granted permanent being [*havaya*] in the world. The reward that these men received for sitting in the ark was that they lived to emerge from it. During the twelve long months on board, Noaḥ's sons worked diligently to feed the cattle and the beasts. Why does the verse list Shem first as if to suggest that he was the oldest son, when in fact Yefet was Noaḥ's firstborn? Because Shem was righteous, whereas Ḥam was the founder of human degradation.

VERSE 19

LEKAḤ TOV

שְׁלֹשָׁה אֵלֶּה בְּנֵי־נֹחַ – *These three were Noaḥ's sons:* All of the earth's people descended from these three men, like the progeny of a huge fish which fill the sea.

וּמֵאֵלֶּה נָפְצָה כָל־הָאָרֶץ – *And from them all the world branched out:* This refers to the seventy nations of the earth.

17 the earth." So said God to Noaḥ: "This is the sign of the covenant that I have established between Me and all flesh that is on
earth."
18 Noaḥ's sons who came out from the ark were Shem, Ḥam, and SHISHI
19 Yefet. Ḥam was the father of Kenaan. These three were Noaḥ's
20 sons; and from them all the world branched out. Noaḥ began
21 to be a man of the land, and he planted a vineyard. He drank
some of the wine, became drunk, and lay uncovered in his tent.

VERSE 20

TANḤUMA

וַיִּטַּע כָּרֶם – *And he planted a vineyard:* Noaḥ introduced four things to the world: planting, drunkenness, cursing, and slavery. With regard to the first, the verse states: *He planted a vineyard.* Following this, Noaḥ *drank some of the wine, became drunk* (9:21). Later *He said, "Cursed be Kenaan! The lowest of the slaves shall he be to his brothers"* (9:25), which represented both the first malediction and the invention of servitude. (Noaḥ 20)

BERESHIT RABBA

וַיָּחֶל – *Began:* With this enterprise, Noaḥ was degraded [*nitḥallel*] and became profane [*ḥullin*]. For the man ought not have planted a vineyard, but rather something useful like a fig tree or an olive tree. Now how did Noaḥ manage to have vines to plant? Rabbi Abba bar Kahana taught: When Noaḥ boarded the ark, he took with him vine shoots and cuttings, as well as fig and olive shoots, as the verse states: *As for you, take all the food to be eaten and store it* (6:21). For people only bother to store things that they will need in the future. (Noaḥ 36:3)

LEKAḤ TOV

אִישׁ הָאֲדָמָה – *A man of the land:* The text here alludes to Adam, the first man, to whom God proclaimed: *Cursed will be the land on your account* (3:17). And this corresponds to the approach which claims that the forbidden tree Adam and Ḥava ate from was a grape vine [since that is what Noaḥ here plants]. For nothing causes as much damage to the world as wine.

VERSE 21

BERESHIT RABBA

וַיֵּשְׁתְּ מִן־הַיַּיִן – *He drank some of the wine:* Noaḥ drank an excessive amount of wine and degraded himself. Rabbi Ḥiyya bar Abba taught: All of this happened on the same day – he planted the vineyard, drank the wine, got drunk, and became humiliated – one step after the other. וַיִּתְגַּל – *And lay uncovered:* Rabbi Yehuda taught in the name of Rabbi Ḥanin, who said in the name of Rabbi Shmuel bar Yitzḥak: Note that the verse does not use the construction *vayiggal* [a simpler word for "uncovered"] but *vayitgal,* which hints that Noaḥ's behavior brought exile [*galut*] upon him and upon future generations.

כב וַיִּתְגַּל בְּתוֹךְ אָהֳלֹה: וַיַּרְא חָם אֲבִי כְנַעַן אֵת עֶרְוַת אָבִיו
כג וַיַּגֵּד לִשְׁנֵי־אֶחָיו בַּחוּץ: וַיִּקַּח שֵׁם וָיֶפֶת אֶת־הַשִּׂמְלָה
וַיָּשִׂימוּ עַל־שְׁכֶם שְׁנֵיהֶם וַיֵּלְכוּ אֲחֹרַנִּית וַיְכַסּוּ אֵת עֶרְוַת

BERESHIT RABBA *(cont.)*

Indeed, the ten tribes of Israel were exiled as a consequence of drink, as the prophet berated them: *Who guzzle wine from bowls* (Amos 6:6), and *Woe for those who rise early to chase ale, whom wine lights up through the night* (Isaiah 5:11). Furthermore, the tribes of Yehuda and Binyamin were similarly driven from their lands because of wine, as the prophet declares: *For these men too have gone astray with wine, they have lost themselves in ale* (Isaiah 28:7). בְּתוֹךְ אָהֳלֹה – *In his tent:* The term *oholo* is written as if it were *oholah* [with a *heh,* meaning "her tent"], referring to Noaḥ's wife's tent. Rav Huna taught in the name of Rabbi Elazar the son of Rabbi Yosei the Galilean: When Noaḥ was leaving the ark, the lion attacked him and injured him [severing his member. However, because Noaḥ was drunk, and forgot that he had been wounded] he approached his wife, attempting to lie with her. His semen was scattered, humiliating him. Rabbi Yoḥanan taught: A person should be extremely cautious regarding his desire for wine. To illustrate the dangers of inebriation, the text uses the sound of *vay* ["woe!"] fourteen times in this passage. [That is, the repeated combination of the letters *vav* and *yod* which produce the sound *vay,* is meant to create an atmosphere of distress for the reader.] The section begins with the statement *Noaḥ began [vayaḥel] to be a man of the land, and he planted [vayitta] a vineyard* (9:20). The narrative continues: *He drank [vayesht]... became drunk [vayishkar], and lay uncovered [vayitgal] in his tent. Ḥam, father of Kenaan, saw [vayar] his father's nakedness and told [vayaged] his two brothers who were outside. Shem and Yefet then took [vayikkaḥ] a cloak and put [vayasimu] it over both their shoulders. They walked [vayelekhu] backward and covered [vaykhasu] their father's nakedness.... Noaḥ woke [vayiketz] from his wine and realized [vayeda] what his youngest son had done to him. He said [vayomer], "Cursed be Kenaan!"* (9:21–25). (Noaḥ 36:4)

VERSE 22

PHILO

וַיַּרְא חָם אֲבִי כְנַעַן אֵת עֶרְוַת אָבִיו – *Ḥam, father of Kenaan, saw his father's nakedness:* Ḥam's behavior is a grim reminder about how certain people live a depraved and malignant life that treats people with derision and contempt. It is a terrible thing for someone to judge the misery of others as though one is a chastising judge. What happened here was even worse, for it is repugnant for any mind to delight in the involuntary misfortune of another.

BERESHIT RABBA

וַיַּגֵּד לִשְׁנֵי־אֶחָיו בַּחוּץ – *And told his two brothers who were outside:* What did Ḥam tell his brothers? He said to Shem and Yefet: "Adam had but two sons, and one of them rose and killed the other. Meanwhile this man [Noaḥ] has three sons and he is intent on making a fourth one!" Thus Ḥam tried to convince his brothers that he had acted appropriately. Rabbi Yaakov bar Zavdi taught: Why does a Canaanite slave go free if his master knocks

22 Ḥam, father of Kenaan, saw his father's nakedness and told his
23 two brothers who were outside. Shem and Yefet then took a
cloak and put it over both their shoulders. They walked backward and covered their father's nakedness, averting their faces

BERESHIT RABBA (cont.)

out his tooth or blinds his eye [as mandated in Exodus 21:26]? It is because Ḥam saw [his father] and told [his two brothers; hence it was Ḥam's eye and mouth which condemned him to servitude]. (Noaḥ 36:5)

LEKAḤ TOV

וַיַּרְא חָם אֲבִי כְנַעַן – *Ham, father of Kenaan saw:* Ḥam eagerly looked at his father instead of averting his gaze. He then proceeded to mock Noaḥ by reporting to his brothers what he had seen.

VERSE 23

TANḤUMA

וַיִּקַּח שֵׁם וָיֶפֶת אֶת־הַשִּׂמְלָה – *Shem and Yefet then took a cloak:* Because the emperor Sanḥeriv employed a messenger [*mal'akh*] to intimidate Yehuda, he was defeated by an angel [*mal'akh*] as the verse states: *And that night, an angel of the Lord went out and struck down 185,000 in the Assyrian camp; by daybreak the next morning, they were all dead bodies* (II Kings 19:35). What did the angel do to Sanḥeriv's army? It is as the prophet states: *And under his frame* [literally, "under his honor"] *a burning will burn as fire burns* (Isaiah 10:16). What does that mean exactly? The soldiers' bodies were burned although their garments remained intact, for an individual's clothes are called "his honor." Why did the Holy One, blessed be He, leave the uniforms unburned? For these people were descendants of Shem, as the verse states: *Shem's sons were Elam, Ashur etc.* [10:22; Sanḥeriv was king of Ashur]. Said the Holy One, blessed be He to Sanḥeriv: "Your ancestor Shem deserves some reward for taking his cloak and covering his father's nakedness, as the verse states: *Shem and Yefet then took a cloak and put it over both their shoulders.*" This is why, when God destroyed the king's army, He left their clothes alone out of respect. (Tzav 3)

BERESHIT RABBA

וַיִּקַּח שֵׁם וָיֶפֶת אֶת־הַשִּׂמְלָה – *Shem and Yefet then took a cloak:* Rabbi Yoḥanan taught: It was Shem who began the act of honoring his father [which is why the verb *vayikkaḥ* is in the singular], and afterward Yefet came along and joined him. This is why Shem was rewarded with a *tallit* [the traditional Jewish fringed garment], whereas Yefet was granted the *pallium* [a Greek cloak. Shem is the direct ancestor of Avraham and hence of the Jewish people, while Yefet's descendants include the Greeks, as mentioned in 10:2]. Now since the verse states that Shem and Yefet *walked backward*, is it not obvious that they did not *see the nakedness of their father*? We are meant to understand that not only did the men walk backward, but that they covered their eyes with their hands as well. They thus exhibited great filial respect. Said the Holy One, blessed be He, to Shem: "Because you covered up

כד אֲבִיהֶם וּפְנֵיהֶם אֲחֹרַנִּית וְעֶרְוַת אֲבִיהֶם לֹא רָאוּ׃ וַיִּיקֶץ
כה נֹחַ מִיֵּינוֹ וַיֵּדַע אֵת אֲשֶׁר־עָשָׂה לוֹ בְּנוֹ הַקָּטָן׃ וַיֹּאמֶר אָרוּר
כו כְּנָעַן עֶבֶד עֲבָדִים יִהְיֶה לְאֶחָיו׃ וַיֹּאמֶר בָּרוּךְ יהוה אֱלֹהֵי
כז שֵׁם וִיהִי כְנַעַן עֶבֶד לָמוֹ׃ יַפְתְּ אֱלֹהִים לְיֶפֶת וְיִשְׁכֹּן בְּאָהֳלֵי־
כח שֵׁם וִיהִי כְנַעַן עֶבֶד לָמוֹ׃ וַיְחִי־נֹחַ אַחַר הַמַּבּוּל שְׁלֹשׁ מֵאוֹת

BERESHIT RABBA *(cont.)*

your father's nakedness, I swear that I will reward you." Thus we read: *So those men were tied up still wearing their mantles, tunics, hats, and clothes and were thrown into the midst of the fiery furnace* [Daniel 3:21. Because Shem provided a covering for Noaḥ, God saved his descendants who were cast into the furnace wearing clothing.] Meanwhile, the Holy One, blessed be He, said to Yefet: Because you covered up your father's nakedness, I swear I will reward you as well. Thus we read concerning Yefet's descendant Gog: *And it will happen on that day: I will grant Gog a burial place there in Israel, the Valley of the Travelers, east of the sea, and it will block the travelers. Here they will bury Gog and his horde; they will call it the Valley of the Horde of Gog* (Ezekiel 39:11). Then the Holy One, blessed be He, said to Ḥam: Because you humiliated your father's nakedness, I swear I will punish you. Thus we read concerning his own descendants: *Just so will it be when the king of Assyria leads away the captives of Egypt, the exiles of Kush, young and old, naked, barefoot, backsides bare, that nakedness of Egypt* (Isaiah 20:4). (Noaḥ 36:6)

VERSE 24

LEKAḤ TOV

וַיִּיקֶץ נֹחַ מִיֵּינוֹ – *Noaḥ woke from his wine:* Noaḥ became sober following his drunkenness. **וַיֵּדַע בְּנוֹ הַקָּטָן** – *His youngest son:* [Alternatively, "his smallest son."] Ḥam was both small minded and of low caliber; for he doomed his descendants to servitude.

VERSE 25

LEKAḤ TOV

וַיֹּאמֶר אָרוּר כְּנָעַן – *He said, "Cursed be Kenaan!":* Granted that Ḥam sinned by disrespecting his father; why was his son Kenaan cursed for his fathers misdeed? Rabbi Yehuda taught: Since God had previously blessed Noaḥ and his sons [as stated in 9:1], Noaḥ could not have cursed Ḥam himself, since he was already blessed. Rabbi Neḥemya suggested: It was Kenaan who had first spied Noaḥ's nakedness and told the others, and that is why he was cursed. Another interpretation: Kenaan was Ḥam's fourth son, as the verse states: *Ḥam's sons were Kush, Mitzrayim, Put, and Kenaan* (10:6). Hence because Ḥam prevented Noaḥ from having a fourth son [according to the approach that the son had in fact castrated his father], Noaḥ cursed Ḥam's fourth son. **עֶבֶד עֲבָדִים יִהְיֶה לְאֶחָיו** – *The lowest of slaves shall he be to his brothers:* Canaanite slaves ought never be freed, as the text orders: *They become hereditary property that you can bequeath to your children* (Leviticus 25:46).

24 so as not to see the nakedness of their father. Noaḥ woke from
his wine and realized what his youngest son had done to him.
25 He said, "Cursed be Kenaan! The lowest of slaves shall he be
26 to his brothers." Then he said, "Blessed be the Lord, God of
27 Shem; Kenaan shall be his slave. May God enlarge Yefet, and let
28 him dwell in the tents of Shem; Kenaan shall be his slave." After

VERSE 26

LEKAḤ TOV

וַיֹּאמֶר בָּרוּךְ יהוה אֱלֹהֵי שֵׁם – *Then he said, "Blessed be the Lord, God of Shem"*: The Divine Presence [represented here by God's unique four-letter name] only rests in the tents of Israel [the descendants of Shem], as the verse states: *Bless God in chorus, the Lord, you of Israel's fountain!* (Psalms 68:27).

VERSE 27

TALMUD YERUSHALMI

יַפְתְּ אֱלֹהִים לְיֶפֶת – *May God enlarge Yefet:* This verse allows the language of Yefet [Greek] to be spoken in the tents of Shem. [That is, we learn from this verse that Jews may learn to speak and read Greek.] (Megilla 1:9)

TALMUD BAVLI

יַפְתְּ אֱלֹהִים לְיֶפֶת – *May God enlarge Yefet:* Rabban Shimon ben Gamliel taught: With regard to Torah scrolls, the Sages permitted these to be written only in Greek. [That is, Greek is the only acceptable language for a Torah scroll other than the original Hebrew.] Rabbi Abbahu said in the name of Rabbi Yoḥanan: The halakha is in accordance with Rabban Shimon ben Gamliel. And Rabbi Yoḥanan said: What is Rabban Shimon ben Gamliel's reasoning? He bases his opinion on an allusion in the Torah, as the verse states: *May God enlarge Yefet, and let him dwell in the tents of Shem*, indicating that the words of Yefet may exist in the tents of Shem. (Megilla 9b)

BERESHIT RABBA

יַפְתְּ אֱלֹהִים לְיֶפֶת – *May God enlarge Yefet:* Reish Lakish taught: this is a blessing for the emperor Cyrus [a descendant of Yefet], who decreed that the Temple be rebuilt. Nevertheless, God will dwell only in the tents of Shem [the people of Israel]. Bar Kappara taught: Let the words of the Torah be recited even in Yefet's language [Greek] within the halls of Shem's academies. Rabbi Yudan taught: This teaches that it is permissible to translate the Torah. (Noaḥ 36:8)

VERSE 28

LEKAḤ TOV

וַיְחִי־נֹחַ אַחַר הַמַּבּוּל – *After the flood Noaḥ lived:* Noaḥ lived an additional 350 years after the flood, which is the sum of the ark's length and its width, as the verse states: *This is how you shall make it: the ark shall be three hundred cubits long, fifty cubits wide, and thirty cubits high* (6:15).

כט שָׁנָה וַחֲמִשִּׁים שָׁנָה: וַיְהִי כָּל־יְמֵי־נֹחַ תְּשַׁע מֵאוֹת שָׁנָה
וַחֲמִשִּׁים שָׁנָה וַיָּמֹת:
י א וְאֵלֶּה תּוֹלְדֹת בְּנֵי־נֹחַ שֵׁם חָם וָיָפֶת וַיִּוָּלְדוּ לָהֶם בָּנִים אַחַר
ב הַמַּבּוּל: בְּנֵי יֶפֶת גֹּמֶר וּמָגוֹג וּמָדַי וְיָוָן וְתֻבָל וּמֶשֶׁךְ וְתִירָס:
ג ד וּבְנֵי גֹּמֶר אַשְׁכְּנַז וְרִיפַת וְתֹגַרְמָה: וּבְנֵי יָוָן אֱלִישָׁה וְתַרְשִׁישׁ
ה כִּתִּים וְדֹדָנִים: מֵאֵלֶּה נִפְרְדוּ אִיֵּי הַגּוֹיִם בְּאַרְצֹתָם אִישׁ
ו לִלְשֹׁנוֹ לְמִשְׁפְּחֹתָם בְּגוֹיֵהֶם: וּבְנֵי חָם כּוּשׁ וּמִצְרַיִם וּפוּט
ז וּכְנָעַן: וּבְנֵי כוּשׁ סְבָא וַחֲוִילָה וְסַבְתָּה וְרַעְמָה וְסַבְתְּכָא וּבְנֵי
ח רַעְמָה שְׁבָא וּדְדָן: וְכוּשׁ יָלַד אֶת־נִמְרֹד הוּא הֵחֵל לִהְיוֹת

CHAPTER 10, VERSE 1

BEMIDBAR RABBA

וְאֵלֶּה תּוֹלְדֹת בְּנֵי־נֹחַ – *These are the descendants of Noaḥ's sons:* When God takes the trouble to build a nation out of an individual and his descendants, He lists the family and introduces the lineage with the word *toledot* ["descendants," or "generations"]. As such we find twelve instances of the term *toledot* in Scripture. The first one appears at the very beginning when we are told: *(1) This is the story [toledot] of the heavens and the earth when they were created* (2:4). This is followed by *(2) This is the book of Adam's descendants [toledot]* (5:1); *(3) This is the story of [toledot] Noaḥ* (6:9); *(4) These are the descendants [toledot] of Noaḥ's sons*; *(5) These are the descendants [toledot] of Shem* (11:10); *(6) These are the descendants [toledot] of Teraḥ* (11:27); *(7) These are the descendants [toledot] of Avraham's son Yishmael* (25:12); *(8) This is the story [toledot] of Yitzḥak, son of Avraham* (25:19); *(9) These are the descendants [toledot] of Esav* (36:1); and *(10) This is the story [toledot] of Yaakov* (37:2). In these ten cases the Holy One, blessed be He, used the word to express His intention to create the world and to establish nations. However there are two other examples where the term *toledot* is used in a slightly different manner. In one instance the word indicates the introduction of the royal dynasty of Israel, and in the other the formation of its priesthood. For in the book of Ruth we read: *(11) This is the line [toledot] of Peretz* [4:18, the ancestor of David and hence] the patriarch of the monarchy; and *(12) These were the descendants [toledot] of Aharon* (Numbers 3:1), a verse which indicates the origins of the priesthood. (Bemidbar 2:21)

LEKAḤ TOV

וְאֵלֶּה תּוֹלְדֹת בְּנֵי־נֹחַ – *These are the descendants of Noaḥ's sons:* [Literally, "and these."] The conjunctive letter *vav* at the start of the verse hints that the descendants of Noaḥ's sons continued their patriarch's contribution to the world; they did not negate it. [Had there been no "and," the text would have suggested a break with Noaḥ's achievements.]

29 the flood Noaḥ lived three hundred and fifty years. Noaḥ lived a
total of nine hundred and fifty years, and he died.
10 1 These are the descendants of Noaḥ's sons, Shem, Ḥam, and
2 Yefet; after the flood, children were born to them. Yefet's sons
were Gomer, Magog, Madai, Yavan, Tuval, Meshekh, and Tiras.
3 4 Gomer's sons were Ashkenaz, Rifat, and Togarma. Yavan's sons
5 were Elisha, Tarshish, Kitim, and Dodanim. From these the
seagoing nations spread out to their territories, each with its
6 own language, by their clans and their nations. Ḥam's sons were
7 Kush, Mitzrayim, Put, and Kenaan. Kush's sons were Seva,
Ḥavila, Savta, Raama, and Savtekha. Raama's sons were Sheva
8 and Dedan. Kush was the father of Nimrod, the first mighty

VERSE 2

LEKAḤ TOV

בְּנֵי יֶפֶת – *Yefet's sons:* The Torah provides Yefet's lineage first because he was Noaḥ's firstborn. **גֹּמֶר וּמָגוֹג וּמָדַי** – *Gomer, Magog, Madai:* Rabbi Shmuel bar Rabbi Ami said: The men listed in this verse founded the lands of North Africa, Germany, Media, Macedonia, Italy, and Antioch. Tiras is Persia.

VERSE 4

YALKUT SHIMONI

וְדֹדָנִים – *And Dodanim:* [Yavan and his descendants are traditionally viewed as the Greek peoples.] Although our verse presents the name of Yavan's son as *Dodanim*, a later text states the name as *Rodanim* [see I Chronicles 1:7]. Rabbi Simon and Rabbi Ḥanin disagreed on this matter. Rabbi Simon argued that this race were called *Dodanim* because their were the uncles [*dodim*] of the Israelite people [since they descended from Yefet, brother of Shem, progenitor of Avraham]. And yet, they were also called *Rodanim* ["tyrants"] because they terrorized Israel. Rabbi Ḥanin maintained: When the people of Israel have the upper hand, the *Dodanim* claim a kinship to them, but when the nation is downtrodden, they come along and oppress [*rodin*] them. (61)

VERSE 8

TANḤUMA

וְכוּשׁ יָלַד אֶת־נִמְרֹד – *Kush was the father of Nimrod:* Why does the text bother to list the lineages of all of these men? Did the Holy One, blessed be He, lack material to include in His Torah? The lesson garnered from these verses is that from the beginning of humanity God paid attention to all the nations of the world. These peoples can never claim their innocence, for God has always known their depraved roots. How so? The text presents Ḥam's lineage with the introduction *Ḥam's sons were Kush, Mitzrayim, Put, and Kenaan.... Kush was the father of Nimrod*. It was Nimrod who first rebelled against God, as the text reports: *The*

ט גִּבֹּר בָּאָרֶץ: הוּא־הָיָה גִבֹּר־צַיִד לִפְנֵי יהוה עַל־כֵּן יֵאָמַר
י כְּנִמְרֹד גִּבּוֹר צַיִד לִפְנֵי יהוה: וַתְּהִי רֵאשִׁית מַמְלַכְתּוֹ בָּבֶל

TANHUMA *(cont.)*

first mighty warrior on earth. The text continues: *Mitzrayim fathered the Ludim…from whom the Philistines descended* (10:13–14). Note that the text does not say that the Patrusim and the Kasluḥim fathered [*holidu*] the Philistines, but that they "emerged" [*yatze'u misham*] as if on their own, hinting that they were born of adultery. However, the Holy One, blessed be He, drew Israel to Himself and took them as His own portion, as the verse states: *The Lord's own share is His people, Yaakov His allotted place* (Deuteronomy 32:9). We further read: *You will be My treasure among all the peoples* (Exodus 19:5), and *I planted you as a choice grape: Perfect and genuine seed* (Jeremiah 2:21). Why does the Holy One, blessed be He, begin the Torah by addressing the lineages of the world's nations? It may be understood through the following metaphor: Consider a king who owns a precious pearl, which he drops into the dirt and grime. In order to locate his gem, the king has to sift through all of the refuse in order to reveal the treasure that is located within the pile. When he finally discovers the lost pearl, he proceeds to ignore all of the trash that he had gone through and focuses all his attention on his beloved treasure. In a similar manner, the Holy One, blessed be He, works His way through all the early personages and lumps them together – *Adam, Shet, Enosh; Keinan, Mahalalel, Yered* (I Chronicles 1:1–2). Then He pays scant attention to the next ten generations of humanity – *Shem, Arpakhshad, Shelaḥ; Ever, Peleg, Reu* (I Chronicles 1:24–25). Indeed when a child reads from the Torah, he speeds through the first ten generations from Adam to Noaḥ in one breath, and again quickly recites the ten representatives of humanity from Noaḥ to Avraham. But suddenly, when he reaches Avraham, Yitzḥak, and Yaakov – the pearls of humanity, he begins to read about their lives in detail. (Vayeshev 1)

BERESHIT RABBA

הוּא הֵחֵל לִהְיוֹת גִּבֹּר בָּאָרֶץ – *The first mighty warrior on earth:* [Literally, "he began to be a mighty warrior on earth."] Rabbi Simon taught: The verb *heḥel* appears three times in the Torah to signify rebellion. The first instance appears in the verse *That was when people began [huḥal] to pray in the name of the Lord* [4:26, signifying the rebellion of the generation of Enosh]. The second is in the verse *Humans began [heḥel] to multiply on earth* [6:1, referring to the corruption of the generation of the flood]. And the third is in the statement [concerning the evil Nimrod] *He began [heḥel] to be a mighty warrior*. (Bereshit 23:7)

VERSE 9

LEKAH TOV

הוּא־הָיָה גִבֹּר־צַיִד – *He was a mighty hunter:* The term "he" [*hu*] is used five times in Scripture to identify men who were wicked, and five times to refer to men who were good. The first one appears in our verse, *He was a mighty hunter*. We next read: *These were the*

9 warrior on earth. He was a mighty hunter before the LORD,
which is why people still say, "Like Nimrod, a mighty hunter
10 before the LORD." His kingdom began with Babylon, Erekh,

LEKAH TOV *(cont.)*

chiefs of Edom – of Esav (36:43). The third instance is in the verse *Eliav's descendants: Nemuel, Datan, and Aviram. These were the same [hu] Datan and Aviram, elect of the community, who rebelled against Moshe* (Numbers 26:9). And later, *In his time of crisis, he still broke faith with the LORD, that [hu] King Aḥaz* (II Chronicles 28:22). The fifth case appears in the verse *It happened in the days of Aḥashverosh – that [hu] Aḥashverosh who ruled 127 provinces from Hodu to Kush* (Esther 1:1). On the other hand, the pronoun is sometimes used with a positive connotation, beginning with the patriarch Avraham: *That is [hu] Avraham* (I Chronicles 1:27). We also find the following texts: *It was they who spoke up to Pharaoh, king of Egypt to bring the Israelites out of Egypt – this same [hu] Moshe and Aharon* (Exodus 6:27); *David was [hu] the youngest, while only the three oldest had left to follow Sha'ul* (I Samuel 17:14); *This was the same [hu] Yeḥizkiyahu who dammed the upper pool of the waters of Giḥon waters* (II Chronicles 32:30); and *This [hu] Ezra ascended from Babylon. He was a scholar, expert in the Torah of Moshe given by the LORD* (Ezra 7:6). To this list Rabbi Berekhya added in the name of the Rabbis: *He [hu] is the LORD, our God; His judgments are throughout the land* (Psalms 105:7) – He is beneficent to all creatures, His compassion endures forever.

MIDRASH AGGADA

הוּא־הָיָה גִבֹּר־צַיִד – *He was a mighty hunter:* Nimrod chased down other people and killed them. **לִפְנֵי יהוה** – *Before the LORD:* Even though Nimrod recognized the existence of God, he made it a point to rebel against Him. **כְּנִמְרֹד גִּבּוֹר צַיִד** – *Like Nimrod, a mighty hunter:* People would say this about Esav, who is referred to later as *a skilled hunter, a man of the field* (25:27).

VERSE 10

BERESHIT RABBA

וְכַלְנֵה בְּאֶרֶץ שִׁנְעָר – *And Kalneh in the land of Shinar:* Shinar is identified with Babylon. Why was it so called? Reish Lakish taught: It was there that the corpses of the flood were deposited [*nin'aru*]. Another interpretation: The place was called Shinar because it is devoid [*menu'eret*] of commandments, lacking the practices of tithes and the Sabbatical year [that are in force in the land of Israel]. Another interpretation: The place was called Shinar because its citizens would suffocate to death [*tashnik*], in darkness [*belo ner*] and unwashed. Another interpretation: The place was called Shinar because its princes died in their youth [as *ne'arim*]. Another interpretation: The place was called Shinar because its princes studied Torah in their youth. Finally: The place was called Shinar because it raised an enemy [*soneh*] who sought to undermine [*le'ar'er*] God in the form of Nevukhadnetzar, king of Babylon. (37:4)

יא וְאֶ֥רֶךְ וְאַכַּ֖ד וְכַלְנֵ֑ה בְּאֶ֖רֶץ שִׁנְעָֽר׃ מִן־הָאָ֥רֶץ הַהִ֖וא יָצָ֣א
יב אַשּׁ֑וּר וַיִּ֙בֶן֙ אֶת־נִ֣ינְוֵ֔ה וְאֶת־רְחֹבֹ֥ת עִ֖יר וְאֶת־כָּֽלַח׃ וְאֶת־
יג רֶ֕סֶן בֵּ֥ין נִֽינְוֵ֖ה וּבֵ֣ין כָּ֑לַח הִ֖וא הָעִ֥יר הַגְּדֹלָֽה׃ וּמִצְרַ֡יִם יָלַ֞ד
יד אֶת־לוּדִ֧ים וְאֶת־עֲנָמִ֛ים וְאֶת־לְהָבִ֖ים וְאֶת־נַפְתֻּחִֽים׃ וְאֶת־
פַּתְרֻסִ֞ים וְאֶת־כַּסְלֻחִ֗ים אֲשֶׁ֨ר יָצְא֥וּ מִשָּׁ֛ם פְּלִשְׁתִּ֖ים וְאֶת־
טו כַּפְתֹּרִֽים׃ וּכְנַ֗עַן יָלַ֛ד אֶת־צִידֹ֥ן בְּכֹר֖וֹ וְאֶת־חֵֽת׃
טז יז וְאֶת־הַיְבוּסִי֙ וְאֶת־הָ֣אֱמֹרִ֔י וְאֵ֖ת הַגִּרְגָּשִֽׁי׃ וְאֶת־הַחִוִּ֥י וְאֶת־
יח הַֽעַרְקִ֖י וְאֶת־הַסִּינִֽי׃ וְאֶת־הָֽאַרְוָדִ֥י וְאֶת־הַצְּמָרִ֖י וְאֶת־
יט הַחֲמָתִ֑י וְאַחַ֣ר נָפֹ֔צוּ מִשְׁפְּח֖וֹת הַֽכְּנַעֲנִֽי׃ וַיְהִ֞י גְּב֤וּל הַֽכְּנַעֲנִי֙
מִצִּידֹ֔ן בֹּאֲכָ֥ה גְרָ֖רָה עַד־עַזָּ֑ה בֹּאֲכָ֞ה סְדֹ֧מָה וַעֲמֹרָ֛ה וְאַדְמָ֥ה
כ וּצְבֹיִ֖ם עַד־לָֽשַׁע׃ אֵ֣לֶּה בְנֵי־חָ֔ם לְמִשְׁפְּחֹתָ֖ם לִלְשֹׁנֹתָ֑ם
כא בְּאַרְצֹתָ֖ם בְּגוֹיֵהֶֽם׃ וּלְשֵׁ֥ם יֻלַּ֖ד גַּם־ה֑וּא אֲבִי֙
כב כָּל־בְּנֵי־עֵ֔בֶר אֲחִ֖י יֶ֥פֶת הַגָּדֽוֹל׃ בְּנֵ֥י שֵׁ֖ם עֵילָ֣ם וְאַשּׁ֑וּר
כג וְאַרְפַּכְשַׁ֖ד וְל֥וּד וַאֲרָֽם׃ וּבְנֵ֖י אֲרָ֑ם ע֥וּץ וְח֖וּל וְגֶ֥תֶר וָמַֽשׁ׃
כד כה וְאַרְפַּכְשַׁ֖ד יָלַ֣ד אֶת־שָׁ֑לַח וְשֶׁ֖לַח יָלַ֥ד אֶת־עֵֽבֶר׃ וּלְעֵ֥בֶר יֻלַּ֖ד
שְׁנֵ֣י בָנִ֑ים שֵׁ֣ם הָֽאֶחָ֞ד פֶּ֗לֶג כִּ֤י בְיָמָיו֙ נִפְלְגָ֣ה הָאָ֔רֶץ וְשֵׁ֥ם אָחִ֖יו

VERSE 11

LEKAḤ TOV

מִן־הָאָרֶץ הַהִוא יָצָא אַשּׁוּר – *From that land, Ashur went out:* It was the wrong-headed ideas of Ashur that our patriarch Avraham left behind. When the Holy One, blessed be He, called on Avraham to go out of his own land, he was seventy years old.

VERSE 15

MEKHILTA DERABBI YISHMAEL

וּכְנַעַן – *Kenaan:* Kenaan was privileged to have the land of Canaan named after him. What did the man do to deserve that? When his descendants heard that Israel was approaching the territory with the intention of conquering it, they evacuated of their own accord. Said the Holy One, blessed be He: Because you abandoned the land on behalf of My children, I will name the area after you, and I will reward you with another home as beautiful as it. This was North Africa. Similarly, we read: *Kenaan fathered Tzidon, his firstborn, and Ḥet*, while a later text states, *The Hittites answered Avraham, "Hear us, my lord. You are a prince of God in our midst* (23:5–6). Said the Holy One, blessed be He, to them: Because you honored My beloved, I will name the land after you, and resettle you in an equally bountiful place. (Massekhta Defisḥa 18)

11 Akad, and Kalneh in the land of Shinar. From that land, Ashur
12 went out and built Nineveh, Reḥovot Ir, Kalaḥ, and Resen be-
13 tween Nineveh and Kalaḥ; that is the great city. Mitzrayim fa-
14 thered the Ludim, Anamim, Lehavim and Naftuḥim, Patrusim,
Kasluḥim – from whom the Philistines descended – and the
15 Kaftorim. Kenaan fathered Tzidon, his firstborn, and
16 17 Ḥet, and the Jebusites, Amorites, and Girgashites, the Hivites,
18 Arkites, and Sinites, the Arvadites, Zemarites, and Hamatites.
19 Later, the Canaanite families were dispersed. The Canaanite
borders were from Sidon toward Gerar near Aza, and toward
20 Sedom, Amora, Adma, and Tzevoyim, near Lasha. These were
the descendants of Ḥam, by their clans and their languages,
21 with their lands and their nations. Sons were also
born to Shem. The older brother of Yefet, he was the ances-
22 tor of all the sons of Ever. Shem's sons were Elam, Ashur, Ar-
23 pakhshad, Lud, and Aram. Aram's sons were Utz, Ḥul, Geter,
24 and Mash. Arpakhshad was the father of Shelaḥ, and Shelaḥ
25 was the father of Ever. To Ever, two sons were born. One was
named Peleg, for in his time the earth was divided. His brother

MEKHILTA DERABBI SHIMON

וּכְנַעַן – *Kenaan:* Why is the land referred to as Canaan when there were five other nations who lived there? We must infer that Kenaan was the ancestor of all of them, as the verse states: *Kenaan fathered Tzidon, his firstborn, and Ḥet.* (13:11)

VERSE 25

BERESHIT RABBA

כִּי בְיָמָיו נִפְלְגָה הָאָרֶץ – *For in his time the earth was divided:* Rabbi Yosei taught: Because the ancients were familiar with their ancestors, they named their children after historical events. However, we do not know our forebears, and hence we name our children after them. [The early generations of humanity lived for so many years that when people became parents, their ancestors were still alive, and it was unnecessary to honor them by naming their progeny after those people.] Rabban Shimon ben Gamliel taught: Because the ancients had access to divine inspiration, they were able to name their children after future events. However, we have no recourse to divine inspiration, and hence we name our children after our ancestors. Rabbi Yosei ben Ḥalafta said: Ever was a great prophet who foresaw the future of his times, as the verse states: *To Ever, two sons were born. One was named Peleg, for in his time the earth was divided. His brother was named Yoktan.* Why was Yoktan so called? It was because he made himself and his business small [*katan*]. How was Yoktan rewarded for his modesty? He was privileged to establish thirteen whole families

כו יָקְטָן: וְיָקְטָן יָלַד אֶת־אַלְמוֹדָד וְאֶת־שָׁלֶף וְאֶת־חֲצַרְמָוֶת
כז כח וְאֶת־יָרַח: וְאֶת־הֲדוֹרָם וְאֶת־אוּזָל וְאֶת־דִּקְלָה: וְאֶת־עוֹבָל
כט וְאֶת־אֲבִימָאֵל וְאֶת־שְׁבָא: וְאֶת־אוֹפִר וְאֶת־חֲוִילָה וְאֶת־
ל יוֹבָב כָּל־אֵלֶּה בְּנֵי יָקְטָן: וַיְהִי מוֹשָׁבָם מִמֵּשָׁא בֹּאֲכָה סְפָרָה
לא הַר הַקֶּדֶם: אֵלֶּה בְנֵי־שֵׁם לְמִשְׁפְּחֹתָם לִלְשֹׁנֹתָם בְּאַרְצֹתָם
לב לְגוֹיֵהֶם: אֵלֶּה מִשְׁפְּחֹת בְּנֵי־נֹחַ לְתוֹלְדֹתָם בְּגוֹיֵהֶם וּמֵאֵלֶּה
נִפְרְדוּ הַגּוֹיִם בָּאָרֶץ אַחַר הַמַּבּוּל:
יא א ב וַיְהִי כָל־הָאָרֶץ שָׂפָה אֶחָת וּדְבָרִים אֲחָדִים: וַיְהִי בְּנָסְעָם ט שביעי

BERESHIT RABBA *(cont.)*

[as told in the following verses]. Now if even a younger son is praised for humbling himself, consider how impressive it is if an important personage exhibits modesty. (Noaḥ 37:7)

VERSE 26

BERESHIT RABBA

וְאֶת־חֲצַרְמָוֶת – *Ḥatzarmavet:* [The name literally means: "Death's Court."] Rabbi Huna said: There is a place called *Ḥatzarmavet*, where people eat only leeks and wear clothes made out of paper. All day long they sit praying for death to take them. Rabbi Shmuel said: They do not even have the luxury of paper garments. (Noaḥ 37:8)

CHAPTER 11, VERSE 1

TALMUD YERUSHALMI

שָׂפָה אֶחָת – *The same language:* Rabbi Elazar and Rabbi Yoḥanan disagreed on the verse's interpretation. One Sage maintained that the people all spoke seventy different languages [and everybody understood each other because they were all multilingual]. The other believed that all of humanity spoke only one language – that of the One Master of the World: Hebrew. (Megilla 1:9)

TANḤUMA

וַיְהִי כָל־הָאָרֶץ שָׂפָה אֶחָת – *The whole world spoke the same language:* Before this chapter begins, the text reports: *These, then, are the clans of the sons of Noaḥ* (10:32). We then read: *The whole world spoke the same language.* King Shlomo teaches: *Even if you crush a fool with a mortar and pestle [ba'eli], together with grain his folly will not depart from him* (Proverbs 27:22). When a fool is being struck in rebuke, he is so lacking in intelligence that he forgets the chastisement in between the lashes! After he manages to rise [*be'oleh*] from the first beating, he unlearns the message before he can be put down again. For his *folly will not depart from him.* [No sooner had the descendants of Noaḥ recovered from the deluge than they began to plot their next rebellion against God.] (Noaḥ 24)

26 was named Yoktan. Yoktan was the father of Almodad, Shelef,
27 28 Ḥatzarmavet, Yeraḥ, Hadoram, Uzal, Dikla, Oval, Avimael,
29 Sheva, Ofir, Ḥavila, and Yovav; all these were Yoktan's sons.
30 Their settlements extended from Mesha toward Sefar, in the
31 eastern hill country. These were the descendants of Shem, by
their clans and their languages, with their lands and their na-
32 tions. These, then, are the clans of the sons of Noaḥ, by their
lines, in their nations. And from these, the nations spread out
across the earth after the flood.
11 1 The whole world spoke the same language, the same words. SHEVI'I
2 And as the people migrated from the east they found a valley

BERESHIT RABBA

וַיְהִי כָל־הָאָרֶץ שָׂפָה אֶחָת – *The whole world spoke the same language:* When Rabbi Elazar son of Rabbi Yosei bar Zimra taught this passage, he opened his lecture by citing the verse *Do not kill them lest my people forget, but send them wandering by Your force, and bring them down* (Psalms 59:12). Said Rabbi Elazar: The verse refers to the generation of the dispersal [the people who constructed the Tower of Babel, the subject of the present chapter]. The nation of Israel petitioned God: Please do not destroy the generation of the dispersal, *lest my people forget*, that is, lest the following generations forget their misdeeds. Rather, *send them wandering* – cast them out, and *bring them down* from the top [of their tower] to the ground. But as for us, *the Lord is our shield* (Psalms 59:12). The following verse states: *For the sins of their mouths* (Psalms 59:13) which refers to the sin that those people uttered. For they argued that every 1,656 years the heavens weaken. [The flood took place in the year 1656 from creation. Subsequently, humanity viewed this as a regular and normal part of nature's cycle, rather than as a divinely ordained punishment.] Said they: Let us construct scaffolding to support the sky. In the future, we will build one structure in the north, and one in the south, and a third in the west. But this first tower will be the eastern foundation. Finally, when that verse concludes: *For the words of their lips, let them be trapped by their own arrogance, by the curses and lies they utter*, that refers to our text: *The whole world spoke the same language, the same words.* (Noaḥ 38:1)

LEKAḤ TOV

שָׂפָה אֶחָת – *The same language:* All of humanity was a single family. Another interpretation: They stirred [*shefot*] a single pot. For these people stirred up trouble in the form of divine retribution for all of humanity. The prophet Yeḥezkel uses this metaphor for evil: *Put the pot onto the fire; stir it, then pour water into it* (Ezekiel 24:3). אֲחָדִים – *The same:* Civilization uttered words against the God, who is unique [*yaḥid*] in the world.

YALKUT SHIMONI

וּדְבָרִים אֲחָדִים – *The same words:* The people of Babylon spoke in veiled speech [*devarim aḥudim*], for the although the sinful behavior of the flood generation was clear, that of their own generation was more subtle. Alternately, the people of that time spoke disparagingly

² מִקֶּ֛דֶם וַֽיִּמְצְא֥וּ בִקְעָ֛ה בְּאֶ֥רֶץ שִׁנְעָ֖ר וַיֵּ֥שְׁבוּ שָֽׁם׃ וַיֹּאמְר֞וּ
אִ֣ישׁ אֶל־רֵעֵ֗הוּ הָ֚בָה נִלְבְּנָ֣ה לְבֵנִ֔ים וְנִשְׂרְפָ֖ה לִשְׂרֵפָ֑ה וַתְּהִ֨י

YALKUT SHIMONI (cont.)

against two who were unique [aḥadim], meaning Avraham, who was an outstanding man, and *the Lord, our God, the Lord is One* (Deuteronomy 6:4). They complained against God, declaring: He has no right to choose the celestial realm for Himself while relegating us to the earth! Let us build a tower and at its summit erect an idol holding a sword. The statue will thus appear to be waging war against the Almighty. (62)

VERSE 2

SIFREI DEVARIM

וַיְהִי בְּנָסְעָם מִקֶּדֶם – *And as the people migrated from the east:* The people who built the Tower of Babel only sinned once they had first satisfied all their earthly needs. For the text states: *And as the people migrated from the east they found a valley in the land of Shinar and settled there* – and "settlement" signifies eating and drinking, as we read later: *The people settled down to eat and drink and then stood up to engage in revelry* (Exodus 32:6). It is that satiety which led to the sin of the golden calf, and it similarly preceded these people's plot, *Come let us build ourselves a city and a tower* (11:4). (Ekev 43)

TALMUD BAVLI

וַיְהִי בְּנָסְעָם – *And as the people migrated:* Rabbi Levi taught: The men of the Great Assembly transmitted the following principle: Whenever Scripture uses the word *vayhi*, it portends some sorrow. (Megilla 10b)

BERESHIT RABBA

וַיְהִי בְּנָסְעָם מִקֶּדֶם – *And as the people migrated from the east:* The people traveled from further east to the nearer east. [Shinar – Babylon – is itself east of the land of Israel. The first settlers arrived in Shinar from even further east.] Rabbi Elazar bar Rabbi Shimon taught: This community purposely distanced themselves from the Ancient God [*kadmon*, evoking *kedem* – "east"]. Said they: We have no interest in the Almighty or His divinity. **וַיִּמְצְאוּ בִקְעָה** – *They found a valley:* Rabbi Yehuda maintains: The world's idolators gathered to locate a spot that could accommodate all of them, and they eventually did find such a place [in Shinar]. Rabbi Neḥemya cited the verse *He scoffs at scoffers* [Proverbs 3:34. That is, God provides sinners the opportunity to indulge their desires. In the current episode, God allowed the people a place to build their ill-advised tower]. **וַיֵּשְׁבוּ שָׁם** – *And settled there:* Rabbi Yitzḥak taught: Wherever we find settlement mentioned, it is not long before Satan [the accusing angel] pounces [to demand divine punishment for the people's wrongs]. Rabbi Ḥelbo taught: Whenever people are complacent, Satan takes the cue to level accusations against them. Rabbi Levi taught: Whenever people are engaged in eating and drinking, Satan files his complaints. (38:7)

3 in the land of Shinar and settled there. They said to each other,
"Come, let us make bricks, let us bake them thoroughly." They

VERSE 3

TANḤUMA

וַיֹּאמְרוּ אִישׁ אֶל־רֵעֵהוּ – *They said to each other:* The Holy One, blessed be He, assisted these people in all their efforts so that He would be able to have the last laugh, as the verse states: *The One who dwells in heaven shall laugh; the Lord will mock them* (Psalms 2:4). For [if God had thwarted their plans] and they had not succeeded in constructing the project, they would have been able to claim: "Had we only managed to finish the tower, we would have climbed up to the heavens and waged war against the Almighty!" Thus the Holy One, blessed be He, helped them begin to realize their scheme, in order to show them their true powerlessness. But ultimately he would humiliate the people of Babylon and exile them, as the subsequent verse states: *From there the Lord scattered them all over the earth* (Genesis 11:8). Consulting with each other, the masses plotted: *Come, let us build ourselves a city and a tower that reaches the heavens, and make a name for ourselves* (11:4). Rabbi Shimon bar Yoḥai taught: Their goal was to hoist an idol to the top of the tower and position it there. For they reasoned: Should the Holy One, blessed be He, decree some punishment against us, our idol will contend with Him and prevent Him from attacking us. Indeed their desire [expressed in the following verse] to *make a name* for themselves was surely an allusion to idolatry, as a later verse states: *Never invoke the names of other gods* (Exodus 23:13). Said God to the people: "You were afraid that you would *be scattered across the face of the earth!* Watch, while I do just that to you!", as the verse reports: *There the Lord scattered them all over the earth* (11:8). Thus was fulfilled the proverb *That which the wicked man dreads will befall him* (Proverbs 10:24). (Noaḥ 28)

BERESHIT RABBA

וַיֹּאמְרוּ אִישׁ אֶל־רֵעֵהוּ – *They said to each other:* Who spoke to whom in this exchange? Rabbi Berekhya taught: It was Mitzrayim who proposed the project to Kush. הָבָה נִלְבְּנָה לְבֵנִים וְנִשְׂרְפָה לִשְׂרֵפָה – *Come let us make bricks, let us bake them thoroughly:* These peoples were themselves destined to be burned out of the world. וַתְּהִי לָהֶם הַלְּבֵנָה לְאָבֶן – *They used bricks for stone:* Rabbi Huna taught: The builders were at first successful in their efforts. (Noaḥ 38:8)

LEKAḤ TOV

הָבָה נִלְבְּנָה לְבֵנִים וְנִשְׂרְפָה לִשְׂרֵפָה – *Come let us make bricks, let us bake them thoroughly:* In an early sign of success, the bricks formed by themselves. As the verse states: *Though the wicked may spring up like grass and all evildoers seem to flourish, they will be destroyed for all eternity* (Psalms 92:8).

ד לָהֶם הַלְּבֵנָה֙ לְאָ֔בֶן וְהַ֣חֵמָ֔ר הָיָ֥ה לָהֶ֖ם לַחֹֽמֶר: וַיֹּאמְר֞וּ הָ֣בָה ׀ נִבְנֶה־לָּ֣נוּ עִ֗יר וּמִגְדָּל֙ וְרֹאשׁ֣וֹ בַשָּׁמַ֔יִם וְנַֽעֲשֶׂה־לָּ֖נוּ

ה שֵׁ֑ם פֶּן־נָפ֖וּץ עַל־פְּנֵ֥י כָל־הָאָֽרֶץ: וַיֵּ֣רֶד יְהֹוָ֔ה לִרְאֹ֥ת אֶת־

VERSE 4

TALMUD BAVLI

הָבָה נִבְנֶה־לָּנוּ עִיר – *Come, let us build ourselves a city:* According to the Mishna, the members of this generation have no share in the World to Come. What sin did they commit? [The nature of the transgression is not stated explicitly in the Torah.] The school of Rabbi Sheila taught that the builders of the Tower of Babel announced: Let us build a tower and ascend to heaven, and we will strike the sky with axes so that its waters will be released. In the land of Israel they laughed at this explanation and asked: If that was their objective, why did they not build their tower on a mountain [instead of in a valley]? Instead, Rabbi Yirmeya bar Elazar taught: The masses were divided into three factions. The first one said: Let us ascend to the top of the tower and dwell there. Another group proposed: Let us ascend to the top of the tower and engage in idol worship there. But the third team had a different plan. They said: Let us ascend to the top of the tower and wage war against God. God dealt with the faction that wished to live in the tower by dispersing them across the land. Those who longed to fight against God were turned into apes, spirits, and demons. And in response to those who were intent on engaging in idolatry, *it was there that the LORD confused the language of all the earth* (11:9). It is taught in a *baraita*: Rabbi Natan says: All of the people were interested in building the tower for the sake of idol worship. For in the current passage we read: *Come, let us…make a name for ourselves* (11:4), whereas later the Torah warns against invoking the "names" of other Gods (Exodus 23:13). Just as the latter reference is to idolatry, so is the former. Rabbi Yoḥanan taught: The uppermost third of the tower was burned, the bottom third of the tower was swallowed into the earth, and the middle third remained intact. Rav said: The atmosphere of the tower causes forgetfulness. [Anyone who goes there forgets what he has learned.] (Sanhedrin 109a)

LEKAḤ TOV

וּמִגְדָּל וְרֹאשׁוֹ בַשָּׁמַיִם – *And a tower that reaches the heavens:* The plan was to construct a tower that was so tall that it could be seen from miles across the countryside. In that way distant people would be able to find the center of the civilization. The masses were thereby trying to avoid their fear of humanity being *scattered across the face of the earth*.

YALKUT SHIMONI

הָבָה נִבְנֶה־לָּנוּ עִיר – *Come, let us build ourselves a city:* The builders managed to construct a tower that was twenty-seven miles high; the structure had one flight of stairs climbing up its east side and another rising on its west side. People who were carrying bricks up took the east staircase, while those who were descending used the west stairs. If a person fell off the tower and died, nobody cared, but if a brick tumbled off the height and was lost, the masses were distraught. "Woe to us!" they would cry, "where will we

4 used bricks for stone and tar for mortar. And they said, "Come,
let us build ourselves a city and a tower that reaches the heavens, and make a name for ourselves. Otherwise we will be scat-
5 tered across the face of the earth." But the LORD came down
to see the city and the tower being built by the children of men.

YALKUT SHIMONI *(cont.)*

ever find another brick just like that one?" But Avraham stood up and mocked and cursed the people in the name of his God, as the verse states: *Thwart them, LORD; divide their speech, for I see violence and strife in the city* (Psalms 55:10). However, the people despised him and ignored his words, treating the prophet like a castoff bit of rock. Thus would be fulfilled the verse *The stone the builders rejected has become the main cornerstone* (Psalms 118:22). (62)

VERSE 5

TANHUMA

וַיֵּרֶד יהוה לִרְאֹת – *But the LORD came down to see:* Is not everything already known to the Holy One, blessed be He? Why then does the verse state: *But the LORD came down to see*? The text is teaching us appropriate human behavior: A judge must always investigate the circumstances in a case before determining a verdict; and a witness must never report evidence based on hearsay. (Noah 28)

AVOT DERABBI NATAN

וַיֵּרֶד יהוה לִרְאֹת אֶת־הָעִיר – *But the LORD came down to see the city:* On ten occasions did the LORD descend to earth. The first time was in the Garden of Eden, regarding which we read: *(1) They heard the sound of the LORD God walking in the garden in the cool of the day* (3:8). The next instance is during the episode of the tower, regarding which the text states: *(2) But the LORD came down to see the city and the tower being built.* God also came down to investigate the evil of Sedom, as the verse states: *(3) I shall go down now and see if they have really done as much as the outcry that has reached Me. If not, I will know* (18:21). God descended to Egypt [to witness Israel's slavery] as He tells Moshe: *(4) So I have come to rescue them from the hand of the Egyptians and bring them up from that land to one that is good* (Exodus 3:8). God also came down to save Israel at the Sea of Reeds, as a later verse describes the incident *(5) He bent the heavens and descended* (II Samuel 22:10), and He descended to address the nation at Mount Sinai, as the Torah states: *(6) And the LORD descended on Mount Sinai, to the top of the mountain* (Exodus 19:20). God descended in a pillar of cloud to communicate with Moshe, as we are told: *(7) Then the LORD came down in the cloud and spoke to him, and took some of the spirit that was upon him and placed it on the seventy elders* (Numbers 11:25). God descended upon the Temple, as the prophet informs us: *(8) God said to me: "This gate will stay shut; it shall not be opened, and no man may enter through it; because the LORD God of Israel entered through it, it shall remain closed"* (Ezekiel 44:2). And God will one day come down once more in the [apocalyptic] time of Gog and Magog, as the text predicts: *(9) On that day His feet will stand upon the Mount of Olives which faces*

ו הָעִיר וְאֶת־הַמִּגְדָּל אֲשֶׁר בָּנוּ בְּנֵי הָאָדָם: וַיֹּאמֶר יהוה
הֵן עַם אֶחָד וְשָׂפָה אַחַת לְכֻלָּם וְזֶה הַחִלָּם לַעֲשׂוֹת וְעַתָּה
ז לֹא־יִבָּצֵר מֵהֶם כֹּל אֲשֶׁר יָזְמוּ לַעֲשׂוֹת: הָבָה נֵרְדָה וְנָבְלָה
ח שָׁם שְׂפָתָם אֲשֶׁר לֹא יִשְׁמְעוּ אִישׁ שְׂפַת רֵעֵהוּ: וַיָּפֶץ יהוה

BERESHIT RABBA *(cont.)*

Jerusalem on the east, and the Mount of Olives will split through its middle – into a great valley – from east to west [Zechariah 14:4; this list omits the tenth reference]. (34)

BERESHIT RABBA

אֲשֶׁר בָּנוּ בְּנֵי הָאָדָם – *Being built by the children of men:* Rabbi Berekhya taught: Why does the verse state that these people were the "children of men" – who else would they be? The children of donkeys and camels? Rather, the text thereby teaches that this civilization were not only the biological descendants of Adam but the bearers of his personality. For just as Adam had displayed ingratitude to God when he said: *The woman you put here with me – she gave me fruit from the tree and I ate* (Genesis 3:12), so were the people of the dispersal equally ungrateful to God for having spared them from the flood. (Noaḥ 38:9)

VERSE 6

TANḤUMA

לֹא־יִבָּצֵר מֵהֶם כֹּל אֲשֶׁר יָזְמוּ – *Nothing they plan to do will be impossible:* Even though the people sinned, said God, "I extend My right hand to them and declare: If you choose to repent, I will accept you, in the spirit of the verse *So now, Israel, what does the Lord your God ask of you? Only this: to revere the Lord your God, to walk in all His ways and love him* (Deuteronomy 10:12)." But the people responded to Him: Even if we be excised [*nivtzarim*, evoking *yibbatzer* – "impossible" – in our verse] from the world, we will never reform! Hence God was forced to *bring back [His] hand again like a grape picker [kevotzer] over his baskets* (Jeremiah 6:9). (Noaḥ 28)

LEKAḤ TOV

לֹא־יִבָּצֵר מֵהֶם כֹּל אֲשֶׁר יָזְמוּ – *Nothing they plan to do will be impossible:* This sentence does not express resignation on God's part, but is rather a rhetorical question: Will nothing be impossible for them? Surely there are things that are impossible for them!

VERSE 7

TALMUD BAVLI

הָבָה נֵרְדָה – *Let us go down:* Rabbi Yoḥanan taught: Although heretics cite Torah verses to support their challenges, each text they quote has its refutation in tow. For example, while the verse states: *Then God said, "Let us make humankind in our image, our likeness"* [1:26 suggesting the existence of multiple deities or creators], this is followed by the statement *So God created humankind in His image: in the image of God He created him* (1:27). Similarly, at

6 The Lord said, "If, as one people with one language, they have
begun to do this, nothing they plan to do will be impossible
7 for them. Let us go down and confuse their language so that
8 one will not understand the speech of another." From there the
Lord scattered them all over the earth, and they abandoned

TANḤUMA *(cont.)*

first we read: *Let us go down and confuse their language*, [in the plural] but the earlier verse states [in the singular]: *But the Lord came down to see the city and the tower being built* (11:5). (Sanhedrin 38b)

TANḤUMA

הָבָה נֵרְדָה – *Let us go down:* The punishment here was meant to confuse the laborers' language and prevent them from communicating effectively with each other. For at first, all the people spoke the holy tongue [Hebrew] – the language that God used to create the world. Now the Holy One, blessed be He, said: In this world, the evil inclination has caused humanity to divide into factions and to split into seventy languages. However, in the next world all nations will address and serve Me as one, as the prophet predicts: *Then I will transform the people's language and turn their words into clear, clean speech so that they may call upon the name of the Lord and serve Him shoulder to shoulder* (Zephaniah 3:9). At that time the nation of Israel will no longer be subservient to the tyranny of the gentiles and will be able to worship God freely and happily, as the verse commands: *Serve the Lord with joy; come before Him in glad song* (Psalms 100:2). The gentiles too will then serve God – out of fear, as the verse states: *Serve the Lord with reverence and tremble as you exalt* (Psalms 2:11). (Noaḥ 24)

BERESHIT RABBA

הָבָה נֵרְדָה – *Let us go down:* This is one of the instances where the Sages altered the text when they were ordered by King Ptolemy to translate the Torah [into Greek, creating the Septuagint]. They rendered this phrase as: "I will go down" [changing the verbs into the singular form to avoid the appearance of polytheism]. (Noaḥ 38:10)

VERSE 8

MISHNA

וַיָּפֶץ יהוה אֹתָם מִשָּׁם – *From there the Lord scattered them:* Nobody from the generation of the flood will ever be admitted into the next world, nor will they be judged in the afterlife, as the verse states: *Then the Lord said, "My spirit will not forever judge man; he is of flesh. His life shall be but one hundred and twenty years"* (6:3), meaning that they would receive neither judgment nor resurrection. And no one from the generation of the Tower of Babel will ever be admitted into the next world, as the verse states: *From there the Lord scattered them all over the earth* – referring to their punishment in this world, and in the following verse: *From there the Lord scattered them all across the face of the earth* (11:9), relating to the eternally wandering souls of these people in the next world. (Sanhedrin 10:3)

ט אֹתָם מִשָּׁם עַל־פְּנֵי כָל־הָאָרֶץ וַיַּחְדְּלוּ לִבְנֹת הָעִיר: עַל־כֵּן
קָרָא שְׁמָהּ בָּבֶל כִּי־שָׁם בָּלַל יהוה שְׂפַת כָּל־הָאָרֶץ וּמִשָּׁם
הֱפִיצָם יהוה עַל־פְּנֵי כָּל־הָאָרֶץ:
י אֵלֶּה תּוֹלְדֹת שֵׁם שֵׁם בֶּן־מְאַת שָׁנָה וַיּוֹלֶד אֶת־אַרְפַּכְשָׁד
יא שְׁנָתַיִם אַחַר הַמַּבּוּל: וַיְחִי־שֵׁם אַחֲרֵי הוֹלִידוֹ אֶת־אַרְפַּכְשָׁד
יב חֲמֵשׁ מֵאוֹת שָׁנָה וַיּוֹלֶד בָּנִים וּבָנוֹת: וְאַרְפַּכְשַׁד
יג חַי חָמֵשׁ וּשְׁלֹשִׁים שָׁנָה וַיּוֹלֶד אֶת־שָׁלַח: וַיְחִי אַרְפַּכְשַׁד
אַחֲרֵי הוֹלִידוֹ אֶת־שֶׁלַח שָׁלֹשׁ שָׁנִים וְאַרְבַּע מֵאוֹת שָׁנָה
יד וַיּוֹלֶד בָּנִים וּבָנוֹת: וְשֶׁלַח חַי שְׁלֹשִׁים שָׁנָה וַיּוֹלֶד
טו אֶת־עֵבֶר: וַיְחִי־שֶׁלַח אַחֲרֵי הוֹלִידוֹ אֶת־עֵבֶר שָׁלֹשׁ שָׁנִים
טז וְאַרְבַּע מֵאוֹת שָׁנָה וַיּוֹלֶד בָּנִים וּבָנוֹת: וַיְחִי־
יז עֵבֶר אַרְבַּע וּשְׁלֹשִׁים שָׁנָה וַיּוֹלֶד אֶת־פָּלֶג: וַיְחִי־עֵבֶר
אַחֲרֵי הוֹלִידוֹ אֶת־פֶּלֶג שְׁלֹשִׁים שָׁנָה וְאַרְבַּע מֵאוֹת שָׁנָה
יח וַיּוֹלֶד בָּנִים וּבָנוֹת: וַיְחִי־פֶלֶג שְׁלֹשִׁים שָׁנָה וַיּוֹלֶד
יט אֶת־רְעוּ: וַיְחִי־פֶלֶג אַחֲרֵי הוֹלִידוֹ אֶת־רְעוּ תֵּשַׁע שָׁנִים

VERSE 9

MEKHILTA DERABBI YISHMAEL

עַל־פְּנֵי כָל־הָאָרֶץ – *All across the face of the earth:* God employed a powerful east wind to punish both the generation of the flood and the people of Sedom, as the verse states: *At the breath of God, they are gone; one gust from His nostrils and they die* (Job 4:9). The first phrase refers to the time of the flood, and the second to the sinners of Sedom. And we similarly find that God employed the same agent to disperse the tower builders of Babel. For the verse describing their fate states: *From there the Lord scattered them all across the face of the earth*, suggesting that they were blown away, as the prophet says: *Like the east wind I will scatter them before the enemy. I will look upon their neck and not upon their face on their fateful day* (Jeremiah 18:17). (Massekhta Devayhi 4)

SIFREI ZUTA

וּמִשָּׁם הֱפִיצָם יהוה – *And from there the Lord scattered them:* When God goes to war, He goes alone, as the verse states: *I have trodden the vat alone; no man of any nation was there with Me* (Isaiah 63:3). And thus, when God punished the generation of the flood, He did it Himself, as the verse states: *And I – I am about to bring floodwaters over the earth to destroy all*

9 the building of the city. That is why it was called Bavel, because
it was there that the LORD confused the language of all the
earth; and from there the LORD scattered them all across the
face of the earth.
10 These are the descendants of Shem. When Shem was one
hundred years old, he had a son, Arpakhshad, two years after
11 the flood. After Arpakhshad was born, Shem lived five hun-
12 dred years and had other sons and daughters. When
Arpakhshad was thirty-five years old, he had a son, Shelaḥ.
13 After Shelaḥ was born, Arpakhshad lived four hundred and
14 three years and had other sons and daughters. When
15 Shelaḥ was thirty years old, he had a son, Ever. After Ever
was born, Shelaḥ lived four hundred and three years and had
16 other sons and daughters. Ever lived thirty-four years
17 and then had a son, Peleg. After Peleg was born, Ever lived
four hundred and thirty years and had other sons and daugh-
18 ters. Peleg lived thirty years and then had a son, Reu.
19 After Reu was born, Peleg lived two hundred and nine years

SIFREI ZUTA *(cont.)*

flesh (6:17). Similarly, did God Himself deal with the generation of the dispersal, as we read: *And from there the LORD scattered them all across the face of the earth.* (6:26)

VERSE 10

LEKAḤ TOV

אֵלֶּה תּוֹלְדֹת שֵׁם – *These are the descendants of Shem:* This passage starts with the word *elleh* ["these," rather than *ve'elleh* – "and these" – suggesting something self-sufficient about this lineage.] The text's intention is to downplay the significance of the descendants of Yefet in contrast. אֵלֶּה תּוֹלְדֹת שֵׁם שֵׁם בֶּן־מְאַת שָׁנָה – *These are the descendants of Shem. When Shem was one hundred years old:* The name Shem appears twice in a row [in the Hebrew] to indicate that the man flourished in both this world and the next, just like Noaḥ. [Noaḥ's name also appears twice in succession, in 6:9.] Shem was one hundred years old two years after the flood, whereas Yefet was two years older, and Ḥam was one year older than him. Thus, at the time of the flood, Shem was ninety-eight years old, and Yefet was then one hundred.

VERSE 14

BERESHIT RABBA

וְשֶׁלַח חַי שְׁלֹשִׁים שָׁנָה – *When Shelaḥ was thirty years old:* [Literally, "and Shelaḥ lived thirty years."] Bar Kappara taught: Whenever the Torah uses the term "lived" [*ḥai*], that indicates that the person in question was righteous. And so encounter this word concerning Shelaḥ [in our verse], and Arpakhshad [in verse 12]. (Bereshit 24)

כ וּמָאתַיִם שָׁנָה וַיּוֹלֶד בָּנִים וּבָנוֹת׃ וַיְחִי רְעוּ
כא שְׁתַּיִם וּשְׁלֹשִׁים שָׁנָה וַיּוֹלֶד אֶת־שְׂרוּג׃ וַיְחִי רְעוּ אַחֲרֵי
הוֹלִידוֹ אֶת־שְׂרוּג שֶׁבַע שָׁנִים וּמָאתַיִם שָׁנָה וַיּוֹלֶד בָּנִים
כב וּבָנוֹת׃ וַיְחִי שְׂרוּג שְׁלֹשִׁים שָׁנָה וַיּוֹלֶד אֶת־נָחוֹר׃
כג וַיְחִי שְׂרוּג אַחֲרֵי הוֹלִידוֹ אֶת־נָחוֹר מָאתַיִם שָׁנָה וַיּוֹלֶד בָּנִים
כד וּבָנוֹת׃ וַיְחִי נָחוֹר תֵּשַׁע וְעֶשְׂרִים שָׁנָה וַיּוֹלֶד
כה אֶת־תָּרַח׃ וַיְחִי נָחוֹר אַחֲרֵי הוֹלִידוֹ אֶת־תֶּרַח תְּשַׁע־עֶשְׂרֵה
כו שָׁנָה וּמְאַת שָׁנָה וַיּוֹלֶד בָּנִים וּבָנוֹת׃ וַיְחִי־תֶרַח
כז שִׁבְעִים שָׁנָה וַיּוֹלֶד אֶת־אַבְרָם אֶת־נָחוֹר וְאֶת־הָרָן׃ וְאֵלֶּה
תּוֹלְדֹת תֶּרַח תֶּרַח הוֹלִיד אֶת־אַבְרָם אֶת־נָחוֹר וְאֶת־הָרָן
כח וְהָרָן הוֹלִיד אֶת־לוֹט׃ וַיָּמָת הָרָן עַל־פְּנֵי תֶּרַח אָבִיו בְּאֶרֶץ

VERSE 27

BERESHIT RABBA

וְאֵלֶּה תּוֹלְדֹת תֶּרַח – *These are the descendants of Teraḥ:* Rabbi Abba bar Kahana taught: Whenever the Torah records an individual's name two times in a row, that indicates that he was successful in this world, and that he will enjoy a share in the World to Come. The Rabbis objected to this principle, citing the verse which states, *These are the descendants of Teraḥ. Teraḥ was the father of Avram*. How could Teraḥ be said to have thrived in this world and to be welcome in the next? [Teraḥ was an idolator, a fact stated in Joshua 24:2.] Rabbi Yoḥanan responded: that verse does not refute the rule. For Rabbi Yudan further taught in the name of Rabbi Abba bar Kahana: When God told Avraham, *As for you, you will join your ancestors in peace; you will be buried in ripe old age* (15:15), God thereby informed Avraham of two things. Firstly, his father did merit a share in the next world; and secondly, that his son Yishmael would repent before his father's demise.

VERSE 28

BERESHIT RABBA

עַל־פְּנֵי תֶּרַח אָבִיו – *While his father Teraḥ was still alive:* [Literally, "in front of Teraḥ his father."] Rabbi Ḥiyya the son of the son of Rav Ada of Jaffa taught: Teraḥ was an idol maker. One day, Teraḥ left on a trip and put his son Avram in charge of the shop. A man came into the store to purchase a statue, and Avram said to him: "Tell me, how old are you?" "I am fifty years old," said the customer. To this Avram responded: "I cannot believe that a fifty-year-old man such as yourself is eager to worship an idol that my father just crafted yesterday." This shamed the man, who left empty handed. Another time a woman arrived at the store bearing a bowl of flour, which she wished to offer in tribute to the idols. Instead, Avram took a piece of wood

20 and had other sons and daughters. Reu lived thir-
21 ty-two years and then had a son, Serug. After Serug was born,
Reu lived two hundred and seven years and had other sons and
22 daughters. Serug lived thirty years and then had a son,
23 Naḥor. After Naḥor was born, Serug lived two hundred years
24 and had other sons and daughters. Naḥor lived twenty-
25 nine years and then had a son, Teraḥ. After Teraḥ was born,
Naḥor lived one hundred and nineteen years and had other
26 sons and daughters. Teraḥ lived seventy years and
27 fathered Avram, Naḥor, and Haran.These are the descendants
of Teraḥ. Teraḥ was the father of Avram, Naḥor, and Haran,
28 and Haran had a son, Lot. While his father Teraḥ was still alive,

BERESHIT RABBA *(cont.)*

and smashed all the statues except for the largest one, into whose hands he placed the club. When Teraḥ came home and saw the disaster that had previously been his showroom, he collared his son and demanded: "What have you done to my wares?!" Said Avram: "Father, I cannot conceal the truth from you. Here is what happened. A woman came into the shop with a gift of flour for the gods that she asked me to distribute to them. But as soon as she left, the idols starting arguing with each other. This one said: 'I will eat first,' and the other one shouted back: 'No, I will eat first!' As they were squabbling, this big statue grabbed a stick and smashed all of the others." Teraḥ was incensed: "What kind of a fool do you take me for? Do these statues have any sort of sentience or self-awareness?" Said Avram to Teraḥ: "Father, listen to what you yourself are saying!" But Teraḥ took hold of his son and brought him to Nimrod [the ruler at the time. The monarch entered into a theological debate with Avram]. "Let us worship fire," said Nimrod. "Why not serve the water instead," proposed Avram, "which can extinguish fire?" "Fine," said Nimrod, "we will worship the water." "But does not water come from clouds," countered Avram, "which makes those even more powerful?" "True," answered Nimrod, "from now on we will serve the clouds." "No," replied Avram, "you would be wise to revere the wind, which scatters the clouds." "Very well, we will accept the wind as our god." "Wrong again," said Avram. "Human beings are the true deities, for they are able to withstand the blowing of the wind." "Enough of these games!" bellowed Nimrod. "I am devoted solely to the fire, who is my god, and to prove it I will throw you into the furnace as an offering. Let your God whom you believe in and worship come and rescue you from that power!" Meanwhile, Avram's brother Haran, who had been following the discussion, remained unsure of his own faith. Said he to himself: "If Avram emerges from the fire victorious, I will side with him; but if Nimrod wins this conflict I will be with him." Now Avram was cast into the fire and was saved [by God]. Turning to Haran, the court asked him: "And what is your position?" Said he: "I'm on Avram's side!" Immediately, Haran was seized and thrown into the fire as well, where he perished in front of his father. (Noaḥ 38:13)

כט מוֹלַדְתּוֹ בְּאוּר כַּשְׂדִּים׃ וַיִּקַּח אַבְרָם וְנָחוֹר לָהֶם נָשִׁים שֵׁם מפטיר
אֵשֶׁת־אַבְרָם שָׂרָי וְשֵׁם אֵשֶׁת־נָחוֹר מִלְכָּה בַּת־הָרָן אֲבִי־
ל לא מִלְכָּה וַאֲבִי יִסְכָּה׃ וַתְּהִי שָׂרַי עֲקָרָה אֵין לָהּ וָלָד׃ וַיִּקַּח
תֶּרַח אֶת־אַבְרָם בְּנוֹ וְאֶת־לוֹט בֶּן־הָרָן בֶּן־בְּנוֹ וְאֵת שָׂרַי

VERSE 29

BERESHIT RABBA

הָרָן אֲבִי־מִלְכָּה וַאֲבִי יִסְכָּה – *Haran, father of Milka and Yiska:* [According to the Sages, the Haran in our verse is the brother of Avram mentioned in verses 27–28. The wording of verse 27 hints that] Avram was one year older than Naḥor, while Naḥor was one year older than Haran. Hence Avram was two years older than Haran. [Furthermore, according to the Midrash, "Yiska" in our verse is another name for Sarai, Avram's wife. Our verse thus informs us that both Avram and Naḥor married their nieces, the daughters of their younger brother Haran. Now Avram was only ten years older than Sara, as stated in the verse *Can a hundred-year-old man become a father?" he said to himself. "Can Sara, at ninety, bear a child?"* (17:17). If Avram was two years older than Haran, Yiska's father, and ten years older than Yiska herself, this means that Haran was only eight years old when his daughter Sara was born, and therefore seven years old when she was conceived! Nevertheless, Sara was not even Haran's first child – Milka was, as our verse indicates. And so,] if we subtract the year that Haran's wife was pregnant with Milka, and the year of pregnancy with Yiska, what emerges is that Haran fathered children when he was only six years old! And yet Avram did not have children for a century! Consider the subsequent verse, *And Sarai was barren – she had no child* (11:30). Commenting on this verse, Rabbi Levi remarked: whenever the Torah remarks that someone "had none" of something, that foreshadows the fact that the person in question would eventually gain what he or she lacked. [And so we should not be disturbed that Haran was a father at such a young age, while his older brother remained childless for decades, since God always planned to one day bless Avram with children.] Thus we eventually read: *The Lord remembered Sara as He had said He would, and acted for Sara as He had promised* (21:1). Similarly, the text introduces Ḥana with the verse *Penina had children, but Ḥana had none* (I Samuel 1:2). And we know that later in that chapter she did have children, as the verse states: *As the Lord took note of Ḥana, she conceived; she bore three sons and two daughters* (I Samuel 2:21). Finally, the prophet bemoans *This Zion, there is none to seek her out* (Jeremiah 30:17). Here we can take heart that one day *a redeemer is coming to Zion* (Isaiah 59:20). As the prophet declares: *Barren woman, never a mother, rejoice; break out in joyful song though you have not given birth, for the children of the forsaken woman will outnumber those of the wife, so says the Lord* (Isaiah 54:1). (Noaḥ 38:14)

LEKAḤ TOV

יִסְכָּה – *Yiska:* Yiska is another name for Sara. Why is she referred to here as Yiska? She was given that nickname because all who saw her would gaze [*sakhin*] at her beauty. Another interpretation: Sara herself looked [*sakha*] into the future using divine inspiration. Thus God could assure Avraham: *Listen to whatever Sara tells you.* (21:12)

29 Haran died in the land of his birth, Ur Kasdim. Avram and MAFTIR
Naḥor married; the name of Avram's wife was Sarai, and the
name of Naḥor's wife was Milka. She was the daughter of Ha-
30 ran, father of Milka and Yiska. And Sarai was barren – she had
31 no child. Teraḥ took his son Avram, and his grandson Lot,
son of Haran, and his daughter-in-law Sarai, his son Avram's
wife, and together they set out from Ur Kasdim to go to the

VERSE 30

YALKUT SHIMONI

וַתְּהִי שָׂרַי עֲקָרָה אֵין לָהּ וָלָד – *And Sarai was barren – she had no child:* [The two phrases seem redundant, hinting at some extreme situation.] Rabba bar Aḥuh taught: Sara even lacked a womb. Rabbi Ami taught: Avraham and Sara were both *tumtumim* [people with concealed or undeveloped genitalia]. Thus the verse states: *Look to the rock you are hewed from, the quarry from which you were carved; look to your father, Avraham, to Sara who gave you birth, for I called him, one alone, and blessed him, made him many* [Isaiah 51:2; the patriarch and matriarch are both compared to stones which are naturally unyielding]. (62)

VERSE 31

YALKUT SHIMONI

וַיִּקַּח תֶּרַח אֶת־אַבְרָם בְּנוֹ – *Teraḥ took his son Avram:* [After Teraḥ surrendered his son Avram to Nimrod for the crime of destroying his idols – see commentary on verse 28,] he was bound and tied and placed on the ground. He was then surrounded on all sides with a pyre – wood piled to a height of five cubits. And still Teraḥ refused to recognize his Creator. At that moment, Teraḥ's friends and neighbors came and goaded him, saying: "You ought to be ashamed of yourself! Do you not recall how you used to boast that your son Avram would inherit the world – both this one and the next? And yet here you are allowing Nimrod to burn him at the stake!" Immediately, the Holy One, blessed be He, felt sympathy for Avram and rushed down to rescue him from death [as recounted above]. Now Teraḥ worried: Perhaps the court will try to execute my son again anyway. Thus he determined to leave the place, as the verse states: *Teraḥ took his son Avram…and together they set out from Ur Kasdim.* As a reward for Teraḥ's recognition of God, the Holy One, blessed be He, granted honor to his son thirty-five years before the old man's death, as the Hittites called him a "prince of God" [23:6, when he came to bury his wife Sara soon after the birth of his son Yitzḥak at the age of 100. Since Teraḥ was seventy years old when Avram was born, as stated in 11:26, and he lived to the age of 205 as we are told in the following verse, he died when Avraham was 135 years old. It follows that Avraham's greatness was first recognized by his neighbors thirty-five years before Teraḥ passed away]. A later verse states: *When a prince sins unintentionally with regard to any of the Lord's commands* [Leviticus 4:22, employing the same word used to laud Avraham]. Just as in the latter text refers to a leader who has only God above him, so too did Avraham have just God as superior to him. (77)

כַּלָּתוֹ אֵשֶׁת אַבְרָם בְּנוֹ וַיֵּצְאוּ אִתָּם מֵאוּר כַּשְׂדִּים לָלֶכֶת
לב אַרְצָה כְּנַעַן וַיָּבֹאוּ עַד־חָרָן וַיֵּשְׁבוּ שָׁם׃ וַיִּהְיוּ יְמֵי־תֶרַח
חָמֵשׁ שָׁנִים וּמָאתַיִם שָׁנָה וַיָּמָת תֶּרַח בְּחָרָן׃

VERSE **32**

BERESHIT RABBA

וַיָּמָת תֶּרַח בְּחָרָן – *And Teraḥ died in Ḥaran:* We subsequently read, *The Lord said to Avram, "Go – from your land"* [12:1, implying that Teraḥ died before Avram left Ḥaran]. Rabbi Yitzḥak stated: If so, the text seems to be missing sixty-five years. [Teraḥ was seventy years old when Avram was born, as stated in verse 26, and Avraham was seventy-five when he moved to Canaan, as reported in 12:4. This means that Teraḥ was 145 at the time of Avram's departure and cannot have died beforehand at the age of 205.] And so, what the text teaches is that the wicked [such as Teraḥ the idol maker] are considered dead even during their lifetimes. Secondly, Avraham was reluctant to abandon his father in Ḥaran

land of Canaan. But when they arrived at Ḥaran, they settled
32 there. Teraḥ lived two hundred and five years, and he died in
Ḥaran.

BERESHIT RABBA *(cont.)*

fearing that the name of God would be profaned – people would say that he followed God's instructions even though that meant leaving his aged father alone. Therefore the Holy One, blessed be He, said to him: I hereby exempt you from the obligation of honoring your father and mother, even though I would never grant such a dispensation to anybody else. Furthermore, I will record your father's death in the text as if it had happened while you were still with him. This is why the Torah first states: *Teraḥ… died in Ḥaran*, and only afterward: *The Lord said to Avram, "Go – from your land"* (12:1). (Lekh Lekha 39:7)

10TH CENTURY

RAV SE'ADYA GAON
882, EGYPT – 942, IRAQ

11TH CENTURY

RASHI, 1040 – 1105, FRANCE

12TH CENTURY

RASHBAM, 1080 – 1160, FRANCE

RABBI AVRAHAM IBN EZRA,
1089, SPAIN – 1164, ENGLAND

RABBI YOSEF BEKHOR SHOR,
12TH CENTURY, FRANCE

13TH CENTURY

RAMBAN, 1194, SPAIN – 1270, ISRAEL

RABBI ḤIZKIYA BEN MANOAḤ – *ḤIZKUNI*,
13TH CENTURY, FRANCE

14TH CENTURY

RABBEINU BAḤYA BEN ASHER,
1255 – 1340, SPAIN

RALBAG, 1288 – 1344, PROVENCE

15TH CENTURY

RABBI YITZḤAK ABARBANEL,
1437, PORTUGAL – 1508, ITALY

16TH CENTURY

RABBI OVADYA SFORNO, 1475 – 1550, ITALY

17TH CENTURY

RABBI SHLOMO EFRAYIM LUNTSCHITZ –
KELI YAKAR, 1550, POLAND – 1619, BOHEMIA

פרשת נח

PARASHAT NOAḤ

THE **CLASSIC** COMMENTATORS

ו ט אֵלֶּה תּוֹלְדֹת נֹחַ נֹחַ אִישׁ צַדִּיק תָּמִים הָיָה בְּדֹרֹתָיו אֶת־ ה
י הָאֱלֹהִים הִתְהַלֶּךְ־נֹחַ: וַיּוֹלֶד נֹחַ שְׁלֹשָׁה בָנִים אֶת־שֵׁם

CHAPTER 6, VERSE 9

RASHI

אֵלֶּה תּוֹלְדֹת נֹחַ נֹחַ אִישׁ צַדִּיק – *This is the story of Noaḥ. Noaḥ was a righteous man:* Because the text began this passage with Noaḥ's name, it proceeds to praise him, as the verse states: *The mention of the righteous is a blessing* [Proverbs 10:7. Rashi is troubled by the gap between the word *toledot* which suggests that the text is about to discuss Noaḥ's lineage, and the actual presentation of his sons which does not occur until the next verse]. Another interpretation: This verse teaches that a person's most important descendants are in fact his good deeds. **בְּדֹרֹתָיו** – *In his generation:* Some of our Rabbis interpret this phrase to Noaḥ's credit: The man was virtuous in his generation [despite living in a negative environment]; imagine how admirable he would have been had he lived in a society with other righteous people. But some scholars see this phrase as critical of Noaḥ: Although Noaḥ was considered exemplary within his own generation, had he lived in the time of Avraham he would not have stood out at all. **אֶת־הָאֱלֹהִים הִתְהַלֶּךְ־נֹחַ** – *Noaḥ walked with God:* In comparison to this description, Avraham said, *The Lord before whom I have walked* (Genesis 24:40). This indicates that Noaḥ required the assistance of God to support him ["with" God], whereas Avraham was strong enough in his virtue to walk by himself ["before" God].

RASHBAM

אֵלֶּה תּוֹלְדֹת נֹחַ – *This is the story of Noaḥ:* The word *toledot* refers to a person's descendants.

IBN EZRA

אֵלֶּה תּוֹלְדֹת נֹחַ – *This is the story of Noaḥ:* The term *toledot* refers to the events of Noaḥ's life. **אִישׁ צַדִּיק** – *A righteous man:* His actions were laudable. **תָּמִים** – *A person of integrity:* His thoughts were noble. **בְּדֹרֹתָיו** – *In his generation:* The term *dorotav* is plural [literally, "generations"] to reflect the fact that Noaḥ's outstanding character spanned several generations, from the time of the flood to the era afterward as well. For Noaḥ lived until his descendant Avraham was fifty-eight years old. The way to remember this is to note that our forefather Avraham was the age of *Noaḥ* [spelled *nun-ḥet* in gematria, for a numerical value of fifty eight] when Noaḥ died.

RAMBAN

אֵלֶּה תּוֹלְדֹת נֹחַ – *This is the story of Noaḥ:* A meaning for this has been put forth by both Ibn Ezra and Radak, who argue that the word *toledot* implies "events," as in the verse *Boast not about tomorrow, for you do not know what might yet occur [yeled] today* (Proverbs 27:1). According to those authors the term introduces the entire narrative of Noaḥ's ordeal. However, this seems incorrect to me, for the story of a person's life is not called his *toledot*. In my opinion the word *toledot* should be understood literally, as in the later verse *These are the descendants [toledot] of Noaḥ's sons, Shem, Ḥam, and Yefet* (10:1), and the verse *These are the*

6 9 This is the story of Noaḥ. Noaḥ was a righteous man, a person
10 of integrity in his generation; Noaḥ walked with God. And

RAMBAN (cont.)

descendants [toledot] of Avraham's son Yishmael (25:12). Hence in the present verse too the text is introducing the sons of Noaḥ: Shem, Ḥam, and Yefet. The next verse repeats the point of Noaḥ's fatherhood when it states: *And Noaḥ had [vayoled] three sons* (6:10), because the initial verse stopped midsentence to inform the reader that *Noaḥ was a righteous man, a person of integrity*, which in turn was to explain why God ordered him specifically to build the ark.

RABBEINU BAḤYA

נֹחַ אִישׁ צַדִּיק – *Noaḥ was a righteous man:* The text presents three praises regarding this man; three ways in which he differed from the rest of his generation. Firstly, Noaḥ acted in "righteous" ways in contrast to the barbarism exhibited by his neighbors, as the verse states: *The earth had become corrupt in God's sight, full of violence* (6:11). Secondly, Noaḥ was *a person of integrity*, meaning that he was perfect in all his attributes, for any deficiency in a person's character is generally repugnant to God. And thus the Torah praises Noaḥ for having no character flaws. In contrast to Noaḥ, all the people around him were deeply flawed and inferior. *Thirdly, Noaḥ walked with God*, a practice that is only exercised by the elite of any generation.

SFORNO

אֶת־הָאֱלֹהִים הִתְהַלֶּךְ־נֹחַ – *Noaḥ walked with God:* Noaḥ walked in the ways of God in the sense that he did good deeds for other people and attempted to rebuke the evil people of his generation.

VERSE 10

RAMBAN

אֶת־שֵׁם אֶת־חָם וְאֶת־יָפֶת – *Shem, Ḥam, and Yefet:* Based on a later verse (10:21), it seems to me that Yefet was the older brother. [The Hebrew of that verse is ambiguous, and can be understood that either Yefet or Shem was the oldest.] Indeed, when the text proceeds to list the brothers' descendants, those of Yefet appear first [starting in 10:2. Ḥam's sons are given in 10:6, and Shem's begin in 10:21]. Ḥam was Noaḥ's youngest son, as the verse states: *Noaḥ woke from his wine and realized what his youngest son had done to him* (9:24). If so Shem is mentioned first in the present verse only because of his superior character. Ḥam is next because he was born after Shem, and that leaves Yefet for the end of the verse [despite his being the oldest]. The Torah did not want to present the sons as Shem, Yefet, and Ḥam [merely switching the older two brothers to show Shem's prominence] because that would have placed all three of them in the wrong position relative to each other. And there was really no greatness to Yefet that would justify upsetting the entire sequence on his behalf. We find a similar phenomenon in the verse *Avraham's sons were Yitzḥak and Yishmael* [I Chronicles 1:28, where Yitzḥak appears before his older brother because he is more significant], and in the verse *To Yitzḥak I granted Yaakov and Esav* [Joshua 24:4; although Esav was the older twin].

יא אֶת־חָם וְאֶת־יָפֶת׃ וַתִּשָּׁחֵת הָאָרֶץ לִפְנֵי הָאֱלֹהִים וַתִּמָּלֵא
יב הָאָרֶץ חָמָס׃ וַיַּרְא אֱלֹהִים אֶת־הָאָרֶץ וְהִנֵּה נִשְׁחָתָה כִּי־

ABARBANEL

אֶת־שֵׁם אֶת־חָם וְאֶת־יָפֶת – *Shem, Ḥam, and Yefet:* Now even though the text above already listed the sons of Noaḥ [in 5:32], it sought fit to mention them again for two reasons. Firstly, because Noaḥ was such an extraordinary and perfect man, the text wished to elaborate his story for reasons which will subsequently become clear. And thus, after Noaḥ and his descendants are listed among all the generations of humankind at the end of Parashat Bereshit, the text returns to relate the life of Noaḥ within his own narrative. In this way, Noaḥ is introduced as the father of all humankind, similar to the way that Adam was presented. Thus the Torah begins: *This is the story of Noaḥ*, as if the book were starting all over again. Secondly, since were told above that *Noaḥ found favor in the Lord's sight* (6:8), foreshadowing that he would be saved from the flood, the verse now explains how God considered Noaḥ to be exceptional, perfect within himself and unusual compared to everybody else. And so the text continues to relate that Noaḥ had just three sons who were all saved along with him from the deluge.

SFORNO

וַיּוֹלֶד נֹחַ – *And Noaḥ had:* As a reward for rebuking his wicked peers, Noaḥ was granted three sons.

VERSE 11

RASHI

וַתִּשָּׁחֵת – *Had become corrupt:* The verb connotes licentiousness and idolatry, as in the warning *not to act in self-destruction [tashḥitun], making yourselves any idol, an image of any shape, any form of man or of woman* (Deuteronomy 4:16), and the following verse: *All flesh corrupting [hishḥit] its ways upon the earth* (6:12). וַתִּמָּלֵא הָאָרֶץ חָמָס – *Full of violence: [Ḥamas* refers specifically to] robbery.

IBN EZRA

וַתִּשָּׁחֵת הָאָרֶץ – *The earth had become corrupt:* Some commentators argue that the accusation in our verse means that the people sinned against God in public [without shame]. Others maintain that they acted corruptly in private, such that only God was aware of their behavior. Nevertheless, in my opinion, the language of the text merely represents the way of common speech so that readers will understand what is implied. The verse means that humanity acted impudently, like a servant who disobeys his master in his very presence, thereby demonstrating that he does not fear him at all.

ABARBANEL

וַתִּשָּׁחֵת הָאָרֶץ – *The earth had become corrupt:* There are two types of violations available to human beings: Those which transgress against fellow people and acts which sin

11 Noaḥ had three sons: Shem, Ḥam, and Yefet. The earth had be-
12 come corrupt in God's sight, full of violence. And when God
saw how corrupt the earth had become, all flesh corrupting its

ABARBANEL *(cont.)*

against God. Thus when the verse states that *the earth had become corrupt in God's sight,* it means that the people of the world were ignoring specifically those rules that govern their relationship with God [for example, they practiced idolatry]. And when the text continues to say that they were "full of violence," that connotes that they were abusing each other by stealing money and fornicating with married women whenever they chose.

VERSE 12

RASHI

כִּי־הִשְׁחִית כָּל־בָּשָׂר – *All flesh corrupting its ways:* [It was not just humans who were misbehaving, but] even cattle, wild beasts, and the birds. For these were copulating with representatives of other species.

BEKHOR SHOR

אֶת־הָאָרֶץ וְהִנֵּה נִשְׁחָתָה – *How corrupt the earth had become:* There was absolutely no sense of justice within society. The more powerful men took advantage of their neighbors, grabbing their daughters, wives, and possessions with impunity. Noaḥ was the only man who acted with any sense of decency; everyone else exercised their personal strength to take whatever they wanted.

RABBEINU BAḤYA

וַיַּרְא אֱלֹהִים אֶת־הָאָרֶץ – *And when God saw the earth:* The name *Elohim* [which can denote a judge] is used in this verse as a sign that God's attribute of Justice was directed at humanity because of their great sin.

KELI YAKAR

וַיַּרְא אֱלֹהִים אֶת־הָאָרֶץ וְהִנֵּה נִשְׁחָתָה – *And when God saw how corrupt the earth had become:* The verse alludes to humanity's practice of idolatry, which was sinful behavior observable only to God. After all, heresy is a matter primarily of the heart. This is why the prophet speaks of regaining *the hearts of the House of Israel, who have all become estranged from me with all their idols* (Ezekiel 14:5), for matters of faith are subject to one's inner thoughts. The verse continues to accuse humanity of *corrupting its ways [darko] upon the earth*. This is an allusion to licentiousness, as the Scripture might speak of a *way [derekh] of a man with a young woman* (Proverbs 30:19). According to our Sages, the men of the time sinned by spilling their seed needlessly. Thus our verse which talks about sins "upon the earth," alludes to the later description of Onan, *Whenever he came to his brother's wife, he let his seed go to waste on the ground* (38:9).

יג הִשְׁחִית כׇּל־בָּשָׂר אֶת־דַּרְכּוֹ עַל־הָאָרֶץ׃ וַיֹּאמֶר
אֱלֹהִים לְנֹחַ קֵץ כׇּל־בָּשָׂר בָּא לְפָנַי כִּי־מָלְאָה הָאָרֶץ חָמָס
יד מִפְּנֵיהֶם וְהִנְנִי מַשְׁחִיתָם אֶת־הָאָרֶץ׃ עֲשֵׂה לְךָ תֵּבַת עֲצֵי־
גֹפֶר קִנִּים תַּעֲשֶׂה אֶת־הַתֵּבָה וְכָפַרְתָּ אֹתָהּ מִבַּיִת וּמִחוּץ

VERSE 13

RASHI

קֵץ כׇּל־בָּשָׂר – *The end of all flesh:* Whenever immorality runs rampant in society, indiscriminate punishment is unleashed against the world, killing both the innocent and the guilty. [This explains the adjective "all".] **כִּי־מָלְאָה הָאָרֶץ חָמָס** – *For the earth is full of violence:* The fate of the world was decreed in response to the robbery. **אֶת־הָאָרֶץ** – *Along with all the earth:* The particle *et* [which has no English equivalent and usually introduces a direct object] should be understood as *min* ["from"]. That is: I am about to destroy them, [removing them] from the earth. We find a similar usage of the term in the verse, *As I leave the city [et ha'ir], I will spread out my hands to the Lord* (Exodus 9:29), suggesting: As I leave from the city; and in the verse, *in his old age, however, he suffered from a foot disease [ḥala et raglav]* (I Kings 15:23), meaning that Asa became ill from his legs. Another interpretation: the phrase *et haaretz* connotes "with the earth" [that is, even the ground itself will be destroyed]. For the soil of the earth was dissolved and washed away to a depth of three handbreadths, which is as far as the plow digs.

BEKHOR SHOR

וְהִנְנִי מַשְׁחִיתָם אֶת־הָאָרֶץ – *I am about to destroy them, along with all the earth:* Because the people of the world have corrupted [*hishḥitu*] their ways, I will soon destroy [*ashḥit*] them. And along with the destruction of humanity, all the cattle, beasts, and birds will drown, and the trees and the grasses will die as well. In short, everything upon the earth will be wiped out, because *the earth is full of violence*, and all the world was created only for the human race. [Since humanity had sinned and was to be obliterated, the other life on earth, which had been made solely to serve human beings, no longer had any purpose.]

RALBAG

מִפְּנֵיהֶם – *Because of them:* [Literally, "in the face of them."] The word *mipeneihem* means "because of them," similar to the verse *Noaḥ, with his sons, his wife, and his sons' wives, came into the ark to escape [i.e., "because of"] the waters of the flood* (7:7). What our verse teaches is that these people made a conscious decision to adopt nasty personalities. For they were born with the choice whether to behave in a praiseworthy manner or to act wickedly.

ABARBANEL

וְהִנְנִי מַשְׁחִיתָם אֶת־הָאָרֶץ – *I am about to destroy them, along with all the earth:* I am destroying the people because they have demonstrated their inability to forge a civil society or dwell peacefully on the land. They do not exercise justice or righteousness. Perhaps this is what our Sages meant [see Sanhedrin 108a] when they said that the verdict was passed on humanity as a result of rampant theft.

13 ways upon the earth, God said to Noaḥ, "The end of
all flesh has come before Me, for the earth is full of violence
because of them. I am about to destroy them, along with all the
14 earth. So make yourself an ark of cypress wood. Make it with

SFORNO

וְהִנְנִי מַשְׁחִיתָם אֶת־הָאָרֶץ – *I am about to destroy them, along with all the earth:* God hereby announced His intention to destroy humanity and the earth simultaneously by changing the climate of the earth and the air. In the world before the flood, the equinox – when the length of the day and the length of the night are equal – was a constant feature of the earth. Afterward, however, the angle of the planet relative to the sun was altered, as God replies to Iyov's complaints [see Job 38:4]. As a result of this shift, in the generations immediately following the flood, human beings began to die at a much younger age. For the climate was no longer ideal, and the fruits of the trees were no longer perfect. This explains why people were granted permission to eat meat at this point in history.

VERSE 14

RASHI

עֲשֵׂה לְךָ תֵּבַת – *So make yourself an ark:* Considering that God has at His disposal many means and methods of rescue, why did He trouble Noaḥ to build the ark? God hoped that during the 120 years that it took Noaḥ to construct the vessel, the people of his time would see him occupied with the project and would ask him what he was doing. Then Noaḥ would say: The Holy One, blessed be He, plans on releasing a flood against the world [to punish you for your sins]. Perhaps when they heard that, they would repent. **עֲצֵי־גֹפֶר** – *Cypress wood:* The name of the tree is *gofer*. Why did God specify that this type of wood be used? The name of the tree was associated with the *gofrit* ["sulfur"] that God would rain down upon the earth to wipe out humankind. **קִנִּים** – *Compartments:* Noaḥ was instructed to build separate chambers for each of the cattle and animal species. **בַּכֹּפֶר** – *In pitch: Kofer* is the Hebrew term for the Aramaic *zefet* [pitch]; in the Talmud, this substance is referred to as *kufra*. [Now, why was Noaḥ ordered to cover both the inside and the outside of his ark with pitch, whereas Yokheved covered] Moshe's ark [with pitch only on the outside]? Since Moshe's life raft was placed in calm waters, it was sufficient to cover the inside of the vessel with clay and the outside with pitch. Furthermore, by reserving the pitch for the exterior of Moshe's ark, his mother ensured that the righteous baby would not have to smell the foul odor of the substance. However, in the current instance, the ark would face strong waves and currents. Therefore, it had to be fully coated on the inside as well as the outside with pitch [in order to prevent leaks].

RABBEINU BAḤYA

עֲשֵׂה לְךָ תֵּבַת עֲצֵי־גֹפֶר – *So make yourself an ark of cypress wood:* Now here the wise son might ask: Considering that Noaḥ was *a righteous man, a person of integrity* (6:9), as the text claims, and given that the man *found favor in the Lord's sight* (6:8), why do we never find Noaḥ praying for the salvation of his generation or urging them to undergo universal

טו בַּכֹּפֶר׃ וְזֶה אֲשֶׁר תַּעֲשֶׂה אֹתָהּ שְׁלֹשׁ מֵאוֹת אַמָּה אֹרֶךְ

RABBEINU BAḤYA *(cont.)*

penitence? Do we not see that our patriarch Avraham expressed sympathy even when God informed him of the impending obliteration of Sedom due to its people's wickedness? How did Avraham react to such news? Several times he begged the Almighty to retract His threat to destroy the city, as the text states: *Now that I have dared to speak to the Lord, though I am mere dust and ashes, what if the righteous are five less than fifty?* (18:27–28). He further petitions God: *Please, may the Lord not be angry, but let me speak. What if only thirty are found there?* (18:30). Such was the custom of the righteous of antiquity and of the prophets; they constantly approached God to pray for the welfare of their generations. Indeed, it is expected and worthy of all leaders to worry about the fate of their communities. Why then was Noaḥ silent when faced with the end of the world? The answer to this difficulty is that Noaḥ's response to God's decree was not one of rebellion against his neighbors, nor did it reflect an attitude of malice. Rather, the man knew that the world is sustained by the number ten, as our Sages maintain (Avot 5:1): God uttered ten statements in His creation of the world. And thus Noaḥ understood that had there been ten virtuous people in the world at that time, God would not have sent a flood to destroy the earth, for the planet would have been able to endure on the merits of those ten individuals. But the good people who were invited onto the ark only numbered eight: Noaḥ, his wife, his three sons, and their three wives. Therefore, because the total of worthy people did not reach ten, Noaḥ knew that the world could not be saved on their behalf. Hence it was God's plan to rescue only Noaḥ, who represented the tenth generation of humanity [counting Adam as the first, Shet as the second, and so on] and the members of his family. Consider that in Avraham's dialogue with God, once the patriarch reached the minimum number of ten righteous people, the Almighty promised: *I will not destroy, for the sake of the ten* (18:32), at which point *the Lord had finished speaking with Avraham, He left* (18:33). At that point God knew that the city of Sedom could not even boast a group of ten respectable people. Meanwhile, Avraham was not permitted to continue praying for a smaller number of citizens, since they were not significant enough to spare their town. This is why Sedom was utterly obliterated. In a similar vein, Noaḥ too was not allowed to pray for a reprieve for the planet since there were fewer than ten people who could support it. Furthermore, God had granted humanity a lengthy period of one hundred and twenty years to repent [the accepted amount of time it took Noaḥ to build the ark]. May the name of the Compassionate One be blessed for not punishing civilization without warning it first of the coming catastrophe.

RALBAG

קִנִּים – *Compartments:* This refers to little rooms and cages to hold each type of bird and animal.

ABARBANEL

עֲשֵׂה לְךָ תֵּבַת עֲצֵי־גֹפֶר – *So make yourself an ark of cypress wood:* God commanded Noaḥ to construct an "ark" rather than a boat or a ship. The vessel he made did not have a mast and

15 compartments and coat it in pitch inside and out. This is how
you shall make it: the ark shall be three hundred cubits long,

ABARBANEL *(cont.)*

sails, but looked instead like a chest. It did not resemble a cube, but was shaped more like a pyramid, with a pointed top to prevent it from capsizing from the water or the wind.

VERSE 15

RABBEINU BAḤYA

וְזֶה אֲשֶׁר תַּעֲשֶׂה אֹתָהּ – *This is how you shall make it:* God directed Noaḥ to construct the ark with these dimensions, even though the space he was creating was much smaller than necessary to house all of the species he would be saving. For Noaḥ would later be required to collect cattle and birds – both kosher and non-kosher types, large and small beasts, two of every kind. Included in this menagerie were some very large animals like elephants and oxen. Had Noaḥ build fifty arks, such a fleet would still not have been able to accommodate all the representatives of the earth's fauna. We must therefore accept that a great miracle occurred to allow the tiny ark to incorporate its myriad passengers. Now the reader might ask: Since God was willing to perform a miracle to stretch the limitations of the ark, why did He even demand that Noaḥ build it according to the dimensions He gave him? Why was it important for Noaḥ to follow the precise length, width, and height that we find in this passage? Why was he required to construct three levels for the ark – *lower, middle, and upper decks* (6:16)? After all, could not the Almighty have saved the animal kingdom without putting Noaḥ to so much bother, simply by allowing all the land species to float on top of the water or hover up in the air? The answer to this problem is as follows. It is the manner of the Torah to command human beings to expend all efforts that they can muster through natural means, and only then will God occasionally intervene miraculously to complete the necessary task. If you look, you will find such an arrangement regarding all the miracles in the Torah. Even the most well-known and explicit acts of providence were accompanied by some dimension of straightforward action. For example, the Torah orders Israel to furnish an army and to send soldiers onto the battlefield armed for conflict. The nation is also expected to follow various military stratagems, as the verse describes in the battle against the Ai: *Lay an ambush to the west of the city* (Joshua 8:2). One might argue that since all of Israel's battles relied on great miracles and divine aid for success, why should the infantry have worried about ambushes in the way that regular armies of other nations do? Hence it is clear that the Israelites too were meant to act as if they were completely on their own; only then would God extend miracles where the people fell short of their goals. Another approach to the same problem is offered by our Sages, of blessed memory. They argue that the construction of the ark took many years, and during all that time Noaḥ's contemporaries saw what he was doing. The neighbors would ask Noaḥ what the ark was for, and he would attempt to persuade them to repent and turn from their evil ways, so there would be no need for the ark at all. But the masses did not heed Noaḥ's rebukes because they possessed little faith, and hence they deserved the verdict of death that they received.

טז הַתֵּבָה חֲמִשִּׁים אַמָּה רָחְבָּהּ וּשְׁלֹשִׁים אַמָּה קוֹמָתָהּ׃ צֹהַר ׀
תַּעֲשֶׂה לַתֵּבָה וְאֶל־אַמָּה תְּכַלֶּנָּה מִלְמַעְלָה וּפֶתַח הַתֵּבָה
יז בְּצִדָּהּ תָּשִׂים תַּחְתִּיִּם שְׁנִיִּם וּשְׁלִשִׁים תַּעֲשֶׂהָ׃ וַאֲנִי הִנְנִי
מֵבִיא אֶת־הַמַּבּוּל מַיִם עַל־הָאָרֶץ לְשַׁחֵת כָּל־בָּשָׂר אֲשֶׁר־
בּוֹ רוּחַ חַיִּים מִתַּחַת הַשָּׁמָיִם כֹּל אֲשֶׁר־בָּאָרֶץ יִגְוָע׃
יח וַהֲקִמֹתִי אֶת־בְּרִיתִי אִתָּךְ וּבָאתָ אֶל־הַתֵּבָה אַתָּה וּבָנֶיךָ

KELI YAKAR

שְׁלֹשׁ מֵאוֹת אַמָּה אֹרֶךְ הַתֵּבָה – *The ark shall be three hundred cubits long:* There are two reasons why the text lists the length, width, and height of the ark. The first purpose of this information is to help us realize that a great miracle defined the structure of the ark – a boat of such limited dimensions was nevertheless able to contain a huge number of animals including some species which are unusually large, such as elephants and bison. Secondly, the measurements of the vessel teach us that the primary reason for the flood was that humanity had become consumed by wanton licentiousness. Thus an earlier verse states: *When the sons of God saw that the daughters of man were lovely, they began to take whomever they chose to be wives to them* (6:2). Our Sages argue that because their sin was great, their punishment was also terrible. It was because of the people's illicit behavior that the name of God – *Yah* – was profaned. For the letters of that name [*yod* and *heh*] are critical for meditating between a man and a woman who are joined in marriage. Without the participation of God, the relationship is consumed by fire. For the word "fire" [*esh*] is spelled *alef-shin*, and when a *yod* is inserted between those two letters the word *ish* – "man" – is created. On the other hand, when a *heh* [the other letter of God's name] is added to the *alef* and the *shin*, the word *isha* – "woman" – is formed. Hence without the presence of God's name in a marriage, the relationship of a husband and wife is destined to burn to the ground. This is why our Sages maintain [see Sanhedrin 108b] that because the people sinned through their boiling passion and desire, they were punished by being drowned in scalding water. It was humanity's own fault for lighting the fire of sin themselves [through unholy relationships]. And hence we find the number fifteen [the numerical value of the divine name *Yah*] appearing throughout this section. For example, the next chapter reads: *Fifteen cubits above them the waters surged as the mountains were covered* (7:20), and *For one hundred and fifty days, the waters surged over the earth* (7:24), that is for fifteen times ten. Although the death sentence against humanity was passed because of robbery [see Rashi on verse 13], humanity was ultimately destroyed because of their sexual immorality and their profanation of God's name.

VERSE 16

RASHI

צֹהַר – *A window:* Some commentators claim that the *tzohar* was a window, whereas other scholars maintain that it was a precious light-producing stone which illuminated

16 fifty cubits wide, and thirty cubits high. Make a window for the
ark, and taper the latter to within a cubit of the top. Put a door
in the side of the ark and make lower, middle, and upper decks.
17 And I – I am about to bring floodwaters over the earth to destroy all flesh that has within it the breath of life under the heav-
18 ens. Everything on earth will die. But I will establish My covenant with you, and you will enter the ark – you, your sons, your

RASHI *(cont.)*

the boat's interior. וְאֶל־אַמָּה תְּכַלֶּנָּה מִלְמַעְלָה – *And taper the latter to within a cubit of the top:* The roof of the ark slanted upward until it narrowed at the top, with a horizontal section of a cubit remaining. In this way the water would run down either side of the roof. בְּצִדָּהּ תָּשִׂים – *Put in the side:* Noah was to build the door on the side of the ark [and not the top] to prevent the rain from falling inside. תַּחְתִּיִּם שְׁנִיִּם וּשְׁלִשִׁים – *Lower, middle, and upper decks:* The ark was divided into three floors, one atop the other. Noaḥ and his family were assigned to the upper story, the middle level was occupied by the animals, and the bottom deck was reserved for waste.

VERSE 17

RASHI

הִנְנִי מֵבִיא – *I am about to bring:* I am now prepared to agree with those [angels] who long ago tried to sway Me [not to create humanity], saying: *What are mortals, that You should be mindful of them; human beings, that You should take note of them?* (Psalms 8:5). מַבּוּל – *Floodwaters:* There are three reasons why the deluge is called a *mabbul*. Firstly, the water destroyed [*billa*] everything; it confused [*bilbel*] the world; and it brought [*hovil*] everything down from a high level to a lower position. Thus, Targum Onkelos renders the word *mabbul* as *tofana*, which means that the waters "swept" everything to Babylonia. That country is a low land, which is also called *Shinar*, since everybody who died in the flood was swept [*nin'aru*] there.

RALBAG

הַמַּבּוּל מַיִם – *Floodwaters:* The term *mabbul* suggests stirring up [*belila*] and turmoil, which is what the deluge would cause.

SFORNO

הַמַּבּוּל מַיִם – *Floodwaters:* The term *mabbul* derives from the word *mappala* ["downfall"] and connotes loss, similar to the term *nevala* ["decay"]. Thus God told Noaḥ: I will soon bring about the downfall of the world, which I presaged when I said, *I am about to destroy them, along with all the earth.* (6:13)

VERSE 18

RASHI

וַהֲקִמֹתִי אֶת־בְּרִיתִי – *But I will establish My covenant:* Noaḥ required an assurance that the fruit he brought aboard would not rot or decay during the flood. God also promised him

יט וְאִשְׁתְּךָ וּנְשֵׁי־בָנֶיךָ אִתָּךְ׃ וּמִכָּל־הָחַי מִכָּל־בָּשָׂר שְׁנַיִם מִכֹּל
כ תָּבִיא אֶל־הַתֵּבָה לְהַחֲיֹת אִתָּךְ זָכָר וּנְקֵבָה יִהְיוּ׃ מֵהָעוֹף
לְמִינֵהוּ וּמִן־הַבְּהֵמָה לְמִינָהּ מִכֹּל רֶמֶשׂ הָאֲדָמָה לְמִינֵהוּ
כא שְׁנַיִם מִכֹּל יָבֹאוּ אֵלֶיךָ לְהַחֲיוֹת׃ וְאַתָּה קַח־לְךָ מִכָּל־מַאֲכָל
כב אֲשֶׁר יֵאָכֵל וְאָסַפְתָּ אֵלֶיךָ וְהָיָה לְךָ וְלָהֶם לְאָכְלָה׃ וַיַּעַשׂ נֹחַ
ז א כְּכֹל אֲשֶׁר צִוָּה אֹתוֹ אֱלֹהִים כֵּן עָשָׂה׃ וַיֹּאמֶר יהוה לְנֹחַ שני

RASHI *(cont.)*

that the wicked men of his time would not kill him. אַתָּה וּבָנֶיךָ וְאִשְׁתְּךָ – *You, your sons, your wife:* The men entered the ark by themselves and the women entered by themselves. We learn from this that sexual intimacy was forbidden on the ark.

IBN EZRA

וַהֲקִמֹתִי אֶת־בְּרִיתִי – *But I will establish My covenant:* [Literally, "I will uphold My covenant."] This statement shows that God had previously guaranteed Noaḥ that he and his sons would survive the flood. The verb *vahakimoti* connotes God's commitment to honor his oath. Still, it seems to me that this verse is an allusion to the covenant of the rainbow [which would be made later, in the aftermath of the flood]. A covenant is an agreement willingly struck between two parties.

RAMBAN

וַהֲקִמֹתִי אֶת־בְּרִיתִי – *But I will establish My covenant:* [Literally, "I will uphold My covenant," which seems to imply the adherence to a covenant already made.] In my opinion, God here is telling Noaḥ that later, during the upheaval of the flood, His covenant with him made now will endure. Noaḥ and his family will enter the ark along with two representatives of every animal species. There they will all remain alive and ride out the flood, emerging safely at the end of the catastrophe. The term "covenant" refers to a divine decree issued by God which He intends to fulfill with no conditions or stipulations. When God speaks of "upholding" a covenant [that He is only making now], it is similar to the verse *They upheld [kiyyemu] and accepted, for themselves and for their children* (Esther 9:27), meaning that the Jews accepted upon themselves something that was to exist in the future.

SFORNO

וַהֲקִמֹתִי אֶת־בְּרִיתִי – *But I will establish My covenant:* I will do so after the flood.

VERSE 19

RASHI

וּמִכָּל־הָחַי – *Of each living creature:* This phrase refers to the demons [who were also rescued on the ark. The Hebrew text contains two phrases: *umikkol haḥai* – of each living creature, and *umikkol basar* – of each animal of flesh. Rashi seems to be explaining the apparent repetition by suggesting that the first term included non-animal creatures.]

19 wife, and your sons' wives with you. And you shall take two of
each living creature, male and female, into the ark to keep alive
20 with you. Of every kind of bird, animal, and wild beast, bring
21 two to keep alive. As for you, take all the food to be eaten and
22 store it: it will be for food for you and for them." Noaḥ did so:
7 1 all that God commanded him, he fulfilled. Then the LORD said SHENI

RASHI *(cont.)*

שְׁנַיִם מִכֹּל – *Two of each:* The least numerous of the creatures were represented by two animals – one male and one female [whereas more than two specimens were brought for the pure species of animal].

VERSE 20

RASHI

מֵהָעוֹף לְמִינֵהוּ – *Of every kind of bird:* All those birds which had mated only with their own kind and had not corrupted their ways. The animals came of their own accord [and did not have to be gathered by Noaḥ]. And Noaḥ took in whichever beasts the ark was willing to accept. [The vessel miraculously rejected those animals that had mated with other species.]

RAMBAN

שְׁנַיִם מִכֹּל יָבֹאוּ אֵלֶיךָ לְהַחֲיוֹת – *Bring two to keep alive:* [Literally, "two of each will come to you to keep alive."] God informed Noaḥ that the animals would arrive in pairs by themselves at the launching site; he would not be required to track them down in the hills or in faraway places. When the beasts arrived, Noaḥ would guide them into the ark. Indeed, when the time came for the animals to assemble, they *came two by two to Noaḥ into the ark, male and female* (7:9). However, when God later commanded Noaḥ to take with him seven pairs of pure animals [see 7:2], He did not indicate that these species would gather on their own, but rather that he would have to catch them. The reason for this discrepancy is that the animals that boarded the ark in order to save their own lives and those of their species came to Noaḥ of their own accord. However, God would not decree that those specimens which would be sacrificed at the end of the flood [see 8:20] should willingly come forward to be slaughtered. Rather, Noaḥ was directed to corral these animals himself for the purpose of bringing sacrifices to God after he had disembarked.

VERSE 22

RASHI

וַיַּעַשׂ נֹחַ – *Noaḥ did so:* This refers to the construction of the ark [as opposed to verse 7:5, which refers to his boarding the vessel].

CHAPTER 7, VERSE 1

RASHI

רָאִיתִי צַדִּיק – *For I have seen you to be righteous:* Here God describes Noaḥ as righteous, whereas above, the text refers to him as *a righteous man, a person of integrity* (6:9). This

CLASSIC COMMENTATORS

בֹּא־אַתָּה וְכׇל־בֵּיתְךָ אֶל־הַתֵּבָה כִּי־אֹתְךָ רָאִיתִי צַדִּיק
ב לְפָנַי בַּדּוֹר הַזֶּה: מִכֹּל ׀ הַבְּהֵמָה הַטְּהוֹרָה תִּקַּח־לְךָ שִׁבְעָה
שִׁבְעָה אִישׁ וְאִשְׁתּוֹ וּמִן־הַבְּהֵמָה אֲשֶׁר לֹא טְהֹרָה הִוא
ג שְׁנַיִם אִישׁ וְאִשְׁתּוֹ: גַּם מֵעוֹף הַשָּׁמַיִם שִׁבְעָה שִׁבְעָה זָכָר

RASHI *(cont.)*

teaches us that it is appropriate to partially compliment a man to his face, but to fully praise him when he is not present.

RAMBAN

וַיֹּאמֶר יהוה לְנֹחַ – *Then the Lord said to Noaḥ:* [The usage of the four letter name of God hints that] God informed Noaḥ that He would employ His attribute of Compassion to rescue him and his household, and that all generations of humankind would descend from him. This is what the verse means when it states: *To keep their kind alive across the earth* (7:3). At first God told Noaḥ: *And you shall take two of each living creature, male and female, into the ark to keep alive with you* (6:19). However, God now used the attribute of Compassion to allude to Noaḥ the matter of the sacrifices. [God instructed Noaḥ to gather seven pairs of pure animals but did not state explicitly that these would be sacrificed at the end of the flood.] It was this tone that intimated to Noaḥ that God would be appeased with the offerings and that the merit of the sacrifices would sustain the world forever after [by invoking God's compassion so that] no flood would ever again destroy the planet's life. Hence the Tetragrammaton is employed here; in fact throughout the Torah, the name *Elohim* [which connotes the attribute of Justice] does not appear in discussions of sacrifices, as I will explain.

SFORNO

כִּי־אֹתְךָ רָאִיתִי צַדִּיק – *For I have seen you alone to be righteous:* God does not praise Noaḥ's family as also being righteous. Nevertheless, God tells Noaḥ: *Enter the ark, you and all your household*, for He was prepared to save Noaḥ's wife and sons for his sake.

KELI YAKAR

כִּי־אֹתְךָ רָאִיתִי צַדִּיק – *For I have seen you alone to be righteous:* The reason God did not compliment Noaḥ in this way when He initially commanded him to construct the ark [in the previous chapter], is that the possibility still existed that civilization would repent. [Had humanity changed its ways Noaḥ would not have been the sole righteous person on the planet.] Furthermore, since Metushelaḥ [who was righteous] was still alive [at God's first communication to Noaḥ], how could God say then: *For I have seen you alone to be righteous*? But then Metushelaḥ died, and God waited for the seven days of his mourning to pass, as the verse states: *For in seven days' time I will send rain on the earth* (7:4). During a period of over a century God had waited for the people to repent, and during the seven days following Metushelaḥ's passing humanity was given a final opportunity to change its wicked ways. For in the process of mourning people often take stock of their own lives. And yet, because the generation maintained its sinful behavior, God now told Noaḥ: *I have seen you alone to be righteous.*

to Noaḥ, "Enter the ark, you and all your household, for I have
seen you alone to be righteous before Me in this generation.
2 Take seven and seven of every pure animal, seven pairs, and
3 two of every animal that is not pure, of each kind a pair. Also
take seven pairs of each kind of bird, male and female, to keep

VERSE 2

RASHI

הַטְּהוֹרָה – *Pure animal:* These are animals that the nation of Israel will eventually refer to as pure [kosher]. This point confirms that Noaḥ learned Torah [and thus knew the distinction between kosher and unkosher animals].

שִׁבְעָה שִׁבְעָה – *Seven and seven:* Noaḥ took multiple pure animals onto the ark so that he could sacrifice them when he exited the ark [following the flood, in 8:20].

RASHBAM

מִכֹּל הַבְּהֵמָה הַטְּהוֹרָה – *Every pure animal:* Even though the Torah had not yet been given to the nation of Israel, the text still refers to the permitted animals as "pure." For it is well known that kosher animals are cleaner and healthier than the forbidden beasts. It is also possible that God detailed for Noaḥ which animals required seven pairs and which two, and that when Moshe recorded this passage [in writing the Torah] he abridged the conversation and referred to these groups merely as the pure animals and those that are not pure.

RALBAG

מִכֹּל הַבְּהֵמָה הַטְּהוֹרָה – *Of every pure animal:* Through a prophetic communication, God revealed to Noaḥ which species required fourteen specimens and which merely two representatives. For the Torah had not yet been given, and it is the later books which detail which animals are pure and hence had to be gathered in seven pairs. Nevertheless, Noaḥ brought aboard even more than fourteen animals of the pure kinds because these are the beasts that are particularly useful to people. **שִׁבְעָה שִׁבְעָה** – *Seven and seven:* God directed Noaḥ to take with him a larger number of pure animals. For God hoped that the people of the generation would see all these sacrificial animals being boarded onto the ark and it would cause them to repent. The Almighty would then have taken pity on humanity and stopped the flood. For as the prophet later writes, *Do I desire the death of the wicked, declares the Lord God, not that he should turn from his ways and live?* (Ezekiel 18:23). However, the sight of the pure animals did not arouse the people's consciences, and they maintained their wicked behavior.

VERSE 3

RASHI

גַּם מֵעוֹף הַשָּׁמַיִם – *Also of each kind of bird:* This instruction was limited to the pure species. We can infer the unstated from the stated. [Even though this verse does not specify that the *seven pairs of each kind of bird* refers to just the pure species, this point which is made obvious with the animals applies to the birds as well.]

ד וּנְקֵבָה לְחַיּוֹת זֶרַע עַל־פְּנֵי כָל־הָאָרֶץ׃ כִּי לְיָמִים עוֹד שִׁבְעָה
אָנֹכִי מַמְטִיר עַל־הָאָרֶץ אַרְבָּעִים יוֹם וְאַרְבָּעִים לָיְלָה
וּמָחִיתִי אֶת־כָּל־הַיְקוּם אֲשֶׁר עָשִׂיתִי מֵעַל פְּנֵי הָאֲדָמָה׃
ה ו וַיַּעַשׂ נֹחַ כְּכֹל אֲשֶׁר־צִוָּהוּ יהוה׃ וְנֹחַ בֶּן־שֵׁשׁ מֵאוֹת שָׁנָה
ז וְהַמַּבּוּל הָיָה מַיִם עַל־הָאָרֶץ׃ וַיָּבֹא נֹחַ וּבָנָיו וְאִשְׁתּוֹ וּנְשֵׁי־
ח בָנָיו אִתּוֹ אֶל־הַתֵּבָה מִפְּנֵי מֵי הַמַּבּוּל׃ מִן־הַבְּהֵמָה
הַטְּהוֹרָה וּמִן־הַבְּהֵמָה אֲשֶׁר אֵינֶנָּה טְהֹרָה וּמִן־הָעוֹף וְכֹל

VERSE 4

RAV SE'ADYA GAON

אֶת־כָּל־הַיְקוּם – *Every living creature:* One of our Jewish writers has suggested that the land of Israel was not inundated by the deluge. This approach is based on the verse *Man, say to [the land of Israel]: You are a land not cleansed, not swept with rain on the day of rage* (Ezekiel 22:24), which is taken to refer to the era of the flood. It behooves us to explain the error in this claim. As a result of the catastrophe described in these chapters, not a single individual survived from earth's inhabited lands. It was only the areas which had no people which were spared the destruction of the waters – God saw no need to drench those regions with water since He stated clearly the purpose of the punishment before it began: *I will send rain on the earth...and I will wipe from the face of the earth every living creature I have made.* What I am trying to say is that the world is covered by a range of different climate zones, some of which – in the south – have no animals or plants due to the tremendous heat, and others – in the north – are devoid of life because of the cold. And since these areas are essentially empty, there was nothing and nobody there for God to wipe out. This should be obvious. Now since the land of Israel does not fall into one of these severe categories, it is equally clear that the waters of the flood affected that place as well.

RASHI

כִּי לְיָמִים עוֹד שִׁבְעָה – *For in seven days' time:* These seven days represent the mourning period over the death of Metushelaḥ the righteous. Because the Holy One, blessed be He, wished to honor that man, He delayed the punishment until the week of mourning had passed. If one works out the age of Metushelaḥ, he will find that this person reached the end of his life when Noaḥ was six hundred years old [which was when the flood occurred]. **כִּי לְיָמִים עוֹד** – *For in...days' time:* What is the significance of the term *od* ["more"]? God added additional time [seven days] to the hundred and twenty years [mentioned in 6:3], after which the decree was meant to be carried out. **אַרְבָּעִים יוֹם** – *For forty days:* The forty-day period corresponds to the time it takes for the formation of a fetus. This alludes to the sin of that generation, which had forced the Creator to fashion illegitimate children.

4 their kind alive across the earth. For in seven days' time I will
send rain on the earth for forty days and forty nights, and I will
wipe from the face of the earth every living creature I have
5 6 made." Noaḥ did all that the Lord commanded him. Noaḥ was
six hundred years old when the floodwaters came upon the
7 earth. Noaḥ, with his sons, his wife, and his sons' wives, came
8 into the ark to escape the waters of the flood. The pure animals,
the animals that were not pure, the birds, and all that walked

BEKHOR SHOR

אַרְבָּעִים יוֹם וְאַרְבָּעִים לָיְלָה – *For forty days and forty nights:* God told Noaḥ how long the rains would last so that during the storm he would not worry that the rain would never cease.

VERSE 5

RASHI

וַיַּעַשׂ נֹחַ – *Noaḥ did:* This verse [as opposed to 6:22] refers to Noaḥ's entry into the ark.

IBN EZRA

וַיַּעַשׂ נֹחַ כְּכֹל אֲשֶׁר־צִוָּהוּ יהוה – *Noaḥ did all the Lord had commanded him:* At this point Noaḥ approached the ark with his family.

VERSE 7

RASHI

נֹחַ וּבָנָיו – *Noaḥ, with his sons:* The verse emphasizes that the men and women entered the ark separately. The two groups kept apart from each other because intimacy was forbidden as long as the outside world was suffering its torments. מִפְּנֵי מֵי הַמַּבּוּל – *To escape the waters of the flood:* Noaḥ was a man of little faith, and even he only partially believed that God was going to flood the entire world. Hence Noaḥ only entered the ark when the rising waters forced him inside.

IBN EZRA

מִפְּנֵי מֵי הַמַּבּוּל – *To escape the waters of the flood:* The family came into the ark because they were afraid of the waters of the flood [that had just begun to fall; not necessarily because the rain was already threatening their lives].

VERSE 8

BEKHOR SHOR

מִן־הַבְּהֵמָה הַטְּהוֹרָה – *The pure animals:* [Even though the Torah had not been given, Noaḥ knew which were pure because] the pure animals are those which people do not find repugnant to eat. Now since the consumption of such animals necessarily reduces their numbers, Noaḥ was commanded to take seven pairs of these beasts onto the boat, *to keep their kind alive across the earth* (7:3). On the other hand, impure animals seem disgusting

ט אֲשֶׁר־רֹמֵשׂ עַל־הָאֲדָמָה: שְׁנַיִם שְׁנַיִם בָּאוּ אֶל־נֹחַ אֶל־
י הַתֵּבָה זָכָר וּנְקֵבָה כַּאֲשֶׁר צִוָּה אֱלֹהִים אֶת־נֹחַ: וַיְהִי
יא לְשִׁבְעַת הַיָּמִים וּמֵי הַמַּבּוּל הָיוּ עַל־הָאָרֶץ: בִּשְׁנַת שֵׁשׁ־
מֵאוֹת שָׁנָה לְחַיֵּי־נֹחַ בַּחֹדֶשׁ הַשֵּׁנִי בְּשִׁבְעָה־עָשָׂר יוֹם
לַחֹדֶשׁ בַּיּוֹם הַזֶּה נִבְקְעוּ כָּל־מַעְיְנוֹת תְּהוֹם רַבָּה וַאֲרֻבֹּת
יב הַשָּׁמַיִם נִפְתָּחוּ: וַיְהִי הַגֶּשֶׁם עַל־הָאָרֶץ אַרְבָּעִים יוֹם

BEKHOR SHOR *(cont.)*

to human beings, who tend to avoid eating them. As such, it was enough for Noaḥ to save a single pair of each of these species [since they were not in danger of being hunted to extinction]. Now the gentiles do eat some of the non-kosher animals, such as the pig, the hare, and the hyrax, but these species reproduce prodigiously.

VERSE 9

RASHI

שְׁנַיִם שְׁנַיִם – *Two by two:* [Although some of the species came in sets of seven pairs, the verse refers to] the lowest number of animals which came from any given species.

בָּאוּ אֶל־נֹחַ – *Came to Noaḥ:* Of their own accord.

BEKHOR SHOR

שְׁנַיִם שְׁנַיִם בָּאוּ אֶל־נֹחַ אֶל־הַתֵּבָה – *Two by to two to Noaḥ into the ark:* Still, one might wonder why Noaḥ was required to save seven males and seven females of the pure species. Consider that when Yaakov dispatched his tribute to Esav, he only sent only one male for every ten ewes and ten does, as the verse states: *Two hundred female goats, twenty male goats, two hundred ewes, twenty rams* (32:14). And Yaakov included cows at a ratio of four to one, as the verse states: *Thirty milk camels and their young, forty cows, ten bulls, twenty female donkeys, and ten male donkeys* (32:15). And of course, it is well known that a single rooster suffices for a coop full of hens. Hence we might surmise that from the large numbers of males, Noaḥ understood God's implication that the pure animals were meant to be sacrificed. And so we later read: *Then Noaḥ built an altar to the Lord and, taking of each of the kinds of pure animals and pure birds, sacrificed burnt offerings on the altar* (8:20). Indeed, the Torah subsequently teaches that burnt offerings may only brought from male animals, as the verse states: *If the offering is a burnt offering from the herd, one must offer a male animal without blemish* (Leviticus 1:3).

VERSE 11

RASHI

בַּחֹדֶשׁ הַשֵּׁנִי – *In the second month:* Rabbi Eliezer taught: This was the month of Marḥeshvan [counting Tishrei as the first month in the year]; whereas Rabbi Yehoshua maintained that this was the month of Iyar [thereby counting Nisan as the first month].

9 the earth came two by two to Noaḥ into the ark, male and fe-
10 male, as God had commanded Noaḥ. Thus, after seven days the
11 floodwaters came upon the earth. In the six hundredth year of
Noaḥ's life, in the second month, on the seventeenth of the
month – on that day, all the wellsprings of the great deep burst,
12 and the heavens' floodgates opened. The rain fell on the earth

RASHI *(cont.)*

נִבְקְעוּ – *Burst:* To release their waters. תְּהוֹם רַבָּה – *Of the great deep:* Humanity's punishment was thus served to them in a manner that was measure for measure: They sinned in a way that was described as *great wickedness* (6:5), and hence they were stricken with water from *the great deep.*

IBN EZRA

נִבְקְעוּ – *Burst:* When *the wellsprings of the great deep burst,* the water surged up from below, and when the *heavens' floodgates opened,* rain streamed down from above. The gushing waters created chaos on earth, and there was no way to distinguish day from night.

RABBEINU BAḤYA

נִבְקְעוּ כָּל־מַעְיְנוֹת תְּהוֹם רַבָּה וַאֲרֻבֹּת הַשָּׁמַיִם נִפְתָּחוּ – *All the wellsprings of the great deep burst, and the heavens' floodgates opened:* Would it not have made more sense for the verse to have first mentioned the opening of the heavens' floodgates and then referred to the bursting of the great deep's wellsprings? For the waters falling from above preceded those rising from below. Perhaps the tone of the text hints that the curse and the punishment essentially came from above, and hence God hesitated to release the rains first. And yet, the upper waters do come before the lower waters when blessing the earth, as the verse states: *Who will bless you with blessings of heaven above, blessings of the deep that lies under* (49:25). Similarly, does Moshe proclaim: *Blessed by the Lord be his land, with the bounty of heaven, with dew, and the deep waters that lie below* (Deuteronomy 33:13). In a similar way we can explain why the text states: *The rain fell on the earth for forty days and forty nights* (7:12), and not "God flooded the earth for forty days and forty nights." For the text wished to avoid directly associating the name of God with punishment, even though it is clear that God was the cause of the deluge, as He informs Noaḥ: *And I – I am about to bring floodwaters over the earth* (6:17). But because all the ways of the Torah are pleasant, and all its paths lead to peace, the text opts to only imply that God is the cause of suffering in the world, rather than to state it outright.

VERSE 12

RASHI

וַיְהִי הַגֶּשֶׁם עַל־הָאָרֶץ – *The rain fell on the earth:* In contrast to this description, a later verse states, the flood came upon the earth [7:17. This difference in terminology is explained as follows]: At the outset of the flood, God brought down rains with a touch

יג וְאַרְבָּעִים לָיְלָה׃ בְּעֶצֶם הַיּוֹם הַזֶּה בָּא נֹחַ וְשֵׁם־וְחָם וָיֶפֶת
בְּנֵי־נֹחַ וְאֵשֶׁת נֹחַ וּשְׁלֹשֶׁת נְשֵׁי־בָנָיו אִתָּם אֶל־הַתֵּבָה׃
יד הֵמָּה וְכָל־הַחַיָּה לְמִינָהּ וְכָל־הַבְּהֵמָה לְמִינָהּ וְכָל־הָרֶמֶשׂ
הָרֹמֵשׂ עַל־הָאָרֶץ לְמִינֵהוּ וְכָל־הָעוֹף לְמִינֵהוּ כֹּל צִפּוֹר
טו כָּל־כָּנָף׃ וַיָּבֹאוּ אֶל־נֹחַ אֶל־הַתֵּבָה שְׁנַיִם שְׁנַיִם מִכָּל־
טז הַבָּשָׂר אֲשֶׁר־בּוֹ רוּחַ חַיִּים׃ וְהַבָּאִים זָכָר וּנְקֵבָה מִכָּל־בָּשָׂר

RASHI *(cont.)*

of compassion so that if the people repented, the precipitation would turn into rains of blessings. However, since humanity did not abandon its wickedness, the rain turned into a flood. **אַרְבָּעִים יוֹם** – *For forty days:* The first day of rains was not included in the period of forty days, since no rain fell during the night preceding it. We know this to be so, since the verse states: *On that day, all the wellsprings of the great deep burst* [7:11. Since a day of twenty-four hours begins with the night and continues during the subsequent daylight, the first full day of the rains began after the daytime when the *great deep burst*]. Now according to Rabbi Eliezer, this meant that the forty days ended on the twenty-eighth of the month of Kislev, because the months of the year alternate between being full months [of thirty days] and incomplete months [of twenty-nine days. Thus, Tishrei was full, and Marḥeshvan was deficient. Now according to verse 11 the rains started on the seventeenth of the month, but as Rashi has argued, the forty days should be counted from the eighteenth of the month.] This leaves twelve days in the month of Marḥeshvan, and twenty-eight days in the month of Kislev [for a total of forty].

VERSE 13

RASHI

בְּעֶצֶם הַיּוֹם הַזֶּה – *On that very day:* The people of Noaḥ's generation boasted that when they would see Noaḥ entering the ark they would break down the door and kill the man. But the Holy One, blessed be He, responded: Watch while I bring Noaḥ into the boat in full view of everybody [that is, in broad daylight], and then we'll see whose plan is realized!

RABBEINU BAḤYA

בְּנֵי־נֹחַ – *His sons:* [Literally, "the sons of Noaḥ"] The verse should have used the simpler phrase "his sons" [since Noaḥ has already been named in the verse]. However, the Torah always takes the opportunity to express a loving relationship, just as human writers choose to emphasize their connections to loved ones. This holds true especially for Noaḥ, who found favor in God's eyes.

13 for forty days and forty nights. On that very day, Noaḥ, his
sons, Shem, Ḥam, and Yefet, Noaḥ's wife, and his sons' three
14 wives entered the ark. With them came every kind of wild
beast, every kind of animal, every creeping, crawling creature
of the land, every kind of flying creature, every bird, and each
15 winged thing. They came to Noaḥ, to the ark, two by two, of all
16 flesh that had within it the breath of life. They came, male and
female of all flesh, as God had commanded him. Then the

VERSE 15

RAMBAN

וַיָּבֹאוּ אֶל־נֹחַ אֶל־הַתֵּבָה – *They came to Noaḥ, to the ark:* The verse emphasizes that the animals did not gather themselves to the boat until the very day when it started to rain and Noaḥ himself entered the ark. For God commanded them all to assemble instantly, as the prophet states: *For it is My mouth that charged them, My spirit that gathered them in* (Isaiah 34:16).

VERSE 16

RASHI

וַיִּסְגֹּר יהוה בַּעֲדוֹ – *Then the Lord shut him in:* God protected Noaḥ by preventing his wicked neighbors from smashing the ark. How did He do so? He surrounded the boat with bears and lions who proceeded to maul any attackers. Nevertheless, the straightforward meaning of *baado* is that God closed the door of the ark against the waters.

IBN EZRA

וַיִּסְגֹּר יהוה בַּעֲדוֹ – *Then the Lord shut him in:* God helped Noaḥ to seal shut the ark so that there were no cracks where the water could leak in. That would have threatened the integrity of the boat and drowned everyone immediately.

BEKHOR SHOR

וַיִּסְגֹּר יהוה בַּעֲדוֹ – *Then the Lord shut him in:* Noaḥ had left the door to the ark open to allow all the various species of animals and birds to flock to it and save themselves. And yet, even once all the beasts had entered the ark, Noaḥ was reluctant to close the door, for he was afraid that perhaps some animals had yet to arrive. For there is no scholar who knows every single species in the world! Hence it was the Holy One, blessed be He, who shut the door to the ark when all of its passengers were aboard. This resembled the gates to the Temple courtyard, which swung shut on their own when the courtyard was full of Israelites on the evening of Passover, as the Talmud in tractate Pesaḥim (64b) reports.

RALBAG

וַיִּסְגֹּר יהוה בַּעֲדוֹ – *Then the Lord shut him in:* The verse is telling us that God protected Noaḥ and his family from any violence that the dangerous animals he had brought with him might inflict.

יז בָּ֣אוּ כַּאֲשֶׁ֨ר צִוָּ֥ה אֹת֖וֹ אֱלֹהִ֑ים וַיִּסְגֹּ֥ר יְהוָ֖ה בַּעֲדֽוֹ: וַיְהִ֧י שלישי
הַמַּבּ֛וּל אַרְבָּעִ֥ים י֖וֹם עַל־הָאָ֑רֶץ וַיִּרְבּ֣וּ הַמַּ֗יִם וַיִּשְׂאוּ֙ אֶת־
יח הַתֵּבָ֔ה וַתָּ֖רָם מֵעַ֥ל הָאָֽרֶץ: וַיִּגְבְּר֥וּ הַמַּ֛יִם וַיִּרְבּ֥וּ מְאֹ֖ד עַל־
יט הָאָ֑רֶץ וַתֵּ֥לֶךְ הַתֵּבָ֖ה עַל־פְּנֵ֥י הַמָּֽיִם: וְהַמַּ֗יִם גָּ֥בְר֛וּ מְאֹ֥ד מְאֹ֖ד
עַל־הָאָ֑רֶץ וַיְכֻסּ֗וּ כָּל־הֶֽהָרִים֙ הַגְּבֹהִ֔ים אֲשֶׁר־תַּ֖חַת כָּל־
כ הַשָּׁמָֽיִם: חֲמֵ֨שׁ עֶשְׂרֵ֤ה אַמָּה֙ מִלְמַ֔עְלָה גָּבְר֖וּ הַמָּ֑יִם וַיְכֻסּ֖וּ
כא הֶהָרִֽים: וַיִּגְוַ֞ע כָּל־בָּשָׂ֣ר ׀ הָרֹמֵ֣שׂ עַל־הָאָ֗רֶץ בָּע֤וֹף וּבַבְּהֵמָה֙
כב וּבַ֣חַיָּ֔ה וּבְכָל־הַשֶּׁ֖רֶץ הַשֹּׁרֵ֣ץ עַל־הָאָ֑רֶץ וְכֹ֖ל הָאָדָֽם: כֹּ֡ל
אֲשֶׁר֩ נִשְׁמַת־ר֨וּחַ חַיִּ֜ים בְּאַפָּ֗יו מִכֹּ֛ל אֲשֶׁ֥ר בֶּחָרָבָ֖ה מֵֽתוּ:

VERSE 17

RASHI

וַתָּרָם מֵעַל הָאָרֶץ – *So that it rose above the land:* The ark sunk eleven cubits beneath the surface of the water like a heavily laden ship, part of which descends below the waves. The following passages will support this calculation.

IBN EZRA

אַרְבָּעִים יוֹם – *Forty days:* Since verse 12 has already stated: *The rain fell on the earth for forty days and forty nights*, why does our verse again say: *For forty days the flood came upon the earth*? We must interpret the verse as meaning: "Only after the flood had been on the earth for forty days and forty nights, did the waters swell, *lifting the ark so that it rose above the land.*" This implies that the ark did not budge at all during the forty days of rainfall.

KELI YAKAR

וַיְהִי הַמַּבּוּל אַרְבָּעִים יוֹם עַל־הָאָרֶץ – *For forty days the flood came upon the earth:* The forty days of rainfall were a punishment for humanity's sin of idolatry. For when people worship other gods it is tantamount to denying the entire Torah, which was delivered over a span of forty days [see Exodus 24:18]. Furthermore, the world was being punished for licentiousness, since those who commit adultery trouble God to create illegitimate children, and a fetus takes forty days to fully form. Lastly, the number forty symbolized the theft that was rampant in society, since the numerical value of the word *gezel* ["robbery" in gematria] is forty.

VERSE 18

RASHI

וַיִּגְבְּרוּ – *Surged:* Of their own accord [independent of the rainfall.]

17 Lord shut him in. For forty days the flood came upon the SHELISHI
earth. The waters swelled, lifting the ark so that it rose above
18 the land. The waters surged, swelling enormously on the earth,
19 and the ark began to drift on the surface of the water. The waters surged ever more, until all the high mountains beneath all
20 the heavens were covered. Fifteen cubits above them the waters
21 surged as the mountains were covered. All flesh that moved
upon the earth perished – birds, animals, wild beasts, and all
22 the creatures that swarm on the earth, and all humankind. Everything on dry land that had breath of life in its nostrils died.

RAMBAN

וַיִּגְבְּרוּ – *Surged:* The choice of the verb *vayigberu* might connote that the water rushed down in a torrent that uprooted trees and brought down buildings. Thus the water pulsed with *gevura* ["strength"]. Our Sages [see Taanit 2a] use the phrase *gevurot geshamim* – "the might of the rains" – to describe a downpour. Perhaps the following verse intends the same meaning: *The span of our life is seventy years – perhaps eighty, if we are strong [bigvurot]* (Psalms 90:10) – if a person has healthy bones, a strong body, and is generally robust, he will live to the age of eighty.

VERSE 20

RASHI

חֲמֵשׁ עֶשְׂרֵה אַמָּה מִלְמַעְלָה – *Fifteen cubits above them:* After the water level had reached the height of the mountains, it continued to rise an additional fifteen cubits. [That is, the figure fifteen should not be calculated from the surface of the ground, but from the top of the mountains.]

IBN EZRA

וַיְכֻסּוּ הֶהָרִים – *The mountains were covered:* Since verse 19 already informed us that *all the high mountains beneath all the heavens were covered,* why does verse 20 need to again report that *the mountains were covered*? The emphasis in the second verse is that the mountains, which were already submerged by water as stated in the previous verse, were now covered to a height of fifteen cubits. Although there are some authors who claim that there is a tall mountain in Greece whose summit escaped the deluge, we will trust the words of our God and reject the foolish ramblings of human beings.

VERSE 22

RASHI

נִשְׁמַת־רוּחַ חַיִּים – *Breath of life:* [The phrase might be understood to mean "living breath." Rashi clarifies that it means:] The breath of life.

אֲשֶׁר בֶּחָרָבָה – *On dry land:* Only the animals on dry land perished; this excludes the fish in the sea.

כג וַיִּ֜מַח אֶֽת־כָּל־הַיְק֣וּם ׀ אֲשֶׁ֣ר ׀ עַל־פְּנֵ֣י הָֽאֲדָמָ֗ה מֵאָדָ֤ם עַד־בְּהֵמָה֙ עַד־רֶ֙מֶשׂ֙ וְעַד־ע֣וֹף הַשָּׁמַ֔יִם וַיִּמָּח֖וּ מִן־הָאָ֑רֶץ וַיִּשָּׁ֧אֶר
כד אַךְ־נֹ֛חַ וַֽאֲשֶׁ֥ר אִתּ֖וֹ בַּתֵּבָֽה: וַיִּגְבְּר֥וּ הַמַּ֖יִם עַל־הָאָ֑רֶץ
ח א חֲמִשִּׁ֥ים וּמְאַ֖ת יֽוֹם: וַיִּזְכֹּ֤ר אֱלֹהִים֙ אֶת־נֹ֔חַ וְאֵ֤ת כָּל־הַֽחַיָּה֙ וְאֶת־כָּל־הַבְּהֵמָ֔ה אֲשֶׁ֥ר אִתּ֖וֹ בַּתֵּבָ֑ה וַיַּֽעֲבֵ֤ר אֱלֹהִים֙ ר֔וּחַ

RAMBAN

מִכֹּל אֲשֶׁר בֶּחָרָבָה מֵתוּ – *Everything on dry land died:* The majority of the fish live in the ocean, which was unaffected by the flood, as the verse states: *The rain fell on the earth* (7:12). This explains why the fish survived the deluge. For all bodies of water are fed by the ocean, and hence all the fish return there. Now no fish were brought onto the ark to keep their species during the deluge. And this is why God tells Noah after the ordeal: *I am about to establish My covenant with you and your descendants after you, and with every living creature that is with you – the birds, the animals, and all the wild beasts of earth that are with you, everything that left the ark, every living creature on earth* (9:9–10). Note that the fish are not mentioned at all.

VERSE 23

RASHI

אַךְ־נֹחַ – *Only Noah:* The straightforward meaning of the word *akh* is "only." However, the Midrash suggests that Noah was groaning and spitting blood because of the trouble that the cattle and wild beasts were giving him. [That is, the word *akh* was Noah's guttural response to his situation.] Some Sages write [in the Midrash] that one day Noah was late serving the lion its food and the big cat bit him. Such does the verse state: *If the righteous person is repaid on earth, certainly the wicked and the sinner will be* [Proverbs 11:31, referring to good people being punished for their infractions].

IBN EZRA

וַיִּמָּחוּ מִן־הָאָרֶץ – *All were wiped from the earth:* Their names were erased from this world because they left no descendants behind. **וַיִּשָּׁאֶר אַךְ־נֹחַ וַאֲשֶׁר אִתּוֹ בַּתֵּבָה** – *Only Noah and those left with him in the ark survived:* This verse argues against some of our ignorant coreligionists who claim that the flood did not cover the entire planet.

CHAPTER 8, VERSE 1

RASHI

וַיִּזְכֹּר אֱלֹהִים – *Then God remembered:* Even though the name *Elohim* is generally associated with God's attribute of Justice, the text uses the term here to indicate that justice can be transformed into mercy by the prayers of the righteous. Conversely, the wickedness of evil people changes God's sense of mercy to that of justice, as the text states: *The Lord saw how great man's wickedness was upon the earth.... The Lord said, "I will erase My creation, humankind, from the face of the land"* (6:5–7). The name "Lord" appears in that verdict despite generally indicating God's compassion. **וַיִּזְכֹּר אֱלֹהִים אֶת־נֹחַ** – *Then God remembered*

23 Every living thing on the face of the earth was wiped out: from
humans to animals, from creeping creatures to winged birds of
the heavens, all were wiped from the earth. Only Noaḥ and
24 those with him in the ark survived. For one hundred fifty days,
8 1 the waters surged over the earth. Then God remembered Noaḥ
and all the wild beasts and animals with him in the ark. God

RASHI *(cont.)*

Noaḥ: [The verse states that God remembered the animals as well.] What did God remember with regard to the animals? God recalled that the animals had not corrupted their ways before the flood, nor did they copulate while in the ark. וַיַּעֲבֵר אֱלֹהִים רוּחַ – *God sent a wind:* A wind of comfort and relief passed before Him. עַל־הָאָרֶץ – *Over the earth:* [The earth was submerged in water. This phrase actually means:] "Because of what had happened on the earth." וַיָּשֹׁכּוּ – *Began to subside:* The verb *vayashokku* is similar to its use in the verse *King Aḥashverosh's rage had subsided [keshokh]* (Esther 2:1), and it connotes the waning of anger.

IBN EZRA

וַיִּזְכֹּר – *Remembered:* God recalled the oath He had sworn to Noaḥ.

RAMBAN

וַיִּזְכֹּר אֱלֹהִים אֶת־נֹחַ – *Then God remembered Noaḥ:* God remembered Noaḥ because he was *a righteous man, a person of integrity* (6:9), and He had forged a covenant to save him. Furthermore, although the verse mentions just Noaḥ by name, it includes his family members who were on the ark as well. His sons and the women are not mentioned explicitly since they were only rescued from drowning on Noaḥ's merits. However, God's remembrance of the beasts and the cattle had nothing to do with their own virtue, since there exists no moral judgment with regard to the animal kingdom – those concepts only apply to people. Rather, what God recalled was His holy word that He employed to create the world. It was God's will, which in the beginning led Him to fashion the earth, that now rose before Him and encouraged Him to sustain all species of life on the ark. Hence God now determined to release the animals out of the boat lest they die inside it. The present verse does not mention the birds or the crawling things which had also been aboard the ark, since the remembrance of them was the same as God's recollection of the beasts, and mentioning one group sufficed for all the passengers.

RABBEINU BAḤYA

וַיִּזְכֹּר אֱלֹהִים אֶת־נֹחַ – *Then God remembered Noaḥ:* The verse lists the wild beasts and the animals who were with Noaḥ on the ark to indicate that God treated all the species equally with regard to general providence. [That is, just because the text lists the beasts and the animals along with Noaḥ, the reader is not to infer that God extended special and individual providence to the animal representatives just as He did to Noaḥ.] God similarly remembered all the birds, even though the verse omits them – God recalled all of the ark's

ב עַל־הָאָ֔רֶץ וַיָּשֹׁ֖כּוּ הַמָּֽיִם׃ וַיִּסָּֽכְרוּ֙ מַעְיְנֹ֣ת תְּה֔וֹם וַאֲרֻבֹּ֖ת
ג הַשָּׁמָ֑יִם וַיִּכָּלֵ֥א הַגֶּ֖שֶׁם מִן־הַשָּׁמָֽיִם׃ וַיָּשֻׁ֧בוּ הַמַּ֛יִם מֵעַ֥ל
הָאָ֖רֶץ הָל֣וֹךְ וָשׁ֑וֹב וַיַּחְסְר֣וּ הַמַּ֔יִם מִקְצֵ֕ה חֲמִשִּׁ֥ים וּמְאַ֖ת יֽוֹם׃
ד וַתָּ֤נַח הַתֵּבָה֙ בַּחֹ֣דֶשׁ הַשְּׁבִיעִ֔י בְּשִׁבְעָֽה־עָשָׂ֥ר י֖וֹם לַחֹ֑דֶשׁ עַ֖ל

RABBEINU BAḤYA *(cont.)*

non-human inhabitants together. Alternatively, perhaps the verse states that God remembered the wild beasts and animals and not the birds because the former have a special kinship with humanity – they too were created on the sixth day, as the verse states: *God made the different kinds of wild animals of the earth, and cattle* (1:25). This is what our verse implies by the words "with him": Not only were the animals in company with Noaḥ on the ark, but their ancestors were fashioned on the same day as the ancestors of their human keepers.

ḤIZKUNI

וַיִּזְכֹּר אֱלֹהִים אֶת־נֹחַ – *Then God remembered Noaḥ:* God remembered that Noaḥ had fed and sustained all of the animals during the twelve months they lived on the ark.

VERSE 2

RASHI

וַיִּסָּכְרוּ מַעְיְנֹת – *The wellsprings of the deep closed:* When the water was released, the text states, *on that day, all the wellsprings of the great deep burst, and the heavens' floodgates opened* (7:11), whereas in the current verse the Torah omits the adjective "all." This is because those springs which are necessary for the world remained open. These include the hot springs of Tiberias and the like. **וַיִּכָּלֵא** – *Were reined in:* The rain was prevented from falling. The verb *vayikkale* appears similarly in the verse *As for You, Lord, do not withhold [tikhla] Your compassion from me* (Psalms 40:12), and in the verse *None of us will refuse [yikhleh] you his tomb to bury your dead"* (Genesis 23:6).

VERSE 3

RASHI

מִקְצֵה חֲמִשִּׁים וּמְאַת יוֹם – *By the end of one hundred fifty days:* The waters began to recede on the first day of the month of Sivan. How is this date calculated? The rains ceased on the twenty-seventh of Kislev. Add to the last three days of Kislev [28–30] the twenty-nine days of Tevet for a total of thirty-two days. The month of Shevat [which is full with thirty days], the month of Adar [which is deficient with twenty-nine days], the month of Nisan [that is full with thirty days], and the month of Iyar [deficient with twenty-nine] add up to one hundred and eighteen days. [With the addition of the thirty-two days from Kislev and Tevet] we reach a total of one hundred and fifty days. [Although Rashi writes here that the rain stopped falling on the twenty-seventh of Kislev, in his explanation to 7:12 he maintains that the rain stopped on the twenty-eighth of that month. Various theories have been offered to reconcile these two positions.]

2 sent a wind over the earth, and the waters began to subside. The
wellsprings of the deep and heavens' floodgates closed, and the
3 heavens' rains were reined in. The water steadily receded from
the earth, and by the end of one hundred fifty days, the water
4 had abated. In the seventh month, on the seventeenth day of
the month, the ark came to rest on the mountains of Ararat.

IBN EZRA

וַיָּשֻׁבוּ הַמַּיִם מֵעַל הָאָרֶץ – *The water steadily receded from the earth:* It was only through prophetic power that the people on the ark calculated these 150 days [since no calendar we possess yields exactly 150 days between the seventeenth of the second month mentioned in 7:11 and the seventeenth of the seventh month noted in 8:4]. Some commentators maintain that this span of time represented five full months of the solar calendar [ostensibly thirty days each]. But this is incorrect, since five solar months would actually total 152 days. [Months on the solar calendar alternate between thirty and thirty-one days, and over the course of 150 days, there must have been at least two months with thirty-one days.] Furthermore, it is also wrong to argue that Noaḥ reckoned a lunar year of intercalated months with Marḥeshvan counted as the second month, and the year being a full one. [Intercalated lunar months alternate between those with twenty-nine days and those with thirty. A lunar year is full if it has 355 days, which will happen if both Marḥeshvan and Kislev have thirty days. The author dismisses this possibility because the months of Tevet and Adar would still have had twenty-nine days each, yielding a total of 148 days.] Indeed, why should the reader strain so? Even if the Torah had stated outright that Noaḥ employed the solar calendar [this should not offend us as adherents of the lunar calendar]. For it was not Noaḥ who instituted the festivals [but the later prophet Moshe]. Now it is possible to explore at length the timing of the ark running aground [as Rashi does]. *But do not turn away to follow futilities that neither help nor save, for they are futile* (I Samuel 12:21).

VERSE 4

RASHI

בַּחֹדֶשׁ הַשְּׁבִיעִי – *In the seventh month:* This refers to the month of Sivan, which is the seventh month counting from Kislev [although Sivan is the ninth month counting from Tishrei] for the rains ceased to fall in the month of Kislev. **בְּשִׁבְעָה־עָשָׂר יוֹם** – *On the seventeenth:* This verse teaches that the ark was submerged beneath the water to a depth of eleven cubits, a fact reached through the following reasoning. The next verse states: *On the first day of the tenth month, the mountaintops became visible* (8:5), referring to the month of Av, which is the tenth month counting from Marḥeshvan, the month when the rains began. [According to 7:11, the rain began to fall on the seventeenth of the second month, Marḥeshvan. Av comes ten months later, although Av is usually considered the eleventh month when counting from Tishrei.] Now because the water rose fifteen cubits above the mountains [as stated in 7:20], and the waters decreased from the first of Sivan [as Rashi argues above] until the

ה הָרֵי אֲרָרָט: וְהַמַּיִם הָיוּ הָלוֹךְ וְחָסוֹר עַד הַחֹדֶשׁ הָעֲשִׂירִי

RASHI *(cont.)*

first of Av, that means that the waters receded fifteen cubits over a span of sixty days. [Adding Sivan's thirty days to Tamuz's twenty-nine days and the first of Av yields a total of sixty.] Hence, the water drained at a rate of one cubit every four days. What emerges is that on the sixteenth of the month of Sivan the water had gone down just four cubits. And since on the next day the ark came to rest [on the mountains of Ararat], we learn that the ark was submerged eleven cubits in the water on top of the mountains. [That is, the bottom of the boat landed on the mountaintop on the seventh of Av, but there were still eleven cubits of water rising from the mountain top to the surface. The water began to recede on the first of Sivan and continued to abate until the first of Av. But in the meantime, the ark came to rest on the seventeenth of Sivan.]

RAMBAN

בַּחֹדֶשׁ הַשְּׁבִיעִי בְּשִׁבְעָה־עָשָׂר יוֹם לַחֹדֶשׁ – *In the seventh month, on the seventeenth day of the month:* The straightforward meaning of the text is that the period of 150 days during which *the waters surged over the earth* (7:24) included the forty days of rainfall at the flood's beginning. It was then that the great torrents took place. According to this approach, the water began to recede on the seventeenth of the month of Nisan. [Counting 150 days from the seventeenth of Marḥeshvan, which was when the rain started, as stated in 7:11, we reach the seventeenth of Nisan.] Thirty days after that, on the seventeenth of Iyar, *the ark came to rest on the mountains of Ararat*. This took place seven months after the start of the rains. [Our verse, which gives the date of Noaḥ's landfall as *the seventh month, on the seventeenth day of the month*, refers not to the month of Nisan, which is the seventh when counting from Tishrei, but Iyar, the seventh when counting from when the flood began in Marḥeshvan.] Seventy–three days after that, on the first of Av, the tops of the mountains became visible. This happened in the tenth month [as stated in 8:5], i.e., the ten month from the onset of the rain in Marḥeshvan. Thus I maintain that a small correction should be made in the interpretation of the text [from Rashi's understanding. According to Ramban all the dates should be reckoned from Marḥeshvan when the rain started. Rashi argues that the seventh month mentioned in 8:4 refers to the seventh month after the rain stopped in Kislev. Thus Rashi believes that the ark came to rest not on the seventeenth of Iyar, but on the seventeenth of Sivan]. Still, my true perspective is slightly otherwise. In my opinion, the 150 days that the water surged began on the seventeenth of the second month, meaning Marḥeshvan [as claimed above], and ran until the seventeenth of the seventh calendar month, which is Nisan. That was when the ark came to rest on the mountains of Ararat. [Here Ramban deviates from his previous interpretation, where he labeled Iyar as the seventh month. In this second reading, there was no lapse of thirty days between the end of the waters roiling the earth, and the end of Noaḥ's voyage.] It was at that point that *the Lord drove the sea back by a strong east wind all night, turning it to dry land and dividing the waters* (Exodus 14:21), meaning that God dried up the land enough for the ark so that the vessel could come to

5 **The water continued to abate until the tenth month, and on the first day of the tenth month, the mountaintops became visible.**

RAMBAN *(cont.)*

rest. Now, the proof for this claim is that the text does give a date for when the waters began to recede. This must be because on the very day that the water began to recede, the ark made landfall [a date with which we are provided]. And hence the sequence of events was as follows. On the day that the downpour began, *all the wellsprings of the great deep burst, and the heavens' floodgates opened* (7:11). This rainfall continued for forty days during which the waters surged and rose above the tops of the mountains to a height of fifteen cubits [as stated in 7:20]. When the rain stopped falling after forty days, the wellsprings of the deep remained opened as did the floodgates of heaven. The atmosphere was extremely humid, and the planet was covered in water; the water did not merely flow downhill like a waterfall, which would have left some areas dry. The flood remained in force for a full 150 days from the start of the rain. At that point, God dispatched a very strong wind across the skies and the lands so that *the wellsprings of the deep…closed* (8:2). Then the water that had been pouring out of these depositories returned to their place, causing the depths to fill up again with water as they had been originally. Simultaneously, the *heavens' floodgates closed* as well, allowing the air to be dried by the wind; the water that had inundated the world was suddenly lapped up. All this activity meant that the water level across the world dropped precipitously on that day, allowing the bottom of the ark, which had been submerged two or three cubits beneath the waves, to strike the mountain. Seventy-three days later, on the tenth month, meaning the month of Tamuz, the tops of the mountains became exposed [as stated in 8:5. Tamuz is the tenth month reckoning from Tishrei]. And after an additional forty days [as reported in 8:6], on the tenth day of the eleventh month [Av], Noaḥ opened the window of the ark to release the raven. The dove was sent out three weeks after that, and thirty days later Noaḥ removed the covering of the ark.

VERSE 5

RASHI

בָּעֲשִׂירִי בְּאֶחָד לַחֹדֶשׁ – *On the first day of the tenth month:* This refers to the month of Av, which is the tenth month counting from Marḥeshvan, when the rain started falling [on the seventeenth. Usually, Av is considered the eleventh month of the year]. Now, one might argue that perhaps this verse refers to Elul, which is the tenth month counting from Kislev, the month when the rain ceased to fall [on the twenty-seventh, as Rashi writes in comments to 8:3]. For one could imagine that just as when verse 4 states that *in the seventh month the ark came to rest*, that reckoning is worked out from Kislev, when the rain ceased to fall, [similarly, in the current verse, the calculation should start from Kislev and hence the tenth month should be Elul. In this way the counting would be uniform throughout the passage. Rashi proceeds to refute this argument.] We cannot say [that both verses count from Kislev]. We must count seven months [mentioned in verse 4] from the end of the rains [in Kislev, and not from their start in Marḥeshvan], since the text

י בָּעֲשִׂירִי֙ בְּאֶחָ֣ד לַחֹ֔דֶשׁ נִרְא֖וּ רָאשֵׁ֥י הֶהָרִֽים: וַֽיְהִ֕י מִקֵּ֖ץ אַרְבָּעִ֣ים י֑וֹם וַיִּפְתַּ֣ח נֹ֔חַ אֶת־חַלּ֥וֹן הַתֵּבָ֖ה אֲשֶׁ֥ר עָשָֽׂה:

ז וַיְשַׁלַּ֖ח אֶת־הָֽעֹרֵ֑ב וַיֵּצֵ֤א יָצוֹא֙ וָשׁ֔וֹב עַד־יְבֹ֥שֶׁת הַמַּ֖יִם מֵעַ֥ל

--- RASHI *(cont.)* ---

has already stated above that the forty days of rainfall combined with the one hundred and fifty days that the water prevailed on the earth take us to the first of Sivan [a conclusion Rashi explains in comments to verse 3. Now if we claim that the seventh month referred to in verse 4 is] the seventh month from when the rains started [on the seventeenth of Marḥeshvan, that] takes us not to Sivan [but to Iyar, the month preceding Sivan, and we cannot argue that the ark came to rest while the waters were still surging over the planet]. Conversely, the tenth month mentioned in verse 5 must be counted from when the rains started [in Marḥeshvan]. For if we suggest that the text means the tenth month from when the rains ceased [in Kislev, and that the mountains became visible on the first of] Elul, the subsequent verse makes no sense when it states: *By the first day of the first month... the water on the earth dried up* (8:13). This is due to the following calculation. *After forty days* (8:6) had elapsed from when the mountaintops had become visible [as stated in 8:5] Noaḥ *sent a raven forth* (8:7), and after waiting twenty-one days he released the dove. [Seven days after Noaḥ sent out the raven, he dispatched the dove for the first time. The dove returned to him and seven days later he sent it out again. This second time it came back with an olive branch. The third mission took place after an additional seven days, for a total of twenty-one days.] This means that sixty full days passed between the time that *the mountaintops became visible* (8:5) and the point that the earth became dry [counting the fortieth day as the first of the subsequent twenty-one days]. Were we to argue that the mountaintops only became visible in Elul [that is, that we should consider the tenth month mentioned in verse 5 as the tenth from Kislev] that would mean that the earth would not have become dry until Marḥeshvan [of the second year, sixty days after the mountaintops had been cleared of water]. Now, why would that month be called the first month in the text? It is only the month of Tishrei which can be referred to the first month, since that is when the world was created – although Rabbi Yehoshua holds that that was Nisan. [Therefore, we must conclude that the mountaintops already became visible in Av, the tenth month after Marḥeshvan, and not in Elul, the tenth month after Kislev, since that would push off the drying of the earth to the second Marḥeshvan, which verse 13 would not have referred to as the first month.]

--- RAMBAN ---

וְהַמַּיִם הָיוּ הָלוֹךְ וְחָסוֹר עַד הַחֹדֶשׁ הָעֲשִׂירִי – *The water continued to abate until the tenth month:* It seems to me that the ark was only seaworthy as long as water streamed up from the deep and was boiling hot, as our Sages maintain [see Sanhedrin 108b]. This allowed the ark to float on the surface of the water. Had the conditions been otherwise, the weight of the boat would have caused it to sink. For the ark was carrying a great many passengers in addition

6 After forty days Noaḥ opened the window he had made in the
7 ark and sent a raven forth. It flew to and fro until the water on

RAMBAN *(cont.)*

to all the food and drinking water that Noaḥ had stored aboard. Now when the water stopped pouring out of the depths, cooled off from its hot temperature, and began to dry up from the wind, the tremendous weight of ark pushed it down into the water, and it hit the top of the mountain.

VERSE 6

RASHI

מִקֵּץ אַרְבָּעִים יוֹם – *After forty days:* The verse refers to forty days after the mountaintops became visible. **אֶת־חַלּוֹן הַתֵּבָה אֲשֶׁר עָשָׂה** – *The window he had made in the ark:* This refers to the *tzohar* window [mentioned in 6:16, which Noaḥ put in the ark to provide light], and not to the door of the vessel made for coming in and going out.

IBN EZRA

אֶת־חַלּוֹן הַתֵּבָה אֲשֶׁר עָשָׂה – *The window he had made in the ark:* It is likely that Noaḥ had built a window into each side of the ark. He now opened the one referred to as the *tzohar* [in 6:16].

VERSE 7

RASHI

יָצוֹא וָשׁוֹב – *To and fro:* The raven flew around and around the ark, refusing to leave on its mission. This was because the bird suspected that Noaḥ had designs on its mate as we learn from the midrash in tractate Sanhedrin (108b). **עַד־יְבֹשֶׁת הַמַּיִם** – *Until the water on earth had dried:* The straightforward meaning of the clause is its literal sense. [The raven continued to fly around until the land dried up.] But the homiletic interpretation is as follows. The raven was selected for a different mission that was required when the earth dried up in the days of Eliyahu. There we read: *The ravens brought [Eliyahu] bread and meat each morning and bread and meat each evening* (I Kings 17:6).

BEKHOR SHOR

וַיֵּצֵא יָצוֹא וָשׁוֹב – *It flew to and fro:* The raven flew back and forth since the flood was still in full force; the bird was afraid to fly too far away from the ark lest it tire and drop into the sea. Nevertheless, the raven was able to eat the flesh off the human and animal carcasses that it found floating on the surface of the water. Subsequently, the raven returned to its nest on the ark. It continued this routine until the waters dried up completely and all of the animals and birds disembarked.

ḤIZKUNI

וַיְשַׁלַּח אֶת־הָעֹרֵב – *And sent a raven forth:* Because it is the raven's practice to eat carrion, Noaḥ understood that if the waters had abated, the bird would be able to feed off the flood's victims which had washed up on the shore. Now one should not ask how

ח הָאָֽרֶץ׃ וַיְשַׁלַּ֥ח אֶת־הַיּוֹנָ֖ה מֵאִתּ֑וֹ לִרְאוֹת֙ הֲקַ֣לּוּ הַמַּ֔יִם מֵעַ֖ל
ט פְּנֵ֥י הָאֲדָמָֽה׃ וְלֹֽא־מָצְאָה֩ הַיּוֹנָ֨ה מָנ֜וֹחַ לְכַף־רַגְלָ֗הּ וַתָּ֤שָׁב
אֵלָיו֙ אֶל־הַתֵּבָ֔ה כִּי־מַ֖יִם עַל־פְּנֵ֣י כָל־הָאָ֑רֶץ וַיִּשְׁלַ֤ח יָדוֹ֙
י וַיִּקָּחֶ֔הָ וַיָּבֵ֥א אֹתָ֛הּ אֵלָ֖יו אֶל־הַתֵּבָֽה׃ וַיָּ֣חֶל ע֔וֹד שִׁבְעַ֥ת יָמִ֖ים
יא אֲחֵרִ֑ים וַיֹּ֛סֶף שַׁלַּ֥ח אֶת־הַיּוֹנָ֖ה מִן־הַתֵּבָֽה׃ וַתָּבֹ֨א אֵלָ֤יו
הַיּוֹנָה֙ לְעֵ֣ת עֶ֔רֶב וְהִנֵּ֥ה עֲלֵה־זַ֖יִת טָרָ֣ף בְּפִ֑יהָ וַיֵּ֣דַע נֹ֔חַ כִּֽי־

HIZKUNI *(cont.)*

Noaḥ could send out the bird into a world that had been plunged into total darkness [in which case, the raven would be unable to find anything], for that was not the case. Even though the constellations – meaning the sun, the moon, and the stars – were not operating in their usual manner to create the cycle of day and nighttime, there was still light over the earth. After all, the verse states, *the mountaintops became visible* (8:5).

VERSE 8

RASHI

וַיְשַׁלַּח אֶת־הַיּוֹנָה – *After that he sent forth a dove:* Seven days after [the raven's flight, Noaḥ released the dove. We can infer that a week had passed because the text subsequently states] *Then he waited another seven days* (8:10). Since the latter verse claims that Noaḥ waited an additional seven days, that implies that he initially waited seven days before first sending out the dove. **וַיְשַׁלַּח** – *After that he sent:* The verb does not mean that Noaḥ sent the bird out on a mission, but that he threw the bird out of the boat to go on its way. As such, Noaḥ would be able to determine *whether the water had subsided*. For if the bird found a place to rest, it would not return to the ark. [In other words, Noaḥ did not send the bird out with the job of ascertaining the state of the world, as the dove was incapable of accepting a mission. Noaḥ just sent the bird out of the ark to fly about naturally, so that Noaḥ himself could learn if the waters had receded.]

SFORNO

וַיְשַׁלַּח אֶת־הַיּוֹנָה – *After that he sent forth a dove:* Noaḥ released all of the doves he had on board – all seven pairs of them. **לִרְאוֹת הֲקַלּוּ** – *To see whether the water had subsided:* If the water had abated, the birds would nest in the mountains and towers as is their custom.

VERSE 9

RAMBAN

וְלֹא־מָצְאָה הַיּוֹנָה מָנוֹחַ – *But the dove found no resting place:* It is not the practice of doves to perch on tall mountaintops where there are no trees, especially when the earth is covered with water. This is why the dove was unable to find an appropriate place to rest. However, once the bird spied the exposed trees, it flew off to build a nest in the branches.

8 the earth had dried. After that he sent forth a dove to see
9 whether the water had subsided from the face of the land. But
the dove found no resting place to plant its foot, and so it returned to him, to the ark, for water still covered the face of the
earth completely. He reached out his hand and brought the
10 dove back to him, into the ark. Then he waited another seven
11 days, and again he sent the dove forth from the ark. The dove
came back to him in the evening – and in its beak was a freshly
picked olive leaf. Noaḥ knew then that the water had subsided

VERSE 10

RASHI

וַיָּחֶל – *Then he waited:* The verb *vayaḥel* connotes waiting, as in the verse *They listened to me and waited [veyiḥellu]* (Job 29:21). There are many such usages in Scripture.

VERSE 11

RASHI

טָרָף בְּפִיהָ – *In its beak, freshly picked:* [The term *befiha,* literally, "in her mouth," suggests that the noun *yona*, dove, is feminine.] Now I maintain that the bird Noaḥ dispatched was a male, which explains why the text sometimes refers to it in the masculine form, and sometimes in the feminine. For every appearance of the term "dove" in Scripture presents it as feminine, as in the verse, *like doves of the valley, crying [homot], all of them* [Ezekiel 7:16; the verb *homot* is a feminine construction, where the masculine would be *homim*], and in the verse, *like an easily wooed, witless [fota] dove* [Hosea 7:11, instead of *foteh.* Rashi is teaching that the species of animal is referred to in the feminine regardless of whether the specimen under discussion is male or female.] טָרָף – *Picked:* The verb *taraf* means that the dove plucked the leaf from the tree [as opposed to finding it lying on the ground or floating on the water]. Now according to the Midrash, the term *taraf* means "food", whereas the word *befiha* connotes "speech" [that is, the bird was asking for food]. For the dove said: I would rather have bitter food like the leaf of an olive tree if it is provided by the Holy One, blessed be He, than food that is sweet like honey but served by human beings.

BEKHOR SHOR

טָרָף – *Freshly picked:* It was clear to Noaḥ that the dove had plucked the leaf from a tree and had not found it floating on the water's surface. For the verb *taraf* connotes something that has been ripped off, as in the verse *Do not eat flesh torn by beasts [terefa] in the wild* (Exodus 22:30).

RAMBAN

וְהִנֵּה עֲלֵה־זַיִת טָרָף בְּפִיהָ – *And in its beak was a freshly picked olive leaf:* Based on this verse, it seems that the trees had not been uprooted nor shattered by the flood waters. For the water did not flow like a raging river, rather the entire world simply became filled with water. Still, in Bereshit Rabba (33:9) our Sages present the following discussion: From where did the

יב קַלּוּ הַמַּיִם מֵעַל הָאָרֶץ׃ וַיִּיָּחֶל עוֹד שִׁבְעַת יָמִים אֲחֵרִים
יג וַיְשַׁלַּח אֶת־הַיּוֹנָה וְלֹא־יָסְפָה שׁוּב־אֵלָיו עוֹד׃ וַיְהִי בְּאַחַת
וְשֵׁשׁ־מֵאוֹת שָׁנָה בָּרִאשׁוֹן בְּאֶחָד לַחֹדֶשׁ חָרְבוּ הַמַּיִם מֵעַל
הָאָרֶץ וַיָּסַר נֹחַ אֶת־מִכְסֵה הַתֵּבָה וַיַּרְא וְהִנֵּה חָרְבוּ פְּנֵי
יד הָאֲדָמָה׃ וּבַחֹדֶשׁ הַשֵּׁנִי בְּשִׁבְעָה וְעֶשְׂרִים יוֹם לַחֹדֶשׁ יָבְשָׁה
טו טז הָאָרֶץ׃ וַיְדַבֵּר אֱלֹהִים אֶל־נֹחַ לֵאמֹר׃ צֵא מִן־ ז רביעי

RAMBAN (*cont.*)

bird bring the olive leaf? Rabbi Levi taught: The dove flew to the Mount of Olives, for the land of Israel was not overwhelmed by the flood. Thus the Holy One, blessed be He, said later to Yeḥezkel: *Man, say to [the Holy Land]: You are a land not cleansed, not swept with rain on the day of rage* (Ezekiel 22:24). However, Rabbi Biryei taught: The gates to the Garden of Eden opened on behalf of the dove, and it brought the leaf from there. Hence according to the Sages, throughout the rest of the world, the trees were either torn out of the ground or broken to pieces from the force of the flood; and surely the leaves disappeared over the course of the ordeal. Similarly, we read in Bereshit Rabba (28:3) that even heavy millstones were crushed by the flood, *as water wears away stones, its torrents scouring the soil* (Job 14:19). Now with regard to the belief that the flood did not affect the land of Israel, what that means is that the rains did not fall on that territory specifically; *the wellsprings of the great deep* (7:11) did not open there. Nevertheless, the waters that originated elsewhere did flow over the entire planet, as the verse states explicitly: *All the high mountains beneath all the heavens were covered* (7:19). And of course there is no wall around the land of Israel that could have kept the deluge at bay. This is why the Sages are quoted in Pirkei Derabbi Eliezer (chapter 23) as saying: No rainwater fell from the skies onto the land of Israel, but still the water that dropped on neighboring lands flowed across its borders into it. Such is the meaning of the verse from Ezekiel. Therefore, according to Rabbi Levi, because no torrential downpour afflicted the land of Israel, the trees that grew there remained standing, while other trees around the world were uprooted and smashed due to the fierceness of the storm.

ABARBANEL

וְהִנֵּה עֲלֵה־זַיִת טָרָף בְּפִיהָ – *And in its beak was a freshly picked olive leaf:* The straightforward meaning of this seems to be that as soon as the peaks of the mountains became visible, there were plenty of olive branches floating along the surface of the water [although all the standing trees had been uprooted by the flood]. Subsequently, when the water abated enough to reveal the mountains, the soil was damp and fertile, which meant that these olive branches could take root in the land. Forty or fifty days later, the plants had already matured enough to produce buds. It was one of these new leaves that the dove plucked and brought in its beak to Noaḥ. On its third excursion, the bird was able to find land where it could rest its legs and eat the vegetation it was accustomed to. This is why the dove did not return again to the ark.

12 from the earth. He waited another seven days and again sent
13 forth the dove – and it returned to him no more. So it was that,
by the first day of the first month of Noaḥ's six hundred and first
year, the water on the earth dried up. Noaḥ removed the cover-
14 ing of the ark and saw that the face of the land was dry. By the
twenty-seventh day of the second month, the earth had dried
15 16 completely. Then God said to Noaḥ, "Leave the ark – REVI'I
you, and your wife, your sons, and your sons' wives with you.

CLASSIC COMMENTATORS

VERSE 12

RASHI

וַיִּיָּחֶל – *He waited:* The term *vayiyyaḥel* means the same as the word *vayaḥel* [in verse 10]. However, that construct represents the simple form ["he waited"], whereas the current word suggests the reflexive ["he made himself wait"]. Thus, *vayaḥel* is the equivalent of *vayamten* ["he waited"], and *vayiyyaḥel* corresponds to *vayitmatten* [in the reflexive *hitpael* form.]

VERSE 13

RASHI

בָּרִאשׁוֹן – *By the first:* According to Rabbi Eliezer, the first month mentioned here refers to Tishrei, whereas Rabbi Yehoshua maintains it is Nisan. **חָרְבוּ** – *Dried up:* The earth became like mud with a hard crust on its surface [while remaining moist beneath.]

IBN EZRA

חָרְבוּ הַמַּיִם – *The water had dried up:* Although the water drained off the surface of the earth, the land was still drenched, which made it too soft to walk on. The drying out of the land took more time.

VERSE 14

RASHI

יָבְשָׁה – *Had dried: By the twenty-seventh day of the second month* the soil had returned to its natural state. Now the rains first started to fall on the seventeenth of the second month [one year before, as reported in 7:11]. The extra eleven days represent the eleven-day difference between the length of the solar year [365 days] and that of the lunar year [354 days], for the punishment meted out to the generation of the flood lasted a full year.

VERSE 16

RASHI

אַתָּה וְאִשְׁתְּךָ – *You and your wife:* Man and wife were permitted to exit the ark together, indicating that once the inhabitants left the boat they were permitted sexual intimacy.

ḤIZKUNI

צֵא מִן־הַתֵּבָה אַתָּה וְאִשְׁתְּךָ – *Leave the ark, you and your wife:* Although God commanded Noaḥ to exit the ark with his wife [which implied that the couple could resume

יז הַתֵּבָה אַתָּה וְאִשְׁתְּךָ וּבָנֶיךָ וּנְשֵׁי־בָנֶיךָ אִתָּךְ: כָּל־הַחַיָּה
אֲשֶׁר־אִתְּךָ מִכָּל־בָּשָׂר בָּעוֹף וּבַבְּהֵמָה וּבְכָל־הָרֶמֶשׂ
הָרֹמֵשׂ עַל־הָאָרֶץ הוצא אִתָּךְ וְשָׁרְצוּ בָאָרֶץ וּפָרוּ וְרָבוּ הַיְצֵא
יח עַל־הָאָרֶץ: וַיֵּצֵא־נֹחַ וּבָנָיו וְאִשְׁתּוֹ וּנְשֵׁי־בָנָיו אִתּוֹ:
יט כָּל־הַחַיָּה כָּל־הָרֶמֶשׂ וְכָל־הָעוֹף כֹּל רוֹמֵשׂ עַל־הָאָרֶץ
כ לְמִשְׁפְּחֹתֵיהֶם יָצְאוּ מִן־הַתֵּבָה: וַיִּבֶן נֹחַ מִזְבֵּחַ לַיהוָה וַיִּקַּח
מִכֹּל ׀ הַבְּהֵמָה הַטְּהֹרָה וּמִכֹּל הָעוֹף הַטָּהֹר וַיַּעַל עֹלֹת

ḤIZKUNI *(cont.)*

cohabitation], he did not do so, as the verse states: *So Noaḥ came out with his sons, his wife, and his sons' wives* (8:18) [the order suggests that he maintained a distance from his wife]. Rabbi Yehuda and Rabbi Neḥemya disagreed on whether that was appropriate. One sage maintained that Noaḥ acted contrary to God's orders and was punished measure for measure when his son Ḥam castrated him. [Such is one interpretation of the episode in 9:20–24.] The other sage argued that by remaining apart from his wife Noaḥ merely continued to follow his initial order [to be celibate while the world was being destroyed], and that he and his sons were rewarded for their sacrifice with a further communication from God, as the verse states: *Then God said to Noaḥ and to his sons with him* (9:8).

ABARBANEL

צֵא מִן־הַתֵּבָה אַתָּה – *Leave the ark, you:* Now just as Noaḥ was the first human to board the ark, followed by his family, and then all of the animals, so too was this sequence maintained when the company disembarked: Noaḥ left first, then his sons, and then finally all of the animal species after them. According to our Sages, it was at this point that the people were again permitted sexual intimacy. Thus Rabbeinu Nissim explains that when God instructed Noaḥ to emerge from the boat He told him: *Leave the ark – you, and your wife, your sons, and your sons' wives with you*, where the order intimates the mixing of the men and women. However, because Noaḥ and his sons were afraid to sleep with their wives and bear children, whom they feared might be killed in a future flood, they decided to leave the ark as they had boarded it: Noaḥ and his sons went out together, followed by the women who kept to themselves [as indicated by the word order of verse 18]. They did not disembark as they had been ordered to – with the men accompanying the women.

VERSE 17

RASHI

הוצא – *Bring them out:* The verb here is written with a *vav* [*hotze*] but it is read as if written with a *yod* [*haytze*]. This anomaly suggests that Noaḥ was to instruct the animals to leave the ark, but if they refused to go out, he was to lead them out – *hotze* – against their will. **וְשָׁרְצוּ בָאָרֶץ** – *Let them swarm again on the earth:* The animals are not permitted to

17 And every living thing with you – birds, animals, and all wild
beasts that walk the earth – bring them out with you. Let them
swarm again on the earth and be fertile and multiply upon it."
18 So Noaḥ came out with his sons, his wife, and his sons' wives.
19 Every beast, creeping thing, winged creature, everything that
20 creeps across the earth, emerged from the ark by families. Then
Noaḥ built an altar to the Lord and, taking of each of the kinds
of pure animals and pure birds, sacrificed burnt offerings on the

RASHI (cont.)

procreate while still on board the ark. We learn from this emphasis that the birds and the animals as well [in addition to the humans] were forbidden to be intimate during the flood.

RALBAG

כָּל־הַחַיָּה אֲשֶׁר־אִתְּךָ – *And every living thing with you:* I imagine that the animals mated when they were on the ark since that is only natural. The nonhuman passengers were not intelligent enough to follow a command to remain celibate during the flood. This is why the animals were invited to exit the ark *by families* (8:19). For while they were on the boat the beasts did not copulate with differing species, but procreated with their own kind and produced young.

VERSE 19

RASHI

לְמִשְׁפְּחֹתֵיהֶם – *By families:* When the animals left the ark, they agreed to God's condition to cleave to their own species.

IBN EZRA

לְמִשְׁפְּחֹתֵיהֶם – *By families:* The animals went out according to their species. Now some commentators maintain that the animals reproduced in the ark, in which case the term means that each animal family left the ark as a group without mixing with other kinds. This approach seems reasonable.

VERSE 20

RAV SE'ADYA GAON

וַיַּעַל עֹלֹת בַּמִּזְבֵּחַ – *He sacrificed burnt offerings on the altar:* It has been said that Noaḥ's sacrifices were a gesture of thanks [for his salvation]. And yet, why did Noaḥ not request anything from God at that time, considering that usually people who bring offerings ask God to continue the beneficence that earned their gratitude? It seems that Noaḥ was so focused on the past that he did not think about the future.

RASHI

מִכֹּל הַבְּהֵמָה הַטְּהֹרָה – *Each of the kinds of pure animals:* Said Noaḥ: The only reason that the Holy One, blessed be He, ordered me to take seven pairs of the pure animals onto the ark, was to later offer them as sacrifices.

כא בַּמִּזְבֵּחַ׃ וַיָּרַח יהוה אֶת־רֵיחַ הַנִּיחֹחַ וַיֹּאמֶר יהוה אֶל־לִבּוֹ
לֹא אֹסִף לְקַלֵּל עוֹד אֶת־הָאֲדָמָה בַּעֲבוּר הָאָדָם כִּי יֵצֶר לֵב
הָאָדָם רַע מִנְּעֻרָיו וְלֹא־אֹסִף עוֹד לְהַכּוֹת אֶת־כָּל־חַי כַּאֲשֶׁר

IBN EZRA

מִכֹּל הַבְּהֵמָה הַטְּהֹרָה – *Each of the kinds of pure animals:* There are ten species of pure animal [as listed in Deuteronomy 14:4–5]. On the other hand, we do not know how many types of pure bird exist, only that they outnumber the impure species. Noaḥ built his altar on one of the mountains of Ararat.

ḤIZKUNI

וַיַּעַל עֹלֹת בַּמִּזְבֵּחַ – *He sacrificed burnt offerings on the altar:* Noaḥ offered sacrifices at the end of his voyage as all seafarers should do. So we see in Psalms (107:22–23): *Let them sacrifice thanksgiving offerings and tell of His deeds with joy. Those who go down to the sea in ships, sailing across the mighty waters.* Noaḥ thanked God for allowing the ark to survive the storm, and for sparing his life when the rest of the world was destroyed. The altar specified here is the same platform previously used by Adam, Kayin, and Hevel.

ABARBANEL

מִכֹּל הַבְּהֵמָה הַטְּהֹרָה – *Each of the kinds of pure animals:* The pure animals and birds are of superior quality compared to the impure species. Now although it was only our teacher Moshe who later designated these animals as pure, Noaḥ was able to identify this special set of beasts and birds on his own, based on his examination of their nature. The purpose of the offerings was to thank God for all of the wonders He had performed on the family's behalf, as the verse states: *For all is from You, and we have given You only what is Yours* (I Chronicles 29:14).

VERSE 21

RASHI

מִנְּעֻרָיו – *From its youth:* The term *mine'urav* ["from his youth"] is written without a *vav* [after the *ayin*] and as such, appears like *mine'arav*. This indicates that when a fetus moves itself [*nin'ar*] to emerge from its mother's womb, its evil inclination has already taken hold. **לֹא אֹסִף... וְלֹא־אֹסִף** – *Never again... never again:* God repeats His determination here as an oath. Thus, when the verse states: *I swore that the waters of Noaḥ would never sweep again over the earth* (Isaiah 54:9), it is referring to this repeated statement, as there was no other explicit oath. This is the interpretation of our Sages in tractate Shevuot (36a).

IBN EZRA

אֶת־רֵיחַ הַנִּיחֹחַ – *The fragrant aroma:* The term *niḥoaḥ* ["fragrant"] derives from the word for rest – *menuḥa*. **וַיֹּאמֶר יהוה אֶל־לִבּוֹ** – *The Lord said in His heart:* [Literally, "to his heart."] The preposition here should be understood as "in" His heart. God then shared His secret rumination with Noaḥ, for the man was a prophet. **לֹא אֹסִף לְקַלֵּל עוֹד אֶת־הָאֲדָמָה** – *Never again will I curse the land:* I will not again curse the land as I did following the sin of Adam, where

21 altar. The Lord smelled the fragrant aroma and said in His
heart, "Never again will I curse the land because of man; the
devisings of the human heart are evil from its youth. And never

IBN EZRA *(cont.)*

the verse states: *Cursed will be the land on your account* (3:17). **יֵצֶר לֵב הָאָדָם** – *The devisings of the human heart:* A person's evil inclination [*yetzer*] reflects his creation [*yetzira*].

BEKHOR SHOR

לֹא אֹסִף לְקַלֵּל עוֹד אֶת־הָאֲדָמָה – *Never again will I curse the land:* God vows never to destroy the vegetation of the earth, the animals, and the beasts. It is only the human sinners who will be killed by the plague or the sword, while the natural world will continue to run its course. Thus God continues: *As long as earth and time endure – sowing time and harvest... will not cease.*

RAMBAN

וַיֹּאמֶר יהוה אֶל־לִבּוֹ – *The Lord said in His heart:* At the time that God made this determination, He did not reveal His decision to the prophet. It was only when He commanded Moshe to write down the Torah that He revealed this principle to man. **בַּעֲבוּר הָאָדָם** – *Because of man:* The world was punished because of humankind, and had people not sinned, the natural world would not have been destroyed, even though the animals too had become corrupt. **כִּי יֵצֶר לֵב הָאָדָם רַע מִנְּעֻרָיו** – *The devisings of the human heart are evil from its youth:* This was a concession to humanity that although people are wicked when they are young, they are better when they mature. These then are two reasons not to obliterate all life on earth. [Firstly, human beings are not responsible for their own natures; secondly, they grow and improve over time.] For according to some commentators, the word *mine'urav* ["from its youth"] can be understood as if written *bin'urav* ["in its youth"].

RALBAG

וַיָּרַח יהוה אֶת־רֵיחַ הַנִּיחֹחַ – *The Lord smelled the fragrant aroma:* The text speaks figuratively and writes using language that is accessible to people. For God does not really have physical senses that can be stimulated.

ABARBANEL

וַיֹּאמֶר יהוה אֶל־לִבּוֹ – *The Lord said in His heart:* This verse uses language descriptive of human speech, for just like human beings mull over an idea before deciding upon one plan instead of another, so too did the Holy One, blessed be He, consult with Himself. As our Sages, of blessed memory, state with regard to creation: With whom did God advise [when He appears to consult with others in 1:26]? He conferred with His own heart. Now, God's advice and determination was *Never again will I curse the land because of man*, as he did by the flood which destroyed the world and cursed it due to humanity's behavior. God reasons that *the devisings of the human heart are evil from its youth*, meaning that from the moment of a person's creation, he has a tendency to sin due to his fundamentally base nature. And so God now decided that if He responded to every transgression by releasing

כב עָשִׂיתִי: עֹד כָּל־יְמֵי הָאָרֶץ זֶרַע וְקָצִיר וְקֹר וָחֹם וְקַיִץ וָחֹרֶף

ABARBANEL *(cont.)*

a deluge against the world, as He had just done, He would have to instigate a flood every year and each month to deal with humanity's recalcitrance. Now should the reader object that such punishment would be no great catastrophe for the land, since soil is insentient, can the same be said for all the animals, which are surely aware of suffering imposed upon them? Should the planet's fauna who are blameless of any wrongdoing be repeatedly wiped out? Hence God determined never again to strike all life forms as He had just done. A better system would surely be to execute retribution against human beings in small doses in ways that do not demand the complete annihilation meted out on the generation of the flood. This is how God would henceforth visit the iniquities of sinners upon them. This might happen during sowing time or harvest when a crop is damaged; or some areas might receive rain while others face drought. Temperature too would play a role, as some locales will become too hot and others too cold, extending the limits of summer and winter beyond their natural dates. Storms would increase, as would diseases and deadly plagues. When God states that *day and night will not cease*, that alludes to the torments of humanity listed in Psalms: *You need not fear terror by night, nor the arrow that flies by day, nor the plague that stalks in darkness, nor disease that ravages at noon* (Psalms 91:5–6). Thus what emerges is not a promise from God that because man is essentially evil from his youth, God will overlook his wicked behavior and forgive him for his sins. Rather, He is declaring that from now on He will punish man in ways other than with a global flood.... Now the substance of the covenant which God struck with humanity was a promise never again to destroy the world with a flood. This was not in fact a response to the merits of Noaḥ, but foreshadowed the nature of humanity in the future. For originally when God *saw how great man's wickedness was upon the earth, and that his thoughts constantly inclined toward evil* (6:5), He declared: *I will erase My creation, humankind, from the face of the land* (6:7). Thus God decided to kill the entire generation of the time because its members had corrupted their ways. However, after the deluge, the Holy One, blessed be He, reached a new decision in His wisdom and said: There is no longer a need *to curse the land because of man* and to send another flood to cleanse the planet. This is because God sent the initial deluge when the world was still young, and man was immature and impetuous. But there was now little fear that humanity would again become so deviant to warrant obliteration. Civilization would be spared that kind of deterioration either because humankind had learned its lesson from the catastrophe, and all people would now direct their hearts toward God, or because all human beings would now branch out from three new patriarchs. Since Shem, Ḥam, and Yefet were three such different personalities, it is unlikely that the temperament of a family that descended from one of these would find common purpose with their cousins – either for good or for evil. As such there never again would arise a situation where all of humanity joined forces in corruption and wickedness, as the generation of the flood had. And there would hence never be a reason for God to obliterate humanity again.

22 again will I destroy all life as I have done. As long as earth and
time endure – sowing time and harvest, cold and heat, summer,

SFORNO

וַיֹּאמֶר יהוה אֶל־לִבּוֹ – *The Lord said in His heart:* Initially, God only expressed this point to Himself. He did not reveal His resolution to Noaḥ and his sons until they had accepted His laws [as listed in 9:1–7] and forged a covenant. **כִּי יֵצֶר לֵב הָאָדָם רַע מִנְּעֻרָיו** – *The devisings of the human heart are evil from its youth:* From now on the earth's climate would be inferior compared to what it had been before the flood. As such, humanity would lack the intellectual capacity that it had before. People would therefore find it even more difficult to withstand the temptations and desires of youth than they did at first.

VERSE 22

RASHI

עֹד כָּל־יְמֵי הָאָרֶץ – *As long as earth and time endure:* The six periods listed here [aside from day and night] represent the entire length of the year – each of the terms signifies two months. This is taught in Bava Metzia (106b): The second half of the month of Tishrei, together with the month of Marḥeshvan and the first half of the month of Kislev comprise the sowing season. The second half of Kislev combined with month of Tevet and the first half of Shevat constitute the cold season, and so forth. **קֹר** – *Cold:* The term *kor* signifies harsher weather than mere winter [*ḥoref*]. **וָחֹרֶף** – *And winter:* During the winter, barley and pungent beans are sown – these ripen quickly. This season begins in the second half of Shevat and runs through Adar and the first half of Nisan. **וְקָצִיר** – *And harvest:* This refers to the second half of Nisan, the entire month of Iyar, and the first half of Sivan. **קַיִץ** – *Summer:* [This is the time covered by the second half of Sivan, the month of Tamuz, and the first half of Av.] During this season, the figs are harvested and laid out to dry in the fields. These fruits are referred to as *kayitz*, as the verse states: *The bread and summer fruit [vehakayitz] are for the young men to eat* (II Samuel 16:2). **חֹם** – *Heat:* This season, *ḥom*, takes place at the end of the summer days [*yemot haḥama*]. It begins in the second half of Av, continues through Elul, and ends with the first half of Tishrei. This period is called *ḥom* because this is when the world is at its hottest [*ḥam*], as the Talmud states in Yoma (29a): The end of the summer is more severe than the summer itself. **וְיוֹם וָלַיְלָה לֹא יִשְׁבֹּתוּ** – *Day and night will not cease:* [God's guarantee promising that day and night will never again cease] implies that the shift from one to the other was interrupted during the flood. This is because during the deluge the celestial spheres were not operative, and hence there was no distinction between day and night. **לֹא יִשְׁבֹּתוּ** – *Will not cease:* These seasons will never stop functioning the way that they are meant to.

IBN EZRA

עֹד כָּל־יְמֵי הָאָרֶץ – *As long as earth and time endure:* [Literally, "all the days of the earth."] We learn from here that the time has been fixed for the end of the earth.

ט א וְיוֹם וָלַיְלָה לֹא יִשְׁבֹּתוּ: וַיְבָרֶךְ אֱלֹהִים אֶת־נֹחַ וְאֶת־בָּנָיו
ב וַיֹּאמֶר לָהֶם פְּרוּ וּרְבוּ וּמִלְאוּ אֶת־הָאָרֶץ: וּמוֹרַאֲכֶם וְחִתְּכֶם
יִהְיֶה עַל כָּל־חַיַּת הָאָרֶץ וְעַל כָּל־עוֹף הַשָּׁמָיִם בְּכֹל אֲשֶׁר

CHAPTER 9, VERSE 1

ABARBANEL

וַיְבָרֶךְ אֱלֹהִים אֶת־נֹחַ וְאֶת־בָּנָיו – *Then God blessed Noaḥ and his sons:* I have no doubt that when Noaḥ and his sons emerged from the ark and saw the utter ruin of the planet they were shocked and distraught. At that point they also feared greatly for the future. There were four reasons for this. Firstly, the surviving family mourned the deaths of all their friends and relatives; everyone they knew had drowned in the relentless waters of the flood. Noaḥ and his sons wandered across a landscape that was wholly desolate. Secondly, the humans were terrified of becoming prey for wild animals. For in the past, when communities existed, a large group of people could band together to fend off an attacking beast and kill it. However, now that the four men could only depend on themselves, they were newly vulnerable. Thirdly, the survivors were desperately anxious over what they would eat. All of the fruit trees that had been given to the first humans for food were now uprooted by the torrents, and the vegetable crops had similarly been washed away and destroyed. Surely the family could not have lasted long enough to depend on a new range of crops and orchards, for these take many days and months, and in some cases years, to produce edible products. What would they eat while they were waiting? Thus Noaḥ and his sons worried that they would sooner die of hunger, and that they would probably have been better off succumbing to the flood! Finally, the family was nervous that dissent amongst them would descend into violence and that fratricide would erupt as had happened between Kayin and Hevel. If that happened, all of humanity would be erased from the world, and there would be nobody left to avenge their deaths. These four matters tormented their souls and convinced them of the futility of reproducing. Thus our Sages tell us that even though God commanded Noaḥ: *Leave the ark – you, and your wife, your sons, and your sons' wives with you* [8:16, which was an invitation to Noaḥ to resume marital relations], Noaḥ refused to do so, saying: Why should I leave the ark and have more children only to see them die? When God saw how despondent Noaḥ and his sons had become over the future, He spoke to the family in a way that addressed each of their concerns, blessing them as follows: In response to their depression at the demise of everyone dear to them, God now told Noaḥ and his sons: *Be fertile, multiply, fill the earth*. In other words, God was instructing Noaḥ to create a new population to replace those who had been lost. These descendants who emerged from his loins would be even more faithful and loving than those acquaintances who had perished. It is as if God promised Noaḥ that He would enhance his fecundity in order to quickly fill the void caused by the disappearance of humanity. Secondly, God allayed Noaḥ's fear of dying at the hands of a ferocious beast by guaranteeing that from now on, *fear and dread of you shall fall upon all beasts of the earth, upon all winged creatures of the heavens*. For the human form is naturally terrifying to animals,

9 1 winter, day, and night will not cease." Then God blessed Noaḥ
and his sons, saying to them, "Be fertile, multiply, fill the earth.
2 Fear and dread of you shall fall upon all beasts of the earth,
upon all winged creatures of the heavens, upon all that creeps
upon the land and all fish of the sea. Into your hand they are

ABARBANEL *(cont.)*

whose instinct is to avoid people. Thus man was granted authority over all life forms. In response to the lack of food in the postdiluvian world, God told Noaḥ and his family: *Every moving thing that lives shall be food for you* (9:3). As such God assured the people that if they could find no produce or vegetation to eat, they might sustain themselves by eating animal flesh. Said God: *I allow them all to you, like green plants*, meaning that meat could serve as a substitute for the plants that humanity had hitherto survived on. It therefore becomes clear why God bestowed upon Noaḥ the same blessings that He had previously granted Adam – the messages that God repeated reflected the concerns that Noaḥ now faced due to the flood. Finally, God recognized that conflict between people remained a true problem. In order to control the possibility of violence, God announced: *And for your own lifeblood I will demand account* (9:5). Noaḥ and his sons worried that one of them might rise and kill his brother, as Kayin had done to Hevel, since Shem, Ḥam, Yefet were alone in the world like those men had been. As such, God warned that the punishment for murder would be severe: *For human life I will demand account*. The taking of a person's life will always be avenged, unlike the slaughter of an animal. Hence when the verse states: *I will demand account of every man toward his fellow man* [*ish aḥiv*, literally, "every man his brother"], it alludes to the homicide of Hevel by his brother. And lest you argue that there could in fact be no justice or vengeance following a murder, since there were no other people alive who could address the crime, know that God has many means of exacting punishment. If a man kills his fellow in the absence of other human beings who can right the wrong, God promises that He *will demand it from every wild beast* (9:5), meaning that justice will be attained by a predatory animal. But if there do exist other people who can respond to the murderer's act, *by man shall his blood be shed* (9:6). In all cases a killer must meet his recompense – either at the hands of human beings, or in some other fashion.

VERSE 2

RASHI

וְחִתְּכֶם – *And dread of you:* The word *ḥatat* means "fear," as in the verse *You see my terror [ḥatat] and stand aghast* (Job 6:21). According to the Midrash, the term is related to *ḥiyyut* ["life"]. Note that as long as even a day-old child is alive, he need not be protected against mice [which are afraid of living people], whereas no mice would fear Og the [giant] king of Bashan were he to be lying dead. Thus, when the verse states: *Fear and dread of you shall fall upon all beasts of the earth*, it means that animals shall flee your presence as long as you are alive.

CLASSIC COMMENTATORS

ג תִּרְמֹ֧שׂ הָאֲדָמָ֛ה וּֽבְכָל־דְּגֵ֥י הַיָּ֖ם בְּיֶדְכֶ֥ם נִתָּֽנוּ׃ כָּל־רֶ֙מֶשׂ֙
אֲשֶׁ֣ר הוּא־חַ֔י לָכֶ֥ם יִהְיֶ֖ה לְאָכְלָ֑ה כְּיֶ֣רֶק עֵ֔שֶׂב נָתַ֥תִּי לָכֶ֖ם
ד ה אֶת־כֹּֽל׃ אַךְ־בָּשָׂ֕ר בְּנַפְשׁ֥וֹ דָמ֖וֹ לֹ֥א תֹאכֵֽלוּ׃ וְאַ֨ךְ אֶת־דִּמְכֶ֤ם
לְנַפְשֹֽׁתֵיכֶם֙ אֶדְרֹ֔שׁ מִיַּ֥ד כָּל־חַיָּ֖ה אֶדְרְשֶׁ֑נּוּ וּמִיַּ֣ד הָֽאָדָ֗ם מִיַּד֙

RALBAG

וּמוֹרַאֲכֶם וְחִתְּכֶם יִהְיֶה עַל כָּל־חַיַּת הָאָרֶץ – *Fear and dread of you shall fall upon all beasts of the earth:* Perhaps God gave humanity this blessing in response to the relationship that people formerly had with the animal kingdom. Previous generations of human beings were so wicked and fearful that God hid the animals from them. Alternatively, maybe the predatory beasts had previously attacked sinners as punishment for their evil deeds, but now God issued this blessing promising humanity dominance.

VERSE 3

RASHI

לָכֶם יִהְיֶה לְאָכְלָה – *Shall be food for you:* I did not allow the first man to eat meat; his diet was restricted to vegetation. However, just as I granted Adam license to eat *green plants*, you may now eat everything.

IBN EZRA

כָּל־רֶמֶשׂ אֲשֶׁר הוּא־חַי – *Every moving thing that lives:* The word *remes* represents a general term for beasts of the field and cattle, and includes all birds and fish as well. Thus human beings were now permitted to eat any type of animal.

BEKHOR SHOR

כְּיֶרֶק עֵשֶׂב – *Like green plants:* Since you saved the animals in the ark, and their salvation was thanks to you, they are now given to you to do with them as you please.

RABBEINU BAḤYA

כְּיֶרֶק עֵשֶׂב נָתַתִּי לָכֶם אֶת־כֹּל – *I allow them all to you, like green plants:* Since God first stated: *I allow them all to you*, we might have thought that the entire animal kingdom was permitted for consumption. This is what the nations believe. And yet the verse continues to say: *like all green plants*, which instructed Noaḥ to treat the fauna like he would the flora. Just as in the world of plants some vegetation is permitted since it is tasty and healthy but other shrubs are harmful and deadly, so too some animals may be eaten (those which the Torah permits) while other beasts should be avoided (those which the Torah forbids). This is the straightforward meaning of the text, for God did not allow the human beings to eat just any animal that they desired.

VERSE 4

RASHI

בְּנַפְשׁוֹ דָמוֹ – *Flesh with its lifeblood:* With this statement God forbade humanity to eat limbs torn from living animals. In other words, people may not eat an animal's flesh as long

3 given. Every moving thing that lives shall be food for you; I
4 allow them all to you, like green plants. But flesh with its life-
5 blood still in it you may not eat. And for your own lifeblood I
will demand account; I will demand it from every wild beast.
For human life I will demand account, of every man toward his

RASHI *(cont.)*

as its soul is still in it. **בְּנַפְשׁוֹ דָמוֹ** – *Flesh with its lifeblood:* As long as its soul is in it. [The emphasis is not on the consumption of blood, but on the presence of life in the animal.] **בָּשָׂר בְּנַפְשׁוֹ לֹא תֹאכֵלוּ** – *But flesh with its lifeblood still in it you may not eat:* The words *basar benafsho lo tokhelu* prohibit eating a limb or flesh from an animal that still lives. [The full clause reads *basar benafasho damo lo tokhelu*, where the middle word *damo* – "its blood" – seems superfluous.] This teaches us that it is also forbidden to drink the blood of an animal while its blood [soul] is still in the animal [that is, while it is still alive. Later, Torah law will forbid to Jews the consumption of animal blood even once its host is dead].

RAMBAN

אַךְ־בָּשָׂר בְּנַפְשׁוֹ דָמוֹ – *But flesh with its lifeblood still in it:* According to Rashi, the verse prohibits eating an animal's flesh while its soul is still in it, meaning consuming of a limb torn from a living animal. Neither may people eat the blood of a living animal. But if that were the sense of the text, it should have read: "Do not eat flesh with its soul in it, nor may you eat blood." This cannot then be the straightforward meaning of the verse, nor is it correct from the perspective of the Midrash. For although the sons of Noaḥ [that is, gentiles] are forbidden to eat a limb from a living animal, as the Sages assert [in Sanhedrin 59a], they face no corresponding prohibition against drinking blood from an animal which is still alive. Such is the opinion of Rabbi Ḥanina ben Gamliel. Rather, the meaning of our verse is: Do not eat flesh when the life of the animal, that is, its blood, is still in it, *for the life of all flesh – its blood is its life* (Leviticus 17:14).

RALBAG

בְּנַפְשׁוֹ דָמוֹ – *Flesh with its lifeblood:* God forbade humans to eat flesh torn from a living animal because that is a repulsive practice and reflects the most awful type of greed. What I mean is that when an individual rips a limb from an animal he has not yet killed, he betrays a fierce gluttony which cannot even wait for proper slaughter before being satisfied.

VERSE 5

RASHI

וְאַךְ אֶת־דִּמְכֶם – *And for your own lifeblood:* Even though I have allowed you to take the lives of animals, *for your own lifeblood I will demand account* – I will demand the blood of a person who takes his own life. The term *lenafshoteikhem* [literally, "for your lives," appearing within the phrase *et dimkhem lenafshoteikhem* – "for your own lifeblood"] emphasizes that God holds an individual accountable for suicide even if he strangles himself and no blood is actually spilled. **מִיַּד כָּל־חַיָּה** – *From every wild beast:* As a consequence of the sins of the generation of the flood, humanity became prey to wild beasts who dominate them, as the verse states: *Like the beasts that perish* [Psalms 49:21; human

ו אִישׁ אָחִיו אֶדְרֹשׁ אֶת־נֶפֶשׁ הָאָדָם׃ שֹׁפֵךְ דַּם הָאָדָם בָּאָדָם
ז דָּמוֹ יִשָּׁפֵךְ כִּי בְּצֶלֶם אֱלֹהִים עָשָׂה אֶת־הָאָדָם׃ וְאַתֶּם פְּרוּ

RASHI *(cont.)*

beings have become like cattle which predators do not fear]. Hence the wild animals need to be specifically warned not to kill people. **וּמִיַּד הָאָדָם** – *Of every man:* I will hold accountable anyone who murders another unobserved. **מִיַּד אִישׁ אָחִיו** – *Toward his fellow man:* [Literally, "his brother."] If a person inadvertently kills his fellow man whom he loves like a brother, I will hold him responsible if he is not exiled [to one of the designated cities of refuge] and does not seek forgiveness for his transgression – for even a person who kills accidentally requires atonement. When there are no witnesses to the event who can testify that it was an accident and have him sentenced to exile, and if he does not willingly submit to justice, the Holy One, blessed be He, will ensure that such punishment shall come about. This is how our Sages in tractate Makkot (10b) interpret the verse *It came about by an act of God* [Exodus 21:13. The Talmud describes a situation where two men have taken the lives of other people: One murdered his victim intentionally, the other killed unintentionally. However, in neither case were witnesses present who could testify to either man's culpability. Hence the first man cannot be executed by the court, nor can the second man be exiled to live in the city of refuge. In order to right these wrongs] the Holy One, blessed be He, arranges for both individuals to visit the same inn at the same time. [While they are there, the murderer finds himself sitting beneath a ladder that the accidental killer is descending. The latter slips and falls, crushing the former to death. Thus, the villain who deserved to be put to death indeed dies, while the negligent man who should have been exiled for his previous mishap is now sentenced to that fate anyway. This is how God ensures that punishment is meted out to one who takes the life *of his fellow man*, even when he had meant no harm.]

IBN EZRA

וְאַךְ אֶת־דִּמְכֶם לְנַפְשֹׁתֵיכֶם – *And for your own lifeblood:* In my opinion, it is unlikely that this phrase refers to the prohibition of suicide [as Rashi suggests].

RAMBAN

מִיַּד כָּל־חַיָּה אֶדְרְשֶׁנּוּ – *I will demand it from every wild beast:* I would be surprised if this phrase is meant to be taken literally and that animals, like people, are to be punished for their behavior. Since animals lack intelligence, it makes little sense to grant them reward or to extract punishment from them. Perhaps what the text means is that when it comes to taking a human life, indeed any beast which mauls a person to death will itself be killed. Such is the decree of the Almighty. Hence we later read: *If an ox gores a man or a woman to death, the ox shall be stoned* (Exodus 21:28). The purpose of that action is not simply to cause the animal's owner a monetary loss [for not properly guarding his ox, but is actually a form of retributory justice against the animal], since we know that even a wild, ownerless animal is also subject to capital punishment [as discussed in Bava Kamma 44b]. The prohibition against murder applies equally to gentiles and to Jews. Now we might attribute the accountability of animals for killing humans to their instinctive aversion to doing so. The secret behind this

6 fellow man: One who sheds the blood of man – by man shall
7 his blood be shed, for in God's image man was made. As for
you, be fertile and multiply, abound on earth and become

RAMBAN *(cont.)*

is as follows: When God created the world He granted human beings a diet of *all these seed-bearing plants on the face of the earth and every tree with seed-bearing fruit* (1:29), while animals were similarly permitted *every green plant for food* (1:30). The latter verse ends with the words "and so it was," indicating that the nature and behavior of the animals was such [that they were vegetarians]. However, now God permitted man to slaughter animals, and corresponding to that altered the instincts of some animals so that they would attack and eat each other. Hence God commanded that although the other living creatures could be eaten by people, the animals would be afraid of humans and not attack them in turn. When God proclaimed that He would demand accountability *from every wild beast*, the emphasis was that He would not hold animals liable for devouring each other. This explains why the text mentions the prohibition of murder here – it is a corollary to the permission now given to people to slaughter animals, that is to spill blood. For according to our Sages [as discussed in Sanhedrin 56b], the first man had already been warned against murder. However, since the killing of animals was now allowed, God repeated that it was permissible to spill the blood of a beast but not that of a fellow human being. It also remained forbidden for animals to take a person's life, for it was still against their nature to do so.

HIZKUNI

מִיַּד כָּל־חַיָּה אֶדְרְשֶׁנּוּ – *I will demand it from every wild beast:* This verse warns an evil person against saying: Rather than kill my enemy with my own hands, I will merely throw him to a pack of wild animals – let them finish him. Hence the verse states: *I will demand it from every wild beast*. [That is, the human who facilitates such a death is held accountable.] Another interpretation: I will demand account from the beast itself, as the verse states: *If an ox gores a man or a woman to death, the ox shall be stoned* (Exodus 21:28).

VERSE 6

RASHI

בָּאָדָם דָּמוֹ יִשָּׁפֵךְ – *By man shall his blood be shed:* If there are witnesses to the murder, you [the court] must put the perpetrator to death [and the matter is taken out of God's hands unlike in the previous case]. Now why is the shedding of human blood so serious? Because *in God's image man was made*. This last clause is missing its subject [literally, "for – made man in God's image"], for it should be understood as: The Maker made man in God's image. There are many such cases of incomplete phrasing in Scripture.

VERSE 7

RASHI

וְאַתֶּם פְּרוּ וּרְבוּ – *As for you, be fertile and multiply:* According to the straightforward meaning of the text, the first appearance of these words [in 9:1] represents a blessing to man to be populous, whereas the current instance suggests a commandment. However,

ח וּרְבוּ שִׁרְצוּ בָאָרֶץ וּרְבוּ־בָהּ׃ וַיֹּאמֶר אֱלֹהִים חמישי
ט אֶל־נֹחַ וְאֶל־בָּנָיו אִתּוֹ לֵאמֹר׃ וַאֲנִי הִנְנִי מֵקִים אֶת־בְּרִיתִי
י אִתְּכֶם וְאֶת־זַרְעֲכֶם אַחֲרֵיכֶם׃ וְאֵת כָּל־נֶפֶשׁ הַחַיָּה אֲשֶׁר

RASHI *(cont.)*

the homiletic interpretation of the repetition teaches that when one ignores his obligation to procreate, that neglect is tantamount to murder.

IBN EZRA

וְאַתֶּם פְּרוּ וּרְבוּ – *As for you, be fertile and multiply:* [After 9:1, this verse seems redundant. According to Ibn Ezra, God here explains that] when you only execute murderers, you will multiply further [as a reward]. According to some commentators [see Rashi], this verse represents the obligation to procreate.

RALBAG

וְאַתֶּם פְּרוּ וּרְבוּ – *As for you, be fertile and multiply:* Now God commanded Noaḥ and his sons to be fertile and multiply, and not to corrupt their ways as did the generation of the flood. That is, their sexual behavior should be geared toward reproduction only. That is why homosexual and bestial activity were forbidden to human beings. God did not also have to warn the people against theft and adultery, since it had already been made clear to Noaḥ that it was those crimes which brought the flood upon humankind. It was similarly obvious that the generation of the flood had been punished for their practice of idolatry, a deviation which began in the time of Enosh [grandson of Adam]. God issued a limited set of rules to the sons of Noaḥ to help them order their community. Still, the Almighty knew that these people were incapable of accepting additional restrictions beyond the seven Noahide laws. The nation of Israel, however, was given the full complement of moral behavior so that they could perfect their society. For they were amenable to such guidance.

VERSE 8

IBN EZRA

וַיֹּאמֶר אֱלֹהִים אֶל־נֹחַ וְאֶל־בָּנָיו – *Then God said to Noaḥ and to his sons:* God conveyed His message to Shem, Ḥam, and Yefet through their father. Still, some commentators maintain that all four men were prophets.

RABBEINU BAḤYA

וַיֹּאמֶר אֱלֹהִים אֶל־נֹחַ וְאֶל־בָּנָיו – *Then God said to Noaḥ and to his sons:* God spoke directly to Noaḥ's sons. In order to emphasize that the communication was not given to Noaḥ alone for him to then transmit to the others, the text includes the word *itto* ["with him"] – God addressed all the men together. This explains why the language of God's communication is in the plural. Nevertheless, God only talked to Shem, and Yefet; Ḥam was not worthy of prophecy.

8 many on it." Then God said to Noaḥ and to his sons ḤAMISHI
9 with him: "I – I am about to establish My covenant with you
10 and your descendants after you, and with every living creature
that is with you – the birds, the animals, and all the wild beasts

ABARBANEL

וַיֹּאמֶר אֱלֹהִים אֶל־נֹחַ וְאֶל־בָּנָיו – *Then God said to Noaḥ and to his sons:* It seems to me that the sons of Noaḥ were not entirely convinced or comforted by God's words and blessings. For even though they believed God's guarantee that the animals would fear and not attack them, and despite being pleased with the license to eat meat and not starve, and feeling safe once murder had been outlawed, they were still anxious that a second flood might once again drown all life on the planet. The survivors understood human nature and knew that it was only a matter of time before everybody sinned in his own way. As such they were reluctant to procreate and bring children into a world which could be destroyed at any moment. This is why He who reads all human thoughts felt it prudent to address the men's concerns. And even though Noaḥ's sons were not primed to receive prophecy, through the guidance of their father, and with God's compassion, He prepared them to hear the voice of the Almighty. This is what the verse means when it states: *Then God said to Noaḥ and to his sons*. This represented a new communication, although it was a continuation of the previous speech begun in verse 1. The first message ended [with verse 7], and now God spoke to Noaḥ and his sons together to assure them that there would never again be a flood that inundated the planet.

CLASSIC COMMENTATORS

VERSE 9

RASHI

הִנְנִי – *I am about:* I sympathize with you. Initially Noaḥ was afraid to have children [lest they be wiped out in a future disaster] unless the Holy One, blessed be He, assured him that He would never again destroy the world. And hence God did so. God reinforced this promise by saying: I hereby agree to establish a covenant and to secure it by giving you a sign to confirm the matter.

SFORNO

אֶת־בְּרִיתִי – *My covenant:* I am prepared to forge this covenant with you on condition that you do not shed innocent blood and thereby cause the land to be destroyed again. For the killing of blameless people corrupts the earth itself, as the verse states: *You shall not pollute the land in which you live: blood pollutes the land. And the land can have no atonement for the blood that is shed in it – except through the blood of the one who shed it* (Numbers 35:33). On the other hand, with all other transgressions the perpetrator himself is punished and the soil is unaffected.

VERSE 10

RASHI

חַיַּת הָאָרֶץ אִתְּכֶם – *The wild beasts of earth that are with you:* This refers to the animals that walk with human beings. מִכֹּל יֹצְאֵי הַתֵּבָה – *Everything that left the ark:* The phrase

אִתְּכֶם בָּעוֹף בַּבְּהֵמָה וּבְכָל־חַיַּת הָאָרֶץ אִתְּכֶם מִכֹּל יֹצְאֵי
יא הַתֵּבָה לְכֹל חַיַּת הָאָרֶץ׃ וַהֲקִמֹתִי אֶת־בְּרִיתִי אִתְּכֶם וְלֹא־
יִכָּרֵת כָּל־בָּשָׂר עוֹד מִמֵּי הַמַּבּוּל וְלֹא־יִהְיֶה עוֹד מַבּוּל
יב לְשַׁחֵת הָאָרֶץ׃ וַיֹּאמֶר אֱלֹהִים זֹאת אוֹת־הַבְּרִית אֲשֶׁר־אֲנִי

RASHI *(cont.)*

includes all detested and crawling creatures. **לְכֹל חַיַּת הָאָרֶץ** – *Every living creature on earth:* These final words include the demons. These entities are not within the category of *every living creature that is with you*, for they do not walk with humans.

VERSE 11

RASHI

וַהֲקִמֹתִי – *I will establish:* "I will give a confirmation [*kiyyum*] of my covenant." And what is that confirmation? The sign of the rainbow, as the verses proceed to describe.

ḤIZKUNI

וַהֲקִמֹתִי אֶת־בְּרִיתִי – *I will establish My covenant:* The text repeats the establishment of a covenant [though this has been stated in verse 9] to emphasize that even if people sin God will not release a second flood.

VERSE 12

RASHI

לְדֹרֹת עוֹלָם – *For all generations to come:* The word *ledorot* is written in deficient form [without the letter *vav* after the *resh*] to indicate that not all generations are served by this sign. Indeed, in eras when completely righteous individuals live, the token in the sky is not required [since it is then clear that there is no threat of destruction]. Such was the time of Ḥizkiyahu, king of Yehuda, and the generation of Rabbi Shimon ben Yoḥai.

RAMBAN

זֹאת אוֹת־הַבְּרִית אֲשֶׁר־אֲנִי נֹתֵן – *This is the sign of the covenant I am making:* The implication from this verse is that the phenomenon of the rainbow had not previously been a feature of creation. It was only now that God fashioned something new and arranged for a rainbow to appear in the sky on cloudy days. In explaining the shape of the rainbow, some commentators argue that had the ends of the bow pointed upward the image would have suggested that the heavens were shooting arrows at the earth, as in the verse *He shot His arrows and scattered them; He hurled lightning bolts and routed them* (Psalms 18:15). Instead, God designed the rainbow with the opposite configuration to demonstrate that the heavens are not at war with the land. Indeed, it is customary for soldiers who wish to convey their peaceful intentions to turn their weapons upside down or backward. Furthermore, since the rainbow is pointed away from us, we can see that there is no bowstring with which

of earth that are with you, everything that left the ark, every liv-
11 ing creature on earth. I will establish My covenant with you, that
never again may all life be destroyed by the waters of a flood;
12 never again will there be a flood to destroy the earth." God said,
"This is the sign of the covenant I am making between Me and

RAMBAN *(cont.)*

to shoot any arrows. Now we must accept the explanation provided by the Greeks that it is the sun's light interacting with moist air which produces a rainbow. For we find that when a barrel of water is placed in the sun, the appearance of a rainbow follows. And in fact, the language of the text supports this understanding, since God declares: *I have laid down My bow in the clouds* [9:13, in the past tense] instead of: "I am laying down My bow in the clouds." [This suggests that in fact at God's creation of the world, He first established the interplay between light and water droplets that allows rainbows to appear.] Nevertheless, God does say: *This is the sign of the covenant I am making* [9:12, meaning that although the phenomenon of the rainbow is old, the pact is new]. Furthermore, the term "My bow" proves that the rainbow was something that God had already possessed. We must therefore interpret the verse as God saying: The rainbow which I laid down in the clouds when I formed the world will from this point on serve as the sign of the covenant between Me and you. Whenever I see the bow in the future, I will remember our agreement of peace. Still, the reader might ask how the rainbow can act as a sign. I would refer him to the verse *This mound is a witness, and the pillar is a witness, that I will not go past this mound on your side and that you will not go past this mound and pillar on my side with intent to do harm* (31:52), as well as the verse *Accept these seven lambs from me as testimony that I dug this well* (21:30). For whenever an object is placed between two parties to remind them of a commitment to each other, that thing is called a "sign, while every agreement is referred to as a "covenant." Similarly, when God commands Avraham regarding circumcision, He declares: *You must circumcise the flesh of your foreskin – this shall be the sign of the covenant between Me and you* (17:11). The procedure is a physical mark that the descendants of Avraham have accepted the mission to serve God together. Plus, as I have said, the shape of the rainbow carries a connotation of peace. And hence, whether the rainbow was just then created, or whether it always existed, its adoption as a sign retains the same value.

ABARBANEL

זֹאת אוֹת־הַבְּרִית – *This is the sign of the covenant:* At this point [after verse 7] Noaḥ and his sons felt assured that God would never again send a flood to destroy the world, and so their communication with God came to an end. Note that the men never asked God for a sign to back up His guarantee, for they believed that He would keep His word. But because of His righteousness, God wanted to provide humanity with a true indication for the future. God therefore initiated another conversation with Noaḥ and his sons [starting in verse 8] wherein He discussed the rainbow. Thus the verse states: *God said, "This is the sign*

נֹתֵן בֵּינִי וּבֵינֵיכֶם וּבֵין כָּל־נֶפֶשׁ חַיָּה אֲשֶׁר אִתְּכֶם לְדֹרֹת
יג עוֹלָם: אֶת־קַשְׁתִּי נָתַתִּי בֶּעָנָן וְהָיְתָה לְאוֹת בְּרִית בֵּינִי וּבֵין
יד הָאָרֶץ: וְהָיָה בְּעַנְנִי עָנָן עַל־הָאָרֶץ וְנִרְאֲתָה הַקֶּשֶׁת בֶּעָנָן:
טו וְזָכַרְתִּי אֶת־בְּרִיתִי אֲשֶׁר בֵּינִי וּבֵינֵיכֶם וּבֵין כָּל־נֶפֶשׁ חַיָּה
בְּכָל־בָּשָׂר וְלֹא־יִהְיֶה עוֹד הַמַּיִם לְמַבּוּל לְשַׁחֵת כָּל־בָּשָׂר:
טז וְהָיְתָה הַקֶּשֶׁת בֶּעָנָן וּרְאִיתִיהָ לִזְכֹּר בְּרִית עוֹלָם בֵּין אֱלֹהִים

ABARBANEL *(cont.)*

of the covenant," meaning: I am now establishing a sign to confirm what I have already promised you. And that is the bow that I will lay down in the clouds.... When God gave man the sign of the rainbow, He described this covenant solely to Noaḥ [unlike the previous communication, which was addressed to his sons as well]. For only Noaḥ was prepared to receive prophecy from God time after time; his sons were unable to manage such interaction with God. Although at first the verse states: *God said, "This is the sign of the covenant,"* giving no indication whom God was addressing, the subsequent verse, *So said God to Noaḥ: "This is the sign of the covenant"* (9:17) indicates that the entire substance of this message was conveyed just to Noaḥ.

VERSE 13

IBN EZRA

אֶת־קַשְׁתִּי נָתַתִּי בֶּעָנָן – *I have laid down My bow in the clouds:* For the first time God now placed a rainbow in the sky. The approach of Rav Se'adya Gaon, that this phenomenon had always existed, is incorrect.

ḤIZKUNI

אֶת־קַשְׁתִּי נָתַתִּי בֶּעָנָן – *I have laid down My bow in the clouds:* Said God: This is a highly significant sign, because it represents an image of Me, so to speak. As a later verse describes: *It was like the appearance of a rainbow in the clouds on a rainy day; the radiance around it had that appearance. This was the appearance of the form of the glory of the Lord* (Ezekiel 1:28). Said God: Were I to ever consider destroying humanity when torrents of rain are falling, would I display before you the form of My glory? No, for it is hardly customary for a king to appear before his servants at a time when they are being chastised. Another interpretation: Why did God select the rainbow from among all His available phenomena as a sign to demonstrate His covenant with the world? For a rainbow presents a vision of both fire and water, a spectacle of red and of green. Just as the water remains at the fire's side without extinguishing it. Similarly, the rainbow is a sign that flooding will never again snuff out the world. Another interpretation: When the rainbow is seen in the sky, its hollow faces downward as an indication of peace. For when archers take aim at their target, they draw the

you – and every living creature with you – for all generations
13 to come. I have laid down My bow in the clouds to be the sign
14 of the covenant between Me and the earth. Whenever I bring
15 clouds over the earth and the rainbow appears in the clouds, I
will remember My covenant that binds Me and you and every
living creature of all flesh so that never again will the waters
16 become a flood to destroy all life. The rainbow will be there in
the cloud, and I will see it, remembering the eternal covenant

ḤIZKUNI *(cont.)*

bowstring toward their faces, which causes the bow to face the enemy. But a rainbow in the sky has the side of its string on earth and the curve facing away from us.

VERSE 14

RASHI

בְּעַנְנִי עָנָן – *When I bring clouds:* When I contemplate bringing darkness [Rashi's interpretation of the word *anan*] and destruction to the world.

IBN EZRA

וְהָיָה בְּעַנְנִי עָנָן עַל־הָאָרֶץ – *Whenever I bring clouds over the earth:* If we are to believe the Greeks, who maintain that the rainbow is caused by the rays of the sun, we must conclude that after the flood God intensified the sun's heat [to create this new phenomenon]. This is the correct way to understand this verse.

RAMBAN

וְהָיָה בְּעַנְנִי עָנָן עַל־הָאָרֶץ – *Whenever I bring clouds over the earth:* God here promises that should He should ever hide the light of His face from the earth in response to the sins of its people, and display His attribute of Justice in the clouds, He will remember the covenant with his attribute of Compassion and show mercy on the planet's children.

ḤIZKUNI

וְנִרְאֲתָה הַקֶּשֶׁת בֶּעָנָן – *The rainbow appears in the clouds:* The rainbow will be seen without its accompanying arrows or bowstring as an indication of peace.

VERSE 16

RASHI

בֵּין אֱלֹהִים וּבֵין כָּל־נֶפֶשׁ חַיָּה – *Between God and every living creature:* The covenant has been forged between the celestial attribute of Justice [alluded to in the word *Elohim*] and you. For this verse could have employed the same phrasing as the previous verse and said: "Between Me" [instead of "between *Elohim*"] and every living creature. However, the choice of wording teaches that when the attribute of Justice levels accusations against you and demands that you be destroyed, I will see the sign and remember our agreement.

יז וּבֵין כָּל־נֶפֶשׁ חַיָּה בְּכָל־בָּשָׂר אֲשֶׁר עַל־הָאָרֶץ: וַיֹּאמֶר
אֱלֹהִים אֶל־נֹחַ זֹאת אוֹת־הַבְּרִית אֲשֶׁר הֲקִמֹתִי בֵּינִי וּבֵין
כָּל־בָּשָׂר אֲשֶׁר עַל־הָאָרֶץ:
יח וַיִּהְיוּ בְנֵי־נֹחַ הַיֹּצְאִים מִן־הַתֵּבָה שֵׁם וְחָם וָיָפֶת וְחָם הוּא אֲבִי ח ששי
יט כ כְנָעַן: שְׁלֹשָׁה אֵלֶּה בְּנֵי־נֹחַ וּמֵאֵלֶּה נָפְצָה כָל־הָאָרֶץ: וַיָּחֶל

VERSE 17

RASHI

זֹאת אוֹת־הַבְּרִית – *This is the sign of the covenant:* God showed Noaḥ the rainbow and said to him: This is the sign that I have been talking about.

VERSE 18

RASHI

וְחָם הוּא אֲבִי כְנָעַן – *Ḥam was the father of Kenaan:* Why is this fact pointed out here? The following passage deals with Noaḥ's drunkenness and the sin perpetrated against him by Ḥam. That act in turn leads to Kenaan being cursed. And so, because the lineage of Ḥam has not yet been recorded and the reader has no idea that Kenaan is Ḥam's son [making Noaḥ's outburst in verse 25 inexplicable], the text saw fit to preface the story with the aside that *Ḥam was the father of Kenaan.*

IBN EZRA

וְחָם הוּא אֲבִי כְנָעַן – *Ḥam was the father of Kenaan:* The text equates father and son to teach that they were both wicked, and that Kenaan followed the evil ways of Ḥam. Now our verse mentions Kenaan but not Kush [listed in 10:6 as Ḥam's firstborn] as the son of Ḥam because it was Kenaan who would be cursed [in verse 25]. The Torah includes the following episode to emphasize that all Canaanites – including their daughters – have been cursed since the time of Noaḥ. Hence Avraham cautions his servant: *Swear by the Lord, God of heaven and earth, that you will not take a wife for my son from among the daughters of the Canaanites among whom I live* (24:3). Similarly does Rivka proclaim: *I loathe my life because of these Hittite women. If Yaakov marries a Hittite woman like them, one of the women of the land, why should I go on living?* [27:46; the Hittites were a subset of the Canaanites].

ABARBANEL

שֵׁם וְחָם וָיָפֶת – *Shem, Ḥam, and Yefet:* We cannot escape the straightforward meaning of the text, which is that Shem was Noaḥ's firstborn son. He was followed by Ḥam, while Yefet was the youngest brother. Do not misinterpret the later verse which reads: *Sons were also born to Shem. The older brother of Yefet* [or alternatively, "The brother of the elder Yefet"], *he was the ancestor of all the sons of Ever* (10:21). For it was not Yefet who was elder, but Shem. Furthermore,

between God and every living creature, all flesh upon the
17 earth." So said God to Noaḥ: "This is the sign of the covenant
that I have established between Me and all flesh that is on
earth."
18 Noaḥ's sons who came out from the ark were Shem, Ḥam, and SHISHI
19 Yefet. Ḥam was the father of Kenaan. These three were Noaḥ's
20 sons; and from them all the world branched out. Noaḥ began

ABARBANEL *(cont.)*

when the current chapter states: *Noaḥ woke from his wine and realized what his youngest son had done to him* (9:24), that does not refer to Ḥam [who was Noaḥ's middle son], but to Kenaan who was Ḥam's youngest son, as I will explain presently.... Later, the Torah will list the descendants of Shem last [starting in 10:21] even though he was the oldest son, because the text wished to conclude with the lineage leading up to Avraham, the founder of our nation [since the rest of the book of Genesis focuses on this family].... I have found written in the literature of the nations the claim that after the flood Noaḥ fathered a fourth son. According to that approach, our verse states, *Noaḥ's sons who came out from the ark were Shem, Ḥam, and Yefet*, to distinguish these men from the next son who was born after the family left the ark. This fourth son was called Yoniko, and he was said to be an exceedingly wise man who discovered astrology in the world after the flood. He was able to foretell the future, with his strongest prediction being the reigns of the four kingdoms as prophesied by Daniel. This Yoniko traveled to the land of Eitan with a company of people, where he became a counselor to Nimrod, advising him on how to rule the entire world. Thus were many tales told about Noaḥ's fourth son. Still, since the Torah omits any mention of this person, we would do best to disbelieve that Noaḥ had a fourth child. For the text says nothing about Yoniko's inheritance among his brothers, while the other sources do not include any information about his sons, grandsons, or any other descendants. This leads me to surmise that the traditions that tell of him are actually concerned with one of Noaḥ's grandsons who is listed in the Torah text. Yoniko might be another name for Ever [introduced in 11:15] who was the wisest man in his generation. And since as a child he was educated by Noaḥ and was a companion to that patriarch in his old age, the tradition arose that this descendant was in fact Noaḥ's son. On occasion one's descendant can be labeled a son [as the Talmud in tractate Yevamot 62b asserts]. The name Yoniko derives from the word *yonek* ["to suckle"], for as a child he soaked up wisdom from Noaḥ and knowledge from his father Shem.

VERSE 20

RASHI

וַיָּחֶל – *Began:* The verb *vayaḥel* means that Noaḥ made himself profane [*ḥullin*, by first planting a vineyard], for he should have begun his agricultural efforts with a different type of crop. **אִישׁ הָאֲדָמָה** – *A man of the land:* The term *ish* connotes "master" of the land, as in the phrase *Naomi's husband [ish]* (Ruth 1:3). **וַיִּטַּע כָּרֶם** – *And he planted a vineyard:* When Noaḥ first entered the ark he took with him vine cuttings and fig shoots.

כא נֹחַ אִישׁ הָאֲדָמָה וַיִּטַּע כָּרֶם: וַיֵּשְׁתְּ מִן־הַיַּיִן וַיִּשְׁכָּר וַיִּתְגַּל
כב בְּתוֹךְ אָהֳלֹה: וַיַּרְא חָם אֲבִי כְנַעַן אֵת עֶרְוַת אָבִיו וַיַּגֵּד

IBN EZRA

אִישׁ הָאֲדָמָה – *A man of the land:* Noaḥ became a devoted farmer, and successful agriculture requires great wisdom. Although the Sages maintain that Noaḥ produced and drank his wine on the same day that he planted the vineyard, that should not be taken literally. Rather, there is a secret significance behind the statement. Similarly, when the verse states: *And she became pregnant and gave birth to a son* (Exodus 2:2), it does not mean that the entire process occurred on the same day [despite the Sages' statements to that effect].

BEKHOR SHOR

אִישׁ הָאֲדָמָה – *A man of the land:* It was on Noaḥ's behalf that the land began to yield its bounty, for the lineage of Kayin [whose act cursed the land] had already died out.

RAMBAN

אִישׁ הָאֲדָמָה – *A man of the land:* The phrase can be contrasted to the term "townsman" [*ish ha'ir*] in the verse *All the townsmen, the men of Sedom...* (19:4), meaning that Noaḥ lived in the countryside. He constructed no town or a state to which he could be linked. Alternatively, Noaḥ was so called because he devoted himself to working the land – sowing and planting, once he saw how desolate the landscape was.

ABARBANEL

וַיָּחֶל נֹחַ אִישׁ הָאֲדָמָה – *Noaḥ began to be a man of the land:* After the flood, and because of his ordeal, Noaḥ was sick of living. This also explains why he decided to create and drink wine – he could no longer bear the sight of water and refused to drink it. Now when our Sages claim that Noaḥ produced and drank the wine on the same day that he planted the vineyard, they are emphasizing that the wine was not an incidental consequence of Noaḥ's vine planting. Rather, Noaḥ's plan all along was to make wine that he could drink – that is what he set out to do.

VERSE 21

BEKHOR SHOR

וַיִּתְגַּל בְּתוֹךְ אָהֳלֹה – *And lay uncovered in his tent:* Somebody else uncovered Noaḥ, although the text does not state directly who that was. However, the curse of Noaḥ implies that it was Kenaan.

VERSE 22

RASHI

וַיַּרְא חָם אֲבִי כְנַעַן – *Ḥam, father of Kenaan, saw:* [Since it was Ḥam who acted inappropriately here, why is the name of his son mentioned at all?] Some of our Sages claim that it was Kenaan who saw his grandfather's nakedness and told his father about it. This explains why

21 to be a man of the land, and he planted a vineyard. He drank
some of the wine, became drunk, and lay uncovered in his tent.
22 Ḥam, father of Kenaan, saw his father's nakedness and told his

RASHI *(cont.)*

Kenaan appears in this verse, and why Noaḥ curses him. וַיַּרְא...אֵת עֶרְוַת אָבִיו – *Saw his father's nakedness:* According to one approach, Ḥam castrated his father, while another opinion claims that he sodomized him.

RAMBAN

וַיַּרְא...אֵת עֶרְוַת אָבִיו – *Saw his father's nakedness:* Ḥam's transgression in this incident was characterized by the son's disrespect for his father. Instead of covering up his father when he saw him lying naked, Ḥam ran off to report what he had seen to his brothers. Furthermore, Ḥam despicably told Shem and Yefet about Noaḥ's shame in front of other people so as to mock his father. This is the significance of the adverb "outside" in verse 22. Indeed, Onkelos translates the word as meaning "in the market." When Noaḥ woke from his drunkenness, he realized what Ḥam *had done to him* by revealing his embarrassment in public.

ABARBANEL

וַיַּרְא חָם אֲבִי כְנַעַן – *Ḥam, father of Kenaan, saw:* It is possible that it was Kenaan who uncovered Noaḥ's nakedness, whereupon both he and his father Ḥam saw Noaḥ lying naked in his tent. Ḥam's sin was that he was not sensitive to his father's dishonor, and did not bother to cover him up. After he undressed Noaḥ, Kenaan continued his violation by rushing off to laugh at his grandfather in front of his brothers, meaning the other sons of Ḥam. Thus, when the verse states: *Ḥam, father of Kenaan, saw his father's nakedness*, that refers to Ḥam's guilt in not covering Noaḥ, whereas the end of the verse, *And told his two brothers who were outside* returns to describe Kenaan's indiscretion. And even though Kenaan actually had three brothers – Kush, Mitzrayim, and Put [as listed in 10:6], Kenaan only found two of them available to hear him boast of his deed. When word of what Kenaan had done reached Shem and Yefet, they did what had to be done to restore Noaḥ's dignity, covering up his nakedness. And since Shem took the initiative in this action, and Yefet followed his lead, the verse presents the act in the singular: *Shem and Yefet then took [vayikkaḥ, instead of the plural vayikḥu]*. This analysis explains why Noaḥ cursed Kenaan: It was either because he uncovered him in the first place, or because he went and talked about Noaḥ's shame with the rest of the family in order to disparage him. But Noaḥ does not actually curse Ḥam, because his transgression was one of passive neglect rather than one of active harm.... Another reason that the Torah includes this whole episode is to demonstrate the righteousness of God, who had previously promised: *Never again will I curse the land because of man* (8:21). Now as I have previously explained, the reason that God made such a guarantee was His knowledge that all the families of humanity would not in the future collaborate in sinful ventures as they had before the flood. For the three sons of Noaḥ now became the patriarchs of a new human race as the world's people spread out across the earth. Consider the simple matter of Noaḥ's drunkenness – the three sons could not even agree on the appropriate response to

כג לִשְׁנֵי־אֶחָיו בַּחוּץ׃ וַיִּקַּח שֵׁם וָיֶפֶת אֶת־הַשִּׂמְלָה וַיָּשִׂימוּ
עַל־שְׁכֶם שְׁנֵיהֶם וַיֵּלְכוּ אֲחֹרַנִּית וַיְכַסּוּ אֵת עֶרְוַת אֲבִיהֶם
כד וּפְנֵיהֶם אֲחֹרַנִּית וְעֶרְוַת אֲבִיהֶם לֹא רָאוּ׃ וַיִּיקֶץ נֹחַ מִיֵּינוֹ
כה וַיֵּדַע אֵת אֲשֶׁר־עָשָׂה לוֹ בְּנוֹ הַקָּטָן׃ וַיֹּאמֶר אָרוּר כְּנָעַן

ABARBANEL *(cont.)*

that incident! For although Ḥam and his son Kenaan sinned in the matter, Shem and Yefet acted differently and charitably toward their father. The story also explains why the descendants of Kenaan are to be perpetually enslaved and would eventually forfeit their land to our patriarch Avraham. A further lesson to emerge from this tale is how careful a person should be to avoid intoxication. Our original ancestor, Adam, who was fashioned by the hand of God, was the first person to sin by eating. And even though Noaḥ was a righteous man who saved all life on earth from disappearing, he sinned through drink. His behavior led to his own shame and brought a curse on many of his descendants.

VERSE 23

RASHI

וַיִּקַּח שֵׁם וָיֶפֶת – *Shem and Yefet then took:* The verse does not use the plural form *vayikḥu* but the singular *vayikkaḥ* to teach that it was Shem who made more of an effort to protect his father's honor than did Yefet. It was because of this devotion that Shem's descendants [that is, the people of Israel] were privileged to wear garments with fringes, whereas, the offspring of Yefet were rewarded with a burial place, as the verse states: *And it will happen on that day: I will grant Gog a burial-place there in Israel* [Ezekiel 39:11. In 10:2 Magog is listed as a son of Yefet, while Gog is the king of Magog]. Meanwhile, Ḥam who disgraced his father will be punished, as the verse states regarding his descendants: *Just so will it be when the king of Assyria leads away the captives of Egypt, the exiles of Kush* [Isaiah 20:4; Kush is named as a son of Ḥam in 10:6]. **וּפְנֵיהֶם אֲחֹרַנִּית** – *Averting their faces:* Why does the verse repeat the description *ufneihem aḥorannit*, literally, "they turned their faces backward," after stating, *they walked backward*? We learn from here that when they approached their father, they were forced to turn around in order to cover him up. They then once again turned their faces backward [away from their father so as not to look at him in his state of shame].

VERSE 24

RASHI

בְּנוֹ הַקָּטָן – *His youngest son:* The adjective *hakatan* describes Ḥam as Noaḥ's rejected and despised son, as in the verse *Look, I have made you small [katon] among nations, scorned by humanity* (Jeremiah 49:15 and Obadiah 1:2).

IBN EZRA

וַיִּיקֶץ נֹחַ מִיֵּינוֹ – *Noaḥ woke from his wine:* The Torah does not clearly state what was done to Noaḥ, only that Kenaan was the perpetrator. What seems to have happened is that Ḥam

23 two brothers who were outside. Shem and Yefet then took a
cloak and put it over both their shoulders. They walked backward and covered their father's nakedness, averting their faces
24 so as not to see the nakedness of their father. Noaḥ woke from
his wine and realized what his youngest son had done to him.
25 He said, "Cursed be Kenaan! The lowest of slaves shall he be

IBN EZRA *(cont.)*

saw his father's nakedness and did not cover him up, as his brothers subsequently did. Instead, Ḥam reported Noaḥ's condition. Kenaan heard about it and did something unspecified to his grandfather.

RABBEINU BAḤYA

וַיֵּדַע אֵת אֲשֶׁר־עָשָׂה לוֹ בְּנוֹ הַקָּטָן – *And realized what his youngest son had done to him:* Ḥam was Noaḥ's youngest son. Now why did Noaḥ curse Kenaan instead of Ḥam, who was the culprit in this episode? There are two reasons why Noaḥ did not curse Ḥam. Firstly, once the Holy One, blessed be He, had blessed Ḥam, as the verse states: *Then God blessed Noaḥ and his sons* (9:1), it was impossible for the man to be cursed directly by his father. Secondly, had Noaḥ cursed Ḥam, that would have only affected Ḥam himself and not his descendants [for the sons he had already existed and were no longer a part of him]. This is why Noaḥ wished to curse Kenaan, who was Ḥam's firstborn son. The power of the curse extended to any future children whom Kenaan would father. As for the verse *Ḥam's sons were Kush, Mitzrayim, Put, and Kenaan* (10:6) which seems to present Kenaan as Ḥam's youngest son, that reflects Kenaan's fall in status after he was cursed; henceforth all of his brothers would be considered superior to him. That is why Kenaan is listed last in that verse. Support for my contention that Kenaan was Ḥam's oldest son comes from the verse *Ḥam, father of Kenaan, saw* (9:22), a description which the text had already provided earlier when it said: *Ḥam was the father of Kenaan* (9:18). Thus it is clear that at the time of this incident Ḥam had no other children save Kenaan, and hence he was the firstborn.

VERSE 25

RASHI

אָרוּר כְּנָעַן – *Cursed be Kenaan:* Said Noaḥ to Ḥam: Because you castrated me and robbed me of the opportunity to father a fourth son who would have served me, it is your fourth son [Kenaan – see 10:6] who is now cursed and destined to serve the descendants of those better men [Shem and Yefet]. For it is because of you that they are now compelled to serve me from now on. Now what drove Ḥam to castrate his father? Said Ḥam to his brothers: You know, the first man had two sons and one of them murdered the other in order to inherit the entire world. Now look – our father already has three sons, and he is intent on having a fourth!

RABBEINU BAḤYA

עֶבֶד עֲבָדִים יִהְיֶה לְאֶחָיו – *The lowest of slaves shall he be to his brothers:* Most straightforwardly, this curse represents a measure for measure response to Ḥam's embarrassment of

כו עֶבֶד עֲבָדִים יִהְיֶה לְאֶחָיו: וַיֹּאמֶר בָּרוּךְ יהוה אֱלֹהֵי שֵׁם
כז וִיהִי כְנַעַן עֶבֶד לָמוֹ: יַפְתְּ אֱלֹהִים לְיֶפֶת וְיִשְׁכֹּן בְּאָהֳלֵי־שֵׁם
כח וִיהִי כְנַעַן עֶבֶד לָמוֹ: וַיְחִי־נֹחַ אַחַר הַמַּבּוּל שְׁלֹשׁ מֵאוֹת
כט שָׁנָה וַחֲמִשִּׁים שָׁנָה: וַיְהִי כָּל־יְמֵי־נֹחַ תְּשַׁע מֵאוֹת שָׁנָה
וַחֲמִשִּׁים שָׁנָה וַיָּמֹת:
י א וְאֵלֶּה תּוֹלְדֹת בְּנֵי־נֹחַ שֵׁם חָם וָיָפֶת וַיִּוָּלְדוּ לָהֶם בָּנִים אַחַר
ב הַמַּבּוּל: בְּנֵי יֶפֶת גֹּמֶר וּמָגוֹג וּמָדַי וְיָוָן וְתֻבָל וּמֶשֶׁךְ וְתִירָס:

RABBEINU BAḤYA *(cont.)*

his father. Ḥam disgraced Noaḥ by looking at his nakedness; not only did he fail to extend himself to cover up his father's shame, but he proceeded to ridicule him by reporting to his brothers what he had seen. And it is commonly known that a slave lives in a state of humiliation. Hence Noaḥ cursed Kenaan, decreeing that he should be a servant for his whole life, as a result of the abasement Ḥam had caused Noaḥ.

VERSE 26

RASHI

בָּרוּךְ יהוה אֱלֹהֵי שֵׁם – *Blessed be the* L*ORD*, *God of Shem:* Blessed be the LORD, who will preserve His promise to the descendants of Shem [Israel] and give them the land of Canaan.

IBN EZRA

בָּרוּךְ יהוה אֱלֹהֵי שֵׁם – *Blessed be the* L*ORD*, *God of Shem:* The sense of the verse is: It is our obligation to express gratitude to the LORD. who is the God of Shem – it is He who will make Kenaan His own slave and that of Shem. The meaning of the curse is that God will force Kenaan to serve Shem. **וִיהִי כְנַעַן עֶבֶד לָמוֹ** – *Kenaan shall be his slave:* Kenaan is to be a servant to Shem, to Yefet, and to Kenaan's own brothers. Hence Kenaan was fated to be a slave for the entire world, since these people were the progenitors of humanity. The fulfillment of this curse and blessing would only come many years after the flood.

BEKHOR SHOR

בָּרוּךְ יהוה אֱלֹהֵי שֵׁם – *Blessed be the* L*ORD*, *God of Shem:* Noaḥ meant: Blessed be the Holy One, blessed be He, who is Shem's master and God. That is, Shem would become so high in rank that above him there would be only the LORD, his God. And thus, because Noaḥ cursed others with being slaves, he emphasizes that this son of his would be forever free. Shem's blessing is appropriate to his name, for "Shem" is the name of the Holy One, blessed be He, as the verse states: *Upon it is the Name [shem] of the* L*ORD of Hosts Enthroned upon the Cherubim* (II Samuel 6:2).

VERSE 27

RASHI

יַפְתְּ אֱלֹהִים לְיֶפֶת – *May God enlarge Yefet:* The Targum renders the verb *yaft* as *yaftei* ["to expand"] – God will extend Yefet's domain. **וְיִשְׁכֹּן בְּאָהֳלֵי־שֵׁם** – *And let him dwell in the*

26 to his brothers." Then he said, "Blessed be the LORD, God of
27 Shem; Kenaan shall be his slave. May God enlarge Yefet, and let
28 him dwell in the tents of Shem; Kenaan shall be his slave." After
29 the flood Noaḥ lived three hundred and fifty years. Noaḥ lived a
total of nine hundred and fifty years, and he died.
10 1 These are the descendants of Noaḥ's sons, Shem, Ḥam, and
2 Yefet; after the flood, children were born to them. Yefet's sons

RASHI *(cont.)*

tents of Shem: God's Divine Presence will rest among Israel. According to the Sages [the entire verse refers to Shem] and this clause means that although God will indeed enlarge Yefet's territory [even so, God will only dwell within Israel's midst.] For when Cyrus, King of Persia, who was a descendant of Yefet [see 10:2], built the Second Temple, God's Divine Presence did not dwell there as it had in the First Temple that Shlomo constructed. And Shlomo of course was a descendant of Shem. **וִיהִי כְנַעַן עֶבֶד** – *Kenaan shall be his slave:* Even if the descendants of Shem are exiled from their land, the sons of Kenaan will still be sold to them as slaves.

IBN EZRA

וְיִשְׁכֹּן בְּאָהֳלֵי־שֵׁם – *And let him dwell in the tents of Shem:* This is actually a blessing for Shem. For the meaning of the text is: "May God live in the tents of Shem." In the previous verse Noaḥ blessed God [and it is He who is the subject of the verb "dwell" here].

VERSE 29

ḤIZKUNI

תְּשַׁע מֵאוֹת שָׁנָה וַחֲמִשִּׁים שָׁנָה – *Nine hundred and fifty years:* The astute reader will note that the flood began *In the six hundredth year of Noaḥ's life* (7:11), whereas the text subsequently states that *after the flood Noaḥ lived three hundred and fifty years*. But the sum of Noaḥ's years seem to be missing a year [that is, the year of the flood itself!] Hence we must conclude that the total number of nine hundred and fifty years does not include the year that Noaḥ spent in the ark.

CHAPTER 10, VERSE 1

RAMBAN

וַיִּוָּלְדוּ לָהֶם בָּנִים אַחַר הַמַּבּוּל – *After the flood, children were born to them:* This verse alludes to the following point. Even though these men could have had children before the flood – since it was usual in those times for men of sixty to father children – Shem, Ḥam, and Yefet only produced sons of their own when they were past the age of one hundred. God prevented them from procreating before the deluge lest their offspring be killed in the catastrophe. Alternatively, had Noaḥ's grandchildren been born before the flood, that would have meant more people whom he had to save.

VERSE 2

RASHI

וְתִירָס – *And Tiras:* This is Persia.

ג ד וּבְנֵי גֹּמֶר אַשְׁכְּנַז וְרִיפַת וְתֹגַרְמָה: וּבְנֵי יָוָן אֱלִישָׁה וְתַרְשִׁישׁ
ה כִּתִּים וְדֹדָנִים: מֵאֵלֶּה נִפְרְדוּ אִיֵּי הַגּוֹיִם בְּאַרְצֹתָם אִישׁ
ו לִלְשֹׁנוֹ לְמִשְׁפְּחֹתָם בְּגוֹיֵהֶם: וּבְנֵי חָם כּוּשׁ וּמִצְרַיִם וּפוּט
ז וּכְנָעַן: וּבְנֵי כוּשׁ סְבָא וַחֲוִילָה וְסַבְתָּה וְרַעְמָה וְסַבְתְּכָא וּבְנֵי
ח רַעְמָה שְׁבָא וּדְדָן: וְכוּשׁ יָלַד אֶת־נִמְרֹד הוּא הֵחֵל לִהְיוֹת

RAMBAN

בְּנֵי יֶפֶת גֹּמֶר וגו׳ – *Yefet's sons were Gomer etc.:* Yefet's sons are listed first because he was the oldest of Noaḥ's sons. Ḥam's progeny are presented next [starting in 10:6, even though he was the youngest according to Ramban], because the text wished to juxtapose the lineage of Shem with the developed account of Avraham's family.

ḤIZKUNI

בְּנֵי יֶפֶת גֹּמֶר וגו׳ – *Yefet's sons were Gomer etc.:* [The text lists the sons of Gomer and Yavan], but ignores the descendants of *Magog, Madai, Tuval, Meshekh, and Tiras* because multiple heads of nations did not emerge from these men; each produced only a single family. The same may be said regarding Ḥam's son Put [whose sons are not mentioned, in contrast to those of his brothers Kush, Mitzrayim, and Kenaan], and Shem's sons Elam, Ashur, and Lud [whereas the text records the names of Arpakhshad's and Aram's sons].

VERSE 5

RAMBAN

אִיֵּי הַגּוֹיִם – *The seagoing nations:* [Literally, "the nations' islands."] The children of Yefet live on islands, each descendant dwelling in a different area, separated by water and distance from the others. Such was the blessing bestowed upon them by their ancestor, who said: *May God enlarge Yefet* (9:27), meaning that they should spread across the vastness of the earth. In contrast to their cousins, the people of Ḥam all remained close to each other, in neighboring countries. Thus we read: *The Canaanite borders were from Sidon toward Gerar… with their lands and their nations* (10:19–20). The descendants of Shem enjoyed a similar arrangement. The purpose of these lists of names is to inform the reader that Avraham descended from Shem, and that the patriarch was granted the land originally settled by Ḥam's children as a result of the sins of their ancestors. Furthermore, the text lists the progeny of Yefet and describes the dispersal of humanity [in the next chapter] in order to explain the existence of multiple languages and the fact that humanity is spread across the far reaches of the earth – a reality that developed relatively soon after the first man was created. An additional message from this chapter is the demonstration of God's promise to Noaḥ that He would not destroy humankind again. Now in his *Guide of the Perplexed* [3:50], the Rambam writes that the Torah's account of human genealogy is evidence that the world was created [and did not always exist]. And he is correct, for Avraham must have related to his descendants the story of Noaḥ and the flood, having heard about it

were Gomer, Magog, Madai, Yavan, Tuval, Meshekh, and Tiras.
3 4 Gomer's sons were Ashkenaz, Rifat, and Togarma. Yavan's sons
5 were Elisha, Tarshish, Kitim, and Dodanim. From these the
seagoing nations spread out to their territories, each with its
6 own language, by their clans and their nations. Ḥam's sons were
7 Kush, Mitzrayim, Put, and Kenaan. Kush's sons were Seva,
Ḥavila, Savta, Raama, and Savtekha. Raama's sons were Sheva
8 and Dedan. Kush was the father of Nimrod, the first mighty

RAMBAN *(cont.)*

from witnesses to the event [which is how the account reached us]. Additionally, Avraham was recipient of a direct line of tradition of witnesses to the creation of the world. For Noaḥ knew his father, who had known Adam, while Yitzḥak and Yaakov saw Shem, who was himself a survivor of the flood. Yaakov related the episode to his children and all those who went down to Egypt, as well as to Pharaoh and that entire generation. Thus the people who live in every era always know their own history at least four or five generations back.

VERSE 7

RAMBAN

וּבְנֵי כוּשׁ סְבָא וַחֲוִילָה – *Kush's sons were Seva, Ḥavila:* Each of these men founded his own nation, while Raama was the father of two peoples [Sheva and Dedan]. Nimrod, on the other hand, did not give rise a nation, which is why the text then states: *Kush was the father of Nimrod* (10:8), separate from all the other sons. Ḥam's son Put developed into a single group rather than multiple nations as did his cousins, the descendants of Mitzrayim and Kenaan. This is why the latter two are further developed [in verses 13–14, and 15–18 respectively], but Put is not.

VERSE 8

RASHI

הוּא הֵחֵל לִהְיוֹת גִּבֹּר – *He was the first mighty warrior:* Nimrod led all of humanity in rebellion [*lehamrid*, evoking *Nimrod*] against the Holy One, blessed be He. For it was he who suggested that they construct the Tower of Babel.

BEKHOR SHOR

הוּא הֵחֵל לִהְיוֹת גִּבֹּר בָּאָרֶץ – *The first mighty warrior on earth:* Nimrod was the first mighty warrior after the flood, whereas before the deluge there were plenty of powerful fighters. These were the strongmen who robbed the weak and were otherwise violent. And this is why God drowned humanity in the first place. In the postdiluvian world, Nimrod began to rebel against God, which is the sense of the phrase "before the Lord." For even though he knew that the Holy One, blessed be He, had punished humankind for their malevolence in the past, he did not care, nor was he cowed before God. Hence the origin of the criticism people level at brazen thugs: So-and-so is like Nimrod who refused to heed God's rebuke, and insists on abusing others.

ט גִּבֹּר בָּאָרֶץ: הוּא־הָיָה גִבֹּר־צַיִד לִפְנֵי יְהוָה עַל־כֵּן יֵאָמַר
י כְּנִמְרֹד גִּבּוֹר צַיִד לִפְנֵי יְהוָה: וַתְּהִי רֵאשִׁית מַמְלַכְתּוֹ בָּבֶל
יא וְאֶרֶךְ וְאַכַּד וְכַלְנֵה בְּאֶרֶץ שִׁנְעָר: מִן־הָאָרֶץ הַהִוא יָצָא
יב אַשּׁוּר וַיִּבֶן אֶת־נִינְוֵה וְאֶת־רְחֹבֹת עִיר וְאֶת־כָּלַח: וְאֶת־
יג רֶסֶן בֵּין נִינְוֵה וּבֵין כָּלַח הִוא הָעִיר הַגְּדֹלָה: וּמִצְרַיִם יָלַד

RAMBAN

הוּא הֵחֵל לִהְיוֹת גִּבֹּר בָּאָרֶץ – *The first mighty warrior on earth:* In my opinion Nimrod was the first person to use force to dominate other people; he was the world's first king. Before Nimrod came along, the world suffered no wars, nor had humanity invented the institution of monarchy. Babylonia was the first region that Nimrod subdued, compelling them to appoint him as their leader. From there the tyrant expanded to Assyria, where he again exercised his power and grew ever stronger. Nimrod used his might to construct fortified cities. This is described in the subsequent verse which states: *His kingdom began with Babylon, Erekh, Akad, and Kalneh in the land of Shinar* (10:10).

ABARBANEL

הוּא הֵחֵל לִהְיוֹת גִּבֹּר בָּאָרֶץ – *The first mighty warrior on earth:* Nimrod was humanity's first overlord.

VERSE 9

RASHI

גִּבֹּר־צַיִד – *A mighty hunter:* This man captured men's imagination with his words, and misled them in revolt against God. **לִפְנֵי יהוה** – *Before the Lord:* It was Nimrod's intention to provoke God to His face. **עַל־כֵּן יֵאָמַר** – *Which is why people still say:* Regarding somebody who brazenly sins, and despite recognizing His Master means to rebel against Him, people say: This man is like Nimrod who was a mighty hunter.

RASHBAM

לִפְנֵי יהוה – *Before the Lord:* This is another way of saying that Nimrod was the toughest man in the world. It is similar to the verse *Nineveh was an immensely* [literally, "to God"] *great city, three days' walk across* (Jonah 3:3), meaning that in all of God's world there was no bigger city than Nineveh.

IBN EZRA

נִמְרֹד – *Nimrod:* In cases where the Torah does not explicate people's names, the reader should not try to determine their meaning. [See Rashi on verse 8.] Nimrod was the first man to exercise dominance over the animals for he was a powerful hunter. **לִפְנֵי יהוה** – *Before the Lord:* Nimrod built altars upon which he sacrificed as burnt offerings to God those animals he caught. Such is the straightforward meaning of the text, although the Midrash takes a different approach.

9 warrior on earth. He was a mighty hunter before the LORD,
which is why people still say, "Like Nimrod, a mighty hunter
10 before the LORD." His kingdom began with Babylon, Erekh,
11 Akad, and Kalneh in the land of Shinar. From that land, Ashur
12 went out and built Nineveh, Reḥovot Ir, Kalaḥ, and Resen
13 between Nineveh and Kalaḥ; that is the great city. Mitzrayim

IBN EZRA

עַל־כֵּן יֵאָמַר – *Which is why people still say:* This was a popular proverb even in Moshe's time. [That is, the adverb "today" refers to Moshe's era, when the Torah was written.]

VERSE 11

RASHI

מִן־הָאָרֶץ – *From that land:* When Ashur saw that his sons were listening to Nimrod's advice by agreeing to rebel against God and build the tower, he moved away from them.

IBN EZRA

מִן הָאָרֶץ – *From that land:* Ashur was the son of Yefet. Nimrod's rise to power took place after the dispersal of the builders of the Tower of Babel, whereupon Nimrod seized power in that locale. Hence Nimrod was the first king in Babylon. According to the history book Seder Olam, Nimrod ruled over the seventy men who constructed the tower, and it was during his reign that the dispersal took place.

VERSE 12

ḤIZKUNI

וְאֶת־רֶסֶן בֵּין נִינְוֵה וּבֵין כָּלַח – *And Resen between Nineveh and Kalaḥ:* The Midrash poses the following question: Why did the Holy One, blessed be He, send a prophet [Yona] to rebuke the people of Nineveh, whereas He did not do so for other [gentile] states? This was due to the merit of Ashur, who was the righteous founder of the city, as the verse states: *From that land, Ashur went out and built Nineveh.* This refers to Ashur's breach with the masses who built the Tower of Babel. He refused to support the enterprise and moved away from society [to found his own city]. Nevertheless, in the end *Assyria [Ashur], too, joined them* [Psalms 83:9, i.e., in fighting against Israel], because he too became corrupt.

VERSE 13

RASHI

לְהָבִים – *Lehavim:* These people were so called because their faces resembled flames [*lehavim*, in their color].

IBN EZRA

וּמִצְרַיִם יָלַד אֶת־לוּדִים – *Mitzrayim fathered the Ludim:* [It is unclear whether *Ludim* is a personal name, the name of a group, or something else. Ibn Ezra proposes:] I believe that each of the names on this list refers to a country peopled by a distinct family group.

יד אֶת־לוּדִ֧ים וְאֶת־עֲנָמִ֛ים וְאֶת־לְהָבִ֖ים וְאֶת־נַפְתֻּחִֽים: וְאֶת־
פַּתְרֻסִ֞ים וְאֶת־כַּסְלֻחִ֗ים אֲשֶׁ֨ר יָצְא֥וּ מִשָּׁ֛ם פְּלִשְׁתִּ֖ים וְאֶת־
טו כַּפְתֹּרִֽים: וּכְנַ֗עַן יָלַ֛ד אֶת־צִידֹ֥ן בְּכֹר֖וֹ וְאֶת־חֵֽת:
טז וְאֶת־הַיְבוּסִי֙ וְאֶת־הָ֣אֱמֹרִ֔י וְאֵ֖ת הַגִּרְגָּשִֽׁי: וְאֶת־הַחִוִּ֥י וְאֶת־

IBN EZRA *(cont.)*

My support for this interpretation comes from the phrase "From where the Philistines came forth," [in verse 14] which alludes to a place [and not to a person; note that the translation of that verse in this edition differs].

RAMBAN

וּמִצְרַיִם יָלַד אֶת־לוּדִים – *Mitzrayim fathered the Ludim:* The Torah reports the lineage of Egypt [*Mitzrayim*] but does mention its location as it does with other peoples. For example, with regard to Yefet's descendants, the text states above: *From these the seagoing nations spread out to their territories* (10:5); and the sons of Kush are associated with the lands of Shinar (10:10) and Ashur (10:11); and the verse details the borders where the descendants of Kenaan lived [in 10:19], as does a later verse with regard to the sons of Shem [in 10:30]. The reason the text does not go into the details of Mitzrayim's homelands is that the land of Egypt was well-known for having been named after this person. All of his progeny lived in the vicinity of Egypt, and their lands too were named after them.

VERSE 14

RASHI

וְאֶת־פַּתְרֻסִים וְאֶת־כַּסְלֻחִים אֲשֶׁר יָצְאוּ מִשָּׁם פְּלִשְׁתִּים – *Patrusim, Kasluḥim – from whom the Philistines descended:* [The Hebrew phrasing gives the impression that] the Philistines descended from both of these peoples. For the Patrusim and Kasluḥim would sleep with each other's wives. The Philistines were born of these women [and their paternity was uncertain].

VERSE 15

RASHBAM

וּכְנַעַן יָלַד אֶת־צִידֹן – *Kenaan fathered Tzidon:* The Torah does not develop the family of Put. [Although Ham had four sons, as listed in verse 6, only the descendants of Kush, Mitzrayim, and Kenaan are presented.] Our Sages explain this lacuna as follows: We might have thought that the family of Put became assimilated into those of his brothers, had not a later verse referred to *Kush and Put and Lud* (Ezekiel 30:5). Rabbi Yosef Kara asked Rabbi Shmuel: Considering that Put's progeny were not absorbed into the rest of his family, why does the Torah not state Put's descendants? The other answered: This passage lists seventy descendants of Noah's sons, and it is from here that we learn that the world is populated by seventy nations. For the text states: *From these the seagoing nations spread out to their territories* (10:5). But Put and his sons represented just a single nation. Had the Torah stated: *And Put fathered so-and-so and so-and-so*, it would have seemed that multiple nations descended from him. And this would have raised the number of human groups and

14 fathered the Ludim, Anamim, Lehavim and Naftuḥim, Patrusim,
Kasluḥim – from whom the Philistines descended – and the Kaf-
15 torim. Kenaan fathered Tzidon, his firstborn, and Ḥet,
16 17 and the Jebusites, Amorites, and Girgashites, the Hivites, Arkites,

RASHBAM *(cont.)*

tongues beyond the accepted total of seventy. Instead, Put's sons remained their own family and hence are not listed here.

RAMBAN

וּכְנַעַן יָלַד – *Kenaan fathered:* These were the ten nations which descended from Kenaan and whose lands were eventually given to our patriarch Avraham. Since all Kenaan's progeny were made slaves for all time [by Noaḥ's curse], they were compelled to give their land to Avraham's children. Most of the names that appear here were changed in the time of Avraham; the appellations provided in our passage were those given to the sons by their father when they were born. Once they spread out to their own lands to form distinct nations, they began to be called by different names. These groups may have even adopted for themselves the names of the locations where they settled. And so, when God later described the gift of land that He was bestowing upon Avraham, He used the new names that the ten nations had taken by that time. As evidence, we can see that although the Hivites are listed here [in verse 17], that name is not mentioned among the peoples whom Avraham's descendants would dispossess [in God's promise of 15:19–21]. And even so, we know that the Hivites did indeed live in the land of Canaan, since they are included later in God's prediction to Israel, which speaks of *Hittites, Girgashites, Amorites, Canaanites, Perizzites, Hivites, and Jebusites* (Deuteronomy 7:1). In fact, the Hivites are included on every such list in the Torah. In the statement that God makes to Avraham, the Canaanites appear as a distinct group [in 15:21] along with the names of the nations that descended from Kenaan. On the other hand, that text mentions only ten nations [in contrast to the eleven names in the present passage, many of them different]. This is because one of Kenaan's sons did not achieve the greatness that his brothers did, and so that son was combined with his brother [the Hivites] to be named after their father [as Canaanites]. It seems that this other brother was Tzidon, Kenaan's firstborn son – it was his children who were subsequently referred to simply as the "Canaanites," along with his brother who also did not amount to a real nation. [Hence the list of eleven individuals in our text is condensed into the ten somewhat altered names appearing in chapter 15, with Tzidon and Hivites becoming one group.] The reader should know that the land of Canaan with its borders was designated for the people of Israel from the time they became a nation, as a later verse states: *When the Highest gave nations their heritage, when He divided humankind, He fixed the boundaries of peoples by the number of Israel's sons* (Deuteronomy 32:8). However, when the earth's people were dispersed, the Holy One, blessed be He, temporarily granted the territory to Kenaan, since he had become a slave, in order to be custodian of the area on behalf of Israel. This may be compared to a wealthy person who deposits the riches intended for his son to a servant for safekeeping. When the son comes of age, he will inherit both the estate and the slave.

יח הָעַרְקִי וְאֶת־הַסִּינִי׃ וְאֶת־הָאַרְוָדִי וְאֶת־הַצְּמָרִי וְאֶת־
יט הַחֲמָתִי וְאַחַר נָפֹצוּ מִשְׁפְּחוֹת הַכְּנַעֲנִי׃ וַיְהִי גְּבוּל הַכְּנַעֲנִי
מִצִּידֹן בֹּאֲכָה גְרָרָה עַד־עַזָּה בֹּאֲכָה סְדֹמָה וַעֲמֹרָה וְאַדְמָה
כ וּצְבֹיִם עַד־לָשַׁע׃ אֵלֶּה בְנֵי־חָם לְמִשְׁפְּחֹתָם לִלְשֹׁנֹתָם
כא בְּאַרְצֹתָם בְּגוֹיֵהֶם׃ וּלְשֵׁם יֻלַּד גַּם־הוּא אֲבִי

VERSE 18

RASHI

וְאַחַר נָפֹצוּ – *Were dispersed:* Many families emerged from these groups.

BEKHOR SHOR

וְאַחַר נָפֹצוּ – *Were dispersed:* It was afterward that one of these groups divided into two, as later happens with the sons of Yosef, who become two separate tribes. Thus the descendants of Kenaan [numbered eleven here] emerged as a set of twelve nations. This is what Moshe referred to when he recounted how God *fixed the boundaries of peoples by the number of Israel's sons* (Deuteronomy 32:8) – the twelve tribes of Israel were about to conquer and settle land that that had been inhabited by the twelve Canaanite nations. Nevertheless, Moshe lists the Canaanites as only seven peoples [in Deuteronomy 7:1], for he mentions the six most significant nations by name and consolidates the other five into one group named after their ancestor Kenaan.

VERSE 19

RASHI

גְּבוּל הַכְּנַעֲנִי – *The Canaanite borders:* The description in this verse details the edge of the Canaanites' territory. For the term *gevul* always refers to the outer reaches of an area, or its end. **בֹּאֲכָה** – *Toward:* The term *boakha* represents the infinitive in noun form ["coming"]. It seems to me that the sense is like the construct used when a person says to his fellow: This border continues until you come to a particular place.

VERSE 20

RASHI

לִלְשֹׁנֹתָם בְּאַרְצֹתָם – *By their languages, with their lands:* Even though these peoples became dispersed into different languages and lands, they were all descendants of Ḥam.

VERSE 21

RASHI

אֲבִי כָּל־בְּנֵי־עֵבֶר – *He was the ancestor of all the sons of Ever:* Shem was the ancestor of all those who lived across [*me'ever*] the river. [According to Rashi, the present verse does not refer to the man named "Ever" who is introduced in 10:24, since this would be stating the obvious. Rather, the word *ever* connotes a preposition, with the phrase *benei ever*

18 and Sinites, the Arvadites, Zemarites, and Hamatites. Later, the
19 Canaanite families were dispersed. The Canaanite borders were
from Sidon toward Gerar near Aza, and toward Sedom, Amora,
20 Adma, and Tzevoyim, near Lasha. These were the descendants
of Ḥam, by their clans and their languages, with their lands and
21 their nations. Sons were also born to Shem. The older
brother of Yefet, he was the ancestor of all the sons of Ever.

RASHI *(cont.)*

meaning: "Those who live across the river."] **אֲחִי יֶפֶת הַגָּדוֹל** – *The older brother of Yefet:* This verse leaves me unsure whether Yefet was the oldest of Noaḥ's sons [and hence the phrase *aḥi Yefet hagadol* should be understood as: "The brother of Yefet the elder"], or whether Shem is the older one [and the verse should be taken as translated in this edition]. However, a later text relates that *when Shem was one hundred years old, he had a son, Arpakhshad, two years after the flood* (11:10). This proves that Yefet was the oldest brother, as follows. Noaḥ was five hundred years old when he first became a father [as attested in 5:32], and the flood began when the man was six hundred years old [as reported in 7:11]. This means that Noaḥ's oldest son was one hundred years old when the rains destroyed the world. But Shem only reached the age of one hundred two years after the flood. [This proves that he could not have been Noaḥ's firstborn.] **אֲחִי יֶפֶת** – *The brother of Yefet:* Shem is described as Yefet's brother and not as Ḥam's. For Shem and Yefet acted respectfully toward their father, while Ḥam disgraced him.

IBN EZRA

אֲבִי כָּל־בְּנֵי־עֵבֶר – *He was the ancestor of all the sons of Ever:* The Torah teaches that Shem was the patriarch of the Hebrews, no one was more exalted than he, and the Lord was his God [as stated in 9:26]. Thus we later find [that Israel, God's people, are named after Ever] in the verse *Thus says the Lord, God of the Hebrews [Ha'ivrim]: How much longer will you refuse to submit to Me?* (Exodus 10:3). In contrast to the praise given to Shem, the text identifies Ḥam as the ancestor of Kenaan to emphasize that there was nobody lower than him. And it is inappropriate for the sacred and the profane to mix together [which is why the lineages are kept separate]. By linking Yefet with Shem in this verse, the text teaches that Yefet was also laudable. The text lists Shem first [in 6:10], even though he was the youngest [see Rashi], out of respect for his character.

ABARBANEL

אֲבִי כָּל־בְּנֵי־עֵבֶר – *The ancestor of all the sons of Ever:* Since Shem had many sons and grandsons as well as two brothers, Ḥam and Yefet, and nephews and grandnephews, the Torah wished to emphasize Shem's upright character. This man thus felt the greatest love for his great-grandson Ever son of Shelaḥ, son of Arpakhshad, and for all of Ever's sons. For Shem saw that Ever was a righteous and wise man that dwelled in tents and study halls like himself. Shem had no great affection for his brother Ḥam or his sons, but He did feel an affinity toward his brother Yefet, who was noble and wholesome. And hence Shem behaved as

כב כָּל־בְּנֵי־עֵבֶר אֲחִי יֶפֶת הַגָּדוֹל׃ בְּנֵי שֵׁם עֵילָם וְאַשּׁוּר
כג וְאַרְפַּכְשַׁד וְלוּד וַאֲרָם׃ וּבְנֵי אֲרָם עוּץ וְחוּל וְגֶתֶר וָמַשׁ׃
כד כה וְאַרְפַּכְשַׁד יָלַד אֶת־שָׁלַח וְשֶׁלַח יָלַד אֶת־עֵבֶר׃ וּלְעֵבֶר יֻלַּד
שְׁנֵי בָנִים שֵׁם הָאֶחָד פֶּלֶג כִּי בְיָמָיו נִפְלְגָה הָאָרֶץ וְשֵׁם אָחִיו
כו יָקְטָן׃ וְיָקְטָן יָלַד אֶת־אַלְמוֹדָד וְאֶת־שָׁלֶף וְאֶת־חֲצַרְמָוֶת
כז כח וְאֶת־יָרַח׃ וְאֶת־הֲדוֹרָם וְאֶת־אוּזָל וְאֶת־דִּקְלָה׃ וְאֶת־עוֹבָל
כט וְאֶת־אֲבִימָאֵל וְאֶת־שְׁבָא׃ וְאֶת־אוֹפִר וְאֶת־חֲוִילָה וְאֶת־
ל יוֹבָב כָּל־אֵלֶּה בְּנֵי יָקְטָן׃ וַיְהִי מוֹשָׁבָם מִמֵּשָׁא בֹּאֲכָה סְפָרָה
לא הַר הַקֶּדֶם׃ אֵלֶּה בְנֵי־שֵׁם לְמִשְׁפְּחֹתָם לִלְשֹׁנֹתָם בְּאַרְצֹתָם
לב לְגוֹיֵהֶם׃ אֵלֶּה מִשְׁפְּחֹת בְּנֵי־נֹחַ לְתוֹלְדֹתָם בְּגוֹיֵהֶם וּמֵאֵלֶּה
נִפְרְדוּ הַגּוֹיִם בָּאָרֶץ אַחַר הַמַּבּוּל׃

ABARBANEL *(cont.)*

if he had no other progeny besides the sons of Ever, and He acted as if he had no other brother save Yefet. Thus when the verse states: *Sons were also born to Shem; he was the ancestor of all the sons of Ever*, it emphasizes that even though Shem had many sons just like his brothers did, he only paid attention to the sons of Ever. He considered himself ancestor of them alone, ignoring his other descendants. Similarly, regarding his own siblings, Shem treated Yefet as his only brother and behaved as if he himself were older [despite being the youngest], for it is common for the oldest child to exercise compassion and concern for his younger brothers as if they were his own offspring. All of this is meant to show that Shem felt nothing for his other brother and sons, or the rest of his family.

SFORNO

אֲבִי כָּל־בְּנֵי־עֵבֶר – *He was the ancestor of all the sons of Ever:* The title of *Ivrim* is assigned to anybody who professes belief in the existence of God, in His abilities, and His providence. This is because Ever attempted to understand and to teach these philosophical principles. Thus we are told: *A fugitive came and reported this to Avram the Hebrew [Ha'ivri]* [14:13; hinting at Avram's faith and saintliness]. When Shem is referred to as "ancestor" [*av*] *of all the sons of Ever*, the term *av* is meant to mean "instructor" as the following verses attest: *His brother's name was Yuval. He was the ancestor [avi] of all who those who play the lyre and the pipe* (4:21); and *Then one man from there retorted, "Well, who is their father [avihem]?"* (I Samuel 10:12). And just as teachers can be referred to as parents, students are sometimes called "children" [*banim*] as in the verse *Now a certain man from the children of the prophets said to another…* (I Kings 20:35).

22 Shem's sons were Elam, Ashur, Arpakhshad, Lud, and Aram.
23 24 Aram's sons were Utz, Ḥul, Geter, and Mash. Arpakhshad was
25 the father of Shelaḥ, and Shelaḥ was the father of Ever. To Ever,
two sons were born. One was named Peleg, for in his time the
26 earth was divided. His brother was named Yoktan. Yoktan was
27 the father of Almodad, Shelef, Ḥatzarmavet, Yeraḥ, Hadoram,
28 29 Uzal, Dikla, Oval, Avimael, Sheva, Ofir, Ḥavila, and Yovav;
30 all these were Yoktan's sons. Their settlements extended from
31 Mesha toward Sefar, in the eastern hill country. These were the
descendants of Shem, by their clans and their languages, with
32 their lands and their nations. These, then, are the clans of the
sons of Noaḥ, by their lines, in their nations. And from these,
the nations spread out across the earth after the flood.

VERSE 25

RASHI

נִפְלְגָה – *Was divided:* In Peleg's time human language became mixed up. The people spread out from the valley where they had settled and were divided [*nitpallegu*] across the world. We learn from this that Ever was a prophet who named his son after future events. [The civilization who built the Tower of Babel is commonly known as *dor hapalaga* – the generation of the dispersal. The father Ever anticipated this upheaval, and so named his son Peleg.] Indeed, the work Seder Olam maintains [in chapter 1] that the scattering of humanity took place only at the end of Peleg's life. Now the incident could not have happened when he was young [and the impetus for his name] due to the following reasoning: Peleg had a younger brother named Yoktan who had fathered several families before the event of the tower. To start, verse 26 reports: *Yoktan was the father of Almodad, Shelef, Ḥatzarmavet, Yeraḥ*, and only then do we read that *the whole world spoke the same language* [11:1, before humanity was dispersed; hence Yoktan was already an adult at the time of the dispersal, and all the more so his older brother Peleg]. And the reader should not suggest that God scattered the people sometime during the middle of Peleg's life [whereupon his name was changed to reflect the event]. For the purpose of the text is not to obscure [the chronology] but to clarify it. We must therefore infer that humanity was scattered in the exact year of his death. **יָקְטָן** – *Yoktan:* Yoktan was so called because he was modest man who belittled [*hiktin*] himself. As a reward for this humility, he was privileged to establish all of these families.

IBN EZRA

וּלְעֵבֶר יֻלַּד שְׁנֵי בָנִים – *To Ever, two sons were born:* According to Seder Olam, our patriarch Avraham was present at the time of dispersal of the builders of the Tower of Babel. This relies on the principle that the historical sequence of events in the Torah is not bound by the order of their appearance. For it is possible that the passage which begins: *The whole world spoke the same language* (11:1), actually took place after the birth of Avraham [in 11:26]. Similarly, when the text states: *Around that time, Yehuda left his brothers and camped near*

יא א ב וַיְהִי כָל־הָאָרֶץ שָׂפָה אֶחָת וּדְבָרִים אֲחָדִים: וַיְהִי בְּנָסְעָם ט שביעי

IBN EZRA *(cont.)*

an Adulamite named Ḥira (38:1), that happened before the sale of Yosef [even though it appears later in the text]. Some commentators maintain that Peleg was a king, and it was "in his time" [i.e., during his reign] that the earth was divided. However, the correct interpretation is that in his time the ages of human beings were halved [*niflegu*], for the people who lived before Peleg and after Noaḥ lived for five hundred years, whereas Peleg's life only lasted half that, as did those of the generations who followed him.

CHAPTER 11, VERSE 1

RASHI

שָׂפָה אֶחָת – *The same language:* The holy tongue [Hebrew].

וּדְבָרִים אֲחָדִים – *The same words:* All of humanity shared the same plan. Everyone came together and said: It is not right that God should retain the upper realm for Himself! Let us ascend to the heavens and wage war against Him. Another interpretation: The people spoke against the single [*yaḥid*] Master of the Universe. Another interpretation: The assembled masses believed that once every 1,650 years the firmament would collapse, as it did during the flood [which took place in the year 1656 after creation]. Thus, they decided to build scaffolding to support the sky. This idea is presented in Bereshit Rabba (38:6).

IBN EZRA

שָׂפָה אֶחָת – *The same language:* This means that everybody spoke the same language, and my guess is that it was Hebrew.

וּדְבָרִים אֲחָדִים – The same words: Avraham was one of the builders of the Tower of Babel. Let this not shock you, for Noaḥ and Shem were there as well. In fact, Shem did not die until Yaakov was past fifty years old.

BEKHOR SHOR

וַיְהִי כָל־הָאָרֶץ שָׂפָה אֶחָת – *The whole world spoke the same language:* What this means is that every person was fluent in seventy languages.

ABARBANEL

וַיְהִי כָל־הָאָרֶץ שָׂפָה אֶחָת – *The whole world spoke the same language:* In my opinion, the sin of the generation of the dispersal resembled the transgression of their ancestor Adam and the crime of his son Kayin. Consider the first man – fashioned directly by the Holy One, blessed be He, in His own image; a person granted the intelligence to perfect himself by recognizing God and learning from His ways. To take care of the first man, God provided him with all of the resources he required: fruit from the garden's trees and water from its rivers. All of this sustenance occurred naturally, such that Adam had no need to work in order to support himself. He could therefore devote all his time and energy to pursuing knowledge of God. After all, that was the reason he was created in the first place. And yet, the man sinned because he was dissatisfied with all the bounty that God had granted him. He was enticed by desires and external pleasures. And so Adam was banished from the Garden of Eden, the paradise where he

11 1 The whole world spoke the same language, the same words. SHEVI'I
2 And as the people migrated from the east they found a valley

ABARBANEL *(cont.)*

had been living. Kayin too chose to busy himself with material things instead of focusing on the spiritual, and this is why he became a tiller of the soil, spending his days plowing the earth, planting, and cultivating it. Eventually, the man's mind became subject to his animal instincts, and he became a man of the earth, a slave to the physical. Hevel, on the other hand, became a shepherd. He was attracted to the natural things in this world and was content with the possessions he already owned. For tending sheep demands no real work or development, just guiding the animals through their natural stages of life. This is why all of our holy patriarchs – Avraham, Yitzḥak, and Yaakov, as well as the sons of Yaakov, Moshe, and David – all worked as shepherds rather than as farmers. Noaḥ too, despite his eventual sin of becoming drunk from his wine, is not referred to by the text as "worker of the land" [like Kayin in 4:2] but as a "man of the land," [in 9:20]. This is because Noaḥ had mastery over the soil, but he was not obsessed with maximizing the bounty that he could coax from it. But because Kayin allowed the animal, physical side of his character to dominate his mental capacities, he is termed a "worker of the land." This is why Kayin built a city and called it Ḥanokh [4:17]: He educated [*ḥinnekh*] and trained his sons in the skills necessary for constructing settlements and assembling communities. And Kayin's descendants persist in his ways, spending their lives in superfluous labor that did not further their spiritual growth.... And then we reach the generation of the dispersal. The sin of these people was very much like the error of Adam, Kayin, and that whole lineage. At the time, God blessed humankind with plenty of natural resources, freeing them from the daily struggle to survive. They had plenty of time to work on perfecting their souls. And yet, this population was not content to enjoy the great gifts that the Almighty had bestowed upon them. They turned their attention to seeking all manner of labor – the construction of a city and a tower which demanded multiple skills and specialties – in order to promote themselves and propagate their society. These people believed that their highest purpose and greatest achievement would be establishing ever-larger communities, where they could perfect the cooperation of society. This was seen as the apex of human development.... And yet, such an enterprise is distracting and disturbing to humanity's true calling, which is his spiritual and intellectual growth. This is why the souls of these people were stricken in punishment, when God confused their language and scattered them across the earth. This retribution paralleled the exile of Adam from the Garden of Eden, the banishment of Kayin from his home, and the erasure of his descendants from the earth during the flood. All these people had sinned in a similar fashion – they all placed their hopes and desires in the Tree of Knowledge while ignoring the Tree of Life, which held the true purpose of existence. Hence they all deserved the same punishment.

VERSE 2

RASHI

וַיְהִי בְּנָסְעָם מִקֶּדֶם – *As the people migrated from the east:* All of humanity had settled in the east, as the earlier verse states: *Their settlements extended from Mesha toward Sefar, in the eastern hill country* (10:30). From there they set out to find a place that could sustain them all, finding only Shinar to be suitable.

ג מִקֶּדֶם וַיִּמְצְאוּ בִקְעָה בְּאֶרֶץ שִׁנְעָר וַיֵּשְׁבוּ שָׁם: וַיֹּאמְרוּ
אִישׁ אֶל־רֵעֵהוּ הָבָה נִלְבְּנָה לְבֵנִים וְנִשְׂרְפָה לִשְׂרֵפָה וַתְּהִי
ד לָהֶם הַלְּבֵנָה לְאָבֶן וְהַחֵמָר הָיָה לָהֶם לַחֹמֶר: וַיֹּאמְרוּ
הָבָה ׀ נִבְנֶה־לָּנוּ עִיר וּמִגְדָּל וְרֹאשׁוֹ בַשָּׁמַיִם וְנַעֲשֶׂה־לָּנוּ
ה שֵׁם פֶּן־נָפוּץ עַל־פְּנֵי כָל־הָאָרֶץ: וַיֵּרֶד יְהוָה לִרְאֹת אֶת־

RAMBAN

וַיְהִי בְּנָסְעָם מִקֶּדֶם – *As the people migrated from the east:* The impetus for building the tower was that these people wanted to make a "name" [*shem*] for themselves (11:4). Now, the reader who recognizes the significance of the term *shem* will understand exactly what their intention was, will grasp the scope of the project they had in mind, and will realize the wickedness of their plan. Furthermore, this motive shows that the punishment that God imposed upon these people by scattering them across the land and confusing their languages was in fact a response in kind to what the masses had plotted. For it had been their design uproot belief in God. In a way, the crime of this generation resembled that of their ancestor Adam. This is perhaps why our Sages discuss this episode as follows: *The Lord came down to see the city and the tower being built by the children of man* (11:5). Rabbi Berekhya taught: Why does the verse refer to these people as "the children of man"? Might we have supposed that they were the offspring of donkeys or camels? Rather, the emphasis is that they were descended from [and shared the effrontery of] the first man. Note that throughout the entire narrative of the flood, the text employs the generic name *Elohim* to refer to God, whereas in the current passage we find only the unique four-letter name of God. This is because the story of the deluge told of humankind's general corruption of the earth, but the episode of the tower is one in which humanity destroyed the principles of faith in God specifically. Hence these rebels were punished with the unique name of God. This explains why God *came down to see*… and the similar retribution against Sedom [see 18:21]. The learned student will understand this.

SFORNO

וַיְהִי בְּנָסְעָם מִקֶּדֶם – *As the people migrated from the east:* The people followed the practice of shepherds, who travel from place to place in search of better pastureland.

VERSE 3

RASHI

אִישׁ אֶל־רֵעֵהוּ – *To each other:* The verse [does not mean that individuals suggested the plan to each other, but that] each nation discussed it with the other groups: Mitzrayim consulted with Kush, who talked it over with Put, who in turned raised the issue with Kenaan. **הָבָה** – *Come:* The people told each other to prepare themselves for the task ahead. The term *hava* represents an invitation [rather than a command] to individuals who arrange themselves into working groups, advisory committees, or to undertake some burden. **לְבֵנִים** – *Bricks:* Since Babylon is situated in a valley, there are no rocks there [that is, there is no quarry from which stones can be hewn]. **וְנִשְׂרְפָה לִשְׂרֵפָה** – *Let us bake them thoroughly:*

3 in the land of Shinar and settled there. They said to each other,
"Come, let us make bricks, let us bake them thoroughly." They
4 used bricks for stone and tar for mortar. And they said, "Come,
let us build ourselves a city and a tower that reaches the heavens, and make a name for ourselves. Otherwise we will be scat-
5 tered across the face of the earth." But the LORD came down

RASHI *(cont.)*

This is the process for producing bricks known as *tiules* ["tiles"] in Old French – the materials are baked in a kiln. לַחֹמֶר – *For mortar:* For plastering the wall.

IBN EZRA

וַיֹּאמְרוּ אִישׁ אֶל־רֵעֵהוּ – *They said to each other:* The people who built the tower were not so foolish as to believe that they could actually reach the heavens with their structure. Nor did they embark on this project because they feared a new flood. For Noaḥ and his sons were present, and they would have testified to God's promise [never again to destroy the world]; the others surely would have listened to them since they were Noaḥ's descendants. Now the Torah does reveal the motives and goals that the builders held: they wished to construct a large city where they could live and erect a tall tower to establish their reputation and glory. This spire would also serve as a beacon to travelers such as shepherds, who would be able to easily locate this metropolitan center. As long as the structure lasted, the names of its builders would be known. This is what the people meant when they boasted: *Let us make a name for ourselves* (11:4). The community hoped that their project would allow them to remain united, but such was not God's will. Still, the builders were unaware of God's desire.

VERSE 4

RASHI

פֶּן־נָפוּץ – *Otherwise we will be scattered:* Let us act to prevent God from striking us with some plague that will force us to disperse from here.

RASHBAM

הָבָה נִבְנֶה־לָּנוּ עִיר – *Let us build ourselves a city:* The text does not seem to explain straightforwardly what the great sin was of this generation of the dispersal. If their transgression was that they planned to build "a tower that reached the heavens," do we not later read regarding the Canaanite fortifications: *The cities are large and walled to the sky* [Deuteronomy 1:28; God did not seem to find those structural achievements offensive in themselves]? The transgression in the present episode actually lay in God's previous command to the people: *Be fertile and multiply. Fill the earth and subdue it* (1:28). But instead, these people chose a single spot to develop out of concern that they *be scattered across the face of the earth*.

VERSE 5

RASHI

וַיֵּרֶד יהוה לִרְאֹת – *But the LORD came down to see:* God did not actually need to descend in order to see the developing project [since He is of course omniscient]. Rather, the language

ו הָעִיר וְאֶת־הַמִּגְדָּל אֲשֶׁר בָּנוּ בְּנֵי הָאָדָם: וַיֹּאמֶר יהוה
הֵן עַם אֶחָד וְשָׂפָה אַחַת לְכֻלָּם וְזֶה הַחִלָּם לַעֲשׂוֹת וְעַתָּה

RASHI (cont.)

of the text is meant to teach judges not to convict a defendant until they have properly investigated and understood the matter. This interpretation is found in Midrash Tanḥuma [chapter 18]. **בְּנֵי הָאָדָם** – *The children of men:* Obviously the people involved in this enterprise were children of men – who else would they be, the offspring of donkeys and camels? The choice of words teaches that these individuals descended from the first man who had similarly expressed ingratitude [and whose character the current society had inherited]. For just as Adam had defended himself by saying: *The woman you put here with me – she gave me fruit from the tree and I ate* (3:12), these people were similarly ungrateful to God for rescuing them from the flood. They were thus perfectly willing to rebel against God who had extended them such grace.

IBN EZRA

וַיֵּרֶד יהוה לִרְאֹת – *But the Lord came down to see:* All activities down on earth are dependent on the forces in the upper realm. In saying that God "came down," the text [does not mean that God has a finite place, but simply] mimics the way people are used to speaking.

RALBAG

וַיֵּרֶד יהוה לִרְאֹת – *But the Lord came down to see:* God had already seen that the gathering of all people in a single location was not conducive to the continuation of humanity. For it was always possible for a disaster to occur at that one site, and such an event would devastate the species. An earthquake might strike in a place, an upheaval caused by the tremendous winds emerging from the center of the planet, or a hurricane powerful enough to split mountains and shatter rocks might descend upon that center of civilization. Alternatively, meteors might fall from the sky, a tsunami might wash away a community, or some other horrible catastrophe could wipe everybody out. Now if all human beings lived together in one place, a natural cataclysm in one part of the land would spell the end for all people. This is why it was critical for humanity to spread out across the earth and to establish multiple cities and settlements. If one area suffered an overwhelming loss, the human species would still survive. This explains why God attempted to thwart the people's plan to localize their society. Through miraculous intervention, God imposed upon the masses the inclination for every family to develop its own language. This resulted in people being unable to understand everyone outside their own family. This in turn led to discord among the groups and caused them to disperse themselves across the land; the construction of the city was thereby halted by popular consent. And hence God exercised His providence in this episode to ensure that human beings would endure. This is the meaning of the story, even though it is not stated explicitly. For God would never have confused the people's language needlessly.

to see the city and the tower being built by the children of men.
6 The LORD said, "If, as one people with one language, they have
begun to do this, nothing they plan to do will be impossible

ABARBANEL

וַיֵּרֶד יהוה לִרְאֹת – *But the LORD came down to see:* God came down to see the people's enterprise even though He certainly had been watching human behavior up to this point, since He manages all affairs of humankind. For God reasoned as follows: Because they have not been content as a single nation that speaks one language, and have embarked on a project that is wholly unnecessary and insignificant, I will conceal My face from them. I will no longer conduct earthly affairs Myself directly but will delegate such responsibilities to celestial ministers. It was to these angels that God addressed His comment: *Let us go down and confuse their language* (11:7); descend with Me to govern the nations of this human race, such that each of you will be given charge of one particular group. And as My personal providence from humanity diminishes, so too will their ability to speak the holy tongue be taken from them. As such, civilization will be divided by languages that emerge from themselves [as opposed to Hebrew which is taught from above]. These forms of communication will connect each nation to a specific guardian angel, just as the holy tongue is unique to God's providence.

SFORNO

וַיֵּרֶד יהוה לִרְאֹת – *But the LORD came down to see:* The language of God coming down to see something reflects a circumstance when a sin has not yet been committed, but the potential for it has arisen. We find a similar situation regarding the rebellious son, whom the Torah anticipates will one day perpetrate more serious infractions than the disobedience and gluttony he practices now. Hence the Sages say [in Sanhedrin 72a] that the Torah "descended to the depths of his motives" [in ascertaining his character and decreeing death upon him based on what it surmises will become of him in the future]. In the subsequent case of Sedom, God says: *I shall go down now and see if they have really done as much as the outcry that has reached Me* (18:21). At that point the wickedness of the people of Sedom had not so exceeded the evil of other cities to warrant the utter destruction that they received. However, their abuse of the poor was inordinate, and that led to the complete breakdown of the society. As the prophet states: *The sin of your sister Sedom was this: pride. She and her daughters had enough bread and an easy tranquility and yet did not aid the hands of the poor and needy* (Ezekiel 16:49). A similar treatment appears regarding the punishment of Israel's exiles, when God vows: *I will hide My face from them, and see what their end will be* (Deuteronomy 32:20).

VERSE 6

RASHI

הֵן עַם אֶחָד – *If, as one people:* Even though these people hold all the benefits of a sound society, as they are united as a single nation with a common language, they still are plotting to do this. לֹא־יִבָּצֵר – *Will be impossible:* The term should be understood as a rhetorical question [that is, "Shall nothing be impossible for them?"], and the verb *lehibbatzer*

ז לֹא־יִבָּצֵר מֵהֶם כֹּל אֲשֶׁר יָזְמוּ לַעֲשׂוֹת: הָבָה נֵרְדָה וְנָבְלָה
ח שָׁם שְׂפָתָם אֲשֶׁר לֹא יִשְׁמְעוּ אִישׁ שְׂפַת רֵעֵהוּ: וַיָּפֶץ יְהוָה
ט אֹתָם מִשָּׁם עַל־פְּנֵי כָל־הָאָרֶץ וַיַּחְדְּלוּ לִבְנֹת הָעִיר: עַל־כֵּן

RASHI *(cont.)*

means "to be prevented," as Targum Onkelos translates it. A similar usage appears in the verse, *He withholds [yivtzor] the spirits of princes* (Psalms 76:13).

IBN EZRA

הֵן עַם אֶחָד וְשָׂפָה אַחַת לְכֻלָּם – *If, as one people with one language:* God addressed this comment to the angels.... God viewed humanity as comprising a single nation, which held one religion. Now it is the plurality of faiths that cause jealousy and hatred among peoples, as does a variety of languages. This is why the king of Persia and Media ordered that *every man must be master in his home, speaking the language of his own people* [Esther 1:22. Uniformity of customs within a household was meant to encourage harmony]. **לֹא־יִבָּצֵר** – *Will be impossible:* The verb means "will be prevented," as in the verse, *And these were all fortress [betzurot] towns* [Deuteronomy 3:5; places where enemies were prevented from entering]. Thus God declared: If I allow the construction to proceed, they will imagine that they can do whatever they want.

ABARBANEL

הֵן עַם אֶחָד וְשָׂפָה אַחַת לְכֻלָּם – *If, as one people with one language:* It was humanity's natural inclination to form a single nation with a common language spoken among them to preserve their unity. Thus nothing was missing from their lives for two thousand years. However, God felt that now the people would start to engage in pointless material pursuits. And there is no doubt that this unbridled drive for physicality would lead to what it always does – endless striving for things. This is what God means when He complains: *Nothing they plan to do will be impossible for them.* Night and day the thoughts of the masses would be occupied with schemes for more building and future development. It is also possible to interpret the verse as meaning: "Now that they have begun to do this" – i.e., have made this error – "should they not now be prevented [*yibbatzer*] from doing everything they plan" – i.e., constructing the city and the tower? As such, *let us go down and confuse their language...*

VERSE 7

RASHI

הָבָה נֵרְדָה – *Let us go down:* Because of His great humility, God now consulted with His court. **הָבָה** – *Let us:* God's response to the human plan represented a measure for measure reaction to the people's proclamation. After the masses had declared: *Let us build ourselves a city and a tower* (11:4), God responded with *Let us go down and confuse their language.* **לֹא יִשְׁמְעוּ** – *So that one will not understand:* [As a result of the confusion] one worker will ask another for a brick, but his colleague will deliver mortar to him. In response, the first man will bash the other's head in.

7 for them. Let us go down and confuse their language so that
8 one will not understand the speech of another." From there the
LORD scattered them all over the earth, and they abandoned
9 the building of the city. That is why it was called Bavel, because
it was there that the LORD confused the language of all the

IBN EZRA

הָבָה נֵרְדָה – *Let us go down:* God dispersed the people for their own good. For God had initially commanded them to *fill the earth and subdue it* [1:28, and not just populate a single area].

VERSE 8

RASHI

וַיָּפֶץ יהוה אֹתָם מִשָּׁם – *From there the Lord scattered them:* The people were spread out across this world. For since they had feared that they would *be scattered across the face of the earth* (11:4), God punished them in just that way. This is an example of what Shlomo writes: *That which the wicked man dreads will befall him* (Proverbs 10:24).

IBN EZRA

וַיַּחְדְּלוּ לִבְנֹת הָעִיר – *And they abandoned the building of the city:* Although part of the city and the tower had been constructed by this point, the project was not completed. Thus the verse states: *But the Lord came down to see the city and the tower being built* [11:5, which indicates that some progress had been made]. Alternatively, that verse might suggest that God intervened based on the plans that the community had devised [but had not yet executed]. In a similar way, a later text states: *Then Balak son of Tzipor, king of Moav, rose up to fight against Israel. He sent for Bilam son of Beor and directed him to curse you* [Joshua 24:9; Balak is viewed as "fighting" even before he brought his armies into the field]. And yet, my first interpretation seems the correct one to me.

VERSE 9

RASHI

וּמִשָּׁם הֱפִיצָם – *And from there He scattered them:* [The previous verse already described the fate of the people in this world. Hence the present sentence] teaches that these people would not receive any share in the next world either. Now which sin was more severe – that of the people of the flood, or that perpetrated by the generation of the dispersal? Note that the first group had not tried to attack God, whereas the later society attempted to wage war against Him, so to speak. And yet, the earlier civilization was wiped off the face of the earth, and the later one was not! However, the people of the deluge were thieves who thrived on conflict amongst themselves, while the tower builders worked together in love and unity, as is attested to in the first verse of the narrative: *The whole world spoke the same language, the same words* (11:1). We learn from here that God despises dissension but values peace.

קָרָא שְׁמָהּ בָּבֶל כִּי־שָׁם בָּלַל יהוה שְׂפַת כָּל־הָאָרֶץ וּמִשָּׁם
הֱפִיצָם יהוה עַל־פְּנֵי כָּל־הָאָרֶץ׃
י אֵלֶּה תּוֹלְדֹת שֵׁם שֵׁם בֶּן־מְאַת שָׁנָה וַיּוֹלֶד אֶת־אַרְפַּכְשָׁד
יא שְׁנָתַיִם אַחַר הַמַּבּוּל׃ וַיְחִי־שֵׁם אַחֲרֵי הוֹלִידוֹ אֶת־אַרְפַּכְשָׁד
יב חֲמֵשׁ מֵאוֹת שָׁנָה וַיּוֹלֶד בָּנִים וּבָנוֹת׃ וְאַרְפַּכְשַׁד
יג חַי חָמֵשׁ וּשְׁלֹשִׁים שָׁנָה וַיּוֹלֶד אֶת־שָׁלַח׃ וַיְחִי אַרְפַּכְשַׁד
אַחֲרֵי הוֹלִידוֹ אֶת־שֶׁלַח שָׁלֹשׁ שָׁנִים וְאַרְבַּע מֵאוֹת שָׁנָה
יד וַיּוֹלֶד בָּנִים וּבָנוֹת׃ וְשֶׁלַח חַי שְׁלֹשִׁים שָׁנָה וַיּוֹלֶד
טו אֶת־עֵבֶר׃ וַיְחִי־שֶׁלַח אַחֲרֵי הוֹלִידוֹ אֶת־עֵבֶר שָׁלֹשׁ שָׁנִים
טז וְאַרְבַּע מֵאוֹת שָׁנָה וַיּוֹלֶד בָּנִים וּבָנוֹת׃ וַיְחִי־
יז עֵבֶר אַרְבַּע וּשְׁלֹשִׁים שָׁנָה וַיּוֹלֶד אֶת־פָּלֶג׃ וַיְחִי־עֵבֶר
אַחֲרֵי הוֹלִידוֹ אֶת־פֶּלֶג שְׁלֹשִׁים שָׁנָה וְאַרְבַּע מֵאוֹת שָׁנָה
יח וַיּוֹלֶד בָּנִים וּבָנוֹת׃ וַיְחִי־פֶלֶג שְׁלֹשִׁים שָׁנָה וַיּוֹלֶד
יט אֶת־רְעוּ׃ וַיְחִי־פֶלֶג אַחֲרֵי הוֹלִידוֹ אֶת־רְעוּ תֵּשַׁע שָׁנִים
כ וּמָאתַיִם שָׁנָה וַיּוֹלֶד בָּנִים וּבָנוֹת׃ וַיְחִי רְעוּ
כא שְׁתַּיִם וּשְׁלֹשִׁים שָׁנָה וַיּוֹלֶד אֶת־שְׂרוּג׃ וַיְחִי רְעוּ אַחֲרֵי
הוֹלִידוֹ אֶת־שְׂרוּג שֶׁבַע שָׁנִים וּמָאתַיִם שָׁנָה וַיּוֹלֶד בָּנִים
כב וּבָנוֹת׃ וַיְחִי שְׂרוּג שְׁלֹשִׁים שָׁנָה וַיּוֹלֶד אֶת־נָחוֹר׃
כג וַיְחִי שְׂרוּג אַחֲרֵי הוֹלִידוֹ אֶת־נָחוֹר מָאתַיִם שָׁנָה וַיּוֹלֶד בָּנִים

RABBEINU BAHYA

כִּי־שָׁם בָּלַל יהוה שְׂפַת כָּל־הָאָרֶץ – *It was there that the Lord confused the language of all the earth:* Surely the reader knows that there exist seventy celestial ministers who represent the leaders of the seventy earthly nations; each guardian angel is a foundation for his group and his language. Now these ministers are members of their respective nations, unlike the Heritage of Israel [God] who is the Creator of all things. And just as the Almighty is God of the heavens, God of all gods, superior and master of them all, so too is His language greater than all other tongues. Therefore our inheritance comprises two equal features – our God who is supreme over everything, and our foundation, our holy language, which is similarly superior to all other languages. This is why our Sages claim (Shabbat 12b): If a person prays in Aramaic, the ministering angels will not assist him, because they do not understand Aramaic.

earth; and from there the LORD scattered them all across the
face of the earth.
10 These are the descendants of Shem. When Shem was one
hundred years old, he had a son, Arpakhshad, two years after
11 the flood. After Arpakhshad was born, Shem lived five hun-
12 dred years and had other sons and daughters. When
Arpakhshad was thirty-five years old, he had a son, Shelaḥ.
13 After Shelaḥ was born, Arpakhshad lived four hundred and
14 three years and had other sons and daughters. When
15 Shelaḥ was thirty years old, he had a son, Ever. After Ever
was born, Shelaḥ lived four hundred and three years and had
16 other sons and daughters. Ever lived thirty-four years
17 and then had a son, Peleg. After Peleg was born, Ever lived
four hundred and thirty years and had other sons and daugh-
18 ters. Peleg lived thirty years and then had a son, Reu.
19 After Reu was born, Peleg lived two hundred and nine years
20 and had other sons and daughters. Reu lived thir-
21 ty-two years and then had a son, Serug. After Serug was born,
Reu lived two hundred and seven years and had other sons
22 and daughters. Serug lived thirty years and then had
23 a son, Naḥor. After Naḥor was born, Serug lived two hundred

CLASSIC COMMENTATORS

VERSE 10

ḤIZKUNI

אֵלֶּה תּוֹלְדֹת שֵׁם – *These are the descendants of Shem:* Whenever the text employs the term *eleh* ["these," in contrast to *ve'eleh* – "and these" – it indicates a disjunction from the previous material]. And so here, unlike the earlier generations [of the flood and Tower of Babel], who were wicked and whose attempts to rebel against God caused them to be lost, these people and their descendants were righteous.

RABBEINU BAḤYA

אֵלֶּה תּוֹלְדֹת שֵׁם – *These are the descendants of Shem:* The present list does not report the deaths of Shem's descendants, unlike the way the text states the deaths of the generations between Adam and Noaḥ [in chapter 5]. Perhaps the reason for this discrepancy is that the royal house of David descended from Shem, and the Messiah son of David will be immortal.

כד וּבָנוֹת׃ וַיְחִי נָחוֹר תֵּשַׁע וְעֶשְׂרִים שָׁנָה וַיּוֹלֶד
כה אֶת־תָּרַח׃ וַיְחִי נָחוֹר אַחֲרֵי הוֹלִידוֹ אֶת־תֶּרַח תְּשַׁע־עֶשְׂרֵה
כו שָׁנָה וּמְאַת שָׁנָה וַיּוֹלֶד בָּנִים וּבָנוֹת׃ וַיְחִי־תֶרַח
כז שִׁבְעִים שָׁנָה וַיּוֹלֶד אֶת־אַבְרָם אֶת־נָחוֹר וְאֶת־הָרָן׃ וְאֵלֶּה
תּוֹלְדֹת תֶּרַח תֶּרַח הוֹלִיד אֶת־אַבְרָם אֶת־נָחוֹר וְאֶת־הָרָן
כח וְהָרָן הוֹלִיד אֶת־לוֹט׃ וַיָּמָת הָרָן עַל־פְּנֵי תֶּרַח אָבִיו בְּאֶרֶץ

VERSE 26

IBN EZRA

וַיּוֹלֶד אֶת־אַבְרָם – *The father of Avram:* Avram was born in a place called Ur Kasdim, a term reminiscent of the verse *So: out of the fires [urim] they will glorify the Lord* (Isaiah 24:15). Now in my opinion it seems that at the time of Avram's birth the locale had a different name, for the Kasdim would only later descend from Naḥor, Avram's brother [as reported in Genesis 22:22]. But when Moshe wrote the Torah, he used this name, because that was how the place was known in his time. We know that Avram was born in Ur Kasdim because when recounting the death of his brother Haran there [in 11:28], and the verse calls it "the land of his birth." It is possible that the Kasdim people established an *ur* [a fire altar] in their town, and that the place was named after the local feature. If so, the term *ur* holds the same meaning as in the verse *Who has a fire [ur] burning in Zion, a furnace in Jerusalem* (Isaiah 31:9). Haran died *al penei* [literally, "before the face of," or "in the presence of"] his father Teraḥ, meaning that Teraḥ saw Haran die. We find similar language in the verse *And Elazar and Itamar served as priests while their father Aharon lived [al penei Aharon]* (Numbers 3:4).

ABARBANEL

וַיּוֹלֶד אֶת־אַבְרָם – *The father of Avram:* On this matter the position of the gentile scholars seems correct to me: The people of Ur Kasdim worshipped fire and the sun, which was considered the lord of fire. This is why the place was called *Ur* ["fire"] *Kasdim*. In any event, the location of Ur Kasdim sat in a region known as *Ever Hanahar* ["Across the River"]. When Yehoshua declares: *From time immemorial, your ancestors – Teraḥ, the father of Avraham and the father of Naḥor – dwelled across the river* (Joshua 24:2), he is referring to the name of a specific region. Proof for this comes from the verse *When they arrived at Ḥaran, they settled there* (11:31), which must have been another town within the same district. Had the family traveled to a new region altogether, the text would have said: They arrived at Ḥaran that is across the river, but the text makes no reference to a new land and region. Thus Ur Kasdim and Ḥaran must have been located in the same district.

VERSE 28

RASHI

עַל־פְּנֵי תֶּרַח אָבִיו – *While Teraḥ his father was still alive:* [Literally, "In the presence of Teraḥ his father."] Haran died while his father was still alive. The Midrash [presents an alternative

24 years and had other sons and daughters. Naḥor lived
25 twenty-nine years and then had a son, Teraḥ. After Teraḥ was
born, Naḥor lived one hundred and nineteen years and had
26 other sons and daughters. Teraḥ lived seventy years
27 and fathered Avram, Naḥor, and Haran.These are the descendants of Teraḥ. Teraḥ was the father of Avram, Naḥor, and Ha-
28 ran, and Haran had a son, Lot. While his father Teraḥ was still

RASHI *(cont.)*

interpretation,] that Haran died because of his father. Teraḥ had brought a complaint against his son Avram before Nimrod for having smashed the father's idols. As a result, Nimrod cast Avram into a fiery furnace. While this was happening, Haran, who was present, said to himself: If Avram emerges victorious from this debate, I will side with him; whereas if Nimrod wins, I will support him. After Avram was rescued from death [having escaped unscathed from the furnace], the court turned to Haran and said: "Well, which do you support [the faith of Avram or that of Nimrod]?" Said Haran: "I am on Avram's side!" Immediately he was thrown into the fiery furnace, where he perished. This is the source of the name *Ur Kasdim* ["the fire of Kasdim"]. Meanwhile, Menaḥem ben Saruq explains the term *ur* as denoting a valley, as in the verse *Out of the crevices [ba'urim] they will glorify the Lord* (Isaiah 24:15), and the verse *And an infant's hand will explore the viper's nest [me'urat]* (Isaiah 11:8). For a hole or a deep fissure is called an *ur*.

RAMBAN

עַל־פְּנֵי תֶּרַח אָבִיו – *While his father Teraḥ was still alive:* The story as transmitted by our Sages is the truth, as I will now explain. Our patriarch Avraham was not born in Ur Kasdim, for his ancestors were the people of Shem, whereas the Kasdim and the entire land of Shinar were territories that belonged to Ḥam [as mentioned in 10:10]. Note that a later verse states: *A fugitive came and reported this to Avram the Hebrew* (14:13); it does not refer to him as "Avram the Kasdi." Furthermore, Yehoshua later claims: *From time immemorial, your ancestors – Teraḥ, the father of Avraham and the father of Naḥor – dwelled across [be'ever] the river* (Joshua 24:2), which emphasizes that Avraham's family always lived there. Additionally, that text continues: *[God] took your forefather Avraham from across the river* (Joshua 24:3). Proof of this point comes from the fact that we later read about Naḥor living in Ḥaran [in Genesis 29:4–5]. Now if Teraḥ's homeland was Ur Kasdim in the land of Shinar, and when he left Ur Kasdim he took with him only Avram and Lot son of Haran, his grandson, and Sarai his daughter-in-law, then Naḥor would have been left behind in Ur Kasdim [and not Ḥaran, where Yaakov subsequently finds his family]. Instead, the fact of the matter is that the birthplace of Avram's family was in Aram [the region containing Ḥaran], which is beyond the Euphrates River. That was where his whole people always lived. And so we read regarding Shem's descendants: *Their settlements extended from Mesha toward Sefar, in the eastern hill country* (10:30). That is a general statement regarding this clan, as the text continues: *With their lands and their nations* (10:31). An additional verse states, *And Bilam took up his oracle and said: "Balak brought me from Aram, the king of Moav from the eastern hills"* [Numbers 23:7, which

כט מוֹלַדְתּוֹ בְּאוּר כַּשְׂדִּים׃ וַיִּקַּח אַבְרָם וְנָחוֹר לָהֶם נָשִׁים שֵׁם מפטיר
אֵשֶׁת־אַבְרָם שָׂרָי וְשֵׁם אֵשֶׁת־נָחוֹר מִלְכָּה בַּת־הָרָן אֲבִי־

RAMBAN *(cont.)*

shows that Aram is in the east]. Hence it is clear that Avraham's family always lived in Aram. Now the Talmud [in Bava Batra 91a] relates that Avraham was jailed in the city of Kuta [after smashing his father's idols], and that town is not in the vicinity of Ur Kasdim [Babylon], as the text proves when it states: *The king of Assyria brought in people from Babylon, Kuta, Ava, Ḥamat* [II Kings 17:24; these were clearly separate regions], and: *The people of Babylon made Sukkot Benot; the people of Kut made Nergal* (II Kings 17:30). It seems that Kuta is a city that is situated beyond the Euphrates River in the land of Aram Naharayim, which was also host to "Ḥaran," as the text later reports: *The servant then took ten of his master's camels, laden with all his master's bounty, and set out to Aram Naharayim, to the city of Naḥor* (Genesis 24:10), which is Ḥaran. Now I have investigated the matter and have learned from many students who have dwelled in that country that Kuta is a large city that sits between Ḥaran and Assyria, a fair distance from the state of Babylonia. And although it is a six day journey between Kuta and Ḥaran it is nevertheless said to be "across the river" because it is found between Aram Naharayim and the Euphrates (which represents the boundary of the land of Israel), "and the Tigris as" *it flows to the east of Assyria* (2:14). And so we must conclude that Teraḥ fathered his older sons Avraham and Naḥor on the eastern side of the Euphrates River, which was the land of his ancestors. He later traveled with his son Avraham to the land of Ur Kasdim, where his youngest son Haran was born. At that time, his son Naḥor was left behind, across the river, in the city of Ḥaran, where he had either been born or moved from Kuta. This is the sense of the verse which states, *Haran died in the land of his birth, Ur Kasdim* – that locale was where Haran alone was born among Teraḥ's children. It was there [in Ur Kasdim] that Avram – who had been born in Kuta – took issue with the popular faith which worshipped the sun. The king of the place imprisoned him, but Avram continued to debate matters of religion with his jailers for many days. Finally, the king began to worry that Avram was corrupting the minds of his people and turning them against their native beliefs. He therefore banished the heretic to the Canaanite border, but not before expropriating all his wealth. And so it was in that land of Ur Kasdim that a miracle was performed on behalf of our patriarch Avraham. It might have been a hidden miracle, in which God imposed upon the king's subconscious that rather than put Avraham to death, he should free him from prison and send him on his way. Alternatively, it might have been a public miracle, when the monarch sentenced Avraham to death in the fiery furnace but he was saved from harm, as the Sages recount. Do not be misled by the questions posed by Rabbi Avraham Ibn Ezra, who wonders why the narrative [regarding Avraham's rescue from the furnace] was not included in the text, for I will explain the reason for its absence as well as that of other miracles: Those other nations [I mentioned] did not describe Avraham's miracle in their books because they argued with his perspective, and they believed that his salvation from a fiery death was a case of witchcraft, just as they believed of the demonstrations that Moshe our teacher performed in Egypt at the start of his mission. Hence the reason that the Torah does not describe the incident is because to do so would have necessitated a detailed account of his disputants' position as well, just as the text

29 alive, Haran died in the land of his birth, Ur Kasdim. Avram MAFTIR
and Naḥor married; the name of Avram's wife was Sarai, and
the name of Naḥor's wife was Milka. She was the daughter of

RAMBAN *(cont.)*

presents the responses of Pharaoh's sorcerers. The difference between the two cases is that Avraham never fully convinced his adversaries of the truth of his claim as our teacher Moshe eventually did. Still, a later verse alludes to the incident when it states: *And [God] told him, "I am the Lord who brought you out from Ur Kasdim to give you this land to possess it"* (15:7). Note the choice of the term "brought you out" [*hotzetikha*] which connotes the performance of a miracle [see Exodus 6:6], instead of "took you" [*lekaḥtikha*]. One is only "brought out" of a situation when he is imprisoned, as in the verse: *I am the Lord your God who brought you out of the land of Egypt, out of the house of slaves* (Exodus 20:2). Once Avraham's life was saved, he and his father Teraḥ were committed to traveling to the land of Canaan, far away from the land of Kasdim, out of fear of that region's king. For their native city of Ḥaran was too close by, and the citizens of the two locales shared a language – their common tongue was Aramaic – and a nationality. Father and son wished to travel to a place where their speech would not be understood by the local king or his people. It was for this reason that the family abandoned Ur Kasdim, as the verse states: *And together they set out from Ur Kasdim to go to the land of Canaan. But when they arrived in Ḥaran, they settled there* (11:31). Since that was where Teraḥ's people and ancestors had always dwelled, they settled among their kin and lived there for a while. While he was there, Avraham received the command to continue what he had planned on doing, and travel onward to Canaan. He left his father, who later died in Ḥaran, his homeland, and journeyed to the land of Canaan.

VERSE 29

RASHI

יִסְכָּה – *Yiska:* Yiska is another name for Sara. She was so called because she would look [*sokha* into the future] using divine inspiration. Alternatively, all people would look [*sokhin*] at her beauty. A third possibility: The name Yiska is connected to nobility [*nesikhut*], just as the term Sara represents authority [*serara*].

IBN EZRA

וְשֵׁם אֵשֶׁת־נָחוֹר מִלְכָּה – *The name of Naḥor's wife was Milka:* The Torah mentions the name of Naḥor's wife in order inform the reader about the lineage of Rivka, Raḥel, and Leah [which will be explored later, in 22:20–23; Raḥel and Leah were Rivka's nieces]. Now according to our Sages, Yiska is another name for Sara; if this idea is based on tradition, then we will accept it [despite the text's silence on this point]. Some commentators maintain that it was Avraham who was sterile; that it was not Sara who was unable to bear children, but this position directly contradicts the text [see 11:30]. Furthermore, Yishmael and the sons of Ketura [Avraham's progeny by other wives, mentioned in 25:2–4] can testify to Avraham's virility. Furthermore, I deny the claim the Sara was Avraham's sister [as suggested by 20:12]. If that were true, the present verse would have made mention of this.

וַאֲבִי יִסְכָּה – *Father of Yiska:* Yiska and Sara are not one and the same person [as Rashi asserts]. For if they were synonymous, the text would

ל לא מִלְכָּה וַאֲבִי יִסְכָּה: וַתְּהִי שָׂרַי עֲקָרָה אֵין לָהּ וָלָד: וַיִּקַּח

IBN EZRA *(cont.)*

have mentioned that Sarai was Teraḥ's granddaughter. Instead, the verse merely mentions her as his daughter-in-law. Furthermore, one should not rely on Avraham's later decision to refer to Sarai as his sister [in 20:12], for Avraham was merely rebuffing the people of Gerar. Similarly we find Avraham misleading his servants to deter them from taking part in the binding of Yitzḥak, as the verse states: *He told his young men, "Stay here with the donkey. I and the boy will go there and worship. Then we will come back to you"* (22:5). In that case Avraham fully planned to sacrifice his son [and hence his statement was not entirely true].... As for the claim that Sara was called Yiska because she saw [*sakha*] into the future with divine inspiration, that idea represents a homily but not tradition; there is no obligation to accept the assertion.... On the other hand, our early Sages maintain that our patriarch Avraham was cast into a fiery furnace, an episode that is not recalled in the Torah. However, if that is part of our tradition, we should acknowledge it as true as if it were included in the Written Law.

ḤIZKUNI

יִסְכָּה – *Yiska:* According to Rashi, Yiska was another name for Sarai. This means, that based on the sequence of their names, Haran must have fathered his first daughter when he was six years old, a position stated explicitly in Bereshit Rabba [see "Time of the Sages"]. The Talmud [in Sanhedrin 69b] maintains that in the early generations of humanity, people regularly became parents at the age of eight. This was also the case with Betzalel, Batsheva, Er and Onan.

VERSE 30

BEKHOR SHOR

וַתְּהִי שָׂרַי עֲקָרָה אֵין לָהּ וָלָד – *And Sarai was barren; she had no child:* The Torah seeks to demonstrate our patriarch Avraham's great love for God, for he relinquished all of his father's inheritance and everything that he owned to follow the divine command. Had Avraham been able to leave either a son or a daughter behind who could take over his portion of Teraḥ's estate, his departure would not have been as much of a sacrifice. However, since Avraham had no children, by obeying the order of the Holy One, blessed be He, he gave up everything he stood to receive from his father.

RABBEINU BAḤYA

וַתְּהִי שָׂרַי עֲקָרָה אֵין לָהּ וָלָד – *And Sarai was barren; she had no child:* There are some women who wait a long time to have children and are considered barren, but they later do give birth. Regarding Sarai, the text tells us both that she "was barren" and that "she had no child," suggesting that she was not biologically suited to ever become a mother. As such, Avram and Sarai agreed to leave their home and to travel to Canaan, hoping that the merit of the holy land would somehow assist them to procreate.

ABARBANEL

וַתְּהִי שָׂרַי עֲקָרָה אֵין לָהּ וָלָד – *And Sarai was barren; she had no child:* The Torah reports that Avram and Naḥor took wives for themselves: *The name of Avram's wife was Sarai, and the name of Naḥor's wife was Milka* (11:29). And although the text reveals that Milka was the

30 Haran, father of Milka and Yiska. And Sarai was barren – she
31 had no child. Teraḥ took his son Avram, and his grandson

ABARBANEL *(cont.)*

daughter of Haran, this was not the same Haran who was Teraḥ's son and Avraham's brother, for he had only one son: Lot. The verse therefore refers to a different man named Haran who had two daughters, Milka and Yiska. The Torah then reports that *Sarai was barren – she had no child*, and this caused Teraḥ great consternation. For out of his three sons, one [Haran] was no more, having died at a young age during his father's lifetime, and his second son Avram had no children at all. Because of this the family was in danger of dying out, and there is no greater tragedy than for the lineage of an important person to end abruptly. Now Avraham certainly did not marry as a young man, for he was perpetually fighting off one evil after another as he contended with the king of that land and his neighbors. These people plagued Avraham with accusations of being a heretic who denied their gods. Rather, it seems to me that Avraham married Sara when he was around forty years old. Thirty-five years later, the patriarch was seventy-five years old [as mentioned in 12:4] when he left Ḥaran at God's command. Thus Teraḥ was distressed that his son Avraham had been married for so long and had yet to produce any offspring. Teraḥ came to believe that perhaps the environment of Ur Kasdim was causing him all these troubles, and he therefore came up with the idea to leave the place. He would travel to the land of Canaan, where the air is wholesome due to the hills and mountains that are there – a climate fertile enough to produce a society of giants [as the spies relate in Numbers chapter 13]. And so, after witnessing the death of Haran and enduring the barrenness of Sarai, *Teraḥ took his son Avram...and his daughter-in-law Sarai* and set out. He did not take Sarai with him because he loved her [since, according to Abarbanel, she was no blood relation of his], but because she was *his son Avram's wife*. Teraḥ also had no way of knowing whether it was Avraham who was sterile or Sara who was infertile. Teraḥ removed his family from the wicked city of Ur Kasdim to alter their fortunes. He also took with him Lot, his grandson, out of compassion and concern lest he meet the same fate as his father. For most children inherit the physical character of their fathers, and Teraḥ worried that a combination of Lot's constitution and the atmosphere of Ur Kasdim would lead to his demise.

VERSE 31

RASHI

וַיֵּצְאוּ אִתָּם – *Together they set out:* The subjects of the verb *vayetze'u*, "set out," are Teraḥ and Avram, who left Ur Kasdim with Lot and Sarai.

IBN EZRA

וַיֵּצְאוּ אִתָּם – *Together they set out:* [Our verse does not mention that Naḥor accompanied Teraḥ and Avram; however, the man's family is later found in Ḥaran, when Yaakov arrives there in chapter 29. Ibn Ezra explains:] It is possible that Naḥor traveled to Ḥaran before his father Teraḥ did, or perhaps he went there later. In my opinion, the divine command that opens Parashat Lekh Lekha [to Avram to travel to Canaan, in 12:1] actually took place before the events of the current verse, *Teraḥ took his son Avram... and together they set out from Ur Kasdim to go to the land of Canaan*. For we find other places where the Torah's narrative is presented out of

תֶּרַח אֶת־אַבְרָם בְּנוֹ וְאֶת־לוֹט בֶּן־הָרָן בֶּן־בְּנוֹ וְאֵת שָׂרַי
כַּלָּתוֹ אֵשֶׁת אַבְרָם בְּנוֹ וַיֵּצְאוּ אִתָּם מֵאוּר כַּשְׂדִּים לָלֶכֶת
לב אַרְצָה כְּנַעַן וַיָּבֹאוּ עַד־חָרָן וַיֵּשְׁבוּ שָׁם׃ וַיִּהְיוּ יְמֵי־תֶרַח
חָמֵשׁ שָׁנִים וּמָאתַיִם שָׁנָה וַיָּמָת תֶּרַח בְּחָרָן׃

IBN EZRA *(cont.)*

chronological order. And we are told here that Teraḥ and Avraham *set out…to go to the land of Canaan*. [That is, Teraḥ and his family left their location in response to God's decree.] However, when Teraḥ arrived in Ḥaran, the place appealed to him, and he settled and then died there. For events in the Torah are not always recorded in chronological order.

RABBEINU BAḤYA

וַיִּקַּח תֶּרַח אֶת־אַבְרָם בְּנוֹ – *Teraḥ took his son Avram:* Even though the text states that *Teraḥ took his son Avram etc.*, really the move was Avram's initiative. However, because the son respected his father and appeared to follow him on the journey, Avram thereby ensured that Teraḥ remained the head of the family and was seen to lead the way. Hence the text gives us the impression that it was Teraḥ who led the family's migration, when in fact Sarai and Lot were traveling to a distant land for Avram's sake. For we see that even after Teraḥ died, Lot continued to journey with Avram.

ḤIZKUNI

וַיִּקַּח תֶּרַח אֶת־אַבְרָם בְּנוֹ – *Teraḥ took his son Avram:* Teraḥ was a descendant of Shem, to whom the land of Canaan was given as an inheritance, as the verse states: *Blessed be the Lord, God of Shem, Kenaan shall be his slave* (9:26). Accompanying Teraḥ were Sarai and Lot, who were brother and sister. [According to the Sages, Yiska, mentioned in verse 29, is Sarai; both she and Lot were children of Haran.] These two figures followed Teraḥ and Avram, who were the heads of the family. **וַיֵּצְאוּ אִתָּם מֵאוּר כַּשְׂדִּים** – *And together they set out from Ur Kasdim:* Teraḥ and Avram embarked on their journey in response to a command from the Holy One, blessed be He, as the verse states: *I am the Lord who brought you out from Ur Kasdim* (15:7). According to this approach, it is unclear where Avram was when he received this divine instruction. [It might have been received in Ur Kasdim or in Ḥaran.]

VERSE 32

RASHI

וַיָּמָת תֶּרַח בְּחָרָן – *And Teraḥ died in Ḥaran:* It was only after Avram left Ḥaran for the land of Canaan [in the following *parasha*] and had lived there for more than sixty years that Teraḥ died. This deduction is based on the following reasoning. The next chapter states: *Avram was seventy-five years old when he left Ḥaran* (12:4). We also know that Teraḥ was seventy years old when Avram was born [as stated in 11:26]. Adding these two facts together, we conclude that Teraḥ was one hundred and forty-five years old when Avram left Ḥaran. And yet, the father still had a long time to live. [Teraḥ lived another sixty years until the age of two hundred and five.] Why then does the text mention Teraḥ's death before Avram's

Lot, son of Haran, and his daughter-in-law Sarai, his son
Avram's wife, and together they set out from Ur Kasdim to go
to the land of Canaan. But when they arrived at Ḥaran, they
32 settled there. Teraḥ lived two hundred and five years, and he
died in Ḥaran.

RASHI *(cont.)*

departure [related at the start of chapter 12]? The goal of the Torah was to avoid publicizing how Avram left Teraḥ when the old man was still alive; the reader might have accused Avram of neglecting his filial obligation to respect his father. Furthermore, the text refers to Teraḥ as a dead man [although he lived for another sixty years], because even when alive, the wicked are considered dead, whereas the righteous are considered alive even when they die. Thus, the verse states: *Benayahu son of Yehoyada was the son of a living man* (II Samuel 23:20).

IBN EZRA

וַיָּמָת תֶּרַח בְּחָרָן – *And Teraḥ died in Ḥaran:* The text reports Teraḥ's death at this point, even though the man lived for an additional sixty years after Avraham's departure. It is common for Scripture to complete its discussion of one topic before moving on [although the subsequent subject overlaps the first chronologically].

RABBEINU BAḤYA

וַיָּמָת תֶּרַח בְּחָרָן – *And Teraḥ died in Ḥaran:* The text refers to Teraḥ as a dead man [even though he died only later – see Rashi] because of his wicked worship of idols; for evil people are called dead even while they are still alive. Now according to our Sages, when God promised Avraham: *You will join your ancestors in peace* (15:15), that implied that Teraḥ too was granted a share in the World to Come thanks to the merits of his son. Still, Teraḥ never strayed from his idolatrous ways throughout his lifetime, and he died still consumed by that wicked behavior. Note that the letter *nun* [the final letter] in the word *Ḥaran* appears upside down in the Torah scroll, hinting that Teraḥ died a sinner, as a result of God's anger [*ḥaron*]. Still, Teraḥ was granted entry into the Next World because of his illustrious son, and hence the fruit managed to save the tree it came from. Similarly, the Midrash states that all types of wood are suitable for fuel on the altar except for olive wood and grape vines. Since olive oil and wine are offered there, the fruit of these plants saved their parent trees from the fire. In a like manner Avraham rescued his father. And this is what God meant when he told Avraham: *You will join your ancestors in peace.*

SFORNO

וַיָּמָת תֶּרַח בְּחָרָן – *And Teraḥ died in Ḥaran:* Teraḥ himself made no attempt to achieve the final purpose of traveling from Ur Kasdim to Ḥaran [i.e., to continue on to Canaan], nor did he ever journey to Canaan to visit Avraham there. He remained away even while Avraham promoted the name of God and became widely known himself. Lot's behavior was the opposite of his grandfather's. He did accompany Avraham for a time, which is why Lot and his descendants merited to receive a portion of the patriarch's gifts [the kingdoms of Amon and Moav]. Meanwhile, Teraḥ's other descendants who were perhaps even more closely related to Avraham inherited nothing from him.

18TH CENTURY

RABBI ḤAYYIM IBN ATTAR – *OR HAḤAYYIM*,
1696, MOROCCO – 1743, ISRAEL

19TH CENTURY

RABBI YAAKOV TZVI MECKLENBURG – *HAKETAV VEHAKABBALA*,
1785 – 1865, GERMANY

SHADAL, 1800 – 1865, ITALY

RABBI SAMSON RAPHAEL HIRSCH,
1808 – 1888, GERMANY

MALBIM, 1809 – 1879, UKRAINE

RABBI NAFTALI TZVI YEHUDA BERLIN – *HAAMEK DAVAR*, 1816, BELARUS – 1893, POLAND

20TH CENTURY

RABBI DAVID TZVI HOFFMAN,
1843, HUNGARY – 1926, GERMANY

RABBI MEIR SIMḤA OF DVINSK – *MESHEKH ḤOKHMA*, 1843, LITHUANIA – 1926, LATVIA

RABBI AHARON KOTLER – *MISHNAT RABBI AHARON*, 1891, BELARUS – 1962, USA

RABBI JOSEPH B. SOLOVEITCHIK,
1903, LITHUANIA – 1993, USA

RABBI MENACHEM MENDEL SCHNEERSON – THE LUBAVITCHER REBBE,
1902, UKRAINE – 1994, USA

NEHAMA LEIBOWITZ,
1905, LATVIA – 1997, ISRAEL

פרשת נח

PARASHAT NOAḤ

CONFRONTING **MODERNITY**

ו ט אֵלֶּה תּוֹלְדֹת נֹחַ נֹחַ אִישׁ צַדִּיק תָּמִים הָיָה בְּדֹרֹתָיו אֶת־ ה
י הָאֱלֹהִים הִתְהַלֶּךְ־נֹחַ: וַיּוֹלֶד נֹחַ שְׁלֹשָׁה בָנִים אֶת־שֵׁם

CHAPTER 6, VERSE 9

OR HAḤAYYIM

אֵלֶּה תּוֹלְדֹת נֹחַ – *This is the story of Noaḥ:* The word *eleh* ["this," seems to rule out something else. It should be understood] in line with what the Sages said: Noaḥ boasted to Moshe: "I am greater than you [for I alone among all people was saved from the flood]." Responded Moshe: "True, you yourself were rescued. And yet, you lacked the power to prevent the destruction of your generation [whereas I managed to deliver Israel from disaster]." Thus when the Torah states: *This is the story of Noaḥ* [alternatively, "these are the generations of Noaḥ"], it means that Noaḥ was of no use to the rest of his generation; his merits sufficed only for his own survival. [The term *eleh* thus excludes the rest of civilization from the label of Noaḥ's generations.] This interpretation helps explain why the name "Noaḥ" appears twice in a row in this verse, [which emphasizes that Noaḥ's goodness benefited only himself.] Furthermore, this understanding extends to the claim that Noaḥ was *a person of integrity in his generation*. These words teach that Noaḥ could not influence the people around him or persuade them to abandon their wicked ways. Only Noaḥ and his sons were able to rely on his character. Noaḥ's sons are not mentioned here [as his "generations"] because they were considered an extension of their father and were essentially included within his name.

RABBI SAMSON RAPHAEL HIRSCH

אֵלֶּה תּוֹלְדֹת נֹחַ – *This is the story of Noaḥ:* This verse recalls an earlier statement which reads: *This is the story of the heavens and the earth when they were created* (2:4), a sentence which introduces the Torah's repeated description of creation. Here too we are about to read about a new beginning of the human race. For humanity had been sentenced to obliteration, and hence Noaḥ was, in a sense a second Adam, a founder of civilization. Now the text does not immediately list Noaḥ's sons, to teach that Noaḥ himself was his own first "descendant." Based on this our Sages declare that an individual's primary progeny, what he is said to leave behind in this world, is the character he has developed.... The text claims that Noaḥ "walked with God" – the people of his time mocked at him, and this led Noaḥ to abandon general society and to cleave only to God. Hence it was through Noaḥ that humankind gained the future that they had squandered.

HAAMEK DAVAR

אֵלֶּה תּוֹלְדֹת נֹחַ – *This is the story of Noaḥ:* [The word *toledot* literally means, "generations." But in this context, the phrase means simply:] These are the events of Noaḥ's life. **תָּמִים הָיָה בְּדֹרֹתָיו** – *A person of integrity in his generation:* The term *tzaddik* ["righteous man"] denotes a person whose behavior toward God is exemplary. A wicked person's character is the exact opposite. However, our verse claims that Noaḥ was a *tzaddik tamim* ["a righteous man of integrity," or "a wholly righteous man"] which indicates that his interactions with other people were also stellar.

6 9 This is the story of Noaḥ. Noaḥ was a righteous man, a person
10 of integrity in his generation; Noaḥ walked with God. And

MESHEKH ḤOKHMA

אִישׁ צַדִּיק תָּמִים הָיָה בְּדֹרֹתָיו – *A righteous man, a person of integrity in his generation:* [The world *bedorotav* is plural, implying two generations. This is because] Noaḥ lived in two separate generations: the world before the flood and the world after it. His character can be compared to that of each generation. According to the Talmud [Avoda Zara 6a], the term *tamim* refers to his character, while the word *tzaddik* refers to his actions. Rashi explains that passage in the Talmud to mean that his character was humble and modest, while his actions were devoid of violence. Now, in the generation that preceded the flood, Noaḥ's nonviolent and chaste actions – that he was a *tzaddik* – were notable, in contrast to the rest of society which was governed by violence and licentiousness. After the flood, however, humanity was chaste and nonviolent [and therefore Noaḥ's nonviolent character was less important]. Before the flood, Noaḥ's humility – that he was *tamim* – was not noteworthy, since others did not view him as righteous [and he therefore had no reason to become haughty] After the flood was over, Noaḥ remained alone and God spoke with him and blessed him, for Noaḥ had essentially saved all life on the planet. Then the verse needed to emphasize that Noaḥ remained humble. This also explains why before the flood God [emphasized only Noaḥ's righteousness, his lack of violence, when He] said to Noaḥ: *For I have seen you alone to be righteous before Me in this generation* (7:1), whereas God does not then mention that Noaḥ was *tamim*, ("modest").

NEHAMA LEIBOWITZ

תָּמִים הָיָה בְּדֹרֹתָיו – *A person of integrity in his generation:* [The language in this verse echoes similar praise used with regard to Avraham. However,] Noaḥ was not charged with the same divine mission to spread the word of God abroad as Avraham, since he only possessed the capacity to save himself, but not others. Regarding him is it not stated: *For I have chosen him* (Genesis 18:19) implying divine choice as in the case of Avraham.

VERSE 10

RABBI SAMSON RAPHAEL HIRSCH

וַיּוֹלֶד נֹחַ שְׁלֹשָׁה בָנִים – *And Noaḥ had three sons:* Noaḥ was five hundred years old when he became a father to three sons. The earlier generations of humanity sired children when they were much younger than that. Hence we must surmise that Noaḥ had intentionally delayed marrying and having children, for he was reluctant to start a family for himself. Noaḥ worried that, at a time when the world around him was corrupt, violent, and heartless, he would be unable to build a pure household and to raise sons who were themselves righteous and characterized by integrity. Only twenty years after God decreed the end of the world, after a five-hundred-year lifetime without a wife and children, during which he trained himself to walk in the ways of God, only then Noaḥ risked becoming a father. אֶת־שֵׁם אֶת־חָם וְאֶת־יָפֶת – *Shem, Ḥam, and Yefet:* The name "Shem" reflects spiritual strengths; the name "Ḥam" [literally, "hot"] suggests the stormy dimension of sensuality;

יא אֶת־חָם וְאֶת־יָפֶת׃ וַתִּשָּׁחֵת הָאָרֶץ לִפְנֵי הָאֱלֹהִים וַתִּמָּלֵא
יב הָאָרֶץ חָמָס׃ וַיַּרְא אֱלֹהִים אֶת־הָאָרֶץ וְהִנֵּה נִשְׁחָתָה כִּי־

RABBI SAMSON RAPHAEL HIRSCH *(cont.)*

and the term "Yefet" refers to the human soul and imagination, that which is attracted to things of beauty [*yofi*].... These three traits incorporate the inner life of human beings. When an individual's soul is healthy, all three dimensions strive together toward a noble purpose. Such was the character of Noaḥ himself. His lofty spiritual strength is expressed in the verse *Noaḥ walked with God* (6:9); that his sensuality was elevated is alluded to in the term *tamim* ["integrity"]; and Noaḥ's [lofty] desires and aspirations are reflected in the word *tzaddik* ["righteous"]. When these three elements are distributed between different people, Shem symbolizes reason, Ḥam represents the senses, and Yefet epitomizes the pursuit of beauty. It is therefore Shem's task to walk with God, Ḥam's mission to be virtuous, and Yefet's job to be righteous, to be guided by the ideal of the good and not that of beauty. In truth, the attribute of Yefet also protects people from overstimulation of the senses, and Yefet's laws serve to limit physical indulgence.... Later on in our commentary we will explore in a more direct way the different attributes that comprised the nations that emerged after the flood.... We accept with perfect faith that all the various branches of humankind were created for the purpose of developing the ideal human being, and for reaching the ultimate and singular goal as stated by the prophet: *For knowledge of the Lord will fill the earth as waters cover the ocean* (Isaiah 11:9).

HAAMEK DAVAR

שְׁלֹשָׁה בָנִים – *Three sons:* The fact that Noaḥ had three sons was another reason why Noaḥ deserved to be the father of the next civilization. Each of these men possessed a different type of strength, just like the three sons of the first man, Adam.

VERSE 11

OR HAḤAYYIM

חָמָס – *Violence:* The term *ḥamas* is a general category for all manner of evil including theft, unlawful sexual unions, murder, and idolatry.

SHADAL

לִפְנֵי הָאֱלֹהִים – *In God's sight:* In God's thought. Even though humanity did not understand that a society wracked with violence could not endure, God knew this very well. We should similarly explain the subsequent verse, *The end of all flesh has come before Me* (6:13).

MALBIM

וַתִּשָּׁחֵת הָאָרֶץ – *The earth had become corrupt:* The text teaches that society had become corrupt regarding all three aspects of the human being, each of which contrasts with Noaḥ's character. First, regarding the spiritual, divine aspect of humans: Noaḥ walked with God, whereas the rest of humanity *had become corrupt in God's sight* (6:11) by promoting the

11 Noaḥ had three sons: Shem, Ḥam, and Yefet. The earth had be-
12 come corrupt in God's sight, full of violence. And when God
saw how corrupt the earth had become, all flesh corrupting its

MALBIM *(cont.)*

decay of their thoughts and beliefs. Second, regarding humans as social animals: Noaḥ is said to have been *a righteous man, a person of integrity* (6:9) who exercised justice and virtue. Others filled the world with violence by committing transgressions against each other, indulging in theft and injustice, undermining interpersonal relations. [Third,] regarding the animal aspect of the human being: Humans should follow natural law and morality, such as the prohibitions of murder or forcefully kidnapping women and the like. [The next verse explains:] *When God saw how corrupt the earth had become, all flesh corrupting its ways upon the earth* (6:12). This refers to the corruption even of natural law.

HAAMEK DAVAR

וַתִּשָּׁחֵת הָאָרֶץ – *The earth had become corrupt:* That is, the people of the earth had become corrupt [and not the earth itself].

RABBI JOSEPH B. SOLOVEITCHIK

וַתִּשָּׁחֵת הָאָרֶץ – *The earth had become corrupt:* Rashi indicates that God's decision to punish the generation of the flood was sealed due to their involvement in thievery. Apparently, the other sins of that generation could have been forgiven. Ramban expands this idea, suggesting that the law against robbery and stealing is a logical one, and awareness of its violation should have been obvious to all. The apparently superfluous words "before God" appear because the prohibition against stealing could result only from open rebellion against God. Along similar lines, the Torah elsewhere describes the sin of a person who was entrusted with a valuable item for safekeeping, and then expropriates it by denying ever having accepted the item to be watched, as *a trespass against God* (Leviticus 5:21). One who truly fears God refrains from sinning against his fellow man.

VERSE 12

HAKETAV VEHAKABBALA

אֶת־דַּרְכּוֹ עַל־הָאָרֶץ – *Its ways upon the earth:* The preposition *al* ["upon"] should be understood as "because of".... For the land itself caused humanity to become corrupt. The soil was blessed and produced great bounties of food, and the wealth led people to sin. This is the sense of the earlier verse *The Lord saw how great man's wickedness was upon the earth* (6:5). As such, the ground was included in the punishment God exacted from the world, as the verse states: *I am about to destroy them, along with all the earth* (6:13). Thus, God planned for the planet to become desolate and feeble. It would no longer have the natural strength to bring forth fruit in great quantities or of the quality it had before.

RABBI DAVID TZVI HOFFMAN

וַיַּרְא אֱלֹהִים – *And when God saw:* The present verse stands in contrast to an earlier verse, *Then God saw all that He had made: and it was very good* (1:31). For just as initially the

יג הִשְׁחִית כָּל־בָּשָׂר אֶת־דַּרְכּוֹ עַל־הָאָרֶץ׃ וַיֹּאמֶר
אֱלֹהִים לְנֹחַ קֵץ כָּל־בָּשָׂר בָּא לְפָנַי כִּי־מָלְאָה הָאָרֶץ חָמָס
יד מִפְּנֵיהֶם וְהִנְנִי מַשְׁחִיתָם אֶת־הָאָרֶץ׃ עֲשֵׂה לְךָ תֵּבַת
עֲצֵי־גֹפֶר קִנִּים תַּעֲשֶׂה אֶת־הַתֵּבָה וְכָפַרְתָּ אֹתָהּ מִבַּיִת
טו וּמִחוּץ בַּכֹּפֶר׃ וְזֶה אֲשֶׁר תַּעֲשֶׂה אֹתָהּ שְׁלֹשׁ מֵאוֹת אַמָּה
אֹרֶךְ הַתֵּבָה חֲמִשִּׁים אַמָּה רָחְבָּהּ וּשְׁלֹשִׁים אַמָּה קוֹמָתָהּ׃

RABBI DAVID TZVI HOFFMAN *(cont.)*

existence of the world was sustained by divine sight, so too did God's sight precede earth's destruction. כָּל־בָּשָׂר – *All flesh:* It is likely that this refers to all life, including the animals and the beasts. Still, the obliteration of the animals was not in response to theft and violence as it was with regard to humanity. Rather, the animals' crimes involved mating with species that were not their own. That corrupted their nature.

VERSE 13

OR HAḤAYYIM

וַיֹּאמֶר אֱלֹהִים לְנֹחַ – *God said to Noaḥ:* God divulged to Noaḥ His plan to destroy all life on earth, so that He could command him to build an ark through which Noaḥ would preserve the human race. Now the question must be asked: Why did Noaḥ squander the opportunity for righteousness by not seeking the Almighty's mercy in sparing the world? This problem becomes even more difficult when we note that, according to the Sages, our patriarch Avraham [who begged God to spare the city of Sedom] learned by example from Noaḥ. They explain that Avraham [realized that despite the righteousness of the eight people on the ark – Noaḥ, his wife, their three sons, and their three wives – God would destroy the entire world. Therefore, Avraham] asked God to save Sedom only if there were at least ten righteous people, i.e. more than had been saved at the time of Noaḥ. This midrash remains problematic, since Noaḥ had actually made no petition whatsoever. Perhaps if Noaḥ had begged God for a reprieve based on the merits of the eight individuals, God would have conceded [and saved the entire world]. It seems that Noaḥ inferred from the language that God used when announcing the end of the world that He was determined to carry through with His threat. When God said to Noaḥ: *The end of all flesh has come before Me.... I am about to destroy them* (6:13), He provided Noaḥ with no opportunity to change God's mind through prayer. In contrast, when God appeared to Avraham regarding Sedom, He spoke less definitively. Instead, God offered Avraham the opportunity to pray on behalf of the city by saying to Avraham: *I shall go down now and see if they have really done as much as the outcry that has reached Me. If not, I will know* (18:21). Even though the decree against Sedom had in fact already been finalized, God still encouraged Avraham to pray for salvation in order to demonstrate His methods of conducting the world.

13 ways upon the earth, God said to Noaḥ, "The end of
all flesh has come before Me, for the earth is full of violence
because of them. I am about to destroy them, along with all the
14 earth. So make yourself an ark of cypress wood. Make it with
15 compartments and coat it in pitch inside and out. This is how
you shall make it: the ark shall be three hundred cubits long,

MALBIM

וַיֹּאמֶר אֱלֹהִים לְנֹחַ – *God said to Noaḥ:* God wanted to save the cluster of grapes that was Noaḥ and his family, and therefore He informed Noaḥ of His plan to destroy the rest of the corrupted vineyard. For God saw that it had become too late to correct humanity and to restore the three aspects of humans. Hence the verse states His ultimate decision: *The end of all flesh has come before Me*, for the planet is overrun with violence. When the people had destroyed natural law and divine law, that affected them only on an individual level, and not on a communal one. In contrast, the cruelty that characterized humankind reflected a collapse of the social laws, the mutual assistance and commitment to the rules that are the foundation of the political community. This was a collective rather than a personal malady. Thus God determined to destroy the whole of society.

VERSE 14

RABBI SAMSON RAPHAEL HIRSCH

עֲשֵׂה לְךָ תֵּבַת עֲצֵי־גֹפֶר – *So make yourself an ark of cypress wood:* The text intentionally spells out for the reader all of the ark's particulars and details, in order to emphasize that Noaḥ himself built the boat following all of God's instructions. Now God could have saved Noaḥ in any number of ways, and questions regarding the dimensions and quality of the ark abound. For example, was the ark as described in our passage truly big enough to contain all the world's animal species? Still, we may ignore those questions, for the message of our text is clear: God chose only one man, in order to save him, his family, and all of the animal life on the planet. Yet, the salvation would only be effected if Noaḥ did exactly as God commanded. We recall the famous rabbinic dictum, as stated in Kiddushin 31a: "Greater is the individual who acts in response to divine command than one who acts when not commanded." This is a fundamental principle in the Torah. Contrary to popular opinion, there can be great value to a person's actions in this world if they align with the will of the Almighty. What one tries to achieve based on his own considerations and imagination can only be said to have a distant, secondary, and perhaps doubtful significance. Noaḥ could have done many things during the 120 years that God granted him before the onset of the flood. He might have spent the time building a hundred little arks. And yet, the text teaches us that Noaḥ did *all that God commanded him* (6:22), leaving God to do the rest.

יט צֹ֣הַר ׀ תַּֽעֲשֶׂ֣ה לַתֵּבָ֗ה וְאֶל־אַמָּה֙ תְּכַלֶּ֣נָּה מִלְמַ֔עְלָה וּפֶ֥תַח הַתֵּבָ֖ה בְּצִדָּ֣הּ תָּשִׂ֑ים תַּחְתִּיִּ֛ם שְׁנִיִּ֥ם וּשְׁלִשִׁ֖ים תַּעֲשֶֽׂהָ: יז וַאֲנִ֗י הִנְנִי֩ מֵבִ֨יא אֶת־הַמַּבּ֥וּל מַ֨יִם֙ עַל־הָאָ֔רֶץ לְשַׁחֵ֣ת כָּל־בָּשָׂ֗ר אֲשֶׁר־בּוֹ֙ ר֣וּחַ חַיִּ֔ים מִתַּ֖חַת הַשָּׁמָ֑יִם כֹּ֥ל אֲשֶׁר־בָּאָ֖רֶץ יִגְוָֽע: יח וַהֲקִמֹתִ֥י אֶת־בְּרִיתִ֖י אִתָּ֑ךְ וּבָאתָ֙ אֶל־הַתֵּבָ֔ה אַתָּ֕ה וּבָנֶ֛יךָ

MALBIM

עֲשֵׂה לְךָ תֵּבַת עֲצֵי־גֹפֶר – *So make yourself an ark of cypress wood:* The ark itself alluded to the nature of the world that would rise anew after the flood. The new world would float above the destructive waters that were washing away the old world, in which materialism had been allowed to dominate spirituality and where the soiled material aspects of existence had become more important than spirituality. But the world after the flood would be built from cypress wood, which floats on water since its spiritual [airy] aspects are greater than its material and dirty earth. God hinted to Noah that in the new world the strength of the spirit would be greater than the power of the material.

VERSE 16

THE LUBAVITCHER REBBE

צֹהַר תַּעֲשֶׂה לַתֵּבָה – *Make a window for the ark:* A window creates no light of its own; it simply allows existing light to enter. A luminous stone, on the other hand, is itself a source of light. Metaphorically, creating light for the ark means bringing divine consciousness into a world that obscures divinity…. This is what it means to make a window: to break through the facade of nature and allow "divine light" to enter…. Once we make the window and allow supernatural Godly light to permeate our awareness, we attain an even higher perspective. We learn to see nature itself as an object of light and revelation.

VERSE 17

RABBI SAMSON RAPHAEL HIRSCH

יִגְוָע – *Will die:* Our Sages have already pointed out that the verb *yigva* refers to the death of righteous people. The Midrash makes this comment while interpreting the verse *Avraham breathed his last [vayigva] and died in his ripe old age, aged and satisfied, and was gathered to his people* (25:8). We find the term similarly used regarding the passing of Yitzhak [in 35:29], and Yaakov [in 49:33]. How surprising that the verb should appear here regarding the obliteration of this wicked generation! The Torah's choice of language is fraught with meaning. For in the present instance, it is not a human who is planning the apocalypse. Instead, the Creator of the world, the merciful and compassionate One, is planning the destruction. Hence the term *gava* is highly significant. When death is preceded by *gevia*, that signifies that the person has left the world without suffering. Thus the Sages explain the term *gevia* as reflecting a sort of dormancy or frozenness. As such, the merciful God exercised compassion even while He was punishing humankind. The survivor Noah would have been unable to bear the thought of millions of lives being snuffed out slowly and painfully. Hence God describes for Noah in advance the sort of death that He will bring to humanity: *Everything on earth will*

16 fifty cubits wide, and thirty cubits high. Make a window for the
ark, and taper the latter to within a cubit of the top. Put a door
in the side of the ark and make lower, middle, and upper decks.
17 And I – I am about to bring floodwaters over the earth to destroy all flesh that has within it the breath of life under the heav-
18 ens. Everything on earth will die. But I will establish My covenant with you, and you will enter the ark – you, your sons, your

RABBI SAMSON RAPHAEL HIRSCH *(cont.)*

die [yigva]. In other words, all consciousness across the world will be frozen before death, reduced painlessly to matter. God will act only on inanimate elements.

MALBIM

וַאֲנִי – *And I:* The Torah emphasizes that God Himself brought the flood. This was to counter the gentile philosophers, who maintain that the deluge was a natural catastrophe, an inevitable occurrence in such a young world. Hence, the verse specifies that God's providence caused the flood.

HAAMEK DAVAR

אֶת־הַמַּבּוּל מַיִם – *Floodwaters:* The term *mabbul* means, "something that leads to destruction," much like the names "Yuval" [mentioned in 4:21] or "Tuval Kayin" [in 4:22], who led [*hovil*] the world to its destruction. The devastation would have been termed a *mabbul* whether the mechanism to affect it had been water or fire. [Hence, the verse had to specify that the *mabbul mayim* consisted of water.]

THE LUBAVITCHER REBBE

אֶת־הַמַּבּוּל מַיִם – *Floodwaters:* The word for flood [*mabbul*] is related to the word confusion [*balal*]. Metaphorically, the waters of the flood drown us, along with our minds, by confusing us as to what is primary and what is secondary in life.

VERSE 18

HAKETAV VEHAKABBALA

וַהֲקִמֹתִי אֶת־בְּרִיתִי – *But I will establish My covenant:* The nature of the covenant is explained by the verses that follow. God tells Noaḥ that He will perform a new and wondrous miracle on the man's behalf, namely that the small boat will nevertheless contain all the collected animals, birds, and beasts.

RABBI SAMSON RAPHAEL HIRSCH

וַהֲקִמֹתִי אֶת־בְּרִיתִי – *But I will establish My covenant:* A covenant represents an unconditional promise. It is to be fulfilled unfettered by external factors, and even in opposition to them. The pledge of a covenant is literally absolute, severed from all influences and stipulations. The nature of such a pact extends to the verb that defines its establishment: *keritat berit* [literally, "the cutting of a covenant"], for something that is torn asunder cannot be easily repaired. In contrast, the phrase *hakamat berit* [literally, "the raising of a covenant"] means the realization of a promise.

יט וְאִשְׁתְּךָ וּנְשֵׁי־בָנֶיךָ אִתָּךְ: וּמִכָּל־הָחַי מִכָּל־בָּשָׂר שְׁנַיִם מִכֹּל
כ תָּבִיא אֶל־הַתֵּבָה לְהַחֲיֹת אִתָּךְ זָכָר וּנְקֵבָה יִהְיוּ: מֵהָעוֹף
לְמִינֵהוּ וּמִן־הַבְּהֵמָה לְמִינָהּ מִכֹּל רֶמֶשׂ הָאֲדָמָה לְמִינֵהוּ
כא שְׁנַיִם מִכֹּל יָבֹאוּ אֵלֶיךָ לְהַחֲיוֹת: וְאַתָּה קַח־לְךָ מִכָּל־מַאֲכָל

HAAMEK DAVAR

וַהֲקִמֹתִי אֶת־בְּרִיתִי – *But I will establish My covenant:* [Literally, "I will uphold My covenant," implying that the covenant had already been made in the past. The Netziv explains:] God refers here to the previous covenant that the world would endure – that is, the blessing bestowed on Adam and Ḥava [in 1:28: *Be fertile and multiply. Fill the earth and subdue it*]. God assures Noaḥ that this covenant will be fulfilled through the survival of him and his sons.

VERSE 19

RABBI SAMSON RAPHAEL HIRSCH

וּמִכָּל־הָחַי – *Each living creature:* According to our Sages, the power of corruption had infected all of the planet's animals [who were sexually engaged with animals of other species], thereby weakening the life force within them as well. Therefore, the verse uses the phrase "each living creature" – only those beasts which have retained their vigor will be invited onto the ark. Similarly, God directs Noaḥ to bring a *male and female* into the ark, He employs the verb *yihyu* ["they will be"] and not *tavi* ["you shall bring"]. This emphasizes that the specimens had to be untainted [i.e., in their original state of "being"] males and females. And it seems to me that this criterion of purity is also alluded to in verse 20 with the repeated usage of the word *minehu* ["its species," which appears three times in the Hebrew]. Only those animals and birds who have been loyal to their species and are still pure representatives of their type shall be saved. Specimens who have mixed with other kinds of beasts are fraudulent and will perish. We find further emphasis on the preservation of animal purity below, when the verse states: *Take seven and seven of every pure animal, seven pairs* [*ish ve'ishto,* literally, "a man and his wife"], *and two of every animal that is not pure, of each kind a pair [ish ve'ishto]* (7:2). The pairs of rescued animals were free of all corruption, and were [referred to with the human terms, husband and wife], because God elevated them at their moment of salvation. The nature of the corruption across the planet was one of sexual deviance, and the character of salvation was defined by chaste behavior.

THE LUBAVITCHER REBBE

לְהַחֲיֹת אִתָּךְ – *To keep alive with you:* Metaphorically, this teaches us that it is our duty to bring anyone and everyone in danger of spiritually "drowning" into the shelter of our personal, spiritual "ark." The doctrine of divine providence implies that when God arranges for us to find out that someone needs help, it is because we are meant to draw him into our lives and bring him closer to Godliness.

19 wife, and your sons' wives with you. And you shall take two of
each living creature, male and female, into the ark to keep alive
20 with you. Of every kind of bird, animal, and wild beast, bring
21 two to keep alive. As for you, take all the food to be eaten and

VERSE 20

SHADAL

יָבֹאוּ אֵלֶיךָ לְהַחֲיוֹת – *Bring to keep alive:* It is your task to sustain the animals and ensure that their lives are not lost.

VERSE 21

MALBIM

וְאַתָּה קַח־לְךָ מִכָּל־מַאֲכָל – *As for you, take all the food:* God said to Noaḥ: Even though the animals will flock to you by themselves, they will not bring their own food. You will have to provide sustenance for all the passengers on the ark, including those who usually store food during summer in advance of winter. Furthermore, you will have to gather food for yourself to eat during the flood. That is the sense of the pronoun emphasized in the expression *kaḥ lekha*, which could be translated literally as, "take for yourself." Noaḥ had to gather diverse kinds of food for all the kinds of animals who would, as it were, eat from Noaḥ's table. Noaḥ's kindness to the animals justified the later permission for humans to eat meat. This was Noaḥ's reward for sharing his food with the creatures, which saved their lives over the course of the year.

HAAMEK DAVAR

וְאַתָּה קַח־לְךָ מִכָּל־מַאֲכָל – *As for you, take all the food:* [The verse uses the expression *kaḥ lekha*, literally, "take for yourself." This means,] take food that is appropriate for your own diet. You need not seek special foods for the benefit of animals who are gathering from distant places [and who have distinctive diets]. Noaḥ imagined that he would be required to send agents to distant lands to gather food that would satisfy the diverse animal species. However, the Almighty did not make such demands of Noaḥ. God allowed him to store whatever provisions he could. The doubling of the language in the verse [*maakhal asher ye'akhel* – "food to be eaten"] is meant to include food that cattle eat raw, as I have explained in comments to Leviticus 11:34. The prediction that *it will be for food for you and for them* promises that whatever food Noaḥ brings on board will be adequate and nourishing for all creatures.

THE LUBAVITCHER REBBE

וְאַתָּה קַח־לְךָ מִכָּל־מַאֲכָל – *As for you, take all the food:* Noaḥ's feeding the animals can be likened to our providing spiritual nourishment to others. When at times we encounter major difficulties in this work we must persevere under all circumstances, as Noaḥ did, especially since the hardships and discomforts that we encounter are rarely so severe that they cause us to groan and spit blood.

כב אֲשֶׁ֤ר יֵֽאָכֵל֙ וְאָסַפְתָּ֣ אֵלֶ֔יךָ וְהָיָ֥ה לְךָ֛ וְלָהֶ֖ם לְאׇכְלָֽה: וַיַּ֖עַשׂ נֹ֑חַ
ז א כְּ֠כֹל אֲשֶׁ֨ר צִוָּ֥ה אֹת֛וֹ אֱלֹהִ֖ים כֵּ֥ן עָשָֽׂה: וַיֹּ֤אמֶר יהוה֙ לְנֹ֔חַ *שני*
בֹּֽא־אַתָּ֥ה וְכׇל־בֵּיתְךָ֖ אֶל־הַתֵּבָ֑ה כִּֽי־אֹתְךָ֥ רָאִ֛יתִי צַדִּ֥יק
ב לְפָנַ֖י בַּדּ֥וֹר הַזֶּֽה: מִכֹּ֣ל ׀ הַבְּהֵמָ֣ה הַטְּהוֹרָ֗ה תִּֽקַּח־לְךָ֛ שִׁבְעָ֥ה
שִׁבְעָ֖ה אִ֣ישׁ וְאִשְׁתּ֑וֹ וּמִן־הַבְּהֵמָ֡ה אֲ֠שֶׁ֠ר לֹ֣א טְהֹרָ֥ה הִ֛וא

VERSE 22

MALBIM

וַיַּעַשׂ נֹחַ – *Noah did so:* Up to now, Noah was commanded to construct the ark and gather the food. These tasks were to be done immediately. Yet, Noah would not have to gather the animals until the day of the storm. Earlier, when God told Noah: *So make yourself an ark of cypress wood* (6:14), that was an immediate command, as was the instruction to *take all the food to be eaten and store it* (6:21). However, the statements *You will enter the ark* (6:18), and *You shall take two of each living creature* (6:19), although expressed early on, were only to be performed much later. This verse, *Noah did so: all that God commanded him, he fulfilled*, refers only to the building of the ark and the storing of the provisions.

CHAPTER 7, VERSE 1

MALBIM

וַיֹּאמֶר יהוה לְנֹחַ – *Then the LORD said to Noah:* The Torah now reports God's communication to Noah that took place seven days before the flood. This instruction was not part of God's earlier message to Noah. Note that this verse refers to God using the unique four-letter name of God, while the earlier verses refer to God as *Elohim*. The divine name *Elohim* connotes God as Creator of the world, He who made the universe and sustains it. Hence, we find only the name *Elohim* in the first chapter of Genesis. Similarly, the name *Elohim* appears early in the Noah story, when speaking of God's global providence over the earth and His plan to preserve the animal species by having Noah save one pair of every species. The name "the LORD" appears here, later in the Noah story, because now God is acting with special providence over Noah. God here protects this righteous man, his possessions, and all his family's needs. Noah was rich with silver, gold, tools, and household goods. He also had his own domesticated livestock — both pure and impure animals — and his own birds such as doves and chickens. Noah did not know whether or not he would be permitted to take these possessions with him on the ark in the same way that he was allowed to take with him the clothes he was wearing. Thus, God now told Noah: *Enter the ark, you and all your household*, meaning that Noah was to pack all his property and store it on the ark before the voyage. That is why God now tells Noah: *For I have seen you alone to be righteous*. God meant that this grace was not due to God's general providence over the world through which He had spoken with him earlier using the name *Elohim*. Rather, the favor was granted to Noah because he was virtuous, and as an expression of the four-letter name of God, which carries connotations of compassion over Noah and his household.

22 store it: it will be for food for you and for them." Noaḥ did so:
7 1 all that God commanded him, he fulfilled. Then the LORD said SHENI
to Noaḥ, "Enter the ark, you and all your household, for I have
seen you alone to be righteous before Me in this generation.
2 Take seven and seven of every pure animal, seven pairs, and

RABBI DAVID TZVI HOFFMAN

בֹּא־אַתָּה וְכָל־בֵּיתְךָ אֶל־הַתֵּבָה – *Enter the ark, you and all your household:* This instruction refers to Noaḥ's household animals, those which are easily domesticated. These species are later defined as "pure" animals, fit for sacrifice. Perhaps Noaḥ received a special revelation regarding this matter [which detailed for him which exactly were the pure animals].

THE LUBAVITCHER REBBE

בֹּא־אַתָּה וְכָל־בֵּיתְךָ אֶל־הַתֵּבָה – *Enter the ark, you and all your household:* Although we have said that "entering the ark" metaphorically signifies immersing ourselves in the words of Torah study and prayer, this does not imply that we should be oblivious to the needs of others. We must not be content with our own self-preservation alone. We are obligated to bring our families, our children, and ultimately the entire world into a wholesome safe haven of Torah study and prayer. The plight of our fellow should give us no rest, for we are all like one organism – if one of us is spiritually ill, we are all affected.

VERSE 2

HAKETAV VEHAKABBALA

מִכֹּל הַבְּהֵמָה הַטְּהוֹרָה תִּקַּח־לְךָ שִׁבְעָה שִׁבְעָה – *Taken seven and seven of every pure animal:* God commanded Noaḥ to take with him more pure animal specimens than those of impure species, because the former are more critical to human life than the latter. Thus, the later verse [7:3] specifies that these animals are *to keep their kind alive across the earth.*

RABBI SAMSON RAPHAEL HIRSCH

מִכֹּל הַבְּהֵמָה הַטְּהוֹרָה – *Of every pure animal:* What is the meaning of the word *tahor* ["pure"]? The term is connected to the word *tzohar* ["window," in that the words share the last two letters of the root]. Indeed, the Aramaic word for *tzohorayim* ["noon," a word related to *tzohar*] is *tihara* [related to *tahor*]. Thus, *tzohar* should be understood as a transparent object which allows light to pass through. I propose that when an item is *tahor*, it is permeable and lets God's light penetrate it. Who is considered a *tahor* person? One who is prepared to receive the Divine Spirit and to allow God's illumination into the soul and body. The opposing state to that is called *tum'a* ["impurity"], for one who is *tamei* is blocked off and closed to the light of God.

HAAMEK DAVAR

מִכֹּל הַבְּהֵמָה הַטְּהוֹרָה – *Of every pure animal:* According to Rashi, the Torah here uses the word *tehora* ["pure"] to mean animals which Israel will be permitted to eat in the future. However, the straightforward meaning of the term is that these animals should be without blemish.

ג שְׁנַיִם אִישׁ וְאִשְׁתּוֹ׃ גַּם מֵעוֹף הַשָּׁמַיִם שִׁבְעָה שִׁבְעָה זָכָר
ד וּנְקֵבָה לְחַיּוֹת זֶרַע עַל־פְּנֵי כָל־הָאָרֶץ׃ כִּי לְיָמִים עוֹד שִׁבְעָה
אָנֹכִי מַמְטִיר עַל־הָאָרֶץ אַרְבָּעִים יוֹם וְאַרְבָּעִים לָיְלָה
וּמָחִיתִי אֶת־כָּל־הַיְקוּם אֲשֶׁר עָשִׂיתִי מֵעַל פְּנֵי הָאֲדָמָה׃

VERSE 3

MALBIM

גַּם מֵעוֹף הַשָּׁמַיִם שִׁבְעָה שִׁבְעָה – *Also take seven pairs of each kind of bird:* This means that Noaḥ is to take seven pairs of each pure species of bird [unlike other impure animals, which God commanded Noaḥ to take two of]. God does not instruct Noaḥ to take only two representatives of the impure birds, because Noaḥ did not have in his household impure birds. In contrast, the impure animals [such as the horse and the donkey] were used to plow and to ride. But the impure birds are birds of prey and are typically not household animals. God tells Noaḥ that the excess pure birds are being saved *to keep their kind alive across the earth*, suggesting that if there remained only a few specimens of these species, there would not be enough for him after the flood. There was another reason for this command. It is well known that all domesticated beasts and household pets were once wild animals. Today we can still find untamed relatives of species which humans have domesticated, such as wild oxen, wild donkeys, and wild geese. At first, all of God's creatures were savage, whereupon humans selected some of the animals, subdued them, and trained them to be used for our own purposes. Civilization was able to change the very nature of these beasts along with their appearance and their diets. In order to preserve undomesticated species of animals, it was sufficient for a single pair to survive aboard the ark. These were creatures which retained the original character that God had imbued them with. In contrast, even though the domesticated animals would be destroyed in the flood, such beasts had not been part of the original creation. Humans after the flood would still have been able to capture and train wild animals, changing their behavior to domesticate them. Therefore, [in chapter 6] God issued the command to save the animals using the name *Elohim*, which relates to the preservation of the world. Hence, God only mandated that Noaḥ take onto the ark one pair each of the wild animals. However, God addressed Noaḥ [at the start of the chapter 7] by using the unique four-letter name of God, which represented His direct providence over Noaḥ and his sons. God, acting on this compassionate dimension, desired that the surviving people would not have to return to the original conditions of nature. Instead, in the transition from the old world to the new, God wanted to preserve the progress that humans had made in domesticating the animals. If humankind was forced to reinvent and redesign all the tools it had developed for plowing and other human labor, it would have set civilization back a thousand years. Hence, God told Noaḥ to take aboard with him everything that he had in his house, for Noaḥ's family possessed all the tools which

3 two of every animal that is not pure, of each kind a pair. Also
take seven pairs of each kind of bird, male and female, to keep
4 their kind alive across the earth. For in seven days' time I will
send rain on the earth for forty days and forty nights, and I will
wipe from the face of the earth every living creature I have

MALBIM *(cont.)*

human beings had devised over the centuries. Similarly, if Noaḥ had not been permitted to salvage the domesticated animals, he and his descendants would have had to start over with the wild creatures, training and teaching them to work with people – achievements that would have taken many years to reproduce. This is why Noaḥ was allowed to put onto the ark the domesticated species he had employed in his household. Still, there was a limit to how many of these work animals could be saved. Only seven pairs of each kind of domesticated beast were granted passage on the ark, a vessel that had a finite amount of space.

VERSE 4

RABBI SAMSON RAPHAEL HIRSCH

אָנֹכִי מַמְטִיר – *I will send rain:* The diligent student of Scripture will recognize the difference between the pronouns *anokhi* ["I"], used in this verse, and *ani* [a different word that means "I"], when God uses these terms in reference to Himself. If God employs the word *anokhi*, it demonstrates a closeness between Him and His creations, and demonstrates that God is treating people with kindness and compassion. In contrast, the term *ani* reflects the divine personality who acts from a distance, while remaining detached from the object of His attention. If this distinction is accurate, the use of *anokhi* here is significant. God is sending the following message to Noaḥ: Although I am about to rain death and destruction upon the world, I remain the Lord. I have not changed My willingness to show kindness and mercy to the earth. I am still *anokhi*, who includes everything, who bears and carries all. Furthermore, the decree I have issued is ultimately for the good of everything. This concept is expressed in the prophetic books, where we often have the four-letter name of God pronounced *Elohim*. That is to say, God's attribute of Compassion [associated with the name *Elohim*] is revealed in His attribute of Justice [hinted at by God's four-letter name]. This term expresses the unity of God within a single word, thereby negating the possibility of a duality of powers in the world.

HAAMEK DAVAR

אַרְבָּעִים יוֹם – *For forty days:* It took only forty days for all life to be obliterated from the planet, even though the water flowed over the earth for one hundred and fifty days, as stated below in verse 8:3.

ה וַיַּ֣עַשׂ נֹ֑חַ כְּכֹ֛ל אֲשֶׁר־צִוָּ֥הוּ יְהוָֽה׃ וְנֹ֕חַ בֶּן־שֵׁ֥שׁ מֵא֖וֹת שָׁנָ֑ה
ו וְהַמַּבּ֣וּל הָיָ֔ה מַ֖יִם עַל־הָאָֽרֶץ׃ וַיָּבֹ֣א נֹ֗חַ וּ֠בָנָיו וְאִשְׁתּ֧וֹ וּנְשֵֽׁי־
ז בָנָ֛יו אִתּ֖וֹ אֶל־הַתֵּבָ֑ה מִפְּנֵ֖י מֵ֥י הַמַּבּֽוּל׃ מִן־הַבְּהֵמָה֙
הַטְּהוֹרָ֔ה וּמִ֨ן־הַבְּהֵמָ֔ה אֲשֶׁ֥ר אֵינֶ֖נָּה טְהֹרָ֑ה וּמִ֨ן־הָע֔וֹף וְכֹ֥ל
ח אֲשֶׁר־רֹמֵ֖שׂ עַל־הָאֲדָמָֽה׃ שְׁנַ֨יִם שְׁנַ֜יִם בָּ֤אוּ אֶל־נֹ֙חַ֙ אֶל־
ט הַתֵּבָ֔ה זָכָ֖ר וּנְקֵבָ֑ה כַּאֲשֶׁ֛ר צִוָּ֥ה אֱלֹהִ֖ים אֶת־נֹֽחַ׃ וַיְהִ֕י

VERSE 5

RABBI JOSEPH B. SOLOVEITCHIK

וַיַּעַשׂ נֹחַ – *Noah did:* Avraham's greatness was based on his firm belief in God's promises. Many events occurred in his life that seemed to contradict the promise that the land would be his and that his children would inherit it. Avraham often found himself in situations where he was ridiculed due to his faith. Therefore, with all of Avraham's accomplishments, the one attribute that God explicitly praises is his pure belief: *Avram put his trust in the* LORD, *He reckoned it to him as righteousness* (15:6). Noah's belief was similarly tested – he built an ark for many years, explaining to onlookers that God was set to destroy the world, while they derisively laughed at him. Despite all the obstacles and the taunts of his contemporaries, Noah did not deviate from God's command. Once Noah clearly demonstrated his belief by completing the ark, God therefore remarked on his righteousness.

VERSE 6

MALBIM

וְנֹחַ – *And Noah:* This verse is a separation between the events that come before and after it. The text first reports that *Noah did all that the* LORD *commanded him* (7:5), an assessment that describes Noah's actions seven days prior to the flood, and which reflects the instructions received from God using His unique four-letter name [with its connotations of divine providence over human beings; see commentary on verse 3]. Subsequently we read that the animals assembled before Noah on the day the flood began, fulfilling a decree that God issued with the name *Elohim* [connoting God's care for the animals], as the text states: *All that walked the earth came two by two…as Elohim had commanded Noah* (7: 8–9). Our verse comes between these two, informing us that [time passed between these two different endeavors:] when Noah was six hundred years old, the flood began, and the rains started to fall upon the earth.

VERSE 8

MESHEKH ḤOKHMA

וּמִן־הָעוֹף – *The birds:* The text does not distinguish here between the pure and the impure birds, [as it had distinguished earlier between pure and impure animals]. This is because Noah had no way to distinguish between pure and impure birds, since the signs of kosher birds include a crop and a gizzard whose lining can be peeled [as described by the Talmud in Ḥullin 59a], and these are internal features. In contrast, kosher mammals are those with

5 6 made." Noaḥ did all that the Lord commanded him. Noaḥ was
six hundred years old when the floodwaters came upon the
7 earth. Noaḥ, with his sons, his wife, and his sons' wives, came
8 into the ark to escape the waters of the flood. The pure animals,
the animals that were not pure, the birds, and all that walked
9 the earth came two by two to Noaḥ into the ark, male and fe-
10 male, as God had commanded Noaḥ. Thus, after seven days the

MESHEKH ḤOKHMA *(cont.)*

divided hoofs, fully split, and which chew the cud (Leviticus 11:3), external signs which Noaḥ could have easily seen. Once all the animals had entered the ark, and Noaḥ spent twelve months taking care of them, he learned that those birds which were represented by just two specimens were the impure birds, and those of which there were fourteen birds were the pure ones. This is how Noaḥ learned the signs of each species.

VERSE 9

RABBI SAMSON RAPHAEL HIRSCH

שְׁנַיִם שְׁנַיִם בָּאוּ אֶל־נֹחַ – *Came two by two to Noaḥ:* The verse reports that the animals arrived in pairs *as God had commanded Noaḥ*. On the one hand, God instructed Noaḥ to collect the animals and birds and to lead them onto the ark. On the other hand, this gathering by twos proceeded independently of Noaḥ's efforts, since he was unable to determine which of the animals had been true to their species [and had not interbreeded with other species]. He also lacked the skills to trap the wild beasts. This reveals a curious truth which is so important to Scripture: Although God consistently demands that human beings obey His commands and take responsibility for their actions, God himself acts as the steward of nature. He governs how its components behave. In other words, "the Lord" is also *Elohim*. Our passage makes this clear: God issued decrees to Noaḥ which he was expected to follow by employing his free will. At the same time God directed the natural world such that the animals would act in a way that would enable Noaḥ to fulfill God's law.

THE LUBAVITCHER REBBE

שְׁנַיִם שְׁנַיִם בָּאוּ אֶל־נֹחַ – *Came two by two to Noaḥ:* Obviously, the fact that the animals came to the ark on their own was miraculous. It was likewise miraculous that no one was able to prevent Noaḥ from entering the ark,. Furthermore, the animals he sheltered dwelled together peacefully. Noaḥ was only required to fulfill God's instructions to the letter; the rest was taken care of by God Himself. Similarly, if we commit ourselves passionately to our divine mission, and act on that commitment, we will be blessed with miraculous success.

VERSE 10

RABBI DAVID TZVI HOFFMAN

וַיְהִי לְשִׁבְעַת הַיָּמִים – *Thus, after seven days:* The narrative of the flood truly begins now. After a further seven-day delay, the flooding of the world begins, an event that had been

יא לְשִׁבְעַ֣ת הַיָּמִ֑ים וּמֵ֣י הַמַּבּ֔וּל הָי֖וּ עַל־הָאָֽרֶץ׃ בִּשְׁנַ֨ת שֵׁשׁ־
מֵא֤וֹת שָׁנָה֙ לְחַיֵּי־נֹ֔חַ בַּחֹ֙דֶשׁ֙ הַשֵּׁנִ֔י בְּשִׁבְעָֽה־עָשָׂ֥ר י֖וֹם
לַחֹ֑דֶשׁ בַּיּ֣וֹם הַזֶּ֗ה נִבְקְעוּ֙ כָּֽל־מַעְיְנֹת֙ תְּה֣וֹם רַבָּ֔ה וַאֲרֻבֹּ֥ת
יב הַשָּׁמַ֖יִם נִפְתָּֽחוּ׃ וַיְהִ֥י הַגֶּ֖שֶׁם עַל־הָאָ֑רֶץ אַרְבָּעִ֣ים י֔וֹם
יג וְאַרְבָּעִ֖ים לָֽיְלָה׃ בְּעֶ֨צֶם הַיּ֤וֹם הַזֶּה֙ בָּ֣א נֹ֔חַ וְשֵׁם־וְחָ֥ם וָיֶ֖פֶת
בְּנֵי־נֹ֑חַ וְאֵ֣שֶׁת נֹ֗חַ וּשְׁלֹ֧שֶׁת נְשֵֽׁי־בָנָ֛יו אִתָּ֖ם אֶל־הַתֵּבָֽה׃
יד הֵ֜מָּה וְכָל־הַֽחַיָּ֣ה לְמִינָ֗הּ וְכָל־הַבְּהֵמָה֙ לְמִינָ֔הּ וְכָל־הָרֶ֛מֶשׂ
הָרֹמֵ֥שׂ עַל־הָאָ֖רֶץ לְמִינֵ֑הוּ וְכָל־הָע֣וֹף לְמִינֵ֔הוּ כֹּ֖ל צִפּ֥וֹר

RABBI DAVID TZVI HOFFMAN *(cont.)*

predicted long ago. Thus, the next verse states: *In the six hundredth year of Noaḥ's life, in the second month etc.* The Sages disagree about the identity of this second month. Rabbi Yehoshua maintains that our verse refers to the month of Iyar [in that Nisan, the preceding month, is the first of the year, as stated in Exodus 12:2]. Rabbi Eliezer argues that the second month is Marḥeshvan [counting Tishrei as the start of the year]. The latter approach is accepted by the scholars of Israel, since the flood took place centuries prior to the revelation of the Torah. At that time, Tishrei was still universally accepted as the first month of the year. Furthermore, the month of Marḥeshvan is the time when the annual rains usually begin to fall in the Middle East. It therefore made sense for God to plan the flood for that season.

VERSE 11

MALBIM

בִּשְׁנַת שֵׁשׁ־מֵאוֹת שָׁנָה – *In the six hundredth year:* Many scholars attribute the global flood of ancient times to the influence of astrology. The heavenly bodies formed a destructive constellation that brought about a flood. Our verse counters that belief by stating: *In the six hundredth year of Noaḥ's life, in the second month, on the seventeenth of the month.* Any competent astrologer acknowledges that such a time does not dictate that the world be flooded. Neither the year, the month, nor even the day are right for such a celestial influence. Furthermore, the reader should not imagine that atmospheric conditions caused the flood through excessive vapor and subsequent precipitation. Nor was it an earthquake splitting the ground and opening the *wellsprings of the great deep*. Even though sometimes clouds will rain great volumes of water across one area of the land, or an earthquake or the shift of one region of the earth would allow subterranean waters to rise to the surface of the earth, we have never found both events happening at the same time. Powerful storms and tectonic shifts are caused by completely different and unrelated forces. In fact, these phenomena are not only incongruous with each other; they oppose one another. Yet, the verse reports: *On that day, all the wellsprings of the great deep burst, and heavens' floodgates opened.*

11 floodwaters came upon the earth. In the six hundredth year of
Noaḥ's life, in the second month, on the seventeenth of the
month – on that day, all the wellsprings of the great deep burst,
12 and the heavens' floodgates opened. The rain fell on the earth
13 for forty days and forty nights. On that very day, Noaḥ, his
sons, Shem, Ḥam, and Yefet, Noaḥ's wife, and his sons' three
14 wives entered the ark. With them came every kind of wild
beast, every kind of animal, every creeping, crawling creature
of the land, every kind of flying creature, every bird, and each

THE LUBAVITCHER REBBE

בַּחֹדֶשׁ הַשֵּׁנִי – *In the second month:* The metaphoric flood also begins in Marḥeshvan. During the month of Tishrei, we spend most of our time in the "ark" of the High Holidays, Sukkot, and Simḥat Torah. Only in the following month, Marḥeshvan, do we return to our ordinary lives. Although this progression appears to be a spiritual descent, there is, in fact, an advantage to the mundane lives we resume in Marḥeshvan, since we fulfill the goal of creating a divine home in this world by infusing mundane existence with divine consciousness.

VERSE 13

THE LUBAVITCHER REBBE

בָּא...אֶל־הַתֵּבָה – *Entered the ark:* One of the lessons we can derive from this part of the narrative is that we should never despair in the face of what is occurring in the world around us. Even when threatened with a devastating flood, we should retain our optimism, for God watches over us. Moreover, we should realize that by entering our spiritual "ark," our prayers and study of Torah can save the entire world and even raise it to a higher level of being, just as Noaḥ beheld a new world when he emerged from the ark.

VERSE 14

MALBIM

הֵמָּה וְכָל־הַחַיָּה לְמִינָהּ – *With them came every kind of wild beast:* Human beings were not the only ones who entered the ark as the rains were beginning, but *every kind of wild beast, every kind of animal* also arrived on that day from their lairs. This demonstrates the divine providence that extended to protect the planet's species. By doing so, God fulfilled His promise, *I will establish My covenant with you, and you will enter the ark* (6:18).

HAAMEK DAVAR

הֵמָּה וְכָל־הַחַיָּה לְמִינָהּ – *With them came every kind of wild beast:* In contrast to the present verse which lists the boarding of *every kind of wild beast [haḥayya], every kind of animal [habehema]*, verse 8 only mentions the animals [*behema*], for it is assumed there that the general category *behema* ["animals"] includes the *ḥayyot* ["wild animals"] as well. Why then does our verse list these as separate groups? The earlier text describes the miraculous gathering of all the animals around the ark. At that moment, the untamed beasts of the field behaved like domesticated animals and allowed themselves to approach human

טו כָּל־כָּנָף׃ וַיָּבֹאוּ אֶל־נֹחַ אֶל־הַתֵּבָה שְׁנַיִם שְׁנַיִם מִכָּל־
טז הַבָּשָׂר אֲשֶׁר־בּוֹ רוּחַ חַיִּים׃ וְהַבָּאִים זָכָר וּנְקֵבָה מִכָּל־בָּשָׂר
יז בָּאוּ כַּאֲשֶׁר צִוָּה אֹתוֹ אֱלֹהִים וַיִּסְגֹּר יהוה בַּעֲדוֹ׃ וַיְהִי שלישי
הַמַּבּוּל אַרְבָּעִים יוֹם עַל־הָאָרֶץ וַיִּרְבּוּ הַמַּיִם וַיִּשְׂאוּ אֶת־
יח הַתֵּבָה וַתָּרָם מֵעַל הָאָרֶץ׃ וַיִּגְבְּרוּ הַמַּיִם וַיִּרְבּוּ מְאֹד עַל־
יט הָאָרֶץ וַתֵּלֶךְ הַתֵּבָה עַל־פְּנֵי הַמָּיִם׃ וְהַמַּיִם גָּבְרוּ מְאֹד מְאֹד
עַל־הָאָרֶץ וַיְכֻסּוּ כָּל־הֶהָרִים הַגְּבֹהִים אֲשֶׁר־תַּחַת כָּל־
כ הַשָּׁמָיִם׃ חֲמֵשׁ עֶשְׂרֵה אַמָּה מִלְמַעְלָה גָּבְרוּ הַמָּיִם וַיְכֻסּוּ
כא הֶהָרִים׃ וַיִּגְוַע כָּל־בָּשָׂר ׀ הָרֹמֵשׂ עַל־הָאָרֶץ בָּעוֹף וּבַבְּהֵמָה

HAAMEK DAVAR *(cont.)*

beings. Hence verse 8 groups both types of animals together and includes the wild beasts within the larger set of *behemot* since they too were acting docile. Here in verse 14, all of the passengers were boarding the ark as the rains started to fall. When wild animals are caught in a downpour it is completely natural for them to become as tame and quiet as cattle. Hence, the wild animals were here acting according to their own nature, which explains why they are identified as their own group.

VERSE 16

HAAMEK DAVAR

כַּאֲשֶׁר צִוָּה אֹתוֹ אֱלֹהִים – *As God had commanded him:* The word order of verse 9 differs slightly from that of the present verse. That clause reads: *As God had commanded Noaḥ* [*kaasher tziva Elohim et Noaḥ*, literally, "as commanded God Noaḥ." In contrast, the current verse reads *kaasher tziva oto Elohim*, literally, "as commanded him God."] The difference in the word order is because the animals assembled around the ark in verse 9 without Noaḥ's efforts. Rather, the spirit of the Lord and His decrees governing the constellations caused the masses of animals to gather around the ark. The command in verse 9 was directed both at Noaḥ and at the animals. Therefore, that verse first states: *As God commanded*, and only then mentions Noaḥ. However, when the animals boarded the ark, God's instruction was issued to Noaḥ alone, which explains the language of our verse – *kaasher tziva oto Elohim*. That command was addressed only to him.

RABBI DAVID TZVI HOFFMAN

וַיִּסְגֹּר יהוה בַּעֲדוֹ – *Then the Lord shut him in:* The term *baado*, [which could be translated as "for him,"] suggests that God shut Noaḥ in for his own benefit, in order to protect him.

15 winged thing. They came to Noaḥ, to the ark, two by two, of all
16 flesh that had within it the breath of life. They came, male and
female of all flesh, as God had commanded him. Then the
17 Lord shut him in. For forty days the flood came upon the SHELISHI
earth. The waters swelled, lifting the ark so that it rose above
18 the land. The waters surged, swelling enormously on the earth,
19 and the ark began to drift on the surface of the water. The waters surged ever more, until all the high mountains beneath all
20 the heavens were covered. Fifteen cubits above them the waters
21 surged as the mountains were covered. All flesh that moved
upon the earth perished – birds, animals, wild beasts, and all
the creatures that swarm on the earth, and all humankind.

VERSE 19

HAKETAV VEHAKABBALA

וַיְכֻסּוּ כׇּל־הֶהָרִים הַגְּבֹהִים – *Until all the high mountains were covered:* First, the high mountains were covered. Afterward, the waters rose another fifteen cubits, [as described in verse 20].

HAAMEK DAVAR

וְהַמַּיִם גָּבְרוּ מְאֹד מְאֹד עַל־הָאָרֶץ – *The waters surged ever more on the earth:* The flood uprooted great tracts of land, creating new hills and mountains that did not exist before the flood. Our passage implies that at that time the mountains of Ararat boasted the planet's tallest peaks. Yet, we know that this is not so today. This is because those mountains which reach higher than Ararat were formed by the flood itself. Similarly, the flood changed the earth's springs. Indeed, Bereshit Rabba states that even though *the wellsprings of the deep closed* (8:2) after the flood, some of these springs remained active. Those springs continue to flow today.

VERSE 21

MALBIM

בָּעוֹף וּבַבְּהֵמָה וּבַחַיָּה – *Birds, animals, wild beasts:* The human soul represents the world's great illumination and includes within it all different types of light. In contrast, the life of an animal contains a small spark compared to that of a person's soul. Hence, the small lights of the animals were snuffed out first, and only later were the great lights of the people extinguished. This verse lists the animals in order of their destruction. First were the birds, which God had fashioned on the fifth day of creation. Next were the animals, which were formed on the sixth day, before human beings. The next verse states: *Everything on dry land that had breath of life in its nostrils died* (7:22), referring to the death of land animals. However, the order in which the creatures' bodies dissolved was the reverse. Because human beings have the weakest constitution their corpses deteriorated first, while the carcasses of the stronger beasts lasted longest. [Hence verse 23 lists the erosion of humans first.]

כב וּבְכָל־הַֽחַיָּ֣ה וּבְכָל־הַשֶּׁ֗רֶץ הַשֹּׁרֵ֛ץ עַל־הָאָ֖רֶץ וְכֹ֣ל הָאָדָ֑ם כֹּ֡ל אֲשֶׁר֩ נִשְׁמַת־ר֨וּחַ חַיִּ֜ים בְּאַפָּ֗יו מִכֹּ֛ל אֲשֶׁ֥ר בֶּחָֽרָבָ֖ה מֵֽתוּ׃

כג וַיִּ֜מַח אֶֽת־כָּל־הַיְק֣וּם ׀ אֲשֶׁ֣ר ׀ עַל־פְּנֵ֣י הָֽאֲדָמָ֗ה מֵאָדָ֤ם עַד־בְּהֵמָה֙ עַד־רֶ֨מֶשׂ֙ וְעַד־ע֣וֹף הַשָּׁמַ֔יִם וַיִּמָּח֖וּ מִן־הָאָ֑רֶץ וַיִּשָּׁ֧אֶר

כד אַךְ־נֹ֛חַ וַֽאֲשֶׁ֥ר אִתּ֖וֹ בַּתֵּבָ֑ה וַיִּגְבְּר֥וּ הַמַּ֛יִם עַל־הָאָ֖רֶץ

ח א חֲמִשִּׁ֥ים וּמְאַ֖ת י֑וֹם׃ וַיִּזְכֹּ֤ר אֱלֹהִים֙ אֶת־נֹ֔חַ וְאֵ֤ת כָּל־הַֽחַיָּה֙ וְאֶת־כָּל־הַבְּהֵמָ֔ה אֲשֶׁ֥ר אִתּ֖וֹ בַּתֵּבָ֑ה וַיַּעֲבֵ֨ר אֱלֹהִ֥ים ר֛וּחַ

VERSE 23

HAKETAV VEHAKABBALA

כָּל־הַיְקוּם – *Every living thing:* According to the commentators, the term *yekum* [translated here as "living thing"] refers to all life, whereas the Sages debate the meaning of the word. Rabbi Berekhya maintains that the word refers to *kiyyumeih* – all the life that populates the world and sustains the planet. Rabbi Avun argues that the term should be understood as *yekuminei*, a Greek word meaning "human habitat," similar in meaning to the Hebrew word *tevel* [usually, "universe"]. This suggestion [with its focus on the inhabitable land] matches the claim that the flood destroyed the ground to a depth of three handbreadths, which is how far a plow digs into the soil. The verse which states: *In the midst of all Israel, how the earth opened its mouth and swallowed them, their families, tents, and every living thing [hayekum] in their households* (Deuteronomy 11:6), fits this approach.

MALBIM

וַיִּשָּׁאֶר אַךְ־נֹחַ וַאֲשֶׁר אִתּוֹ בַּתֵּבָה – *Only Noaḥ and those with him in the ark survived:* This verse describes the fulfillment of God's earlier vow *I will erase My creation, humankind, from the face of the land* – *man, even animals and creeping things, even birds of the heavens* (6:7). Even though some remnants of the animal kingdom survived on the ark, these were all considered an appendage to Noaḥ, who had found favor in God's eyes. And Noaḥ himself was not included in God's oath of destruction, since he was promised at the time: *I will establish My covenant with you, and you will enter the ark* (6:18). And so God's promise was fulfilled in that *only Noaḥ and those with him in the ark survived*, meaning that God saved only Noaḥ and those people and creatures who accompanied him. Furthermore, none of these creatures had remained on "the land," but only in the ark floating above it. For the original decree [in verse 6:7] related to the population on the land and not to those creatures who were on the water.

HAAMEK DAVAR

וַיִּמַח אֶת־כָּל־הַיְקוּם אֲשֶׁר עַל־פְּנֵי הָאֲדָמָה – *Every living thing on the face of the earth was wiped out:* The bodies of all the people and creatures decayed. The verse emphasizes that the corpses which lay *on the face of the earth* decomposed. Other bodies were buried under the upheaval of soil caused by the surging waters, and these corpses were preserved from

22 Everything on dry land that had breath of life in its nostrils
23 died. Every living thing on the face of the earth was wiped out:
from humans to animals, from creeping creatures to winged
birds of the heavens, all were wiped from the earth. Only Noaḥ
24 and those with him in the ark survived. For one hundred fifty
8 1 days, the waters surged over the earth. Then God remembered
Noaḥ and all the wild beasts and animals with him in the
ark. God sent a wind over the earth, and the waters began to

HAAMEK DAVAR *(cont.)*

decay. This explains the fossils that are unearthed by paleontologists and which come from creatures unknown in our times. In contrast, some suggest that fossils come from previous worlds which God had created and destroyed. Indeed, on several occasions, Bereshit Rabba claims that when the Torah states: *Then God saw all that He had made: and it was very good* (1:31), the text reflects the fact that God had created and destroyed multiple worlds. Nevertheless, I find such an approach difficult since Shemot Rabba states that God returned those previous worlds to chaos and desolation. This means that absolutely no remnants were left from God's initial formations, [including any fossil record]. Instead, it seems to me that the skeletons which are being unearthed in our times were those of creatures who lived before the flood. Though these animals have been discovered in climates normally foreign to them, before the flood these creatures had different characters which allowed them to live in those regions. Regarding the strange animals with which we are not currently familiar, these can be explained as the products of hybridization between disparate species, such as a mule which is the offspring of a donkey and a horse. God wished that the bones of these deviant creatures would remain intact for later generations to discover and learn how nature had been corrupted. At the time of the flood, however, God desired that these creatures should not be discovered and instead be eradicated from the surface of the earth, lest people find them and be tempted to cross breed different species in an effort to recreate those odd animals. Hence the text again states: *All were wiped from the earth*. For divine providence concealed from that generations and several subsequent generations the strange and aberrant fossils, lest these breeders strive to reproduce such objectionable creatures.

THE LUBAVITCHER REBBE

וַיִּמַח אֶת־כָּל־הַיְקוּם – *Every living thing was wiped out:* The flood served not only as a punishment but also as a spiritual cleansing for a world that had become spiritually contaminated. That is why the waters of the flood are called "the waters of Noaḥ" [in Isaiah 54:9] meaning "the waters of divine *nahat* [pleasure and satisfaction]."

CHAPTER 8, VERSE 1

OR HAḤAYYIM

וַיִּזְכֹּר אֱלֹהִים אֶת־נֹחַ וְאֵת כָּל־הַחַיָּה – *Then God remembered Noaḥ and all the wild beasts:* Why was it insufficient for God to remember Noaḥ, such that the text also says that the Almighty

בּ עַל־הָאָ֑רֶץ וַיָּשֻׁ֖כּוּ הַמָּֽיִם: וַיִּסָּֽכְרוּ֙ מַעְיְנֹ֣ת תְּה֔וֹם וַאֲרֻבֹּ֖ת
ג הַשָּׁמָ֑יִם וַיִּכָּלֵ֥א הַגֶּ֖שֶׁם מִן־הַשָּׁמָֽיִם: וַיָּשֻׁ֧בוּ הַמַּ֛יִם מֵעַ֥ל
הָאָ֖רֶץ הָל֣וֹךְ וָשׁ֑וֹב וַיַּחְסְר֣וּ הַמַּ֔יִם מִקְצֵ֕ה חֲמִשִּׁ֥ים וּמְאַ֖ת יֽוֹם:
ד וַתָּ֤נַח הַתֵּבָה֙ בַּחֹ֣דֶשׁ הַשְּׁבִיעִ֔י בְּשִׁבְעָה־עָשָׂ֥ר י֖וֹם לַחֹ֑דֶשׁ עַ֖ל
ה הָרֵ֥י אֲרָרָֽט: וְהַמַּ֗יִם הָיוּ֙ הָל֣וֹךְ וְחָס֔וֹר עַ֖ד הַחֹ֣דֶשׁ הָֽעֲשִׂירִ֑י

OR HAḤAYYIM (cont.)

recalled the animals aboard the ark? Perhaps the text is informing us that God did not merely end the flood for Noah's sake, but also because of *the wild beasts and animals [who] were with him*. These creatures were remembered for their own sake. The Torah lists the ark's occupants as if to say: Not only did God remember Noah, but also the animals who were aboard. Additionally, by mentioning the animals the verse indicates that because God recalled Noah, He also considered all the effort that Noah had expended in caring for, and feeding, the animals during the months at sea.

RABBI SAMSON RAPHAEL HIRSCH

וַיִּזְכֹּר אֱלֹהִים אֶת־נֹחַ – *Then God remembered Noah:* According to our Sages, even the rescue of Noah was an expression of God's justice [as reflected in the divine name *Elohim*, used in the verse]. God saved the world and returned it to its former state of grandeur because the planet deserved it. The salvation did not reflect only God's merciful concern for the future of humankind. This explains the repetition of the name *Elohim* throughout this narrative.

RABBI DAVID TZVI HOFFMAN

וַיִּזְכֹּר אֱלֹהִים אֶת־נֹחַ – *Then God remembered Noah:* Since the forces of nature had been released, a special effort of divine providence was required to rein in these powers and to set the world straight again. Such corrective measures would only be extended on behalf of humanity. This is why the text states: *Then God remembered Noah*. That was the first step in returning things to their natural state. **וַיָּשֻׁכּוּ הַמַּיִם** – *And the waters began to subside:* The term *vayashokku* ["began to subside"] derives from the verb *shakhakh*, meaning "to calm down." The stormy conditions of the flood which carried the ark over the waters settled down, thereby saving the boat from any danger of capsizing in the turbulence.

RABBI JOSEPH B. SOLOVEITCHIK

וַיִּזְכֹּר אֱלֹהִים אֶת־נֹחַ – *Then God remembered Noah:* Just as God exhibits both universal and individual concern, so too should people; one should not dedicate all of one's efforts on behalf of communal needs while ignoring individual needs. God is concerned with infinity itself, both in the historical sense, regarding all generations of humankind, and in the physical sense, regarding the boundless cosmos. At the same time, He remains concerned as well with each and every individual. Noah was rescued from the flood for two reasons. First,

2 subside. The wellsprings of the deep and heavens' floodgates
3 closed, and the heavens' rains were reined in. The water steadily
received from the earth, and by the end of one hundred fifty
4 days, the water had abated. In the seventh month, on the seventeenth day of the month, the ark came to rest on the mountains
5 of Ararat. The water continued to abate until the tenth month,
and on the first day of the tenth month, the mountaintops

RABBI JOSEPH B. SOLOVEITCHIK *(cont.)*

through Noaḥ, humanity itself was saved. Second, Noaḥ was saved because as an individual he was deserving. Even had humanity been saved by another means, Noaḥ himself would have been spared on his own merits.

VERSE 2

MALBIM

וַיִּסָּכְרוּ מַעְיְנֹת תְּהוֹם – *The wellsprings of the deep closed: The waters began to subside* (8:1) because *the wellsprings of the deep and heavens' floodgates closed*. Furthermore, the rain stopped falling from the skies. Since the entire planet was covered with water, it would have been natural for evaporation to increase, which in turn would lead to additional rainfall. However, the winds scattered the clouds to prevent more precipitation. The word *vayyikale* ["reined in"] means that the wind forcefully prevented the rain.

VERSE 3

OR HAḤAYYIM

מִקְצֵה חֲמִשִּׁים וּמְאַת יוֹם – *By the end of one hundred fifty days:* The waters started to flow out to the oceans and *receded from the earth* 150 days after the start of the flood.

SHADAL

וַיַּחְסְרוּ הַמָּיִם – *The water had abated:* The root *ḥet-samekh-resh* from the word *vayaḥseru* does not mean that something has diminished, but that it is lacking. In this context, the verb indicates that some places, namely the highest mountains, were left completely without water. However, I disagree with Rashi's assertion that the water simply sat on the earth for five months after the rains stopped, with no decrease at all. That would have been completely unnatural, and since the Torah does not state that this occurred, we need not accept that it did.

VERSE 5

MALBIM

וְהַמַּיִם הָיוּ הָלוֹךְ וְחָסוֹר – *The water continued to abate:* Once the ark ran aground it was possible to measure the decline of the water level using the boat itself as a ruler. According to the Sages, the ark's hull sat ten cubits below the surface, which was a third of the vessel's total height. Thus, each day the passengers could see how much more of the ark's exterior was exposed. Noaḥ's family watched the water going down until the tenth month, Tamuz, when the peaks of the Ararat mountains became visible.

ו בַּעֲשִׂירִי בְּאֶחָד לַחֹדֶשׁ נִרְאוּ רָאשֵׁי הֶהָרִים: וַיְהִי מִקֵּץ
אַרְבָּעִים יוֹם וַיִּפְתַּח נֹחַ אֶת־חַלּוֹן הַתֵּבָה אֲשֶׁר עָשָׂה:
ז וַיְשַׁלַּח אֶת־הָעֹרֵב וַיֵּצֵא יָצוֹא וָשׁוֹב עַד־יְבֹשֶׁת הַמַּיִם מֵעַל

VERSE 6

OR HAḤAYYIM

וַיְהִי מִקֵּץ אַרְבָּעִים יוֹם – *After forty days:* The following question must be asked: How did Noaḥ know that it was safe to open the ark's window and that water would not come surging through the opening and sink the vessel? Perhaps Noaḥ was assured that the flood would last no longer than twelve months [and hence he was sure that the waters had started to recede]. Furthermore, in preparation for the ordeal, Noaḥ had stored on the boat just enough food to feed its occupants for a year. He was therefore able to measure the passage of time by the diminishing provisions.

VERSE 7

OR HAḤAYYIM

וַיְשַׁלַּח אֶת־הָעֹרֵב – *He sent a raven forth:* According to our Sages [see Sanhedrin 108b], during the yearlong stay on the ark the raven violated the injunction against sexual intercourse and copulated with its mate. Noaḥ became aware of this, and when he eventually opened the vessel's window, he immediately expelled the raven from the ark. This explains why the present verse merely states: *He sent the raven forth,* and does not continue: "to see whether the water had subsided," as it does in the subsequent verse regarding the dispatch of the dove [for Noaḥ simply wanted to be rid of the bird]. Now the text reports that the raven *flew to and fro until the water on the earth had dried*, meaning that after Noaḥ threw it out of the boat, the bird circled back to him, only to be chased away again. This routine carried on until the water had abated and the raven was able to land on the ground. Afterward, when describing Noaḥ's release of the dove, why does the verse specify that *he sent forth a dove from him [me'itto]* (8:8)? This superfluous word emphasizes that Noaḥ released the dove out of his own motivation, in order *to see whether the water had subsided* [in contrast to the raven]. Furthermore, Noaḥ could not have learned the information he sought from the raven, because that bird was removed from the ark as a punishment and not as an agent. [And hence when the raven flew back to the ark that was no indication that the water was still covering the earth, only that the creature longed to return home.] Noaḥ's attitude to the dove was altogether different. When that bird could find *no resting place to plant its foot* (8:9), Noaḥ willingly received it back into the safety of the vessel, as that verse states: *He reached out his hand and brought the dove back to him, into the ark.* The last words of that clause emphasize that Noaḥ granted the dove refuge and protection after its mission. But the raven was not welcomed back despite its difficulty over the open water – every time it tried to return to the ark Noaḥ shooed it away again.

RABBI SAMSON RAPHAEL HIRSCH

וַיְשַׁלַּח אֶת־הָעֹרֵב – *He sent a raven forth:* The raven [*orev*] is not the sort of bird which seeks human company; its natural habitat is the wilderness [*arava*]. Thus Noaḥ knew that if a

6 became visible. After forty days Noaḥ opened the window he
7 had made in the ark and sent a raven forth. It flew to and fro

RABBI SAMSON RAPHAEL HIRSCH *(cont.)*

raven flew back to him, that would be a clear sign that the planet was still desolate [and that the bird only returned out of desperation]. This explains the difference between the present verse, *He sent a raven forth*, and the next sentence which adds a word, *He sent forth the dove from him [me'itto]*. The dove is accustomed to the presence of people, and hence when it returned to the boat, Noaḥ *reached out his hand and brought the dove back to him*. Noaḥ was certain that if the dove did not come back, he would have proof that the world was normal once again.

MALBIM

וַיְשַׁלַּח אֶת־הָעֹרֵב – *He sent a raven forth:* Noaḥ did not release the raven in order to determine whether the floodwaters had receded, as he subsequently does with the dove, for verse 7 does not state that as the man's motive. Rather, in antiquity the raven was used as a mechanism for foretelling the future. Special houses were built for this bird and priests would interpret its behavior as useful portents. Whether a raven flew off to the right or the left, climbed high or descended, cawed as it went or moved silently, all had significance for believers in the powers of this species. The bird possesses other telling signs and movements, and indeed our Sages maintain that the verse *Never curse a king, not even in your mind, nor a rich man, even in your bedchamber, for a bird of the sky will carry that voice; a winged creature will repeat the word* (Ecclesiastes 10:20) refers specifically to this species. Hence Noaḥ sent the bird out to fly freely, in order to then discern from its flight pattern the nature of the air and the water. Watching the raven fly to and fro, Noaḥ was able to understand the conditions of the planet outside the ark.

HAAMEK DAVAR

וַיְשַׁלַּח אֶת־הָעֹרֵב – *He sent a raven forth:* Why does Noaḥ choose to employ the raven and the dove as his agents to test the waters on the earth? After all, aboard the ark there was a range of birds – including specimens who were better flyers – that Noaḥ could have used. Furthermore, did Noaḥ even have permission to remove some of the rescued species from the ark before all the occupants were released together? I must therefore infer that the raven and the dove whose missions are describe in this chapter did not belong to the pairs of their respective kinds whom Noaḥ was charged with preserving for the renewed world. [Those had to remain protected until the flood was over.] However, before the deluge Noaḥ had been one of those important personages who raises ravens and doves, as the Talmud mentions [see Shabbat 128a]. Some of his stock were brought into the ark before the rains began, under the rubric of God's instruction *Enter the ark, you and all your household* (7:1), as I discussed above in comments to that verse. Now it is not the custom of domesticated ravens to fly very far away from home, unlike doves, which can be trained to carry messages great distances and to return with objects in their mouths. This explains the flight path of the raven when it was released from the ark: It immediately saw that the ark remained surrounded by water and refused to fly off in any direction. Instead,

ח הָאָרֶץ׃ וַיְשַׁלַּח אֶת־הַיּוֹנָה מֵאִתּוֹ לִרְאוֹת הֲקַלּוּ הַמַּיִם מֵעַל
ט פְּנֵי הָאֲדָמָה׃ וְלֹא־מָצְאָה הַיּוֹנָה מָנוֹחַ לְכַף־רַגְלָהּ וַתָּשָׁב
אֵלָיו אֶל־הַתֵּבָה כִּי־מַיִם עַל־פְּנֵי כָל־הָאָרֶץ וַיִּשְׁלַח יָדוֹ
י וַיִּקָּחֶהָ וַיָּבֵא אֹתָהּ אֵלָיו אֶל־הַתֵּבָה׃ וַיָּחֶל עוֹד שִׁבְעַת יָמִים
יא אֲחֵרִים וַיֹּסֶף שַׁלַּח אֶת־הַיּוֹנָה מִן־הַתֵּבָה׃ וַתָּבֹא אֵלָיו
הַיּוֹנָה לְעֵת עֶרֶב וְהִנֵּה עֲלֵה־זַיִת טָרָף בְּפִיהָ וַיֵּדַע נֹחַ כִּי־
יב קַלּוּ הַמַּיִם מֵעַל הָאָרֶץ׃ וַיִּיָּחֶל עוֹד שִׁבְעַת יָמִים אֲחֵרִים

HAAMEK DAVAR *(cont.)*

it flew back and forth several times in the vicinity of the vessel. However, the dove was accustomed to carrying items in its beak even from substantial distances. Hence the verse states: *After that he sent forth a dove* (8:8), suggesting that Noaḥ wished the bird to remove itself very far from its master.

VERSE 8

MALBIM

וַיְשַׁלַּח אֶת־הַיּוֹנָה מֵאִתּוֹ – *He sent forth the dove from him:* The dove is a domesticated bird and is pure [kosher] as well. On board the ark was a pair of wild doves which were preserved on the vessel, along with seven pairs of domesticated doves which belonged to Noaḥ himself before the deluge. It was one of these fourteen birds which Noaḥ dispatched from the boat. This explains the superfluous term "from him" – this specimen was from Noaḥ's own collection of possessions that he had brought along.

THE LUBAVITCHER REBBE

לִרְאוֹת הֲקַלּוּ הַמַּיִם – *To see whether the water had subsided:* Noaḥ did not leave the ark until God instructed him to do so. What, then, was the purpose of seeing if the land was dry? The answer is that since God has entrusted him with the survival of life, Noaḥ felt responsible to take whatever natural steps would encourage God to hasten the renewal of life on earth. And indeed, Noaḥ's efforts – which revealed his great yearning to fulfill the task that God had given him – expedited God's command to leave the ark.... Like the flood, only God can end the exile. But, like Noaḥ, we can hasten the redemption by actively yearning for it and doing all in our power to hasten its arrival.

VERSE 9

OR HAḤAYYIM

וַיִּשְׁלַח יָדוֹ וַיִּקָּחֶהָ – *He reached out his hand and brought the dove:* Upon its return to the ark, the dove was exhausted since it had *found no resting place to plant its foot*. Noaḥ feared that the bird was completely sapped of its strength and might even fall into the water. He was therefore solicitous and, reaching out his hand, helped the dove back into the shelter of the ark.

8 until the water on the earth had dried. After that he sent forth a
dove to see whether the water had subsided from the face of the
9 land. But the dove found no resting place to plant its foot, and
so it returned to him, to the ark, for water still covered the face
of the earth completely. He reached out his hand and brought
10 the dove back to him, into the ark. Then he waited another
11 seven days, and again he sent the dove forth from the ark. The
dove came back to him in the evening – and in its beak was a
freshly picked olive leaf. Noaḥ knew then that the water had
12 subsided from the earth. He waited another seven days and

HAAMEK DAVAR

וַיָּבֵא אֹתָהּ אֵלָיו אֶל־הַתֵּבָה – *And brought the dove back to him, into the ark:* [The verse appears to contain several redundancies. Firstly, the sentence begins by stating that the dove returned "to him." Is it not superfluous to then continue with the phrase "to the ark"? Secondly, why does the second half of the verse state that Noaḥ *brought the dove back to him, into the ark* – was the bird not there already?] We must explain that when the dove returned from its maiden voyage it did not actually enter the ark, but merely approached the vessel. The bird was reluctant to enter the boat because it had nothing in its beak to offer Noaḥ as it had been trained to do. Hence the dove imagined that its owner would refuse it admittance to the ark, since it had returned bearing no gift. This is why it flew around the exterior of the ark and did not attempt to return to its place. Noaḥ however took pity on the bird, and *he reached out his hand and brought the dove back to him* with the intention of warming the bird and calming it from its trip. This compassionate action of Noaḥ teaches us a valuable lesson: When a messenger returns from an unsuccessful mission and cannot supply the desired information or response due to no fault of his own, he must nevertheless be treated with respect, just as if he had succeeded. It was only then, once the bird was held and assuaged, that Noaḥ *brought the dove back to him, into the ark.*

VERSE 11

SHADAL

עֲלֵה־זַיִת טָרָף – *A freshly picked olive leaf:* Naftali Hertz Wessely [18th century] and Rabbi Isaac Samuel Reggio [19th century] maintain that the term *aleh* describes a tree's leaf even once it has fallen to the ground. But the word *taraf* is used only when the leaf is still attached to the branch or has been recently plucked off and remains fresh. Now when Noaḥ saw that the leaf supplied by the dove was fresh (for the olive tree maintains its leaves throughout the year), he understood that the bird had not found it floating on the surface of the water. Rather, it was clear that the leaf had been picked from its place of growth. This told Noaḥ that the trees were not covered by water anymore, that the flood had receded.

VERSE 12

MALBIM

וְלֹא־יָסְפָה שׁוּב־אֵלָיו עוֹד – *And it returned to him no more:* Experts maintain that unless a dove has become accustomed to its nest it must be guarded against flying away. On the

יג וַיְשַׁלַּח֙ אֶת־הַיּוֹנָ֔ה וְלֹֽא־יָסְפָ֥ה שׁוּב־אֵלָ֖יו עֽוֹד: וַ֠יְהִ֠י בְּאַחַ֨ת וְשֵׁשׁ־מֵא֜וֹת שָׁנָ֗ה בָּֽרִאשׁוֹן֙ בְּאֶחָ֣ד לַחֹ֔דֶשׁ חָֽרְב֥וּ הַמַּ֖יִם מֵעַ֣ל הָאָ֑רֶץ וַיָּ֤סַר נֹ֙חַ֙ אֶת־מִכְסֵ֣ה הַתֵּבָ֔ה וַיַּ֕רְא וְהִנֵּ֥ה חָֽרְב֖וּ פְּנֵ֥י הָאֲדָמָֽה: יד וּבַחֹ֙דֶשׁ֙ הַשֵּׁנִ֔י בְּשִׁבְעָ֧ה וְעֶשְׂרִ֛ים י֖וֹם לַחֹ֑דֶשׁ יָבְשָׁ֖ה הָאָֽרֶץ: טו וַיְדַבֵּ֥ר אֱלֹהִ֖ים אֶל־נֹ֥חַ לֵאמֹֽר: ז צֵא רביעי

MALBIM (cont.)

other hand, once the bird has laid eggs in a spot it will become committed to that place. The dove in the current narrative had not left any eggs behind on the ark, and therefore it had no compunction about flying off forever, even though it was a trained bird.

HAAMEK DAVAR

וְלֹא־יָסְפָה שׁוּב־אֵלָיו עוֹד – *And it returned to him no more:* [Why did the dove never again come back to Noaḥ? Was it not a homing bird, as the author argues above in comments to verse 7?] Unlike during its previous sortie, when it managed to find something to bring back to Noaḥ, the dove was now unable to locate a satisfactory object to carry to its master. The bird was therefore afraid to show its face before Noaḥ as it had been trained to do, and hence it stayed away from then on. According to my interpretation of the story, we understand why the dove did not attempt to rejoin its mate. Such behavior is not only unusual for birds in general, but more so with this species, which is monogamous. And yet, as I have written, the dove which Noaḥ dispatched for this mission was one that had been specially trained for the task, and it did not have a special mate aboard the ark. [That is, this dove was not one of the fourteen doves that Noaḥ was commanded to take onto the vessel to preserve their species, but was brought specifically for the job at hand.]

VERSE 14

HAAMEK DAVAR

יָבְשָׁה הָאָרֶץ – *The earth had dried completely:* This verse reports two developments. Firstly, all the land had been cleared of the floodwaters [not just the area surrounding the ark]. And secondly, the ground was now completely dry. *By the first day of the first month* [the date given in verse 13] the land around the ark was free of water as far as the eye could see. However at that point the soil remained muddy and swampy. Now, *by the twenty-seventh day of the second month* [roughly two months later] the ground was thoroughly dried out.

VERSE 15

HAAMEK DAVAR

וַיְדַבֵּר אֱלֹהִים – *Then God said:* I have already explained [in comments to 7:1] that the text employs the name *Elohim* throughout the flood narrative. For that appellation shows God as creator of the natural world and as sustainer of all life.

13 again sent forth the dove – and it returned to him no more. So
it was that, by the first day of the first month of Noaḥ's six hundred and first year, the water on the earth dried up. Noaḥ removed the covering of the ark and saw that the face of the land
14 was dry. By the twenty-seventh day of the second month, the
15 earth had dried completely. Then God said to Noaḥ, REVI'I
16 "Leave the ark – you, and your wife, your sons, and your sons'

VERSE 16

OR HAḤAYYIM

צֵא מִן־הַתֵּבָה אַתָּה וְאִשְׁתְּךָ – *Leave the ark – you, and your wife:* [Why did God specify both Noaḥ and his wife?] With this command God now permitted to Noaḥ and the other passengers what had been forbidden to them upon boarding the ark months previously [that is, sexual intimacy]. Indeed, regarding the animal species, the following verse states: *Let them swarm again on the earth and be fertile and multiply upon it* [granting permission to the world's creatures to resume mating]. Now God was careful to utter the command to "leave" first, before listing the males and the females who could now be together. By this He implied that as long as the occupants remained on the boat they would be forbidden from cohabiting even though the catastrophe was essentially over. This is why the subsequent verse states: *So Noaḥ came out with his sons, his wife, and his sons' wives* (8:18), where the men departed together and the women too left as a group. For no physical contact was permitted until all the passengers were clear of the ark. Noaḥ thereby carefully observed God's instruction and disembarked before reuniting with his wife.

MALBIM

צֵא מִן־הַתֵּבָה – *Leave the ark:* The fact that God had to instruct Noaḥ to leave the ark suggests that he and his family were reluctant to leave it, even though the land had dried up. This hesitation can be explained as follows: The salvation that the ark provided the people and the animals under their care was not effected through natural means. Had the boat not been protected by divine providence it surely would have been smashed and sunk by the force of the great storm. Indeed, the boat lacked a mast, sails, or even oars to propel or steer it. Of course, God could have devised some simpler and less miraculous mechanism for rescuing the life forms that He wished to preserve. For example, He could have deposited all the animal representatives on an isolated island and shielded that land mass from the flood! Hence the plan that God executed was a divine mystery. For after God decided to destroy the planet and all life that roamed it – including Noaḥ – He then needed to save the righteous man in a way that did not violate that vow. This God did by keeping Noaḥ afloat on the waters which were not subject to the decree [to erase all life "on the land," as expressed in 6:7]. Hence God commanded Noaḥ and his household to enter the ark seven days before the onset of the rains to become accustomed to the place and to establish the vessel as their home. As such, the family would no longer be considered residents of the earth, but as seagoing people. In this way they joined the community of fish who were also not fated for destruction. Now since Noaḥ did not know how long the earth

יז מִן־הַתֵּבָה אַתָּה וְאִשְׁתְּךָ וּבָנֶיךָ וּנְשֵׁי־בָנֶיךָ אִתָּךְ׃ כָּל־
הַחַיָּה אֲשֶׁר־אִתְּךָ מִכָּל־בָּשָׂר בָּעוֹף וּבַבְּהֵמָה וּבְכָל־הָרֶמֶשׂ
הָרֹמֵשׂ עַל־הָאָרֶץ הוצא אִתָּךְ וְשָׁרְצוּ בָאָרֶץ וּפָרוּ וְרָבוּ הַיְצֵא
יח עַל־הָאָרֶץ׃ וַיֵּצֵא־נֹחַ וּבָנָיו וְאִשְׁתּוֹ וּנְשֵׁי־בָנָיו אִתּוֹ׃ כָּל־ יט
הַחַיָּה כָּל־הָרֶמֶשׂ וְכָל־הָעוֹף כֹּל רוֹמֵשׂ עַל־הָאָרֶץ
כ לְמִשְׁפְּחֹתֵיהֶם יָצְאוּ מִן־הַתֵּבָה׃ וַיִּבֶן נֹחַ מִזְבֵּחַ לַיהוָה וַיִּקַּח
מִכֹּל ׀ הַבְּהֵמָה הַטְּהֹרָה וּמִכֹּל הָעוֹף הַטָּהֹר וַיַּעַל עֹלֹת

MALBIM *(cont.)*

was meant to remain desolate, he could not exit the ark and resettle on land until God had informed him that the period of darkness had ended; that the planet was once again available for human habitation and would never be destroyed again.

THE LUBAVITCHER REBBE

צֵא מִן־הַתֵּבָה – *Leave the ark:* It may be tempting to remain in this protective spiritual atmosphere, and its serene perfection might delude us into thinking that there really is no need to perfect the world around us. We are nevertheless instructed to leave it, for the true purpose of entering the ark is to ultimately emerge from it, enter the world, and transform it into God's home. We should not view our departure from our personal ark as self-sacrifice for the sake of others, since leaving the ark benefits and completes us, as well. As lofty as the levels we can attain in our own arks may be, they are nonetheless finite. Such levels are incomparable to the levels we can reach through our work in the "real world," in which God provides us with the opportunity to share in the experience of infinity by creating a home for His infinite essence.

VERSE 17

MALBIM

כָּל־הַחַיָּה אֲשֶׁר־אִתְּךָ – *And every living thing with you:* Said God to Noaḥ: The salvation of the animal kingdom was thanks to your merit; it was only because of your righteousness that these representative creatures even boarded the ark. And hence, it is similarly due to your virtue that they are granted permission to disembark. Thus the verse states: *Bring them out with you*. This statement also hints at how the human soul includes within it all the forces of nature and represents each of the distinct animal attributes. For example, people have the capacity to display the zeal of the ant, the modesty of the cat, the strength of the lion, and the boldness of the leopard. And when people perfect the spirits within themselves, so too will they perfect the spirit of the animal world.

HAAMEK DAVAR

הוצא אִתָּךְ – *Bring them out with you:* Noaḥ was not meant to merely open the door of the ark and release all of the birds and animals. Rather, he was to guide them safely from the vessel and prevent the beasts from trampling or attacking each other.

17 wives with you. And every living thing with you – birds, animals, and all wild beasts that walk the earth – bring them out
with you. Let them swarm again on the earth and be fertile and
18 multiply upon it." So Noaḥ came out with his sons, his wife, and
19 his sons' wives. Every beast, creeping thing, winged creature,
everything that creeps across the earth, emerged from the ark by
20 families. Then Noaḥ built an altar to the LORD and, taking of
each of the kinds of pure animals and pure birds, sacrificed

VERSE 18

MALBIM

וַיֵּצֵא־נֹחַ וּבָנָיו – *So Noaḥ came out with his sons:* [The word order in the verse hints that the men and women left the ark separately, contravening God's command in verse 16.] Our Sages maintain that Noaḥ was afraid to resume sexual relations with his wife, lest they produce more children who would subsequently be killed in a new flood. The new generation of people would therefore be wiped out alongside the animal families that would be created after the flood.

VERSE 19

MALBIM

לְמִשְׁפְּחֹתֵיהֶם יָצְאוּ מִן־הַתֵּבָה – *Emerged from the ark by families:* This emphasizes that throughout the duration of the deluge all the animal species were cooped up on the ark, and yet they refrained from attacking each other. But once the vessel's passengers were released, they formed their own distinct groups: The herbivores spread out across the savannahs, and the carnivores gathered into packs to hunt them. For the latter only now suddenly became carnivorous; they had not been before the deluge, as God had commanded: *And to all the beasts of the earth and birds of the heavens and everything that crawls over the earth and has within it living spirit – I give every green plant for food* (1:30). However, in the postdiluvian world predators started eating the flesh of other animals. And so all the animals divided themselves into different families, meaning categories of beast.

RABBI DAVID TZVI HOFFMAN

לְמִשְׁפְּחֹתֵיהֶם יָצְאוּ מִן־הַתֵּבָה – *Emerged from the ark by families:* The Torah means that the animals disembarked according to their different species. The term "family" is used here in the same sense of the word "kind" in the text's description of creation [for example in 1:24 – *Let the land produce every kind of living thing*]. The animal occupants left the ark by their own accord, just as they had entered the vessel of their own volition [and did not have to be dragged or coerced].

VERSE 20

RABBI SAMSON RAPHAEL HIRSCH

וַיִּבֶן נֹחַ מִזְבֵּחַ – *Then Noaḥ built an altar:* This verse, which is the first in the Torah to mention altars and burnt offerings, shows the great significance of the sacrificial system. It stands as

כא בַּמִּזְבֵּחַ: וַיָּרַח יהוה אֶת־רֵיחַ הַנִּיחֹחַ וַיֹּאמֶר יהוה אֶל־לִבּוֹ

RABBI SAMSON RAPHAEL HIRSCH *(cont.)*

a stark refutation to those who denounce the concept of animal sacrifice and mock its power. Consider the following apparent contradiction: For an entire year Noaḥ devoted his life and all of his energy to saving and caring for the vast range of animals he had brought onto the ark. And now, at the end of the ordeal, when his salvation was complete, Noaḥ takes some of those very same creatures that he had labored to protect, and slaughters them for sake of a sacrifice to the Almighty! Furthermore, this gesture bears tremendous importance for the history of the world, for the subsequent verses proclaim that the development of the earth and of civilization even until today are a consequence of the offerings that Noaḥ brought upon his emergence from the ark. What was Noaḥ's intention when he built the altar and sacrificed the burnt offerings? What was he thinking, and what was he trying to express? Did God guarantee the eternal endurance of the world as a reward for Noaḥ's actions? There are many rabbinic texts arguing that the very first altar was actually first erected by Adam. Its structure and form hints at elevation, an attempt as it were to reach outward and upward toward God. It is because of this that the altar is referred to as *harel* ["Mountain of God"] in the book of Ezekiel (43:15). Now the Jewish perception of a temple differs from that held by the gentile world. Israel is permitted to sacrifice only on an altar built of separate stones; we are forbidden to offer our animals on an altar set up as a pillar – that is, a single piece of rock hewn out of the ground. On the contrary, we are commanded to *build* an altar. Nor are we allowed to balance a platform atop arches and pillars. The Torah refers to the object as an "altar of earth" (Exodus 20:21), regarding which the Sages state [see Zevaḥim 58a] that this means it must be attached to the ground, as sort of an extension of the land. For that is the essential quality of the altar – the raising of the earth toward God through the efforts of human beings. If people simply remove a slab of stone out of the ground and use it for sacrifices, they have not in any way altered that piece of nature which God Himself created. But if the community first constructs an altar out of stones, that symbolizes their own development, progression and ascension toward the deity they are trying to communicate with. And so, when Noaḥ built his altar to honor God, using soil that had now been gifted to humanity a second time, he thereby dedicated all of the planet's earth and transformed it into a temple. It is similarly the mission of humankind to place one stone atop another in a project that turns all of the land into an "altar of earth" and a mountain of God. Now when other nations attempt to approach their gods, they necessarily abandon the precincts of human life and experience, for they believe that a deity can exist only within untamed nature. Of course, God can be found in the realm of the outdoors too, but the primary essence of His divinity is directed at the sphere of human existence. It is in the wilds that the greatness of the Lord is revealed, but it is in the company of humanity that we witness His righteousness. This explains the superior sanctity inherent in a constructed altar compared to the simple character of a pillar quarried straight out of a hill. This idea encapsulates the essence of a temple. In a similar vein it was prohibited to plant trees anywhere near the altar, and no beams of wood were visible in the proximity of the sacred platform [see Deuteronomy 16:21 and Sifrei].... Note that Scripture employs the four-letter name of God [translated here

21 burnt offerings on the altar. The Lord smelled the fragrant

RABBI SAMSON RAPHAEL HIRSCH *(cont.)*

as Lord] when discussing sacrifices, but never the name *Elohim*. Our Sages explain that this choice of words is an intentional argument against heretics who might accuse Israel itself of idolatry and of sacrificing to various forces of nature. [The former name is a specific name for the God of Israel, while the latter is a more general term that reflects God's relationship with the entire world. Indeed the word *elohim* is occasionally used to refer to false deities, as in Exodus 20:3.] Furthermore, usage of the unique name is also meant to deny the false claims that animal sacrifice is nothing more than death and destruction, an attempt to satisfy a vengeful and bloodthirsty God. Our opponents therefore delight in how the sacrificial system has been suspended in our times. They thank God that we have come to our senses and have moved past the need to serve the Almighty by spilling blood unnecessarily. To counter such positions, the Torah employs the name "the Lord." Noaḥ too addressed these concerns when he built his altar to God. In fact, the four-letter name was inscribed on the head plate of the High Priest precisely to argue against those who would disparage the sacrifices. We bring offerings specifically to the Lord, to the divine force who has no interest in the death of the wicked, but only in their repentance.

HAAMEK DAVAR

וַיִּבֶן נֹחַ מִזְבֵּחַ – *Then Noaḥ built an altar:* Noaḥ built an altar because he sought a blessing from God. He offered sacrifices to propitiate God and secure His benediction.

RABBI DAVID TZVI HOFFMAN

וַיִּבֶן נֹחַ מִזְבֵּחַ – *Then Noaḥ built an altar:* An altar is an elevated site, and when the supplicant climbs up to its height and raises his sacrifice to the platform he physically demonstrates his aspiration to approach the divine. Such a person seeks to become close to his Creator, and hence he literally pulls himself up to a height. This is why Noaḥ's sacrifice is referred to here as an *ola* [literally, "that which rises"]. On the other hand, the offerings that Kayin and Hevel brought to God are described as *menaḥot* [in 4:3–4, a term meaning "gift"], and their sacrifices simply signified their acknowledgement of thanks to the Almighty. Noaḥ, on the other hand, offers up his *ola* to God in flames reaching to the heavens. This gesture illustrated the man's willingness to dedicate his life to God and to purify and refine his character by divine fire.

VERSE 21

SHADAL

כִּי יֵצֶר לֵב הָאָדָם רַע מִנְּעֻרָיו – *The devisings of the human heart are evil from its youth:* God came to the following conclusion: It would be inappropriate for Me to destroy all life whenever man becomes corrupt, since human beings have a tendency to sin. Considering that *the devisings of the human heart are evil from its youth*, were I to wipe out all life on the planet due to humanity's behavior, I would have to bring a flood upon the world in every generation. I have also seen this interpretation offered by Abarbanel. Note that the previous verse states that people tend toward evil in their youth specifically, and not that the nature

לֹא אֹסִף לְקַלֵּל עוֹד אֶת־הָאֲדָמָה בַּעֲבוּר הָאָדָם כִּי יֵצֶר לֵב
הָאָדָם רַע מִנְּעֻרָיו וְלֹא־אֹסִף עוֹד לְהַכּוֹת אֶת־כָּל־חַי כַּאֲשֶׁר

SHADAL (cont.)

of human beings is essentially degenerate. Rather, starting from when they are young, people entertain wicked thoughts – but this is neither natural nor inevitable.

RABBI SAMSON RAPHAEL HIRSCH

כִּי יֵצֶר לֵב הָאָדָם רַע מִנְּעֻרָיו – *The devisings of the human heart are evil from its youth:* The original meaning of the word *naar* ["youth"] is to shake or to cast off [as in the verb *lena'er*]. Thus the word *ne'urim* refers to young people who are eager to shake their youthfulness and to develop into adulthood. Such youngsters are not influenced to any great degree by good or ill impressions; these are basically children who remain absorbed in their natural character. Nobody has yet taught these youths the art of hypocrisy, and hence they are able to brush off anybody or any opinion that does not support their approaches to life. Young people cannot be characterized as either righteous or wicked. Woe to the observer who maintains that the average child is essentially nefarious. Whoever truly understands boys and girls will attest that such an evaluation is folly; young people are not naturally corrupt, nor are the devisings of the human heart evil from its youth! For no villain chooses a life of vice by drawing upon his young years and limited experience. In normal times, the number of reprobate adults far outnumbers the population of wayward adolescents. Make no mistake: misguided children are fully capable of misconduct, for they have yet to submit to the framework of the commandments. But it is the personal independence that is granted to every human being which eventually structures a person's ethical character. Consider that when the Holy One, blessed be He, chose the people of Israel, He did not pick them because they were a nation easily swayed and subdued, but specifically because they were of stiff-necked stock. For it was clear and known to the Almighty that Israel would eventually master their obstinacy and adopt a righteous path through life. And then their stubbornness and their self-determination would be forces for good, keeping them on the straight and narrow. In a similar manner, the Holy One, blessed be He, planted in every newborn the yearning for independence so that he may eventually strengthen his resolve toward the service of God. This freedom to choose first manifests itself in a person's youthfulness: A child appears eager to shake off all restraints that the adult world imposes upon him, to cast off the burdens that are meant to restrict his options and limit his liberty. However, once the Jew arrives at the recognition that the essence of the law is in fact freedom and not constraint, he is filled with the enthusiasm that is characteristic of childhood. He then vows to devote his life to the exalted ideals just discovered.... Now let us return to our narrative. When life was reintroduced to the desolate world following the flood, human personalities began to diverge dramatically from one another. Even more than that, different nations emerged with significantly varied attributes. The division of the land into continents and countries prevented all natural communication between communities. It would be millennia before technology could help overcome such barriers. Meanwhile the distances and other obstacles that arose across the earth served to stifle the spread of evil throughout humanity. And so thousands of years have passed without the

aroma and said in His heart, "Never again will I curse the land because of man; the devisings of the human heart are evil from its youth. And never again will I destroy all life as I have done.

RABBI SAMSON RAPHAEL HIRSCH *(cont.)*

entire world becoming corrupt as it had been in Noaḥ's time. The passing of generations has led to the changing of behavior. Younger and more vigorous nations supplant older and degenerate people. If we combine all of these points, we reach an understanding that this verse heralds a new beginning in the development of humanity and in its education. Thus does God declare: Even if the heart of human beings tends toward wickedness already from their youth, still *never again will I curse the land because of man.. and never again will I destroy all life as I have done*. Instead, of all of these contrasts – *cold and heat, summer, winter, day, and night* – will continue to exist in concert and will rule the earth simultaneously across the days and years.

HAAMEK DAVAR

וַיֹּאמֶר יהוה אֶל־לִבּוֹ – *The Lord said in His heart:* The term "heart" as used here is an allusion to the constellations that govern people's lives, just as a person's heart moderates his existence. Thus the "heart of the world" is referred to as "the heart of God" so to speak, as I have written in comments on the verse *Then the Lord regretted that He had made man on earth, and His heart was touched with sorrow* (6:6).

RABBI JOSEPH B. SOLOVEITCHIK

לֹא אֹסִף לְקַלֵּל – *Never again will I curse:* The building of the ark is symbolic of the call issued to Noaḥ, the summons to build and create a new society. Yet those who survived and came after this natural cataclysm did not improve; man was not redeemed. He remained as wicked as antediluvian man. Punishment, however severe, did not achieve the desired effect. Man still led a brute existence, and his intention remained wicked. God therefore decided that ruthless punishment would no longer be employed to purge creation of evil.

יֵצֶר לֵב הָאָדָם רַע – *The devisings of the human heart are evil:* God justifies the flood by suggesting that every imagination of his heart was *constantly inclined toward evil* (6:5). Yet here, using a similar rationale, God states that He will no longer bring about this kind of catastrophe upon the world. How can the same idea justify both the punishment and the assertion that no such punishment will again be leveled? The key difference between the two statements is the word "constantly," suggesting that before the flood, all man's instincts and talents were directed to complete evil. Such a person could become entirely impure, with no hope of redemption. After the flood, the "constantly" was removed, and every person had the capacity for repentance.

THE LUBAVITCHER REBBE

יֵצֶר לֵב הָאָדָם רַע – *The devisings of the human heart are evil:* This statement employed in this verse as an argument why human beings should not be destroyed appears earlier as an argument for precisely the opposite, i.e., why they should be destroyed [in 6:5]. The explanation of this seeming contradiction is as follows: Noaḥ's sacrificial offerings caused

כב עָשִׂיתִי׃ עֹד כָּל־יְמֵי הָאָרֶץ זֶרַע וְקָצִיר וְקֹר וָחֹם וְקַיִץ וָחֹרֶף
ט א וְיוֹם וָלַיְלָה לֹא יִשְׁבֹּתוּ׃ וַיְבָרֶךְ אֱלֹהִים אֶת־נֹחַ וְאֶת־בָּנָיו

THE LUBAVITCHER REBBE *(cont.)*

the selfsame argument that called for God's use of His attribute of Justice and now dictate implying His aspect of Compassion. In this lies the incredible spiritual power of sacrifice.

VERSE 22

HAAMEK DAVAR

עֹד כָּל־יְמֵי הָאָרֶץ – *As long as earth and time endure:* Idleness leads to misbehavior, and licentiousness is a product of the great abundance and superlative health that humanity enjoyed in the world before the flood. However, from now on, *sowing time and harvest, cold and heat, summer, winter, day, and night will not cease.* People will now be compelled to work, and the constantly changing atmosphere will necessarily lead to sickness and frailty. As such, man will become less inclined to sin. Now the Holy One, blessed be He, used the phrase "as long as earth and time endure" instead of the more direct "forever." The phrase relates specifically to the natural condition of the universe, as opposed to the messianic period when all humanity will recognize the rule of God. In those times there will exist no danger that humanity will transgress divine commands. As such, nature will change again, and the world will be completely governed by direct providence from heaven. There will then be no sowing or harvest, as the prophets predict.

RABBI JOSEPH B. SOLOVEITCHIK

זֶרַע וְקָצִיר וְקֹר וָחֹם – *Sowing time and harvest, cold and heat:* What is the connection between the preceding verse about the evil nature of man and this verse, about the unalterable, steady routine of nature? Just as there are no leaps or sudden transformations within the cosmic process, there are no leaps in human nature. A catastrophe, even of such enormous proportions as the deluge, did not have a redeeming effect upon man, who is by his very nature wicked.

CHAPTER 9, VERSE 1

MALBIM

פְּרוּ וּרְבוּ – *Be fertile, multiply:* Our teacher Abarbanel describes the scene upon Noaḥ's emergence from the ark. The survivor looked around at the desolate world and was seized by anxiety regarding four separate issues. Firstly, Noaḥ was struck by the near complete destruction of humanity that had left just four men alive. In response to this, God blessed Noaḥ, telling him: *Be fertile, multiply, fill the earth.* Secondly, Noaḥ was terrified that the absence of a human population would embolden the animals to encroach on his family and attack them. To counter this, God promised him: *Fear and dread of you shall fall upon all beasts of the earth* (9:2). Next, Noaḥ worried about feeding his wife and sons. Now that all the trees and vegetation had been uprooted, ruined, and smashed, what would the people eat? To relieve this concern God permitted human beings to eat animal flesh [in verse 3]. And lastly, Noaḥ feared that the hatred that arose between Kayin and Hevel when they had the whole world laid out before them would similarly grip his own sons.

22 As long as earth and time endure – sowing time and harvest,
cold and heat, summer, winter, day, and night will not cease."
9 1 Then God blessed Noaḥ and his sons, saying to them, "Be

MALBIM *(cont.)*

Fratricide would inevitably follow. In an effort to prevent that, God declared: *One who sheds the blood of man – by man shall his blood be shed* (9:6). Note that when God granted Adam dominance over nature, He told him: *Fill the earth and subdue it* (1:28), a detail which God does not feature in God's command to Noaḥ now. Because Adam had not yet truly risen above his animal character, he was not allowed to eat meat. [That is, Adam was virtually an equal with the rest of the animal kingdom.] Instead, Adam was forced to fight against the animals and to capture them as an act of self-defense, which is why God tells him to conquer nature. However, Noaḥ's personality stood at a different level – he was a fully realized human being with the power of speech. As such, the animals felt a natural timidity in the face of his superiority. No war or conquest would now be necessary to subdue the animal species. Now there is a difference between the terms "fear" [*mora*] and "dread" [*ḥitta*]. When an animal feels fear, it is terrified that it will come to harm. On the other hand, "dread" describes the total and natural submission such as a weak person feels in the face of the powerful. When the predatory animals in the postdiluvian world began to eat meat, Noaḥ was suddenly afraid of them. This is why God blessed Noaḥ by assuring him that those beasts would fear him instead. They would do their best to conceal themselves in forests and barren lands, fleeing for their lives from humans.

HAAMEK DAVAR

פְּרוּ וּרְבוּ – *Be fertile, multiply:* This verse is only a blessing but not a commandment – the commandment to reproduce appears at the end of this passage: *As for you, be fertile and multiply* (9:7). Such is also the position of the Talmud [see Sanhedrin 59a]. This explains why the word "God" is not repeated in the middle of the verse as it is in the commandment to Adam. [A verse at the start of the Torah relates God's first communication to humans after their creation, *God blessed them, saying, "Be fertile and multiply. Fill the earth and subdue it"* (1:28). In that instance God both blessed the people and ordered them to procreate – the repetition of the term "God" proves that there were two different messages. However, in the present verse, the word "God" appears just once. Hence the sense of the text is: *God blessed Noaḥ and his sons, saying to them, "Be fertile, multiply."* There is no command in this verse separate from the blessing.] Nevertheless, the verse includes the words "saying to them" [literally, "and He said to them," when it could have just said: "saying"; this seems to imply that there were separate components to the message]. This is because God's speech to the men conveyed additional material [verses 2–7] which did not comprise blessings at all [and hence the text demanded an additional verb].

THE LUBAVITCHER REBBE

פְּרוּ וּרְבוּ – *Be fertile, multiply:* The very first commandment with which humanity was entrusted after having experienced mass destruction was to "be fertile and multiply," to populate the world anew.... The same holds true for our spiritual procreation, i.e.,

ב וַיֹּאמֶר לָהֶם פְּרוּ וּרְבוּ וּמִלְאוּ אֶת־הָאָרֶץ׃ וּמוֹרַאֲכֶם וְחִתְּכֶם
יִהְיֶה עַל כָּל־חַיַּת הָאָרֶץ וְעַל כָּל־עוֹף הַשָּׁמָיִם בְּכֹל אֲשֶׁר
ג תִּרְמֹשׂ הָאֲדָמָה וּבְכָל־דְּגֵי הַיָּם בְּיֶדְכֶם נִתָּנוּ׃ כָּל־רֶמֶשׂ
אֲשֶׁר הוּא־חַי לָכֶם יִהְיֶה לְאָכְלָה כְּיֶרֶק עֵשֶׂב נָתַתִּי לָכֶם

THE LUBAVITCHER REBBE *(cont.)*

educating our pupils. We should not be satisfied with having taught pupils in our younger years, we must continue to educate new pupils as we grow older.

VERSE 2

RABBI SAMSON RAPHAEL HIRSCH

עַל כָּל־חַיַּת הָאָרֶץ – *Upon all beasts of the earth:* Man's initial relationship with the earth was defined in his responsibilities toward the Garden of Eden where he was placed *to work it and safeguard it* (2:15). That set of obligations now lapsed as the people became occupied with working to preserve their own lives. Indeed, the earlier closeness which humanity felt to the animal world had been supplanted by a new state wherein the animal kingdom now lived in fear and dread of human beings.... The previous verses described the world after the flood as a time for education, as Noaḥ was given the mandate to prevent evil from conquering human society. Such a mission would be possible because people would now be inherently different from one another [and would not band together to corrupt all civilization]. A shorter life span would also ensure the rapid turnover of the generations, which in turn would allow a greater acceptance of the kingdom of God as the youth rejuvenate the world. As such, individuals and nations would strive ever harder toward the eternal goal of humanity. Now if this assessment is correct, it means that humanity's mission is no longer to dominate the earth in an effort to perfect nature. Rather, the aim of our efforts is in fact the human project – we must work to improve and purify ourselves in order to return to the true and noble relationship with God for which we were destined.

HAAMEK DAVAR

וּמוֹרַאֲכֶם – *Fear of you:* Animals will flee from you and will be afraid to attack human beings. **וְחִתְּכֶם** – *And dread of you:* Creatures of the world will be terrified if a person approaches them. **בְּכֹל אֲשֶׁר תִּרְמֹשׂ הָאֲדָמָה** – *Upon all that creeps upon the land:* [The verse lists four categories of creatures – beasts, birds, creeping things, and fish. One way to read the verse is to understand that the "fear and dread" mentioned at its start will inhere only in the first two groups, while only the latter two will be given "into your hand," the phrase that closes the verse. But the Netziv disagrees:] Creeping animals too will fear and dread you. For if the latter two kinds of beast related only to the words *Into your hand they are given*, the text should have prefaced the creeping animals with the word *kol* ["all," without the prefix *bet*, which would have signaled the start of a new idea]. Rather, it is clear that these beasts are included in the prediction that the image of man will strike fear in animal hearts. Now the Holy One, blessed be He, slightly altered the language regarding the fear felt by the beasts of the earth and the birds of the skies [introduced with the words *al kol* – "upon all"], to that

2 fertile, multiply, fill the earth. Fear and dread of you shall fall
upon all beasts of the earth, upon all winged creatures of the
heavens, upon all that creeps upon the land and all fish of the
3 sea. Into your hand they are given. Every moving thing that
lives shall be food for you; I allow them all to you, like green

HAAMEK DAVAR *(cont.)*

regarding the creeping animals and the fish [*bekhol*] because there is a difference between the first pair of creatures and the second. The distinction lies in the type of trepidation that these animals experience in the presence of humans. Animals and birds will fly as soon as they catch sight of people, even though a great distance might separate them. Creeping things and fish however remain oblivious to the threat humans pose until the hunter reaches out his hand to touch them. It is only then that they are alerted to the danger and recoil and hide. Thus the preposition *be* ["in"] reflects the nearness at which a thing can be touched. **בְּיֶדְכֶם נִתָּנוּ** – *Into your hand they are given:* Even though all of these animals run from human beings, with diligence and effort people are still capable of catching them.

RABBI JOSEPH B. SOLOVEITCHIK

וּמוֹרַאֲכֶם וְחִתְּכֶם – *Fear and dread of you:* A new relationship is established here between man and animal, a tension engendered by fear and dread. Animal is afraid of man and flees before him. Why? Because instinctively, the animal senses man's animosity and evil designs. Man-animal becomes a life-killer, an animal eater. He becomes bloodthirsty and flesh-hungry. Is the Torah happy about this change? Somehow we intuitively feel the silent tragic note that pervades this whole chapter. The Torah was compelled to concede defeat to human nature that was corrupted by man.

VERSE 3

OR HAḤAYYIM

לָכֶם יִהְיֶה לְאָכְלָה – *Shall be food for you:* The question bears asking why Adam was not permitted to eat meat but Noaḥ was. It seems to me that Noaḥ was granted this license because when they were on the ark, the animals Noaḥ was caring for ate food that he supplied them. [That is, Noaḥ essentially took possession of the animals and was now allowed to do with them as he pleased. Adam, on the other hand, was given no such ownership.] There are three ways in which Noaḥ was considered to own the animal kingdom. Firstly, it was through the agency of Noaḥ that God chose to preserve each of the animal species. Had it not been for Noaḥ not a single living thing would have survived. Furthermore, had humanity not been carried over to the new world, the animals would not have been rescued at all. [This follows the rabbinic belief that once God decreed that humanity should be destroyed, the animal world was also slated for death, because the beasts were only made to serve humans.] Secondly, Noaḥ devoted the entire year on the ark to toiling and caring for the animal passengers. Consider the description of Noaḥ's efforts presented by the Sages who associate with him the verse *You shall eat the fruit of your labor* [Psalms 128:2; since Noaḥ worked to protect and feed the animals, he was later entitled to eat them]. And thirdly, by offering sacrifices to God, Noaḥ appeased the Almighty and led God to vow:

ד ה אֶת־כֹּל׃ אַךְ־בָּשָׂר בְּנַפְשׁוֹ דָמוֹ לֹא תֹאכֵלוּ׃ וְאַךְ אֶת־דִּמְכֶם
לְנַפְשֹׁתֵיכֶם אֶדְרֹשׁ מִיַּד כָּל־חַיָּה אֶדְרְשֶׁנּוּ וּמִיַּד הָאָדָם מִיַּד

OR HAḤAYYIM *(cont.)*

Never again will all life be destroyed by the waters of a flood (9:11). As a reward, God allowed Noaḥ to partake of the animals whose continued endurance he had secured.

RABBI SAMSON RAPHAEL HIRSCH

לָכֶם יִהְיֶה לְאָכְלָה – *Shall be food for you:* Since the conditions of humans' lives had been altered, so too was their diet. It seems that the new allowance of eating meat was related to the shortened lifespan humans were to experience. Whatever people previously had seven or eight hundred years to accomplish, now had to be done in seventy or eighty years. As such, the faster speed of life demanded richer sources of energy. Furthermore, changes in temperature and climate and the progression of the seasons must have also been connected to the new license to eat animals. For the constant shifts in the natural world meant it would be harder to depend on agriculture for survival. Now our Sages put forth an argument that is supported by geologists, namely that before the flood, the planet's temperature was far more stable, and vegetation existed in greater supply than after the deluge. Thus an all-plant diet was easier to sustain in the antediluvian world, and there was no need for people to resort to animal flesh to survive. Note that the Torah does not wish its adherents to be vegetarians, nor is it averse to the consumption of meat. In fact, the opposite is true: there exists an obligation to eat meat on the festivals [see Sifrei on Deuteronomy 16:11]. Of course, if we existed in humanity's original state, we would be forbidden to eat meat. However, currently meat is essential to human well-being. As soon as God allowed people to indulge their desire for flesh, He also instituted laws regarding forbidden food [such as that stated in verse 4]. Indeed, we later find that when Israel was given the Torah, every single food restriction relates to animals. Hence we can map the following progression: At first, meat was off limits altogether, and when it was allowed there were laws governing its enjoyment [for all people, and even more rules for the Jewish people]. On the other hand, there exists not a single plant species which is inherently forbidden. And while the Torah introduces laws of *ḥadash* [regulating the time when a new wheat crop may be consumed], *orla* [which states that fruit trees may not be harvested until their fourth year], and *kil'ayim* [forbidding the planting together of disparate seeds], these are issues that are imposed upon the cultivation and enjoyment of the plants – they do not define the permissibility of particular species. The next verse in our passage describes the prohibition of eating a limb from a living animal, thereby introducing the first food-related prohibition. This law is incumbent upon all human beings and is not restricted to the community of Israel.

VERSE 4

MALBIM

אַךְ־בָּשָׂר בְּנַפְשׁוֹ דָמוֹ – *But flesh with its lifeblood still in it:* I am only permitting you to eat meat from an animal that is no longer alive. Only then will the animal be served in being elevated to be part of a human body. But you may not eat *flesh with its lifeblood still in it,* when the animal's life still courses through its bloodstream. This constitutes murder and cruelty.

4 plants. But flesh with its lifeblood still in it you may not eat.
5 And for your own lifeblood I will demand account; I will demand it from every wild beast. For human life I will demand

RABBI DAVID TZVI HOFFMAN

אַךְ־בָּשָׂר בְּנַפְשׁוֹ דָמוֹ – *But flesh with its lifeblood still in it:* The blood of a creature represents the organ of life through which its vital functions are carried out. It is only once the blood has been drained from an animal through slaughter that its life force also leaves its body. While an animal is still alive its blood is tied to its soul. And since the physical substance is inherently connected to the spiritual, it is the latter which animates the former and hence consumption of blood is forbidden. For life is an exalted affair, and even animal lives belong to God and may not be consumed by people. Only once the life of a creature has been completely extracted from the flesh, when there no longer exists any possibility that the animal can act as it had previously, then its flesh may be consumed. This leads us to the prohibition of eating the limb from a living animal. Now the text could not have presented this law in an abridged form by simply stating: "Do not eat flesh from a living animal." For even though that is essentially the commandment, such phrasing could have easily been misconstrued and thought to forbid a limb only from an animal that is completely alive. But when a creature has been mortally wounded and is no longer fully functional, we might have thought it permissible to eat a part of it already before its demise. Hence the precise language of our verse emphasizes that even if the animal has already been slaughtered, eating it remains forbidden if the creature is still convulsing. Limbs and blood extracted from the animal in such a state may not be consumed, for the life force of the beast is still active through its blood. Still, this verse does not mean that it is forbidden for gentiles to eat blood [once an animal is dead] since that would have been a straightforward prohibition to enunciate, as the Torah later does [regarding Jews, in Leviticus 7:26. That is, our text forbids all people eating blood or limbs before an animal is dead, but not afterward].

RABBI JOSEPH B. SOLOVEITCHIK

לֹא תֹאכֵלוּ – *You may not eat:* The mere fact that God begins to legislate a moral norm and teaches man how to actualize it bears witness to God's confidence in man's ability to fulfill the law and to establish himself as a moral being. If God gave man a moral code, apparently He thought that man still had a great potential for good, despite his malicious, evil actions.

VERSE 5

HAKETAV VEHAKABBALA

מִיַּד אִישׁ אָחִיו – *Of every man toward his fellow man:* The verse features the synonyms *adam* and *ish* [both meaning "man"] and appends the word *aḥiv* [literally, "his brother"; the wording seems strangely diverse]. Thus it seems to me that the verse recognizes two types of murder. Usually the killing of a person is to his detriment and is perpetrated by somebody seeking vengeance, or as the result of a robbery or some other violent encounter. And yet, on occasion the victim of such a crime benefits from his death, such as when he is mired in severe depression or physical torment and would rather die than live.... Such was the case with King Sha'ul, whom the Amalekite quotes as saying: *Stand over me and finish*

ו אִישׁ אָחִיו אֶדְרֹשׁ אֶת־נֶפֶשׁ הָאָדָם׃ שֹׁפֵךְ דַּם הָאָדָם בָּאָדָם
ז דָּמוֹ יִשָּׁפֵךְ כִּי בְּצֶלֶם אֱלֹהִים עָשָׂה אֶת־הָאָדָם׃ וְאַתֶּם פְּרוּ

HAKETAV VEHAKABBALA *(cont.)*

me off, for I am wracked with convulsions, but my life still lingers (II Samuel 1:9). The present verse addresses both types of murder: That which is cruel and committed by the lowest kind of person, is referred to by calling the perpetrator *adam* [with its base connotations of earth – *adama*]. But the Torah also forbids the murder of a person who wants to die and would consider it a favor if somebody took his life. The sort of individual who would honor such a request may be an otherwise upstanding person – an *ish* [with connotations of nobility]. He might even be the victim's friend who believes he is doing something meritorious by killing, and putting him out of his misery. Nevertheless, the text warns that such mercy killing is equally forbidden. Thus even though the Torah distinguishes between spilling the blood of an enemy and that of a friend, it finds both actions abhorrent.

HAAMEK DAVAR

מִיַּד אִישׁ אָחִיו – *Of every man toward his fellow man:* The Holy One, blessed be He, explains that an murderer is prosecuted for taking a human life when he ought to have treated the other with fellowship [*aḥva*]. On the other hand, during the course of a war, it is permitted to kill the enemy for such is the way of the world. Regarding this Scripture acknowledges: *There is a time to kill, a time to heal… A time to love, a time to hate; a time for war and a time for peace* (Ecclesiastes 3:3, 3:8).… Furthermore, the king of Israel is permitted to wage a war of choice [to conquer territory] even though some of his subjects will necessarily be killed in the process.

RABBI DAVID TZVI HOFFMAN

אֶת־דִּמְכֶם לְנַפְשֹׁתֵיכֶם – *Your own lifeblood:* Since humanity had been granted permission to spill the blood of animals in order to eat them, it now had to be emphasized that no such latitude is allowed regarding the murder of people. This is because each human life is sacred within the community of human beings, and certainly when compared to the animal world.… At first the text makes a general statement: Anybody who murders a person must be punished. The passage then proceeds to specify that such accountability will be demanded regardless of the perpetrator's identity – whether he be a fellow human or a predatory beast. Our Sages, of blessed memory, infer from the initial clause of this text – *And for your own lifeblood I will demand account* – that the prohibition of murder extends to one's own suicide as well, and includes cases of hanging [where one's blood is not actually drawn]. Thus the term *lenafshoteikhem* ["to your own souls"] is added after *dimkhem* ["your blood," to emphasize that even bloodless murder is proscribed].

VERSE 6

SHADAL

שֹׁפֵךְ דַּם הָאָדָם – *One who sheds the blood of man:* It is perfectly clear – both from the Torah and the Mishna – that it is forbidden to murder a gentile. For all human beings were created in the image of God, not just Jews.

6 account, of every man toward his fellow man: One who sheds
the blood of man – by man shall his blood be shed, for in God's
7 image man was made. As for you, be fertile and multiply,

RABBI JOSEPH B. SOLOVEITCHIK

בְּצֶלֶם אֱלֹהִים – *In God's image:* Rabbi Akiva is quoted in Pirkei Avot (3:18) as saying: Beloved is man, for he was created in the image of God, as it is said: *For in God's image man was made.* The proof text cited by Rabbi Akiva is this verse here in Parashat Noaḥ. But why didn't Rabbi Akiva cite an earlier verse containing the same idea: *So God created humankind in His image* (1:27)? This verse was selected because it is prefaced by the prohibition to murder. Rabbi Akiva was concerned with finding a scriptural confirmation for the basic principle of human dignity, which is based on the fact that man was created in God's image. The fact that man's blood cannot be shed with impunity is a manifestation of the principle of human dignity, the basis of Rabbi Akiva's idea.

VERSE 7

HAAMEK DAVAR

שִׁרְצוּ בָאָרֶץ – *Abound on earth:* Settle the reaches of the earth quickly in an effort to rapidly develop human civilization. If you do that, you will necessarily multiply your population, since expansion of space is always accompanied by increase in people. However, when a community is tied to the same place, its numbers remain stagnant.... Now it seems to me that in the phrase "be fertile and multiply" [*peru urvu*], the second verb should not be understood as meaning "become many," but rather "become great" in stature. The command here is for Noaḥ's descendants to create governments and monarchies that will prevent society from devouring itself.

MESHEKH ḤOKHMA

וְאַתֶּם פְּרוּ וּרְבוּ – *As for you, be fertile and multiply:* The Talmud in Bava Batra (60b) makes the remarkable suggestion that when the Roman government rose to power and imposed cruel decrees against us forbidding the study of Torah and observance of the commandments such as circumcision, perhaps it would have been better for us not to marry and produce children. Better that the descendants of our patriarch Avraham merely die out on their own than for them to be brought to an end by idol worshippers! To counter such an approach, our text assures us that even in violent times, when our nation faces murder and unspeakable bloodshed, we must not yield to defeatism. For God will exact punishment from those who murder; people who spill blood will have their own lives taken from them. Our mission is to continue to *be fertile and multiply*. We therefore read in a responsa of Rav Aḥai Gaon [8th century] commenting on Parashat Vezot Haberakha, that the Jewish people have a positive commandment to marry and to raise children. That author cites as support the following verse: *Take wives, and beget sons and daughters. Take wives for your sons and give your daughters to husbands so that they may give birth to sons and daughters. Multiply there; do not be diminished* (Jeremiah 29:6). Rav Aḥai's message was that even during a period of oppressive decrees and exile, the obligation to procreate remains in place, just as the prophet Yirmeyahu encouraged the Israelites living in

ח וּרְבוּ שִׁרְצוּ בָאָרֶץ וּרְבוּ־בָהּ׃ וַיֹּאמֶר אֱלֹהִים חמישי
ט אֶל־נֹחַ וְאֶל־בָּנָיו אִתּוֹ לֵאמֹר׃ וַאֲנִי הִנְנִי מֵקִים אֶת־בְּרִיתִי
י אִתְּכֶם וְאֶת־זַרְעֲכֶם אַחֲרֵיכֶם׃ וְאֵת כָּל־נֶפֶשׁ הַחַיָּה אֲשֶׁר
אִתְּכֶם בָּעוֹף בַּבְּהֵמָה וּבְכָל־חַיַּת הָאָרֶץ אִתְּכֶם מִכֹּל יֹצְאֵי
יא הַתֵּבָה לְכֹל חַיַּת הָאָרֶץ׃ וַהֲקִמֹתִי אֶת־בְּרִיתִי אִתְּכֶם וְלֹא־
יִכָּרֵת כָּל־בָּשָׂר עוֹד מִמֵּי הַמַּבּוּל וְלֹא־יִהְיֶה עוֹד מַבּוּל
יב לְשַׁחֵת הָאָרֶץ׃ וַיֹּאמֶר אֱלֹהִים זֹאת אוֹת־הַבְּרִית אֲשֶׁר־אֲנִי
נֹתֵן בֵּינִי וּבֵינֵיכֶם וּבֵין כָּל־נֶפֶשׁ חַיָּה אֲשֶׁר אִתְּכֶם לְדֹרֹת

MESHEKH ḤOKHMA *(cont.)*

the foreign land of Babylonia. **פְּרוּ וּרְבוּ** – *Be fertile and multiply:* It is reasonable to assume that the Torah exempted women from the obligation to procreate, while demanding that men fulfill this requirement. Regarding God's commandments, the verse states: *Its ways are the ways of pleasantness, and all of its paths are peaceful* (Proverbs 3:17). As such, God will never burden anyone with a duty that is too onerous for his body to perform. Indeed, the Talmud points out [see Ḥullin 109b] that all prohibitions mandated by the Torah are matched by parallel pleasures that Jews may enjoy. [For example, although it is forbidden to consume animal blood, it is permissible to eat liver which bears a similar taste.] And so no human being is compelled to be celibate. Moshe our teacher [who famously distanced himself from his wife] represented an exceptional case: due to his greatness and exalted state he had to maintain an ever-pure body.… And therefore, because pregnancy necessarily puts a woman in mortal danger of childbirth, the Torah does not obligate women to have children. [Even though a man requires a wife in order to fulfill this duty, there is no requirement for every woman or any particular woman to bear young. Such is not the case with men; every man is commanded to father children.]

VERSE 8

HAAMEK DAVAR

וַיֹּאמֶר אֱלֹהִים אֶל־נֹחַ – *Then God said to Noaḥ:* Compare the present verse to God's communications to Noaḥ before the flood. We read earlier: *God said to Noaḥ [Lenoaḥ]* (6:13), and *Then the Lord said to Noaḥ [Lenoaḥ]* [7:1; here, on the other hand we have the phrase *el Noaḥ*]. In my comments to the book of Exodus [see 8:21] I show that the word *el* demonstrates a greater degree of familiarity and friendliness than the abbreviated *le*. Furthermore, when the text employs the bare form *le,* it indicates that the speaker has not addressed the other by name, but is calling him to come forward to speak. On the other hand, usage of the word *el* shows that the speaker has first affectionately pronounced his listener's name before beginning to converse with him. In other words, here God introduced the current message by saying: "Noaḥ, I – I am about to establish My covenant etc." On the other hand, at the start

8 abound on earth and become many on it." Then God ḤAMISHI
9 said to Noaḥ and to his sons with him: "I – I am about to establish My covenant with you and your descendants after you,
10 and with every living creature that is with you – the birds, the
animals, and all the wild beasts of earth that are with you, ev-
11 erything that left the ark, every living creature on earth. I will
establish My covenant with you, that never again may all life be
destroyed by the waters of a flood; never again will there be a
12 flood to destroy the earth." God said, "This is the sign of the
covenant I am making between Me and you – and every living

HAAMEK DAVAR *(cont.)*

of the flood, the world was in turbulence, and hence God addressed Noaḥ curtly, with the short form *le*. After the deluge, the Holy One, blessed be He, was on closer terms with Noaḥ, who greatly benefited from his obedience to all of God's commands. This is why we now find the preposition *el*.

VERSE 11

OR HAḤAYYIM

וְלֹא־יִכָּרֵת כָּל־בָּשָׂר עוֹד – *Never again may all life be destroyed:* God would never again send a flood to totally destroy all life on the planet. However, the Almighty reserved the right to release water to drown a particular area of the world if the wicked people there deserve to be punished. The verse continues: *Never again will there be a flood to destroy the earth,* meaning: Even if a deluge does inundate a particular region, there will never be such a global catastrophe as the one just unleashed that destroyed the earth itself. That second clause would not have been sufficient by itself, since it is just a guarantee protecting the land, but not a promise that humanity will be forever safe from such all-encompassing retribution. Hence God also promises that *never again will all life be destroyed.*

VERSE 12

MALBIM

זֹאת אוֹת־הַבְּרִית – *This is the sign of the covenant:* God spoke these words to Noaḥ after striking the covenant with him. For the pact itself was effected by God's vow never again to flood the world with water [in the previous verse]. The forging of an agreement is always characterized by a vow. And now God provided Noaḥ with a sign that He meant to uphold the covenant; a sign is some symbol chosen by parties to a pact to help them remember the agreement. This is what God meant when He stated: *This is the sign of the covenant.*

HAAMEK DAVAR

זֹאת אוֹת־הַבְּרִית – *This is the sign of the covenant:* The usage of the demonstrative pronoun "this" suggests that the Holy One, blessed be He, actually pointed out the rainbow to Noaḥ when discussing its significance.

יג עוֹלָם: אֶת־קַשְׁתִּי נָתַתִּי בֶּעָנָן וְהָיְתָה לְאוֹת בְּרִית בֵּינִי וּבֵין
יד הָאָרֶץ: וְהָיָה בְּעַנְנִי עָנָן עַל־הָאָרֶץ וְנִרְאֲתָה הַקֶּשֶׁת בֶּעָנָן:
טו וְזָכַרְתִּי אֶת־בְּרִיתִי אֲשֶׁר בֵּינִי וּבֵינֵיכֶם וּבֵין כָּל־נֶפֶשׁ חַיָּה
בְּכָל־בָּשָׂר וְלֹא־יִהְיֶה עוֹד הַמַּיִם לְמַבּוּל לְשַׁחֵת כָּל־בָּשָׂר:
טז וְהָיְתָה הַקֶּשֶׁת בֶּעָנָן וּרְאִיתִיהָ לִזְכֹּר בְּרִית עוֹלָם בֵּין אֱלֹהִים
יז וּבֵין כָּל־נֶפֶשׁ חַיָּה בְּכָל־בָּשָׂר אֲשֶׁר עַל־הָאָרֶץ: וַיֹּאמֶר
אֱלֹהִים אֶל־נֹחַ זֹאת אוֹת־הַבְּרִית אֲשֶׁר הֲקִמֹתִי בֵּינִי וּבֵין
כָּל־בָּשָׂר אֲשֶׁר עַל־הָאָרֶץ:

RABBI DAVID TZVI HOFFMAN

זֹאת אוֹת־הַבְּרִית – *This is the sign of the covenant:* Why did God choose this particular phenomenon as His sign of the covenant? The rainbow represents an upside-down weapon, namely the bow used to shoot arrows. When this image appears in the sky, its feet are pointed downward; if it were facing the other direction, it would seem as if arrows were being shot out of the heavens toward earth. But the current configuration projects the opposite message – God is not directing missiles of death toward the planet's inhabitants. For there is no longer animosity between God and humans; the light representing affection has superseded the darkness of the clouds.

VERSE 13

SHADAL

אֶת־קַשְׁתִּי נָתַתִּי בֶּעָנָן – *I have laid down My bow in the clouds:* Rainbows are only seen occasionally and unpredictably in the sky. The ancients believed that the phenomenon was a message of the god Iris and attached many foolish ideas to its occurrence. But the Torah has cleansed this matter from all such harmful nonsense and offered it a positive association. It also seems to me that ancient cultures saw the rainbow as a message from the gods and a portent for future events, employing it within their divination practices. The Torah dismisses all these claims and declares the rainbow to be nothing more than a sign of God's commitment never to flood the world again.

RABBI SAMSON RAPHAEL HIRSCH

אֶת־קַשְׁתִּי נָתַתִּי בֶּעָנָן – *I have laid down My bow in the clouds:* This is the nature of the rainbow: The phenomenon is built on a pure ray of light that is broken into seven different colors – from the red which is closest to the light, to the band of purple which is farthest from the light blending with the darkness. And yet, all these stripes of color can be recombined to create a single ray of white light, shining brightly and purely. Thus does the rainbow symbolize the spectrum of living souls in our world – ranging from humans, represented by the red, who are closest to the divine, to the dimmest and lowliest animals such as the worm. All of earth's creatures are essentially made of flesh. Furthermore, it is

13 creature with you – for all generations to come. I have laid
down My bow in the clouds to be the sign of the covenant be-
14 tween Me and the earth. Whenever I bring clouds over the
15 earth and the rainbow appears in the clouds, I will remember
My covenant that binds Me and you and every living creature
of all flesh so that never again will the waters become a flood to
16 destroy all life. The rainbow will be there in the cloud, and I will
see it, remembering the eternal covenant between God and ev-
17 ery living creature, all flesh upon the earth." So said God to
Noaḥ: "This is the sign of the covenant that I have established
between Me and all flesh that is on earth."

RABBI SAMSON RAPHAEL HIRSCH *(cont.)*

the wide variety within the family of humankind – from the brightest and most spiritual people to the most opaque and physical with barely a glimmer of the Divine – who are all united in the life that God has granted the human race. Each of us shines with the refracted light of the Divine Spirit, including those who seem to barely shine with it at all. Every soul burns with the lamp of God's light.

VERSE 14

MALBIM

וְהָיָה בְּעַנְנִי עָנָן עַל־הָאָרֶץ – *Whenever I bring clouds over the earth:* In the future, the world surely will need rain. God is informing Noaḥ that when the rainclouds gather, he is not to fear for his life or for the safety of the planet. For God forged a covenant with the world never again to enlist a flood to punish the earth. After God provided Noaḥ with a sign to confirm His promise and finished speaking with him, clouds filled the sky, and with them the rainbow appeared for the first time. God immediately said to Noaḥ: Look up and see the rainbow I have placed in the heavens – *This is the sign of the covenant;* such is its design and its configuration.

VERSE 15

HAKETAV VEHAKABBALA

וְזָכַרְתִּי אֶת־בְּרִיתִי – *I will remember My covenant:* The remembrance mentioned in this verse refers to human beings who need small reminders to prevent them from forgetting things. It does not relate to God, before whom no knowledge is ever erased. Surely God does not require a sign to help Him recall anything.

VERSE 17

HAAMEK DAVAR

וַיֹּאמֶר אֱלֹהִים אֶל־נֹחַ – *So God said to Noaḥ:* God repeats this message to Noaḥ alone lest he make the following error: Noaḥ might have thought that humanity would only be safe from destruction when the sign of the rainbow appears in the sky. However, on a stormy day when the mark of the covenant is not visible, that might suggest that the world is at

יח וַיִּהְיוּ בְנֵי־נֹחַ הַיֹּצְאִים מִן־הַתֵּבָה שֵׁם וְחָם וָיָפֶת וְחָם הוּא ח ששי
יט אֲבִי כְנָעַן׃ שְׁלֹשָׁה אֵלֶּה בְּנֵי־נֹחַ וּמֵאֵלֶּה נָפְצָה כָל־הָאָרֶץ׃

HAAMEK DAVAR *(cont.)*

risk of obliteration. Perhaps Noaḥ asked God about this distinction, or prayed regarding it. God therefore repeated His assertion: *This is the sign of the covenant* – this rainbow that I am showing you merely represents the sign *of the covenant that I have established between Me and all flesh*. God does not again mention His remembrance or the rainbow. [That is, the covenant remains in force independent of the sign that recalls it.] When a rainbow appears in the clouds, it indicates that the generation living beneath it actually deserves to be wiped out [but God is withholding punishment]. But even when the rainbow is not visible in the sky, the world is also guaranteed its safety based on God's word alone.

VERSE 18

RABBI SAMSON RAPHAEL HIRSCH

וַיִּהְיוּ בְנֵי־נֹחַ הַיֹּצְאִים מִן־הַתֵּבָה – *Noaḥ's sons who came out from the ark:* The Torah is divided into two genres, each comprising roughly half of the text: the legal sections and the narrative passages. When a student learns the legal portions of the Torah he must always bear in mind that the Oral Law preceded the Written Law. In other words, at first the nation of Israel was taught all the Torah's statutes orally, and only then were they given the written summary of that corpus to help them recall the totality of the law. Thus the Written Law comprises short lists which are based on the more developed oral version of the material. The same relationship exists between the oral presentation of the Torah's stories and their written form. Take for example the current chapters. The story of Noaḥ and the flood was surely not recorded during the lifetime of the tale's hero, but centuries later when the Israelites were already familiar with the Canaanite peoples who descended from Noaḥ's grandson. These nations had long descended to the depths of moral depravity, and the land of Israel was ready to discharge its degenerate inhabitants when the Israelites came along to supplant them. And although the covenant that God forged with Noaḥ would spare humankind from total destruction, it would guarantee no reprieve for groups of the man's descendants who corrupted their ways. Thus did nation after nation exit the stage of world history, and when the Canaanites had pushed their fortunes too far, a much younger people was allowed to take their place. This is where the progeny of Kenaan stood when their Israelite cousins received the current story in its written form, stating that Ḥam, one of the survivors of the flood founded that people. It was important for Israel to hear about the sin of Ḥam from God's mouth, just as it is crucial that we learn the root of his nation's wickedness which later sprouted into full-fledged societal corruption.

MALBIM

וְחָם הוּא אֲבִי כְנָעַן – *Ham was the father of Kenaan:* We learn from this that Noaḥ, Shem, and Yefet refrained from sexual intercourse with their wives during their time on the ark. Ḥam alone violated the ban against intimacy – he impregnated his wife and Kenaan

18 Noaḥ's sons who came out from the ark were Shem, Ḥam, and SHISHI
19 Yefet. Ḥam was the father of Kenaan. These three were Noaḥ's

MALBIM *(cont.)*

was born during the flood. The verse means to emphasize that the only descendants of Noaḥ to emerge from the ark were those listed here – Shem and Yefet had no sons, just as they had none when they boarded the vessel. For the same men are listed entering the ark as leaving it. And yet, the verse continues to state that *Ḥam was the father of Kenaan*, because he was born during the deluge.

HAAMEK DAVAR

וַיִּהְיוּ בְנֵי־נֹחַ הַיֹּצְאִים מִן־הַתֵּבָה – *Noaḥ's sons who came out from the ark:* The verse emphasizes that Shem, Ḥam, and Yefet were Noaḥ's sons who left the ark, in contrast to other sons whom Noaḥ surely fathered after the flood. These other progeny are not mentioned in the text, and the Torah here maintains that just as the world was originally founded by three types of men represented by Kayin, Hevel, and Shet (as I have written above in my commentary to chapter 4), so too was the new human civilization established by three personalities – Shem, Ḥam, and Yefet. The text further develops the point that these three men symbolized three different types of character. For it was the will of the Holy One, blessed be He, that the affairs of humanity would be conducted by three kinds of person. The first sort are the simple farmers who are not particularly sensitive; the second group comprises intellectuals, who have a keen understanding of the human mind. The third type of person is the spiritual leader who cleaves to God and serves as the divine chariot of his historical time and place. This is the sense of the claim that *from them all the world branched out* (9:19). And of course some descendants of Shem and Yefet lived within the community of Ḥam, which is why there can be found in that community wise and spiritual men. The opposite arrangement was also found. And it also happened that some children were born with temperaments that differed from their parents' personalities.

RABBI DAVID TZVI HOFFMAN

וְחָם הוּא אֲבִי כְנָעַן – *Ḥam was the father of Kenaan:* The text provides this information now in order to make the subsequent episode clear, when Noaḥ curses Ḥam [mentioning Kenaan, in verse 25].

THE LUBAVITCHER REBBE

וְחָם – *Ḥam:* Ḥam means "hot." Metaphorically, Ḥam alludes to the soul's ardent desire and yearning to draw near and cleave to God. "Kenaan," which is sometimes translated as "merchant," alludes to the soul's pursuit of the profit it earns by studying the Torah and observing the commandments: its increased connection to God. Ḥam was the father of Kenaan: When the soul descends into this world and clothes itself in the body and the animating soul, it experiences an intense longing for Godliness and an ardent yearning for God's presence – it becomes Ḥam. This longing inspires it to earn the reward of increased connection to God by studying the Torah and performing the commandments to become Kenaan.

כ כא וַיָּחֶל נֹחַ אִישׁ הָאֲדָמָה וַיִּטַּע כָּרֶם׃ וַיֵּשְׁתְּ מִן־הַיַּיִן וַיִּשְׁכָּר
כב וַיִּתְגַּל בְּתוֹךְ אָהֳלֹה׃ וַיַּרְא חָם אֲבִי כְנַעַן אֵת עֶרְוַת אָבִיו

VERSE 20

MALBIM

וַיָּחֶל נֹחַ אִישׁ הָאֲדָמָה – *Noaḥ began to be a man of the land:* Noaḥ did not plant his vineyard with the intention of getting drunk. Rather, Noaḥ was *a man of the land*, meaning a master of the soil who had the ground completely under his control. As owner of the earth, Noaḥ was required to work with it and prepare it for production. This man of the sea subsequently became expert in agriculture and viticulture, planting grapes for the benefit of society. For the vine is an important plant that bestows its own blessing upon the community.

MESHEKH ḤOKHMA

וַיָּחֶל נֹחַ אִישׁ הָאֲדָמָה – *Noaḥ began to be a man of the land:* In Bereshit Rabba (36:3), Noaḥ is compared to Moshe: Rabbi Berekhya taught: Moshe was more beloved to God than Noaḥ. At first Noaḥ is termed a "righteous man" (6:9) and is later demoted to "a man of the land." In contrast, Moshe is first called an "Egyptian man" (Exodus 2:19) but is subsequently given the honorific "man of God" (Deuteronomy 33:1). This contrast is based on the fact that there are two different ways to serve God Almighty. In the first approach, a person is so devoted to divine service that he secludes himself so as to better focus on that effort. Other people, however, occupy themselves with communal needs while foregoing their own requirements, essentially sacrificing their lives for others. On first consideration it would be natural to assume it is the first type of devotee who reaches great heights of spirituality, while the second sort relinquishes some of his own development by having to do deal with human beings. Indeed, the Midrash Kohelet Rabba analyzes the verse from Ecclesiastes, *Lucre turns a wise man delirious, and a gift makes him lose his wisdom* (7:7) in this way: Since Rabbi Yehoshua ben Levi was busy tending to the masses he forgot eighty separate laws. However, during the account of Noaḥ we find the man keeping to himself, not bothering to rebuke the people of his generation. And the Sages maintain that for this oversight Noaḥ deserved to die in the flood along with everybody else. Because he isolated himself, he who was first called a "righteous man" fell from that lofty perch and became only "a man of the land." Meanwhile, Moshe's development grew in the opposite direction. At first, Moshe was identified as an "Egyptian man" – and he went into exile for the sake of society at large, intervening in the beating of the Israelite. His willingness to sacrifice his freedom on behalf of Israel by killing the Egyptian is what ultimately led to his title as a "man of God," For Moshe eventually reached the highest level of perfection available to humanity.

MISHNAT RABBI AHARON

אִישׁ הָאֲדָמָה – *Man of the land:* Until now, Noaḥ had accomplished great things. He had saved all of creation through his righteousness and extended unceasing kindness and care toward the animal kingdom all the time they were on the ark. Now, however, he made the small misstep of planting a vineyard, and suddenly the Torah insists on describing him

20 sons; and from them all the world branched out. Noaḥ began
21 to be a man of the land, and he planted a vineyard. He drank
some of the wine, became drunk, and lay uncovered in his tent.
22 Ḥam, father of Kenaan, saw his father's nakedness and told his

MISHNAT RABBI AHARON *(cont.)*

with the word *vayaḥel* ["began"], hinting that he had become profane [*ḥulin*]. This seemingly insignificant act debased the prophet, turning him utterly into a "man of the land." This is because he declined to continue his spiritual ascent after the flood. The idea expressed here is that any change a person makes in their life becomes a defining feature of his personality. Thus, a small diversion toward materialism on Noaḥ's part now ended up devaluing all the work he had done until this point. And so, for example, a person might diligently study Torah for eighteen hours every day. Every hour of his study stands at a level of divine service inherent in a person whose every waking hour is devoted to that pursuit. But if that person should reduce his study regimen to ten hours every day, he has not lost only those hours no longer spent in the study hall. Every remaining hour that he still spends in study has descended to a much lower level as well.

VERSE 21

MALBIM

וַיֵּשְׁתְּ מִן־הַיַּיִן – *He drank some of the wine:* However, once Noaḥ indulged in some of his wine he ended up drinking too much and became inebriated. When Noaḥ became uncovered he resembled Adam, whose unlawful eating of the Tree of Knowledge similarly had repercussions of a sexual nature.

RABBI JOSEPH B. SOLOVEITCHIK

וַיִּשְׁכָּר – *Became drunk:* Noaḥ did not grasp the divine message regarding the covenant. Right after being shown the rainbow, Noaḥ planted a vineyard, drank of the wine, became intoxicated and was uncovered within his tent. The covenant was defiled, Noaḥ's household was divided, and the great vision of a united covenantal community faded. The selection of Noaḥ was a failure. Avraham was the first human with whom God formed a partnership. God prepared the blueprint for redemption; man was the engineer who put redemption into effect by actualizing his potential, drawing out of himself whatever was hidden in the recesses of his personality. The redemptive act is not instantaneous but piecemeal – it may take millennia to complete. Yet man should always behold the rainbow in the dark cloud, the great divine light in the darkness of the existential night of human fall and corruption.

VERSE 22

RABBI SAMSON RAPHAEL HIRSCH

וַיַּרְא חָם אֲבִי כְנַעַן – *Ḥam, father of Kenaan, saw:* When this episode took place Ḥam was already father to several children. And hence, if he had considered the relationship that he had with his children, that should have made him sensitive to how he treated his own father. Yet, instead of just telling [*lemor*] his brothers what he had seen, he related the sight in detail

כג וַיַּגֵּ֥ד לִשְׁנֵֽי־אֶחָ֖יו בַּחֽוּץ׃ וַיִּקַּח֩ שֵׁ֨ם וָיֶ֜פֶת אֶת־הַשִּׂמְלָ֗ה
וַיָּשִׂ֙ימוּ֙ עַל־שְׁכֶ֣ם שְׁנֵיהֶ֔ם וַיֵּֽלְכוּ֙ אֲחֹ֣רַנִּ֔ית וַיְכַסּ֕וּ אֵ֖ת עֶרְוַ֣ת
כד אֲבִיהֶ֑ם וּפְנֵיהֶם֙ אֲחֹ֣רַנִּ֔ית וְעֶרְוַ֥ת אֲבִיהֶ֖ם לֹ֥א רָאֽוּ׃ וַיִּ֥יקֶץ

RABBI SAMSON RAPHAEL HIRSCH *(cont.)*

[hence the verb *vayagged*]. Ḥam described the whole episode before Shem and Yefet, painting a picture of the episode for them. Ḥam delighted in the event, believing that this report would amuse the others. Now I have already explained that the words "father of Kenaan" allude to the nation that would eventually emerge from this line and become sinful and corrupt. Centuries later, Israel found itself positioned between two nations from the line of Ḥam [Egypt and Canaan]: While in Egypt, they witnessed the social deterioration widespread in that land; and when they returned to Canaan they saw the ethical perversions manifested among the peoples there as well. Thus, when Israel witnessed the downfall of these nations, it became clear that a slight, almost insignificant incident was the root of all of this corruption – namely, Ḥam's disregard for his father's dignity. For all human success is predicated on the relationship of the family and the attitudes that children have for their parents.

HAAMEK DAVAR

וַיַּגֵּד לִשְׁנֵי־אֶחָיו – *And told his two brothers:* The verb *vayagged* always connotes the conveyance of a story, not simply a verbal report. Here, the text relates that Ḥam not only let his brothers know that Noaḥ was lying uncovered – which is not actually a story – but discussed with Shem and Yefet the entire account of Kenaan's abuse of his grandfather [see Rashi].

VERSE 23

MALBIM

וַיִּקַּח שֵׁם וָיֶפֶת – *Shem and Yefet then took:* After the text reports that Ḥam chose the abominable ways of the Canaanites, who behaved like animals, it describes that Shem was the first one to act in a contrary way. For Shem was a godly person. Yefet then followed his brother's lead, for he understood that proper manners dictate the preservation of a parent's honor. Thus did the two cover their father's nakedness.

RABBI JOSEPH B. SOLOVEITCHIK

וַיְכַסּוּ אֵת עֶרְוַת אֲבִיהֶם – *And covered their father's nakedness:* Shem and Yefet had differing motivations for their action; Shem was motivated by ethics, while Yefet was motivated by etiquette. Ethics as a value obligates man to do what is proper, even when there is no one to witness and appreciate his action. Upon seeing Noaḥ's nakedness, Shem immediately acted to save his father from embarrassment. His descendants were thus given the commandment of fringes on their garments, because according to the basic halakha, the garment should be worn under one's clothing, with only the fringes exposed. The commandment of donning a piece of clothing not readily visible is a reflection of Shem's emphasis on ethics in the private domain. In contrast, Yefet was motivated by appearance and peer

23 two brothers who were outside. Shem and Yefet then took a
cloak and put it over both their shoulders. They walked backward and covered their father's nakedness, averting their faces
24 so as not to see the nakedness of their father. Noaḥ woke from
his wine and realized what his youngest son had done to him.

RABBI JOSEPH B. SOLOVEITCHIK *(cont.)*

pressure. Yefet helped cover Noaḥ only after Shem had taken the initiative, acting only because Shem would appreciate this help. As a result, Yefet's reward was the burial of his progeny [see Rashi], as burial reflects the concept of human dignity, a religious category that dictates how one person should relate to another.

THE LUBAVITCHER REBBE

וַיֵּלְכוּ אֲחֹרַנִּית – *They walked backward:* If indeed they walked backward, it is obvious that they did not see their father's nakedness. Rather, the verse's closing words teach that Shem and Yefet did not focus on their father's shameful behavior, but instead on what they had to do to correct the situation. Ḥam in contrast *saw his father's nakedness* (9:22). Not only did he not remedy the situation; he focused on his father's shortcoming and even told his brothers about it. Why the dissimilar reactions among the brothers? The Baal Shem Tov taught that the people we encounter in our lives are like mirrors. If we see evil in them, we are really seeing a reflection of the evil within ourselves. Since we are generally blind to our own faults, God arranges for us to notice them in someone else, expecting us to take the cue and recognize that we possess these same faults so we can correct them in ourselves. Thus, since Shem and Yefet did not share Noaḥ's weakness for drunkenness, they did not focus on it. In contrast, Ḥam did share Noaḥ's weakness; therefore he focused on his father's shame rather than how he could be of help.

VERSE 24

RABBI SAMSON RAPHAEL HIRSCH

אֵת אֲשֶׁר־עָשָׂה לוֹ בְּנוֹ הַקָּטָן – *What his youngest son had done to him:* We must interpret this phrase literally and identify Ḥam as Noaḥ's youngest son, even though he is listed second [in verse 18]. Indeed, we subsequently find Yefet referred to as the oldest son [a possible reading of 10:21] even though he is mentioned third in our chapter. Thus Noaḥ's sons were born in this order: Yefet, Shem, and Ḥam, and notwithstanding they are presented in a different sequence here: Shem, Ḥam, and Yefet. This matter will be made clear if we recall that all the Torah's tales are directed primarily at Jewish readers. Thus Shem is given prominence in the text as the *ancestor of all the sons of Ever* (10:21), making him the most important of these three brothers to the Hebrews, who descend from Ever. Ḥam appears next on the list because his progeny – Egypt and Canaan [Mitzrayim and Kenaan of 10:6] represent the opposite of what Israel stands for. In the future, Israel is destined to overcome the descendants of Ḥam; such a victory encompasses the entire historical development of the Jewish people. It is only after such an achievement that Israel will encounter the descendants of Yefet. And thus, Shem and Ḥam stand as competing and contrasting nations, with Yefet positioned as the intermediary between the two poles. Now we should not be surprised that Noaḥ [in the next verse] curses

נֹחַ מִיֵּינוֹ וַיֵּדַע אֵת אֲשֶׁר־עָשָׂה לוֹ בְּנוֹ הַקָּטָן׃ וַיֹּאמֶר אָרוּר כה
כְּנָעַן עֶבֶד עֲבָדִים יִהְיֶה לְאֶחָיו׃ וַיֹּאמֶר בָּרוּךְ יְהוָה אֱלֹהֵי כו
שֵׁם וִיהִי כְנַעַן עֶבֶד לָמוֹ׃ יַפְתְּ אֱלֹהִים לְיֶפֶת וְיִשְׁכֹּן בְּאָהֳלֵי־ כז
שֵׁם וִיהִי כְנַעַן עֶבֶד לָמוֹ׃ וַיְחִי־נֹחַ אַחַר הַמַּבּוּל שְׁלֹשׁ מֵאוֹת כח
שָׁנָה וַחֲמִשִּׁים שָׁנָה׃ וַיְהִי כָּל־יְמֵי־נֹחַ תְּשַׁע מֵאוֹת שָׁנָה כט
וַחֲמִשִּׁים שָׁנָה וַיָּמֹת׃
וְאֵלֶּה תּוֹלְדֹת בְּנֵי־נֹחַ שֵׁם חָם וָיָפֶת וַיִּוָּלְדוּ לָהֶם בָּנִים אַחַר י א

RABBI SAMSON RAPHAEL HIRSCH *(cont.)*

Kenaan rather than Ḥam. For in truth, the curse he issues has little to do with Kenaan himself, just as the blessing does not truly relate to the person of Shem. It is not the individual Ḥam who is cursed, and not historical figure of Shem who is blessed. Rather, the blessing and the curse refer to the ideas these personalities represent and the influence that they will have on humanity through the development of their descendants. Note that Noaḥ does not declare: "Blessed is Shem," but *Blessed be the Lord, God of Shem....* And so the text lays out before us the founders of three great streams of humankind, each of which symbolizes the character of those peoples. Shem represents spirituality; it is he who pronounces the name of God. Ḥam epitomizes human sensuality and is identified with those who treat everything as objects. Yefet exists between those two opposites, whose soul and emotions stand at the meeting point between spirituality and physicality. These three tendencies are all present in the human heart, and they are further characterized by entire nations. The truth is that there is no single people in the world that bears just one of these traits, that thrives only with its spirit or its soul. In this sense a nation is like a person who is dominated by one attribute of another, while sometimes giving expression to the opposing tendencies.

VERSE 27

HAAMEK DAVAR

יַפְתְּ אֱלֹהִים לְיֶפֶת – *May God enlarge Yefet:* In contrast to Noaḥ's blessing for Shem in the previous verse which employs God's unique four-letter name [translated here as "Lord"], now [in a blessing for the gentiles] we find the name *Elohim*. The latter term is employed here to reflect the fact that the nations of the world are directed by various celestial powers whom God has assigned to them. [The word *elohim* literally means, "powers."] For the gentiles are unfamiliar with the special name of God, as the Talmud attests [in Sanhedrin 60a]. Hence they achieve divine beneficence [by understanding God's will not through revelation] but by using their own intellectual faculties. **וְיִשְׁכֹּן בְּאָהֳלֵי־שֵׁם** – *And let him dwell in the tents of Shem:* Noaḥ blessed Yefet with the hope that his descendants would achieve wisdom and welcome the people of Shem into their midst. It is Shem's progeny who represent the divine expression in this world, spirituality that is limitless and which has much to teach Yefet's offspring, as the verse states: *By me do kings reign, and chieftains legislate*

25 He said, "Cursed be Kenaan! The lowest of slaves shall he be
26 to his brothers." Then he said, "Blessed be the Lord, God of
27 Shem; Kenaan shall be his slave. May God enlarge Yefet, and let
28 him dwell in the tents of Shem; Kenaan shall be his slave." After
29 the flood Noaḥ lived three hundred and fifty years. Noaḥ lived a
total of nine hundred and fifty years, and he died.
10 1 These are the descendants of Noaḥ's sons, Shem, Ḥam, and

HAAMEK DAVAR *(cont.)*

righteousness (Proverbs 8:15). Furthermore, the prophet Yeshayahu declares: *I shall form you and make you a covenant people, make you a light unto nations* (Isaiah 42:6), meaning that Israel was created in order to help develop the faith of any nation willing to accept God's covenant [that is, belief in God]. It is the task of the Jewish people to light the path for these groups. An additional element in this blessing to Yefet is alluded to by the words *May God enlarge Yefet*: When the people of Yefet expand their lives they will advance *the tents of Shem*. Thus we find in the tractate Avoda Zara (2b): The Holy One, Blessed be He, says to the Romans: "With what did you occupy yourselves?" They say in response: "Master of the Universe, we have established many marketplaces, we have built many bathhouses, and we have increased much silver and gold. And we did all of this only for the sake of the Jewish people, so that they would be free to engage in Torah study." As such, the development of Yefet's descendants will effectively benefit the tents of Shem. Meanwhile, Onkelos interprets this verse differently, writing that it is through Yefet's efforts that the Divine Presence will dwell in the tent of Shem, for it was the king of Persia [Cyrus, who descended from Yefet] who gave the order to build the Second Temple in Jerusalem.

RABBI JOSEPH B. SOLOVEITCHIK

יַפְתְּ אֱלֹהִים לְיֶפֶת – *May God enlarge Yefet:* The word *Yefet* carries the connotation of beauty. Noaḥ blessed Yefet with an appreciation for beauty, style and etiquette. The Divine Presence however would reside in the tents of Shem. A concern for externals alone is insufficient to attain the Divine Presence. In order to merit the Divine Presence, man must act ethically and morally, in the private as well as public realm.

CHAPTER 10, VERSE 1

SHADAL

וְאֵלֶּה תּוֹלְדֹת בְּנֵי־נֹחַ – *These are the descendants of Noaḥ's sons:* The term *toledot* ["history," or "generations"] here refers to the sons that were born to Shem, Ḥam, and Yefet. Now the names that are listed in the following verses – as pointed out by Johannes Clericus (18th century) and Ernst Rosenmueller (19th century) – are mostly those of nations rather than of individuals. Many of these names appear in the plural form, such as *the Ludim, Anamim, Lehavim, and Naftuḥim* (10:13), while others are given in the relative form such as *the Jebusites, Amorites, and Girgashites* (10:16). As such it is clearly not the aim of this passage to relate which personality fathered which individual. Rather, the intention of our chapter is to link various nations to their ancestors. An exception to this general approach is Nimrod, who is

ב הַמַּבּוּל: בְּנֵי יֶפֶת גֹּמֶר וּמָגוֹג וּמָדַי וְיָוָן וְתֻבָל וּמֶשֶׁךְ וְתִירָס:
ג ד וּבְנֵי גֹּמֶר אַשְׁכְּנַז וְרִיפַת וְתֹגַרְמָה: וּבְנֵי יָוָן אֱלִישָׁה וְתַרְשִׁישׁ
ה כִּתִּים וְדֹדָנִים: מֵאֵלֶּה נִפְרְדוּ אִיֵּי הַגּוֹיִם בְּאַרְצֹתָם אִישׁ
ו לִלְשֹׁנוֹ לְמִשְׁפְּחֹתָם בְּגוֹיֵהֶם: וּבְנֵי חָם כּוּשׁ וּמִצְרַיִם וּפוּט
ז וּכְנָעַן: וּבְנֵי כוּשׁ סְבָא וַחֲוִילָה וְסַבְתָּה וְרַעְמָה וְסַבְתְּכָא וּבְנֵי
ח רַעְמָה שְׁבָא וּדְדָן: וְכוּשׁ יָלַד אֶת־נִמְרֹד הוּא הֵחֵל לִהְיוֹת
ט גִּבֹּר בָּאָרֶץ: הוּא־הָיָה גִבֹּר־צַיִד לִפְנֵי יהוה עַל־כֵּן יֵאָמַר

SHADAL *(cont.)*

mentioned as a specific individual [in 10:8–10]. Still, even he is only singled out as the founder of a nation and a kingdom. Since we do not know the particular traditions or customs of each of these peoples, nor their corrupted beliefs, it is difficult to say what exactly the purpose is of identifying all of these lineages. It is true that many ancient nations believed that a local deity drew their folk out of the ground in a miraculous fashion and that is how their state was born, or that their people descended from their god himself. Hence the Torah's overall aim here is to counter such absurdities, and to establish the correct faith, which is that all of humanity descends from a single man, and that we were all created by the one God.

HAAMEK DAVAR

אַחַר הַמַּבּוּל – *After the flood:* According to our Sages, of blessed memory, Shem, Ḥam, and Yefet had sons before the flood as well. [And yet, the present verse seems to imply that these men only fathered children after the flood.] Thus we must understand our verse as meaning that they now had even more sons. This is similar to the repeated phrase *And he had other sons and daughters*, that appears throughout our text. [We find this language for example, in 11:11, 11:13, and 11:15. Thus the principal characters are named in these verses, but there lived many other people who are not identified by the text.]

VERSE 8

MALBIM

הוּא הֵחֵל לִהְיוֹת גִּבֹּר בָּאָרֶץ – *The first mighty warrior on earth:* At first Nimrod's strength was manifested in his superior hunting abilities, for the world was swarming with animals at that time. Whoever demonstrated the ability to subdue the wild beasts was treated like a god by his peers and neighbors. This explains the phrase *He was a mighty hunter before the Lord* (10:9). Because of his skill, people flocked to Nimrod and followed him. This led to the man's eventual dominance of other men.

HAAMEK DAVAR

הוּא הֵחֵל לִהְיוֹת גִּבֹּר בָּאָרֶץ – *The first mighty warrior on earth:* Nimrod introduced the institution of monarchy and began to dominate other people. Indeed it was the will of God for kings to one day rule the world, as I have written above in comments to the verse *As*

2 Yefet; after the flood, children were born to them. Yefet's sons
were Gomer, Magog, Madai, Yavan, Tuval, Meshekh, and Tiras.
3 4 Gomer's sons were Ashkenaz, Rifat, and Togarma. Yavan's sons
5 were Elisha, Tarshish, Kitim, and Dodanim. From these the
seagoing nations spread out to their territories, each with its
6 own language, by their clans and their nations. Ḥam's sons were
7 Kush, Mitzrayim, Put, and Kenaan. Kush's sons were Seva,
Ḥavila, Savta, Raama, and Savtekha. Raama's sons were Sheva
8 and Dedan. Kush was the father of Nimrod, the first mighty
9 warrior on earth. He was a mighty hunter before the Lord,
which is why people still say, "Like Nimrod, a mighty hunter

HAAMEK DAVAR *(cont.)*

for you, be fertile and multiply, abound on earth and become many on it (9:7). The world can only survive if it is run by powerful leaders, since otherwise society would devour itself. And it was Nimrod who was the first to realize this, as the next verse states: *He was a mighty hunter before the Lord*. This means that Nimrod's reign fulfilled God's desire that there be human monarchs. The strongman was considered the servant of God, just as, centuries later the emperor Nevukhadnetzar is referred to as *My [God's] servant* (Jeremiah 25:9). And even though Nevukhadnetzar was a tyrant, he was still labeled God's agent because he acted as the disciplinary rod of the Holy One, blessed be He [against Israel]. It was through the Babylonian king that God acted in this world. The wicked Nimrod served the same function.

RABBI DAVID TZVI HOFFMAN

נִמְרֹד – *Nimrod:* The name *Nimrod* derives from the word *mered* ["rebellion"], for this man was a rebel. Everybody referred to him as such since he relied on his strength to turn against God. At that time, God was still widely recognized by humanity, and people prayed to Him as their savior and redeemer. But Nimrod imagined that he could dispense with divine assistance, believing that he was powerful enough to revolt against the Almighty. **הוּא הֵחֵל לִהְיוֹת גִּבֹּר בָּאָרֶץ** – *The first mighty warrior on earth:* Nimrod was the first warrior in the world, meaning that he was a capable hunter. Thus the following verse develops the brief statement made in here.

VERSE 9

RABBI SAMSON RAPHAEL HIRSCH

הוּא־הָיָה גִבֹּר־צַיִד לִפְנֵי יהוה – *He was a mighty hunter before the Lord:* The phrase "before the Lord" never alludes to an person acting against the will of God. In fact, the term appears to represent the opposite sentiment: a man or a group performing "before the Lord" is doing what God wants them to do. Consider the verse regarding the tribes of Gad and Reuven [the tribes who wished to settle on the east side of the Jordan], *Moshe replied to them, "If you do this – if you arm yourselves for battle before the Lord"* (Numbers 32:20). The same must be said regarding the present usage: Nimrod *was a mighty hunter before the Lord*, meaning

י כְּנִמְרֹד גִּבּוֹר צַיִד לִפְנֵי יְהוָה: וַתְּהִי רֵאשִׁית מַמְלַכְתּוֹ בָּבֶל
יא וְאֶרֶךְ וְאַכַּד וְכַלְנֵה בְּאֶרֶץ שִׁנְעָר: מִן־הָאָרֶץ הַהִוא יָצָא
יב אַשּׁוּר וַיִּבֶן אֶת־נִינְוֵה וְאֶת־רְחֹבֹת עִיר וְאֶת־כָּלַח: וְאֶת־
יג רֶסֶן בֵּין נִינְוֵה וּבֵין כָּלַח הִוא הָעִיר הַגְּדֹלָה: וּמִצְרַיִם יָלַד
יד אֶת־לוּדִים וְאֶת־עֲנָמִים וְאֶת־לְהָבִים וְאֶת־נַפְתֻּחִים: וְאֶת־
פַּתְרֻסִים וְאֶת־כַּסְלֻחִים אֲשֶׁר יָצְאוּ מִשָּׁם פְּלִשְׁתִּים וְאֶת־
טו כַּפְתֹּרִים: וּכְנַעַן יָלַד אֶת־צִידֹן בְּכֹרוֹ וְאֶת־חֵת:
טז יז וְאֶת־הַיְבוּסִי וְאֶת־הָאֱמֹרִי וְאֵת הַגִּרְגָּשִׁי: וְאֶת־הַחִוִּי וְאֶת־
יח הַעַרְקִי וְאֶת־הַסִּינִי: וְאֶת־הָאַרְוָדִי וְאֶת־הַצְּמָרִי וְאֶת־
יט הַחֲמָתִי וְאַחַר נָפֹצוּ מִשְׁפְּחוֹת הַכְּנַעֲנִי: וַיְהִי גְּבוּל הַכְּנַעֲנִי
מִצִּידֹן בֹּאֲכָה גְרָרָה עַד־עַזָּה בֹּאֲכָה סְדֹמָה וַעֲמֹרָה וְאַדְמָה

RABBI SAMSON RAPHAEL HIRSCH *(cont.)*

that through his actions he fulfilled the will of God. And yet, Nimrod's appropriation of the name of God was his great corruption. When properly understood, the name of God grants freedom and equality to all men. This name extends compassion and righteousness throughout the world. At the time of Nimrod's rise, this name still burned brightly in the consciousness of humankind, something that Nimrod used to his advantage. For Nimrod began to subjugate society, all along claiming that his domination of civilization was being done in the name of God. And hence Nimrod was the first person to fly the banner of God for wicked purposes. He cloaked his tyranny behind the holy mantle of God's will, declaring that his rule was mandated by God Himself. Such an approach developed as time went by. Subsequent kings did not only claim to rule with divine imprimatur and pretend to shine with holy favor and authority, but eventually determined that they themselves were deities! It is specifically among Ḥam's descendants that we find the Pharaohs kneeling in respect before their own divine images. Nimrod served as the model for all such lying tyrants who crown themselves with an imaginary halo of holiness. The power, politics, and the very positions of these despots are the subject of the saying: *Like Nimrod, a mighty hunter before the Lord.*

RABBI DAVID TZVI HOFFMAN

לִפְנֵי יהוה – *Before the Lord:* Nimrod acted against the will of God. His early offense was the wanton hunting of animals. From that he graduated to instigating wars against a humanity that had been relatively peaceful beforehand. Now God is always interested in teaching people to act righteously and humanely. As such, God does not permit humans to hunt animals and to kill them cruelly for sport. **עַל־כֵּן יֵאָמַר** – *Which is why people still say:* Nimrod's behavior led to the creation of a proverb which seems to have still been in use

10 before the Lord." His kingdom began with Babylon, Erekh,
11 Akad, and Kalneh in the land of Shinar. From that land, Ashur
12 went out and built Nineveh, Reḥovot Ir, Kalaḥ, and Resen be-
13 tween Nineveh and Kalaḥ; that is the great city. Mitzrayim fa-
14 thered the Ludim, Anamim, Lehavim and Naftuḥim, Patrusim,
Kasluḥim – from whom the Philistines descended – and the
15 Kaftorim. Kenaan fathered Tzidon, his firstborn, and
16 17 Ḥet, and the Jebusites, Amorites, and Girgashites, the Hivites,
18 Arkites, and Sinites, the Arvadites, Zemarites, and Hamatites.
19 Later, the Canaanite families were dispersed. The Canaanite
borders were from Sidon toward Gerar near Aza, and toward

RABBI DAVID TZVI HOFFMAN *(cont.)*

in the time of our teacher Moshe [who wrote this verse]. Thus people would refer to a tyrant who rebels against God and who initiates wars between nations as being like Nimrod.

VERSE 11

RABBI SAMSON RAPHAEL HIRSCH

מִן־הָאָרֶץ הַהִוא יָצָא אַשּׁוּר – *From that land, Ashur went out:* Ashur was one of Shem's descendants. It seems that Nimrod only excelled at his hunting within his own domain. For it is only in the absence of moral freedom that people can be pressed into subjugation. That is where the unethical can thrive as hunters of men. Now Nimrod was only able to exercise his power against the descendants of Ḥam, whereas Ashur managed to escape Nimrod's authority and moved to a different land. And while Nimrod developed into a cruel tyrant, Ashur built towns and paved intercity roads – this is what the verse refers to by the term "*Reḥovot Ir*" [literally, "city squares"]. Nimrod gloried in his conquests, but Ashur took pride in what he built. Still, these impressions are only guesses.

VERSE 19

MESHEKH ḤOKHMA

וַיְהִי גְּבוּל הַכְּנַעֲנִי – *The Canaanite borders:* The text here delineates the borders of all the cities in the area of Sedom, with the exception of Tzoar [listed in 19:22 among the towns in that region, and the only one to be saved from destruction]. This omission explains why God spared that location from destruction; the operative principle was His commitment to *hold the descendants to account for the sins of the fathers* (Exodus 20:5) when the children maintain their parents' sinful ways. For the previous chapter describes Kenaan's sodomy of Noaḥ [see Rashi], and his descendants in Sedom continued that path by demanding: *Where are the men who came to you tonight? Bring them out to us so that we may know them* (19:5). And hence the people of Sedom were wiped out for perpetuating their ancestor's wicked behavior. But the town of Tzoar was not included in Kenaan's territory; and since its citizens there were not descendants of Kenaan, despite being wicked they could not be considered as mimicking their forebear's sin. That is why they were spared.

וּצְבִ֖ים עַד־לָ֑שַׁע אֵ֣לֶּה בְנֵי־חָ֗ם לְמִשְׁפְּחֹתָ֛ם לִלְשֹׁנֹתָ֖ם ⟨כ⟩
בְּאַרְצֹתָ֖ם בְּגוֹיֵהֶֽם: וּלְשֵׁ֥ם יֻלַּ֖ד גַּם־ה֑וּא אֲבִי֙ ⟨כא⟩
כָּל־בְּנֵי־עֵ֔בֶר אֲחִ֖י יֶ֥פֶת הַגָּדֽוֹל: בְּנֵ֥י שֵׁ֖ם עֵילָ֣ם וְאַשּׁ֑וּר ⟨כב⟩
וְאַרְפַּכְשַׁ֖ד וְל֥וּד וַֽאֲרָֽם: וּבְנֵ֖י אֲרָ֑ם ע֥וּץ וְח֖וּל וְגֶ֥תֶר וָמַֽשׁ: ⟨כג⟩
וְאַרְפַּכְשַׁ֖ד יָלַ֣ד אֶת־שָׁ֑לַח וְשֶׁ֖לַח יָלַ֥ד אֶת־עֵֽבֶר: וּלְעֵ֥בֶר יֻלַּ֖ד ⟨כד/כה⟩
שְׁנֵ֣י בָנִ֑ים שֵׁ֣ם הָֽאֶחָ֞ד פֶּ֗לֶג כִּ֤י בְיָמָיו֙ נִפְלְגָ֣ה הָאָ֔רֶץ וְשֵׁ֥ם אָחִ֖יו
יָקְטָֽן: וְיָקְטָ֣ן יָלַ֔ד אֶת־אַלְמוֹדָ֖ד וְאֶת־שָׁ֑לֶף וְאֶת־חֲצַרְמָ֖וֶת ⟨כו⟩
וְאֶת־יָֽרַח: וְאֶת־הֲדוֹרָ֥ם וְאֶת־אוּזָ֖ל וְאֶת־דִּקְלָֽה: וְאֶת־עוֹבָ֛ל ⟨כז/כח⟩
וְאֶת־אֲבִֽימָאֵ֖ל וְאֶת־שְׁבָֽא: וְאֶת־אוֹפִ֥ר וְאֶת־חֲוִילָ֖ה וְאֶת־ ⟨כט⟩
יוֹבָ֑ב כָּל־אֵ֖לֶּה בְּנֵ֥י יָקְטָֽן: וַיְהִ֥י מֽוֹשָׁבָ֖ם מִמֵּשָׁ֑א בֹּאֲכָ֥ה סְפָ֖רָה ⟨ל⟩
הַ֥ר הַקֶּֽדֶם: אֵ֣לֶּה בְנֵי־שֵׁ֔ם לְמִשְׁפְּחֹתָ֖ם לִלְשֹׁנֹתָ֑ם בְּאַרְצֹתָ֖ם ⟨לא⟩
לְגוֹיֵהֶֽם: אֵ֣לֶּה מִשְׁפְּחֹ֧ת בְּנֵי־נֹ֛חַ לְתוֹלְדֹתָ֖ם בְּגוֹיֵהֶ֑ם וּמֵאֵ֜לֶּה ⟨לב⟩
נִפְרְד֧וּ הַגּוֹיִ֛ם בָּאָ֖רֶץ אַחַ֥ר הַמַּבּֽוּל:

VERSE 21

HAKETAV VEHAKABBALA

וּלְשֵׁם יֻלַּד גַּם־הוּא – *Sons were also born to Shem:* The [seemingly superfluous] phrase *gam hu* ["also"], hints that the man Shem was a superlative character compared to all the people of his generation. A similar connotation attaches to the verse *And Shet too [gam hu] had a son, and named him Enosh* (4:26), for Shet was also an exceptional human being. The text testifies to this when it states: *Adam lived one hundred and thirty years and then had a son in his own likeness and image, and named him Shet* (5:3). Commenting on this, the Vilna Gaon writes that even though all people are created in the image of God, really only Adam and Shet truly represented that quality. According to the Talmud [see Bava Batra 58a], this point was confirmed by a heavenly voice. However, starting with Enosh, all future human beings looked like monkeys compared to Adam. This is why people are referred to as *anashim*, which is the plural of the name *Enosh*, in his honor…. Now because Shet's likeness was so true to the divine image, the text refers to him as *gam hu* ["also he," more impressive than just "he"]. Regarding Shem, the text states that *he was the ancestor of all the sons of Ever*, meaning that he taught and instructed all of the students who gathered to learn in the study hall of Ever. It was Shem who strove to educate these pupils in the correct matters of faith.

RABBI SAMSON RAPHAEL HIRSCH

וּלְשֵׁם יֻלַּד גַּם־הוּא – *Sons were also born to Shem:* The destiny of humankind rested on Shem's shoulders, and he too produced children. There are two reasons why the text

20 Sedom, Amora, Adma, and Tzevoyim, near Lasha. These were
the descendants of Ḥam, by their clans and their languages,
21 with their lands and their nations. Sons were also
born to Shem. The older brother of Yefet, he was the ancestor of
22 all the sons of Ever. Shem's sons were Elam, Ashur, Arpakhshad,
23 Lud, and Aram. Aram's sons were Utz, Ḥul, Geter, and Mash.
24 Arpakhshad was the father of Shelaḥ, and Shelaḥ was the father
25 of Ever. To Ever, two sons were born. One was named Peleg, for
in his time the earth was divided. His brother was named Yok-
26 tan. Yoktan was the father of Almodad, Shelef, Ḥatzarmavet,
27 28 Yeraḥ, Hadoram, Uzal, Dikla, Oval, Avimael, Sheva, Ofir,
29 30 Ḥavila, and Yovav; all these were Yoktan's sons. Their settlements extended from Mesha toward Sefar, in the eastern hill
31 country. These were the descendants of Shem, by their clans
32 and their languages, with their lands and their nations. These,
then, are the clans of the sons of Noaḥ, by their lines, in their
nations. And from these, the nations spread out across the earth
after the flood.

RABBI SAMSON RAPHAEL HIRSCH *(cont.)*

emphasizes this point. Firstly, Shem *was the ancestor of all the sons of Ever*. Now actually, Ever was Shem's great-grandson, and it was only Ever's sons who began to fulfill Noaḥ's blessing, *May God enlarge Yefet, and let him dwell in the tents of Shem* (9:27). Still, Shem was the spiritual ancestor of this clan. Even Yaakov learned Torah at the feet of Shem [according to the Midrash]. It is due to Shem that Avraham emerged from the house of Teraḥ, Avraham who was able to transmit to his children the message for humankind that God had entrusted to his family. All of that was only possible because of Shem. On occasion a person will mock his ancestors and disparage the traditions that they have bequeathed to the next generations. But such an ingrate remains ignorant of the merit and the meaning that his elders of the past have maintained as the family legacy on his behalf. Secondly, Shem's older brother was Yefet, the oldest of Noaḥ's three sons. [The Hebrew of our verse is ambiguous as to whether Yefet or Shem was older.] It was Yefet's mission to precede his younger brother and to prepare humanity to accept the lessons that Shem was ready to impart. It was natural that Shem was not immediately accepted as a luminary, for people find the art and the science of Yefet more palatable and accessible. On the other hand, the hidden light that Shem carries and offers to the world, the truth that he preaches, is that the Torah's commandments must be either observed or rejected; there is no middle way. It necessarily takes a long time for such ideas to find universal recognition.

VERSE 25

SHADAL

כִּי בְיָמָיו נִפְלְגָה הָאָרֶץ – *For in his time the earth was divided:* All of languages were mixed up [in the story of the Tower of Babel].

יא א ב וַיְהִי כָל־הָאָרֶץ שָׂפָה אֶחָת וּדְבָרִים אֲחָדִים׃ וַיְהִי בְּנָסְעָם ט שביעי
ג מִקֶּדֶם וַיִּמְצְאוּ בִקְעָה בְּאֶרֶץ שִׁנְעָר וַיֵּשְׁבוּ שָׁם׃ וַיֹּאמְרוּ
אִישׁ אֶל־רֵעֵהוּ הָבָה נִלְבְּנָה לְבֵנִים וְנִשְׂרְפָה לִשְׂרֵפָה וַתְּהִי

CHAPTER 11, VERSE 1

OR HAḤAYYIM

שָׂפָה אֶחָת – *The same language:* Because the entire world spoke the same language, all humanity wanted to live together as a single collective; they had no desire to spread out. They decided to construct one settlement, one city where they could all live. And since they were afraid that they might anyway end up scattered to various lands, they built a tower which could serve as a beacon for everybody to be able to find the center of civilization. Should anyone stray from society's place, he would be able to easily find his way back by traveling toward the structure. This fear of theirs is expressed in the phrase *Otherwise we will be scattered across the face of the earth* (11:4). It was their greatest concern that humanity would be divided into small communities distant from and unconnected with each other. But God disapproved of such a scheme, even though He recognized that human beings blessed with free will might want to order society in this way. In response to their project, God set out to thwart humanity's plan and to confuse its languages. That would divide the people and force the different groups to diverge and found their own settlements. And this He achieved, as we read: *From there the Lord scattered them all over the earth* (11:8). The dispersal proves my interpretation that God's motive for stopping the construction [was not just that He did not wish a tower to be built], but that He wanted the earth to be populated, for reasons known only to Him.

RABBI SAMSON RAPHAEL HIRSCH

וַיְהִי כָל־הָאָרֶץ שָׂפָה אֶחָת – *The whole world spoke the same language:* Natural causes led to humanity splitting into different groups. And this in turn allowed the rise of multiple languages. Nevertheless, the different tongues were not completely different from each other. There was a single language, but it was divided into different dialects.

MALBIM

וַיְהִי כָל־הָאָרֶץ שָׂפָה אֶחָת – *The whole world spoke the same language:* The episode of the Tower of Babel took place during the lifetime of Peleg, who was born 101 years after the flood. Now Noaḥ and his sons certainly all spoke the same language – Hebrew, according to our Sages. They also used the same "words" [*devarim*], a word which sometimes refers to speech, and sometimes to matters or ideas.... Between the time of Noaḥ and this story, humanity lived a quiet and peaceful life, their needs were limited and their possessions few. Additionally, people were generally concerned with all of the same issues. Such is the sense of the phrase "the same [*aḥadim*] words" as in the verse *Stay with him a few [aḥadim] years, until your brother's rage subsides* (27:44). Here too, the adjective *aḥadim* refers to a series of things that are alike.

11 1 The whole world spoke the same language, the same words. SHEVI'I
2 And as the people migrated from the east they found a valley
3 in the land of Shinar and settled there. They said to each other,
"Come, let us make bricks, let us bake them thoroughly." They

VERSE 2

SHADAL

מִקֶּדֶם – *From the east:* Humanity traveled from the east, that is from the Mountains of Ararat, where the ark had come to rest at the end of the flood.

RABBI SAMSON RAPHAEL HIRSCH

וַיִּמְצְאוּ בִקְעָה בְּאֶרֶץ שִׁנְעָר – *They found a valley in the land of Shinar:* The community congregated in the valley, where they attempted to create something out of nothing, based solely on the power of the human being and the strength of his determination. It was there that they discovered the potential of a mass movement – they realized that they had the ability to dominate nature if they could only harness all of the latent energy it stored. Humankind then decided to construct an edifice for the generations, an eternal memorial to the power of the community and its superiority over the individual. Now the Holy One, blessed be He, founded His world on the collective, *and established His myriad forces upon the earth* (Amos 9:6). For the range of human thoughts and opinions is as great as the number of individuals in our species, and we must work together to complement each other's abilities. And while every individual with his limited powers will eventually leave this world, only the community survives forever. As our Sages assert: The community does not die, nor does the whole ever become impoverished. Great and enduring values are only created through the united efforts of the many. The collective can be seen as the completion of the individual only when the group's aims before God are not at odds with the goals of each person. When the will of the community is sublimated to the will of God, if its united forces are dedicated and sanctified to His service, then the person who shares those desires will draw strength and encouragement from the whole. But herein lies the danger. At the end of the day, the individual will be forced to acknowledge his own limitations; but the community never faces that sobering realization. For the state possesses almost unlimited strength, and as such, it might come to see itself as representing a superior, lofty, and perhaps divine entity. The group might then come to view the collective value as far more significant to that of the individual, and forget that the primary task of the community is to aid the lone man and woman, and to finish what they cannot achieve by themselves. The individual must never become secondary to the collective.

THE LUBAVITCHER REBBE

בְּנָסְעָם מִקֶּדֶם – *Migrated from the east:* The incident of the Tower of Babel occurred in the aftermath of the flood. The survivors sought to ensure their self-preservation and protect themselves from destruction but overlooked the flood's lessons that we must look to God to ensure our well-being.

ד לָהֶם הַלְּבֵנָה לְאָבֶן וְהַחֵמָר הָיָה לָהֶם לַחֹמֶר׃ וַיֹּאמְרוּ
הָבָה ׀ נִבְנֶה־לָּנוּ עִיר וּמִגְדָּל וְרֹאשׁוֹ בַשָּׁמַיִם וְנַעֲשֶׂה־לָּנוּ
ה שֵׁם פֶּן־נָפוּץ עַל־פְּנֵי כָל־הָאָרֶץ׃ וַיֵּרֶד יהוה לִרְאֹת אֶת־

VERSE 4

HAKETAV VEHAKABBALA

הָבָה נִבְנֶה־לָּנוּ עִיר וּמִגְדָּל – *Come, let us build ourselves a city and a tower:* When the generation of the dispersal considered how the world had been destroyed by the flood, they devised mechanisms – which have been lost to us today – to build a structure capable of absorbing celestial powers into itself. This object would serve to protect all future generations from any catastrophe which might strike the world. The word *ir* ["city"] has protective connotations, as in the verse *I am asleep; but my heart is watchful [er]* (Song of Songs 5:2).

MALBIM

הָבָה נִבְנֶה־לָּנוּ עִיר וּמִגְדָּל – *Come, let us build ourselves a city and a tower:* The new generation decided to abandon the old ways and the institution of the family, a determination alluded to in the verse *The people migrated from the east [mikedem]* (11:2). Interpreting this phrase, our Sages suggest that humankind had decided to abandon God, who was the first thing ever to exist [*kadmon*]. The people then found a valley where they attempted to establish a great and powerful kingdom and appoint a monarch to rule them. Our Sages maintain that Nimrod was humanity's leader at that point; it was he who rebelled against God. The first stage in the construction project was to build houses with walls to replace the tents they had dwelled in previously. They managed to find soil that was perfectly suitable for the fashioning of bricks. This made it easy for them to raise their buildings with minimum toil. But this entire project stood in opposition to the divine will, since it was God's wish for humankind to spread out and populate the land. The community's subsequent plan to construct a tower shows that they had forgotten all about God. They had started to believe that earth's bounty was bequeathed to them by the constellation Orion.

RABBI JOSEPH B. SOLOVEITCHIK

וְנַעֲשֶׂה־לָּנוּ שֵׁם – *And make a name for ourselves:* The generation tried to create a new social and world order. In order to realize this ideal, they destroyed individual freedom, dictating to everyone what to do and how to live. Man became a slave in a rigid, inflexible world. He was disciplined, believing in a system contrived by man. This society gave preference to doctrine over preserving life, to utopian ideas over human reality. The value of man was not based upon his spiritual essence, but rather, the number of bricks he could carry to the top of the tower.

VERSE 5

MALBIM

וַיֵּרֶד יהוה לִרְאֹת – *But the Lord came down to see:* God predicted what this construction project would lead to. He understood that the collective settlement of humanity would be

4 used bricks for stone and tar for mortar. And they said, "Come,
let us build ourselves a city and a tower that reaches the heavens, and make a name for ourselves. Otherwise we will be scat-
5 tered across the face of the earth." But the LORD came down
to see the city and the tower being built by the children of men.

MALBIM *(cont.)*

accompanied by violence, theft, and murder. Cruelty and the rise of tyrants were inevitable consequences of such communal development. Furthermore, the planned tower would defy the towering strength of God's name and reputation. For the people's design was to raise this structure with the intention of worshipping idols there. This motive is alluded to in the statement in the previous verse: *Let us make a name for ourselves*. Such a plan would eventually cause the corruption of all humankind.

HAAMEK DAVAR

וַיֵּרֶד יהוה לִרְאֹת – *But the Lord came down to see:* God's intention to descend here is not similar to His later declaration *So I have come down to rescue them from the hand of the Egyptians and bring them up from that land* (Exodus 3:8), or like the subsequent description, *The Lord came down in a column of cloud* (Numbers 12:5) in the story of Miriam. In those cases, the text means that God revealed His divine presence. However, in the current instance there was no such communion with human beings. The verse uses the language of God "descending" for the following reason: At that time the affairs of man were conducted only through natural means and not through private or direct providence, since humanity was not acting in accord with the Torah's directives or engaged in the service of God. And it is beneath the dignity of the Holy One, blessed be He, to interact with such simple people. Nevertheless, when the collective began to construct the city and the tower which impinged on God's plans, He descended from [i.e., suppressed] His honor with the intent of examining the behavior of humankind and whether it would do to punish them.

RABBI DAVID TZVI HOFFMAN

וַיֵּרֶד יהוה לִרְאֹת – *But the Lord came down to see:* Were God not the educator and the savior of the human race, He would have paid no attention to this group's petty and foolish project to build a tower. But because God feels great compassion toward human beings, He is unable to merely stand by while His creations act stupidly, or to allow them to proceed toward utter destruction. Instead, God seeks ways to interrupt people's sinful ways in time to guide the errant along more productive paths. This is the sense of the verse *But the Lord came down to see* – the exalted God who dwells in the heavens descended from His detached position in order to consider the actions of humanity and to watch its behavior. The second expression of God's descent – in verse 7: *Let us go down and confuse their language* – similarly expresses God's willingness to intervene in the fate of humanity. Each time that God gets directly involved in human history, it should be understood as a new instance of descent to earth out of love.

ו הָעִיר וְאֶת־הַמִּגְדָּל אֲשֶׁר בָּנוּ בְּנֵי הָאָדָם: וַיֹּאמֶר יהוה
הֵן עַם אֶחָד וְשָׂפָה אַחַת לְכֻלָּם וְזֶה הַחִלָּם לַעֲשׂוֹת וְעַתָּה
ז לֹא־יִבָּצֵר מֵהֶם כֹּל אֲשֶׁר יָזְמוּ לַעֲשׂוֹת: הָבָה נֵרְדָה וְנָבְלָה
ח שָׁם שְׂפָתָם אֲשֶׁר לֹא יִשְׁמְעוּ אִישׁ שְׂפַת רֵעֵהוּ: וַיָּפֶץ יהוה

VERSE 6

RABBI SAMSON RAPHAEL HIRSCH

הֵן עַם אֶחָד – *If, as one people:* After the people had traveled from the east together and gathered in a single location, they found themselves in complete unity. And yet the first thought that occurred to the masses, once they came to recognize the importance of the community, was not to sanctify the name of God, or to join forces in common worship of the Almighty, but rather *Let us make a name for ourselves* (11:4).! The project they embarked upon represented the first group effort in history to realize the power of the collective. But humankind organized itself for an evil purpose. The congregation held a precious treasure in its hands, namely the value of the individuals who comprised the whole. Now surely it is the obligation of every man and woman to proclaim the name of God. But in this episode the people preferred to establish a name only for themselves and to thereby subjugate the individual to the aims of the collective. It is then that each person feels it his right to stand up and declare: I do not recognize the authority or the worth of the state; it is only myself in whom I believe. That is how a man ends up severing himself from God, from whom he derives all human wisdom. He becomes a creature governed by subjectivity, whose perspective is based not on the good of the community but on a selfish view of what is good for him alone. The individual then becomes the new foundation of a society of one. In the end everyone will determine his own goals. One person might argue: Let us maintain fealty to the old ways and the law system that has governed us. But another will decide: No, I have no interest in your communal rules; whatever I am able to gain for myself I will take. Such is the confusion of subjectivity that caused the deterioration of this community.

HAAMEK DAVAR

לֹא־יִבָּצֵר מֵהֶם כֹּל אֲשֶׁר יָזְמוּ לַעֲשׂוֹת – *Nothing they plan to do will be impossible for them:* If the people continue to act with a single purpose and are allowed to complete their tower, they will move on to their next tyrannical plan: to control people's thoughts. Anybody who thinks differently than the collective will be subject to theft and murder, which will completely destroy all human settlement. The fact that the people are currently of one mind does not bode well for the future.

VERSE 7

HAAMEK DAVAR

אֲשֶׁר לֹא יִשְׁמְעוּ אִישׁ שְׂפַת רֵעֵהוּ – *So that one will not understand the speech of another:* It is occasionally possible for two people who speak different languages to nevertheless be able to communicate. But God now planned to confuse their language so thoroughly that there would be no understanding at all between the builders.

6 The LORD said, "If, as one people with one language, they have
begun to do this, nothing they plan to do will be impossible
7 for them. Let us go down and confuse their language so that
8 one will not understand the speech of another." From there the
LORD scattered them all over the earth, and they abandoned

VERSE 8

RABBI SAMSON RAPHAEL HIRSCH

וַיָּפֶץ יהוה אֹתָם מִשָּׁם – *From there the LORD scattered them:* With the dispersal of humanity across the earth, an event which God alluded to in His covenant with Noaḥ, the preface to the Torah effectively comes to an end. These introductory chapters demonstrate to Israel the early history of humankind. And now the Torah paves the way for the history of the nation of Israel. Indeed, the special mission of the Jews is grounded in the first twenty generations of humankind. From this point forward the Torah will no longer concern itself with the history of the world in general. Humanity is now given the freedom to develop on its own; it is only later that the prophets will turn their attention to the world's other nations. As the great edifices that humankind erects for itself crumble one by one, all people will eventually acknowledge that there is but one name worthy of being exalted and sanctified. It is the obligation of every human being to enlist all the power of the individual and the collective to cry out for the glorification of the name of God throughout our lives and that of the community. It is only thus that we shall find peace and tranquility on earth. It is regarding that process that the prophet announces: *Then I will transform the people's language and turn their words into clear [berura], clean speech so that they may call upon the name of the LORD and serve Him shoulder to shoulder* (Zephaniah 3:9). Indeed, it seems to me that this much later verse serves as a support for my interpretation of the present passage. The adjective *berura* ["clear"] represents the exact opposite of the term *balul* ["confused," in the next verse]. This is the only way to understand the connection between the clear speech in the cited verse and the willingness of all humanity to *call upon the name of the LORD*. When the language of the human race becomes clear, we will stop referring to things by names that are subjective, based on our own personal aims, and with a desire to promote ourselves, and will start naming things based on their role in the service of God. All of humanity will then frame their desire in objective terms, an untainted world view which recognizes the will of God as everything. All men and women will then view everything from the perspective of its designation for the service of God. And when humanity submits completely to the divine will, the spiritual and social cohesion that was lost with the building of the tower will be regained.

HAAMEK DAVAR

וַיַּחְדְּלוּ לִבְנֹת הָעִיר – *And they abandoned the building of the city:* Note that God's treatment of humankind caused them to cease building the city but not, it seems, the tower. For even if the community had completed that structure, the purpose for which it was designed would now be void. The structure would no longer be used to supervise humanity, which had become fractured and dispersed due to their various languages. And yet, even if the people

ט אֹתָ֛ם מִשָּׁ֖ם עַל־פְּנֵ֣י כָל־הָאָ֑רֶץ וַֽיַּחְדְּל֖וּ לִבְנֹ֥ת הָעִֽיר׃ עַל־כֵּ֞ן
קָרָ֤א שְׁמָהּ֙ בָּבֶ֔ל כִּי־שָׁ֛ם בָּלַ֥ל יְהוָ֖ה שְׂפַ֣ת כָּל־הָאָ֑רֶץ וּמִשָּׁם֙
הֱפִיצָ֣ם יְהוָ֔ה עַל־פְּנֵ֖י כָּל־הָאָֽרֶץ׃

י אֵ֚לֶּה תּוֹלְדֹ֣ת שֵׁ֔ם שֵׁ֚ם בֶּן־מְאַ֣ת שָׁנָ֔ה וַיּ֖וֹלֶד אֶת־אַרְפַּכְשָׁ֑ד
יא שְׁנָתַ֖יִם אַחַ֥ר הַמַּבּֽוּל׃ וַֽיְחִי־שֵׁ֗ם אַֽחֲרֵי֙ הוֹלִיד֣וֹ אֶת־אַרְפַּכְשָׁ֔ד
יב חֲמֵ֥שׁ מֵא֖וֹת שָׁנָ֑ה וַיּ֥וֹלֶד בָּנִ֖ים וּבָנֽוֹת׃ וְאַרְפַּכְשַׁ֣ד
יג חַ֔י חָמֵ֥שׁ וּשְׁלֹשִׁ֖ים שָׁנָ֑ה וַיּ֖וֹלֶד אֶת־שָֽׁלַח׃ וַֽיְחִ֣י אַרְפַּכְשַׁ֗ד
אַֽחֲרֵי֙ הוֹלִיד֣וֹ אֶת־שֶׁ֔לַח שָׁלֹ֣שׁ שָׁנִ֔ים וְאַרְבַּ֥ע מֵא֖וֹת שָׁנָ֑ה
יד וַיּ֥וֹלֶד בָּנִ֖ים וּבָנֽוֹת׃ וְשֶׁ֥לַח חַ֖י שְׁלֹשִׁ֣ים שָׁנָ֑ה וַיּ֖וֹלֶד
טו אֶת־עֵֽבֶר׃ וַֽיְחִי־שֶׁ֗לַח אַֽחֲרֵי֙ הוֹלִיד֣וֹ אֶת־עֵ֔בֶר שָׁלֹ֣שׁ שָׁנִ֔ים
טז וְאַרְבַּ֥ע מֵא֖וֹת שָׁנָ֑ה וַיּ֥וֹלֶד בָּנִ֖ים וּבָנֽוֹת׃ וַֽיְחִי־
יז עֵ֕בֶר אַרְבַּ֥ע וּשְׁלֹשִׁ֖ים שָׁנָ֑ה וַיּ֖וֹלֶד אֶת־פָּֽלֶג׃ וַֽיְחִי־עֵ֗בֶר
אַֽחֲרֵי֙ הוֹלִיד֣וֹ אֶת־פֶּ֔לֶג שְׁלֹשִׁ֣ים שָׁנָ֔ה וְאַרְבַּ֥ע מֵא֖וֹת שָׁנָ֑ה
יח וַיּ֥וֹלֶד בָּנִ֖ים וּבָנֽוֹת׃ וַֽיְחִי־פֶ֕לֶג שְׁלֹשִׁ֖ים שָׁנָ֑ה וַיּ֖וֹלֶד
יט אֶת־רְעֽוּ׃ וַֽיְחִי־פֶ֗לֶג אַֽחֲרֵי֙ הוֹלִיד֣וֹ אֶת־רְע֔וּ תֵּ֥שַׁע שָׁנִ֖ים
כ וּמָאתַ֣יִם שָׁנָ֑ה וַיּ֥וֹלֶד בָּנִ֖ים וּבָנֽוֹת׃ וַֽיְחִ֣י רְע֔וּ
כא שְׁתַּ֥יִם וּשְׁלֹשִׁ֖ים שָׁנָ֑ה וַיּ֖וֹלֶד אֶת־שְׂרֽוּג׃ וַֽיְחִ֣י רְע֗וּ אַֽחֲרֵי֙
הוֹלִיד֣וֹ אֶת־שְׂר֔וּג שֶׁ֥בַע שָׁנִ֖ים וּמָאתַ֣יִם שָׁנָ֑ה וַיּ֖וֹלֶד בָּנִ֥ים
כב וּבָנֽוֹת׃ וַֽיְחִ֣י שְׂר֔וּג שְׁלֹשִׁ֖ים שָׁנָ֑ה וַיּ֖וֹלֶד אֶת־נָחֽוֹר׃
כג וַֽיְחִ֣י שְׂר֗וּג אַֽחֲרֵי֙ הוֹלִיד֣וֹ אֶת־נָח֔וֹר מָאתַ֥יִם שָׁנָ֑ה וַיּ֖וֹלֶד בָּנִ֥ים
כד וּבָנֽוֹת׃ וַֽיְחִ֣י נָח֔וֹר תֵּ֥שַׁע וְעֶשְׂרִ֖ים שָׁנָ֑ה וַיּ֖וֹלֶד
כה אֶת־תָּֽרַח׃ וַֽיְחִ֣י נָח֗וֹר אַֽחֲרֵי֙ הוֹלִיד֣וֹ אֶת־תֶּ֔רַח תְּשַֽׁע־עֶשְׂרֵ֥ה

HAAMEK DAVAR (cont.)

were unable to understand each other, they might still have lived together. Hence the text affirms that the construction of the city ended, and its inhabitants all moved away.

9 the building of the city. That is why it was called Bavel, because
it was there that the Lord confused the language of all the
earth; and from there the Lord scattered them all across the
face of the earth.
10 These are the descendants of Shem. When Shem was one
hundred years old, he had a son, Arpakhshad, two years after
11 the flood. After Arpakhshad was born, Shem lived five hun-
12 dred years and had other sons and daughters. When
Arpakhshad was thirty-five years old, he had a son, Shelaḥ.
13 After Shelaḥ was born, Arpakhshad lived four hundred and
14 three years and had other sons and daughters. When
15 Shelaḥ was thirty years old, he had a son, Ever. After Ever
was born, Shelaḥ lived four hundred and three years and had
16 other sons and daughters. Ever lived thirty-four years
17 and then had a son, Peleg. After Peleg was born, Ever lived
four hundred and thirty years and had other sons and daugh-
18 ters. Peleg lived thirty years and then had a son, Reu.
19 After Reu was born, Peleg lived two hundred and nine years
20 and had other sons and daughters. Reu lived thir-
21 ty-two years and then had a son, Serug. After Serug was born,
Reu lived two hundred and seven years and had other sons and
22 daughters. Serug lived thirty years and then had a son,
23 Naḥor. After Naḥor was born, Serug lived two hundred years
24 and had other sons and daughters. Naḥor lived twenty-
25 nine years and then had a son, Teraḥ. After Teraḥ was born,
Naḥor lived one hundred and nineteen years and had other

VERSE 10

RABBI SAMSON RAPHAEL HIRSCH

אֵלֶּה תּוֹלְדֹת שֵׁם – *These are the descendants of Shem:* Our chapter culminates with a listing of Shem's descendants, at the end of which we find Avraham. The patriarch was a member of the generation [of the Tower of Babel] which proclaimed: *Let us make a name for ourselves* (11:4). And yet this man's life was guided by a single principle, that of *calling out in the name of the Lord* (4:26). Avraham bequeathed this practice of promoting God's name to his sons and founded his nation on its importance. It is through this concept that humankind will eventually find the meaning in life and will emerge from its millennia of aimless wandering and despair. Our patriarch Avraham showed the way for all of humanity; he roused, beckoned, and warned us that we must never forget this fundamental ideal.

כו שָׁנָה וּמְאַת שָׁנָה וַיּוֹלֶד בָּנִים וּבָנוֹת׃ וַיְחִי־תֶרַח
כז שִׁבְעִים שָׁנָה וַיּוֹלֶד אֶת־אַבְרָם אֶת־נָחוֹר וְאֶת־הָרָן׃ וְאֵלֶּה
תּוֹלְדֹת תֶּרַח תֶּרַח הוֹלִיד אֶת־אַבְרָם אֶת־נָחוֹר וְאֶת־הָרָן
כח וְהָרָן הוֹלִיד אֶת־לוֹט׃ וַיָּמָת הָרָן עַל־פְּנֵי תֶּרַח אָבִיו בְּאֶרֶץ
כט מוֹלַדְתּוֹ בְּאוּר כַּשְׂדִּים׃ וַיִּקַּח אַבְרָם וְנָחוֹר לָהֶם נָשִׁים שֵׁם מפטיר
אֵשֶׁת־אַבְרָם שָׂרָי וְשֵׁם אֵשֶׁת־נָחוֹר מִלְכָּה בַּת־הָרָן אֲבִי־
ל לא מִלְכָּה וַאֲבִי יִסְכָּה׃ וַתְּהִי שָׂרַי עֲקָרָה אֵין לָהּ וָלָד׃ וַיִּקַּח
תֶּרַח אֶת־אַבְרָם בְּנוֹ וְאֶת־לוֹט בֶּן־הָרָן בֶּן־בְּנוֹ וְאֵת שָׂרַי

VERSE 26

RABBI JOSEPH B. SOLOVEITCHIK

אֶת־אַבְרָם – *Avram:* Through devious ways and zigzag channels Providence began to realize a new human personality: the charismatic. Avraham was born, chosen, and charged with a mission by God. Avraham was selected to rehabilitate man and to reinstate him to the ideal which he was destined to occupy. **וַיּוֹלֶד אֶת־אַבְרָם** – *And fathered Avram:* The significance of Avraham's birth consists in the certitude that greatness in a human being could no longer be suppressed or destroyed no matter how fiendish the circumstances; however corrupt or wicked society may be, genuine holiness and greatness eventually triumph over satanic opposition. Once Avraham was born, it was quite certain that he would redeem the world. The expectation on the part of Providence was that the great courageous spirit which entered the frail body of a crying infant would ultimately defy and defeat the power of pagan tyranny.

VERSE 27

RABBI DAVID TZVI HOFFMAN

וְאֵלֶּה תּוֹלְדֹת תֶּרַח – *These are the descendants of Teraḥ:* Playing the role of an introduction to the story of Avraham is a description of Teraḥ's family. All three of Teraḥ's sons are important to the history of Israel. Naḥor is the father of Rivka, and Haran is the father of Lot. It is also important to know where exactly Avraham was born, for the Torah wishes to emphasize that the first patriarch was not a product of the corrupt and sinful Canaanite society. Nor did these men marry women who emerged from that despicable milieu; rather their wives came from their own lands and families. This group preserved a strong faith in the existence of God, even though some of its members embraced idolatry [as attested to by Joshua 24:2]. It is even likely that the emigration of this clan resulted from theological disputes that they had with their neighbors.

VERSE 28

SHADAL

בְּאוּר כַּשְׂדִּים – *In Ur Kasdim:* It seems to me that Ur Kasdim was not situated in Babylonia. Rather, there occurred some event, whose nature has since been lost, that led to the place

26 sons and daughters. Teraḥ lived seventy years and
27 fathered Avram, Naḥor, and Haran.These are the descendants
of Teraḥ. Teraḥ was the father of Avram, Naḥor, and Haran,
28 and Haran had a son, Lot. While his father Teraḥ was still alive,
29 Haran died in the land of his birth, Ur Kasdim. Avram and MAFTIR
Naḥor married; the name of Avram's wife was Sarai, and the
name of Naḥor's wife was Milka. She was the daughter of Ha-
30 ran, father of Milka and Yiska. And Sarai was barren – she had
31 no child. Teraḥ took his son Avram, and his grandson Lot,
son of Haran, and his daughter-in-law Sarai, his son Avram's

SHADAL *(cont.)*

being named after the Chaldeans [Kasdim, or Babylonians]. The site was actually located in Aram Naharayim [Upper Mesopotamia, mentioned in 24:10], also known as "Ever Hanahar" ["Across the River"] as in the verse *From time immemorial, your ancestors – Teraḥ, the father of Avraham and the father of Naḥor – dwelled across the river and worshipped other gods* (Joshua 24:2). As Samuel Bochart [17th century] points out, it is clear that if Avraham had started off in Chaldea [Lower Mesopotamia] he would not have had to travel through Ḥaran in order to get to the land of Canaan. Based on this interpretation, the convoluted travels mapped out by Ramban and Netivot Hashalom become unnecessary.

VERSE 30

SHADAL

וַתְּהִי שָׂרַי עֲקָרָה – *And Sarai was barren:* The information is relevant now since God is about to tell Avraham: *I will make you a great nation* (12:2).

MALBIM

וַתְּהִי שָׂרַי עֲקָרָה – *And Sarai was barren:* The text points out the barrenness of Sarai even though her sister Milka also did not have children until several decades later, when Yitzḥak was thirty-seven years old, as we read: *Some time later, Avraham was told, "Milka too has had children with your brother Naḥor"* (22:20). And yet Milka was not actually barren during all those years, since she did give birth to girls and also suffered miscarriages. On the other hand, Sarai did not conceive at all, and hence it was clear that she was barren.

VERSE 31

OR HAḤAYYIM

וַיִּקַּח תֶּרַח – *Teraḥ took:* Unbeknownst to him, Teraḥ was following the advice offered by our Sages, of blessed memory: If one suffers misfortune, he should move, since a different location improves one's luck. Now when Teraḥ saw that no children were born to his son Avram, he hoped that moving the family to a new country would improve its fate. The text informs us that Avraham was held in such high regard by his relatives that they all agreed to accompany him on his journey toward a better destination and a more promising destiny. This is the sense of the verse.

כַּלָּתוֹ אֵשֶׁת אַבְרָם בְּנוֹ וַיֵּצְאוּ אִתָּם מֵאוּר כַּשְׂדִּים לָלֶכֶת
לב אַרְצָה כְּנַעַן וַיָּבֹאוּ עַד־חָרָן וַיֵּשְׁבוּ שָׁם׃ וַיִּהְיוּ יְמֵי־תֶרַח
חָמֵשׁ שָׁנִים וּמָאתַיִם שָׁנָה וַיָּמָת תֶּרַח בְּחָרָן׃

MALBIM

וַיִּקַּח תֶּרַח – *Teraḥ took:* All of the information provided so far regarding this family serves to explain why Teraḥ pulled up stakes and set off for Canaan. Since Haran had died, and Avraham had no children, the family was a small one. In those days, the patriarch of a clan who lacked many sons was considered weak and ineffectual. As such, Teraḥ was perceived as insignificant compared to his father Naḥor, about whom the verse states: *He had other sons and daughters* (11:25). Furthermore, Teraḥ was distressed that his son Avram was hounded by the king Nimrod. And even though the lad was saved once from the fiery furnace, Teraḥ could not count on additional miracles to keep his son alive. He therefore decided to relocate to the land of Canaan, where the descendants of Shem were then living. For these men had split from the family of Ḥam and Nimrod their king. As well, the people of Shem were kin to Teraḥ's father. This is why Teraḥ chose to flee to their land in order to escape Nimrod and his tyranny.

HAAMEK DAVAR

וַיִּקַּח תֶּרַח – *Teraḥ took:* Even though God had not yet commanded Avram to emigrate to the land of Canaan, a foreshadow of that decree had already emanated from heaven. From

wife, and together they set out from Ur Kasdim to go to the
land of Canaan. But when they arrived at Ḥaran, they settled
32 there. Teraḥ lived two hundred and five years, and he died in
Ḥaran.

HAAMEK DAVAR *(cont.)*

a distance Avram had seen the shimmer of holiness glowing off the promised land, as I will discuss below in comments to 15:7. The text relates that *Teraḥ took his son Avram etc.* which gives the impression that it was the father who initiated the move. Nevertheless, the journey was really undertaken due to Avram's insight and advice [for he was the one who had detected the unusual nature of the far-off land]. Because Avram's mind and soul were immersed in lofty thoughts and intellectual musings, he was not really suitable to lead such a difficult journey. As such, Teraḥ took charge of the migration. He took Avram, Lot, and Sarai in hand and is therefore given credit for the move.

VERSE 32

SHADAL

וַיִּהְיוּ יְמֵי־תֶרַח – *Teraḥ lived:* The text wraps up the story of Teraḥ's life in order to then devote itself fully to the narrative of Avraham. Thus, the Torah mentions this detail now, even though Teraḥ only died sixty years after Avram left Ḥaran for Canaan [as described in the next chapter].

פרשת נח
PARASHAT NOAḤ

THE **BIBLICAL**
IMAGINATION

RABBI SHAI FINKELSTEIN

THE FLOOD AND ITS SIGNIFICANCE

Parashat Bereshit ends with a pessimistic description of the state of the world. God's earth, and especially the crowning achievement of His creation – its people – have become sinful and corrupt. The entire planet stands on the brink of destruction, as God has decided to wipe out all animal and human life and to start over afresh. God expresses His desire to annihilate everything: "I will erase My creation, humankind, from the face of the land – man, even animals and creeping things, even birds of the heavens – for I regret having made them" (6:7). And yet, for those readers encountering this tale for the first time, the divine declaration seems somewhat obscure: God has not yet detailed exactly *how* He plans on obliterating the life He has made. Nevertheless, very early in Parashat Noaḥ we learn of His method: "And I – I am about to bring floodwaters over the earth to destroy all flesh that has within it the breath of life under the heavens. Everything on earth will die" (6:17). A deluge will drown all creatures on land, and a new world will arise upon the ruins with Noaḥ as its founding father.

God's scheme to bring the first iteration of the world to an end by means of a *mabbul* ["flood"] has led many of the commentators to investigate the origin of this Hebrew term. Scholars have attempted to understand the literal significance of the word, and to consider how that relates to the nature of the deluge and to God's chosen method of destruction.

In his commentary to 6:17, Rashi offers two interpretations for the word *mabbul*. The first suggests destruction, for the water destroyed *(billa)* everything it covered. The flood wiped out all life on the planet, and because of the effect that the waters had on its victims, the event became known as a *mabbul*. Rashi's second offering differs: The word *mabbul* is linked to the word for "confused" – *bilbel*. As the waters rose across the earth and its swells washed away everything in their path, the resulting chaos mixed up the entire planet – no distinctions could be made between animate and inanimate objects when all were submerged beneath the waves. One of the features that sets human beings apart from the rest of the animal kingdom is our ability to comprehend nuanced distinctions. Human children are taught early on to differentiate between truth and falsehood. Our need to name the things we find in our environment is an expression of the way that we make sense and order of the world. However, the first humans craved more power than they were at first allotted, believing that if they ate the fruit from the Tree of Knowledge their "eyes would

be opened, and [they would] be like God, knowing good and evil" (3:5). In fact, the disobedience of Adam and Ḥava represented the first step in the downfall of humanity. When the pair misappropriated the fruit of the forbidden tree, they demonstrated their inability or unwillingness to distinguish between their property and that which belongs to somebody else. As humankind descended deeper into pandemonium, people began to accept theft as a completely natural and reasonable mechanism for acquiring possessions that rightfully belonged to others. This eventually developed into shameless and unchecked rapaciousness: "When the sons of God saw that the daughters of man were lovely, they began to take whomever they chose to be wives to them" (6:2). In another bizarre manifestation of blurred boundaries, animals began to copulate with members of other species. In short, a complete lack of order and justice descended upon the carefully crafted and categorized world God had bequeathed to His creations. As such, the deluge which followed was merely a continuation of the confusion that the planet's creatures had begun; the watery erasure of limits and definitions was a punishment in kind, a phenomenon that appears often in Tanakh. Since humanity was so eager to ignore the designations that God had ingrained in His world, He assisted them by further washing away all remaining distinctions and order that the people had not yet managed to dismantle.

As a final point, Rashi maintains that during the flood the corpses were all swept away toward Mesopotamia, which was also called Shinar since everybody who perished in the deluge was shaken out (*nin'aru)* there. This point is a play on the word connecting the word *mabbul* with the name of the land of Babylonia [*Bavel*]. As the penultimate story in our *parasha* will recount, it was in Babylonia that God mixed up [*bilbel*] human language in the process of thwarting the people's plan to build their tower. The story of the tower is also one of jumbled priorities: according to our Sages, the men constructing it had such high hopes for their project that they considered the loss of materials to be more severe than the deaths of laborers. In summation, the flood narrative reflects the twisted perspectives that pervaded society during the time of Noaḥ, and how that world was wiped away by a flood sent to cleanse the planet of its deviations.

The Lubavitcher Rebbe develops this point with the following comment: "The word for flood (*mabbul*) is related to the word confusion (*balal*). Metaphorically, the waters of the flood drown us, along with our minds, by confusing us as to what is primary and what is secondary in life." The Rebbe maintains that water in general holds the power to wash people along with it as it flows along its way. Those who allow themselves to be carried with the current stop thinking for themselves or plotting any new or alternate paths across the sea of life. They do not take the time or opportunity to fight against the tide or to evaluate the decisions they are making for their futures. Surely, water is a positive force in

this world and a critical substance for all earthly life. However, hidden within it is an ability to dampen or fade human identity. It is not coincidental that Pharaoh's daughter names Moshe after her having drawn him out of the water (Exodus 2:10) – Moshe's life destiny was to pull his people out of the murkiness of the Egyptian waves that threatened to wash away the Israelite character. In this way Moshe followed in the footsteps of his ancestor Avraham who, crossing the Euphrates River, left a community intent on assimilating him into its culture of idolatry. But Avraham refused to drown in the face of that onslaught; it was his role to influence the world, not to be swamped by his neighbors trying to dissolve his faith.

Noaḥ had the misfortune of living in a generation that was impervious to his cries to reform. When nature took over the task of cleansing humanity, the waters rose above the mountaintops and threatened to sweep Noaḥ away as well, and they might have, had he not been ensconced in the ark. God chose water as His mechanism of destruction to educate humankind. The message of the Almighty was powerful and relentless: human beings must not permit their identity to be eroded or lost amid the crashing waves of human society. One must resist the urge to go with the flow if one's destiny lies in the opposite direction. God expects each of us to take advantage of the divine image we been invested with, to identify our own unique characters, to fix our priorities, and to chart a course through the turbulent streams of existence.

It is true that the flood could be seen as simply perpetuating the confusion that humankind had initiated, but it is only we who experience anarchy and disorder. The Creator of the world maintains a steady vision of the universe's structure and destiny. This steadiness of hand can be seen, for example, in God's insistence in preserving his attribute of Compassion even at the time of His most potent anger at the world. Rabbi Samson Raphael Hirsch (nineteenth century) takes this approach in commenting on the phrase "everything on earth will die [*yigva*]" (6:17) which we cited above:

> Our Sages have already pointed out that the verb *yigva* refers to the death of righteous people. The Midrash makes this comment while interpreting the verse "Avraham breathed his last [*vayigva*] and died in his ripe old age, aged and satisfied, and was gathered to his people" (25:8). We find the term similarly used regarding the passing of Yitzḥak [in 35:29], and Yaakov [in 49:33]. How surprising that the verb should appear here regarding the obliteration of this wicked generation! The Torah's choice of language is fraught with meaning. For in the present instance, it is not a human who is planning the apocalypse. Instead, the Creator of the world, the merciful and compassionate One, is planning the destruction. Hence the term *gava*

> is highly significant. When death is preceded by *gevia,* that signifies that the person has left the world without suffering. Thus the Rabbis explain the term *gevia* as reflecting a sort of dormancy or frozenness. As such, the merciful God exercised compassion even while He was punishing humankind. The survivor Noaḥ would have been unable to bear the thought of millions of lives being snuffed out slowly and painfully. Hence God describes for Noaḥ in advance the sort of death that He will bring to humanity: "Everything on earth will die [*yigva*]." In other words, all consciousness across the world will be frozen before death, reduced painlessly to lifeless matter. The only remaining step will be for the dead bodies to be broken down into and dissolved into the swirling floodwaters.

Rabbi Hirsch introduces a psychological element to the story which the Torah itself does not describe. God chooses Noaḥ and his family to be humanity's only survivors of the impending doom that He is unleashing against the world. From their vessel of salvation, the family is destined to witness the complete destruction of their home. The thoughts of such annihilation would cause any person with a modicum of sensitivity to feel horror and distress. To help Noaḥ keep his senses, God assures him that although everybody he has ever known is about to die, their deaths will be instantaneous and painless. And thus divine compassion finds expression even during times of God's utmost anger. Thus all God's faculties are constantly, steadily in play; his character knows no change or caprice, for the Almighty is not influenced by external factors or the passage of time.

For our part, the concept of *imitato dei* defines our mission to find the same confidence and equanimity in our own personal identities. We must fortify ourselves to resist those societal currents that threaten to drag us into their undertow. One must never mindlessly allow one's character to be eroded in the face of communal forces and influences.

And so, the *mabbul* is not merely a title of a particular sort of punishment given to the generation that perished in Noaḥ's time. Rather, the term represents a spiritual concept and God's expectations from humanity: The individual must strive unceasingly to preserve the image of God he or she has been granted, while struggling to withstand the relentless waves constantly trying to drag us down. We must each learn how to haul ourselves out of the seas, and in so doing rescue others who are at risk of drowning. It is only thus that our unique character can be saved and developed, it is only thus that each of us can live to sail into the peaceful waters of our future.

THE ETERNAL DIALECTIC

The Torah portrays Noaḥ as a wholly good and virtuous person, bordering on the perfect. The description that the Torah provides for this man is unmatched in biblical literature: "Noaḥ was a righteous man, a person of integrity in his generation; Noaḥ walked with God" (6:9). And yet, despite such glowing praise, the Sages make repeated efforts to diminish Noaḥ's greatness by comparing him, usually unfavorably, to the achievements of other generations and other superlative figures who populate our national history. For example, according to the Rabbis, Noaḥ is given an exceedingly long time to build the ark – over a century – time he is meant to use to rebuke his neighbors and to try to reform the people of his era. Does he? Since the text itself lacks any evidence of such efforts, the Sages criticize Noaḥ for his inaction and his insensitivity. They blame Noaḥ for not trying to save the world or to prevent its destruction.

Many commentators characterize Noaḥ as "an average sort of hero" who cared only for himself and his own survival; worrying not one whit for his friends and neighbors of six hundred years. Our Sages pull no punches as they seize the somewhat cryptic phrase "Noaḥ walked with God" and explain it to Noaḥ's detriment. They compare this seemingly approving statement to a similar description of Avraham, "the LORD before whom I have walked" (Genesis 24:40). Quoting the Midrash, Rashi explains that although Noaḥ needed God's assistance to progress through the world, and hence walked "with" God, Avraham was confident enough to walk by himself, "before" the Almighty. Similarly, when dealing with the verse "Noaḥ, with his sons, his wife, and his sons' wives, came into the ark to escape the waters of the flood" (7:7), the Sages argue that Noaḥ did not actually believe that God was going to destroy the world, and so he waited until the last minute before boarding the ark. Now this sort of analysis raises two questions:

1. Why do the Sages feel the need to level such stinging judgments against Noaḥ considering the absence of such negativity in the text of the Torah itself?
2. What precisely is the message that the Sages are trying to impart with this attitude toward the figure of Noaḥ?

Perhaps the Sages believed that Noaḥ squandered his potential to become the father of all humanity. Instead, as we read in the closing chapter of Noaḥ's life,

he chose to wallow drunk in his tent. Noaḥ had begun his career by inventing the plow (according to Bereshit Rabba 25), taking aim at the curse given to his ancestor Adam, "By the sweat of your brow will you eat bread" (3:19). This is a man who could have changed the world and redirected the fate of humankind. And yet, Noaḥ did not share the faith in himself that God had when He told him: "I have seen you alone to be righteous before Me in this generation" (7:1). Noaḥ was satisfied with his lot and failed to seize the opportunity to develop a better future for his children. He simply sat and waited for the world to change itself – and this is a critical error in life and a miscalculation of what God wants from us. Our Sages, of blessed memory, belittled Noaḥ for the poor results that emerged from his life and actions. Not only was Noaḥ unable to make a radical difference in the ways that people conduct themselves, but he neglected to transmit his values and plans to his own sons. While Noaḥ may have saved the world, he simultaneously managed to lose himself.

The message that our Sages are trying to impart is that people must have confidence in their own abilities and trust in themselves to direct their lives to the highest possible degree. Woe to one who allows inertia to become the guiding force in one's life! Noaḥ epitomizes the actor who strides onto the stage with great fanfare and shouts of fantastic promise but leaves the spotlight with muffled mumblings of mediocrity. His career opened with tremendous hope for the future of humankind, but the second chapter of his life was characterized by inaction and the failure to pave any meaningful paths open to the human race.

The accusation that Noaḥ refused to believe in his own self-worth can be illuminated by the words of the Rambam in his *Guide of the Perplexed* (1:5). The Rambam quotes the introduction to Aristotle's *On the Heavens*, wherein the author begs the reader not to view him as a haughty know-it-all. Rather, Aristotle humbly asks his audience to accept that he has done his best and taxed all his mental faculties to reach the conclusions his book presents.

The Rambam adopts a similar approach for students of Judaism and the Torah. No individual should boastfully claim that he understands everything when he or she is just starting out. Rather, every man or woman should practice a system of constant self-improvement with regard to learning and ethical behavior as a prerequisite to expressing any type of opinion. The Rambam directs the reader to the verse describing Moshe's encounter with the burning bush: "Then Moshe hid his face, for he was afraid to look at God" (Exodus 3:6), to explain that it reflects Moshe's unwillingness to circumvent the usual educational steps toward the creation of a prophet. How could he jump ahead in one great leap to the highest level of prophecy and revelation when he had not prepared for it? It was only later, when Moshe felt he had graduated to the position of God's confidant, that he was prepared to "look upon the Lord's form" (Numbers 12:8). In

contrast to Moshe, who intuitively understood that matters must progress naturally, the Israelite nobles were overeager to view God (as described in Exodus chapter 24) and burst through the barriers at a time when they were not quite ready. As such, the sight that they glimpsed was incomplete, and these people were eventually burned in the conflagration described in Numbers chapter 11.

This idea presented in the *Guide of the Perplexed* is worth serious contemplation, for it touches upon a whole range of personal decisions which we face in our lives. At what point is a man or woman certain that he or she is ready for action or to assume a leadership role? Conversely, when is a person right to refuse the responsibility of a position, knowing that that the time is not yet ripe?

The Talmud (Sota 22a) cites Rav's interpretation of the verse that allegorically warns against the harlot, "For she has turned many into corpses, and numerous are her victims" (Proverbs 7:26). According to Rav, the first clause in this verse refers to a disciple who has not yet attained the qualification to pronounce legal rulings, but makes such decisions anyway. The second half of the sentence conversely describes a student who has mastered the material necessary for issuing rulings, and yet refuses to do so. The Talmud thus identifies two categories of misguided students. The first type believes he is ready to lead a congregation and rule on matters of halakha, when really his confidence in his abilities and knowledge is misplaced. Meanwhile, the second kind of personality is too humble or insecure to recognize what he knows, and so he withholds his learning from the community. Both types of unawareness are dangerous and can lead to the destruction of society.

How do people know when they are qualified to teach? What is the best way to test such abilities? When are we deluding ourselves into believing that God thinks of us as the "righteous man in his generation," worthy of issuing fateful decisions for our neighbors? This dialectic between a sense of readiness and natural self-doubt might stem from the individual's humility and honesty. This in turn leads to intense inner conflict that keeps the person from acting or choosing a future. The Torah thus portrays two personalities faced with this difficulty who acted in opposite ways. Noaḥ allowed his lack of surety to dominate his life, whereas Avraham chose to lead the world as the father of great nations and founder of the Israelite people. No human decision is graced with any sort of guarantee. But indecision and inaction also do not offer any safety or tranquility for the person who indulges them.

What we have been describing is confrontation with one of humanity's greatest challenges, that which constantly plagues men and women struggling to find their ways in this life. The tension that ensues forces us to engage in much self-reflection, to learn to understand our personalities, and to honestly gauge our talents, abilities, and qualifications. That is the only way in which a person

can ever feel ready to take the bold step into the unknown future; self-awareness is the sole attribute that can produce faith in one's heart and trust in one's decisions. That, combined with the help of the Creator, can lead us toward realizing our dreams and fulfilling our destiny.

Unfortunately, humanity has yet to discover a mathematical formula to aid in our decision making. Instead, we are forced to undergo much trial and error, to fortify ourselves with courage and submission, strength and modesty. The person who is created in the image of God has been assigned the tremendous burden of imitating our Maker, tasked with forming worlds of his or her own. God calls upon us to fashion new realities based on an understanding of our inner selves, and an awareness that the future will be influenced by our decisions and consequent actions.

EDUCATIONAL CHALLENGES IN THE MODERN WORLD

Noaḥ's generation was a mess of cruelty, barbarism, and violence, as the Torah itself describes: "The earth had become corrupt in God's sight, full of violence.... God saw how corrupt the earth had become, all flesh corrupting its ways upon the earth" (6:11–12). In response to this ethical deterioration, the Almighty determined to destroy all life on earth and to restart the project of humanity. Noaḥ and his family were chosen to lead the new era of the postdiluvian world and to guide the human race toward a better future. The family's salvation was dependent on their construction of an ark, as God commands: "So make yourself an ark of cypress wood. Make it with compartments and coat it in pitch inside and out" (6:14). And included in God's design for this vessel was a feature He refers to as a *tzohar* in 6:16.

Our Sages, of blessed memory, debate the precise nature and purpose of the *tzohar*. A midrash in Bereshit Rabba (31:11) offers two approaches to the identity of the *tzohar*. According to Rabbi Abba bar Kahana, the *tzohar* was simply a window in the side of the ark. Rabbi Levi on the other hand, claims that it was a miraculous precious jewel. The first interpretation is based on the similarity of language between the term *tzohar* and the word *tzhoharayim* ["noon"] with connotations of light. The second understanding suggests that Noaḥ brought into the ark a light-emitting gem that illuminated the boat's interior for its passengers. According to Rabbi Levi, no outside light could enter the vessel during the flood. With this debate as our starting point, let us pose two questions: one exegetical and one conceptual.

The observant reader might ask Rabbi Abba bar Kahana why the Torah in chapter 6 uses the word *tzohar* to mean "window" when in chapter 8 the standard term *ḥalon* appears for just that purpose: "After forty days Noaḥ opened the window [*ḥalon*] he had made in the ark" (8:6). Why would the text use two different words to represent the same thing? Rabbi Levi, on the other hand, would have to explain why Noaḥ was required to fix an artificial light source inside the ark when it is clear that the window we encounter in chapter 8 was suitable for that need. On a different level of analysis, we must ask what the philosophical differences are between the two approaches. What message is each position attempting to convey?

In his popular commentary to Rashi's work known as *Siftei Ḥakhamim* (published in 1680), Rabbi Shabtai Bass addresses these problems. That author suggests that even though it is clear that the ark was equipped with a window, as the

text reports in chapter 8 upon Noaḥ's release of the raven, it would seem that the *tzohar* was constructed not to admit light but simply to provide the circulation of air. Based on this theory, it is quite likely that the ark held *two* windows: one of the openings was for letting light into the boat, and this is the window through which the raven and the dove later exit. The second window – which the text refers to as a *tzohar* – was there strictly to improve the ark's ventilation. And hence there is no contradiction or repetition in the Torah's descriptions of these two features, which served different functions.

Let us now examine the conceptual differences between the two rabbinic positions, as well as attempt to identify their common denominator. In the process we will seek the underlying lessons that these rabbis have hidden within their theories.

Tragically for him, Noaḥ lived in an era that was saturated with corruption, bereft of morality or altruistic behavior. In their interpretation of the Torah's use of the term "violence" [*ḥamas*], the Sages write as follows (Bereshit Rabba 31:6): "Rabbi Levi taught: When the verse states: 'For the earth is full of violence' (6:13), it means that humanity practiced idolatry, engaged in licentiousness, and committed murder." Creation had thus lost its way completely and was intent on abusing the image of God that people had been endowed with. As such, God decided to wipe humanity from the face of the earth and destroy the world that He had created in six days, and to create life all over again. For the survival of Noaḥ and his family, this meant that they had to build a large vessel to protect them from the deadly waters of the deluge. Furthermore, once the doors to the vessel were sealed shut, there was no way that anybody who was undeserving of salvation could be rescued from the divine punishment.

One way of looking at this is that God ordered Noaḥ to build for himself a box in which to shelter himself, and through which he would escape the retribution that had been decreed against his generation. Once God "shut him in" the ark (7:16), Noaḥ was essentially cut off from the outside world, which was about to undergo a terrible transformation. Now let us ask ourselves: at that moment was it permitted to keep open a window that might allow some connection to the external world to penetrate the safe haven inside? Or was it critical that the vessel remained hermetically sealed against the sin and the suffering that covered the world that Noaḥ was leaving behind? Perhaps no measure of influence could be allowed to seep into the floating refuge. If that were the case, Noaḥ would have had to suspend a light source from the ceiling of the ark in order to allow its inhabitants to see each other.

Perhaps this problem forms the basis of the debate between Rabbi Abba bar Kahana and Rabbi Levi: Once the ark's construction was complete, could Noaḥ maintain some small link to the world he had been born into, an earth that was

to be obliterated before his tightly shut eyes? Or perhaps God had determined that Noaḥ's contact and connection with that world needed to be wholly severed. If that were the case, then the light shining from the gem provided the sole illumination on an earth that was clouded over, just as Noaḥ's righteousness shone brightly and alone among the dreary companions of his race.

This question regarding Noaḥ floats downstream to us across the generations, representing a fundamental difficulty for Jews who have remained faithful to the Torah and commandments in these turbulent times. The Orthodox community simultaneously embraces the societal advances around us and partakes of the modern achievements that the greater world provides us all. At the same time, we must surely recognize that society at large often adopts perspectives and positions that run contrary to our traditions and to our age-old beliefs. Any parent who has tried to raise his or her children in a world of conflicting values knows how treacherous these waters are to navigate.

Such a complex reality forces each individual to build his or her own metaphoric ark that can shield his or her family from external and unwanted influences. Strange, foreign, and startling ideas constantly bombard our personal ships as we bob to and fro through the waves. And so, how can we, as captains of these vessels, provide light for our passengers? How are we to balance the light seeping through the cracks of our windows with that which shines from our ancient texts and practices? Shall we open a *tzohar* to our private arks so that we can simply breathe, or affix a picture window in our walls so that those inside can see everything that the outside world has to offer? The insular among us will insist on providing all their family's light themselves while refusing to make use of general society's flashy offerings.

On the other hand, some Jews keep an open window in their arks, encouraging the infiltration of external ideas from the wider world beyond their shelter. These men and women believe that we have a great deal to learn from others – Jewish or not – and every value and culture should be assessed fairly, truthfully, and accurately. Occasionally, this window can be kept fully open, and other times it must be firmly locked. However, the attitude of families with a window is based on the trust they put in their ability to mix and to reconcile the light streaming in from outside with the illumination emanating from within.

In order to properly balance the values of the Torah with the world of science and general art and culture, we must thoroughly study the Torah and understand its messages. Full immersion in the service of God, intellectual development, and sensitivity toward others are all prerequisites to engaging with the outside world. Ideally, the Modern Orthodox Jew believes in combining the two interpretations which we have seen in the Midrash. We must understand that God long ago provided us with the Torah – an illuminating gem. Meanwhile

great wisdom has been achieved and continues to flourish beyond the four walls of the Beit Midrash. There is certainly much to be gained from scientific and cultural advances that can enrich our own religious lives. And so we must adopt a lifestyle that switches back and forth between the gas and the brakes, that constantly opens the window a little bit more, but later closes it when something incompatible with our values floats by. This is not a simple existence; it is a complicated and never-ending series of decisions. The devoted Jew is forever evaluating the world and how it affects his or her life, influences the nation as a whole, and affects our mission to lead humankind by example.

Nevertheless, we possess the powers necessary to navigate our arks through stormy seas to safe shores. We can educate our children to adopt Jewish lifestyles defined by an understanding of our national mission within the world at large. And so, when God told Noaḥ: "Make a *tzohar* for the ark," He was speaking to us as well.

*For commentaries and the Biblical Imagination
turn to the left side of this volume.*